Technical
COMMUNICATION

Technical
COMMUNICATION

THIRTEENTH EDITION

Mike Markel
Boise State University

Stuart A. Selber
Penn State University

bedford/st.martin's
Macmillan Learning
Boston | New York

Vice President: Leasa Burton
Program Director, English: Stacey Purviance
Senior Program Manager: Laura Arcari
Director of Content Development: Jane Knetzger
Executive Manager, Development: Maura Shea
Senior Development Editor: Sherry Mooney
Assistant Editor: Annie Campbell
Director of Media Editorial: Adam Whitehurst
Media Editor: Julia Domenicucci
Executive Marketing Manager: Joy Fisher Williams
Senior Director, Content Management Enhancement: Tracey Kuehn
Senior Managing Editor: Michael Granger
Senior Manager of Publishing Services and Content Project Manager: Andrea Cava
Lead Digital Asset Archivist and Senior Workflow Project Manager: Jennifer Wetzel
Production Supervisor: Brianna Lester
Director of Design, Content Management: Diana Blume
Interior Design: Maureen McCutcheon Design
Cover Design: William Boardman
Director of Rights and Permissions: Hilary Newman
Photo Permissions Editors: Angie Boehler; Krystyna Borgen, Lumina Datamatics, Inc.
Director of Digital Production: Keri deManigold
Advanced Media Project Manager: Sarah O'Connor Kepes
Project Management: Lumina Datamatics, Inc.
Project Managers: Gunjan Chandola Bhatt, Misbah Ansari/Lumina Datamatics, Inc.
Composition: Lumina Datamatics, Inc.
Cover and Title Page Image: Copyright Xinzheng. All Rights Reserved./Moment/
   Getty Images
Printing and Binding: LSC Communications

Library of Congress Control Number: 2020935176
ISBN 978-1-319-24500-9 (paperback)
ISBN 978-1-319-35414-5 (Loose-leaf Edition)

Printed in the United States of America.
2 3 4 5 6   25 24 23 22

Acknowledgments
*Acknowledgments and copyrights appear on the same page as the text and art selections they
cover; these acknowledgments and copyrights constitute an extension of the copyright page.*

For information, write: Bedford/St. Martin's, 75 Arlington Street, Boston, MA 02116

Preface for Instructors

TECHNICAL COMMUNICATION has, by definition, always involved technology in fundamental ways, from the tools people use to produce and access workplace documents to the subject matter of those documents and the contexts in which they are implemented. Previous editions of *Technical Communication* have responded to this reality by providing a variety of valuable tools for students on how to use technology in effective ways. Tech Tips, examples from a variety of media, and the inclusion of the LaunchPad platform with its suite of additional resources helped to train generations of students in how to take advantage of the affordances of technology. When considering the changes needed for the thirteenth edition, however, we acknowledged that the concerns of today's learners are less a matter of how to use a particular tool—though support in that area is still a key to success—and more a question of why and when to use what tools to achieve a specific rhetorical goal. Which is to say that with a vast array of technology available, we felt that it was most important for students to appreciate the context and implications of their digital choices, developing an evaluative perspective that will serve them through generations of technological evolution.

In technical-communication situations, however, that evolution is a multidimensional process with both social and technical aspects. A new feature, Strategies for Online Communication, has been added to the thirteenth edition to address this process. Professionals from a diverse array of fields provide models of their writing to showcase key digital skills they employ in their work. Annotations provided by those professionals highlight the rhetorical moves and technical considerations they made while developing the document. This new feature explores the complex factors in digital-specific situations, including how to effectively implement recurring content, how to crowd-source data and information, and how to integrate multiple modalities into a single end-product. These real-world models present technology in all its possibility and complexity and truly speak to the decisions available to today's technical communicators.

Finally, although it doesn't always feel this way, technology tends to be more evolutionary than revolutionary in nature. Although the web has enabled people to communicate in new and different ways, it involves practices and perspectives that derive from earlier media. For better or worse, the page metaphor still has a notable impact on website design and use, and techniques from film, television, and music production help inform the creation of digital content for technical communication. The new edition embraces this sort of change and continues to provide thorough guidance on traditional, still-valuable approaches to writing while making clear connections to emerging approaches. A great example of this in the thirteenth edition is our newly enhanced coverage on résumé writing in Chapter 15, Applying for a Job. Along with a complete explanation of the elements and variations for print-based résumés and cover letters, the new edition presents students with the fuller range of options that technology makes available, including a new visually enhanced résumé, an infographic résumé, and a video résumé. This new coverage showcases the evolution of this particular genre and equips students to make effective decisions based on their specific rhetorical needs.

Keeping technology in perspective is not a new task for the field, but it has become intensified in an age of digital everything. In each and every project, technical communicators need to be alert to the benefits and consequences of technology for their own work and for the work of users and their communities. Being alert requires a critical eye, but not in a negative sense: a technological integration of nearly any sort is a nuanced process with a range of options to explore. As opposed to being either a cynic or an evangelist for technology, technical communicators should be curious professionals who are interested in what might be gained, lost, and reproduced, and in how technology can advance the goals, approaches, and values of the field.

We have revised the new edition of *Technical Communication* to give students even more support for navigating this changing technological landscape. The practice of technical communication, in fact, has never been more dynamic or complex, in large part because of the ongoing evolution and reinvention of technology and work. Today's professionals face an ever-increasing set of challenges in the development of documents, from analyzing global contexts to designing digital content. This book will help prepare students to address such challenges—in their courses and in their careers—and will help them to become effective, responsible communicators in a technologically saturated world.

New to This Edition

The Thirteenth Edition has been revised to help students stay current with a changing technical-communication environment. We have created a new feature, Strategies for Online Communication, that introduces an emergent topic or issue of digital communication and explores how it is handled by workplace professionals, who share their strategies and insights with students. The new feature appears in Chapters 3, 4, 11, and 20, and the professionals discuss managing recurring content, crowdsourcing data and information, using multiple modalities in technical communication documents, and moderating user forums. They all provide instructive examples from their work and annotate the examples to illustrate the most salient points.

The chapter on applying for a job now includes coverage of nontraditional résumé formats, including infographic-based résumés and video résumés, giving students tips on how to create them and, crucially, when to consider using them. This chapter also adds new material on preparing for and participating in online job interviews, which are increasingly common because they save companies money and time.

The chapter on designing print and online documents now discusses the possibility of leveraging the affordances of both media in the same end-user context. We have also updated our discussion in Chapter 1 of how employers rank the value of technical-communication skills and abilities, and we have added new Tech Tips in the chapters on designing print and online documents and creating graphics. The Tech Tips continue to reflect not just *how* to create different parts of documents using different kinds of software, but *why* to use these tools in the first place. In fact, in all of our revisions, we work to bridge research and practice at the level of document production and use.

Updated examples, both in the print text and in Achieve, provide opportunities for students to analyze the types of documents they will need to produce or contribute to, such as comparison-based data visualizations about education and the earnings gap and a video-based tutorial about selling into international markets.

Achieve with *Technical Communication* is an exciting, new, and comprehensive set of interconnected teaching and assessment tools. It integrates the most effective elements from Bedford/St. Martin's market-leading digital solutions you may be familiar with—including LaunchPad, LearningCurve, and iClicker—in a single, powerful, easy-to-use platform. We are proud to present **Achieve with *Technical Communication***, which rests on three core values: *engaging students for better outcomes*, *supporting students of all levels*, and *partnering with teachers and learners*.

Achieve with *Technical Communication* comes with a curated course option that you can adapt to fit your needs; add, hide, and rearrange resources and assignments—conveniently available in a searchable library—until the course works for you. Resources in Achieve with *Technical Communication* include:

- *An interactive e-book* with *Technical Communication* brings together the resources students need to prepare for your class. Students can download the e-book to read offline, or to have read aloud to them.

- *LearningCurve adaptive quizzing* offers personalized question sets and feedback for each student based on correct and incorrect responses. Questions are conveniently tied back to the e-book to encourage students to access help when they need it.

- *Pre-built writing assignments and other activities* have been developed to support the *Technical Communication* approach, designed to deliver a coherent learning experience, and will make prep, practice, and review easy and engaging.

- *Source Check plagiarism detection* allows students to scan their papers for potential plagiarism *before* they submit them for review, allowing students to learn academic writing habits and citation practices in the context of their own writing.

- *Diagnostics and study plans* help establish a baseline for student performance—a mark from which students can make progress throughout the course. Promoting personalized learning, Achieve helps students create actionable study plans to strengthen their skills and build their confidence.

- *Reporting and insights* that do the heavy lifting for you with powerful analytics that highlight student engagement, provide opportunities for intervention, and allow you to visualize trends in student progress across assignments.

Based on leading scholars' work on writer development, the pre-built writing assignments in Achieve with *Technical Communication* give teachers deeper visibility into students' writing processes so they can target instruction and feedback to help writers grow and develop across drafts, across assignments, and across courses. Students do the work of the course in a contained and active writing space that includes a suite of powerful writing tools. Actionable insights make students' progress toward outcomes clear and measurable.

- *Revision.* The Revision Plan helps writers turn feedback into concrete strategies and take ownership of their revision planning. For students, the Revision Plan creates accountability; for teachers, it provides insights about how well students understand the feedback they receive.

- *Reflection.* The writing tools increase students' rhetorical awareness and promote the transfer of skills and habits from draft to draft. How? By prompting students to articulate the choices they make as writers and to communicate their confidence in the drafts they write. You can choose and customize reflection prompts to fit your course and assignment goals.

- *Instructor feedback tools.* Powerful and customizable commenting tools allow you to focus your feedback on success criteria—draft goals that you set—and efficiently mark patterns of error. Feedback links to e-book content to give students point-of-need support in the context of their own writing.

- *Peer review tools.* When you empower students to seek feedback from and offer feedback to one another, you invite them to become *writers*, not just students of writing. Achieve's tools scaffold and support students' development as peer reviewers—and allow you to easily facilitate and monitor the process.

- *Pre-built assignments and units that make your life easier.* A flexible assignment building tool allows you to assign ready-made writing prompts or create your own.

Get ready for insights and *aha!* moments. Get ready to **achieve more**.

The following table describes the updates made to each chapter in the Thirteenth Edition.

CHAPTER	WHAT'S NEW
Chapter 1 Introduction to Technical Communication	• Updated coverage of the current state of technical communication in the job market
Chapter 3 Writing Technical Documents	• New Strategies for Online Communication feature on managing recurring content
Chapter 4 Writing Collaboratively	• New Strategies for Online Communication feature on crowdsourcing platforms
Chapter 6 Researching Your Subject	• New model of a social media search engine • Updated Team Exercise
Chapter 7 Organizing Your Information	• Updated coverage of cause and effect
Chapter 8 Communicating Persuasively	• Updated Table 8.1 on logical fallacies
Chapter 11 Designing Print and Online Documents	• New coverage on combining print and online documents • New Strategies for Online Communication feature on Using Multiple Modalities • Tech Tip: Why and How To Set Up Pages
Chapter 12 Creating Graphics	• Tech Tip: Why and How To Use Drawing Tools
Chapter 15 Applying for a Job	• New coverage on nontraditional résumés • Updated coverage of interviewing • New Guidelines box on Preparing for an Online Job Interview
Chapter 17 Writing Informational Reports	• Updated Focus on Process: Informational Reports
Chapter 20 Writing Definitions, Descriptions, and Instructions	• Strategies for Online Communication: Moderating User Forums
Appendix Reference Handbook	• Updated coverage of 2019 APA Style guidelines

Acknowledgments

The Thirteenth Edition of *Technical Communication* has benefited greatly from the perceptive observations and helpful suggestions of our fellow instructors throughout the country. We thank Lisa Abney, Northwestern State University of Louisiana; Eleanor Allen, Central New Mexico Community College; Mikayla Beaudrie, University of North Florida; Shavawn Berry, Arizona State University; Josh Chase, Michigan Technological University; Sara DiCaglio, Texas A&M University; Robert Haynes, Arizona State University; Lori Hughes, Lone Star College-Montgomery; Amber Lancaster, Oregon Institute of Technology; Terri Pantuso, Texas A&M University–College Station Campus; Heather Pristash, Western Wyoming Community College; Elizabeth Weiser, Ohio State University; Tammy Wolf, Central New Mexico Community College; and several anonymous reviewers.

We have been fortunate, too, to work with a terrific team at Bedford/St. Martin's. Stacey Purviance and Laura Arcari assembled the first-class team that has worked so hard on this edition, including Andrea Cava, Sherry Mooney, and Annie Campbell, and from Lumina Datamatics, Inc., Gunjan Chandola Bhatt and Misbah Ansari. For us, Bedford/St. Martin's continues to exemplify the highest standards of professionalism in publishing. The people there have been endlessly encouraging and helpful. We hope they realize the value of their contributions to this book.

Stuart would like to thank his family, Kate Latterell and Avery and Griffin Selber, for their ongoing support and encouragement.

A Final Word

We are more aware than ever before of how much we learn from our students, our fellow instructors, and our colleagues in industry and academia. If you have comments or suggestions for making this a better book, please contact us through the publisher. We hope to hear from you.

Mike Markel and Stuart A. Selber

Bedford/St. Martin's Puts You First

From day one, our goal has been simple: to provide inspiring resources that are grounded in best practices for teaching reading and writing. For more than 35 years, Bedford/St. Martin's has partnered with the field, listening to teachers, scholars, and students about the support writers need. We are committed to helping every writing instructor make the most of our resources.

How Can We Help *You*?

- Our editors can align our resources to your outcomes through correlation and transition guides for your syllabus. Just ask us.
- Our sales representatives specialize in helping you find the right materials to support your course goals.
- Our Bits blog on the Bedford/St. Martin's English Community (**community .macmillan.com**) publishes fresh teaching ideas weekly. You'll also find easily downloadable professional resources and links to author webinars on our community site.

Contact your Bedford/St. Martin's sales representative or visit **macmillanlearning .com** to learn more.

Print and Digital Options for *Technical Communication*

Choose the format that works best for your course, and ask about our packaging options that offer savings for students.

Print

- *Paperback.* To order the paperback edition, use ISBN 978-1-319-24500-9.
- *Loose-leaf edition.* This format does not have a traditional binding; its pages are loose and hole punched to provide flexibility and a lower price to students. It can be packaged with our digital space for additional savings. To order the loose-leaf packaged with Achieve, use ISBN 978-1-319-38531-6.

Digital

- *Achieve with* Technical Communication. Achieve puts student writing at the center of your course and keeps revision at the core, with a dedicated composition space that guides students through drafting, peer review, source check, reflection, and revision. Developed to support best practices in commenting on student drafts, Achieve is a flexible, integrated suite of tools for designing and facilitating writing assignments, paired with actionable insights that make students' progress toward outcomes clear and measurable. Fully editable pre-built assignments support the book's approach and an e-book is included. For details, visit **macmillanlearning .com/college/us/englishdigital**.

- *Popular e-book formats.* For details about our e-book partners, visit **macmillanlearning.com/ebooks**.

- *Inclusive Access.* Enable every student to receive their course materials through your LMS on the first day of class. Macmillan Learning's Inclusive Access program is the easiest, most affordable way to ensure all students have access to quality educational resources. Find out more at **macmillanlearning.com/inclusiveaccess**.

Your Course, Your Way

No two writing programs or classrooms are exactly alike. Our Curriculum Solutions team works with you to design custom options that provide the resources your students need. (Options below require enrollment minimums.)

- *ForeWords for English.* Customize any print resource to fit the focus of your course or program by choosing from a range of prepared topics, such as Sentence Guides for Academic Writers.

- *Macmillan Author Program (MAP).* Add excerpts or package acclaimed works from Macmillan's trade imprints to connect students with prominent authors and public conversations. A list of popular examples or academic themes is available upon request.

- *Mix and Match.* With our simplest solution, you can add up to 50 pages of curated content to your Bedford/St. Martin's text. Contact your sales representative for additional details.

- *Bedford Select.* Build your own print handbook or anthology from a database of more than 800 selections, and add your own materials to create your ideal text. Package with any Bedford/St. Martin's text for additional savings. Visit **macmillanlearning.com/bedfordselect**.

Select Value Packages

Add value to your text by packaging one of the following resources with *Technical Communication*.

Document-Based Cases for Technical Communication, Second Edition, by Roger Munger (Boise State University), offers realistic writing tasks based on seven context-rich scenarios, with more than 50 examples of documents that students are likely to encounter in the workplace. To order the print book packaged with *Document-Based Cases for Technical Communication*, contact your sales representative.

Team Writing, by Joanna Wolfe (Carnegie Mellon University), is a print supplement with online videos that provides guidelines and examples of collaborating to manage written projects by documenting tasks, deadlines, and team goals. Two- to five-minute videos corresponding with the chapters in *Team Writing* gives students the opportunity to analyze team interactions and learn about communication styles. Practical troubleshooting tips show students how best to handle various types of conflicts within peer groups. To order the print book packaged with *Team Writing,* contact your sales representative.

Instructor Resources

You have a lot to do in your course. We want to make it easy for you to find the support you need—and to get it quickly.

Instructor's Resource Manual for Technical Communication, Thirteenth Edition, is available as a PDF that can be downloaded from macmillanlearning. com. Visit the instructor resources tab for *Technical Communication.* In addition to chapter overviews and teaching tips, the instructor's manual includes sample syllabi, essays on teaching the technical communication course, and suggested responses to all of the Document Analysis Activities, Exercises, and Cases.

Test Bank for Technical Communication, Thirteenth Edition, offers a convenient way to provide additional assessment to students and is available in Achieve with *Technical Communication.* Instructors using Achieve will find the test bank material there, where they can add pre-built quizzes to any unit or build their own tests from the test bank questions. **Lecture slides** are available from **macmillanlearning.com** to download and adapt for each chapter.

Introduction for Writers

THE THIRTEENTH EDITION of *Technical Communication* offers a wealth of support to help you complete your technical communication projects. For quick reference, many of these features are indexed on the last book page and inside back cover of this book.

Annotated Examples make it easier for you to learn from the many model documents, illustrations, and screen shots throughout the text.

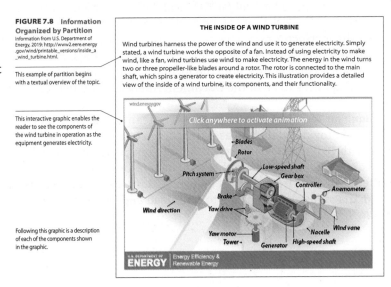

FIGURE 7.8 Information Organized by Partition
Information from U.S. Department of Energy, 2019: http://www2.eere.energy.gov/wind/printable_versions/inside_a_wind_turbine.html.

This example of partition begins with a textual overview of the topic.

This interactive graphic enables the reader to see the components of the wind turbine in operation as the equipment generates electricity.

Following this graphic is a description of each of the components shown in the graphic.

Tech Tips explain why and how to use widely available digital tools for common writing tasks such as collaborating on documents, inserting graphics, and formatting documents.

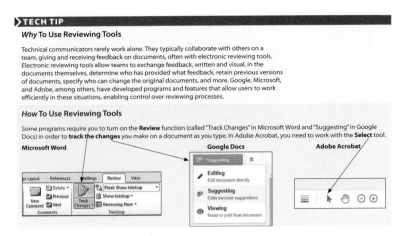

> **TECH TIP**

Why **To Use Reviewing Tools**

Technical communicators rarely work alone. They typically collaborate with others on a team, giving and receiving feedback on documents, often with electronic reviewing tools. Electronic reviewing tools allow teams to exchange feedback, written and visual, in the documents themselves, determine who has provided what feedback, retain previous versions of documents, specify who can change the original documents, and more. Google, Microsoft, and Adobe, among others, have developed programs and features that allow users to work efficiently in these situations, enabling control over reviewing processes.

How **To Use Reviewing Tools**

Some programs require you to turn on the **Review** function (called "Track Changes" in Microsoft Word and "Suggesting" in Google Docs) in order to **track the changes** you make on a document as you type. In Adobe Acrobat, you need to work with the **Select** tool.

DOCUMENT ANALYSIS ACTIVITY

Analyzing Evidence in an Argument

In this excerpt from an article on the job service Monster .com, the writer presents an argument about hiring a social-media officer. The questions below ask you to consider the nature of the evidence this writer presents.

1. In the first two paragraphs, the writer tells a story. Which kind of evidence is this, and how effective is it?

2. In paragraph 3, we learn the occupation of the person on that unpleasant flight. How does this new information add to the effectiveness of the argument?

3. Does paragraph 4 present any evidence? If not, what function does it serve?

Social Media Strategy: Is It Time to Hire a Social Media Officer?

① When Ted Rubin (@tedrubin) touched down in Asheville, NC after a particularly unpleasant flight with a carrier he rarely uses, he immediately posted an update to his 54,000 Twitter followers. "Just landed … boy do I miss @JetBlue."

A few minutes later, a representative from Jet Blue responded to say thanks. While Rubin tagged the other airline in his original tweet, he never heard back from them. "Guess who I'll be flying next?" he laughs.

② Rubin, who serves as Chief Social Marketing Officer for the shopping Web site Collective Bias, says this type of personal engagement isn't a novelty anymore — customers have come to expect it. "Social media is way deeper than most companies understand," he says. "It's time to recognize that social isn't just campaign-based, it's an integrated part of your ongoing business strategy."

③ Let's face it — your social media strategy is about more than monitoring social media — it touches customer service, vendor relations, social media recruiting and more. Thus many organizations are bringing in new staff to handle their social media strategy.

Document Analysis Activities in every chapter prompt you to apply what you have just read as you analyze a real business or technical document.

CASE 5: Focusing on an Audience's Needs and Interests

You're interning in the marketing department of a cell-phone service provider, and your supervisor has asked you to perform research into a competing provider's products and services for the over-65 market, paying special attention to the ways in which the company successfully appeals to the needs and interests of its audience. She then asks you to prepare an oral presentation about your findings. If your instructor has assigned it, go to Achieve to begin your project.

Cases for every chapter present real-world writing scenarios built around common workplace documents that you can download, critique, and revise.

◢
GUIDELINES Communicating Professionally

When you communicate in the workplace, model the behavior of successful professionals.

▶ **Be honest.** Successful communicators tell the truth. They don't promise what they know they can't deliver, and they don't bend facts. When they make mistakes, they admit them and work harder to solve the problem.

▶ **Be willing to learn.** Successful communicators know that they don't know everything — not about what they studied in college, what their company does, or how to write and speak. Every professional is a lifelong learner.

▶ **Display emotional intelligence.** Successful communicators understand their own emotions and those of others. Because they can read people — through body language, facial expression, gestures, and words — they can work effectively in teams, helping to minimize interpersonal conflict and encouraging others to do their best work.

▶ **Be generous.** Successful communicators reply to requests for information, and they share information willingly. (Of course, they don't share confidential information, such as trade secrets, information about new products being developed, or personal information about colleagues.)

Guidelines boxes throughout the book summarize crucial information and provide strategies related to key topics.

Focus on Process boxes point out key steps in the process of writing different kinds of technical documents.

FOCUS ON PROCESS: Writing Proposals

When writing a proposal, pay special attention to these steps in the writing process.

PLANNING
Consider your readers' knowledge about and attitudes toward what you are proposing. Use the techniques discussed in Chapters 5 and 6 to learn as much as you can about your readers' needs and about the subject. Also consider whether you have the personnel, facilities, and equipment to do what you propose to do.

DRAFTING
Collaboration is critical for large proposals because no one person has the time and expertise to do all the work. See Chapter 4 for more about collaboration. In writing the proposal, follow the instructions in any request for proposal (RFP) or information for bid (IFB) from the prospective customer. If there are no instructions, follow the structure for proposals outlined in this chapter.

REVISING
External proposals usually have a firm deadline. Build in time to revise, edit, and proofread the proposal thoroughly and still get it to readers on time. See the Writer's Checklist at the end of this chapter.

EDITING
See Chapter 10 for advice on writing correct and effective sentences.

PROOFREADING
See Appendix, Part C, for proofreading tips.

Ethics Notes in every chapter remind you to think about the ethical implications of your writing and communication choices, encouraging the highest standards of professionalism.

ETHICS NOTE

PULLING YOUR WEIGHT ON COLLABORATIVE PROJECTS

Collaboration involves an ethical dimension. If you work hard and well, you help the other members of the team. If you don't, you hurt them.

You can't be held responsible for knowing and doing everything, and sometimes unexpected problems arise in other courses or in your private life that prevent you from participating as actively and effectively as you otherwise could. When problems occur, inform the other team members as soon as possible. For instance, call the team leader as soon as you realize you will have to miss a meeting. Be honest about what happened. Suggest ways you might make up for missing a task. If you communicate clearly, the other team members are likely to cooperate with you.

If you are a member of a team that includes someone who is not participating fully, keep records of your attempts to get in touch with that person. When you do make contact, you owe it to that person to try to find out what the problem is and suggest ways to resolve it. Your goal is to treat that person fairly and to help him or her do better work, so that the team will function more smoothly and more effectively.

Writer's Checklists at the end of most chapters summarize important concepts and act as handy reminders as you draft and revise your work.

WRITER'S CHECKLIST

Following is a checklist for analyzing your audience and purpose. Remember that your document might be read by one person, several people, a large group, or several groups with various needs.

☐ Did you fill out an audience profile sheet for your primary and secondary audiences? *(p. 91)*

In analyzing your audience, did you consider the following questions about each of your most important readers:

☐ What is your reader's educational background? *(p. 93)*

☐ What is your reader's professional experience? *(p. 93)*

☐ What is your reader's job responsibility? *(p. 93)*

☐ economic? *(p. 101)*

☐ social? *(p. 101)*

☐ religious? *(p. 101)*

☐ educational? *(p. 102)*

☐ technological? *(p. 102)*

☐ linguistic? *(p. 102)*

In planning to write for an audience from another culture, did you consider other cultural variables:

☐ focus on individuals or groups? *(p. 102)*

☐ distance between business life and private life? *(p. 103)*

Brief Contents

Contents

4   Writing Collaboratively   62

Part 2 Planning the Document   *87*

5   Analyzing Your Audience and Purpose   *88*

Part 3 Developing and Testing the Verbal and Visual Information   **175**

8   Communicating Persuasively   *176*

9   Emphasizing Important Information *197*

10   Writing Correct and Effective Sentences *218*

Part 4 Learning Important Applications *371*

14 Corresponding in Print and Online *372*

15 Applying for a Job *399*

16 Writing Proposals   *436*

17 Writing Informational Reports   *462*

21 Making Oral Presentations   *593*

Understanding the Role of Oral Presentations   *594*

Understanding the Process of Preparing and Delivering an Oral Presentation   *595*

Preparing the Presentation   *595*

Delivering the Presentation   *616*

Answering Questions After a Presentation   *620*

Sample Evaluation Form   *620*

APPENDIX Reference Handbook *624*

Part 1

Understanding the Technical Communication Environment

Introduction to Technical Communication

THIS TEXTBOOK EXPLORES how people in the working world find, create, and deliver technical information. Even if you do not plan on becoming a *technical communicator* (a person whose main job is to produce documents such as manuals, reports, and websites), you will often find yourself creating documents on your own, participating in teams that create them, and contributing technical information to others who use and create them. The purpose of *Technical Communication* is to help you learn the skills you need to communicate more effectively and more efficiently in your professional life.

What Is Technical Communication?

Technical information is frequently communicated through documents such as proposals, emails, reports, podcasts, computer help files, blogs, and wikis. Although these documents are a key component of technical communication, so too is the *process*: writing and reading tweets and text messages, for example, or participating in videoconference exchanges with colleagues. Technical communication encompasses a set of *activities* that people do to discover, shape, and transmit information.

When you produce technical communication, you use the four basic communication modes—listening, speaking, reading, and writing—to analyze a problem, find and evaluate evidence, and draw conclusions. These are the same skills and processes you use when you write in college, and the principles you have studied in your earlier writing courses apply to technical communication. The biggest difference between technical communication and the other kinds of writing you have done is that technical communication has a somewhat different focus on *purpose* and *audience*.

Four Basic Modes of Communication

| Listening | Speaking | Reading | Writing |

UNDERSTANDING PURPOSE

Technical communication begins with identifying a problem and thinking about how to solve it. Because of the variety of problems and solutions in the working world, people communicate technical information for a number of *purposes*, many of which fall into one of the two categories:

- **Communication that helps others learn about a subject, carry out a task, or make a decision.** For instance, administrators with the International Trade Administration might hire a media production company to make

FIGURE 1.1
A Communication
That Helps Others
Carry Out a Task
The purpose of this online
video at Export.gov is to help
businesses learn how to make
sales in a foreign market.
U.S. Commercial Service.

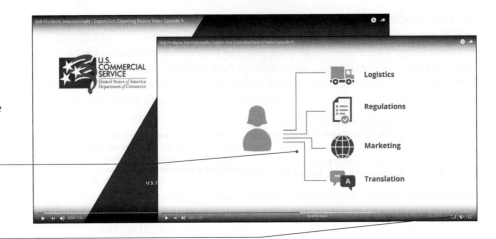

The visual in the video lists
the four key elements that the
voiceover discusses in greater
detail.

The closed captioning aids
the hearing impaired.

a video that explains to companies how to make sales in a foreign market. The president of a manufacturing company might write an article in the company newsletter to explain to employees why the management decided to phase out production of one of the company's products. The board of directors of a community-service organization might produce a grant proposal to submit to a philanthropic organization in hopes of being awarded a grant. Figure 1.1 shows a screen capture from a video that explains how to sell products internationally.

- **Communication that reinforces or changes attitudes and motivates readers to take action.** A wind-energy company might create a website with videos and text intended to show that building wind turbines off the coast of a tourist destination would have many benefits and few risks. A property owners' association might create a website to make the opposite argument: that the wind turbines would have few benefits but many risks. In each of these two cases, the purpose of communicating the information is to persuade people to accept a point of view and encourage them to act—perhaps to contact their elected representatives and present their views about this public-policy issue. Figure 1.2 shows an excerpt from a website that promotes the building of wind turbines off the coast of Massachusetts.

UNDERSTANDING AUDIENCE

When you communicate in the workplace, you have not only a clear purpose—what you want to achieve—but also a clearly defined *audience*—one or more people who are going to read the document, attend the oral presentation, visit the website, or view the video you produce. Sometimes audience members share the same purpose, but not always. It's possible, even likely, that a piece of technical communication will have multiple audiences with different purposes.

BENEFITS OF VOTING

BENEFITS FOR VOTERS

Voting is connected with a host of positive benefits for the individual voter. Compared to non-voters, voters are more likely to volunteer, contact their elected officials, and stay informed about local affairs. Voting is associated with:

Active Citizenship
Registered voters are more likely to engage in civic and political activities than those who are not registered. They are also more likely to talk to elected officials and be an advocate for themselves and their families. Voters are more likely to be active and engaged citizens who connect with their neighbors and participate in community activities.

Social Connections
Voters tend to have stronger social connections, leading to a greater quality of life and longevity. Census surveys suggest that registered voters are, compared to non-voters, more strongly connected with their neighbors and family members. They are more likely to discuss political issues with family or do favors for their neighbors.[1]

Personal Agency
Voters have the satisfaction of knowing that they have expressed their opinions. Voting is a form of personal empowerment that gives you the opportunity to voice your opinion on issues that matter to you, your family, and your community.

Other Benefits
- **Better health outcomes.** Voters have higher levels of self-reported health and voting could also potentially boost mental health.[2]
- **Reduced unemployment.** Voting and other forms of civic engagement have been tied to lower unemployment rates.[3]
- **Lower recidivism rates.** Ex-offenders who have their civil rights restored are less likely to return to prison. The Florida Parole Commission reported that over a two year period ex-offenders who had their voting rights restored were three times less likely to end up back in custody.[4]

> Even if the winner of an election was not their preferred choice, "people are happier with the outcome and they feel more in control of their lives, if they voted."
>
> —*Psychologist Marc Zimmerman, professor at the University of Michigan's School of Health*

[1] CIRCLE. "Civic Engagement among Registered Citizens and Non-Registered Eligible Citizens," http://www.civicyouth.org/civic-engagement-among-registered-voters-and-non-registered-eligible-citizens/
[2] Huffington Post. "Voting and Health: Five Reasons Why It's Good For You." http://www.huffingtonpost.com/2012/11/06/voting-good-for-health-election-day_n_2078569.html
[3] NCoC. *Civic Health and Unemployment.* http://www.ncoc.net/unemployment
[4] Florida Parole Commission. "Status Update: Restoration of Civil Rights Cases Granted 2009 and 2010," https://fpc.state.fl.us/docs/reports/2009-2010ClemencyReport.pdf

Nonprofit VOTE
www.nonprofitvote.org

FIGURE 1.2

A Communication That Aims to Change Attitudes

The purpose of this flyer is to help not-for-profit agencies encourage their clients to view voting as a positive civic obligation with many benefits. Nonprofit.org.

The color scheme is congruent with the message, and the color combination of red, white, and blue also creates strong contrast, contributing to readability.

The flyer uses headings and subheadings to emphasize the benefits of voting.

The flyer uses a pull quote to highlight a compelling point from an expert.

In most of your previous academic writing, your audience has been your instructor, and your purpose has been to show your instructor that you have mastered some body of information or skill. Typically, you have not tried to create new knowledge or motivate the reader to take a particular action—except to give you an "A" for that assignment.

By contrast, in technical communication, your audience will likely include peers and supervisors in your company, as well as people outside your company.

For example, suppose you are a public-health scientist working for a federal agency. You and your colleagues just completed a study showing that, for most adults, moderate exercise provides as much health benefit as strenuous exercise. After participating in numerous meetings with your colleagues and after drafting, critiquing, and revising many drafts, you produce four different documents:

- a journal article for other scientists
- a press release to distribute to popular print and online publications
- an infographic for use in doctors' offices
- an animated blog post for your agency to share on social media

In each of these documents, you present the key information in a different way to meet the needs of a particular audience.

Why Technical Communication Skills Are Important in Your Career

Many college students believe that the most important courses they take are those in their major. Some biology majors think, for example, that if they just take that advanced course in genetic analysis, employers will conclude that they are prepared to do more advanced projects and therefore will hire them.

But knowledge in a particular field is not the only thing employers are looking for. It's not even the most important skill or ability. Surveys over the past several decades have shown consistently that employers want to hire people who can communicate. Look at it this way: when employers hire a biologist, they want a person who can communicate effectively about biology. When they hire a civil engineer, they want a person who can communicate effectively about civil engineering.

A 2013 survey of 500 business executives found that almost half—44 percent—think that recent hires are weak in soft skills (including communication and collaboration), whereas only 22 percent think recent hires are weak in technical skills (Adecco Staffing, 2013). According to another 2013 survey, by the Workforce Solutions Group at St. Louis Community College, more than 60 percent of employers believe that job seekers are weak in communication and interpersonal skills. This figure is up 10 percentage points from 2011 (*Time*, 2013).

Job Outlook 2019, a report produced by the National Association of Colleges and Employers, found that written communication skills, problem-solving skills, and teamwork skills top the list of skills employers seek on a job candidate's resume. The report's main data point about written communication skills is that 80 percent of employers consider it to be a top priority (National Association, 2019, p. 30). Here are the top ten skills and attributes, according to employers, and the percentage of respondents in the study who ranked the skills and attributes:

SKILL OR ATTRIBUTE	PERCENTAGE
Communication skills (written)	82.0
Problem-solving skills	80.9
Ability to work in a team	78.7
Initiative	74.2
Analytical/quantitative skills	71.9
Strong work ethic	70.8
Communication skills (verbal)	67.4
Leadership	67.4
Detail oriented	59.6
Technical skills	59.6

Most of these skills relate to the technical communication process introduced in this chapter and described in greater detail throughout the book.

A study of more than 400 employers suggests that technical communication is even more important for professionals now than it ever has been in the past (Hart Research Associates, 2015, pp. 1–4). Over 80 percent of the employers surveyed said that their top priority in hiring new employees is finding people with excellent writing, speaking, and problem-solving skills. They also emphasized the ability to work in groups and make ethical decisions. Some reports estimate that large companies spend nearly $20 million annually to train employees (The Industry Report, 2018, p. 20). Would companies rather not have to spend that money on writing training? Yes.

You're going to be producing and contributing to a lot of technical documents. The facts of life in the working world are simple: the better you communicate, the more valuable you are. This textbook can help you learn and practice the skills that will make you a better communicator.

The Challenges of Producing Technical Communication

One of the most challenging activities you will engage in as a professional is communicating your ideas to audiences. Why? Because communication is a higher-order skill that involves many complex factors.

The good news is that there are ways to think about these complex factors, to think *through* them, that will help you communicate better. No matter what document you produce or contribute to, you need to begin by considering five sets of factors.

AUDIENCE-RELATED FACTORS

What problem or problems are your audience trying to solve? Does your audience know enough about your subject to understand a detailed discussion, or do you need to limit the scope, the amount of technical detail, or the type of graphics you use? Does your audience already have certain attitudes or expectations about your subject that you wish to reinforce or change? Does your audience speak English well, or should you present the information in more than one language? Does your audience share your cultural assumptions about such matters as how to organize and interpret documents, or do you need to adjust your writing approach to match a different set of assumptions? Does your audience include people with disabilities (of vision, hearing, movement, or cognitive ability) who have requirements you need to meet?

PURPOSE-RELATED FACTORS

Before you can write, you need to determine your purpose: what do you want your audience to know or believe or do after having read your document? Do you have multiple purposes? If so, is one more important than the others? Although much technical communication is intended to help people perform tasks, such as configuring privacy settings in a social-media environment, many organizations large and small devote significant communication resources to the increasingly vital purpose of branding: creating an image that helps customers distinguish the company from competitors. Most companies now employ community specialists as technical communicators to coordinate the organization's day-to-day online presence and its social-media campaigns. These specialists publicize new products and initiatives and respond to questions and new developments. They also manage all of the organization's documents—from tweets to blog posts to Facebook fan pages and company-sponsored discussion forums.

SETTING-RELATED FACTORS

What is the situation surrounding the problem you are trying to solve? Is there a lot at stake in the situation, such as the budget for a project, or is your document a more routine communication, such as technical notes for a software update? What is the context in which your audience will use your document? Will the ways in which they use it—or the physical or digital environment in which they use it—affect how you write? Will the document be used in a socially or politically charged setting? Does the setting include established norms of ethical behavior? Is the setting formal or informal? Settings can have a great deal of influence over how audiences think about and use technical communication.

DOCUMENT-RELATED FACTORS

What type of content will the document include? How will the content aid problem solving? Does your subject dictate what kind of document (such as a report or a blog post) you choose to write? Does your subject dictate what medium (print or digital) you choose for your document? Do you need to provide audiences with content in more than one medium? If you're using a document template, how should you modify it for your audiences and purposes? Does the application call for a particular writing style or level of formality? (For the sake of convenience, we will use the word *document* throughout this book to refer to all forms of technical communication, from written documents to oral presentations and online forms, such as podcasts and wikis.)

PROCESS-RELATED FACTORS

What process will you use to produce the document? Is there an established process to support the work, or do you need to create a new one? Do you have sufficient time for planning tasks, such as analyzing your audience and purpose, choosing writing tools, and researching and reading background information? Does your budget limit the number of people you can enlist to help you or limit the size or shape of the document? Does your schedule limit how much information you can include in the document? Does your schedule limit the type or amount of document testing you can do? Will the document require updating or maintenance?

Because all these factors interact in complicated ways, every technical document you create involves a compromise. If you are writing a set of printed instructions for installing a water heater and you want those instructions to be easily understood by people who speak only Spanish, you will need more time and a bigger budget to have the document translated, and it will be longer and thus a little bit harder to use, for both English and Spanish speakers. You might need to save money by using smaller type, smaller pages, and cheaper paper, and you might not be able to afford to print the instructions in full color. In technical communication, you do the best you can with your resources of time, information, and money. The more carefully you think through your options, the better able you will be to use your resources wisely and make a document that will get the job done.

Characteristics of a Technical Document

Technical communication shares certain general characteristics with other types of communication. For example, both technical communication and journalism report data and information in an organized and efficient manner. Technical communication, however, isn't journalism or investigative reporting. It's communication produced in workplace settings to help people in both professional and personal contexts accomplish tasks.

Almost every technical document that gets the job done has six major characteristics:

- **It addresses particular readers.** Knowing who the readers are, what they understand about the subject, how well they speak a particular language, and how they will use the document will help you decide what kind of document to write, how to structure it, how much detail to include, and what sentence style and vocabulary to use.

- **It helps readers solve problems.** For instance, you might produce a video that explains to your company's employees how to select their employee benefits, or you might write a document spelling out the company's policy on using social media in the workplace.

- **It reflects the organization's goals and culture.** For example, a state government department that oversees vocational-education programs submits an annual report to the state legislature in an effort to secure continued funding, as well as a lot of technical information to the public in an effort to educate its audience. Although the connection may not be obvious, technical documents also reflect the organization's culture. For example, many organizations encourage their employees to blog about their areas of expertise to create a positive image of the organization.

- **It is produced collaboratively.** No one person has all the information, skills, or time needed to create a large document. You will work with subject-matter experts—the various technical professionals—to create a better document than you could have made working alone. You will routinely post questions to networks of friends and associates—both inside and outside your own organization—to get answers to technical questions.

- **It uses design to increase readability.** Technical communicators use design features—such as typography, spacing, and color—to make a document not only more attractive but also more usable, so that it creates a positive impression and is easy to navigate and understand.

- **It consists of words or images or both.** Images—both static and moving—can make a document more interesting and appealing to readers and can help the writer communicate and reinforce difficult concepts, communicate instructions and descriptions of objects and processes, communicate large amounts of quantifiable data, and communicate with nonnative speakers.

Although most technical documents share the characteristics listed above, their quality can vary widely. How can you recognize a well-made document? Consider the characteristics described in the Guidelines box on page 11.

◢
GUIDELINES Measures of Excellence
in Technical Documents

Several key elements help to distinguish excellent technical documents:

▶ **Honesty.** The most important measure of excellence in a technical document is
honesty. You need to tell the truth and not mislead the reader, not only because it
is the right thing to do but also because readers can get hurt if you are dishonest.
Also, if you are dishonest, you and your organization could face serious
legal charges. If a court finds that your document's failure to provide honest,
appropriate information caused a substantial injury or loss, your organization
might have to pay millions of dollars.

▶ **Clarity.** Your goal is to produce a document that conveys a single meaning the
reader can understand easily. An unclear technical document can be dangerous.
A carelessly drafted building code, for example, could tempt contractors to use
inferior materials or techniques. In addition, an unclear technical document is
expensive. Handling a telephone call to a customer-support center costs $5–10
for a simple question but about $20–45 for a more complicated problem — and
about a third of the calls are the more expensive kind (Carlaw, 2010). Clear
technical communication in a product's documentation (its user instructions) can
greatly reduce the number and length of such calls.

▶ **Accuracy.** A slight inaccuracy can confuse and annoy your readers; a major
inaccuracy can be dangerous and expensive. In another sense, accuracy is a
question of ethics. Technical documents must be as objective and unbiased as
you can make them. If readers suspect that you are slanting information — by
overstating or omitting facts — they will doubt the validity of the entire document.

▶ **Comprehensiveness.** A good technical document provides all the information
readers need. It describes the background so that readers unfamiliar with the
subject can understand it. It contains sufficient detail so that readers can follow
the discussion and carry out any required tasks. It refers to supporting materials
clearly or includes them as attachments. A comprehensive document provides
readers with a complete, self-contained discussion that enables them to use the
information safely, effectively, and efficiently.

▶ **Accessibility.** A good technical document can be accessed and used by
people with varying physical abilities. Although accessibility is important in
all documents, it is of particular concern with online materials. For example,
instructional videos should include closed captioning for the visually impaired.
Documents designed with accessibility in mind tend to function better for
everyone. For more about designing accessible documents, see Chapter 11.

▶ **Usability.** In technical communication, *usability* measures how successfully a
document achieves its purposes and meets its audience's needs. For more about
testing for usability, see Chapter 13.

▶ **Conciseness.** A document must be concise enough to be useful to a busy
reader. You can shorten most writing by 10 to 20 percent simply by eliminating
unnecessary phrases, choosing shorter words, and using economical grammatical
forms. Your job is to figure out how to convey a lot of information economically.

(*continued*)

▸ **Professional appearance.** You start to communicate before anyone reads the first word of the document. If the document looks neat and professional, readers will form a positive impression of it and of you. Your document should adhere to the format standards of your organization or your professional field, and it should be well designed. For example, a letter should follow one of the traditional letter formats and have generous margins.

▸ **Correctness.** A correct document is one that adheres to the conventions of grammar, punctuation, spelling, mechanics, and usage. Sometimes, incorrect writing can confuse readers or even make your writing inaccurate. The more typical problem, however, is that incorrect writing makes you look unprofessional. If your writing is full of errors, readers will wonder if you were also careless in gathering, analyzing, and presenting the technical information. If readers doubt your professionalism, they will be less likely to accept your conclusions or follow your recommendations.

Skills and Qualities Shared by Successful Workplace Communicators

People who are good at communicating in the workplace share a number of skills. Three of them relate to the problem-solving skills you have been honing in school and will continue to develop in your career:

- **Ability to perform research.** Successful communicators know how to perform primary research (discovering new information through experiments, observations, interviews, surveys, and calculations) and secondary research (finding existing information by reading what others have written or said). Successful communicators seek out information from people who *use* the products and services, not just from the manufacturers. Therefore, although successful communicators would visit the Toyota website to learn about the technical specifications of a Prius if they wanted to find out what it was like to drive, own, or repair a Prius, they would be sure to search the internet for information from experts not associated with Toyota, as well as *user-generated content*: for example, information from owners presented in discussion forums and blogs.

- **Ability to analyze information.** Successful communicators know how to identify the best information—most accurate, relevant, recent, and unbiased—and then figure out how it can help them in understanding a problem and ways to solve it. Successful communicators know how to sift through mountains of data, identifying relationships among apparently unrelated facts. They know how to evaluate a situation, look at it from other people's perspectives, and zero in on the most important issues.

- **Ability to speak and write clearly.** Successful communicators know how to express themselves clearly and simply, both to audiences that know a lot about the subject and to audiences that do not. They take care to revise, edit, and proofread their documents so that the documents present accurate information, are easy to read, and make a professional impression. And they know how to produce different types of documents, from tweets to memos to presentations.

In addition to the skills just described, successful workplace communicators have several qualities that relate to professional attitudes and work habits. These qualities are outlined in the following Guidelines box.

GUIDELINES Communicating Professionally

When you communicate in the workplace, model the behavior of successful professionals.

▶ **Be honest.** Successful communicators tell the truth. They don't promise what they know they can't deliver, and they don't bend facts. When they make mistakes, they admit them and work harder to solve the problem.

▶ **Be willing to learn.** Successful communicators know that they don't know everything — not about what they studied in college, what their company does, or how to write and speak. Every professional is a lifelong learner.

▶ **Display emotional intelligence.** Successful communicators understand their own emotions and those of others. Because they can read people — through body language, facial expression, gestures, and words — they can work effectively in teams, helping to minimize interpersonal conflict and encouraging others to do their best work.

▶ **Be generous.** Successful communicators reply to requests for information, and they share information willingly. (Of course, they don't share confidential information, such as trade secrets, information about new products being developed, or personal information about colleagues.)

▶ **Monitor the best information.** Successful communicators seek out opinions from others. They monitor the best online sources for new approaches that can spark their own ideas. They use searching and filtering tools to help them stay on top of the torrent of new information on the internet. They know how to use social media and can represent their organization online.

▶ **Be self-disciplined.** Successful communicators are well organized and diligent. They finish what they start, and they always do their best on any document, from the least important text message to the most important report.

▶ **Prioritize and respond quickly.** Successful communicators know that the world doesn't always conform to their own schedules. Because social media never sleeps, communicators sometimes need to put their current projects aside in order to respond immediately to a problem or request. And even though speed is important, they know that quality is, too; therefore, they make sure every document is fully professional before it goes out.

DOCUMENT ANALYSIS ACTIVITY

Analyzing a Technical Document

This two-page publication was produced by the Centers for Disease Control and Prevention (CDC). The following questions ask you to think about the various factors that contributed to the content and design of this document.

1. Who is the audience for this document? Where do you think the authors intended for the document to be displayed?

2. With which of the two general purposes does this document more closely align? Does it help others to learn about a subject, carry out a task, or make a decision, or does it reinforce or change attitudes and motivate readers to take action? If the document appears to have some combination of these purposes, which seems to be the most important? How can you tell?

Information from Centers for Disease Control and Prevention, 2016: www.cdc.gov/physicalactivity/downloads/healthy-strong-america.pdf.

Analyzing a Technical Document (*continued*)

PHYSICAL ACTIVITY SAVES LIVES AND PROTECTS HEALTH

1 IN 10 **premature deaths** could be prevented by getting enough physical activity.

It could also prevent:

1 IN 8
cases of
breast cancer

1 IN 8
cases of
colorectal cancer

1 IN 12
cases of
diabetes

1 IN 15
cases of
heart disease

Physical activity is the closest thing we have to a wonder drug.

Dr. Tom Frieden, CDC Director

INVESTING IN PHYSICAL ACTIVITY MAKES SENSE

BENEFITS FOR CHILDREN
- Improves aerobic fitness
- Improves muscular fitness
- Improves bone health
- Promotes favorable body composition
- Improves attention and some measures of academic performance (with school physical activity programs)

BENEFITS FOR ADULTS
- Lowers risk of high blood pressure
- Lowers risk of stroke
- Improves aerobic fitness
- Improves mental health
- Improves cognitive function
- Reduces arthritis symptoms
- Prevents weight gain

BENEFITS FOR HEALTHY AGING
- Reduces risk of falling
- Improves balance
- Improves joint mobility
- Extends years of active life
- Helps prevent weak bones and muscle loss
- Delays onset of cognitive decline

PHYSICAL ACTIVITY BENEFITS COMMUNITIES

ECONOMIC
Building active and walkable communities can help:
- Increase levels of retail economic activity and employment
- Increase property values
- Support neighborhood revitalization
- Reduce health care costs

SAFETY
Walkable communities can improve safety for people who walk, ride bicycles, and drive.

WORKFORCE
Physically active people tend to take fewer sick days.

CDC
U.S. Department of Health and Human Services
Centers for Disease Control and Prevention

FOR MORE INFORMATION PLEASE VISIT:
Division of Nutrition, Physical Activity, and Obesity
www.cdc.gov/nccdphp/dnpao

266093-C

3. What problem is the document addressing? Does the document provide clear solutions?

4. Has the document been designed to facilitate usability? How does it use words and images to communicate information? Does it create a positive impression? Is it easy to navigate and understand? Does it address readers with various physical abilities?

5. Is the document concise? How well does it communicate a lot of information in an economical manner? Can busy readers scan it and grasp the main point?

6. Does the document appear professional? Why or why not?

EXERCISES

1. Form small groups and study the home page of your college or university's website. Focus on three measures of excellence in technical communication: clarity, accessibility, and professional appearance. How effectively does the home page meet each of these measures of excellence? Be prepared to share your findings with the class.

2. Locate an owner's manual for a consumer product, such as a coffee maker, bicycle, or hair dryer. In a memo to your instructor, discuss at least three decisions the writers and designers of the manual appear to have made to address audience-related factors, purpose-related factors, setting-related factors, document-related factors, or process-related factors. For instance, if the manual is printed only in English, the writers and designers presumably decided either that it was not necessary to create versions in other languages or that they didn't have the resources to do so. For more about memos, see Ch. 14, p. 386.

3. Using a job site such as Indeed.com or Monster.com, locate three job ads for people in your academic major. In each ad, identify references to writing and communication skills, and then identify references to professional attitudes and work habits. Be prepared to share your findings with the class.

CASE 1: Using the Measures of Excellence in Evaluating a Résumé

Your technical-communication instructor is planning to invite guest speakers to deliver presentations to the class on various topics throughout the semester, and she has asked you to work with one of them to tailor his job-application presentation to the "Measures of Excellence" discussed in this chapter. If your instructor has assigned it, go to Achieve to access relevant documents and complete your writing assignment.

Understanding Ethical and Legal Considerations

ETHICAL AND LEGAL ISSUES are all around you in your work life. If you look at the website of any bike manufacturer, for example, you will see that bicyclists are always shown wearing helmets. Is this because bike manufacturers care about safety? Certainly. But bike makers also care about product liability. If a company website showed cyclists without helmets, an injured cyclist might sue, claiming that the company was suggesting it is safe to ride without a helmet.

Ethical and legal pitfalls lurk in the words and graphics of many kinds of documents. In producing a proposal, you might be tempted to exaggerate or lie about your organization's past accomplishments, pad the résumés of the project personnel, list as project personnel some workers who will not be contributing to the project, or present an unrealistically short work schedule. In drafting product information, you might feel pressured to exaggerate the quality of the products shown in catalogs or manuals or to downplay the hazards of using those products. In creating graphics, you might be asked to hide an item's weaknesses by manipulating a photo of a product.

One thing is certain: there are many serious ethical and legal issues related to technical communication, and all professionals need a basic understanding of them. Keep in mind that decisions and actions can be legal but not ethical, or vice versa. You will need to think carefully about both aspects of any technical communication you create and address any conflicts that arise.

A Brief Introduction to Ethics

Ethics is the study of the principles of conduct that apply to an individual or a group. For some people, ethics is a matter of intuition—what their gut feelings tell them about the rightness or wrongness of an act. Others see ethics in terms of their own religion or the Golden Rule: treat others as you would like them to treat you. Ethicist Manuel G. Velasquez outlines four moral standards that are useful in thinking about ethical dilemmas (2011):

- **Rights.** This standard concerns individuals' basic needs and welfare. Everyone agrees, for example, that people have a right to a reasonably safe workplace. When we buy a product, we have a right to expect that the information that accompanies it is honest and clear. However, not everything that is desirable is necessarily a right. For example, in some countries, high-quality health care is considered a right. That is, the government is required to provide it, regardless of whether a person can afford to pay for it. In other countries, health care is not considered a right.

- **Justice.** This standard concerns how the costs and benefits of an action or a policy are distributed among a group. For example, the cost of maintaining a high-speed broadband infrastructure should be borne, in part, by people who use it. However, because everyone benefits from the infrastructure, the standard of justice suggests that general funds can also be used to pay for it. Another example: justice requires that people doing the same job receive the same pay, regardless of gender or race.

- **Utility.** This standard concerns the positive and negative effects that an action or a policy has, will have, or might have on others. For example, if a company is considering closing a plant, the company's leaders should consider not only the money they would save but also the financial hardship of laid-off workers and the economic effects on the community. One tricky issue in thinking about utility is figuring out the time frame to examine. An action such as laying off employees can have one effect in the short run—improving the company's quarterly balance sheet—and a very different effect in the long run—hurting the company's productivity or the quality of its products.

- **Care.** This standard concerns the relationships we have with other individuals. We owe care and consideration to all people, but we have greater responsibilities to people in our families, our workplaces, and our communities. The closer a person is to us, the greater care we owe that person. Therefore, we have greater obligations to members of our family than we do to others in our community.

Although these standards provide a vocabulary for thinking about how to resolve ethical conflicts, they are imprecise and often conflict with each other. Therefore, they cannot provide a systematic method of resolving ethical conflicts. Take the case of a job opportunity in your company. You are a member of the committee that will recommend which of six applicants to hire to redesign a customer portal that hosts tutorials and documentation. One of the six is a friend of yours who has been unable to secure a professional job since graduating from college two years ago. She therefore does not have as much website design experience as the other five candidates. However, she is enthusiastic about gaining experience in this particular field—and eager to start paying off her student loans.

How can the four standards help you think through the situation? According to the *rights* standard, lobbying for your friend or against the other applicants would be wrong because all applicants have an ethical right to an evaluation process that considers only their qualifications to do the job. Looking at the situation from the perspective of *justice* yields the same conclusion: it would be wrong to favor your friend. From the perspective of *utility*, lobbying for your friend would probably not be in the best interests of the organization, although it might be in your friend's best interests. Only according to the *care* standard does lobbying for your friend seem reasonable.

As you think about this case, you have to consider a related question: should you tell the other people on the hiring committee that one of the applicants is your friend? Yes, because they have a right to know about your personal relationship so that they can better evaluate your contributions to the discussion. You might also offer to *recuse* yourself (that is, not participate in the discussion of this position), leaving it to the other committee members to decide whether your friendship with a candidate represents a conflict of interest.

Here is one more complication in thinking about this case: let's say your friend is one of the top two candidates for the job. In your committee, which is made up of seven members, three vote for your friend, but four vote for the other candidate, who already has a very good job. She is a young, highly skilled employee with a degree from a prestigious university. In other words, she is likely to be very successful in the working world, regardless of whether she is offered this particular job. Should the fact that your friend has yet to start her own career affect your thinking about this problem? Some people would say no: the job should be offered to the most qualified applicant. Others would say yes: society does not adequately provide for its less-fortunate members, and because your friend needs the job more and is almost as qualified as the other top applicant, she should get the offer. In other words, some people would focus on the narrow, technical question of determining the best candidate for the job, whereas others would see a much broader social question involving human rights.

Most people do not explore the conflict among rights, justice, utility, and care when they confront a serious ethical dilemma; instead, they simply do what they think is right. Perhaps this is good news. However, the depth of ethical thinking varies dramatically from one person to another, and the consequences of superficial ethical thinking can be profound. For these reasons, ethicists have described a general set of principles that can help people organize their thinking about the role of ethics within an organizational context. These principles form a web of rights and obligations that connect an employee, an organization, and the world in which the organization is situated.

For example, in exchange for their labor, employees enjoy three basic rights: fair wages, safe and healthy working conditions, and due process in the handling of such matters as promotions, salary increases, and firing. Although there is still serious debate about the details of employee rights, such as whether employees have the right to freedom from surreptitious surveillance and unreasonable searches in drug investigations, the debate almost always concerns the extent of employees' rights, not the existence of the basic rights themselves. For instance, ethicists disagree about whether hiring undercover investigators to identify drug users at a job site is an unwarranted intrusion on employees' rights, but there is no debate about employees' right to freedom from unwarranted intrusion.

Your Ethical Obligations

In addition to enjoying rights, an employee assumes obligations, which can form a clear and reasonable framework for discussing the ethics of technical communication. The following discussion outlines three sets of obligations that you have as an employee: to your employer, to the public, and to the environment.

OBLIGATIONS TO YOUR EMPLOYER

You are hired to further your employer's legitimate aims and to refrain from any activities that run counter to those aims. Specifically, you have the following obligations:

- **Competence and diligence.** *Competence* refers to your skills; you should have the training and experience to do the job adequately. *Diligence* simply means working hard. Unfortunately, a survey of over 1,000 workers revealed that more than half of employees waste up to one hour of their eight-hour day surfing the web, socializing with co-workers, and doing other tasks unrelated to their jobs (Salary.com, 2013).

- **Generosity.** Although *generosity* might sound like an unusual obligation, you are obligated to help your co-workers and stakeholders outside your organization by sharing your knowledge and expertise. What this means is that if you are asked to respond to appropriate questions or provide recommendations on some aspect of your organization's work, you should do so. If a customer or supplier contacts you, make the time to respond helpfully. Generosity shows professionalism and furthers your organization's goals.

- **Honesty and candor.** You should not steal from your employer. Stealing includes such practices as embezzlement, "borrowing" office supplies, and padding expense accounts. *Candor* means truthfulness; you should report to your employer problems that might threaten the quality or safety of the organization's product or service.

Issues of honesty and candor include what Sigma Xi, the Scientific Research Society, calls trimming, cooking, and forging (Sigma Xi, 2000, p. 11). *Trimming* is the smoothing of irregularities to make research data look extremely accurate and precise. *Cooking* is retaining only those results that fit the theory and discarding the others. And *forging* is inventing some or all of the data or even reporting experiments that were never performed. In carrying out research, employees must resist any pressure to report only positive findings.

- **Confidentiality.** You should not divulge company business outside of the company. If a competitor finds out that your company is planning to introduce a new product, it might introduce its own version of that product, robbing your company of its competitive advantage. Many other kinds of privileged information—such as information on quality-control problems, personnel matters, relocation or expansion plans, and financial restructuring—also could be used against the company. A well-known confidentiality problem involves *insider information*: an employee who knows about a development that will increase (or decrease) the value of the company's stock, for example, buys (or sells) the stock before the information is made public, thus unfairly—and illegally—reaping a profit (or avoiding a loss).

- **Loyalty.** You should act in the employer's interest, not in your own. Therefore, it is unethical to invest heavily in a competitor's stock, because that could jeopardize your objectivity and judgment. For the same reason, it is unethical (and illegal) to accept bribes or kickbacks. It is unethical to devote considerable time to moonlighting (performing an outside job, such as private consulting), because the outside job could lead to a conflict of interest and because the heavy workload could make you less productive in your primary position. However, you do not owe your employer absolute loyalty; if your employer is acting unethically, you have an obligation to try to change that behavior—even, if necessary, by blowing the whistle.

For more about whistle-blowing, see The Role of Corporate Culture in Ethical and Legal Conduct on page 30.

OBLIGATIONS TO THE PUBLIC

Every organization that offers products or provides services is obligated to treat its customers fairly. As a representative of an organization, and especially as an employee communicating technical information, you will frequently confront ethical questions.

In general, an organization is acting ethically if its product or service is both *safe* and *effective*. The product or service must not injure or harm the consumer, and it must fulfill its promised function. However, these commonsense principles provide little guidance in dealing with complicated ethical problems that arise routinely.

The U.S. Consumer Product Safety Commission (2017) estimates that around 42,000 deaths and more than 16 million injuries occurred in the United States in a single year because of consumer products—not counting automobiles and medications. Even more common, of course, are product and service failures: products or services don't do what they are supposed to do, products are difficult to assemble or operate, they break down, or they require more expensive maintenance than the product information indicates.

Who is responsible for injuries and product failures: the company that provides the product or service or the consumer who purchases it? In individual cases, blame is sometimes easy enough to determine. A person who operates a chainsaw without reading the safety information and without seeking any instruction in how to use it is to blame for any injuries caused by the normal operation of the saw. But a manufacturer that knows that the chain on the saw is liable to break under certain circumstances and fails to remedy this problem or warn the consumer is responsible for any resulting accidents.

Unfortunately, these principles do not outline a rational theory that can help companies understand how to act ethically in fulfilling their obligations to the public. Today, most court rulings are based on the premise that the manufacturer knows more about its products than the consumer does and therefore has a greater responsibility to make sure the products comply with all of the manufacturer's claims and are safe. Therefore, in designing, manufacturing, testing, and communicating about a product, the manufacturer has to make sure the product will be safe and effective when used according to the instructions. However, the manufacturer is not liable when something goes wrong that it could not have been foreseen or prevented.

OBLIGATIONS TO THE ENVIRONMENT

One of the most important lessons we have learned in recent decades is that we are polluting and depleting our limited natural resources at an unacceptably high rate. Our excessive use of fossil fuels not only deprives future generations of them but also causes possibly irreversible pollution problems, such as climate change. Everyone—government, businesses, and individuals—must work to preserve the environment to ensure the survival not only of our own species but also of the other species with which we share the planet.

But what does this have to do with you? In your daily work, you probably do not cause pollution or deplete the environment in any extraordinary way. Yet you will often know how your organization's actions affect the environment. For example, if you work for a manufacturing company, you might be aware of the environmental effects of making or using your company's products. Or you might help write an environmental impact statement.

As communicators, we should treat every actual or potential occurrence of environmental damage seriously. We should alert our supervisors to the situation and work with them to try to reduce the damage. The difficulty, of course, is that protecting the environment can be expensive. Clean fuels usually cost more than dirty ones. Disposing of hazardous waste properly costs more (in the short run) than merely dumping it. Organizations that want to reduce costs may be tempted to cut corners on environmental protection.

Your Legal Obligations

Ethical and legal obligations are closely related. In fact, our ethical values have shaped many of our laws. For this reason, professionals should know the basics of four different bodies of law: copyright, trademark, contract, and liability.

COPYRIGHT LAW

As a student, you are frequently reminded to avoid plagiarism. A student caught plagiarizing would likely fail the assignment and possibly the course and might even be expelled from school. A medical researcher or a reporter caught plagiarizing would likely be fired or at least find it difficult to publish in the future. But plagiarism is an ethical, not a legal, issue. Although a plagiarist might be expelled from school or be fired, he or she will not be fined or sent to prison.

By contrast, copyright is a legal issue. Copyright law is the body of law that relates to the appropriate use of a person's intellectual property: written documents, pictures, musical compositions, and the like. Copyright literally refers to a person's *right* to *copy* the work that he or she has created.

The most important concept in copyright law is that only the copyright holder—the person or organization that owns the work—can copy it. For instance, if you work for Zipcar, you can legally copy information from the Zipcar website and use it in other Zipcar documents. This reuse of information is routine in business, industry, and government because it helps ensure that the information a company distributes is both consistent and accurate.

However, if you work for Zipcar, you cannot simply copy information that you find on the Car2Go website and put it in Zipcar publications. Unless you obtained written permission from Car2Go to use its intellectual property, you would be infringing on Car2Go's copyright.

Why doesn't the Zipcar employee who writes the information for Zipcar own the copyright to that information? The answer lies in a legal concept known as *work made for hire*. Anything written or revised by an employee on the job is the company's property, not the employee's.

Although copyright gives the owner of the intellectual property some rights, it doesn't give the owner all rights. You can place small portions of copyrighted text in your own document without getting formal permission from the copyright holder. When you quote a few lines from an article, for example, you are taking advantage of a part of copyright law called *fair use*. Under fair-use guidelines, you have the right to use a portion of a published work, without

◢
GUIDELINES Determining Fair Use

Courts consider four factors in disputes over fair use:

▶ **The purpose and character of the use, especially whether the use is for profit.** Profit-making organizations are scrutinized more carefully than nonprofits.

▶ **The nature and purpose of the copyrighted work.** When the information is essential to the public — for example, medical information — the fair-use principle is applied more liberally.

▶ **The amount and substantiality of the portion of the work used.** A 200-word passage would be a small portion of a book but a large portion of a 500-word brochure.

▶ **The effect of the use on the potential market for the copyrighted work.** Any use of the work that is likely to hurt the author's potential to profit from the original work would probably not be considered fair use.

getting permission, for purposes such as criticism, commentary, news reporting, teaching, scholarship, or research. Because fair use is based on a set of general guidelines that are meant to be interpreted on a case-by-case basis, you should still cite the source accurately to avoid potential plagiarism.

A new trend is for copyright owners to stipulate which rights they wish to retain and which they wish to give up. You might see references to Creative Commons, a not-for-profit organization that provides symbols for copyright owners to use to communicate their preferences. Figure 2.1 shows four of the Creative Commons symbols. A benefit of using materials with Creative Commons licenses is that you don't have to track down the copyright holder to ask for permission. Note that some internet search engines allow you to search for Creative Commons materials.

 Attribution. You must attribute the work in the manner specified by the author or licensor (but not in any way that suggests that they endorse you or your use of the work).

 Noncommercial. You may not use this work for commercial purposes.

 No Derivative Works. You may not alter, transform, or build upon this work.

 Share Alike. If you alter, transform, or build upon this work, you may distribute the resulting work only under the same or similar license to this one.

FIGURE 2.1 **Selected Licensing Symbols from Creative Commons**

The organization has created a number of symbols to represent rights that copyright owners can retain or release.

Licensed under a Creative Commons Attribution 4.0 International License, https://creativecommons.org/licenses/by/4.0/.

For more about documenting your sources, see Appendix, Part B.

◢ GUIDELINES Dealing with Copyright Questions

Consider the following advice when using material from another source.

▶ **Abide by the fair-use concept.** Do not rely on excessive amounts of another source's work (unless the information is your company's own boilerplate).

▶ **Seek permission.** Write to the source, stating what portion of the work you wish to use and the publication you wish to use it in. The source is likely to charge you for permission.

▶ **Cite your sources accurately.** Citing sources fulfills your ethical obligation and strengthens your writing by showing the reader the range of your research.

▶ **Consult legal counsel if you have questions.** Copyright law is complex. Don't rely on instinct or common sense.

ETHICS NOTE

DISTINGUISHING PLAGIARISM FROM ACCEPTABLE REUSE OF INFORMATION

Plagiarism is the act of using someone else's words or ideas without giving credit to the original author. It doesn't matter whether the writer intended to plagiarize. Obviously, it is plagiarism to borrow or steal graphics, video or audio media, written passages, or entire documents and then use them without attribution. Web-based sources are particularly vulnerable to plagiarism, partly because people mistakenly think that if information is on the web it is free to borrow and partly because this material is so easy to copy, paste, and reformat.

However, writers within a company often reuse one another's information without giving credit—and this is completely ethical. For instance, companies publish press releases when they wish to publicize news. These press releases typically conclude with descriptions of the company and how to get in touch with an employee who can answer questions about the company's products or services. These descriptions, sometimes called *boilerplate*, are simply copied and pasted from previous press releases. Because these descriptions are legally the intellectual property of the company, reusing them in this way is completely honest. Similarly, companies often *repurpose* their writing. That is, they copy a description of the company from a press release and paste it into a proposal or an annual report. This reuse is also acceptable.

When you are writing a document and need a passage that you suspect someone in your organization might already have written, ask a more experienced co-worker whether the culture of your organization permits reusing someone else's writing. If the answer is yes, check with your supervisor to see whether he or she approves of what you plan to do.

TRADEMARK LAW

Companies use *trademarks* and *registered trademarks* to ensure that the public recognizes the name or logo of a product.

- A *trademark* is a word, phrase, name, or symbol that is identified with a company. The company uses the ™ symbol after the product name to claim the design or device as a trademark. However, using this symbol does not grant the company any legal rights. It simply sends a message to other organizations that the company is claiming a trademark.

GUIDELINES Protecting Trademarks

Use the following techniques to protect your client's or employer's trademark.

▶ **Distinguish trademarks from other material.** Use boldface, italics, a different typeface, a different type size, or a different color to distinguish the trademarked item.

▶ **Use the trademark symbol.** At least once in each document — preferably the first time the name or logo appears — use the appropriate symbol after the name or logo, followed by an asterisk. At the bottom of the page, include a statement such as the following: "*COKE is a registered trademark of the Coca-Cola Company."

▶ **Use the trademarked item's name as an adjective, not as a noun or verb.** Trademarks can become confused with the generic term they refer to. Use the trademarked name along with the generic term, as in Xerox® photocopier or LaserJet® printer.

| DOES NOT PROTECT TRADEMARK | buy three LaserJets® |
| PROTECTS TRADEMARK | buy three LaserJet® printers |

▶ **Do not use the possessive form of the trademarked name.** Doing so reduces the uniqueness of the item and encourages the public to think of the term as generic.

| DOES NOT PROTECT TRADEMARK | iPad's® fine quality |
| PROTECTS TRADEMARK | the fine quality of iPad® tablets |

- A *registered trademark* is a word, phrase, name, or symbol that the company has registered with the U.S. Patent and Trademark Office. The company can then use the ® symbol after the trademarked item. Registering a trademark, a process that can take years, ensures much more legal protection than a simple trademark throughout the United States, as well as in other nations. Although a company is not required to use the symbol, doing so makes it easier for the company to take legal action against another organization that it believes has infringed on its trademark.

All employees are responsible for using trademark and registered trademark symbols accurately when referring to a company's products.

CONTRACT LAW

Contract law deals with agreements between two parties. In most cases, disputes concern whether a product lives up to the manufacturer's claims. These claims take the form of express warranties or implied warranties.

An *express warranty* is a written or oral statement that the product has a particular feature or can perform a particular function. For example, a statement in a printer manual that the printer produces 17 pages per minute is an express warranty. An *implied warranty* is one of two kinds of nonwritten guarantees:

- The *merchantability warranty* guarantees that the product is of at least average quality and appropriate for the ordinary purposes it was intended to serve.

- The *fitness warranty* guarantees that the product is suitable for the buyer's purpose if the seller knows that purpose. For example, if a car salesperson knows that a buyer wishes to pull a 5,000-pound trailer but also knows that a car cannot pull such a load, the salesperson is required to inform the buyer of this fact.

LIABILITY LAW

Under product-liability law, a manufacturer or seller of a product is liable for injuries or damages caused by the use of that product. Liability is an important concern for technical communicators, because courts frequently rule that manufacturers are responsible for providing adequate operating instructions and for warning consumers about the risks of using their products. Figure 2.2 shows a warning label used to inform people of how to avoid a safety risk.

Manufacturers of products used in the United States have a legal *duty to warn* users by providing safety labels on products (and the same information in their accompanying instructions) and by explaining in the instructions how to use the products safely. According to intellectual-property attorney Kenneth Ross (2011), the manufacturer has this duty to warn when all four of these characteristics apply:

1. The product is dangerous.

2. The danger is or should be known by the manufacturer.

3. The danger is present when the product is used in the usual and expected manner.

4. The danger is not obvious to or well known by the user.

The complication for technical communicators is that one set of guidelines regarding duty to warn is used in the United States (the American National Standards Institute's ANSI Z535, last revised in 2011) and another set is used in the European Union (the International Organization for Standardization's ISO 3864, which is updated periodically). Both sets of guidelines are relatively vague, and they contradict each other in important ways. Therefore, before publishing labels or instructions for products that can be dangerous, consult with an attorney who specializes in liability issues.

FIGURE 2.2   A Warning Label

This warning label uses symbols — such as the orange box, the red circle with the slash, and the image of the heart and pacemaker — and words to visually and verbally warn people with pacemakers to stay away from a device that can hurt them. The warning helps the company do the right thing — and avoid product-liability lawsuits.

Reproduced with permission from www.safetylabelsolutions.com.

◢
| **GUIDELINES** | Abiding by Liability Laws

Pamela S. Helyar summarizes the communicator's obligations and offers 10 guidelines for abiding by liability laws (1992):

▶ **Understand the product and its likely users.** Learn everything you can about the product and its users.

▶ **Describe the product's functions and limitations.** Help people determine whether it is the right product to buy. In one case, a manufacturer was found liable for not stating that its electric smoke alarm does not work during a power outage.

▶ **Instruct users on all aspects of ownership.** Include assembly, installation, use and storage, testing, maintenance, first aid and emergencies, and disposal.

▶ **Use appropriate words and graphics.** Use common terms, simple sentences, and brief paragraphs. Structure the document logically, and include specific directions. Make graphics clear and easy to understand; where necessary, show people performing tasks. Make the words and graphics appropriate to the educational level, mechanical ability, manual dexterity, and intelligence of intended users. For products that will be used by children or nonnative speakers of your language, include graphics illustrating important information.

▶ **Warn users about the risks of using or misusing the product.** Warn users about the dangers of using the product, such as chemical poisoning. Describe the cause, extent, and seriousness of the danger. A car manufacturer was found liable for not having warned consumers that parking a car on grass, leaves, or other combustible material could cause a fire. For particularly dangerous products, explain the danger and how to avoid it, and then describe how to use the product safely. Use *mandatory language*, such as *must* and *shall*, rather than *might*, *could*, or *should*. Use the words *warning* and *caution* appropriately.

For a discussion of danger, warning, and caution, see Ch. 20, p. 579.

▶ **Include warnings along with assertions of safety.** When product information says that a product is safe, readers tend to pay less attention to warnings. Therefore, include detailed warnings to balance the safety claims.

▶ **Make directions and warnings conspicuous.** Safety information must be in large type and easily visible, appear in an appropriate location, and be durable enough to withstand ordinary use of the product.

▶ **Make sure that the instructions comply with applicable company standards and local, state, and federal laws.**

▶ **Perform usability testing.** Test the product (to make sure it is safe and easy to use) and test the instructions (to make sure they are accurate and easy to understand).

For a discussion of usability testing, see Ch. 13.

▶ **Make sure users receive the information.** If you discover a problem after the product has been shipped to retailers, tell users by direct mail or email, if possible, or newspaper and online advertising if not. Automobile-recall notices are one example of how manufacturers contact their users.

The Role of Corporate Culture in Ethical and Legal Conduct

Most employees work within organizations, such as corporations and government agencies. We know that organizations exert a powerful influence on their employees' actions. According to a study by the Ethics Resource Center of more than 6,500 employees in various businesses (2014), organizations that value ethics and build strong cultures experience fewer ethical problems than organizations with weak ethical cultures. In organizations with strong ethical cultures, far fewer employees feel pressure to commit misconduct, far fewer employees observe misconduct, far more employees report the misconduct that they see, and there is far less retaliation against employees who report misconduct.

Companies can take specific steps to improve their ethical culture:

- The organization's leaders can set the right tone by living up to their commitment to ethical conduct.
- Supervisors can set good examples and encourage ethical conduct.
- Peers can support those employees who act ethically.
- The organization can use additional communication to reinforce the formal policies, such as those presented in a company code of conduct.

In other words, it is not enough for an organization to issue a statement that ethical and legal behavior is important. The organization has to create a culture that values and rewards ethical and legal behavior. That culture starts at the top and extends to all employees, and it permeates the day-to-day operations of the organization.

An important element of a culture of ethical and legal conduct is a formal code of conduct. Most large corporations in the United States have one, as do almost all professional societies. (U.S. companies that are traded publicly are required to state whether they have a code of conduct—and if not, why not.) Figure 2.3 shows some excerpts from the Texas Instruments code of conduct. Codes of conduct vary greatly from organization to organization, but most of them address such issues as the following:

- adhering to local laws and regulations, including those intended to protect the environment
- avoiding discrimination
- maintaining a safe and healthy workplace
- respecting privacy
- avoiding conflicts of interest
- protecting the company's intellectual property
- avoiding bribery and kickbacks in working with suppliers and customers

Code of Conduct
Our values and ethics

Our values

Integrity — Do the right thing | Be honest

Innovation — Solve problems | Create boldly | Challenge the impossible

our communities

STRUMENTS

SZZA066A

Ethics quick test

When confronted with an ethical choice use this checklist as a guide. If you need help, please contact the Ethics Office.

The ethics quick test:

Our Code of Conduct

Our **Code of Conduct** is grounded in our **values**. It lists specific behaviors that we expect from every TIer around the world. While it is expansive, it is not exhaustive. Employees are expected to use sound judgment and seek advice through their chain of leadership or through the TI Ethics Office regarding situations not covered here. Violations of the code may be punishable by reprimand or termination, and in some ... waived for any director,

TEXAS INSTRUMENTS

Reporting a concern

Any TI employee, contractor, supplier, distributor or customer who has reason to believe that TI or a TI employee, contractor or other person(s) acting on TI's behalf has violated a law, statutory regulation, TI's Code of Conduct or corporate policy should report the suspected violation. Concerns may be reported to:

- Managers or supervisors;
- Human Resources representatives;
- TI's Ethics Office (see box on next page);
- TI's Law Department;
- Individuals identified in the Standard Policies and Procedures (SP&P) covering the relevant subject matter of the suspected violation.

Investigations into reported concerns shall be conducted according to SP&P 04-05-05: Complaint Procedures and Investigations.

SP&P link is only accessible within TI.

TEXAS INSTRUMENTS

TEXAS INSTRUMENTS

FIGURE 2.3   A Code of Conduct

These sample pages from the Texas Instruments (TI) code of conduct illustrate the importance of ethics and values to the company's culture. The full code of conduct — which is over 30 pages long — includes detailed information about company policy and practices for resolving complaints. TI has earned praise for its commitment to ethical and legal conduct.

Information from Texas Instruments, 2015: ti.com/lit/ml/szza066a/szza066a.pdf. Courtesy Texas Instruments.

A code of conduct focuses on behavior, including adhering to the law. Many codes of conduct are only a few paragraphs long; others are lengthy and detailed, some consisting of several volumes.

An effective code has three major characteristics:

- **It protects the public rather than members of the organization or profession.** For instance, the code should condemn unsafe building practices but not advertising, which increases competition and thus lowers prices.

- **It is specific and comprehensive.** A code is ineffective if it merely states that people must not steal or if it does not address typical ethical offenses such as bribery in companies that do business in other countries.

- **It is enforceable.** A code is ineffective if it does not stipulate penalties, including dismissal from the company or expulsion from the profession.

Although many codes are too vague to be useful in determining whether a person has violated one of their principles, writing and implementing a code can be valuable because it forces an organization to clarify its own values and fosters an increased awareness of ethical issues. Texas Instruments, like many organizations, encourages employees to report ethical problems to a committee or a person (sometimes called an *ethics officer* or an *ombudsperson*) who investigates and reaches an impartial decision.

If you think there is a serious ethical problem in your organization, find out what resources your organization offers to deal with it. If there are no resources, work with your supervisor to solve the problem.

What do you do if the ethical problem persists even after you have exhausted all the resources at your organization and, if appropriate, the professional organization in your field? The next step will likely involve *whistle-blowing*—the practice of going public with information about serious unethical conduct within an organization. For example, an engineer is blowing the whistle when she tells a regulatory agency or a newspaper that quality-control tests on a company product were faked.

Ethicists such as Velasquez (2011) argue that whistle-blowing is justified if you have tried to resolve the problem through internal channels, if you have strong evidence that the problem is hurting or will hurt other parties, and if the whistle-blowing is reasonably certain to prevent or stop the wrongdoing. But Velasquez also points out that whistle-blowing is likely to hurt the employee, his or her family, and other parties. Whistle-blowers can be penalized through negative performance appraisals, transfers to undesirable locations, or isolation within the company. The Ethics & Compliance Initiative (2018) reports that more than one in three workers in the private sector who reported misconduct experienced some form of retaliation.

Understanding Ethical and Legal Issues Related to Social Media

There is probably some truth to this comment from social-media consultant Peter Shankman: "For the majority of us, social media is nothing more than a faster way to screw up in front of a larger number of people in a shorter amount of time" (Trillos-Decarie, 2012). As social media have become more prevalent and important in the workplace, we're starting to get a better idea of both the rewards and risks. Certainly, social media have created many new and exciting ways for people in the workplace to connect with each other and with other stakeholders outside the organization. However, the wide-spread use of social media by employees in the workplace and in their private lives also presents challenges.

User-generated content, whether it is posted to Facebook, Twitter, LinkedIn, YouTube, Instagram, Yelp, Pinterest, or any of the many other online services, presents significant new ethical and legal issues. Just as employers are trying to produce social-media policies that promote the interests of the organization without infringing on employees' rights of free expression, all of us need to understand the basics of ethical and legal principles related to these new media.

A 2014 report by the law firm Proskauer Rose LLP, "Social Media in the Workplace Around the World 3.0," surveyed over 100 companies from the United States and many other countries. Here are some of the survey findings (Proskauer Rose LLP, 2014, p. 2):

- Almost 80 percent of employers have social-media policies.
- More than one-third of employers block employee access to social media.
- More than half of the employers reported problems caused by misuse of social media by employees. Over 70 percent of businesses have had to take disciplinary action against an employee for misuse of social media.

And in a 2016 report by the Pew Research Center, employees indicated that they use social media on the job to take a break from work, help solve work-related problems, and learn about someone they work with (Pew Research Center, 2016).

Over the next few years, organizations will revise their policies about how employees may use social media in the workplace, just as courts will clarify some of the more complicated issues related to social media and the law. For these reasons, what we now see as permissible and ethical is likely to change. Still, it is possible to identify a list of best practices that can help you use social media wisely—and legally—in your career.

Finally, a related suggestion: avoid criticizing your employer online. Although defamation laws forbid making untrue factual statements about your employer, you are in fact permitted to criticize your employer, online or offline. The National Labor Relations Board has ruled that doing so is legal because it is protected discussion about "working conditions." Our advice: if you're angry, move away from the keyboard. Once you post something, you've lost control of it.

However, if you think your employer is acting illegally or unethically, start by investigating the company's own resources for addressing such problems. Then, if you are still dissatisfied, consider whistle-blowing, which is discussed on p. 32 under The Role of Corporate Culture in Ethical and Legal Conduct.

GUIDELINES Using Social Media Ethically and Legally

These guidelines can help you use social media to your advantage in your career.

▶ **Keep your private social-media accounts separate from your company-sponsored accounts.** After you leave a company, you don't want to get into a dispute over who "owns" an account. Companies can argue, for example, that your collection of Twitter followers is in fact a customer list and therefore the company's intellectual property. Regardless of whether you post from the workplace or at home, post only about business on your company-sponsored accounts.

▶ **Read the terms of service of every service to which you post.** Although you retain the copyright on original content that you post, most social-media services state that they can repost your content wherever and whenever they want, without informing you, getting your permission, or paying you. Many employers would consider this policy unacceptable.

▶ **Avoid revealing unauthorized news about your own company.** A company that wishes to apply for a patent for one of its products or processes has, according to the law, only one year to do so after the product or process is first mentioned or illustrated in a "printed publication." Because courts have found that a photo on Facebook or a blog or even a tweet is equivalent to a printed publication (Bettinger, 2010), you could inadvertently start the clock ticking. Even worse, some other company could use the information to apply for a patent for the product or process that *your* company is developing. Or suppose that on your personal blog, you reveal that your company's profits will dip in the next quarter. This information could prompt investors to sell shares of your company's stock, thereby hurting everyone who owns shares — including you and most of your co-workers.

▶ **Avoid self-plagiarism.** Self-plagiarizing is the act of publishing something you have already published. If you write an article for your company newsletter and later publish it on a blog, you are violating your company's copyright, because your newsletter article was a work made for hire and therefore the company's intellectual property.

▶ **Avoid defaming anyone.** Defamation is the legal term for making false statements of fact about a person that could harm that person. Defamation includes libel (making such statements in writing, as in a blog post) and slander (making them in speech, as in a video posted online). In addition, you should not repost libelous or slanderous content that someone else has created.

(continued)

▶ **Don't live stream or quote from a speech or meeting without permission.** Although you may describe a speech or meeting online, you may not stream video or post quotations without permission.

▶ **Avoid false endorsements.** The Federal Trade Commission has clear rules defining false advertising. The most common type of false advertising involves posting a positive review of a product or company in exchange for some compensation. For instance, some unscrupulous software companies give reviewers a copy of the software to be reviewed (which is perfectly legal) loaded on an expensive computer that the reviewers can keep. Unless the reviewer explicitly notes in the review the compensation from the software company, posting the positive review is considered false advertising. Similarly, you should not endorse your own company's products without stating your relationship with the company (U.S. Federal Trade Commission, 2017).

▶ **Avoid impersonating someone else online.** If that person is real (whether alive or dead), you could be violating his or her right of publicity (the right to control his or her name, image, or likeness). If that person is a fictional character, such as a character on a TV show or in a movie, you could be infringing on the copyright of whoever created that character.

▶ **Avoid infringing on trademarks by using protected logos or names.** Don't include copyrighted or trademarked names, slogans, or logos in your posts unless you have received permission to do so. Even if the trademark owner likes your content, you probably will be asked to stop posting it. If the trademark owner dislikes your content, you are likely to face a more aggressive legal response.

Communicating Ethically Across Cultures

The United States exports more than $2.2 trillion worth of goods and services to the rest of the world (U.S. Census Bureau, 2016). U.S. companies do not necessarily have the same ethical and legal obligations when they export as when they sell in the United States. For this reason, technical communicators should understand the basics of two aspects of writing for people in other countries: communicating with cultures with different ethical beliefs and communicating in countries with different laws.

COMMUNICATING WITH CULTURES WITH DIFFERENT ETHICAL BELIEFS

Companies face special challenges when they market their products and services to people in other countries (and to people in their home countries who come from other cultures). Companies need to decide how to deal with situations in which the target culture's ethical beliefs clash with those of their own culture. For instance, in many countries, sexual discrimination makes it difficult for women to assume responsible positions in the workplace. If a U.S. company that sells cell phones, for example, wishes to present product information in such a country, should it reinforce this discrimination by excluding women from photographs of its products? Ethicist Thomas Donaldson argues that doing so is wrong (1991). According to the principle

DOCUMENT ANALYSIS ACTIVITY

Presenting Guidelines for Using Social Media

This excerpt is from a corporate social-media policy statement. The questions below ask you to think about how to make the policy statement clearer and more useful.

1. The "Overview" section discusses the company's social-media policy guidelines in terms of etiquette. In what way is "etiquette" an appropriate word to describe the policy? In what way is it inappropriate?

2. The "What Are Social Media?" section provides little useful information. What other information might it include to make the document more useful to Paragon employees?

3. The bulleted guidelines are vague. Revise any two of them to include more specific information.

① *Overview*

In today's world, just about everything we do online can be traced back to us and can have an impact (for better or worse) on a company. Paragon wants to remind you that the company policies on anti-harassment, ethics, and company loyalty extend to all media. There is a certain etiquette you should abide by when you participate online. This document is not intended to be restrictive, but to provide some guidelines on proper social-networking etiquette.

② *What Are Social Media?*

Social media are the tools and content that enable people to connect online, share their interests, and engage in conversations.

Guidelines

These policies apply to individuals who want to participate in social-media conversations on behalf of Paragon. Please be mindful that your behavior at all times reflects on Paragon as a whole. Do not write or post anything that might reflect negatively on Paragon.

③
- Always use your best judgment and be honest.
- Be respectful of confidential information (such as clients, financials).
- Always be professional, especially when accepting criticism.
- Participate, don't promote. Bring value. Give to get.
- Write only about what you know.
- When in doubt, ask for help/clarification.
- Seek approval before commenting on any articles that portray Paragon negatively.

he calls the *moral minimum*, companies are ethically obligated not to reinforce patterns of discrimination in product information.

However, Donaldson also argues that companies are not obligated to challenge the prevailing prejudice directly. A company is not obligated, for example, to include photographs that show women performing roles they do not normally perform within a particular culture, nor is it obligated to portray women wearing clothing, makeup, or jewelry that is likely to offend local standards. But there is nothing to prevent an organization from adopting a more activist stance. Organizations that actively oppose discrimination are acting admirably.

COMMUNICATING IN COUNTRIES WITH DIFFERENT LAWS

When U.S. companies export goods and services to other countries, they need to adhere to those countries' federal and regional laws. For instance, a company that wishes to export to Germany must abide by the laws of Germany and of the European Union, of which it is a part. In many cases, the target region will not allow goods and services to be imported that do not conform to local laws. The hazardous-product laws of the European Union, in particular, are typically more stringent than those of the United States.

Because exporting goods to countries with different laws is such a complex topic, companies that export devote considerable resources to finding out what they need to do, not only in designing and manufacturing products but also in writing the product information. For an introduction to this topic, see Lipus (2006).

Principles for Ethical Communication

Although it is impossible to state principles for ethical communication that will guide you through all the challenges you will face communicating in the workplace, the following provide a starting point.

ABIDE BY RELEVANT LAWS

You must adhere to the laws governing intellectual property, contracts, and liability. Here are some examples:

- **Do not violate copyright.** When you want to publish someone else's copyrighted material, such as graphics you find on the web, get written permission from the copyright owner.
- **Honor the laws regarding trademarks.** For instance, use the trademark symbol (™) and the registered trademark symbol (®) properly.
- **Live up to the express and implied warranties on your company's products.**
- **Abide by all laws governing product liability.** Helyar's (1992) guidelines, presented on page 29, are a good introduction for products to be sold in the United States. Lipus's (2006) guidelines are useful for products to be sold outside the United States.

COMPLY WITH ACCESSIBILITY STANDARDS

The federal government has outlined standards for making websites and other forms of technical communication accessible to all users, including people with disabilities, who make up about 12.8 percent of the population (Institute on Disability, 2017). Government sites are required to comply with Section 508 of the Rehabilitation Act, and the Department of Health and Human Services encourages all private and commercial sites to do the same.

For more on accessibility, see Ch. 11, pp. 287–90.

In some cases, companies can be held liable for not making their communication accessible. For example, Target was sued (and lost) for not making its website accessible for blind customers, a violation of the Americans with Disabilities Act (Miranda-Hess, 2013).

ABIDE BY THE APPROPRIATE PROFESSIONAL CODE OF CONDUCT

Your field's professional organization, such as the American Society of Civil Engineers, is likely to have a code that goes beyond legal issues to express ethical principles, such as telling the truth, reporting information accurately, respecting the privacy of others, and avoiding conflicts of interest.

ABIDE BY YOUR ORGANIZATION'S POLICY ON SOCIAL MEDIA

If your employer has a written policy about how employees may use social media, study it. If there is no written policy, check with Human Resources or your supervisor for advice. If you think that you will be unable to abide by the employer's policy—whether written or not—you should not work there, or you should abide by it while you try to change it.

TAKE ADVANTAGE OF YOUR EMPLOYER'S ETHICS RESOURCES

Your employer is likely to have a code of conduct, as well as other resources, such as an Ethics Office, which can help you find information to guide you in resolving ethical challenges you encounter. Your employer will likely have a mechanism for anonymously registering complaints about unethical conduct.

TELL THE TRUTH

Sometimes, employees are asked to lie about their companies' products or about those of their competitors. Obviously, lying is unethical. Your responsibility is to resist this pressure, going over your supervisor's head if necessary.

DON'T MISLEAD YOUR READERS

A misleading statement—one that invites or even encourages the reader to reach a false conclusion—is ethically no better than lying. Avoid these four common kinds of misleading technical communication:

For a more detailed discussion of misleading writing, see Ch. 10. For a discussion of avoiding misleading graphics, see Ch. 12.

- **False implications.** If, as an employee of SuperBright, you write "Use only SuperBright batteries in your new flashlight," you imply that only that brand will work. If that is untrue, the statement is misleading. Communicators sometimes use clichés such as *user-friendly*, *ergonomic*, and *state-of-the-art* to make a product sound better than it is; use specific, accurate information to back up your claims about a product.

- **Exaggerations.** If you say, "Our new Operating System 2500 makes system crashes a thing of the past" when the product only makes them less likely, you are exaggerating. Provide specific technical information on the reduction of crashes. Similarly, do not write "We carried out extensive market research" if all you did was make a few phone calls.

- **Legalistic constructions.** It is unethical to write "The 3000X was designed to operate in extreme temperatures, from –40 degrees to 120 degrees Fahrenheit" if the product does not operate reliably in those temperatures. Although the statement might technically be accurate—the product was *designed* to operate in those temperatures—it is misleading.

- **Euphemisms.** If you refer to someone being fired, say *fired*, not *granted permanent leave* or *offered an alternative career opportunity*.

USE DESIGN TO HIGHLIGHT IMPORTANT ETHICAL AND LEGAL INFORMATION

Courts have found that burying information in footnotes or printing it in very small type violates a company's obligation to inform consumers and warn them about hazards in using a product. When you want to communicate safety information or other facts that readers need to know, use design features to make that information easy to see and understand. Figure 2.4 shows how design principles can be used to communicate nutritional information on food labels.

BE CLEAR

Clear writing helps your readers understand your message easily. Your responsibility is to write as clearly as you can to help your audience understand what you are saying. For instance, if you are writing a product warranty, make it as simple and straightforward as possible. Don't hide behind big words and complicated sentences. Use tables of contents, indexes, and other accessing devices to help your readers find what they need.

AVOID DISCRIMINATORY LANGUAGE

Don't use language that discriminates against people because of their sex, religion, ethnicity, race, sexual or gender orientation, or physical or mental abilities. Employees have been disciplined or fired for sending inappropriate jokes through the company email system.

ACKNOWLEDGE ASSISTANCE FROM OTHERS

Don't suggest that you did all the work yourself if you didn't. Cite your sources and your collaborators accurately and graciously. For more about citing sources, see Appendix, Part B.

For techniques for writing clearly, including avoiding discriminatory language, see Ch. 10.

FIGURE 2.4 Using Design to Emphasize Important Information
This nutritional labeling system is called "traffic-light labeling" because it uses red and green to indicate how healthful a food is.
Shaun Finch — Coyote-Photography .co.uk/Alamy.

WRITER'S CHECKLIST

☐ Did you abide by relevant laws? *(p. 37)*

☐ Did you comply with accessibility standards? *(p. 38)*

☐ Did you abide by the appropriate corporate or professional code of conduct? *(p. 38)*

☐ Did you abide by your organization's policy on social media? *(p. 38)*

☐ Did you take advantage of your company's ethics resources? *(p. 38)*

☐ Did you tell the truth? *(p. 38)*

Did you avoid using

☐ false implications? *(p. 38)*

☐ exaggerations? *(p. 39)*

☐ legalistic constructions? *(p. 39)*

☐ euphemisms? *(p. 39)*

☐ Did you use design to highlight important ethical and legal information? *(p. 39)*

☐ Did you write clearly? *(p. 39)*

☐ Did you avoid discriminatory language? *(p. 39)*

☐ Did you acknowledge any assistance you received from others? *(p. 39)*

EXERCISES

1. It is late April, and you need a summer job. On your town's news website, you see an ad for a potential job. The only problem is that the ad specifically mentions that the job is "a continuing, full-time position." You know that you will be returning to college in the fall. Is it ethical for you to apply for the job without mentioning this fact? Why or why not? If you believe it is unethical to withhold that information, is there any ethical way you can apply? Be prepared to share your ideas with the class.

2. You serve on the Advisory Committee of your college's bookstore, which is a private business that leases space on campus and donates 10 percent of its profits to student scholarships. The head of the bookstore wishes to stock Simple Study Guides, a popular series of plot summaries and character analyses of classic literary works. In similar bookstores, the sale of Simple Study Guides yields annual profits of over $10,000. Six academic departments have signed a statement condemning the idea. Should you support the bookstore head or the academic departments? Be prepared to discuss your answer with the class.

3. Using the search term "social media policy examples," find a corporate policy statement on employee use of social media. In a 500-word memo to your instructor, explain whether the policy statement is clear, specific, and comprehensive. Does the statement include a persuasive explanation of why the policy is necessary? Is the tone of the statement positive or negative? How

would you feel if you were required to abide by this policy? If appropriate, include a copy of the policy statement (or a portion of it) so that you can refer to it in your memo. For more about memos, see Ch. 14.

4. **TEAM EXERCISE** Form small groups. Study the website of a company or other organization that has a prominent role in your community or your academic field. Find information about the organization's commitment to ethical and legal conduct. Often, organizations present this information in sections with titles such as "information for investors," "about the company," or "values and principles of conduct."

   • One group member could identify the section that states the organization's values. How effective is this section in presenting information that goes beyond general statements about the importance of ethical behavior?

   • A second group member could identify the section that describes the organization's code of conduct. Does the organization seem to take principles of ethical and legal behavior seriously? Can you get a clear idea from the description whether the organization has a specific, well-defined set of policies, procedures, and resources available for employees who wish to discuss ethical and legal issues?

   • A third group member could identify any information related to the organization's commitment to the environment. What does the organization do, in its normal operations, to limit its carbon footprint and otherwise encourage responsible use of natural resources and minimize damage to the environment?

- As a team, write a memo to your instructor presenting your findings. Attach the organization's code of conduct to your memo.

CASE 2: The Ethics of Requiring Students to Subsidize a Plagiarism-Detection Service

The provost of your university has sent a letter to you and other members of the Student Council proposing that the university subscribe to a plagiarism-detection service, the cost of which would be subsidized by students' tuition. You and other council members have some serious concerns about the proposal and decide to write to the provost, analyzing the ethical implications of requiring students to subsidize such a program. If your instructor has assigned it, go to Achieve to read the provost's letter and begin drafting your response.

3

Writing Technical Documents

3

THIS CHAPTER PRESENTS a writing process that focuses on the techniques and tools most useful for technical communicators. Should you use the process described here? If you don't already have a process that works for you, yes. But your goal should be to devise a process that enables you to write *effective* documents (that is, documents that accomplish your purpose) *efficiently* (without taking more time than necessary). At the end of this chapter, you will find a Writer's Checklist. After you try implementing some of the techniques described in this chapter, you can start to revise the Writer's Checklist to reflect the techniques that you find most effective.

The writing process consists of five steps: planning, drafting, revising, editing, and proofreading. The challenging part of writing, however, is that these five steps are not linear. That is, you don't plan the document, then check off a box, and go on to drafting. At any step, you might double back to do more planning, drafting, or revising. Even when you think you're almost done — when you're proofreading — you still might think of something that would improve the document. That means you'll need to go back and rethink all five steps.

As you backtrack, you will have one eye on the clock, because the deadline is sneaking up on you. That's the way it is for all writers. A technical communicator stops working on a user manual because she has to get it off to the print shop. An engineer stops working on a set of slides for a conference presentation because it's time to head for the airport. So, when you read about how to write, remember that you are reading about a messy process that goes backward as often as it goes forward and that, most likely, ends only when you run out of time.

Remember, too, that many of the documents you produce will never truly be "finished." Many types of documents posted online are called *living documents* because they are meant to be revised as new information becomes available or policies change. Policy manuals, for example, keep changing.

Planning

Planning, which can take more than a third of the total time spent on a writing project, is critically important for every document, from an email message to a book-length manual. Start by thinking about your writing situation.

CONSIDERING YOUR WRITING SITUATION

Your writing situation includes factors that will affect your communication: your audience, purpose, setting, document type, and process. Considering the opportunities and challenges presented by these factors is an important part of the planning process.

For more about analyzing your audience, see Ch. 5, p. 90.

Analyzing Your Audience If you are lucky, you can talk with your audience before and during your work on the document. These conversations can help you learn what your readers already know, what they want to know, and how they would like the information presented. You can test out drafts, making changes as you go.

Even if you cannot consult your audience while writing the document, you still need to learn everything you can about your readers so that you can determine the best scope, organization, and style for your document. Then, for each of your most important readers, try to answer the following three questions:

- **Who is your reader?** Consider such factors as education, job experience and responsibilities, skill in reading English, cultural characteristics, and personal preferences.

- **What are your reader's attitudes and expectations?** Consider the reader's attitudes toward the topic and your message, as well as the reader's expectations about the kind of document you will be presenting.

- **Why and how will the reader use your document?** Think about what readers will do with the document. This includes the physical environment in which they will use it, the techniques they will use in reading it, and the tasks they will carry out after they finish reading it.

For more about analyzing your purpose, see Ch. 5, p. 110.

Analyzing Your Purpose You cannot start to write until you can state the purpose (or purposes) of the document. Ask yourself these two questions:

1. After your readers have read your document, what do you want them to know or do?

2. What beliefs or attitudes do you want them to hold?

A statement of purpose might be as simple as this: "The purpose of this report is to recommend whether the company should adopt a health-promotion program." Although the statement of purpose might not appear in this form in the final document, you want to state it clearly now to help you stay on track as you carry out the remaining steps.

Analyzing Your Setting Your setting includes both the situation surrounding the problem you are trying to solve and the context in which your audience will use your document. Before you begin to draft, consider the following setting-related issues:

- **High stakes vs. low stakes.** For example, will your document determine the budget for a large project, or will it be used in a more routine manner, such as to help users understand a software update?

- **Physical vs. digital.** In what type of environment will your audience use your document, and how will that environment affect the way you write it?

- **Formal vs. informal.** The setting's level of formality—which differs significantly, for example, from a blog post to a proposal—will dictate the style and tone you will use in your writing. It will also affect the length of and detail provided in your document.

- **Mundane vs. socially or politically charged.** Depending on your field or subject matter, you may be writing about a topic that some readers will find sensitive. For example, you may be writing about replacing fossil-fuel technology with renewable energy in a region where many people have jobs in coal mining or oil refining.

- **Established vs. undefined norms of ethical behavior.** If norms of ethical behavior have been established for your subject area, by all means follow them. If you are unsure about the ethical norms for a particular setting, look for those of an appropriate professional organization, such as the Council of Biology Editors (CBE) or the Institute of Electrical and Electronics Engineers (IEEE).

Settings can have a great deal of influence over how audiences think about and use technical communication.

Selecting Your Document Application, Design, and Delivery Method

Once you know to whom you are writing and why, you need to select an application (the type of document), a design, and a delivery method. You have a number of questions to consider:

- **Has the application already been chosen for me?** If you are writing a proposal to submit to the U.S. Department of the Interior, for example, you must follow the department's specifications for what the proposal is to look like and how it is to be delivered. For most kinds of communication, however, you will likely have to select the appropriate application yourself, such as a set of instructions or a manual. Sometimes, you will deliver an oral presentation or participate in a phone conference or a videoconference.

For more about application types, see Part 4. For more about design, see Ch. 11.

- **What will my readers expect?** If your readers expect a written set of instructions, you should present a set of instructions unless some other application, such as a report or a manual, is more appropriate. If they expect to see the instructions in a simple black-and-white booklet—and there is no good reason to design something more elaborate than that—your choice is obvious. For instance, instructions for installing and operating a ceiling fan in a house are generally presented in a small, inexpensive booklet with the pages stapled together or on a large, folded sheet of paper. However, for an expensive home-theater system, readers might expect a glossy, full-color manual.

- **What delivery method will work best?** Related to the question of reader expectations is the question of how you will deliver the document to your readers. For instance, you would likely mail an annual report to your readers, in addition to posting it on your company website. You might present industry forecasts on a personal blog or on one sponsored by your employer. You might deliver a user's manual for a new type of photo-editing program online rather than in print because the program—and therefore the manual—will change.

It is important to think about these questions during the planning process, because your answers will largely determine the scope, organization, style, and design of the information you will prepare. As early as the planning step, you need to imagine your readers using your information.

Analyzing the Writing Process

The process you use to create your document will depend on several key factors:

- **Existing process.** In some cases, just as with the choice of applications, an existing process will be available for you to follow as you produce your document. In other cases, you may need to create your own process. As explained in this chapter, every writing process should include time for planning, drafting, revising, editing, and proofreading.

- **Time.** Be sure to consider the amount of time you have available to plan, research, and create your document. In some cases, you may need to allow time for additional steps, including collaboration and testing, both of which are discussed below.

- **Budget.** Your budget will influence almost every aspect of your document: the amount of time you spend on it, the number of people you can enlist to help you, the size and shape of the document, the design of the document, and the production quality.

- **Tools.** Before you begin a big project, consider which type of writing tool will best meet your project's needs. You probably do most of your writing with commercial software such as Microsoft Office or open-source software such as Google Docs, and you will likely continue to do much of your writing with these tools. Because of the rapid increase in the number of sophisticated tools such as Adobe InDesign and free web-based tools such as Wordpress, however, keeping up with all your options and being sure to choose the one that best meets your needs can help you create a more effective document.

  Specialized tools built for professional writers can be particularly useful for long, complicated projects that require extensive research. Scrivener, for example, lets you gather your research data in a single location and easily reorganize your document at the section or chapter level. Composition programs optimized for tablets, such as WritePad, convert handwriting into text, translate text into a number of languages, and allow cloud-based storage.

- **Collaboration.** Are you expected to collaborate with others when producing your document? If so, be sure to allow enough time for others to review your work and for you to review theirs. For more on collaboration, see Chapter 4.

- **Document testing.** Part of your writing process may involve testing the document before, during, or after creating it to be sure it fulfills its purpose for users. Chapter 13 discusses document testing.

- **Ongoing maintenance.** The audience for most digital documents and some print documents will expect updates and revisions. For example, periodic updates are necessary on the Consumer Product Safety Commission's website to inform the public of product recalls and other safety hazards.

GENERATING IDEAS ABOUT YOUR SUBJECT

Generating ideas is a way to start mapping out the information you will need to include in the document, deciding where to put it, and identifying additional information that may be required.

First, find out what you already know about the topic by using any of the techniques shown in Table 3.1.

RESEARCHING ADDITIONAL INFORMATION

For more about conducting research, see Ch. 6.

Once you have a good idea of what you already know about your topic, you must obtain the rest of the information you will need. You can find and evaluate what other people have already written by reading reference books, scholarly books, articles, websites, and reputable blogs and discussion forums. In addition, you might compile new information by interviewing experts, distributing surveys and questionnaires, making observations, sending inquiries, and conducting experiments. Don't forget to ask questions and gather opinions from your own network of associates, both inside and outside your organization.

DEVISING A SCHEDULE AND A BUDGET

For more about progress reports, see Ch. 17, p. 468. For more about project management, see Ch. 4, p. 66.

During the planning stage, you also must decide when you will need to provide the information and how much you can spend on the project. For instance, for the project on health-promotion programs, your readers might need a report to help them decide what to do before the new fiscal year begins in two months. In addition, your readers might want a progress report submitted halfway through the project. Making a schedule is often a collaborative process: you meet with your main readers, who tell you when they need the information, and you estimate how long the different tasks will take.

You also need to create a budget. In addition to the time you will need to do the project, you need to think about expenses you might incur. For example, you might need to travel to visit companies with different kinds of health-promotion programs. You might need to conduct specialized database searches, create and distribute questionnaires to employees, or conduct interviews at remote

TABLE 3.1 Techniques for Generating Ideas About Your Topic

TECHNIQUE	EXPLANATION	EXAMPLE
Asking the six journalistic questions	Asking *who, what, when, where, why,* and *how* can help you figure out how much more research you need to do. Note that you can generate several questions from each of these six words.	• *Who* would be able to participate? • *Who* would administer it? • *What* would the program consist of?
Brainstorming	Spending 15 minutes listing short phrases and questions about your subject helps you think of related ideas. Later, when you construct an outline, you will rearrange your list, add new ideas, and toss out some old ones.	• Why we need a program • Lower insurance rates • On-site or at a club? • Who pays for it? • What is our liability? • Increase our productivity
Freewriting	Writing without plans or restrictions, without stopping, can help you determine what you do and do not understand. And one phrase or sentence might spark an important idea.	A big trend today in business is sponsored health-promotion programs. Why should we do it? Many reasons, including boosting productivity and lowering our insurance premiums. But it's complicated. One problem is that we can actually increase our risk if a person gets hurt. Another is the need to decide whether to have the program — what exactly is the program . . .
Talking with someone	Discussing your topic can help you find out what you already know about it and generate new ideas. Simply have someone ask you questions as you speak. Soon you will find yourself in a conversation that will help you make new connections from one idea to another.	You: One reason we might want to do this is to boost productivity. Co-worker: What exactly are the statistics on increased productivity? And who has done the studies? Are they reputable? You: Good point. I'm going to have to show that putting money into a program is going to pay off. I need to see whether there are unbiased recent sources that present hard data.
Clustering and branching	One way to expand on your topic is to write your main idea or main question in the middle of the page and then write second-level and third-level ideas around it, branching out with connecting lines.	*(diagram)* Institute a health-promotion program? — When? (study it first?, pilot program?); What? (company sponsored?, commercial program?); Who? (?, ?, ?); How? (retain a consultant?, advice from insurance co.?); Why? (reduce illness, injury; reduce premiums); Where? (on-site?, at health club?)

locations. Some projects call for *usability testing*—evaluating the experiences of prospective users as they try out a system or a document. The cost of this testing needs to be included in your budget.

For more about usability testing, see Ch. 13.

Drafting

You can begin drafting your document at any point in the planning process. You might jot down some key information for an executive summary as you are thinking about your audience and purpose. Very likely, you will come up with some compelling evidence you want to include in your document during the research phase. But at some point, you need to organize your information into a complete draft of the document. Working with organizational patterns and outlines is a good place to start.

ORGANIZING AND OUTLINING YOUR DOCUMENT

For more about organizing your information, see Ch. 7.

Although each document has its own requirements, you can use existing organizational patterns or adapt them to your own situation. For instance, the compare-and-contrast pattern might be an effective way to organize a discussion of different health-promotion programs. The cause-and-effect pattern might work well for a discussion of the effects of implementing such a program.

At first, your organization is only tentative. When you start to draft, you might find that the pattern you chose isn't working well or that you need additional information that doesn't fit into the pattern.

Once you have a tentative plan, write an outline to help you stay on track as you draft. To keep your purpose clearly in mind as you work, you may want to write it at the top of your page before you begin your outline.

Some writers like to draft within the outline created by their word-processing program. Others prefer to place a paper copy of their outline on the desk next to their keyboard and begin drafting a new document that follows that outline. Whichever method you prefer, you can begin drafting by filling out the sections of your outline. You don't need to work in a particular order, but keep an eye out for sections that are too skimpy and may need more content, and watch for sections that get overloaded and may need further dividing with new headings, paragraphs, or both. Keep in mind, too, that you may choose to reorder or eliminate sections of your outline as you draft. When you do, make sure you make changes deliberately, so that nothing gets moved or left out by mistake.

USING TEMPLATES

For more about design, see Ch. 11.

For your draft, you might consider using an existing template or modifying one to meet your needs. Templates are preformatted designs for different types of documents, such as letters, memos, newsletters, and reports. Templates incorporate the design specifications for the document, including typeface, type size, margins, and spacing. Once you have selected a template, you just type in the information.

Using templates, however, can lead to three problems:

- **They do not always reflect the best design principles.** For instance, most letter and memo templates default to 10-point type, even though 12-point type is easier to read.

- **They bore readers.** Readers get tired of seeing the same designs.

- **They cannot help you answer the important questions about your document.** Although templates can help you format information, they cannot help you figure out how to organize and write a document. Sometimes, templates can even send the wrong message for your particular audience and purpose. For example, résumé templates in word processors present a set of headings that might work better for some job applicants than for others.

In addition, the more you rely on existing templates, the less likely you are to learn how to use the software to make your documents look professional.

STRATEGIES FOR ONLINE COMMUNICATION

Cosmo and Lorenzo Rossi on Managing Recurring Content

Technical communicators can save time and energy by systematically managing recurring content. Recurring content is data and information that companies reuse to support routine tasks, such as communicating with audiences. Recurring content is a type of organizational boilerplate, but it must be updated and customized for particular situations (rather than reused more or less verbatim). Cosmo and Lorenzo Rossi are the founding owners of Bad Habit Media, a start-up company focused on recurring content creation for social media. Using their own template as a model (Figure 3.1), they explain how this strategy can keep you from wasting time re-creating similar material while still attending to key issues of audience and purpose.

COSMO ROSSI
Courtesy Cosmo and Lorenzo Rossi

LORENZO ROSSI
Courtesy Cosmo and Lorenzo Rossi

At Bad Habit Media, Cosmo and Lorenzo Rossi create recurring online content for their clients, including tutorials, podcasts, interviews, teaser videos, and other elements of social media posts. Part of their ongoing process is finding new customers, and they themselves use recurring content in email correspondence to communicate their products and services. In this example of an email message used for making "cold calls" to potential clients, Rossi and Rossi establish both standardized and customized elements, distinguishing which elements need to be tailored from those that can be used for everyone.

Instead of creating a new message for each potential client, Rossi and Rossi begin with recurring content and adapt it, focusing on what is required to successfully customize the communication.

Last Updated: 2020-05-13

Cold Contact
Subject: Let's make something cool–Bad Habit
Body:

Hi **ARTIST_NAME,**

My name is **MY_NAME.** My brother, **BROTHER'S_NAME** and I just started a social content agency called Bad Habit focusing on producing unique recurring content for emerging artists. We heard about you **HOW_WE_HEARD_ABOUT_YOU** and we'd love to work with you!

Even though most people understand that posting regularly on social media is a crucial step to standing out online, not many artists have the time, energy, resources, or creative space to continuously deliver content they're proud of.

That's where we come in: first we get to know your brand, your audience, and your goals, then we work with you to create a simple and effective system so you can release unique, creative, and consistent content that resonates with your fans.

Ultimately, we want to create content that excites you, tells your story, and helps build your audience, but here are some examples of what we can do:

USE_RELEVANT_ITEMS_IN_A_RELEVANT_ORDER
— Live performance videos in unique locations
— Online broadcast (live steams)
— "Making of" or process videos
— Teaser videos for upcoming projects
— Interview series
— Tutorials
— Podcasts
— Dance videos, animation, puppets, and more!

We'd love to meet up sometime and talk more about how we can work together – what is your availability over the next few weeks?

Thanks for your time and talk soon,

MY_NAME
Co-founder
Bad Habit Media

The text that needs to be customized is in all caps and bold, making it easy to identify. Recurring content is in regular type.

The first paragraph of the email includes customized material, which helps Rossi and Rossi connect immediately with potential clients, increasing the likelihood that they will keep reading the message.

The message includes an editable list of the products and services offered by Bad Habit Media. Rossi and Rossi grow the list but also edit it for specific situations.

Rossi and Rossi reorder the edited list. All of the remaining items are relevant for a specific situation, but they are organized from the most to least important to appeal to a potential client.

Any of the recurring content can also be edited and revised as needed.

FIGURE 3.1   Bad Habit Media Recurring Content for Email Correspondence

◢
GUIDELINES Drafting Effectively

Try the following techniques when you begin to draft or when you get stuck in the middle of drafting.

▶ **Get comfortable.** Choose a good chair, set at the right height for the keyboard, and adjust the light so that it doesn't reflect off the screen.

▶ **Start with the easiest topics.** Instead of starting at the beginning of the document, begin with the section you most want to write.

▶ **Draft quickly.** Try to make your fingers keep up with your brain. Turn the phrases from your outline into paragraphs. You'll revise later.

▶ **Don't stop to get more information or to revise.** Set a timer, and draft for forty-five minutes without stopping. When you come to an item that requires more research, skip to the next item. Don't worry about sentence structure or spelling.

▶ **Try invisible writing.** Darken the screen or turn off the monitor so that you can look only at your hard-copy outline or the keyboard. That way, you won't be tempted to stop typing to revise what you have just written.

▶ **Stop in the middle of a section.** When you stop, do so in the middle of a paragraph or even in the middle of a sentence. You will find it easy to conclude the idea you were working on when you begin writing again. This technique will help you avoid writer's block, the mental paralysis that can set in when you stare at a blank screen.

There are also templates that include not only design specifications and elements but also actual content for users. These more involved templates help organizations repurpose content and extend the value of work, but the content still needs to be customized for specific situations. Keep in mind that templated content is just a starting point for drafting.

▶**TECH TIP**

Why To Modify Templates

Templates provided by Microsoft Word offer ready-made formats for documents such as letters, memos, newsletters, and reports, but these templates probably don't exactly match your writing situation. The template designers couldn't know, for example, your particular purpose or anything about your audience, your word limit, or the tone you want to strike. If you work with a pre-existing template, it's usually necessary to customize it to meet your specific needs.

How To Modify Templates

1. To locate an existing template, select **File** and then select **New**. This will open the **Available Templates** window. Within this window, you can study templates already installed on your computer as well as ones available for download.

2. You can start with a Blank Document or with one of the many available templates. First, choose a template, and then select **Create**. If you click on a folder of templates, such as **Sample templates**, you can select a template and then save it as a document or a template. Select the format you want (**Document** or **Template**), then select **Create**. If you want to save the changes you make for future use, be sure to select Template.

3. After making changes to the design of the template, select **File** and then select **Save**. Your modified template will be stored in a file you can access later through the **My Templates** tab in the Available Templates window.

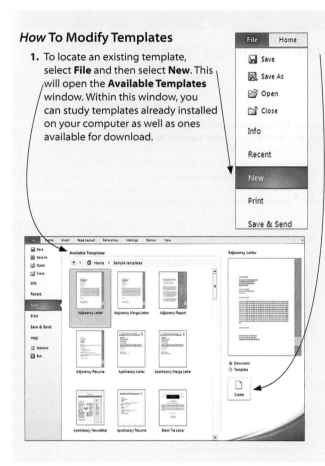

USING STYLES

Styles are like small templates that apply to the design of smaller elements, such as headings and lists. Like templates, styles save you time. For example, as you draft your document, you don't need to add all the formatting each time you want to designate an item as a first-level heading. You simply highlight the text you want to be a first-level heading and use a pull-down menu or ribbon at the top of your screen to select that style. The text automatically incorporates all the specifications of that style.

If you decide to modify a style—by italicizing a heading, for instance—you need to change it only once; the software automatically changes every instance of that style in the document. In collaborative documents, styles make it easier for collaborators to achieve a consistent look.

DOCUMENT ANALYSIS ACTIVITY

Identifying the Strengths and Weaknesses of a Commercial Template

The template from Microsoft Word shown here presents one approach to writing a résumé. The questions below ask you to think about the assumptions underlying this template.

1. How well does the explanation of how to use the template (located under "Objective") help you understand how to write an effective résumé?

2. How well does the template explain how to reformat the elements, such as your name?

3. Does the template clearly describe what you should do if you wish, for instance, to include a list of references, rather than use the phrase "References are available upon request"?

Your Name

> [Job Title]
> [Job Title]

OBJECTIVE
Getting the perfect job might be challenging, but a great-looking résumé doesn't have to be! We've provided a few quick tips to help you get started. To replace any tip text with your own, just click it and start typing.

Need another experience or education entry? You got it. Just click in the sample entries below and then click the plus sign that appears. Looking for a matching cover letter? All you had to do was ask! On the Insert tab, click Cover Page.

EXPERIENCE
[Dates From - To]
[Company]

[Position Held]
> Click here to enter text.
> Click here to enter text
> Click here to enter text

EDUCATION
[Dates From - To]
[School Name, Location]

[Degree]
> Click here to enter text.
> Click here to enter text

REFERENCES
References are available upon request.

[Address 1]
[Address 2]
[City, ST ZIP Code]

[Telephone]
[Email]
[Website]

Why To Use the Styles Group

As you draft your document, you can save time by using Microsoft Word's Styles group to apply styles to elements such as headings, lists, and body text. Using styles helps to ensure consistency, especially in collaborative documents, and makes it easy to automatically change every instance of a style in your document when you revise.

How To Use the Styles Group

1. To apply a style, select the text you want to format, then select a style from the **Quick Styles** gallery in the **Styles** group on the **Home** tab.

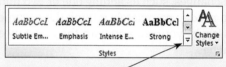

If you do not see the style you want in the gallery, you can access additional styles by using the up and down arrows.

You can also apply a **Quick Style Set** to your entire document by selecting the **Change Styles** icon.

2. Another way to apply a **style** is to select the Styles dialog box launcher and then select the style you wish to use.

If you do not see the style options you want, select **Options** to display the **Style Pane Options** dialog box.

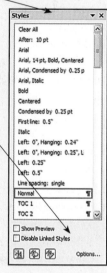

Revising

Revising is the process of looking again at your draft to see whether it works. After you revise, you will carry out two more steps—editing and proofreading—but at this point you want to focus on three large topics:

For more about audience and purpose, see Ch. 5.

- **Audience.** Has your understanding of your audience changed? Will you be addressing people you hadn't considered before? If so, how will that change what you should say and how you should say it?

- **Purpose.** Has your understanding of your purpose changed? If so, what changes should you make to the document?

- **Subject.** Has your understanding of the subject changed? Should you change the scope—that is, should you address more or fewer topics? Should you change the organization of the document? Should you present more evidence or different types of evidence?

On the basis of a new look at your audience, purpose, and subject, you might decide that you need to make small changes, such as adding one or two minor topics. Or you might decide that you need to completely rethink the document.

There are two major ways to revise: by yourself and with the assistance of others. If possible, use both approaches.

STUDYING THE DRAFT BY YOURSELF

The first step in revising is to read and reread your document, looking for different things each time. For instance, you might read it once just to see whether the information you have presented is appropriate for the various audiences you have identified. You might read it another time to see whether each of your claims is supported by appropriate and sufficient evidence.

Start with the largest, most important issues first; then work on the smaller, less important ones. That way, you don't waste time on awkward paragraphs you might eventually decide to delete. Begin by reviewing the document as a whole (for organization, development, and content), saving the sentence-level concerns (such as grammar, punctuation, and spelling) for later.

One effective way to review your whole document for coherence is to study its outline. If you have used Word's style tools to insert heading levels, you can view the outline of your document on screen, as shown in Figure 3.2. If you haven't used style tools, you can still sketch an outline of your document based on its headings and content.

SEEKING HELP FROM OTHERS

For technical documents, it is best to turn to two kinds of people for help. Subject-matter experts (SMEs) can help you determine whether your facts and explanations are accurate and appropriate. If, for instance, you are writing about fuel-cell automobiles, you could ask an automotive expert to review your document. Important documents are routinely reviewed by technical experts before being released to the public.

The writer has set the outline view to show the first two levels of his report.

Using the outline view, it is easy to identify organization problems:

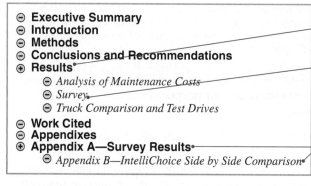

- ⊖ **Executive Summary**
- ⊖ **Introduction**
- ⊖ **Methods**
- ⊖ **Conclusions and Recommendations**
- ⊕ **Results**
  - ⊖ *Analysis of Maintenance Costs*
  - ⊖ *Survey*
  - ⊖ *Truck Comparison and Test Drives*
- ⊖ **Work Cited**
- ⊖ **Appendixes**
- ⊕ **Appendix A—Survey Results**
  - ⊖ *Appendix B—IntelliChoice Side by Side Comparison*

- The results section should precede the conclusions and recommendations section.

- In the results section, the second item — survey — seems to be different from the other two items, both of which seem to relate to the topic of the vehicles, not to the methods the writer used.

- Appendix A and Appendix B should both be second-level headings.

FIGURE 3.2 **Studying the Organization of a Document Using the Outline View**

◢| GUIDELINES Revising the Draft

After you finish your draft, look through it to make sure the writing is well organized, well developed, and coherent. The following questions can help you study the draft yourself; they can also be used as a helpful guide for your reviewers.

▶ **Does the draft meet readers' expectations?** If, for instance, the readers of a report expect a transmittal letter, they might be confused if they don't see one. Check to make sure that the draft includes the information readers expect and looks the way they expect it to. Be especially careful if the document or site will be used by people from other cultures, who might have different expectations. For more on writing for multicultural readers, see Chapter 5, page 101.

▶ **Has anything been left out in turning the outline into a draft?** Check the original outline to see that all the topics are included in the document itself. Review the outline of the final draft to focus on the headings. Is anything missing?

▶ **Is the organization logical?** The document is likely to reflect several different organizational patterns. For instance, the overall pattern might be chronological. Within that pattern, sections might be organized from more important to less important. When you look at the headings, are these patterns visible, and do they seem to work well? For more on organizational patterns, see Chapter 7.

▶ **Are the arguments well developed?** Have claims been presented clearly and emphatically? Has sufficient and appropriate research been done to gather evidence that supports the claims effectively? Is the reasoning valid and persuasive? For more on conducting research, see Chapter 6. For more on using evidence effectively, see Chapter 8, page 184.

▶ **Is the emphasis appropriate throughout the draft?** If a major point is treated only briefly, mark it for possible expansion. If a minor topic is treated at great length, mark it for possible condensing.

(continued)

▶ **Is the draft honest, and does it adhere to appropriate legal standards?** Is the information presented honestly? Is any information misleading? Has any critical information that might counter the argument been omitted? Does the document adhere to appropriate legal standards of intellectual property, such as copyright law? Does it comply with relevant accessibility standards? For more on ethical and legal issues, see Chapter 2.

▶ **Does the document come across as reliable and helpful?** Check to see that the writing style is fully professional: modest, understated, and cooperative. For more on a professional persona, see Chapter 8, page 193.

The second category of reviewers includes both actual users of your existing document and prospective users of the next version of the document. These people can help you see problems you or other knowledgeable readers don't notice. For instance, a prospective user of a document on fuel-cell technologies might point out that she doesn't understand what a fuel cell is because you haven't defined the term.

For more about these techniques, as well as usability testing, see Ch. 13.

How do you learn from SMEs and from users and prospective users? Here are a few techniques:

- surveying, interviewing, or observing readers as they use the existing document
- interviewing SMEs about a draft of the document
- conducting focus groups to learn users' or prospective users' opinions about an existing or proposed document
- uploading the document to an online writing space, such as Microsoft SharePoint or Google Drive, and authorizing people to revise it

It is important to revise all drafts, but it is especially important to revise drafts of documents that will be read and used by people from other cultures. If your readers come from another culture, try to have your draft reviewed by someone from that culture. That reviewer can help you see whether you have made correct assumptions about how readers will react to your ideas and whether you have chosen appropriate kinds of evidence and design elements. As discussed in Chapters 11 and 12, people from other cultures might be surprised by some design elements used in reports, such as marginal comments.

ETHICS NOTE
ACKNOWLEDGING REVIEWERS RESPONSIBLY

When you write on the job, take advantage of the expertise of others. It is completely ethical to ask subject-matter experts and people who are similar to the intended audience of your document to critique a draft of it. If your reviewer offers detailed comments and suggestions on the draft or sends you a multipage review — and you use some or many of the ideas — you are ethically bound to acknowledge that person's contributions. This acknowledgment can take the form of a one- or two-sentence statement of appreciation in the introduction of the document or in a transmittal letter. Or you could write a letter or memo of appreciation to the reviewer; he or she can then file it and use it for a future performance evaluation.

Editing

Having revised your draft and made changes to its content and organization, it's time for you to edit. Editing is the process of checking the draft to improve its grammar, punctuation, style, usage, diction (word choice), and mechanics (such as use of numbers and abbreviations). You will do most of the editing by yourself, but you might also ask others for assistance, especially writers and editors in your organization. One technology that enables people at different locations to work together is a wiki, a website that lets authorized readers edit a document (also referred to as a wiki) and archives all the previous versions of the document.

The resources devoted to editing will vary depending on the importance of the document. An annual report, which is perhaps the single most important document that people will read about your organization, will be edited rigorously because the company wants it to look perfect. A biweekly employee newsletter also will be edited, but not as rigorously as an annual report. What about the routine emails you write every day? Edit them, too. It's unprofessional not to.

For a discussion of using wikis to create collaborative documents, see Ch. 4.

GUIDELINES Editing the Draft

After you address the big-picture revision issues, consider these five questions related to the verbal and visual elements of the draft:

▶ **Are all paragraphs well developed?** Does each paragraph begin with a clear topic sentence that previews or summarizes the main point? Are all claims validated with appropriate and sufficient support? For more on paragraph development, see Chapter 9.

▶ **Are all sentences clear and correct?** Make sure each sentence is easy to understand, is grammatically correct, and is structured to emphasize the appropriate information. For more on writing effective sentences, see Chapter 10.

▶ **Are all the elements presented consistently?** Check to see that parallel items are presented consistently. For example, are all headings on the same level structured the same way (perhaps as noun phrases or as gerunds, ending in *-ing*)? And check for grammatical parallelism, particularly in lists, but also in traditional sentences. For more on parallelism, see Chapter 10, page 230.

▶ **Is the design effective?** Does the document or site look professional and attractive, and is it easy to navigate? Do readers find it easy to locate the information they want? For more on design, see Chapter 11.

▶ **Are graphics used appropriately?** Are there opportunities to translate verbal information into graphics to make the communication easier to understand and more emphatic? Are the graphic types appropriate and effective? Are the graphics linked to the text? For more on graphics, see Chapter 12.

Proofreading

For more about proofreading, see Appendix, Part C.

Proofreading is the process of checking to make sure you have typed what you meant to type. You are looking for minor problems caused by carelessness or haste. For instance, have you written *filename* on one page and *file name* on another? Have you been consistent in expressing quantities in numerals or in words? Have you been consistent in punctuating citations in your list of works cited?

Look particularly for problems in word endings. For instance, a phrase such as "we studying the records from the last quarter" is likely a careless error left over from an earlier draft of the sentence. Change it to "we studied the records from the last quarter." Also look for missing and repeated words: "We studied the from the last quarter" or "We studied the the records from the last quarter."

Although your software can help you with some of these chores, it isn't sophisticated enough to do it all. The following sentence contains three errors that you should catch in proofreading:

There are for major reasons we should implementing health-promotion program.

Here they are:

1. "For" is the wrong word. The word should be "four."
2. "Implementing" is the wrong verb form. The verb should be "implement." This mistake is probably left over from an earlier version of the sentence.
3. The article "a" is missing before the phrase "health-promotion program." This is probably just a result of carelessness.

By the way, a spell-checker and grammar-checker didn't flag any of these errors.

Although some writers can proofread effectively on the screen, others prefer to print a copy of the text. These writers say that because the text looks different on the page than it does on the screen, they are more likely to approach it with fresh eyes, as their eventual readers will, and therefore more likely to see errors.

Proofreading is vital to producing a clear, well-written document that reflects your high standards and underscores your credibility as a professional. Don't insult yourself and your readers by skipping this step. Reread your draft carefully and slowly, perhaps out loud, and get a friend to help. You'll be surprised at how many errors you'll find.

WRITER'S CHECKLIST

In planning the document, did you

☐ analyze your audience? *(p. 44)*

☐ analyze your purpose? *(p. 44)*

☐ analyze your setting? *(p. 44)*

☐ select an appropriate document application, design, and delivery method? *(p. 45)*

☐ analyze your writing process? *(p. 46)*

☐ generate ideas about your subject? *(p. 47)*

☐ research additional information? *(p. 47)*

☐ devise a schedule and a budget? *(p. 47)*

In drafting the document, did you

☐ organize and outline your document? *(p. 49)*

☐ use templates, if appropriate? *(p. 49)*

☐ use styles? *(p. 53)*

In revising the draft, did you

☐ study the draft by yourself? *(p. 56)*

☐ seek help from others? *(p. 56)*

☐ Did you edit the document carefully? *(p. 59)*

☐ Did you proofread the document carefully? *(p. 60)*

EXERCISES

1. Read your word processor's online help about using the outline view. Make a file with five headings, each of which has a sentence of body text below it. Practice using the outline feature to do the following tasks:

   a. change a first-level heading to a second-level heading

   b. move the first heading in your outline to the end of the document

   c. hide the body text that goes with one of the headings

2. Your word processor probably contains a number of templates for such applications as letters, memos, and résumés. Evaluate one of these templates. Is it clear and professional looking? Does it present a design that will be effective for all users or only for some? What changes would you make to the template to improve it? Write a memo to your instructor presenting your findings, and attach a copy of the template. For more about memos, see Ch. 14, p. 386.

3. Proofread the following paragraph. For information on writing effective sentences, see Chapter 10 and Appendix, Part C.

   People who have a federal student loan can apply for a program from the Department of Education that is intended to give relief to former students with moderate incomes by sketching the payments out over a longer period. The program calculates monthly payments on the basis of income. In addition, the program forgave balances after 25 years (10 years if the the person chooses employment in public service). The monthly-payment calculation, called income-based repayment (IBR), is determined by the size of the loan and the person's income. For some 90 percent of the more than one million people who have already enrolled, the IRB works out to less than 10 percent of their income. The program also caps the payments at 15 percent of a person's income over $16,000 a year (and eliminates payments for people who earn less than $16,000).

CASE 3: Understanding Why Revision Software Cannot Revise and Edit Your Document

You are an engineer who has been asked to write a project report regarding a defect in a wireless heart-rate monitor for bicyclists. Your supervisor has some concerns about the quality of the writing in the draft of the report you submitted and has asked you to rework the introduction. If your instructor has assigned it, go to Achieve to get started revising the report.

Writing Collaboratively

4

THE EXPLOSIVE GROWTH of digital media has greatly expanded the scope of workplace collaboration, reducing barriers of time and space. Today, people routinely collaborate not only with members of their project teams but also with others within and outside their organization, as shown in Figure 4.1.

But how exactly does this sort of collaboration work? In every possible way. For example, you and other members of your project team might use collaboration tools primarily to gather information that you will use in your research. You bring this information back to your team, and then you work exclusively with your team in drafting, revising, and proofreading your document. In a more complex collaboration pattern, you and other members of your team might use collaboration tools to gather information from sources around the globe and then reach out to others in your organization to see what they think of your new ideas. Later in the process, you create the outline of your document, in the form of a wiki, and authorize everyone in your own organization to draft sections, pose questions and comments, and even edit what others have written. In short, you can collaborate with any number of people at one or at several stages of the writing process.

For more about the writing process, see Ch. 3.

Every document is unique and will therefore call for a unique kind of collaboration. Your challenge is to think creatively about how you can work effectively with others to make your document as good as it can be. Being aware of the strengths and limitations of collaborative tools can prompt you to find people in your community and around the world who can help you think about your subject and write about it compellingly and persuasively.

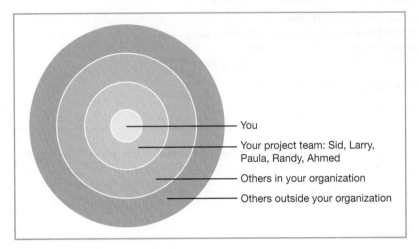

FIGURE 4.1   Collaboration Beyond the Project Team

Using digital collaboration tools such as messaging technologies, videoconferencing, shared document workspaces, and wikis, you can tap into the world's knowledge for ideas and information.

Advantages and Disadvantages of Collaboration

As a student, you have probably already worked collaboratively on course projects. As a professional, you will work collaboratively on many more projects. In the workplace, the stakes might be higher. Effective collaboration can make you look like a star, but ineffective collaboration can ruin an important project—and hurt your reputation. The best way to start thinking about collaboration is to understand its main advantages and disadvantages.

ADVANTAGES OF COLLABORATION

According to a study conducted by the Institute for Corporate Productivity in collaboration with Professor Rob Cross from Babson College (2017), companies that promoted collaborative working were five times as likely to be high performing than companies that did not. Writers who collaborate can create a better document and improve the way an organization functions:

- **Collaboration draws on a wider knowledge base.** Therefore, a collaborative document can be more comprehensive and more accurate than a single-author document.

- **Collaboration draws on a wider skills base.** No one person can be an expert manager, writer, editor, graphic artist, and production person.

- **Collaboration provides a better idea of how the audience will read the document.** Because each collaborator acts as an audience, working with collaborators produces more questions and suggestions than one person could while writing alone.

- **Collaboration improves communication among employees.** Because you and your collaborators share a goal, you learn about each other's jobs, responsibilities, and frustrations.

- **Collaboration helps acclimate new employees to an organization.** New employees learn how things work—which people to see, which forms to fill out, and so forth—as well as what the organization values, such as ethical conduct and the willingness to work hard and sacrifice for an important initiative.

- **Collaboration motivates employees to help an organization grow.** New employees bring new skills, knowledge, and attitudes that can help the organization develop. More experienced employees mentor the new employees as they learn. Everyone teaches and learns from everyone else, and the organization benefits.

DISADVANTAGES OF COLLABORATION

Collaboration can also have important disadvantages:

- **Collaboration takes more time than individual writing.** It takes longer because of the time needed for the collaborators to communicate. In addition, meetings—whether they are live or remote—can be difficult to schedule.

- **Collaboration can lead to groupthink.** When collaborators value getting along more than thinking critically about the project, they are prone to *groupthink*. Groupthink, which promotes conformity, can result in an inferior document, because no one wants to cause a scene by asking tough questions.

- **Collaboration can yield a disjointed document.** Sections can contradict or repeat each other or be written in different styles. To prevent these problems, writers need to plan and edit the document carefully.

- **Collaboration can lead to inequitable workloads.** Despite the project leader's best efforts, some people will end up doing more work than others.

- **Collaboration can reduce a person's motivation to work hard on the document.** A collaborator who feels alienated from the team can lose motivation to make the extra effort.

- **Collaboration can lead to interpersonal conflict.** People can disagree about the best way to create the document or about the document itself. Such disagreements can hurt working relationships during the project and long after.

Managing Projects

At some point in your career, you will likely collaborate on a project that is just too big, too technical, too complex, or too difficult for your team to complete successfully without some advance planning and careful oversight.

Often, collaborative projects last several weeks or months, and the efforts of several people are required at scheduled times for the project to proceed. For this reason, collaborators need to spend time managing the project to ensure that it not only meets the needs of the audience but also is completed on time and, if relevant, within budget.

◢ GUIDELINES Managing Your Project

These seven suggestions can help you keep your project on track.

▶ **Break down a large project into several smaller tasks.** Working backward from what you must deliver to your client or manager, partition your project into its component parts, making a list of what steps your team must take to complete the project. This task is not only the foundation of project management but also a good strategy for determining the resources you will need to complete the project successfully and on time. After you have a list of tasks to complete, you can begin to plan your project, assign responsibilities, and set deadlines.

▶ **Plan your project.** Planning allows collaborators to develop an effective approach and reach agreement before investing a lot of time and resources. Planning prevents small problems from becoming big problems with a deadline looming. Effective project managers use planning documents such as *needs analyses*, *information plans*, *specifications*, and *project plans*.

▶ **Create and maintain an accurate schedule.** An accurate schedule helps collaborators plan ahead, allocate their time, and meet deadlines. Update your schedule when changes are made, and either place the up-to-date schedule in an easily accessible location (for example, on a project website) or send the schedule to each team member. If the team misses a deadline, immediately create a new deadline. Team members should always know when tasks must be completed.

▶ **Put your decisions in writing.** Writing down your decisions, and communicating them to all collaborators, helps the team remember what happened. In addition, if questions arise, the team can refer easily to the document and, if necessary, update it.

▶ **Monitor the project.** By regularly tracking the progress of the project, the team can learn what has already been accomplished, whether the project is on schedule, and if any unexpected challenges exist.

▶ **Distribute and act on information quickly.** Acting fast to get collaborators the information they need helps ensure that the team makes effective decisions and steady progress toward completing the project.

▶ **Be flexible regarding schedule and responsibilities.** Adjust your plan and methods when new information becomes available or problems arise. When tasks are held up because earlier tasks have been delayed or need reworking, the team should consider revising responsibilities to keep the project moving forward.

Conducting Meetings

Collaboration involves meetings. Whether you are meeting live in a room or using videoconferencing tools, the five aspects of meetings discussed in this section can help you use your time productively and produce the best possible document.

LISTENING EFFECTIVELY

Participating in a meeting involves listening and speaking. If you listen carefully to other people, you will understand what they are thinking and will be able to speak knowledgeably and constructively. Unlike hearing, which involves receiving and processing sound waves, listening involves understanding what the speaker is saying and interpreting the information.

◀

GUIDELINES Listening Effectively

Follow these five steps to improve your effectiveness as a listener.

▶ **Pay attention to the speaker.** Look at the speaker, and don't let your mind wander.

▶ **Listen for main ideas.** Pay attention to phrases that signal important information, such as "What I'm saying is . . ." or "The point I'm trying to make is. . . ."

▶ **Don't get emotionally involved with the speaker's ideas.** Even if you disagree, continue to listen. Keep an open mind. Don't stop listening in order to plan what you are going to say next.

▶ **Ask questions to clarify what the speaker said.** After the speaker finishes, ask questions to make sure you understand. For instance, "When you said that each journal recommends different protocols, did you mean that each journal recommends several protocols or that each journal recommends a different protocol?"

▶ **Provide appropriate feedback.** The most important feedback is to look into the speaker's eyes. You can nod your approval to signal that you understand what he or she is saying. Appropriate feedback helps assure the speaker that he or she is communicating effectively.

SETTING YOUR TEAM'S AGENDA

It's important to get your team off to a smooth start. In the first meeting, start to define your team's agenda.

Figure 4.2 shows a work-schedule form. Figure 4.3 on p. 70 shows a team-member evaluation form, and Figure 4.4 on p. 71 shows a self-evaluation form.

◢

GUIDELINES Setting Your Team's Agenda

Carrying out these tasks will help your team work effectively and efficiently.

▶ **Define the team's task.** Every team member has to agree on the task, the deadline, and the approximate length of the document. You also need to agree on more conceptual points, including the document's audience, purpose, and scope.

▶ **Choose a team leader.** This person serves as the link between the team and management. (In an academic setting, the team leader represents the team in communicating with the instructor.) The team leader also keeps the team on track, leads the meetings, and coordinates communication among team members.

▶ **Define tasks for each team member.** There are three main ways to divide the tasks: according to technical expertise (for example, one team member, an engineer, is responsible for the information about engineering), according to stages of the writing process (one team member contributes to all stages, whereas another participates only during the planning stage), or according to sections of the document (several team members work on the whole document, but others work only on, say, the appendixes). People will likely assume informal roles, too. One person might be good at clarifying what others have said, another at preventing arguments, and another at asking questions that force the team to reevaluate its decisions.

▶ **Establish working procedures.** Before starting to work, collaborators need answers — in writing, if possible — to the following questions:

— When and where will we meet?

— What procedures will we follow in the meetings?

— What tools will we use to communicate with other team members, including the leader, and how often will we communicate?

▶ **Establish a procedure for resolving conflict productively.** Disagreements about the project can lead to a better product. Give collaborators a chance to express ideas fully and find areas of agreement, and then resolve the conflict with a vote.

▶ **Create a style sheet.** A style sheet defines the characteristics of the document's writing style. For instance, a style sheet states how many levels of headings the document will have, whether it will have lists, whether it will have an informal tone (for example, using "you" and contractions), and so forth. If all collaborators draft using a similar writing style, the document will need less revision. And be sure to use styles, as discussed in Chapter 3, to ensure a consistent design for headings and other textual features and to save time.

▶ **Establish a work schedule.** For example, for a proposal to be submitted on February 10, you might aim to complete the outline by January 25, the draft by February 1, and the revision by February 8. These dates are called *milestones*.

▶ **Create evaluation materials.** Team members have a right to know how their work will be evaluated. In college, students often evaluate themselves and other team members. In the working world, managers are more likely to do the evaluations.

WORK-SCHEDULE FORM

Name of Project:	*VoIP feasibility study*
Principal Reader:	*Joan*
Other Readers:	*Carlton, Wendy*
Group Members:	*Saada, Larry, Randy, Ahmed*
Type of Document Required:	*recommendation report*

Milestones	Responsible Member	Status	Date
Deliver Document	*Saada*		*May 19*
Proofread Document	*all*		*May 18*
Send Document to Print Shop	*n/a*		*n/a*
Complete Revision	*Randy*		*May 17*
Review Draft Elements	*all*	*Done*	*May 16*
Assemble Draft	*Ahmed*	*Done*	*May 13*
Establish Tasks	*Larry*	*Done*	*May 9*

Progress Reports	Responsible Member	Status	Date
Progress Report 3	*n/a*		
Progress Report 2	*n/a*		
Progress Report 1	*Randy*	*Done*	*May 15*

Meetings	Agenda	Location	Date	Time
Meeting 3	*Review final draft*	*Room C*	*May 18*	*3:30*
Meeting 2	*Review draft elements*	*Room B*	*May 16*	*2:00*
Meeting 1	*Kickoff meeting*	*Room C*	*May 9*	*3:00*

Notes

FIGURE 4.2
Work-Schedule Form

Notice that milestones are sometimes presented in reverse chronological order; the delivery-date milestone, for instance, comes first. On other forms, items are presented in normal chronological order.

The form includes spaces for listing the person responsible for each milestone and progress report and for stating the progress toward each milestone and progress report.

For printable versions of Figs. 4.2, 4.3, and 4.4, see the downloadable forms in Achieve.

ETHICS NOTE

PULLING YOUR WEIGHT ON COLLABORATIVE PROJECTS

Collaboration involves an ethical dimension. If you work hard and well, you help the other members of the team. If you don't, you hurt them.

You can't be held responsible for knowing and doing everything, and sometimes unexpected problems arise in other courses or in your private life that prevent you from participating as actively and effectively as you otherwise could. When problems occur, inform the other team members as soon as possible. For instance, call the team leader as soon as you realize you will have to miss a meeting. Be honest about what happened. Suggest ways you might make up for missing a task. If you communicate clearly, the other team members are likely to cooperate with you.

If you are a member of a team that includes someone who is not participating fully, keep records of your attempts to get in touch with that person. When you do make contact, you owe it to that person to try to find out what the problem is and suggest ways to resolve it. Your goal is to treat that person fairly and to help him or her do better work, so that the team will function more smoothly and more effectively.

FIGURE 4.3
Team-Member Evaluation Form

TEAM-MEMBER EVALUATION FORM

Your name: _____Mackenzie Hopkins_____

Title of the project: _____4-wheel-drive feasibility report_____

Date: _____October 14, 2017_____

Instructions

Use this form to evaluate the other members of your group. Write the name of each group member other than yourself in one of the columns, then assign a score of 0 to 10 (0 being the lowest grade, 10 the highest) to each group member for each criterion. Then total the scores for each member. Because each group member has different strengths and weaknesses, the scores you assign will differ. On the back of this sheet, write any comments you wish to make.

Criteria	Team Members			
	Vinh-Thuy	Karina	Bob	
1. Regularly attends meetings	1. 10	1. 9	1. 6	1.
2. Is prepared at meetings	2. 9	2. 8	2. 5	2.
3. Meets deadlines	3. 9	3. 9	3. 2	3.
4. Contributes good ideas in meetings	4. 9	4. 10	4. 9	4.
5. Contributes ideas diplomatically	5. 8	5. 9	5. 9	5.
6. Submits high-quality work	6. 9	6. 9	6. 7	6.
7. Listens to other members	7. 8	7. 10	7. 6	7.
8. Shows respect for other members	8. 9	8. 10	8. 6	8.
9. Helps to reduce conflict	9. 9	9. 10	9. 5	9.
10. Your overall assessment of this person's contribution	10. 9	10. 9	10. 7	10.
Total Points	89	93	62	

Mackenzie gives high grades to Vinh-Thuy and Karina but low grades to Bob. If Vinh-Thuy and Karina agree with Mackenzie's assessment of Bob's participation, the three of them should meet with Bob to discuss why his participation has been weak and to consider ways for him to improve.

CONDUCTING EFFICIENT MEETINGS

Much of human communication is nonverbal. That is, although people communicate through words and through the tone, rate, and volume of their speech, they also communicate through body language. For this reason, meetings provide the most information about what a person is thinking and feeling—and the best opportunity for team members to understand one another.

To help make meetings effective and efficient, team members should arrive on time and stick to the agenda. One team member should serve as secretary, recording the important decisions made at the meeting. At the end of the meeting, the team leader should summarize the team's accomplishments and state the tasks each team member is to perform before the next meeting. If possible, the secretary should give each team member this informal set of meeting minutes.

For a discussion of meeting minutes, see Ch. 17, p. 481.

FIGURE 4.4
Self-Evaluation Form

SELF-EVALUATION FORM

Your name: _Lucas Barnes_   Date: _April 12, 2017_

Title of the project: _digital-camera study progress report_

Instructions

On this form, record and evaluate your own involvement in this project. In the Log section, record the activities you performed as an individual and those you performed as part of the team. For all activities, record the date and the number of hours you spent. In the Evaluation section, write two brief statements, one about aspects of your contribution you think were successful and one about aspects you want to improve.

Log Individual Activities	Date	Number of Hours
Reviewed proposal and analyzed the Simmons article	April 9	1.5
Wrote a draft of the progress report	April 10	2.5
Revised a draft of the progress report	April 11	1

Activities as Part of Team	Date	Number of Hours
Met to discuss test research	April 10	1
Emailed group and replied to questions about draft	April 11	2.5
Met to discuss revision of progress report	April 11	1.5

Evaluation
Aspects of My Participation That Were Successful

I think I did a good job in reviewing the proposal and critiquing the research. I had the draft ready on time, although there were some rough parts in it. I participated effectively in the group meeting about the revision. I think I'm getting a little better about being less sensitive when the team suggests revisions.

Aspects of My Participation That I Want to Improve in the Future

I still need to get better at completing my work early enough so I can set it aside before getting it out to the other group members. I get embarrassed when they point out superficial mistakes that I should have caught. I need to practice using styles so that my drafts are easier to incorporate into the group's draft. The other members remembered to use them. I didn't.

The evaluation section of the form is difficult to fill out, but it can be the most valuable section for you in assessing your skills in collaborating. When you get to the second question, be thoughtful and constructive. Don't merely say that you want to improve your skills in using the software. And don't just write "None."

COMMUNICATING DIPLOMATICALLY

Because collaborating can be stressful, it can lead to interpersonal conflict. People can become frustrated and angry with one another because of personality clashes or because of disputes about the project. If the project is to succeed, however, team members have to work together productively. When you speak in a team meeting, you want to appear helpful, not critical or overbearing.

CRITIQUING A TEAM MEMBER'S WORK

In your college classes, you probably have critiqued other students' writing. In the workplace, you will do the same sort of critiquing of notes and drafts written by other team members. Knowing how to do it without offending the writer is a valuable skill.

◢ GUIDELINES: Communicating Diplomatically

These suggestions for communicating diplomatically will help you communicate effectively.

▶ **Listen carefully, without interrupting.** See the Guidelines box on page 67.

▶ **Give everyone a chance to speak.** Don't dominate the discussion.

▶ **Avoid personal remarks and insults.** Be tolerant and respectful of other people's views and working methods. Doing so is right—and smart: if you anger people, they will go out of their way to oppose you.

▶ **Don't overstate your position.** A modest qualifier such as "I think" or "it seems to me" is an effective signal to your listeners that you realize that everyone might not share your views.

> OVERBEARING   My plan is a sure thing; there's no way we're not going to kill Allied next quarter.

> DIPLOMATIC   I think this plan has a good chance of success: we're playing off our strengths and Allied's weaknesses.

Note that in the diplomatic version, the speaker says "this plan," not "my plan."

▶ **Don't get emotionally attached to your own ideas.** When people oppose you, try to understand why. Digging in is usually unwise—unless it's a matter of principle—because, although it's possible that you are right and everyone else is wrong, it's not likely.

▶ **Ask pertinent questions.** Bright people ask questions to understand what they hear and to connect it to other ideas. Asking questions also encourages other team members to examine what they hear.

▶ **Pay attention to nonverbal communication.** Bob might *say* that he understands a point, but his facial expression might show that he doesn't. If a team member looks confused, ask him or her about it. A direct question is likely to elicit a statement that will help the team clarify its discussion.

◢ GUIDELINES: Critiquing a Colleague's Work

People can be sensitive about their writing. Following these three suggestions for critiquing writing will increase the chances that your colleague will consider your ideas positively.

▶ **Start with a positive comment.** Even if the work is weak, say, "You've obviously put a lot of work into this, Joanne. Thanks." Or, "This is a really good start. Thanks, Joanne."

(continued)

▶ **Discuss the larger issues first.** Begin with the big issues, such as organization, development, logic, design, and graphics. Then work on smaller issues, such as paragraph development, sentence-level matters, and word choice. Leave editing and proofreading until the end of the process.

▶ **Talk about the document, not the writer.**

RUDE	You don't explain clearly why this criterion is relevant.
BETTER	I'm having trouble understanding how this criterion relates to the topic.

Your goal is to improve the quality of the document you will submit, not to evaluate the writer or the draft. Offer constructive suggestions.

RUDE	Why didn't you include the price comparisons here, as you said you would?
BETTER	I wonder if the report would be stronger if we included the price comparisons here.

In the better version, the speaker focuses on the goal (to create an effective report) rather than on the writer's draft. Also, the speaker qualifies his recommendation by saying, "I wonder if. . . ." This approach sounds constructive rather than boastful or annoyed.

DOCUMENT ANALYSIS ACTIVITY

Critiquing a Draft Clearly and Diplomatically

This is an excerpt from the Methods section of a report about computer servers. In this section, the writer is explaining the tasks he performed in analyzing different servers. In a later section, he explains what he learned from the analysis. The comments in the balloons were inserted into the document by the author's colleague.

The questions in the margin ask you to think about techniques for critiquing.

The first task of the on-site evaluations was to set up and configure each server. We noted the relative complexity of setting up each system to our network.

Comment: Huh? What exactly does this mean?

After we had the system configured, we performed a set of routine maintenance tasks: add a new memory module, swap a hard drive, swap a power supply, and perform system diagnostics.

Comment: Okay, good. Maybe we should explain why we chose these tests.

We recorded the time and relative difficulty of each task. Also, we tried to gather a qualitative feeling for how much effort would be involved in the day-to-day maintenance of the systems.

Comment: What kind of scale are you using? If we don't explain it, it's basically useless.

Comment: Same question as above.

After each system was set up, we completed the maintenance evaluations and began the benchmark testing. We ran the complete WinBench and NetBench test suites on each system. We chose several of the key factors from these tests for comparison.

Comment: Will readers know these are the right tests? Should we explain?

1. What is the tone of the comments? How can they be improved?

2. How well does the collaborator address the larger issues?

3. How well does the collaborator address the writing, not the writer?

4. How well do the collaborator's comments focus on the goal of the document, rather than judging the quality of the writing?

▶ TECH TIP

Why To Use Reviewing Tools

Technical communicators rarely work alone. They typically collaborate with others on a team, giving and receiving feedback on documents, often with electronic reviewing tools. Electronic reviewing tools allow teams to exchange feedback, written and visual, in the documents themselves, determine who has provided what feedback, retain previous versions of documents, specify who can change the original documents, and more. Google, Microsoft, and Adobe, among others, have developed programs and features that allow users to work efficiently in these situations, enabling control over reviewing processes.

How To Use Reviewing Tools

Some programs require you to turn on the **Review** function (called "Track Changes" in Microsoft Word and "Suggesting" in Google Docs) in order to **track the changes** you make on a document as you type. In Adobe Acrobat, you need to work with the **Select** tool.

Microsoft Word   **Google Docs**   **Adobe Acrobat**

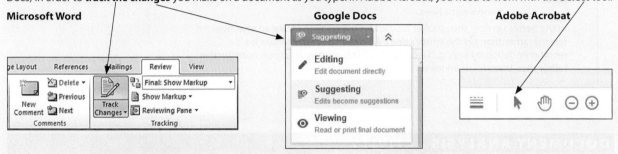

You can insert **comments** (or "Sticky Notes" in Adobe Acrobat) in places where you want to ask questions or provide further information without disrupting the text. You can also use the **highlight** feature to emphasize words and passages. And you can **reply to** or **resolve** others' comments.

Commenting with Microsoft Word

Replying with Google Docs

Highlighting and Commenting with Adobe Acrobat

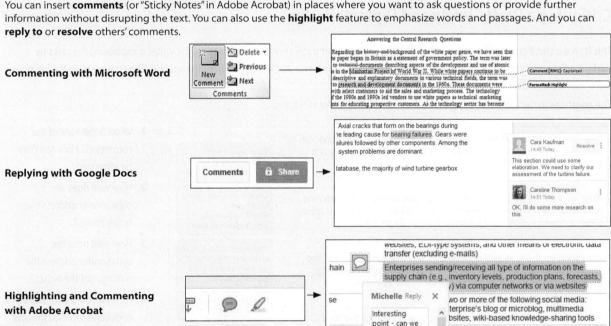

(continued)

You can review the tracked changes and comments of others, accepting or rejecting their changes. If you are not the owner of the document, make sure the owner has authorized you to **accept**, **reject**, **resolve**, **undo**, or **delete** the changes of others. If you are unsure, insert a note indicating any places you make changes that might otherwise go unnoticed.

Microsoft Word

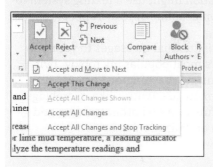

Google Docs

Adobe Acrobat

Using Electronic Tools in Collaboration

Professionals use many types of electronic tools to exchange information and ideas as they collaborate. The following discussion highlights the major technologies that enable collaboration: word-processing tools, messaging technologies, videoconferencing, wikis and shared document workspaces, and virtual worlds.

WORD-PROCESSING TOOLS

Most word processors offer three powerful features that are useful in collaborative work:

- The *comment feature* lets readers add electronic comments to a file.
- The *revision feature* lets readers mark up a text by deleting, revising, and adding words and indicates who made which suggested changes.
- The *highlighting feature* lets readers use different "highlighting pens" to call the writer's attention to a particular passage.

MESSAGING TECHNOLOGIES

Two messaging technologies that have been around for decades are instant messaging and email. *Instant messaging (IM)*, or chat functionality, is real-time, text-based communication between two or more people. In the working world, IM enables people in different locations to communicate textual information at the same time. *Email* is an asynchronous medium for sending brief textual messages and for transferring files such as documents, spreadsheets, images, and videos.

For more about writing email, see Ch. 14, p. 388.

For use on mobile devices such as phones, the two most popular messaging technologies are text messaging and microblogging.

Text messaging enables people to use mobile devices to send messages that can include text, audio, images, and video. Texting is the fastest-growing technology for exchanging messages electronically because most people keep their phones nearby. Organizations use text messaging for such purposes as sending a quick update or alerting people that an item has been delivered or a task completed. On your campus, the administration might use a texting system to remind students of an upcoming registration deadline or to alert people about a campus emergency.

Microblogging is a way of sending very brief textual messages to your personal network. You probably use the world's most popular microblog, Twitter, which now has more than 300 million users (Washington Post, 2019). Although some organizations use Twitter, many use Twitter-like microblogs such as Yammer, which includes a search function and other features and which can be administered from within an organization.

VIDEOCONFERENCING

Videoconferencing technology allows two or more people at different locations to simultaneously see and hear one another as well as exchange documents, share data on computer displays, and use electronic whiteboards. Systems such as Skype are simple and inexpensive, requiring only a webcam and some free software. However, there are also large, dedicated systems that require extensive electronics, including cameras, servers, and a fiber-optic network or high-speed telephone lines. Figure 4.5 shows a videoconference in progress.

FIGURE 4.5

A Videoconference

Videoconferencing systems range from sophisticated ones like this, to inexpensive cameras attached to individual workstations, to systems that work on smartphones. Most videoconferencing systems can display more than one window to accommodate several sets of participants.

Courtesy Cisco Systems, Inc.

GUIDELINES Participating in a Videoconference

Follow these six suggestions for participating effectively in a videoconference.

▶ **Practice using the technology.** For many people, being on camera is uncomfortable, especially the first time. Before participating in a high-stakes videoconference, become accustomed to the camera by participating in a few informal videoconferences.

▶ **Arrange for tech support at each site.** Participants can quickly become impatient or lose interest when someone is fumbling to make the technology work. Each site should have a person who can set up the equipment and troubleshoot if problems arise.

▶ **Organize the room to encourage participation.** If there is more than one person at the site, arrange the chairs so that they face the monitor and camera. Each person should be near a microphone. Before beginning the conference, check that each location has adequate audio and video as well as access to other relevant technology such as computer monitors. Finally, remember to introduce everyone in the room, even those off camera, to everyone participating in the conference.

▶ **Make eye contact with the camera.** Eye contact is an important element of establishing your professional persona. The physical setup of some videoconferencing systems means you will likely spend most of your time looking at your monitor and not directly into the camera. However, this might give your viewers the impression that you are avoiding eye contact. Make a conscious effort periodically to look directly into the camera when speaking.

▶ **Dress as you would for a face-to-face meeting.** Wearing inappropriate clothing can distract participants and hurt your credibility.

▶ **Minimize distracting noises and movements.** Sensitive microphones can magnify the sound of shuffling papers, fingers tapping on tables, and whispering. Likewise, depending on your position in the picture frame, excessive movements can be distracting.

WIKIS AND SHARED DOCUMENT WORKSPACES

In the not-too-distant past, people would collaborate on a document by using email to send it from one person to another. One person would write or assemble the document and then send it to another person, who would revise it and send it along to the next person, and so forth. Although the process was effective, it was inefficient: only one person could work on the document at any given moment. Today, two new technologies—wikis and shared document workspaces—make collaborating on a document much simpler and more convenient.

A *wiki* is a web-based document that authorized users can write and edit. The best-known wiki is Wikipedia, an online encyclopedia that contains millions of articles written and edited by people around the world. In the working world, people use software such as MediaWiki and Confluence to host wikis used for creating many kinds of documents, such as instructions, manuals, lists of frequently asked questions, and policy documents. For instance, many organizations create their policies on social media by setting up wikis and inviting employees to write and edit what others have written. The concept is that a wiki draws on the expertise and insights of people throughout the organization and, sometimes, outside the organization. Figure 4.6 shows a portion of a wiki.

A *shared document workspace* makes it convenient for a team of users to edit a file, such as a Prezi or PowerPoint slide deck or a Word document. A shared document workspace such as Microsoft SharePoint or Google Drive archives all the revisions made by each of the team members, so that the team can create a single document that incorporates selected revisions. Some shared document workspaces enable a user to download the document, revise it on his or her computer, and then upload it again. This feature is extremely convenient because the user does not need to be connected to the internet to work on the document.

TASER, a company that manufactures law-enforcement products, uses the shared document workspace Quip to collaborate on press releases and other documents. Figure 4.7 shows one of those press releases in development. In

This portion of a screen from wikiHow shows an excerpt from an article about how to add an HP printer to a wireless network. Users can click on the Edit tab or Edit buttons to edit the article and on the Discuss tab to post questions and answers.

FIGURE 4.6   A Wiki

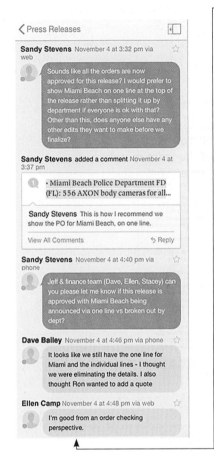

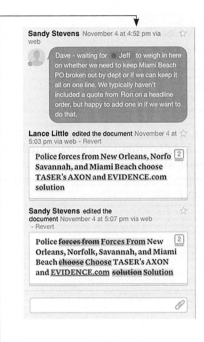

FIGURE 4.7   A Quip Document and Chat Thread

TASER employees collaborate in Quip on final edits to a press release announcing the purchases of products by several municipal police forces. The chat thread, which is located directly to the left of the document, serves as a single space where all communication about a project is recorded, such as approvals from other departments, as well as communication about the document itself. Here, team members discuss how to format information about purchases from multiple departments within a single police force, and they quickly resolve the questions. See the following page for the press release under discussion.

Quip, team members can edit a single version of a document simultaneously. Those edits are recorded in a chat thread, where team members can also add comments and questions. TASER PR Director Sydney Siegmeth notes that Quip helps the company overcome one of collaboration's biggest disadvantages: inefficiency.

Although this section has discussed various collaboration tools as separate technologies, software companies are bundling programs in commercial products such as IBM Sametime, Adobe Creative Cloud, and Skype for Business, which are suites of voice, data, and video services. These services usually share four characteristics:

- **They are cloud based.** That is, organizations lease the services and access them over the internet. They do not have to acquire and maintain special hardware. This model is sometimes called *software as a service.*

TASER's press releases are developed by many teams, including some from outside the company. Before using Quip, Siegmeth's team had to consolidate edits made to various versions of the document by other teams and make sure all of the contributors received updates about the progress of the press release. Quip's chat thread streamlines all communication regarding the document in a single place, ensuring that all parties are kept in the loop. TASER has also found that Quip motivates employees to make their contributions more quickly than they did when working with email and a word processor. "I've found that once someone goes in to make an edit or a comment, others will jump in there too and offer their approval or other edits," Siegmeth says.

FIGURE 4.7 **A Quip Document and Chat Thread** (*continued*)

- **They are integrated across desktop and mobile devices.** Because employees can access these services from their desktops or mobile devices, they are free to collaborate in real time even if they are not at their desks. Some services provide *presence awareness*, the ability to determine a person's online status, availability, and geographic location.

- **They are customizable.** Organizations can choose whichever services they wish and then customize them to work effectively with the rest of the organization's electronic infrastructure, such as computer software and telephone systems.

- **They are secure.** Organizations store the software behind a firewall, providing security: only authorized employees have access to the services.

CROWDSOURCING PLATFORMS

Some problems in technical communication can only be solved by enlisting the help of a large number of people. Crowdsourcing platforms like GitHub allow computer programmers from around the world to collaborate on a library of open-source code that can be downloaded and edited for any purpose. The distributed programmers bring a broad range of expertise from different professional settings, providing widely varying perspectives on coding problems and their solutions. On Zooniverse, nearly 2 million registered volunteers help researchers solve problems by collecting, transcribing, and interpreting data and information. For example, over 5,000 volunteers help monitor the health and behavior of penguin populations by counting penguins in aerial photographs taken with drones and planes. This data helps researchers understand the size and shape of penguin colonies and how penguins use their natural habitat. Answers to these questions are critical to writing policies for marine protected areas (MPAs) in the Antarctic Peninsula.

STRATEGIES FOR ONLINE COMMUNICATION

Jenny Gilbert, Crowdsourcing Data and Information

Technical communicators can crowdsource data and information to help them with the research process. Crowdsourcing is a technique by which customers, stakeholders, and other audiences are asked to contribute their own perspectives and resources to a project. This technique is particularly valuable in large-scale projects for online settings, where problem solving can be distributed and managed over digital networks. Jenny Gilbert is the director of institutional advancement at Mount Auburn Cemetery, a national historic landmark and the country's first rural cemetery. She explains how a crowdsourcing strategy can bring audiences together to help answer certain types of research questions in technical communication contexts.

Mount Auburn Cemetery

JENNY GILBERT

At Mount Auburn Cemetery, Jenny Gilbert writes grants and annual reports and communicates in a variety of ways with donors. The cemetery's database of crowdsourced materials about the deceased, both notables and everyday people from local communities, can be accessed from a website; however, most visitors use the database optimized as a mobile app because it also helps them to navigate the 175-acre site. The app was designed by an interdisciplinary team of professionals, but there are regularly scheduled "digitization days" where people from the community learn how to populate the app with personal artifacts. People who don't need help can simply upload contributions on their own at any time. This example from the mobile app shows part of the entry for Sgt. Nathaniel Preston Harris of Brookline, Massachusetts (1841–1863), who died of disease while serving in the Civil War. The artifacts were provided by family members.

There are over 100,000 people buried and commemorated at Mount Auburn Cemetery. The large-scale task of populating the database could only be accomplished by involving community members.

The database is organized around different types of memories, including family memories, relationship memories, education memories, and career memories.

People can upload letters, photographs, videos, written memories, and more.

All content uploaded to the database must be verified and approved by Mount Auburn Cemetery, to provide quality control.

The people uploading content must have the lawful right to do so. If the content is copyrighted, then they must either own the copyright themselves or have permission to share the content.

The entry of Sgt. Nathaniel Preston includes a personal photograph and the shipping papers that were used to return his remains to Brookline, Massachusetts. Through this crowdsourcing effort, Mount Auburn Cemetery can share important historical artifacts with the general public that would otherwise be unavailable.

FIGURE 4.8 Crowdsourcing Content for a Database

Mount Auburn Cemetery

For more about maintaining a professional presence online, see Ch. 2, p. 38.

ETHICS NOTE

MAINTAINING A PROFESSIONAL PRESENCE ONLINE

According to a report from Cisco Systems (2010), half of the surveyed employees claim to routinely ignore company guidelines that prohibit the use of social media for non-work-related activities during company time. If you use your organization's social media at work, be sure to act professionally so that your actions reflect positively on you and your organization. Be aware of several important legal and ethical issues related to social media.

Although the law has not always kept pace with recent technological innovations, a few things are clear. You and your organization can be held liable if you make defamatory statements (statements that are untrue and damaging) about people or organizations, publish private information (such as trade secrets) or something that publicly places an individual "in a false light," publish personal information, harass others, or participate in criminal activity.

In addition, follow these guidelines to avoid important ethical pitfalls:

- Don't waste company time using social media for nonbusiness purposes. You owe your employer diligence (hard work).
- Don't divulge secure information, such as a login and password that expose your organization to unauthorized access, and don't reveal information about products that have not yet been released.
- Don't divulge private information about anyone. Private information relates to such issues as religion, politics, and sexual orientation.
- Don't make racist or sexist comments or post pictures of people drinking.

If your organization has a written policy on the use of social media, study it carefully. Ask questions if anything in it is unclear. If the policy is incomplete, work to make it complete. If there is no policy, work to create one.

For an excellent discussion of legal and ethical aspects of using your organization's social media, see Kaupins and Park (2010).

You can find a more popular example of crowdsourcing in disaster-response situations. Technical communication researcher Liza Potts studied how citizens used social media during Hurricane Katrina, the London bombings, and the Mumbai attacks to help officials manage critical emergencies that were chaotic and often unpredictable (Potts, 2014). Her findings revealed that social media content shared by the many citizens who were in and around the emergencies was essential to communicating what was going on and what needed to be done to help the victims. The content included written descriptions, photographs, and videos, which were uploaded to digital networks and then circulated across the globe.

Gender and Collaboration

Effective collaboration involves two related challenges: maintaining the team as a productive, friendly working unit and accomplishing the task. Scholars of gender and collaboration see these two challenges as representing the socialized perspectives of women and men.

This discussion should begin with a qualifier: in discussing gender, we are generalizing. The differences in behavior between two people who share a gender are likely to be just as great as the differences in behavior between people of different genders.

The differences in how men and women tend to communicate and work in teams have been traced to each culture's traditional family structure. Because women were traditionally the primary caregivers in American culture, they learned to value nurturing, connection, growth, and cooperation; because men were the primary breadwinners, they learned to value separateness, competition, debate, and even conflict (Karten, 2002). In collaborative teams, women appear to value consensus and relationships more than men do, to show more empathy, and to demonstrate superior listening skills. Women talk more about topics unrelated to the task (Duin, Jorn, & DeBower, 1991), but this talk is central to maintaining team coherence. Men appear to be more competitive than women. Scholars of gender recommend that all professionals strive to achieve an androgynous mix of the skills and aptitudes commonly associated with both women and men.

Culture and Collaboration

For more about multicultural issues, see Ch. 5, p. 107.

Most collaborative teams in industry and in the classroom include people from other cultures. The challenge for all team members is to understand the ways in which cultural differences can affect team behavior. People from other cultures:

- might find it difficult to assert themselves in collaborative teams;
- might be unwilling to respond with a definite "no";
- might be reluctant to admit when they are confused or to ask for clarification;
- might avoid criticizing others;
- might avoid initiating new tasks or performing creatively.

Even the most benign gesture of friendship on the part of a U.S. student can cause confusion. If a U.S. student casually asks a Japanese student about her major and the courses she is taking, the Japanese student might find the question too personal—yet she might consider it perfectly appropriate to talk about her family and her religious beliefs (Lustig & Koester, 2012). Therefore, you should remain open to encounters with people from other cultures without jumping to conclusions about what their actions might or might not mean.

WRITER'S CHECKLIST

In managing your project, did you

☐ break it down into several smaller tasks if it was large? *(p. 66)*

☐ create a plan? *(p. 66)*

☐ create and maintain an accurate schedule? *(p. 66)*

☐ put your decisions in writing? *(p. 66)*

☐ monitor progress? *(p. 66)*

☐ distribute and act on information quickly? *(p. 66)*

☐ act flexibly regarding schedule and responsibilities? *(p. 66)*

At your first team meeting, did you

☐ define the team's task? *(p. 68)*

☐ choose a team leader? *(p. 68)*

☐ define tasks for each team member? *(p. 68)*

☐ establish working procedures? *(p. 68)*

☐ establish a procedure for resolving conflict productively? *(p. 68)*

☐ create a style sheet? *(p. 68)*

☐ establish a work schedule? *(p. 68)*

☐ create evaluation materials? *(p. 68)*

To help make meetings efficient, do you

☐ arrive on time? *(p. 70)*

☐ stick to the agenda? *(p. 70)*

☐ make sure that a team member records important decisions made at the meeting? *(p. 70)*

☐ make sure that the leader summarizes the team's accomplishments and that every member understands what his or her tasks are? *(p. 70)*

To communicate diplomatically, do you

☐ listen carefully, without interrupting? *(p. 72)*

☐ give everyone a chance to speak? *(p. 72)*

☐ avoid personal remarks and insults? *(p. 72)*

☐ avoid overstating your position? *(p. 72)*

☐ avoid getting emotionally attached to your own ideas? *(p. 72)*

☐ ask pertinent questions? *(p. 72)*

☐ pay attention to nonverbal communication? *(p. 72)*

In critiquing a team member's work, do you

☐ start with a positive comment? *(p. 72)*

☐ discuss the larger issues first? *(p. 73)*

☐ talk about the document, not the writer? *(p. 73)*

☐ use the comment, revision, and highlighting features of your word processor, if appropriate? *(p. 74)*

When you participate in a videoconference, do you

☐ first practice using videoconferencing technology? *(p. 77)*

☐ arrange for tech support at each site? *(p. 77)*

☐ organize the room to encourage participation? *(p. 77)*

☐ make eye contact with the camera? *(p. 77)*

☐ dress as you would for a face-to-face meeting? *(p. 77)*

☐ minimize distracting noises and movements? *(p. 77)*

EXERCISES

For more about memos, see Ch. 14, p. 386.

1. Experiment with the comment, revision, and highlighting features of your word processor. Using online help if necessary, learn how to make, revise, and delete comments; make, undo, and accept revisions; and add and delete highlights.

2. Locate free videoconferencing software on the internet. Download the software, and install it on your computer at home. Learn how to use the feature that lets you send attached files.

3. Using a wiki site such as wikiHow.com, find a set of instructions on a technical process that interests you. Study one of the revisions to the instructions, noting the types of changes made. Do the changes relate to the content of the instructions, to the use of graphics, or to the correctness of the writing? Be prepared to share your findings with the class.

4. **TEAM EXERCISE** If you are enrolled in a technical-communication course that calls for you to do a large collaborative project, such as a recommendation report or an oral presentation, meet with your team members. Study the assignment for the project, and then fill out the work-schedule form. (You can download the form from Achieve.) Be prepared to share your completed form with the class.

5. You have probably had a lot of experience working in collaborative teams in previous courses or on the job. Brainstorm for five minutes, listing some of your best and worst experiences participating in collaborative teams. Choose one positive experience and one negative experience. Think about why the positive experience went well. Was there a technique that a team member used that accounted for the positive experience? Think about why the negative experience went wrong. Was there a technique or action that accounted for the negative experience? How might the negative experience have been prevented — or fixed? Be prepared to share your responses with the class.

6. **TEAM EXERCISE** Your college or university wishes to update its website to include a section called "For Prospective International Students." Along with members of your team, first determine whether your school already has information of particular interest to prospective international students. If it does, write a memo to your instructor describing and evaluating the information. Is it accurate? Comprehensive? Clear? Useful? What kind of information should be added to the site to make it more effective?

If the school's site does not have this information, perform the following two tasks:

- *Plan.* What kind of information should this new section include? Does some of this information already exist elsewhere on the web, or does it all have to be created from scratch? For example, can you create a link to an external site with information on how to obtain a student visa? Write an outline of the main topics that should be covered.

- *Draft.* Write the following sections: "Where To Live on or near Campus," "Social Activities on or near Campus," and "If English Is Not Your Native Language." What graphics could you include? Are they already available? What other sites should you link to from these three sections?

In a memo, present your suggestions to your instructor.

CASE 4: Accommodating a Team Member's Scheduling Problems

Your technical-communication instructor has organized you into groups of three in which you will collaborate on a series of projects throughout the semester. Before your first assignment is due, you learn that one team member must deal with a family emergency that will interfere with his ability to participate in the project for some time. Now, you and your other teammate must devise a plan to proceed with the project. You also decide to propose a class-wide policy for communicating with teammates when problems arise. If your instructor has assigned it, go to Achieve to get started on your assignment.

Part 2

Planning the Document

Analyzing Your Audience and Purpose

➡

5

DIGITAL STRATEGIST Jason Falls writes frequently about how companies can use social media to develop relationships with customers. What does he say is the key to using social media for business? Knowing your audience. The analytics report shown in Figure 5.1 provides basic information about the people who have visited a specific Facebook page in the previous four weeks: their gender, age, and geographic location. If you want more detailed information, you can purchase sophisticated tools and software that allow you to analyze the data on your own, or you can hire an expert to do it for you. Understanding your followers — your audience — can help you tailor your page to the people who are already visiting and broaden or adjust your content to reach more people.

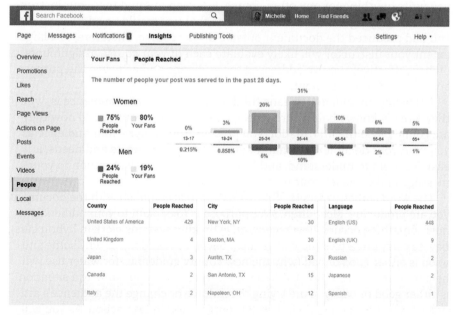

FIGURE 5.1   **Analysis of Facebook Users**

Organizations of all sorts, not just businesses, analyze their audiences. Government agencies that want to appeal to the general public — to urge people to eat better, get vaccinated, or sign up for health insurance, to name just a few activities — start by analyzing their audiences to learn how to motivate them. Political campaigns analyze voters to determine the issues they want to see addressed. Charities such as the March of Dimes analyze their audiences to improve the effectiveness of their communications.

Understanding Audience and Purpose

Projects of all sizes and types succeed only if they are based on an accurate understanding of the needs and desires of their audiences and have a clear, focused purpose. Because the documents and other communication you produce in the workplace will, more often than not, form the foundations of these projects, they too will succeed only if they are based on an accurate understanding of your audience and have a clear purpose.

Although you might not realize it, you probably consider audience in your day-to-day communication. For example, when you tell your parents about a new job you've landed, you keep the discussion general and focus on the job details you know they care most about: its location, its salary and benefits, and your start date. But when you email a former internship supervisor with the same news, you discuss your upcoming duties and projects in more detail.

As you produce documents for this technical-communication course, you will of course consider your instructor's expectations, just as you do when you write anything for any other course. But keep in mind that your instructor is also playing the role of the audience that you would be addressing if you had produced the document outside of this course. Therefore, to a large extent your instructor will likely evaluate each of your course assignments on how effectively you've addressed the audience and achieved the purpose specified in the assignment.

Analyzing an audience means thinking about who your audience is, what they already know about your subject, how they feel about it, and how they are going to use the information you present. You analyze your audience as you plan your document so that it appeals to their interests and needs, is easy for them to understand, and motivates them to pay attention to your message and consider your recommendations.

The word *purpose* refers to what you want to accomplish with the document you are producing. Most often, your purpose is to explain to your audience how something occurs (how regenerative braking systems work in hybrid cars), how to carry out a task (how to set up a Skype connection), or why some situation is either good or bad (why the new county guidelines for water use will help or hurt your company). When your purpose is to explain why a situation is either good or bad, you are trying to reinforce or change the audience's attitudes toward the situation and perhaps urge them to take action. As you will see, in many cases your technical communication will have multiple purposes.

Before you can start to think about writing about your *subject*, analyze your audience and purpose. Doing so will help you meet your readers' needs—and your own. For instance, you're an engineer working for a consulting company. One document to which you might contribute is a report to the city planning board about how building a housing development would affect the natural environment as well as the city's roads, schools, and sanitation infrastructure. That's the *subject* of the report. The *purpose* is to motivate the planning board to approve the project so that it can begin. How does the audience affect how you analyze your purpose? Think about who the board members are. If most of them are not engineers, you don't want to use specialized vocabulary and advanced engineering graphics and concepts. You don't want to dwell on the technical details. Rather, you want to use general vocabulary, graphics, and concepts. You want to focus on the issues the board members are concerned about. Would the development affect the environment negatively? If so, is the developer including a plan to offset that negative effect? Can the roads handle the extra traffic? Can the schools handle the extra kids? Will the city have to expand its police force? Its fire department? Its sewer system?

In other words, when you write to the planning board, you focus on topics they are most interested in, and you write the document so that it is easy for them to read and understand. If the project is approved and you need to communicate with other audiences, such as architects and contractors, you will have different purposes, and you will adjust your writing to meet each audience's needs.

What can go wrong when you don't analyze your audience? McDonald's Corporation found out when it printed takeout bags decorated with flags from around the world. Among them was the flag of Saudi Arabia, which contains scripture from the Koran. This was extremely offensive to Muslims, who consider it sacrilegious to throw out items bearing sacred scripture. As a result, McDonald's lost public credibility.

Throughout this chapter, the text will refer to your *reader* and your *document*. But all of the information refers as well to oral presentations, which are the subject of Chapter 21, as well as to documents in various media, such as podcasts or videos.

Using an Audience Profile Sheet

As you read the discussions in this chapter about audience characteristics and techniques for learning about your audience, you might think about using an audience profile sheet: a form that prompts you to consider various audience characteristics as you plan your document. For example, the profile sheet can help you realize that you do not know much about your primary reader's work history and what that history can tell you about how to shape your document. Figure 5.2 shows an audience profile sheet that provides important information about one of a writer's most important readers.

FIGURE 5.2 Audience Profile Sheet

Assume that you work in the drafting department of an architectural engineering firm. You know that the company's computer-assisted design (CAD) software is out of date and that recent CAD technology would make it easier and faster for the draftspeople to do their work. You want to persuade your company to authorize buying a CAD workstation that costs about $4,000. Before getting started with your document, you fill out an audience profile sheet for your primary reader, Harry Becker, the manager of your company's Drafting and Design Department.

You should modify this form to meet your own needs and those of your organization. For a printable version of Fig. 5.2, see the downloadable forms in Achieve.

AUDIENCE PROFILE SHEET

Reader's Name: Harry Becker

Reader's Job Title: Manager, Drafting and Design Department

Kind of Reader: Primary __X__ Secondary ____

Education: BS, Architectural Engineering, Northwestern, 1998. CAD/CAM Short Course, 1998; Motivating Your Employees Seminar, 1997; Writing on the Job Short Course, 2008

Professional Experience: Worked for two years in a small architecture firm. Started here 16 years ago as a draftsperson. Worked his way up to Assistant Manager, then Manager. Instrumental in the Wilson project, particularly in coordinating personnel and equipment.

Job Responsibilities: Supervises a staff of 12 draftspeople. Approves or denies all requests for capital expenditures over $2,000 coming from his department. Works with employees to help them make the best case for the purchase. After approving or denying the request, forwards it to Tina Buterbaugh, Manager, Finance Dept., who maintains all capital expenditure records.

Personal Characteristics: N/A

Personal Preferences: Likes straightforward documents, lots of evidence, clear structure. Dislikes complicated documents full of jargon.

Cultural Characteristics: Nothing of note.

Attitude Toward the Writer: No problems.

Attitude Toward the Subject: He understands and approves of my argument.

Expectations About the Subject: Expects to see a clear argument with financial data and detailed comparisons of available systems.

Expectations About the Document: Expects to see a report, with an executive summary, of about 10 pages.

Reasons for Reading the Document: To offer suggestions and eventually approve or deny the request.

Way of Reading the Document:

Skim it ____   Study it __X__ Read a portion of it ____   Which portion?

Modify it and submit it to another reader ____

Attempt to implement recommendations ____

Use it to perform a task or carry out a procedure ____

Use it to create another document ____

Other ____   Explain.

Reading Skill: Excellent

Reader's Physical Environment: N/A

If your document has several readers, you must decide whether to fill out only one sheet (for your most important reader) or several sheets. One technique is to fill out sheets for one or two of your most important readers and one for each major category of other readers. For instance, you could fill out one sheet for your primary reader, Harry Becker; one for managers in other areas of your company; and one for readers from outside your company.

When do you fill out an audience profile sheet? Although some writers like to do so at the start of the process as a way to prompt themselves to consider audience characteristics, others prefer to do so at the end of the process as a way to help themselves summarize what they have learned about their audience. Of course, you can start to fill out the sheet before you begin and then complete it or revise it at the end.

Determining the Important Characteristics of Your Audience

When you analyze the members of your audience, you are trying to learn what you can about their background and knowledge, their reasons for reading or listening to you, their attitudes and expectations, and how they will use the information you provide.

WHO ARE YOUR READERS?

For each of your most important readers, consider seven factors:

- **The reader's education.** Consider the person's degree as well as any formal education or training the person completed while on the job. Also keep in mind when the education and training occurred, since methods and practices can change over time.

  Knowing your readers' educational background helps you determine how much supporting material to provide, what level of vocabulary to use, what kind of sentence structure to use, what types of graphics to include, how long your document should be, and whether to provide such elements as a glossary or an executive summary.

- **The reader's professional experience.** A nurse with a decade of experience might have represented her hospital on a community committee to encourage citizens to give blood and might have contributed to the planning for the hospital's new delivery room. These experiences would have provided several areas of competence or expertise that you should consider as you plan your document.

- **The reader's job responsibility.** Consider the major job responsibility of your reader and how your document will help that person accomplish it. For example, if you are writing a feasibility study on ways to cool the air for a new office building and you know that your reader, an upper-level

For advice on finding information about your readers, see Techniques for Learning about Your Audience, pp. 97–100.

manager, oversees operating expenses, you should explain how you are estimating future utility costs.

- **The reader's reading skill.** Consider whether you should be writing at all or whether it would be better to use another medium, such as a video, an oral presentation, or a podcast. If you decide to write, consider whether your reader will be able to understand how to use the type of document you have selected, handle the level of detail you will present, and easily comprehend your graphics, sentence structure, and vocabulary.

- **The reader's cultural characteristics.** Understanding cultural characteristics can help you appeal to your reader's interests and avoid confusing or offending him or her. As discussed later in this chapter in Communicating Across Cultures (pp. 101–107), cultural characteristics can affect virtually every aspect of a reader's comprehension of a document and perception of the writer.

- **The reader's personal characteristics.** Does your reader have any other personal characteristics that you should consider as you write and design your document? One important consideration is accessibility. For example, in your videos you may need to provide closed captioning to accommodate the hearing impaired, or in a diagram you may want to use not just various colors but also various shapes to accommodate those with color vision problems.

- **The reader's personal preferences.** One person might hate to see the first-person pronoun *I* in technical documents. Another might find the word *interface* distracting when the writer isn't discussing computers. Does your reader prefer one type of application (such as blogs or memos) over another? Try to accommodate as many of your reader's preferences as you can.

WHY IS YOUR AUDIENCE READING YOUR DOCUMENT?

For each of your most important readers, consider why he or she will read your document. Some writers find it helpful to classify readers into categories—such as primary, secondary, and tertiary—that identify each reader's distance from the writer. Here are some common descriptions of these three categories of readers:

- A *primary audience* consists of people to whom the communication is directed; they may be inside or outside the writer's own organization. For example, they might include the writer's team members, who assisted in carrying out an analysis of a new server configuration for the IT department; the writer's supervisor, who reads the analysis to decide whether to authorize its main recommendation to adopt the new configuration; and an executive, who reads it to determine how high a priority the server project should have on a list of projects to fund. If you were producing text or videos for the Hewlett-Packard website, your primary audience would include customers, vendors, and suppliers who visit the site.

- A *secondary audience* consists of people more distant from the writer who need to stay aware of developments in the organization but who will not directly act on or respond to the document. Examples include managers of other departments, who are not directly involved in the project but who need to be aware of its broad outlines, and representatives from the marketing and legal departments, who need to check that the document conforms to the company's standards and practices and with relevant legal standards, such as antidiscrimination or intellectual-property laws. External readers who are part of a secondary audience might include readers of your white paper who are not interested in buying your product but who need to stay current with the new products in the field.

- A *tertiary audience* consists of people even further removed from the writer who might take an interest in the subject of the report. Examples include interest groups (such as environmental groups or other advocacy organizations); local, state, and federal government officials; and, if the report is made public, the general public. Even if the report is not intended to be distributed outside the organization, given today's climate of information access and the ease with which documents can be distributed, chances are good that it will be made available to outsiders.

Regardless of whether you classify your readers using a scheme such as this, think hard about why the most important audience members will read your document. Don't be content to list only one purpose. Your direct supervisor, for example, might have several purposes that you want to keep in mind:

- to learn what you have accomplished in the project

- to determine whether to approve any recommendations you present

- to determine whether to assign you to a follow-up team that will work on the next stage of the project

- to determine how to evaluate your job performance next month

You will use all of this information about your audience as you determine the ways it affects how you will write your document or plan your presentation. In the meantime, write the information down so that you can refer to it later.

WHAT ARE YOUR READERS' ATTITUDES AND EXPECTATIONS?

In thinking about the attitudes and expectations of each of your most important readers, consider these three factors:

- **Your reader's attitude toward you.** Most people will like you because you are hardworking, intelligent, and cooperative. Some won't. If a reader's animosity toward you is irrational or unrelated to the current project, try to earn that person's respect and trust by meeting him or her on some neutral ground, perhaps by discussing other, less volatile projects or some shared interest, such as gardening, skiing, or science-fiction novels.

For tips on critiquing a team member's draft diplomatically, see Ch. 4, p. 72.

- **Your reader's attitude toward the subject.** If possible, discuss the subject thoroughly with your primary readers to determine whether they are positive, neutral, or negative toward it. Table 5.1 provides some basic strategies for responding to different attitudes.

- **Your reader's expectations about the document.** Think about how your readers expect to see the information treated in terms of scope, organizational pattern, and amount of detail. Consider, too, the application. If your reader expects to see the information presented as a memo, use a memo unless some other format would clearly work better.

HOW WILL YOUR READERS USE YOUR DOCUMENT?

In thinking about how your reader will use your document, consider the following three factors:

- **The way your reader will read your document.** Will your reader
  — file it?
  — skim it?
  — read only a portion of it?
  — study it carefully?

TABLE 5.1   Responding to Different Attitudes

IF . . .	TRY THIS . . .
Your reader is neutral or positively inclined toward your subject.	Write the document so that it responds to the reader's needs; make sure that vocabulary, level of detail, organization, and style are appropriate.
Your reader is hostile to the subject or to your approach to it.	• Find out what the objections are, and then answer them directly. Explain why the objections are not valid or are less important than the benefits. For example, you want to hire an online-community manager to coordinate your company's social-media efforts, but you know that one of your primary readers won't like this idea. Try to find out why. Does this person think social media are a fad? That they are irrelevant and can't help your company? If you understand the objections, you can explain your position more effectively. • Organize the document so that your recommendation follows your explanation of the benefits. This strategy encourages the hostile reader to understand your argument rather than to reject it out of hand. • Avoid describing the subject as a dispute. Seek areas of agreement and concede points. Avoid trying to persuade readers overtly; people don't like to be persuaded, because it threatens their egos. Instead, suggest that there are new facts that need to be considered. People are more likely to change their minds when they realize this.
Your reader was instrumental in creating the policy or procedure that you are arguing is ineffective	In discussing the present system's shortcomings, be especially careful if you risk offending one of your readers. When you address such an audience, don't write, "The present system for logging customer orders is completely ineffective." Instead, write, "While the present system has worked well for many years, new developments in electronic processing of orders might enable us to improve logging speed and reduce errors substantially."

—modify it and submit it to another reader?

—try to implement its recommendations?

—use it to perform a test or carry out a procedure?

—use it as a source document for another document?

If only 1 of your 15 readers will study the document for details such as specifications, you don't want the other 14 people to have to wade through them. Therefore, put this information in an appendix. If you know that your reader wants to use your status report as raw material for a report to a higher-level reader, try to write it so that it can be reused with little rewriting. Make sure the reader has access to the electronic file so that passages can be merged into the new document without needing to be retyped.

- **The physical environment in which your reader will read your document.** Often, technical documents are formatted in a special way or constructed of special materials to improve their effectiveness. Documents used in poorly lit places might be printed in larger-than-normal type. If documents are to be used on ships, on aircraft, or in garages, where they might be exposed to wind, water, and grease, you might have to use special waterproof bindings, oil-resistant or laminated paper, color coding, and unusual-sized paper.

- **The digital environment in which your reader will read your document.** If you are writing a document that will be viewed online, consider the platforms on which it will be accessed. Will readers be viewing it on mobile devices? Desktop computers? Both? How can you design the document so that it is easy to access—easy to get to, to see, to navigate, and to use—in these environments?

For more about designing a document for use in different environments, see Ch. 11, p. 256.

Techniques for Learning About Your Audience

To learn about your audience, you figure out what you do and do not already know, interview people, read about them, and read documents they have written. Of course, you cannot perform extensive research about every possible reader of every document you write, but you should learn what you can about your most important readers of your most important documents.

DETERMINING WHAT YOU ALREADY KNOW ABOUT YOUR AUDIENCE

Start by asking yourself what you already know about your most important readers: their demographics (such as age, education, and job responsibilities); their expectations and attitudes toward you and the subject; and the ways they will use your document. Then list the important factors you *don't* know. That is where you will concentrate your energies. The audience profile sheet shown in Figure 5.2 (p. 92) can help you identify gaps in your knowledge about your readers.

INTERVIEWING PEOPLE

For your most important readers, make a list of people who you think have known them and their work the longest or who are closest to them on the job. These people might include those who joined the organization at about the same time your readers did; people who work in the same department as your readers; and people at other organizations who have collaborated with your readers.

For a discussion of interviewing, see Ch. 6, p. 140.

Prepare a few interview questions that are likely to elicit information about your readers and their preferences and needs. For instance, you are writing a proposal for a new project at work. You want to present return-on-investment calculations to show how long it will take the company to recoup what it invested, but you're not sure how much detail to present because you don't know whether an important primary reader has a background in this aspect of accounting. Several of this reader's colleagues will know. Interview them in person, on the phone, or by email.

READING ABOUT YOUR AUDIENCE ONLINE

If you are writing for people in your own organization, start your research there. If your primary reader is a high-level manager or executive, search the organization's website or internal social network. Sections such as "About Us," "About the Company," and "Information for Investors" often contain a wealth of biographical information, as well as links to other sources.

In addition, use a search engine to look for information on the internet. You are likely to find newspaper and magazine articles, industry directories, websites, and blog posts about your audience.

SEARCHING SOCIAL MEDIA FOR DOCUMENTS YOUR AUDIENCE HAS WRITTEN

Documents your readers have written can tell you a lot about what they like to see with respect to design, level of detail, organization and development, style, and vocabulary. If your primary audience consists of those within your organization, start searching for documents they've produced within the company. Then broaden the search to the internet.

Although some of your readers might have written books or articles, many or even most of them might be active users of social media, such as Facebook and Twitter. Pay particular attention to LinkedIn, a networking site for professionals. LinkedIn profiles are particularly useful because they include a person's current and former positions and education, as well as recommendations from other professionals. Figure 5.3 is an excerpt from the LinkedIn entry written by Mike Markley, a technical communicator at Aquent.

Markley begins his LinkedIn profile with this summary:

Professional and Technical Communication: Serving as consultant, practitioner, project manager, university instructor, and senior manager. I have managed large and small teams; recruited, trained, and supervised professionals at all levels; and

FIGURE 5.3   A LinkedIn Bio
Michael Markley.

directed strategy for large consulting engagements with P&L responsibility. I am a lifelong learner and active in my community. I have a passion for innovative projects that expand the capacity of organizations and communities, provide opportunities for youth and emerging professionals, create enterprise, and increase quality of life.

This paragraph suggests that Markley has an extensive background, not only in technical communication but also in various levels of management. You can expect that he knows project management, budgeting, and human resources. He understands both how to make documents and how to lead teams that make documents. The summary also indicates the types of projects that interest him most as a manager and consultant. You can guess that he has a strong interest in working with community organizations.

A typical LinkedIn entry directs you to a person's websites and blogs and to the LinkedIn groups to which the person belongs. You can also see the person's *connections* (his or her personal network). And if you are a LinkedIn member, you can see whether you and the person share any connections.

In addition, the person you are researching might have a social-media account on which he or she posts about matters related to his or her job. Reading a person's recent posts will give you a good idea of his or her job responsibilities and professionalism, as shown in Figure 5.4.

This summary is followed by a much more detailed description of Mike Markley's professional history and education. Even this brief summary suggests that Markley has extensive experience.

This excerpt from Mike Markley's tweet history shows a variety of types of posts: a tweet about a course taught by his company, another about a job opening at his company, and a rare personal tweet, urging his followers to donate to community radio. Also in Markley's history are tweets about news items and thank-you tweets to speakers at conferences.

FIGURE 5.4 **Excerpt from a List of Tweets**
Reprinted by permission of Mike Markley.

ANALYZING SOCIAL-MEDIA DATA

Private companies and public agencies alike analyze social media to better understand their audiences. Private companies use these data primarily to determine who their customers are, how they feel about various marketing messages, and how these messages influence their buying behavior. Public agencies use these data to help them refine their own messages.

For instance, the Centers for Disease Control and Prevention (CDC), a U.S. federal agency, analyzes social media to improve the quality and effectiveness of its public health information. The agency starts by classifying people into various categories by age (such as tweens, teens, baby boomers) and determining which media each group uses most. On the basis of these data, the agency designs and implements health campaigns on such topics as cancer screening, HIV/AIDS prevention and treatment, vaccines, and smoking cessation.

Then the CDC monitors social media to determine how many people are seeing the agency's information, how they are engaging with the information (whether they share the information or follow links to other sites), and whether the information is changing their behavior (Centers for Disease Control, 2013). Among the data the CDC analyzes each month are the following:

- the number of visitors to each of the CDC web pages
- the most popular keywords searched on CDC pages as well as on selected other sites and popular search engines such as Google
- the numbers of Facebook fans and Twitter followers
- the number of click-throughs to CDC web pages from Facebook and Twitter

On the basis of these data, the CDC adjusts its social-media campaigns to use its resources most effectively.

Communicating Across Cultures

Our society and our workforce are becoming increasingly diverse, both culturally and linguistically, and businesses are exporting more goods and services. As a result, professionals often communicate with individuals from different cultural backgrounds, many of whom are nonnative speakers of English, both in the United States and abroad, and with speakers of other languages who read texts translated from English into their own languages.

The economy of the United States depends on international trade. In 2015, the United States exported over $3.1 trillion of goods and services (U.S. Census Bureau, 2019). In addition, the population of the United States itself is truly multicultural. Each year, the United States admits about a million immigrants (U.S. Department of Homeland Security, 2019).

Effective communication requires an understanding of culture: the beliefs, attitudes, and values that motivate people's behavior.

UNDERSTANDING THE CULTURAL VARIABLES "ON THE SURFACE"

Communicating effectively with people from another culture requires understanding a number of cultural variables that lie on the surface. You need to know, first, what language or languages to use. You also need to be aware of political, social, religious, and economic factors that can affect how readers will interpret your documents. Understanding these factors is not an exact science, but it does require that you learn as much as you can about the culture of those you are addressing.

A brief example: Microsoft's search engine had trouble catching on in China, in part because of its name—*Bing*—which means "sickness" in Chinese (Yan, 2015).

In *International Technical Communication*, Nancy L. Hoft (1995) describes seven major categories of cultural variables that lie on the surface:

- **Political.** This category relates to trade issues and legal issues (for example, some countries forbid imports of certain foods or chemicals) and laws about intellectual property, product safety, and liability.

- **Economic.** A country's level of economic development is a critical factor. In many developing countries, most people cannot afford devices for accessing the internet.

- **Social.** This category covers many issues, including gender roles and business customs. In most Western cultures, women play a much greater role in the workplace than they do in many Middle Eastern and Asian cultures. Business customs—including forms of greeting, business dress, and gift giving—vary from culture to culture.

- **Religious.** Religious differences can affect diet, attitudes toward individual colors, styles of dress, holidays, and hours of business.

- **Educational.** In the United States, 40 million people are only marginally literate. In other countries, the rate can be much higher or much lower. In some cultures, classroom learning with a teacher is considered the most acceptable way to study; in others, people tend to study on their own.
- **Technological.** If you sell high-tech products, you need to know whether your readers have the hardware, the software, and the technological infrastructure to use them.
- **Linguistic.** In some countries, English is taught to all children starting in grade school; in other countries, English is seen as a threat to the national language. In many cultures, the orientation of text on a page and in a book is not from left to right.

In addition to these basic differences, you need to understand dozens of other factors. For instance, the United States is the only major country that has not adopted the metric system. Whereas Americans use periods to separate whole numbers from decimals, and commas to separate thousands from hundreds, much of the rest of the world reverses this usage.

UNITED STATES	3,425.6
EUROPE	3.425,6

Also, in the United States, the format for writing out and abbreviating dates is different from that of most other cultures:

UNITED STATES	March 2, 2020	3/2/20
EUROPE	2 March 2020	2/3/20
JAPAN	2020 March 2	20/3/2

These cultural variables are important in obvious ways: for example, you can't send an electronic file to a person who doesn't have access to the internet. However, there is another set of cultural characteristics—those beneath the surface—that you also need to understand.

UNDERSTANDING THE CULTURAL VARIABLES "BENEATH THE SURFACE"

Scholars of multicultural communication have identified cultural variables that are less obvious than those discussed in the previous section but just as important. Writing scholars Elizabeth Tebeaux and Linda Driskill (1999) explain five key variables and how they are reflected in technical communication.

- **Focus on individuals or groups.** Some cultures, especially in the West, value individuals more than groups. The typical Western employee doesn't see his or her identity as being defined by the organization for which he or she works. Other cultures, particularly those in Asia, value groups more than individuals. The typical employee in such cultures sees himself or herself more as a representative of the organization than as an individual who happens to work there.

  Communication in individualistic cultures focuses on the writer's and reader's needs rather than on those of their organizations. Writers use the pronoun *I* rather than *we*. Letters are addressed to the principal reader and signed by the writer.

Communication in group-oriented cultures focuses on the organization's needs by emphasizing the benefits to be gained through a cooperative relationship between organizations. Writers emphasize the relationship between the writer and the reader rather than the specific technical details of the message. Writers use *we* rather than *I*. They might use their organization's name, not their own, in the complimentary close.

- **Distance between business life and private life.** In some cultures, especially in the West, many people separate their business lives from their private lives. When the workday ends, they are free to go home and spend their time as they wish. Although many employees are increasingly expected to be available by email or phone outside official working hours, those in the West still usually think of themselves primarily as individuals rather than as part of an organizational body. In other cultures, particularly in Asia, people see a much smaller distance between their business lives and their private lives. Even after the day ends, they still see themselves as employees of their organization.

  Cultures that value individualism tend to see a great distance between business and personal lives. In these cultures, communication focuses on technical details, with relatively little reference to personal information about the writer or the reader.

  Cultures that are group oriented tend to see a smaller distance between business life and private life. In these cultures, communication contains much more personal information—about the reader's family and health—and more information about general topics—for example, the weather and the seasons. The goal is to build a formal relationship between the two organizations. Both the writer and the reader are, in effect, on call after business hours and are likely to transact business during long social activities such as elaborate dinners or golf games.

- **Distance between ranks.** In some cultures, the distance in power and authority between workers within an organization is small. This small distance is reflected in a close working relationship between supervisors and their subordinates. In other cultures, the distance in power and authority between workers within an organization is great. Supervisors do not consult with their subordinates. Subordinates use formal names and titles—"Mr. Smith," "Dr. Perez"—when addressing people of higher rank.

  Individualistic cultures that separate business and private lives tend to have a smaller distance between ranks. In these cultures, communication is generally less formal. Informal documents (emails and memos) are appropriate, and writers often sign their documents with their first names only. Keep in mind, however, that many people in these cultures resent what they view as inappropriate informality, such as letters or emails addressed "Dear Jim" when they have never met the writer.

In cultures with a great distance between ranks, communication is generally formal. Writers tend to use their full professional titles and to prefer formal documents (such as letters) to informal ones (such as memos and emails). Writers make sure their documents are addressed to the appropriate person and contain the formal design elements (such as title pages and letters of transmittal) that signal their respect for their readers.

- **Need for details to be spelled out.** Some cultures value full, complete communication. A written text must be comprehensive, containing all the information a reader needs to understand it. These cultures are called *low-context cultures*. Other cultures value documents in which some of the details are merely implied. This implicit information is communicated through other forms of communication that draw on the personal relationship between the reader and the writer, as well as social and business norms of the culture. These cultures are called *high-context cultures*.

  Low-context cultures tend to be individualistic; high-context cultures tend to be group oriented. In low-context cultures, writers spell out all the details. Documents are like contracts in that they explain procedures in great detail and provide specific information that indicates the rights and responsibilities of both the writer and the readers. In high-context cultures, writers tend to omit information that they consider obvious because they don't want to insult the reader. For example, a manual written for people in a high-context culture might not explain why a cell-phone battery needs to be charged because everyone already knows why.

- **Attitudes toward uncertainty.** In some cultures, people are comfortable with uncertainty. They communicate less formally and rely less on written policies. In many cases, they rely more on a clear set of guiding principles, as communicated in a code of conduct or a mission statement. In other cultures, people are uncomfortable with uncertainty. Businesses are structured formally, and employees use explicit procedures for communicating.

  In cultures that tolerate uncertainty, written communication tends to be less detailed. Oral communication is used to convey more of the information that is vital to the relationship between the writer and the readers. In cultures that value certainty, communication tends to be detailed. Policies are lengthy and specific, and forms are used extensively. Roles are firmly defined, and there is a wide distance between ranks.
  As you consider this set of cultural variables, keep four points in mind:

- **Each variable represents a spectrum of attitudes.** Terms such as *high-context* and *low-context*, for instance, represent the opposite end points on a scale. Most cultures occupy a middle ground.

- **The variables do not line up in a clear pattern.** Although the variables sometimes correlate—for example, low-context cultures tend to be individualistic—in any one culture, the variables do not form a consistent pattern. For example, the dominant culture in the United States is highly individualistic rather than group oriented but only about midway along the scale in terms of tolerance of uncertainty.

- **Different organizations within the same culture can vary greatly.** For example, one software company in Germany might have a management style that does not tolerate uncertainty, whereas another software company in that country might tolerate a lot of uncertainty.

- **An organization's cultural attitudes are fluid, not static.** How an organization operates is determined not only by the dominant culture but also by its own people. As new people join an organization, its culture changes. The IBM of 2020 is not the IBM of 2000.

For you as a communicator, this set of variables therefore offers no answers. Instead, it offers a set of questions. You cannot know in advance the attitudes of the people in an organization. You have to interact with them before you can reach even tentative conclusions. The value of being aware of the variables is that they can help you study the communication from people in that organization and become more aware of underlying values that affect how they will interpret your documents.

CONSIDERING CULTURAL VARIABLES AS YOU WRITE

The challenge of communicating effectively with a person from another culture is that you are communicating with a person, not a culture. You cannot be sure which cultures have influenced that person. For example, a 50-year-old Japanese-born manager at the computer manufacturer Fujitsu in Japan has been shaped by the Japanese culture, but he also has been influenced by the culture of his company and of the Japanese computer industry in general. Because he works on an export product, it is also likely that he has traveled extensively outside of Japan and has absorbed influences from other cultures.

A further complication is that when you communicate with a person from another culture, to that person *you* are from another culture, and you cannot know how much that person is trying to accommodate your cultural patterns. As writing scholar Arthur H. Bell (1992) points out, the communication between the two of you is carried out in a third, hybrid culture. When you write to a large audience, the complications increase. A group of managers at Fujitsu represents a far more complex mix of cultural influences than one manager at Fujitsu.

No brief discussion of cultural variables can answer questions about how to write for a particular multicultural audience. You need to study your readers' culture and, as you plan your document, seek assistance from someone native to the culture who can help you avoid blunders that might confuse or offend your readers.

Start by reading some of the basic guides to communicating with people from cultures other than your own, and then study guides to the particular culture you are investigating. In addition, numerous sites on the internet provide useful guidelines that can help you write to people from another culture. If possible, study documents written by people in your audience. If you don't have access to these, try to locate documents written in English by people from the culture you are interested in.

For books and other resources about writing to people from cultures other than your own, see the Selected Bibliography, p. 710.

Figures 5.5 and 5.6 show excerpts from documents that provide useful glimpses into cultural variables. Figure 5.5 is part of a management-philosophy statement from a Japanese electronics company. Figure 5.6, from a training manual used by Indian Railways, describes a medical exam that prospective applicants are required to take.

Notice how the writers describe the company philosophy in terms of ever-expanding circles: from employees to society to humankind. This philosophy attempts to relate a fulfilling workplace environment to the "pursuit of mental riches as a human being."

The Management Rationale of the Kyocera Group is: "To provide opportunities for the material and intellectual growth of all our employees, and through our joint efforts, contribute to the advancement of society and humankind." The "material and intellectual growth" that we aim for includes the pursuit of economic stability, and entails the pursuit of mental riches as a human being, in the shape of life with purpose and job satisfaction through self-fulfillment in the workplace.

Individual goals and growth are placed in service to the success of society. This interdependence of the individual and society — and a balanced life of work and recreation — is deeply ingrained in many Asian cultures.

FIGURE 5.5   Statement of Management Philosophy by a Japanese Electronics Company

Advancing Kyocera Philosophy Education. © 2019 by KYOCERA Corporation. Used by permission of Kyocera Corporation.

The passage sounds as if it were written a hundred years ago, full of complicated sentences and formal vocabulary. The writing style is closer to that of the British (who colonized India) than that of the United States.

However, the explanation of why the exam is used is particularly candid: to save the government from having to support employees who become ill and therefore cannot perform the tasks for which they were hired.

The wording of this note, which follows a table showing the minimum height requirements for male and female applicants, would likely be considered offensive in most cultures. In India, a culture made of many ethnic groups and with a rigid caste system, most readers would not be offended.

501. Introduction: (1) The standards of physical fitness to be adopted should make due allowance for the age and length of service, if any, of the candidate concerned.

(2) No person will be deemed qualified for admission to the public service who shall not satisfy the Government, or the appointing authority, as the case may be, that he has no disease, constitutional affliction or bodily infirmity unfitting him, or likely to unfit him for that service.

(3) It should be understood that the question of fitness involves the future as well as the present and that one of the main objectives of medical examination is to secure continuous effective service, and in the case of candidates for permanent appointment, to prevent early pension or payment in case of premature death.

...

Note: The minimum height prescribed can be relaxed in case of candidates belonging to races such as Gorkhas, Garhwalis, Assamese, Nagaland tribal, whose average height is distinctly lower.

FIGURE 5.6   Statement from an Indian Railways Training Manual

◢ GUIDELINES Writing for Readers from Other Cultures

The following suggestions will help you communicate more effectively with readers from a variety of cultures.

▶ **Limit your vocabulary.** Every word should have only one meaning and you should avoid complex sentence constructions.

▶ **Keep sentences short.** There is no magic number, but try for an average sentence length of no more than 20 words.

▶ **Define abbreviations and acronyms in a glossary.** Don't assume that your readers know what a particular acronym means; these will naturally vary across languages.

▶ **Avoid jargon unless you know your readers are familiar with it.** For instance, your readers might not know what malware is.

▶ **Avoid idioms and slang. These terms are culture specific.** If you tell your Japanese readers that your company plans to put on a "full-court press," most likely they will be confused.

▶ **Use the active voice whenever possible.** The active voice is easier for nonnative speakers to understand than the passive voice.

▶ **Be careful with graphics.** The shopping cart icon on e-commerce websites does not translate well, because outside of the United States people are used to a bag or basket icon.

▶ **Be sure someone from the target culture reviews your document.** Even if you have had help in planning the document, have it reviewed before you publish and distribute it.

For a discussion of Simplified English, see Ch. 10, p. 247.

For more about voice, see Ch. 10, p. 235.

For more about graphics, see Ch. 12, p. 301.

USING GRAPHICS AND DESIGN FOR MULTICULTURAL READERS

One of the challenges of writing to people from another culture is that they are likely to be nonnative speakers. One way to overcome the language barrier is to use effective graphics and appropriate document design.

However, the most appropriate graphics and design can differ from culture to culture. Business letters written in Australia use a different size paper and a different format than those in the United States. A series of graphics arranged left to right could confuse readers from the Middle East, who read from right to left. For this reason, you should study samples of documents written by people from the culture you are addressing to learn the important differences.

For more about design for multicultural readers, see Ch. 11, p. 290. For more about graphics for international readers, see Ch. 12, p. 341.

Applying What You Have Learned About Your Audience

You want to use what you know about your audience to tailor your communication to their needs and preferences. Obviously, if your most important reader does not understand the details of DRAM technology, you cannot use

Examining Cultural Variables in a Business Letter

These two versions of the same business letter were written by a sales manager for an American computer company. The first letter was addressed to a potential customer in the United States; the second version was addressed to a potential customer in Japan. The questions in the margin ask you to think about how cultural variables affect the nature of the evidence, the structure of the letters, and their tone (see pp. 101–107).

Server Solutions
Cincinnati, OH 46539

Nadine Meyer
Director of Marketing

July 3, 2019

Mr. Philip Henryson, Director of Purchasing
Allied Manufacturing
1321 Industrial Boulevard
Boise, ID 83756

1 Dear Mr. Henryson:

Thank you for your inquiry about our PowerServer servers. I'm happy to answer your questions.

The most popular configuration is our PowerServer 3000. This model is based on the Intel® Xeon ES-4600 processor, ServerSure High-End UltraLite chipset with quadpeer PCI architecture, and embedded RAID. The system comes with our InstallIt system-management CD, which lets you install the server and monitor and manage your network with a simple graphical interface. With six PCI slots, the PowerServer 3000 is equipped with redundant cooling as well as redundant power, and storage expandability to 1.0TB. I'm taking the liberty of enclosing the brochure for this system to fill you in on the technical details.

The PowerServer 3000 has performed extremely well on a number of industry benchmark tests. I'm including with this letter copies of feature articles on the system from *PC World, CIO,* and *DigiTimes*.

It would be a pleasure for me to arrange for an on-site demo at your convenience. I will phone you on Monday to see what dates would be best for you. In the meantime, please do not hesitate to get in touch with me directly if you have any questions about the PowerServer line.

I look forward to talking with you next week.

Sincerely,

Nadine Meyer

Nadine Meyer
Director of Marketing

Attachments:
"PowerServer 3000 Facts at a Glance"
"Another Winner from Server Solutions"
"Mid-Range Servers for 2017"
"Four New Dual-Processor Workhorses"

Examining Cultural Variables in a Business Letter (*continued*)

Server Solutions
Cincinnati, OH 46539

Mr. Kato Kirisawa, Director of Purchasing
Allied Manufacturing
3-7-32 Kita Urawa
Saitama City, Saitama Pref. 336-0002
Japan

Nadine Meyer
Director of Marketing

1 Dear Sir:

2 It is my sincere hope that you and your loved ones are healthy and enjoying the pleasures of summer. Here in the American Midwest, the warm rays of the summer sun are accompanied by the sounds of happy children playing in the neighborhood swimming pools. I trust that the same pleasant sounds greet you in Saitama City.

3 Your inquiry about our PowerServer 3000 suggests that your company is growing. Allied Manufacturing has earned a reputation in Japan and all of Asia for a wide range of products manufactured to the most demanding standards of quality. We are not surprised that your company requires new servers that can be expanded to provide fast service for more and more clients.

4 For more than 20 years, Server Solutions has had the great honor of manufacturing the finest computer servers to meet the needs of our valued customers all over the world. We use only the finest materials and most innovative techniques to ensure that our customers receive the highest-quality, uninterrupted service that they have come to expect from us.

5 One of my great pleasures is to talk with esteemed representatives such as yourself about how Server Solutions can help them meet their needs for the most advanced servers. I would be most gratified if our two companies could enter into an agreement that would be of mutual benefit.

Sincerely,

Nadine Meyer

Nadine Meyer
Director of Marketing

Attachments:
    "PowerServer 3000 Facts at a Glance"
    "Another Winner from Server Solutions"
    "Mid-Range Servers for 2017"
    "Four New Dual-Processor Workhorses"

2019 July 3

1. How does the difference in the salutations (the "Dear..." part of the letter) reflect a cultural difference?

2. Does the first paragraph of the second letter have any function beyond delaying the discussion of business?

3. What is the point of telling Mr. Kirisawa about his own company? How does this paragraph help the writer introduce her own company's products?

4. To a reader from the United States, the third paragraph of the second letter would probably seem thin. What aspect of Japanese culture makes it effective in the context of this letter?

5. Why doesn't the writer make a more explicit sales pitch at the end of the second letter?

the concepts, vocabulary, and types of graphics used in that field. If she uses one-page summaries at the beginning of her documents, decide whether they will work for your document. If your primary reader's paragraphs always start with clear topic sentences, yours should, too.

The samples of technical communication shown in Figure 5.7 illustrate some of the ways writers have applied what they know about their audiences in text and graphics.

> ### ETHICS NOTE
> **MEETING YOUR READERS' NEEDS RESPONSIBLY**
>
> A major theme of this chapter is that effective technical communication meets your readers' needs. What this theme means is that as you plan, draft, revise, and edit, you should always be thinking of who your readers are, why they will read your document, and how they will read the document. For example, if your readers include many nonnative speakers of English, you will adjust your vocabulary, sentence structure, and other textual elements so that readers can understand your document easily. If your readers will be accessing the document on a mobile device, you will ensure that the design is optimized for their screen.
>
> Meeting your readers' needs does *not* mean writing a misleading or inaccurate document. If your readers want you to slant the information, omit crucial data, or downplay bad news, they are asking you to act unethically. You should not do so. For more information on ethics, see Chapter 2.

Writing for Multiple Audiences

Many documents are addressed to more than one reader. Often, an audience consists of people with widely different backgrounds, needs, and attitudes.

If you think your document will have a number of readers, consider making it *modular*: break the document up into components addressed to different readers. A modular report might contain an executive summary for managers who don't have the time, knowledge, or desire to read the whole report. It might also contain a full technical discussion for expert readers, an implementation schedule for technicians, and a financial plan in an appendix for budget officers. Figure 5.8 shows the table of contents for a modular report.

Determining Your Purpose

Once you have identified and analyzed your audience, it is time to examine your purpose. Ask yourself this: "What do I want this document to accomplish?" When your readers have finished reading what you have written, what do you want them to *know* or *believe*? What do you want them to *do*? Your writing should help your readers understand a concept, adopt a particular belief, or carry out a task.

In defining your purpose, think of a verb that represents it. (Sometimes, of course, you have several purposes.) The following list presents verbs in two

What is XSLT?

XSL Transformations (XSLT 2.0) is a language for transforming XML documents into other XML documents, text documents or HTML documents. You might want to format a chapter of a book using XSL-FO, or you might want to take a database query and format it as HTML.

With XSLT 2.0, processors can operate not only on XML but on anything that can be made to look like XML: relational database tables, geographical information systems, file systems, anything from which your XSLT processor can build an XDM instance. In some cases an XSLT 2.0 processor might also be able to work directly from a database of XDM instances. This ability to operate on multiple input files in multiple formats, and to treat them all as if they were XML files, is very powerful. It is shared with XQuery, and with anything else using XPath 2.0:

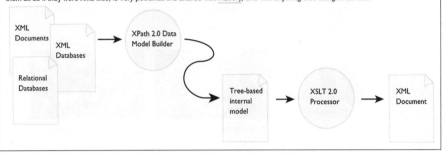

a. Document presenting technical information to an expert audience

Information from World Wide Web Consortium, 2015: www.w3.org/standards/xml/transformation.html.

This excerpt from a technical description of a web coding language appears on the site of the World Wide Web Consortium (W3C).

Because the readers are coding experts, the writers use highly technical language and refer to advanced topics. Note, however, that the nontechnical information is written simply and directly.

Notice that the graphic is based on a simple flowchart and basic icons. Why? Because the readers are interested only in understanding the logic of the process illustrated in the flowchart.

Axon Blog

Struggling to Organize Terabytes of Evidence? We Can Help.

Adopting new technology can place an enormous burden on law enforcement agencies. Managing the massive amounts of data digital technology can produce is a time-consuming and complex task. Many agencies are already struggling to keep up with the demand, and most don't have long-term storage plans in place.

READ MORE →

b. Document motivating decision makers to learn about a product

Information from Axon, 2016: www.axon.io/blog.

This blog post, from Axon, focuses on a problem facing law enforcement agencies: the need to store large amounts of digital information efficiently. The post is addressed to law enforcement officers who need to access information quickly and remotely.

The writer aims to connect with the reader by acknowledging the "enormous burden" police officers face trying to keep up with new digital technologies and by pointing out that many agencies find themselves in a similar situation. The headline offers to help those who are struggling, and the photograph suggests that help will come in the form of a program that keeps terabytes of data organized and readily available at the tap of a finger. Although the solution isn't given on this page, the reader is led to believe that details can be found by clicking the "Read More" link.

FIGURE 5.7   Using Text and Graphics to Appeal to Readers' Needs and Interests (*continued*)

This excerpt from the Stay Healthy section of the American Cancer Society website shows several techniques for providing information to a general audience.

The page begins with brief text intended to motivate readers to find out more about how to stay healthy. The tone throughout — from the words to the colorful images designed to make the links more appealing — is encouraging: it says, "You can do this."

The page includes a set of six links to detailed information on more specific topics about preventing cancer.

The "Sign Up for Email" button is placed in the center of the page, inviting visitors with a way to stay engaged in cancer prevention even after they leave the site.

Notice that the writers use simple, direct language, as well as the second person (*you*), to maintain an informal tone.

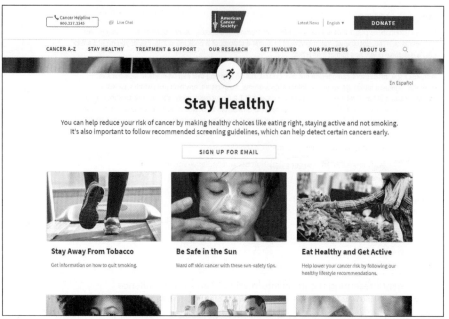

c. Document presenting educational resources to a general audience
Information from American Cancer Society, 2019: www.cancer.org/healthy/index.

The online transportation network company Uber faces opposition from some who believe that it is unsafe and illegal for drivers to provide what they call "pirate" taxi services without a special license. This page from the Uber website is part of the company's attempt to project a positive message.

The text emphasizes the less concrete benefits that Uber provides: people can get rides, not just across town, but "towards their dreams." Connections are forged. Opportunities are created. These are all difficult points to argue with. The smiling faces of Uber drivers ("partners") and riders in the video that opens this page show the human side of the company. The reader is made to feel like a part of this global mission to connect people across cultures.

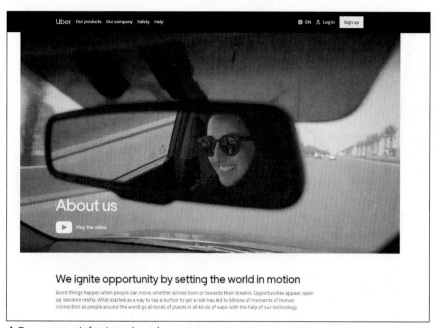

d. Document reinforcing a brand
Information from Uber, 2019: https://www.uber.com/us/en/about/.

FIGURE 5.7 **Using Text and Graphics to Appeal to Readers' Needs and Interests** (*continued*)

Contents

Foreword	v
Preface	vii
Summary for Policymakers	1
Technical Summary	19
1 Historical Overview of Climate Change Science	93
2 Changes in Atmospheric Constituents and Radiative Forcing	129
3 Observations: Atmospheric Surface and Climate Change	235
4 Observations: Changes in Snow, Ice and Frozen Ground	337
5 Observations: Ocean Climate Change and Sea Level	385
6 Palaeoclimate	433
7 Coupling Between Changes in the Climate System and Biogeochemistry	499
8 Climate Models and Their Evaluation	589
9 Understanding and Attributing Climate Change	663
10 Global Climate Projections	747
11 Regional Climate Projections	847
Annex I: Glossary	941
Annex II: Contributors to the IPCC WGI Fourth Assessment Report	955
Annex III: Reviewers of the IPCC WGI Fourth Assessment Report	969
Annex IV: Acronyms	981
Index	989

This table of contents shows the organization of a modular document.

Few readers will want to read the whole document — it's almost 1,000 pages long.

Most readers will want to read the 18-page summary for policymakers.

Some readers will want to read selected sections of the technical summary or "annexes" (appendixes).

FIGURE 5.8 Table of Contents for a Modular Report

Source: Figure 5.8 from Bindoff, N.L., J. Willebrand, V. Artale, A, Cazenave, J. Gregory, S. Gulev, K. Hanawa, C. Le Quéré, S. Levitus, Y. Nojiri, C.K. Shum, L.D. Talley and A. Unnikrishnan, 2007: Observations: Oceanic Climate Change and Sea Level. In: Climate Change 2007: The Physical Science Basis. Contribution of Working Group I to the Fourth Assessment Report of the Intergovernmental Panel on Climate Change [Solomon, S., D. Qin, M. Manning, Z. Chen, M. Marquis, K.B. Averyt, M. Tignor and H.L. Miller (eds.)]. Cambridge University Press, Cambridge, United Kingdom and New York, NY, USA.

categories: those used to communicate information to your readers and those used to convince them to accept a particular point of view.

Communicating Verbs	**Convincing Verbs**
authorize	analyze
define	argue
describe	assess
explain	conclude
illustrate	determine
inform	evaluate
outline	forecast
present	propose
review	recommend
summarize	request

This classification is not absolute. For example, *review* could in some cases be a *convincing verb* rather than a *communicating verb*: one writer's review of a complicated situation might be very different from another's.

Here are a few examples of how you can use these verbs to clarify the purpose of your document (the verbs are italicized).

- This wiki *presents* the draft of our policies on professional use of social media within the organization.

- This letter *authorizes* the purchase of six new tablets for the Jenkintown facility.

- This report *recommends* that we revise the website as soon as possible.

Sometimes your real purpose differs from your expressed purpose. For instance, if you want to persuade your reader to lease a new computer system rather than purchase it, you might phrase the purpose this way: *to explain the advantages of leasing over purchasing.* As mentioned earlier, many readers don't want to be *persuaded* but are willing to learn new facts or ideas.

In situations like this, stick to the facts. No matter how much you want to convince your readers, it is unacceptable to exaggerate or to omit important information. Trust that the strength and accuracy of your writing will enable you to achieve your intended purpose.

Gaining Management's Approval

After you have analyzed your audience and purpose, consider gaining the approval of management before you proceed. The larger and more complex the project and the document, the more important it is to be sure that you are on the right track before you invest too much time and effort.

For example, suppose you are planning a proposal to upgrade your company's computer-assisted-design (CAD) equipment. You already know your audience and purpose, and you are drafting a general outline in your mind. But before you actually start to write an outline or gather the information you will need, spend another 10 or 15 minutes making sure your primary reader, your supervisor, agrees with your thinking by submitting to him a brief description of your plans. You don't want to waste days or even weeks working on a document that won't fulfill its purpose. If you have misunderstood what your supervisor wants, it is far easier to fix the problem at this early stage.

Your description can also serve another purpose: if you want your reader's views on which of two strategies to pursue, you can describe each one and ask your reader to state a preference.

Choose an application that is acceptable to your reader, and then clearly and briefly state what you are trying to do in the project. Here is an example of the description you might submit to your boss about the CAD equipment. In composing this description of her plan, the writer drew on audience profile sheets for her two principal readers. She describes a logical, rational strategy for proposing the equipment purchase.

> Juan:
>
> Please tell me if you think this is a good approach for the proposal on CAD equipment.
>
> Outright purchase of the complete system will cost more than $1,000, so you would have to approve it and send it on for Tina's approval. (I'll provide leasing costs as well.) I want to show that our CAD hardware and software are badly out of date and need to be replaced. I'll be thorough in recommending new equipment, with independent evaluations in the literature, as well as product demonstrations. The proposal should specify what the current equipment is costing us and show how much we can save by buying the recommended system.
>
> I'll call you later today to get your reaction before I begin researching what's available.
>
> Renu

The purpose of the memo

A statement of the audience for the proposal

A statement of the purpose, followed by early statements of the scope of the document

A statement of how the writer intends to follow up on this memo

Once you have received your primary reader's approval, you can feel confident about starting to gather information.

Revising Information for a New Audience and Purpose

Chapter 2 introduced the concept of boilerplate information: standard text or graphics that are plugged into various documents published by your organization (see p. 26). Often, however, when you write to a new audience or have a new purpose, you need to revise the information.

Figure 5.9 shows an excerpt from a press release by Google (2013) about Project Loon. Figure 5.10 is an excerpt from an article based on the press release.

INTRODUCING PROJECT LOON: BALLOON-POWERED INTERNET ACCESS

The Internet is one of the most transformative technologies of our lifetimes. But for 2 out of every 3 people on earth, a fast, affordable Internet connection is still out of reach. And this is far from being a solved problem.

There are many terrestrial challenges to Internet connectivity—jungles, archipelagos, mountains. . . .

Solving these problems isn't simply a question of time: it requires looking at the problem of access from new angles. So today we're unveiling our latest moonshot from Google: balloon-powered Internet access.

A press release is a statement distributed by a company to the news media to promote a new development at the company. The company hopes the news media will print the news release, thereby publicizing the development.

The writer sketches in the technical problems.

The writer then announces his belief that his company has solved the problem by looking at it from a new angle. His use of the word moonshot *suggests that Google is proud of how ambitious the program is.*

FIGURE 5.9   Press Release (*continued*)

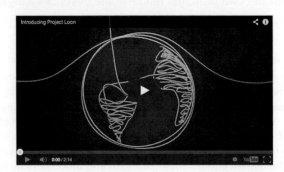

We believe that it might actually be possible to build a ring of balloons, flying around the globe on the stratospheric winds, that provides Internet access to the earth below. It's very early days, but we've built a system that uses balloons, carried by the wind at altitudes twice as high as commercial planes, to beam Internet access to the ground at speeds similar to today's 3G networks or faster. As a result, we hope balloons could become an option for connecting rural, remote, and underserved areas, and for helping with communications after natural disasters. The idea may sound a bit crazy—and that's part of the reason we're calling it <u>Project Loon</u>—but there's solid science behind it.

The writer refers to previous attempts to use high-altitude platforms and explains why the new approach is different.

Balloons, with all their effortless elegance, present some challenges. Many projects have looked at high-altitude platforms to provide Internet access to fixed areas on the ground, but trying to stay in one place like this requires a system with major cost and complexity. So the idea we pursued was based on freeing the balloons and letting them sail freely on the winds. All we had to do was figure out how to control their path through the sky. We've now found a way to do that, using just wind and solar power: we can move the balloons up or down to catch the winds we want them to travel in. . . .

Now we need some help—this experiment is going to take way more than our team alone. This week we started a pilot program in the <u>Canterbury area of New Zealand</u> with 50 testers trying to connect to our balloons. This is the first time we've launched this many balloons (30 this week, in fact) and tried to connect to this many receivers on the ground, and we're going to learn a lot that will help us improve our technology and balloon design. . . .

The writer describes the role his company hopes the public will play. The tone throughout this press release is that this is an ambitious project to address a problem that we can solve if we all work together.

This is still highly experimental technology and we have a long way to go—we'd love your support as we keep trying and keep flying! <u>Follow our Google+ page</u> to keep up with Project Loon's progress.

Onward and upward.

FIGURE 5.9   Press Release (*continued*)
Alphabet

GOOGLE'S LOON PROJECT PUTS BALLOON TECHNOLOGY IN SPOTLIGHT

Google's Project Loon aims to bring remote parts of the globe online with a ring of floating balloons. The balloons will drift through the stratosphere—which is about twice as high as commercial planes fly—to deliver 3G service to off-the-grid areas.

> The writer begins with a description of the project, largely based on the information from the Google press release, as well as a link to the press release.

The ambitious project's recent test launch on New Zealand's South Island has generated a lot of media buzz, but it turns out that high-altitude platforms (HAP) have been around for a while.

A decade ago, the European Union funded the CAPANINA project to deliver broadband from high-altitude platforms in the stratosphere. Back in 2005, it successfully produced broadband wireless access at distances of up to 37 miles (60 kilometers) from a free-floating balloon in the stratosphere over northern Sweden.

> The press release referred briefly to earlier attempts to use HAP. These earlier attempts will be a focus of this article.

Tim Tozer, an expert on wireless, satellite, and HAP communications at the University of York in Great Britain, was part of that effort. He spoke with National Geographic about the current state of the science—and the promising future beyond Google's balloons.

> The writer introduces Tim Tozer, a HAP pioneer. The writer's interview with Tozer provides the focus of this article: an outsider's perspective on Project Loon.

Google's Loon Project has already been valuable in terms of getting people interested in what might be possible, says Tozer. "I'd be pretty amazed if this system developed into anything *per se*," he says. "I think projects like this are great in terms of encouraging somebody, somewhere, to get very serious about this and dedicate the funds to developing the kind of aerial craft that can do it properly.

"Many folks jumped the gun 15 years ago postulating about types of HAPs—'wonder craft' that could stay up, roughly in one place, for months or years and carry all types of payloads and instruments. The problem is that as an aerospace project these things don't really exist yet. So what everybody has since realized is that you can't start big. It would be nice if you could, but you'll have to get there in an incremental way with small demonstrator and development projects which can kind of prove the technology."

> The article presents much more analysis by Tozer. His philosophy of technological progress—that it works best if scientists take small, incremental steps—is very different from that of Google, which prefers to take giant steps.

FIGURE 5.10 Article Based on a Press Release

From Brian Handwerk, "Google's Loon Project Puts Ballon Technology in Spotlight," National Geographic Daily News, June 18, 2013. Reprinted by permission of National Geographic.

WRITER'S CHECKLIST

Following is a checklist for analyzing your audience and purpose. Remember that your document might be read by one person, several people, a large group, or several groups with various needs.

☐ Did you fill out an audience profile sheet for your primary and secondary audiences? *(p. 91)*

In analyzing your audience, did you consider the following questions about each of your most important readers:

☐ What is your reader's educational background? *(p. 93)*

☐ What is your reader's professional experience? *(p. 93)*

☐ What is your reader's job responsibility? *(p. 93)*

☐ What is your reader's reading skill? *(p. 94)*

☐ What are your reader's cultural characteristics? *(p. 94)*

☐ What are your reader's personal characteristics? *(p. 94)*

☐ What are your reader's personal preferences? *(p. 94)*

☐ Why will the reader read your document? *(p. 94)*

☐ What is your reader's attitude toward you? *(p. 95)*

☐ What is your reader's attitude toward the subject? *(p. 96)*

☐ What are your reader's expectations about the document? *(p. 96)*

☐ How will your reader read your document? *(p. 96)*

☐ What is the physical environment in which your reader will read your document? *(p. 97)*

☐ What is the digital environment in which your reader will read your document? *(p. 97)*

In learning about your readers, did you

☐ determine what you already know about them? *(p. 97)*

☐ interview people? *(p. 98)*

☐ read about your audience online? *(p. 98)*

☐ search social media for documents your audience has written? *(p. 98)*

☐ analyze social-media data, if available? *(p. 100)*

In planning to write for an audience from another culture, did you consider the following cultural variables:

☐ political? *(p. 101)*

☐ economic? *(p. 101)*

☐ social? *(p. 101)*

☐ religious? *(p. 101)*

☐ educational? *(p. 102)*

☐ technological? *(p. 102)*

☐ linguistic? *(p. 102)*

In planning to write for an audience from another culture, did you consider other cultural variables:

☐ focus on individuals or groups? *(p. 102)*

☐ distance between business life and private life? *(p. 103)*

☐ distance between ranks? *(p. 103)*

☐ need for details to be spelled out? *(p. 104)*

☐ attitudes toward uncertainty? *(p. 104)*

In writing for a multicultural audience, did you

☐ limit your vocabulary? *(p. 107)*

☐ keep sentences short? *(p. 107)*

☐ define abbreviations and acronyms in a glossary? *(p. 107)*

☐ avoid jargon unless you knew that your readers were familiar with it? *(p. 107)*

☐ avoid idioms and slang? *(p. 107)*

☐ use the active voice whenever possible? *(p. 107)*

☐ use graphics carefully? *(p. 107)*

☐ have the document reviewed by someone from the reader's culture? *(p. 107)*

☐ In writing for multiple audiences, did you consider creating a modular document? *(p. 110)*

☐ Did you state your purpose in writing and express it using a verb or verbs? *(p. 110)*

☐ Did you get management's approval of your analysis of audience and purpose? *(p. 114)*

☐ If you are reusing a document with a new audience or purpose, did you revise the information accordingly? *(p. 115)*

EXERCISES

1. Choose a 200-word passage from a technical article related to your major course of study and addressed to an expert audience. (You can find a technical article on the web by using Google Scholar or the Directory of Open Access Journals. In addition, many federal government agencies publish technical articles and reports on the web.) Rewrite the passage so that it will be clear and interesting to a general reader. Submit

the original passage to your instructor along with your revision.

2. The following passage is an advertisement for a translation service. Revise the passage to make it more appropriate for a multicultural audience. Submit the revision to your instructor.

> If your technical documents have to meet the needs of a global market but you find that most translation houses are swamped by the huge volume, fail to accommodate the various languages you require, or fail to make your deadlines, where do you turn?

> Well, your search is over. Translations, Inc. provides comprehensive translations in addition to full-service documentation publishing.

> We utilize ultrasophisticated translation programs that can translate a page in a blink of an eye. Then our crack linguists comb each document to give it that personalized touch.

> No job too large! No schedule too tight! Give us a call today!

3. Study the website of a large manufacturer of computer products, such as Hewlett-Packard, Acer, Dell, or Lenovo. Identify three different pages that address different audiences and fulfill different purposes. Here is an example:

> Name of the page: Lenovo Group Fact Page

> Audience: prospective investors

Purpose: persuade the prospective investor to invest in the company

Be prepared to share your findings with the class.

4. **TEAM EXERCISE** Form small groups and study two websites that advertise competing products. For instance, you might choose the websites of two car makers, two television shows, or two music producers. Have each person in the group, working *alone*, compare and contrast the two sites according to these three criteria:

   a. the kind of information they provide: hard, technical information or more emotional information

   b. the use of multimedia such as animation, sound, or video

   c. the amount of interactivity they invite — that is, the extent to which you can participate in activities while you visit the site

After each person has separately studied the sites and taken notes about the three criteria, come together as a group. After each person shares his or her findings, discuss the differences as a group. Which aspects of these sites caused the most difference in group members' reactions? Which aspects seemed to elicit the most consistent reactions? In a brief memo to your instructor, describe and analyze how the two sites were perceived by the different members of the group.

CASE 5: Focusing on an Audience's Needs and Interests

You're interning in the marketing department of a cell-phone service provider, and your supervisor has asked you to perform research into a competing provider's products and services for the over-65 market, paying special attention to the ways in which the company successfully appeals to the needs and interests of its audience. She then asks you to prepare an oral presentation about your findings. If your instructor has assigned it, go to Achieve to begin your project.

Researching Your Subject

➡️

6

IN THE WORKPLACE, you will often conduct research to support your technical communication. As a buyer for a clothing retailer, for example, you might need to conduct research to help you determine whether a new line of products would be successful in your store. As a civil engineer, you might need to perform research to determine whether to replace your company's current surveying equipment with 3D-equipped stations. And as a pharmacist, you might need to research whether a prescribed medication might have a harmful interaction with another medication a patient is already taking.

In the workplace, you will conduct research using a variety of methods. You will consult websites, blogs, and discussion forums, and you might listen to podcasts or watch videos. Sometimes you will interview people, and you will likely distribute surveys electronically to acquire information from customers and suppliers. Regardless of which technique you use, your challenge will be to sort the relevant information from the irrelevant, and the accurate from the bogus.

This chapter focuses on conducting primary research and secondary research. *Primary research* involves discovering or creating technical information yourself. *Secondary research* involves finding information that other people have already discovered or created. This chapter presents secondary research first. Why? Because you will probably do secondary research first. To design the experiments or the field research that goes into primary research, you need a thorough understanding of the information that already exists about your subject.

Understanding the Research Process

In most cases, whether you are conducting academic research or workplace research, your main goal is to answer a question.

In *academic research*, your goal is to find information that will help answer a scholarly question: "To what extent do standardized tests contribute to the success of public elementary schools?" or "What effects do violent media have on teenagers?" Academic research questions are often more abstract than applied. That is, they seek information regarding the principles underlying a phenomenon. Academic research usually requires extensive secondary research: reading scholarly literature in academic journals and books. If you do primary research, as scientists do in labs, you do so only after you have conducted extensive secondary research.

In *workplace research*, your goal is to find information to help you answer a practical question: "Should we replace our sales staff's notebook computers with tablets?" or "What would be the advantages and disadvantages to our company of adopting a European-style privacy policy for customer information?" Workplace research questions frequently focus on improving a situation at a particular organization. These questions call for considerable primary research because they require you to learn about your own organization's processes and how the people in your organization would respond to your ideas. Sometimes, workplace research questions address the needs of customers or other stakeholders. You will need a thorough understanding of your organization's external audiences in order to effectively align your products or services with their needs.

Regardless of whether you are conducting academic or workplace research, the basic research methods—primary and secondary research—are fundamentally the same, as is the goal: to find answers to your questions effectively and efficiently. The following Guidelines box provides an overview of planning for the research process, and the Guidelines: Researching a Topic box below reviews important points to consider while conducting research.

GUIDELINES Planning for the Research Process

These eight steps can help you develop a research plan.

▸ **Analyze your audience.** Who are your most important readers? What are their personal characteristics, their attitudes toward your subject, their motivations for reading? If you are writing to an expert audience that might be skeptical about your message, you need to do a lot of research to gather the evidence for a convincing argument. See Ch. 5.

▸ **Analyze your purpose.** Why are you writing? Understanding your purpose helps you understand the types of information readers will expect. Think in terms of what you want your readers to know or believe or do after they finish reading your document. See Ch. 5.

▸ **Analyze your subject.** What do you already know about your subject? What do you still need to find out? Using techniques such as freewriting and brainstorming, you can determine those aspects of the subject you need to investigate. See Ch. 3.

▸ **Consider the document type.** What application will you need to deliver: a proposal, a report, a website? What kind of oral presentation will you need to deliver? See Ch. 3.

▸ **Work out a schedule and a budget for the project.** When is the document due? Do you have a budget for phone calls, database searches, or travel to libraries or other sites? See Ch. 3.

▸ **Determine what information will need to be part of the document.** Draft an outline of the contents, focusing on the kinds of information that readers will expect to see in each part. See Ch. 3.

▸ **Determine what information you still need to acquire.** Make a list of the pieces of information you don't yet have.

▸ **Create questions you need to answer in your document.** Writing the questions in a list forces you to think carefully about your topic. One question suggests another, and soon you have a lengthy list that you need to answer.

◢
GUIDELINES Researching a Topic

Follow these seven guidelines as you gather information to use in your document.

▶ **Conduct secondary research.** Study journal articles and web-based sources such as discussion forums, blogs, and podcasts.

▶ **Conduct primary research.** You can answer some of your questions by consulting company records, interviewing experts in your organization, distributing questionnaires, and interviewing other people in the industry. Other questions call for using social media to gather information from your customers, suppliers, and other stakeholders.

▶ **Be persistent.** Don't be discouraged if a research method doesn't yield useful information. Even experienced researchers fail at least as often as they succeed. Be prepared to rethink how you might find the information. Don't hesitate to ask reference librarians for help or to post questions on discussion forums.

▶ **Evaluate your information.** Once you have your information, you need to evaluate its quality: is it accurate, comprehensive, unbiased, and current?

▶ **Record your data carefully.** Prepare the materials you will need. Write information down, on paper or electronically. Record interviews (with the respondents' permission). Paste the URLs of the sites you visit into your notes. Bookmark sites so that you can return to them easily.

▶ **Triangulate your research methods.** *Triangulating* your research methods means using more than one or two methods. If a manufacturer's website says a printer produces 17 pages per minute, an independent review in a reputable magazine also says 17, and you get 17 in a demo at your office with your documents, the printer probably will produce 17 pages per minute. When you need to answer important questions, don't settle for only one or two sources.

▶ **Do more research.** If the information you have acquired doesn't sufficiently answer your questions, do more research. And if you have thought of additional questions that need to be answered, do more research. When do you stop doing research? You stop only when you think you have enough high-quality information to create your document.

For more about evaluating information, see the Guidelines box "Evaluating Print and Online Sources," on pp. 134–35.

Remember that you might also need to perform additional research as you draft, revise, edit, and proofread the technical communication that results from your research. Whenever you need additional information to help you make your argument clear and persuasive, do more research.

Choosing Appropriate Research Methods

Different research questions require different research methods. Once you have determined the questions you need to answer, think about the various research techniques you could use to answer them.

For example, your research methods for finding out how a current situation is expected to change would differ from your research methods for finding out how well a product might work for your organization. That is, if you want to know how outsourcing will change the computer-support industry over the next 10 to 20 years, you might search for long-range predictions in journal and magazine articles and on reputable websites and blogs. By contrast, if you want to figure out whether a specific scanner will produce the quality of scan that you need and will function reliably, you might do the same kind of secondary research and then observe the operation of the scanner at a vendor's site, schedule product demos at your site, follow up by interviewing others in your company, and perform an experiment in which you try two different scanners and analyze the results.

Table 6.1 provides a good starting point for thinking about how to acquire the information you need. You are likely to find that your research plan changes as you conduct your research. You might find, for instance, that you need more than one method to get the information you need or that the one method you thought would work doesn't. Still, having a plan can help you discover the most appropriate methods more quickly and efficiently.

If you are doing research for a document that will be read by people from other cultures, think about what kinds of evidence your readers will consider appropriate. In many non-Western cultures, tradition or the authority

TABLE 6.1 Research Questions and Methods

TYPE OF QUESTION	EXAMPLE OF QUESTION	APPROPRIATE RESEARCH TECHNIQUE
What is the theory behind this process or technique?	How do greenhouse gases contribute to global warming?	**Encyclopedias**, **handbooks**, and **journal articles** present theory. Also, you can find theoretical information on **websites** of reputable professional organizations and universities. Search using keywords such as "greenhouse gases" and "global warming."
What is the history of this phenomenon?	When and how did engineers first try to extract shale oil?	**Encyclopedias** and **handbooks** present history. Also, you can find historical information on **websites** of reputable professional organizations and universities. Search using keywords such as "shale oil" and "petroleum history."
What techniques are being used now to solve this problem?	How are companies responding to the federal government's laws on health-insurance portability?	If you need recent information, you will have better luck using digital resources such as **websites** and **social media** than using traditional print media. Search using keywords and tags such as "health-insurance portability." Your search will be most effective if you use standard terminology, such as "HIPAA" for the health-insurance law.

(continued)

TABLE 6.1 Research Questions and Methods (*continued*)

TYPE OF QUESTION	EXAMPLE OF QUESTION	APPROPRIATE RESEARCH TECHNIQUE
How is a current situation expected to change?	What changes will outsourcing cause in the computer-support industry over the next 10 to 20 years?	For long-range predictions, you can find information in **journal articles** and **magazine articles** and on reputable **websites**. Experts might write forecasts on **discussion forums** and **blogs**.
What products are available to perform a task or provide a service?	Which vendors are available to upgrade and maintain our company's website?	For products and services, search **websites**, **discussion forums**, and **blogs**. Reputable vendors — manufacturers and service providers — have sites describing their offerings. But be careful not to assume vendors' claims are accurate. Even the specifications they provide might be exaggerated.
What are the strengths and weaknesses of competing products and services?	Which portable GPS system is the lightest?	Search for benchmarking articles from experts in the field, such as a **magazine article** (either in print or on the web) about camping and outfitting that compares the available GPS systems according to reasonable criteria. Also check **discussion forums** for reviews and **blogs** for opinions. If appropriate, do **field research** to answer your questions.
Which product or service do experts recommend?	Which four-wheel-drive SUV offers the best combination of features and quality for our needs?	Experts write **journal articles**, **magazine articles**, and sometimes **blogs**. Often, they participate in **discussion forums**. Sometimes, you can **interview** them, in person or on the phone, or write them **inquiries**.
What do our stakeholders think about a current or proposed product or service?	Would the public like to see us add a plug-in hybrid version to our line of small SUVs? How would we market it to distinguish it from the existing hybrid small SUVs?	Study **journal** and **magazine articles** or influential **blogs** or post a question on a **company blog** or on a **microblogging site** such as Twitter and ask for responses. Also consider analyzing social-media data, using software to capture and measure keywords from social-media platforms.
What are the facts about how we do our jobs at this company?	Do our chemists use gas chromatography in their analyses?	Sometimes, you can **interview** someone, in person or on the phone, to answer a simple question. To determine whether your chemists use a particular technique, start by asking someone in the relevant department.
What can we learn about what caused a problem in our organization?	What caused the contamination in the clean room?	You can **interview** personnel who were closest to the problem and **inspect** the scene to determine the cause of the problem.
What do our personnel think we should do about a situation?	Do our quality-control analysts think we need to revise our sampling quotient?	If there are only a few personnel, **interview** them. If there are many, use **questionnaires** to get the information more quickly.
How well would this product or service work in our organization?	Would this scanner produce the quality of scan that we need and interface well with our computer equipment?	Read product reviews on reputable **websites**. Study **discussion forums**. **Observe** the use of the product or service at a vendor's site. Schedule product **demos** at your site. Follow up by **interviewing** others in your company to get their thinking. Do an **experiment** in which you try two different solutions to a problem and then analyze the results.

of the person making the claim can be extremely important, in some cases more important than the kind of scientific evidence that is favored in Western cultures.

And don't forget that all people pay particular attention to information that comes from their own culture. If you are writing to European readers about telemedicine, for instance, try to find information from European authorities and about European telemedicine. This information will interest your readers and will likely reflect their cultural values and expectations.

Conducting Secondary Research

When you conduct secondary research, you are trying to learn what experts have to say about a topic. Whether an expert is a world-famous scientist revising an earlier computer model about the effects of climate change on agriculture in Europe or the head of your human-resources department checking company records to see how a new health-care law changed the way your company hired part-time workers last year, your goal is the same: to acquire the best available information — the most accurate, most unbiased, most comprehensive, and most current.

Sometimes you will do research in a library, particularly if you need specialized handbooks or access to online subscription services that are not freely available on the internet. Sometimes you will do your research on the web. As a working professional, you might find much of the information you need in your organization's information center. An *information center* is an organization's library, a resource that collects different kinds of information critical to the organization's operations. Many large organizations have specialists who can answer research questions or who can get articles or other kinds of data for you.

UNDERSTANDING RESEARCH TOOLS

Most technical information — whether it exists in print or electronic form or both — can be tracked down using search tools available in your library, many of which are also available on your personal computer.

Library Catalogs A library's catalog contains electronic records of its physical holdings — all of the books, journals, reports, and other print documents the library contains, as well as its nonprint materials such as audio and video recordings. To search for an item, consult the catalog's instructions, which explain how to limit your search by characteristics such as types of media, date of publication, and language. The instructions also explain how to use punctuation and words such as *and*, *or*, and *not* to focus your search effectively.

Online Databases Most libraries subscribe to services, such as LexisNexis, ProQuest, InfoTrac, Gale Virtual Reference, and ERIC, that provide access to large databases of full-text journal articles, conference proceedings, newspapers, and other documents. Some databases have a specific focus within a field or subject matter. Check with a reference librarian—either in person or through a virtual chat—for guidance on the most useful and relevant databases for your needs.

Newspaper and Periodical Indexes Indexes are similar to databases, but they typically contain only citation information for articles. If you locate an article title that sounds promising, you then need to track down the periodical through other means in order to access the full article. There are periodical indexes in any number of fields. The following brief list will give you a sense of the diversity of titles:

- *Applied Science & Technology Index*
- *Business Source Premier*
- *Engineering Village*
- *National Newspaper Index*
- *Readers' Guide to Periodical Literature*

Abstract Services Abstract services are like indexes but also provide abstracts: brief technical summaries of the articles. In most cases, reading the abstract will enable you to decide whether to seek out the full article. Some abstract services, such as Chemical Abstracts Service, cover a broad field, but many are specialized rather than general.

For more about abstracts, see "Abstract" in Ch. 18 on p. 495.

Web Search Engines If you search the web effectively and efficiently, you can find reference materials such as dictionaries and encyclopedias that don't exist in print, online versions of magazines and journals, conversion calculators and other statistical software, current survey data, government documents, animations, audio and video podcasts, and many other kinds of information.

Reference Works Reference works include general dictionaries and encyclopedias, biographical dictionaries, almanacs, atlases, and dozens of other research tools. These print and online works are especially useful when you are beginning a research project because they provide an overview of the subject and often list the major works in the field.

TYPES OF SECONDARY RESEARCH SOURCES

Using the search tools described above, you will uncover a wide variety of information from a multitude of source types.

Books Printed (and electronic) books continue to be useful and popular. Most are edited and published by reputable organizations, some of them with a scientific or academic affiliation. Books provide in-depth background information on a wide range of subjects.

Periodicals: Journals and Magazines Usually published weekly, monthly, or quarterly, periodicals typically focus on a specific subject area and provide recent findings on a variety of issues. Journals tend to be more scholarly and scientific, and their articles are often reviewed by experts in the field; magazines are intended for a more general audience. Many periodicals are available in both print and digital formats.

Newspapers and Online News Sources Three of the most important indexed U.S. newspapers are the following:

- the *New York Times*, a reputable U.S. newspaper for national and international news
- the *Christian Science Monitor*, another highly regarded general newspaper
- the *Wall Street Journal*, the most authoritative news source on business, finance, and the economy

Many newspapers available on the web can be searched electronically, although sometimes there is a charge for archived articles. In addition, important news sites such as APnews.com have become reliable sources for breaking news.

Government Documents The U.S. government is the world's biggest publisher. In researching any field of science, engineering, or business, you are likely to find that a federal agency or department has produced a relevant brochure, report, or book.

Government publications are cataloged and shelved separately from other kinds of materials. They are classified according to the Superintendent of Documents system, not the Library of Congress system. A reference librarian or a government documents specialist at your library can help you use government publications. You can also access various government sites and databases on the internet. For example, if your company wishes to respond to a request for proposals (RFP) published by a federal government agency, you will find that RFP on a government site. The major entry point for federal government sites is USA.gov, which links to hundreds of millions of pages of government information and services. It also features tutorials, a topical index, online transactions, and links to state and local government sites.

For more about RFPs, see "Solicited Proposals" in Ch. 16 on p. 439.

Websites and Social Media Web searches can yield many sources that exist only on the internet, from company-sponsored sites to online archives. Social-media sources include discussion forums, blogs, and wikis. Because social-media sites typically provide user-generated content, they must be used with caution, as detailed in the next section.

USING SOCIAL MEDIA AND OTHER INTERACTIVE RESOURCES

Social media and other interactive resources enable people to collaborate, share, link, and generate content in ways that traditional websites offering static content cannot. However, the ease and speed with which new content can be posted, as well as the lack of formal review of the content, create challenges for online researchers. Everyone using social-media resources must be extra cautious in evaluating and documenting sources.

This discussion covers three categories of social-media and web-based resources used by researchers—discussion forums, wikis, and blogs—as well as two techniques for streamlining the process of using these resources: tagged content and RSS feeds.

Discussion Forums Online discussion forums sponsored by professional organizations, private companies, and others enable researchers to tap a community's information. Discussion forums are especially useful for presenting quick, practical advice. However, the advice might or might not be authoritative, so it should be checked against other sources whenever possible.

Wikis A wiki is a website that makes it easy for members of a community, company, or organization to create and edit content collaboratively. Often, a

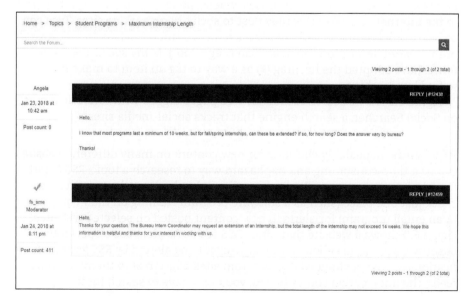

FIGURE 6.1
A Discussion Board Exchange

If you use a search engine to find this interchange, you are performing secondary research: discovering what has already been written or said about a topic. If you post a question to a discussion forum (or comment on a blog post) and someone responds, you are performing primary research, just as if you were interviewing that person. But don't worry too much about whether you are doing primary or secondary research; worry about whether the information is accurate and useful.

wiki contains articles, information about student and professional conferences, reading lists, annotated sets of links, book reviews, and documents used by members of the community. You might have participated in creating and maintaining a wiki in one of your courses or as a member of a community group outside of your college.

Wikis are popular with researchers because they contain information that can change from day to day, on topics in fields such as medicine or business. As members make changes to the content, the wiki keeps track of who made the changes and when they were made. In addition, because wikis rely on information contributed voluntarily by members of a community, they represent a much broader spectrum of viewpoints than media that publish only information that has been approved by editors. For this reason, however, you should be especially careful when you use wikis; the information they contain might not be trustworthy. It's a good idea to corroborate any information you find on a wiki by consulting other sources. To find a wiki in your subject area, use a specialized search engine such as wiki.com.

For more about blogs, see "Writing Microblogs" in Ch. 14 on p. 391.

Blogs Many technical and scientific organizations, universities, and private companies sponsor blogs that offer useful information for researchers.

Keep in mind that bloggers are not always independent voices. A Hewlett-Packard employee writing on a company-sponsored blog will likely be presenting the company's viewpoint on the topic. Don't count on that blogger to offer objective views about products. Blogs sponsored by government and nonprofit agencies are more likely to be trustworthy.

Tagged Content Tags are descriptive keywords people use to categorize and label content such as blog entries, videos, podcasts, and images they post to the internet or bookmarks they post to social-bookmarking sites. Tags can be one-word descriptors without spaces or punctuation (such as "sandiegozoo") or multiword descriptors (such as "San Diego Zoo"). Many social-media platforms have adopted the hashtag (#) as a way to tag an item to make it easier to find by searching.

Figure 6.2 shows search results for web pages tagged with "driverless cars" on Social Searcher, a search engine that tracks social-media sites.

RSS Feeds Repeatedly checking for new content on many different websites can be a time-consuming and haphazard way to research a topic. *RSS* (short for *rich site summary* or *really simple syndication*) *technology* allows readers to check just one place (such as a software program running on their computer or an email program) for alerts to new content posted on selected websites. Figure 6.3 shows a website that offers RSS feeds. Readers use a special type of software program called an *RSS aggregator* to be alerted by *RSS feeds* (notifications of new or changed content from sites of interest to them). With RSS feeds, the information comes to you; you don't have to search for it.

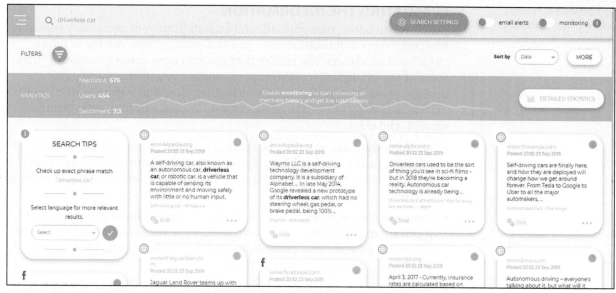

FIGURE 6.2   Search Results for Pages Tagged with "Driverless Cars"

This search returned numerous pages that relate to the topic of driverless cars. You could also search for individual posts about the topic on other social media and get even more results.

Social Searcher.com.

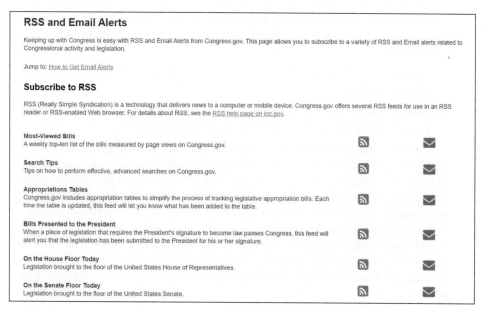

**FIGURE 6.3
A Website Offering RSS Feeds**

This pop-up menu is from a congressional website that offers RSS subscriptions. The orange feed icon is used on many websites to indicate RSS. Congress.gov.

For more about taking notes, paraphrasing, and quoting, see Appendix, Part A.

EVALUATING THE INFORMATION

You've taken notes, paraphrased, and quoted from your secondary research. Now, with more information than you can possibly use, you try to figure out what it all means. You realize that you still have some questions—that some of the information is incomplete, some contradictory, and some unclear. There is no shortage of information; the challenge is to find information that is accurate, unbiased, comprehensive, appropriately technical, current, and clear.

- **Accurate.** Suppose you are researching whether your company should consider flextime scheduling. If your research returns conflicting results, you will want to find additional sources on the subject to help you make a decision.

- **Unbiased.** You want sources that have no financial stake in your project. A private company that transports workers in vans is likely to be a biased source because it could profit from flextime, making extra trips to bring employees to work at different times.

- **Comprehensive.** You want information from different kinds of people—in terms of gender, cultural characteristics, and age—and from people representing all viewpoints on the topic.

- **Appropriately technical.** Good information is sufficiently detailed to respond to the needs of your readers, but not so detailed that they cannot understand it or do not need it. For the flextime study, you need to find out whether opening your building an hour earlier and closing it an hour later would significantly affect your utility costs. You can get this information by interviewing people in the Operations Department; you do not need to do a detailed inspection of all the utility records of the company.

- **Current.** If your information is 10 years old, it might not accurately reflect today's situation.

- **Clear.** You want information that is easy to understand. Otherwise, you'll waste time figuring it out, and you might misinterpret it.

The most difficult kind of material to evaluate is user-generated content from the internet—such as information on discussion forums or in blogs—because it rarely undergoes the formal review procedure used for books and professional journals. A general principle for using any information you find on the internet is to be extremely careful. Because content is unlikely to have been reviewed before being published on a social-media site, use one or more trusted sources to confirm the information you locate. Some instructors do not allow their students to use blogs or wikis for their research. Check with your instructor to learn his or her policies.

Why To Use Social Media in Research

Social media such as discussion forums, wikis, and blogs can provide up-to-the-minute content and collaboration opportunities for researchers. Discussion forums can offer quick, practical advice on specific issues; wikis are typically created by community volunteers who have the latest information in their field; and blogs can be found on a wide range of topics. In all three cases, however, the information provided is not necessarily authoritative or unbiased, so it should be corroborated by other sources whenever possible. Finally, consider fulfilling your ethical obligation of generosity by contributing your own expertise and findings on social-media sites to benefit others in your company or field.

How To Use Social Media in Research

Discussion Forum

Use a search engine to find a discussion forum thread. Then search within a forum for a specific subject, or post your own question to the forum.

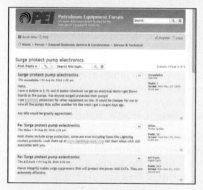

Wiki

Search wiki.com or other search engines to find specialized wikis on your topic. Then search the wiki to find specific information.

Government-Sponsored Blog

Search for and within government-sponsored blogs to find authoritative information in a range of subject areas such as climate, economics, and immigration.

Illustration reprinted by permission of John Cook.

Company-Sponsored Blog

Search blogs sponsored by private organizations to get helpful information, product reviews, and opinions, but watch for author bias.

▲ GUIDELINES Evaluating Print and Online Sources

FOR PRINTED SOURCES	FOR ONLINE SOURCES
▶ **Authorship**	
Do you recognize the name of the author? Does the source describe the author's credentials and current position? If not, can you find this information in a "who's who" or by searching for other books or other journal articles by the author?	If you do not recognize the author's name, is the site mentioned on another reputable site? Does the site contain links to other reputable sites? Does it contain biographical information — the author's current position and credentials? Can you use a search engine to find other references to the author's credentials? Be especially careful with unedited sources such as Wikipedia; some articles in it are authoritative, others are not. Be careful, too, with blogs, some of which are written by disgruntled former employees with a score to settle.
▶ **Publisher**	
What is the publisher's reputation? A reliable book is published by a reputable trade, academic, or scholarly publisher; a reliable journal is sponsored by a professional association or university. Are the editorial board members well known?	Can you determine the publisher's identity from headers or footers? Is the publisher reputable? If the site comes from a personal account, the information it offers might be outside the author's field of expertise. Many internet sites exist largely for public relations or advertising.
Trade publications — magazines about a particular industry or group — often promote the interests of that industry or group. For example, information in a trade publication for either loggers or environmentalists might be biased. If you doubt the reliability of a book or journal, ask a reference librarian or a professor.	For instance, websites of corporations and other organizations are unlikely to contain self-critical information. For blogs, examine the *blogroll*, a list of links to other blogs and websites. Credible blogs are likely to link to blogs already known to be credible. If a blog links only to the author's friends, blogs hosted by the same corporation, or blogs that express the same beliefs, be very cautious.
▶ **Knowledge of the literature**	
Does the author appear to be knowledgeable about the major literature on the topic? Is there a bibliography? Are there notes throughout the document?	Analyze the internet source as you would any other source. Often, references to other sources will take the form of links.

(continued)

▶ **Accuracy and verifiability of the information**

Is the information based on reasonable assumptions? Does the author clearly describe the methods and theories used in producing the information, and are they appropriate to the subject? Has the author used sound reasoning? Has the author explained the limitations of the information?

Is the site well constructed? Is the information well written? Is it based on reasonable assumptions? Are the claims supported by appropriate evidence? Has the author used sound reasoning? Has the author explained the limitations of the information? Are sources cited? Online services such as Clicky help you evaluate how active a blog is, how the blog ranks compared to other blogs, and who is citing the blog. Active, influential blogs that are frequently linked to and cited by others are more likely to contain accurate, verifiable information.

▶ **Timeliness**

Does the document rely on recent data? Was the document published recently?

Was the document created recently? Was it updated recently? If a site is not yet complete, be wary.

Conducting Primary Research

Although the library and the internet offer a wealth of authoritative information, in the workplace you will often need to conduct primary research because you need new information. There are eight major categories of primary research: analysis of social-media data, observations and demonstrations, inspections, experiments, field research, interviews, inquiries, and questionnaires.

ANALYSIS OF SOCIAL-MEDIA DATA

Every hour, tens of millions of posts are made on social media. A torrent of information is continuously coming online, and many organizations are working hard to sift through it to find useful insights.

Businesses are spending the most time on social-media research, trying to figure out what customers like and dislike about their products and services, learn what they want, and reinforce brand loyalty. Take the case of Nielsen, which for 50 years has been monitoring the TV viewing habits of Americans by distributing questionnaires and attaching devices to their TVs, and then selling the data it collects to TV networks and producers, who use the information to determine how much to charge advertisers. The problem at Nielsen is that many people don't watch TV on a TV, or they don't watch shows when they are broadcast. Now Nielsen also uses social-media analysis: gathering data by monitoring social media to listen in on what people are saying on Twitter, Facebook, and other services about different TV programs (DeVault, 2013).

DOCUMENT ANALYSIS ACTIVITY

Evaluating Information from Internet Sources

This information appears on the website of the Corn Refiners Association. The questions below ask you to consider the guidelines for evaluating internet sources (pp. 134–35).

1. Given the association's name and the product being discussed, what potential bias might exist on the part of the authors of this document?

2. What main point are the authors making in "The Science of Sugar"? How do they use comparisons between high fructose corn syrup and regular sugar to try to persuade readers of their point of view?

3. If you were considering using this source in a document you were writing, what information would you want to discover about the site and the organization that publishes it? How would you locate the information you needed?

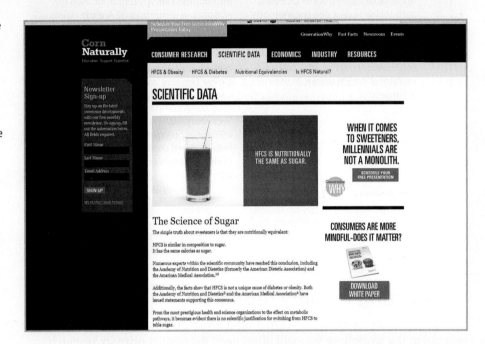

But organizations other than businesses are analyzing social-media data, too. For instance, the U.S. Geological Survey created the Twitter Earthquake Detector (TED), a program to monitor Twitter for the use of the word *earthquake*. Why? Because they realized that when people experience earthquakes, a lot of them tweet about it. The Centers for Disease Control, a U.S. federal agency, analyzes keywords on social media to monitor the spread of diseases, such as the Zika virus, in the United States and around the world. According to one scientist, "The world is equipped with human sensors—more than 7 billion and counting. It's by far the most extensive sensor network on the planet. What can we learn by paying attention?" (McCaney, 2013).

How do you perform social-media data analysis? There are many software programs that can help you devise searches. Among the most popular is HootSuite, which includes tools for listening in on what people are saying about your company on social media such as Twitter, Facebook, LinkedIn, and many other services. In addition, HootSuite helps you monitor and manage your company's social-media presence and provides *analytics*: demographic data about who is following your company, their attitudes, and their behaviors. Figure 6.4 shows a HootSuite dashboard, the screen that lets you view and manage all the information.

Like other similar tools for managing social media, HootSuite enables you to view all of your social-media accounts from a single dashboard and post content to multiple accounts at once. Here we see a person's Facebook, Twitter, and Instagram streams.

Clicking the analytics button provides access to tools you can use to view various metrics such as growth in numbers of followers during a specific period of time or frequency of readers' interactions with your posts.

FIGURE 6.4 A HootSuite Dashboard
Hootsuite.

OBSERVATIONS AND DEMONSTRATIONS

Observation and demonstration are two common forms of primary research. When you *observe*, you simply watch some activity to understand some aspect of it. For instance, if you were trying to determine whether the location of the break room was interfering with work on the factory floor, you could observe the situation, preferably at different times of the day and on different days of the week. If you saw workers distracted by people moving in and out of the room or by sounds made in the room, you would record your observations by taking notes, taking photos, or shooting video of events. An observation might lead to other forms of primary research. You might, for example, follow up by interviewing some employees who could help you understand what you observed.

When you witness a *demonstration* (or *demo*), you are watching someone carry out a process. For instance, if your company was considering buying a conveyor belt sorter for its warehouse, you could arrange to visit a manufacturer's facility, where technicians would show how the sorter works. If your company was considering a portable machine, such as a laptop computer, manufacturers or dealers could demo their products at your facility.

When you plan to observe a situation or witness a demo, prepare beforehand. Write down the questions you need answered or the factors you want to investigate. Prepare interview questions in case you have a chance to speak with someone. Think about how you are going to incorporate the information you acquire into the document you will write. Finally, bring whatever equipment you will need (pen and paper, computer, camera, etc.) to the site of the observation or demo.

INSPECTIONS

Inspections are like observations, but you participate more actively. For example, a civil engineer can determine what caused a crack in a foundation by inspecting the site: walking around, looking at the crack, photographing it and the surrounding scene, examining the soil. An accountant can determine the financial health of an organization by inspecting its financial records, perhaps performing calculations and comparing the data she finds with other data.

These professionals are applying their knowledge and professional judgment as they inspect a site, an object, or a document. Sometimes inspection techniques are more complicated. A civil engineer inspecting foundation cracking might want to test his hunches by bringing soil samples back to the lab for analysis.

When you carry out an inspection, do your homework beforehand. Think about how you will use the data in your document: will you need photographs or video files or computer data? Then prepare the materials and equipment you'll need to capture the data.

EXPERIMENTS

Learning to conduct the many kinds of experiments used in a particular field can take months or even years. This discussion is a brief introduction. In many cases, conducting an experiment involves four phases.

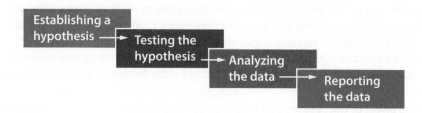

- **Establishing a hypothesis.** A hypothesis is an informed guess about the relationship between two factors. In a study relating gasoline octane and miles per gallon, a hypothesis might be that a car will get 5 percent better mileage with 89-octane gas than with 87-octane gas.

- **Testing the hypothesis.** Usually, you need an experimental group and a control group. These two groups should be identical except for the condition you are studying: in the above example, the gasoline. The control group would be a car running on 87 octane. The experimental group would be an identical car running on 89 octane. The experiment would consist of driving the two cars over an identical course at the same speed—preferably in some sort of controlled environment—over a given distance, such as 1,000 miles. Then you would calculate the miles per gallon. The results would either support or refute your original hypothesis.

- **Analyzing the data.** Do your data show a correlation—one factor changing along with another—or a causal relationship? For example, we know that sports cars are involved in more fatal accidents than sedans (there is a stronger correlation for sports cars), but we don't know what the causal relationship is—whether the car or the way it is driven is the important factor.

- **Reporting the data.** When researchers report their findings, they explain what they did, why they did it, what they saw, what it means, and what ought to be done next.

For more about reports, see Chs. 17–19.

FIELD RESEARCH

Whereas an experiment yields quantitative data that typically can be measured precisely, most field research is qualitative; that is, it yields data that typically cannot be measured precisely. Often in field research, you seek to understand the quality of an experience. For instance, you might want to understand how a new seating arrangement affects group dynamics in a classroom. You could design a study in which you observed and shot video of classes and interviewed the students and the instructor about their reactions to the new arrangement. Then you could do the same in a traditional class-room and compare the results.

Some kinds of studies have both quantitative and qualitative elements. In the case of classroom seating arrangements, you could include some quantitative measures, such as the number of times students talked with one another. You could also distribute questionnaires to elicit ratings by the students and the instructor. If you used these same quantitative measures on enough classrooms, you could gather valid quantitative information.

When you are doing quantitative or qualitative research on the behavior of animals—from rats to monkeys to people—try to minimize two common problems:

- **The effect of the research on the behavior you are studying.** In studying the effects of the classroom seating arrangement, minimize the effects of your own presence. For instance, if you observe in person, avoid drawing attention to yourself. Also, make sure that the video camera is placed unobtrusively and that it is set up before the students arrive, so they don't see the process. Still, any time you bring in a camera, you cannot be sure that what you witness is typical.

- **Bias in the recording and analysis of the data.** Bias can occur because researchers want to confirm their hypotheses. In an experiment to determine whether students write differently on physical keyboards than on touch screens, a researcher might see differences where other people don't. For this reason, the experiment should be designed so that it is *double blind*. That is, the students shouldn't know what the experiment is about so that they don't change their behavior to support or negate the hypothesis, and the data being analyzed should be disguised so that researchers don't know whether they are examining the results from the control group or the experimental group. For example, the documents produced on keyboards and touch screens should be printed out the same way.

Conducting an experiment or field research is relatively simple; the hard part is designing your study so that it accurately measures what you want it to measure.

INTERVIEWS

Interviews are extremely useful when you need information on subjects that are too new to have been discussed in the professional literature or are too narrow for widespread publication (such as local political questions).

In choosing a respondent—a person to interview—answer three questions:

- **What questions do you want to answer?** Only when you know this can you begin to search for a person who can provide the information.

- **Who could provide this information?** The ideal respondent is an expert willing to talk. Unless there is an obvious choice, such as the professor carrying out the research you are studying, use directories, such as local industrial guides, to locate potential respondents. You may also be able to find experts through your social-media network.

- **Is the person willing to be interviewed?** Contact the potential respondent by phone or in writing and describe what kind of information you are seeking. If the person is not able to help you, he or she might be willing to refer you to someone who can. Explain why you have decided to ask him or her. (A compliment works better than admitting that the person you really

▲
GUIDELINES Conducting an Interview

Follow these suggestions for preparing for and conducting an interview—and for following up after the interview.

PREPARING FOR THE INTERVIEW

▶ **Do your homework.** If you ask questions that have already been answered in the professional literature, the respondent might become annoyed and uncooperative.

▶ **Prepare good questions.** Good questions are clear, focused, and open.

— **Be clear.** The respondent should be able to understand what you are asking.

UNCLEAR	Why do you sell Trane products?
CLEAR	What are the characteristics of Trane products that led you to include them in your product line?

The unclear question can be answered in a number of unhelpful ways: "Because they're too expensive to give away" or "Because I'm a Trane dealer."

— **Be focused.** The question must be narrow enough to be answered briefly. If you want more information, you can ask a follow-up question.

UNFOCUSED	What is the future of the computer industry?
FOCUSED	What will the American microchip industry look like in 10 years?

— **Ask open questions.** Your purpose is to get the respondent to talk. Don't ask a lot of questions that have yes or no answers.

CLOSED	Do you think the federal government should create industrial partnerships?
OPEN	What are the advantages and disadvantages of the federal government's creating industrial partnerships?

▶ **Check your equipment.** If you will be recording the interview, test your voice recorder or video camera to make sure it is operating properly.

BEGINNING THE INTERVIEW

▶ **Arrive on time.**

▶ **Thank the respondent for taking the time to talk with you.**

▶ **State the subject and purpose of the interview and what you plan to do with the information.**

▶ **If you wish to record the interview, ask permission.**

(continued)

CONDUCTING THE INTERVIEW

▶ **Take notes.** Write down important concepts, facts, and numbers, but don't take such copious notes that you can't make eye contact with the respondent or that you are still writing when the respondent finishes an answer.

▶ **Start with prepared questions.** Because you are likely to be nervous at the start, you might forget important questions. Have your first few questions ready.

▶ **Be prepared to ask follow-up questions.** Listen carefully to the respondent's answer and be ready to ask a follow-up question or request a clarification. Have your other prepared questions ready, but be willing to deviate from them if the respondent leads you in unexpected directions.

▶ **Be prepared to get the interview back on track.** Gently return to the point if the respondent begins straying unproductively, but don't interrupt rudely or show annoyance. Do not say, "Whoa! I asked about layoffs in this company, not in the whole industry." Rather, say, "On the question of layoffs at this company, do you anticipate . . . ?"

CONCLUDING THE INTERVIEW

▶ **Thank the respondent.**

▶ **Ask for a follow-up interview.** If a second meeting would be useful, ask to arrange one.

▶ **Ask for permission to quote the respondent.** If you think you might want to quote the respondent by name, ask for permission now.

AFTER THE INTERVIEW

▶ **Write down the important information while the interview is fresh in your mind.** (This step is unnecessary, of course, if you have recorded the interview.) If you will be printing a transcript of the interview, make the transcript now.

▶ **Send a brief thank-you note.** Within a day or two, send a note showing that you appreciate the respondent's courtesy and that you value what you have learned. In the note, confirm any previous offers you have made, such as to send the respondent a copy of your final document.

wanted to interview is out of town.) Explain what you plan to do with the information, such as write a report or present a talk. Then, if the person is willing to be interviewed, set up an appointment at his or her convenience.

When you wish to present the data from an interview in a document you are preparing, include a transcript of the interview (or an excerpt from the interview). You will probably present the transcript as an appendix so that readers can refer to it but are not slowed down when reading the body of the document. You might decide to present brief excerpts from the transcript in the body of the document as evidence for points you make.

Figure 6.5 is from a transcript of an interview with an attorney specializing in information technology. The interviewer is a student who is writing about legal aspects of software ownership.

Q. Why is copyright ownership important in marketing software?

A. If you own the copyright, you can license and market the product and keep other people from doing so. It could be a matter of millions of dollars if the software is popular.

Q. Shouldn't the programmer automatically own the copyright?

A. If the programmer wrote the program on personal time, he or she should and does own the copyright.

Q. So "personal time" is the critical concept?

A. That's right. We're talking about the "work-made-for-hire" doctrine of copyright law. If I am working for you, anything I make under the terms of my employment is owned by you.

Q. What is the complication, then? If I make the software on my machine at home, I own it; if I'm working for someone, my employer owns it.

A. Well, the devil is in the details. Often the terms of employment are casual, or there is no written job description or contract for the particular piece of software.

Q. Can you give me an example of that?

A. Sure. There was a 1992 case, *Aymes v. Bonelli*. Bonelli owned a swimming pool and hired Aymes to write software to handle record keeping on the pool. This was not part of Bonelli's regular business; he just wanted a piece of software written. The terms of the employment were casual. Bonelli paid no health benefits, Aymes worked irregular hours, usually unsupervised — Bonelli wasn't a programmer. When the case was heard, the court ruled that even though Bonelli was paying Aymes, Aymes owned the copyright because of the lack of involvement and participation by Bonelli. The court found that the degree of skill required by Aymes to do the job was so great that, in effect, he was creating the software by himself, even though he was receiving compensation for it.

Q. How can such disagreements be prevented? By working out the details ahead of time?

A. Exactly. The employer should have the employee sign a statement that the project is being carried out as work made for hire and should register the copyright with the U.S. Copyright Office in Washington. Conversely, employees should try to have the employer sign a statement that the project is not work made for hire and should try to register the copyright themselves.

Q. And if agreement can't be reached ahead of time?

A. Then stop right there. Don't do any work.

The student prompts the attorney to expand her answers.

The student responds to the attorney's answers, making the interview more of a discussion.

FIGURE 6.5 **Excerpt from an Interview**

INQUIRIES

A useful alternative to a personal interview is to send an inquiry. This inquiry can take the form of a letter, an email, or a message sent through an organization's website. If you are lucky, your respondent will provide detailed and helpful answers. However, the respondent might not clearly understand what you want to know or might choose not to help you. Although the strategy of the inquiry is essentially that of a personal interview, inquiries can be less successful because the recipient has not already agreed to provide information and might not respond. Also, an inquiry, unlike an interview, gives you little opportunity to follow up by asking for clarification.

For more about inquiry letters, see "Common Types of Letters," Ch. 14, p. 380.

To find software for conducting surveys, search for "survey software."

QUESTIONNAIRES

Questionnaires enable you to solicit information from a large group of people. You can send questionnaires through the mail, email them, present them as forms on a website, or use survey software (such as SurveyMonkey).

Unfortunately, questionnaires rarely yield completely satisfactory results, for three reasons:

- **Some of the questions will misfire.** Respondents will misinterpret some of your questions or supply useless answers.
- **You won't obtain as many responses as you want.** The response rate will almost never exceed 50 percent. In most cases, it will be closer to 10 to 20 percent.
- **You cannot be sure the respondents are representative.** People who feel strongly about an issue are much more likely to respond to questionnaires than are those who do not. For this reason, you need to be careful in drawing conclusions based on a small number of responses to a questionnaire.

When you send a questionnaire, you are asking the recipient to do you a favor. Your goal should be to construct questions that will elicit the information you need as simply and efficiently as possible.

Asking Effective Questions To ask effective questions, follow two suggestions:

- **Use unbiased language.** Don't ask, "Should U.S. clothing manufacturers protect themselves from unfair foreign competition?" Instead, ask, "Are you in favor of imposing tariffs on men's clothing?"
- **Be specific.** If you ask, "Do you favor improving the safety of automobiles?" only an eccentric would answer no. Instead, ask, "Do you favor requiring automobile manufacturers to equip new cars with electronic stability control, which would raise the price by an average of $300 per car?"

Table 6.2 explains common types of questions used in questionnaires.

Include an introductory explanation with the questionnaire. This explanation should clearly indicate who you are, why you are writing, what you plan to do with the information from the questionnaire, and when you will need it.

For more about testing documents, see Ch. 13.

Testing the Questionnaire Before you send out *any* questionnaire, show it and its accompanying explanation to a few people who can help you identify any problems. After you have revised the materials, test them on people whose backgrounds are similar to those of your intended respondents. Revise the materials a second time, and, if possible, test them again. Once you have sent the questionnaire, you cannot revise it and resend it to the same people.

Administering the Questionnaire Determining who should receive the questionnaire can be simple or difficult. If you want to know what the residents of a particular street think about a proposed construction project, your job is easy. But if you want to know what mechanical-engineering students in colleges across the country think about their curricula, you will need a background in sampling techniques to identify a representative sample.

Make it easy for respondents to present their information. For mailed questionnaires, include a self-addressed, stamped envelope.

TABLE 6.2	Common Types of Questions Used in Questionnaires	
TYPE OF QUESTION	**EXAMPLE**	**COMMENTS**
Multiple choice	Would you consider joining a company-sponsored sports team? Yes _____ No _____	The respondent selects one of the alternatives.
Likert scale	The flextime program has been a success in its first year. strongly disagree _ _ _ _ _ _ strongly agree	The respondent ranks the degree to which he or she agrees or disagrees with the statement. Using an even number of possible responses (six, in this case) increases your chances of obtaining useful data. With an odd number, many respondents will choose the middle response.
Semantic differential	Logging on to the system simple _ _ _ _ _ _ difficult The description of the new desalinization process interesting _ _ _ _ _ _ boring	The respondent registers a response along a continuum between a pair of opposing adjectives. Usually, these questions measure a person's feelings about a task, an experience, or an object. As with Likert scales, an even number of possible responses yields better data.
Ranking	Please rank the following work schedules in order of preference. Put a 1 next to the schedule you would most like to have, a 2 next to your second choice, and so on. 8:00–4:30 _____ 8:30–5:00 _____ 9:00–5:30 _____ flexible _____	The respondent indicates the priority of a number of alternatives.
Short answer	What do you feel are the major advantages of the new parts-requisitioning policy? 1. _____ 2. _____ 3. _____	The respondent writes a brief answer using phrases or sentences.
Short essay	The new parts-requisitioning policy has been in effect for a year. How well do you think it is working? _____ _____ _____ _____ _____ _____	Although essay questions can yield information you never would have found using closed-ended questions, you will receive fewer responses to them because answering them requires more effort. Also, essays cannot be quantified precisely, as data from other types of questions can.

Figure 6.6 on page 146 shows a sample questionnaire.

Presenting Questionnaire Data in Your Document To decide where and how to present the data that you acquire from your questionnaire, think about your audience and purpose. Start with this principle: important information is presented and analyzed in the body of a document, whereas less important information is presented in an appendix (a section at the end that only some of your audience will read). Most often, different versions of the same information appear in the two places.

September 6, 2019

To: All employees
From: William Bonoff, Vice President of Operations
Subject: Evaluation of the Lunches Unlimited food service

As you may know, every two years we evaluate the quality and cost of the food service that caters our lunchroom. We would like you to help in our evaluation by sharing your opinions about the food service. Please note that your responses will remain anonymous. Please drop the completed questionnaires in the marked boxes near the main entrance to the lunchroom.

1. Approximately how many days per week do you eat lunch in the lunchroom?

   0 _____   1 _____   2 _____   3 _____   4 _____   5 _____

2. At approximately what time do you eat in the lunchroom?

   11:30–12:30 _____   12:00–1:00 _____   12:30–1:30 _____   varies _____

3. A clean table is usually available.

   strongly disagree _____ _____ _____ _____ _____ _____ strongly agree

4. The Lunches Unlimited personnel are polite and helpful.

   strongly disagree _____ _____ _____ _____ _____ _____ strongly agree

5. Please comment on the quality of the different kinds of food you have eaten in the lunchroom.
   a. Daily specials
      excellent _____ good _____ satisfactory _____ poor _____
   b. Hot dogs and hamburgers
      excellent _____ good _____ satisfactory _____ poor _____
   c. Other entrées
      excellent _____ good _____ satisfactory _____ poor _____

6. What *foods* would you like to see served that are not served now?

   _____

   _____

   _____

7. What *beverages* would you like to see served that are not served now?

   _____

   _____

   _____

8. Please comment on the prices of the foods and beverages served.
   a. Hot meals (daily specials): too high _____   fair _____   a bargain _____
   b. Hot dogs and hamburgers: too high _____   fair _____   a bargain _____
   c. Other entrées: too high _____   fair _____   a bargain _____

9. Would you be willing to spend more money for a better-quality lunch if you thought the price was reasonable?

   yes, often _____   sometimes _____   not likely _____

10. On the other side of this sheet, please provide whatever comments you think will help us evaluate the catering service.

   _____

Thank you for your assistance.

Likert-scale questions 3 and 4 make it easy for the writer to quantify data about subjective impressions.

Short-answer questions 6 and 7 are best for soliciting ideas from respondents.

FIGURE 6.6 Questionnaire

Typically, the full questionnaire data are presented in an appendix. If you can, present the respondents' data—the answers they provided—in the questionnaire itself, as shown here:

1. Approximately how many days per week do you eat lunch in the lunchroom?

   0 **12**   1 **16**   2 **18**   3 **12**   4 **9**   5 **4**

2. At approximately what time do you eat in the lunchroom?

   11:30–12:30 **3**   12:00–1:00 **26**   12:30–1:30 **7**   varies **23**

If you think your reader will benefit from analyses of the data, present such analyses. For instance, you could calculate the percentage for each response: for question 1, "12 people—17 percent—say they do not eat in the cafeteria at all." Or you could present the percentage in parentheses after each number: "12 (17%)."

Selected data might then be interpreted in the body of the document. For instance, you might devote a few sentences or paragraphs to the data for one of the questions. The following example shows how a writer might discuss the data from question 2.

> Question 2 shows that 26 people say that they use the cafeteria between noon and 1:00. Only 10 people selected the two other times: 11:30–12:30 or 12:30–1:30. Of the 23 people who said they use the cafeteria at various times, we can conclude that at least a third—8 people—use it between noon and 1:00. If this assumption is correct, at least 34 people (26 + 8) use the cafeteria between noon and 1:00. This would explain why people routinely cannot find a table in the noon hour, especially between 12:15 and 12:30. To alleviate this problem, we might consider asking department heads not to schedule meetings between 11:30 and 1:30, to make it easier for their people to choose one of the less-popular times.

The body of a document is also a good place to discuss important non-quantitative data. For example, you might wish to discuss and interpret several representative textual answers to open-ended questions.

ETHICS NOTE

REPORTING AND ANALYZING DATA HONESTLY

When you put a lot of time and effort into a research project, it's frustrating if you can't find the information you need or if the information you find doesn't help you say what you want to say. As discussed in Chapter 2, your responsibility as a professional is to tell the truth.

If the evidence suggests that the course of action you propose won't work, don't omit that evidence or change it. Nor should you hide it in a place where readers may not see it. Rather, try to figure out why the evidence does not support your proposal. Present your explanation honestly and visibly.

If you can't find reputable evidence to support your claim that one device works better than another, don't just keep silent and hope your readers won't notice. Explain why you think the evidence is missing and how you propose to follow up by continuing your research.

If you make an honest mistake, you are a person. If you cover up a mistake, you're a dishonest person. If you get caught fudging the data, you could be an unemployed dishonest person. If you don't get caught, you're still a smaller person.

WRITER'S CHECKLIST

☐ Did you determine the questions you need to answer for your document? *(p. 121)*

Did you plan before beginning the research process, considering the following important issues:

☐ audience? *(p. 122)*

☐ purpose? *(p. 122)*

☐ subject? *(p. 122)*

☐ document type? *(p. 122)*

☐ schedule and budget? *(p. 122)*

☐ information needed? *(p. 122)*

Did you choose appropriate research tools to find sources, including

☐ library catalogs? *(p. 126)*

☐ online databases? *(p. 127)*

☐ newspaper and periodical indexes? *(p. 127)*

☐ abstract services? *(p. 127)*

☐ web search engines? *(p. 127)*

☐ reference works? *(p. 127)*

Did you find appropriate secondary-research sources to answer your questions, including

☐ books? *(p. 128)*

☐ journal and magazine articles? *(p. 128)*

☐ newspaper and online news articles? *(p. 128)*

☐ government documents? *(p. 128)*

☐ websites? *(p. 129)*

☐ social media? *(p. 129)*

In evaluating information, did you carefully assess

☐ the author's credentials? *(p. 134)*

☐ the publisher? *(p. 134)*

☐ the author's knowledge of literature in the field? *(p. 134)*

☐ the accuracy and verifiability of the information? *(p. 135)*

☐ the timeliness of the information? *(p. 135)*

Did you choose appropriate primary-research methods to answer your questions, including, if appropriate,

☐ social-media data analysis? *(p. 135)*

☐ observations and demonstrations? *(p. 138)*

☐ inspections? *(p. 138)*

☐ experiments? *(p. 139)*

☐ field research? *(p. 139)*

☐ interviews? *(p. 140)*

☐ inquiries? *(p. 143)*

☐ questionnaires? *(p. 144)*

☐ Did you report and analyze the data honestly? *(p. 147)*

EXERCISES

For more about memos, see Ch. 14, p. 386.

1. Imagine you are an executive working for a company that distributes books to bookstores in the Seattle, Washington, area. Your company, with a 20,000-square-foot warehouse and a fleet of 15 small delivery vans, employs 75 people. The following are three questions that an academic researcher specializing in energy issues might focus on in her research. Translate each of these academic questions into a workplace question that your company might need to answer.

   a. What are the principal problems that need to be resolved before biomass (such as switchgrass) can become a viable energy source for cars and trucks?

   b. How much money will need to be invested in the transmission grid before windmills can become a major part of the energy solution for business and residential customers in the western United States?

   c. Would a federal program that enables companies to buy and sell carbon offsets help or hurt industry in the United States?

2. For each of the following questions, select a research technique that is likely to yield a useful answer. For instance, if the question is "Which companies within a 20-mile radius of our company headquarters sell recycled paper?" a search of the web is likely to provide a useful answer.

   a. Does the Honda CR-V include traction control as a standard feature?

   b. How much money has our company's philanthropic foundation donated to colleges and universities in each of the last three years?

c. How does a 3D printer work?

d. Could our Building 3 support a rooftop green space?

e. How can we determine whether we would save more money by switching to LED lighting in our corporate offices?

3. Using a search engine, answer the following questions. Provide the URL of each site that contains information for your answer. If your instructor requests it, submit your answers in an email to him or her.

   a. What are the three largest or most important professional organizations in your field? (For example, if you are a construction management major, your field is construction management, civil engineering, or industrial engineering.)

   b. What are three important journals read by people in your field?

   c. What are three important online discussion forums or bulletin boards read by people in your field?

   d. What are the date and location of an upcoming national or international professional meeting for people in your field?

   e. Name and describe, in one paragraph for each, three major issues being discussed by practitioners or academics in your field. For instance, nurses might be discussing the effect of managed care on the quality of medical care delivered to patients.

4. Revise the following interview questions to make them more effective. In a brief paragraph for each, explain why you have revised the question as you have.

   a. What is the role of communication in your daily job?

   b. Do you think it is better to relocate your warehouse or go to just-in-time manufacturing?

   c. Isn't it true that it's almost impossible to train an engineer to write well?

d. Where are your company's headquarters?

e. Is there anything else you think I should know?

5. Revise the following questions from questionnaires to make them more effective. In a brief paragraph for each, explain why you have revised the question as you have.

   a. Does your company provide tuition reimbursement for its employees? Yes_____ No_____

   b. What do you see as the future of bioengineering?

   c. How satisfied are you with the computer support you receive?

   d. How many employees work at your company? 5–10_____ 10–15_____ 15 or more_____

   e. What kinds of documents do you write most often? memos_____ letters_____ reports_____

6. **TEAM EXERCISE** Form small groups, and describe and evaluate your college or university's website. A different member of the group might carry out each of the following tasks:

   • Analyze the kinds of information the site contains, and determine what sort of research would be necessary to find that information.

   • In an email to the site's webmaster, ask questions about the process of researching content for the site. For example, how involved was the webmaster with the research for the site? What process did the webmaster or website contributors go through to find the content?

   • What kind of ongoing research would be needed to keep the university's website up to date? What additional topics could be researched and added to the site?

In a memo to your instructor, present your findings and recommend ways to improve the site.

CASE 6: Revising a Questionnaire

You're a marketing director at a real-estate company. You are trying to determine whether it would be cost-effective to have the company's agents take property photos instead of having the photos taken by the professional photographers employed by the supplier with which you currently contract. You ask one of your agents to develop a questionnaire to gauge agents' reactions to and opinions about the possibility of adding photography to their responsibilities, but you find that her questionnaire needs considerable revising before it will be an effective tool. If your instructor has assigned it, go to Achieve to access the questionnaire and begin assessing it.

Organizing Your Information

➡

7

DURING THE PLANNING PHASE of your writing process, you need to organize the information that will go into a document. Writers draw on a number of organizational patterns to deliver information to their audiences. But how do you know which organizational patterns will work best for a given project? Is it a question of the information you want to communicate? The audience you are addressing? The purpose you are trying to achieve? The culture in your own company? Short answer: to varying degrees, all of these factors will influence the pattern you choose. To get some ideas, talk with experienced co-workers, study other similar documents, and read this chapter.

At this point, you should know for whom you are writing and why, and you should have completed most of your research. Now it is time to start organizing the information that will make up the body of your document, whether it is a print or online document.

Understanding Three Principles for Organizing Technical Information

In organizing your information, analyze your audience and purpose, use conventional patterns of organization, and display your organizational pattern prominently.

As with any important writing task, you might want to discuss your ideas about how to organize the document with others in your network. They might identify other factors that you should consider or suggest other patterns of organization that might work better for your audience, purpose, and subject.

ANALYZING YOUR AUDIENCE AND PURPOSE

Although you thought about your audience and purpose as you planned and researched your subject, your analyses of audience and purpose are likely to change as you continue. Therefore, it is useful to review your initial assessment of audience and purpose before you proceed.

Will your audience like the message you will present? If so, announce your main point early in the document. If not, consider a pattern that presents your important evidence before your main point. Is your audience used to seeing a particular pattern in the application (the kind of document you will be writing)? If they are, you will probably want to use that pattern, unless you have a good reason to use a different one.

For more about audience and purpose, see Ch. 5.

What is your purpose in writing the document? Do you want your audience to understand a body of information or to accept a point of view and perhaps act on it? One purpose might call for a brief report without any appendixes; the other might require a detailed report, complete with appendixes.

If you are addressing people from other cultures, remember that organizational patterns can vary from culture to culture. If you can, study documents written by people from the culture you are addressing to see whether they favor an organizational pattern different from the one you are considering. As you do so, ask yourself the following four questions:

1. **Does the document follow expected organizational patterns?** For example, this chapter discusses the general-to-specific pattern. Does the document you are studying present the specific information first?

2. **Do the introduction and conclusion present the kind of information you would expect?** In the United States, main findings are often presented in the introduction; in some other cultures, the main findings are not presented until late in the document.

3. **Does the document appear to be organized linearly?** Is the main idea presented first in a topic sentence or thesis statement? Does supporting information follow? In some cultures, main ideas are withheld until the end of the paragraph or document.

4. **Does the document use headings?** If so, does it use more than one level?

If documents from the culture you plan to address are organized very differently from those you're used to seeing, take extra steps to ensure that you don't distract readers by using an unfamiliar organizational pattern.

USING CONVENTIONAL PATTERNS OF ORGANIZATION

This chapter presents a number of conventional, or commonly used, patterns of organization, such as the chronological pattern and the spatial pattern. You should begin by asking yourself whether a conventional pattern for presenting your information already exists. Using a conventional pattern makes things easier for you as a writer and for your audience.

For you, a conventional pattern serves as a template or checklist, helping you remember which information to include and where to put it. In a proposal, for example, you include a budget, which you put near the end or in an appendix. For your audience, a conventional pattern makes your document easier to read and understand. Readers who are familiar with proposals can find the information they want because you have put it where others have put similar information.

Does this mean that technical communication is merely a process of filling in the blanks? No. You need to assess the writing situation continuously as you work. If you think you can communicate your ideas better by modifying a conventional pattern or by devising a new pattern, do so. However, you gain nothing if an existing pattern would work just as well.

DISPLAYING YOUR ORGANIZATIONAL PATTERN PROMINENTLY

Make it easy for your readers to understand your organizational pattern. Displaying your pattern prominently involves three main steps:

- **Create a detailed table of contents.** If your document has a table of contents, including at least two levels of headings helps readers find the information they seek.

- **Use headings liberally.** Headings break up the text, making your pages more interesting visually. They also communicate the subject of the section and improve readers' understanding.

- **Use topic sentences at the beginnings of your paragraphs.** The topic sentence announces the main point of a paragraph and helps the reader understand the details that follow.

For more about tables of contents, see "Table of Contents," Ch. 18, p. 496. For more about headings and topic sentences, see "Writing Clear, Informative Headings," Ch. 9, p. 199 and "The Topic Sentence," Ch. 9, p. 207.

Understanding Conventional Organizational Patterns

Every argument calls for its own organizational pattern. Table 7.1 explains the relationship between organizational patterns and the kinds of information you want to present.

Long, complex arguments often require several organizational patterns. For instance, one part of a document might be a causal analysis of the problem you are writing about, and another might be a comparison and contrast of

TABLE 7.1 Organizational Patterns and the Kinds of Information You Want To Present

IF YOU WANT TO ...	CONSIDER USING THIS ORGANIZATIONAL PATTERN	FOR EXAMPLE ...
Explain events that occurred or might occur or tasks that the reader is to carry out	**Chronological** (p. 154). Most of the time, you present information in chronological order. Sometimes, however, you use reverse chronology.	You describe the process used to diagnose the problem with the accounting software. Or, in a résumé, you describe your more recent jobs before your earlier ones.
Describe a physical object or scene, such as a device or a location	**Spatial** (p. 154). You choose an organizing principle such as top-to-bottom, east-to-west, or inside-to-outside.	You describe the three main buildings that will make up the new production facility.
Explain a complex situation, such as the factors that led to a problem or the theory that underlies a process	**General to specific** (p. 157). You present general information first, then specific information. Understanding the big picture helps readers understand the details.	You explain the major changes and the details of a law mandating the use of a new refrigerant in cooling systems.
Present a set of factors	**More important to less important** (p. 158). You discuss the most important issue first, then the next most important issue, and so forth. In technical communication, you don't want to create suspense. You want to present the most important information first.	When you launch a new product, you discuss market niche, competition, and then pricing.

(continued)

TABLE 7.1   Organizational Patterns and the Kinds of Information You Want To Present (*continued*)

IF YOU WANT TO . . .	CONSIDER USING THIS ORGANIZATIONAL PATTERN	FOR EXAMPLE . . .
Present similarities and differences between two or more items	**Comparison and contrast** (p. 160). You choose from one of two patterns: (1) discuss all the factors related to one item, then all the factors related to the next item, and so forth; (2) discuss one factor as it relates to all the items, then another factor as it relates to all the items, and so forth.	You discuss the strengths and weaknesses of three companies bidding on a contract your company is offering. You discuss everything about Company 1, then everything about Company 2, and then everything about Company 3. Or you discuss the management structure of Company 1, of Company 2, and of Company 3; then you address the engineering expertise of Company 1, of Company 2, and of Company 3; and so forth.
Assign items to logical categories or discuss the elements that make up a single item	**Classification or partition** (p. 163). Classification involves placing items into categories according to some criterion. Partition involves breaking a single item or a group of items into major elements.	For classification, you group the motors your company manufactures according to the fuel they burn: gasoline or diesel. For partition, you explain the operation of each major component of one of your motors.
Discuss a problem you encountered, the steps you took to address the problem, and the outcome or solution	**Problem–methods–solution** (p. 166). You can use this pattern in discussing the past, the present, or the future. Readers understand this organizational pattern because they use it in their everyday lives.	In describing how your company is responding to a new competitor, you discuss the problem (the recent loss in sales), the methods (how you plan to examine your product line and business practices), and the solution (which changes will help your company prosper).
Discuss the factors that led to (or will lead to) a given situation, or the effects that a situation led to or will lead to	**Cause and effect** (p. 167). You can start from causes and speculate about effects, or you can start with the effect and try to determine which factors were the causes of that effect.	You discuss factors that you think contributed to a recent sales dip for one of your products. Or you explain how you think changes to an existing product will affect its future sales.

two options for solving that problem. Figure 7.1, an excerpt from a user's manual, shows how different patterns might be used in a single document.

CHRONOLOGICAL

The chronological—or timeline—pattern is commonly used to describe events. In an *accident report*, you describe the events in the order in which they occurred. In the background section of a *report*, you describe the events that led to the present situation. In a set of slides for an *oral presentation*, you explain the role of social media in U.S. presidential elections by discussing each of the presidential elections, in order, since 2000.

Figure 7.2, a timeline presented on the website of the U.S. Patent and Trademark Office, is organized chronologically.

SPATIAL

The spatial pattern is commonly used to describe objects and physical sites. In an *accident report*, you describe the physical scene of the accident. In a *feasibility study* about building a facility, you describe the property

CONTENTS

Chapter 1: Setting Up Your Susamu Tablet
9 Opening the Box
9 Setting Up Your Susamu Tablet
15 Shutting Down Your Susamu Tablet

Chapter 2: Using Your Susamu Tablet
20 Basic Features of the Susamu Tablet
22 Using the Touch Screen Keyboard
26 Using the Ports on the Susamu Tablet
29 Using the Susamu Tablet Battery

Chapter 3: If You Have Problems
34 Troubleshooting Tips
39 Finding Other Resources
43 Contacting Susamu

Different sections of this manual use different organizational patterns.

Chapter 1 is organized *chronologically*: you take the product out of the box before you set it up and run it and before you shut it down.

In Chapter 1, the section called "Opening the Box" uses *partition* by showing and naming the various items that are included in the package.

Chapter 2 is organized from *general to specific*: you want to understand the basic features of the product before you study the more specialized features.

Chapter 3 is organized according to the *problem–methods–solution* pattern. The reader tries to solve the problem by reading the troubleshooting tips, locating other resources, and contacting the manufacturer.

FIGURE 7.1 Using Multiple Organizational Patterns in a Single Document

GUIDELINES Organizing Information Chronologically

These three suggestions can help you write an effective chronological passage.

- **Provide signposts.** If the passage is more than a few hundred words long, use headings. Choose words such as *step*, *phase*, *stage*, and *part*, and consider numbering them. Add descriptive phrases to focus readers' attention on the topic of the section:

  Phase One: Determining Our Objectives

  Step 3: Installing the Lateral Supports

  At the paragraph and sentence levels, transitional words such as *then*, *next*, *first*, and *finally* will help your reader follow your discussion.

For more about transitions, see "Adding Transitional Words and Phrases," Ch. 9, p. 212.

- **Consider using graphics to complement the text.** Flowcharts, in particular, help you emphasize chronological passages for all kinds of readers, from the most expert to the general reader.

For more about graphics, see Ch. 12.

- **Analyze events where appropriate.** When you use chronology, you are explaining what happened in what sequence, but you are not necessarily explaining why or how an event occurred or what it means. For instance, the largest section of an accident report is usually devoted to the chronological discussion, but the report is of little value unless it explains what caused the accident, who bears responsibility, and how such accidents can be prevented.

156

FIGURE 7.2   Information Organized Chronologically

Information from United States Patent and Trademark Office, 2016: www.uspto.gov/patent/initiatives.

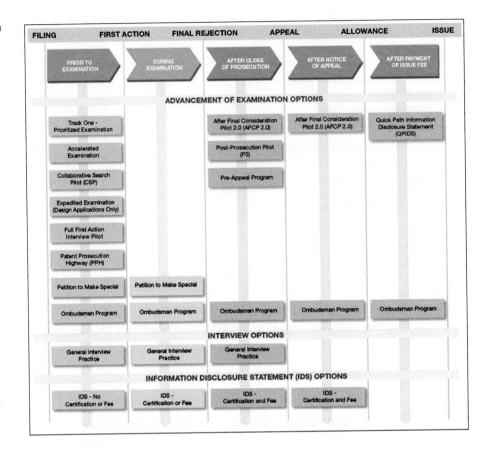

The U.S. Patent and Trademark Office created this timeline to display the various programs and initiatives that are available to applicants during each phase of the application process. In the live version of this document on the USPTO website, each program title links to more specific information about objectives and participation requirements.

on which it would be built. In a *proposal* to design a new microchip, you describe the layout of the new chip. The Guidelines box below can help you organize information spatially. Figure 7.3 shows the use of spatial organization.

◢❙ **GUIDELINES** Organizing Information Spatially

These three suggestions can help you write an effective spatial passage.

▶ **Provide signposts.** Help your readers follow the argument by using words and phrases that indicate location (*to the left, above, in the center*) in headings, topic sentences, and support sentences.

▶ **Consider using graphics to complement the text.** Diagrams, drawings, photographs, and maps clarify spatial relationships.

▶ **Analyze events where appropriate.** A spatial arrangement doesn't explain itself; you have to do the analysis. A diagram of a floor plan cannot explain why the floor plan is effective or ineffective.

FIGURE 7.3 Information Organized Spatially
Energy Star.

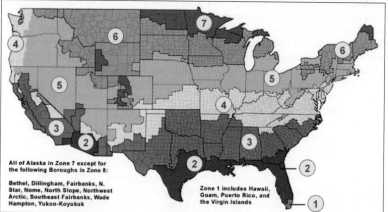

Recommended Home Insulation R– Values

Insulation level are specified by R-Value. R-Value is a measure of insulation's ability to resist heat traveling through it. The higher the R-Value the better the thermal performance of the insulation. The table below shows what levels of insulation are cost-effective for different climates and locations in the home.

Recommended insulation levels for retrofitting existing wood-framed buildings

All of Alaska in Zone 7 except for the following Boroughs in Zone 8:

Bethel, Dillingham, Fairbanks, N. Star, Nome, North Slope, Northwest Arctic, Southeast Fairbanks, Wade Hampton, Yukon-Koyukuk

Zone 1 includes Hawaii, Guam, Puerto Rico, and the Virgin Islands

Zone	Add Insulation to Attic		Floor
	Uninsulated Attic	**Existing 3–4 Inches of Insulation**	
1	R30 to R49	R25 to R30	R13
2	R30 to R60	R25 to R38	R13 to R19
3	R30 to R60	R25 to R38	R19 to R25
4	R38 to R60	R38	R25 to R30
5 to 8	R49 to R60	R38 to R49	R25 to R30

Wall Insulation: *Whenever exterior siding is removed* on an

Uninsulated **wood-frame wall:**

- Drill holes in the sheathing and blow insulation into the empty wall cavity before installing the new siding, and
- Zones 3–4: Add R5 insulative wall sheathing beneath the new siding
- Zones 5–8: Add R5 to R6 insulative wall sheathing beneath the new siding.

Insulated **wood-frame wall:**

- For Zones 4 to 8: Add R5 insulative sheathing before installing the new siding.

This information is addressed to homeowners who want to add insulation to their attics or floors. To help readers understand how much insulation they need based on their climate, the writers could have used an alphabetical list of cities or states or zip codes. Instead, the writers chose a map because it enables readers to quickly and easily "see" the climate in their region.

GENERAL TO SPECIFIC

The general-to-specific pattern is useful when your readers need a general understanding of a subject to help them understand and remember the details. For example, in a *report*, you include an executive summary—an overview for managers—before the body of the report. In a set of *instructions*, you provide general information about the necessary tools and materials and about safety measures before presenting the step-by-step instructions. In a *blog*, you describe the topic of the blog before presenting the individual blog posts.

Figure 7.4 (on p. 158), from the U.S. Department of State, explains the principles underlying the nation's cybersecurity policy.

The first paragraph is an *advance organizer*: a general summary of the topics that will be addressed in more detail.

The three topics are announced in the italicized phrases.

These phrases are used at the start of the three sections.

The United States will confront these [cyberterrorism] challenges—while preserving our core principles. Our policies flow from a commitment to both preserving the best of cyberspace and safeguarding our principles. Our international cyberspace policy reflects our core commitments to *fundamental freedoms, privacy,* and the *free flow of information.*

Fundamental Freedoms. Our commitment to freedom of expression and association is abiding, but does not come at the expense of public safety or the protection of our citizens. Among these civil liberties, recognized internationally as "fundamental freedoms," the ability to seek, receive and impart information and ideas through any medium and regardless of frontiers has never been more relevant. As a nation, we are not blind to those Internet users with malevolent intentions, but recognize that exceptions to free speech in cyberspace must also be narrowly tailored. For example, child pornography, inciting imminent violence, or organizing an act of terrorism have no place in any society, and thus, they have no place on the Internet. Nonetheless, the United States will continue to combat them in a manner consistent with our core values—treating these issues specifically, and not as referenda on the Internet's value to society.

Privacy. Our strategy marries our obligation to protect our citizens and interests with our commitment to privacy. As citizens increasingly engage via the Internet in their public and private lives, they have expectations for privacy: individuals should be able to understand how their personal data may be used, and be confident that it will be handled fairly. Likewise, they expect to be protected from fraud, theft, and threats to personal safety that lurk online—and expect law enforcement to use all the tools at their disposal, pursuant to law, to track and prosecute those who would use the Internet to exploit others. The United States is committed to ensuring balance on both sides of this equation, by giving law enforcement appropriate investigative authorities it requires, while protecting individual rights through appropriate judicial review and oversight to ensure consistency with the rule of law.

Free Flow of Information. States do not, and should not have to choose between the free flow of information and the security of their networks. The best cybersecurity solutions are dynamic and adaptable, with minimal impact on network performance. These tools secure systems without crippling innovation, suppressing freedom of expression or association, or impeding global interoperability. In contrast, we see other approaches—such as national-level filters and firewalls—as providing only an illusion of security while hampering the effectiveness and growth of the Internet as an open, interoperable, secure, and reliable medium of exchange. The same is true commercially; cyberspace must remain a level playing field that rewards innovation, entrepreneurship, and industriousness, not a venue where states arbitrarily disrupt the free flow of information to create unfair advantage. The United States is committed to international initiatives and standards that enhance cybersecurity while safeguarding free trade and the broader free flow of information, recognizing our global responsibilities, as well as our national needs.

FIGURE 7.4 **Information Organized from General to Specific**
The White House.

MORE IMPORTANT TO LESS IMPORTANT

The more-important-to-less-important organizational pattern recognizes that readers often want the bottom line—the most important information— first. For example, in an *accident report*, you describe the three most important

◢|
GUIDELINES Organizing Information from
General to Specific

These two suggestions can help you use the general-to-specific pattern effectively.

▶ **Provide signposts.** Explain that you will address general issues first and then move on to specific concerns. If appropriate, incorporate the words *general* and *specific* or other relevant terms in the major headings or at the start of the text for each item you describe.

▶ **Consider using graphics to complement the text.** Diagrams, drawings, photographs, and maps help your reader understand both the general information and the fine points.

factors that led to the accident before describing the less important factors. In a *feasibility study* about building a facility, you present the major reasons that the proposed site is appropriate, then the minor reasons. In a *proposal* to design a new microchip, you describe the major applications for the new chip, then the minor applications.

For most documents, this pattern works well because readers want to get to the bottom line as soon as possible. For some documents, however, other patterns work better. People who write for readers outside their own company often reverse the more-important-to-less-important pattern because

◢|
GUIDELINES Organizing Information from More
Important to Less Important

These three suggestions can help you write a passage organized from more important to less important.

▶ **Provide signposts.** Tell your readers how you are organizing the passage. For instance, in the introduction of a proposal to design a new microchip, you might write, "The three applications for the new chip, each of which is discussed below, are arranged from most important to least important."

In creating signposts, be straightforward. If you have two very important points and three less important points, present them that way: group the two important points and label them something like "Major Reasons to Retain Our Current Management Structure." Then present the less important factors as "Other Reasons to Retain Our Current Management Structure." Being straightforward makes the material easier to follow and enhances your credibility.

▶ **Explain why one point is more important than another.** Don't just say that you will be arranging the items from more important to less important. Explain why the more important point is more important.

▶ **Consider using graphics to complement the text.** Diagrams and numbered lists often help to suggest levels of importance.

Writers of technical communication often have to explain why some information is more important than other information. To do so, they typically present the more important information first and use words and phrases to signal the importance of the points they present. This paragraph sketches the background of the Forest Service's strategy for combatting the damage done by bark beetles. Notice that the problem the paragraph focuses on first is the health and safety risks posed by the falling trees. The next point, about the environmental impacts, is less important, as suggested by the word "also" in the final sentence.

FIGURE 7.5 Information Organized from More Important to Less Important
U.S . Forest Service.

WESTERN BARK BEETLE STRATEGY OVERVIEW

Across six states of the interior west, over 17.5 million acres of forested lands are infested by bark beetles. The infestation is growing at an estimated 600,000 acres a year with the potential to affect the majority of our western pine, fir and spruce forests. It is estimated that 100,000 beetle-killed trees are currently falling daily, posing a serious health and safety threat to forest visitors, residents and employees. The epidemic is also causing unprecedented environmental impacts.

The Western Bark Beetle Strategy (PDF, 7.0 MB) developed in 2011 identifies how the Forest Service is responding to and will respond to the western bark beetle epidemic over the next five years (FY 2011–2016). The extent of the epidemic requires prioritization of treatments, first providing for human safety in areas threatened by standing dead hazard trees, and second, addressing dead and down trees that create hazardous fuels conditions adjacent to high value areas. After the priority of safety, forested areas with severe mortality will be reforested with the appropriate species (recovery). Forests will also be thinned to reduce the number of trees per acre and create more diverse stand structures to minimize extensive epidemic bark beetle areas (resiliency). This is a modest strategy that reflects current budget realities, but focuses resources in the most important places that can make a big difference to the safety of the American public.

Here the writer uses the words "first" and "second" to signal priority. Safety is the most important issue; reforestation is less important, as suggested by the phrase "After the priority of safety." Thinning the forests is a lower priority, as suggested by the word "also" in the phrase "Forests will also be thinned."

they want to make sure their audience reads the whole discussion. This reversed pattern is also popular with writers who are delivering bad news. For instance, if you want to justify recommending that your organization *not* go ahead with a popular plan, the reverse sequence lets you explain the problems with the popular plan before you present the plan you recommend. Otherwise, readers might start to formulate objections before you have had a chance to explain your position.

Figure 7.5 from the U.S. Department of Agriculture, shows the more-important-to-less-important organizational structure.

COMPARISON AND CONTRAST

Typically, the comparison-and-contrast pattern is used to describe and evaluate two or more items or options. For example, in a *memo*, you compare and contrast the credentials of three finalists for a job. In a *proposal* to design a new microchip, you compare and contrast two different strategies for designing the chip. In a *video* explaining different types of low-emissions vehicles, you compare and contrast electric cars and hybrids.

The first step in comparing and contrasting two or more items is to determine the *criteria*: the standards or needs you will use in studying the items. For example, if a professional musician who plays the piano in restaurants was looking to buy a new portable keyboard, she might compare and contrast available instruments using the number of keys as one criterion. For this person, 88 keys would be better than 64. Another criterion might be weight: lighter is better than heavier.

Almost always, you will need to consider several or even many criteria. Start by deciding whether each criterion represents a *necessary* quality or merely a *desirable* one. In studying keyboards, for instance, the number of keys might be a necessary quality. If you need an 88-key instrument to play your music, you won't consider any instruments without 88 keys. The same thing might be true of touch-sensitive keys. But a MIDI interface might be less important, a merely desirable quality; you would like MIDI capability, but you would not eliminate an instrument from consideration just because it doesn't have MIDI.

Two typical patterns for organizing a comparison-and-contrast discussion are *whole-by-whole* and *part-by-part*. The following example illustrates the difference between them. The example shows how two printers—Model 5L and Model 6L—might be compared and contrasted according to three criteria: price, resolution, and print speed.

The whole-by-whole pattern provides a coherent picture of each option: Model 5L and Model 6L. This pattern works best if your readers need an overall assessment of each option or if each option is roughly equivalent according to the criteria.

Whole-by-whole	Part-by-part
Model 5L • price • resolution • print speed	Price • Model 5L • Model 6L
Model 6L • price • resolution • print speed	Resolution • Model 5L • Model 6L
	Print Speed • Model 5L • Model 6L

The part-by-part pattern lets you focus your attention on the criteria. If, for instance, Model 5L produces much better resolution than Model 6L, the part-by-part pattern reveals this difference more effectively than the whole-by-whole pattern does. The part-by-part pattern is best for detailed comparisons and contrasts.

You can have it both ways. You can begin with a general description of the various items and then use a part-by-part pattern to emphasize particular aspects.

Once you have chosen the overall pattern—whole-by-whole or part-by-part—you decide how to order the second-level items. That is, in a whole-by-whole passage, you have to sequence the aspects of the items or options being compared; in a part-by-part passage, you have to sequence the items or options themselves.

Figure 7.6 (p. 162) shows a comparison-and-contrast table about employment in the labor force.

FIGURE 7.6
Information Organized by Comparison and Contrast
U.S. Census Bureau.

Men & Women, Money & Work

MAY 29, 2019

Men & Women, Money & Work
Does education narrow the earnings gap?

Overall, women workers earn about 80 cents for every dollar men earn. This difference widens with more education to 74 cents among workers with a bachelor's degree, down from 78 cents for workers without the college degree. Use this visualization to compare median earnings differences between men and women workers by occupation. Presented here are estimates of full-time, year-round workers, aged 25 and older. Each circle represents a detailed occupation. Circle size represents the number of workers in that group. A value of zero indicates too few workers to calculate an estimate.

Select options:

Education level	Women's to men's earnings ratio	Occupation size	Percentage of women in occupation	Who's older?
⦿ (All)	⦿ (All)	⦿ (All)	⦿ (All)	⦿ (All)
○ Bachelor's degree +	○ Over 1.0	○ 1,000,000+	○ Mostly women (more than 75%)	○ Women older
○ < Bachelor's degree	○ No earnings difference	○ 500,000-999,999	○ Mostly men (fewer than 25%)	○ Men older
	○ .80-.99	○ 10,000-499,999	○ Mixed (25% to 75%)	○ No age difference
	○ .60-.79			
	○ Less than .60			

Look up occupation

Highlight Occupation

Or, select major occupation group

(All)

This graphic shows **Median Earnings** and **Median Age** for men and women at **(All)** education levels with an earnings ratio of **All**, in occupations where the majority of full-time workers are **All**, and the median age difference shows **All**, with an occupation size of **All** workers.

This chart published by the federal government presents a lot of information about earning power across a variety of ages. The main theme is the comparison between men and women: how gender impacts relative pay at different ages. Because the main basis of comparison and contrast is the perceived gender of workers, the writers chose a side-by-side graph structure, with data about men in one column and data about women in the other.

◢
GUIDELINES Organizing Information by
Comparison and Contrast

These four suggestions can help you compare and contrast items effectively.

▶ **Establish criteria for the comparison and contrast.** Choose criteria that are consistent with the needs of your audience.

▶ **Evaluate each item according to the criteria you have established.** Draw your conclusions.

▶ **Organize the discussion.** Choose either the *whole-by-whole* or the *part-by-part* pattern or some combination of the two. Then order the second-level items.

▶ **Consider using graphics to complement the text.** Graphics can clarify and emphasize comparison-and-contrast passages. Diagrams, drawings, and tables are common ways to provide such clarification and emphasis.

ETHICS NOTE

COMPARING AND CONTRASTING FAIRLY

Because the comparison-and-contrast organizational pattern is used frequently in evaluating items, it appears often in product descriptions as part of the argument that one company's products are better than a competitor's. There is nothing unethical in this. But it is unethical to misrepresent items, such as when writers portray their own product as better than it is or portray their competitor's as worse than it is.

Obviously, lying about a product is unethical. But some practices are not so easy to characterize. For example, suppose your company makes tablet computers and your chief competitor's model has a longer battery life than yours. In comparing and contrasting the two tablets, are you ethically obligated to mention battery life? No, you are not. If readers are interested in battery life, it is their responsibility to figure out what your failure to mention battery life means and seek further information from other sources. If you do mention battery life, however, you must do so honestly, using industry-standard techniques for measuring it. You cannot measure your tablet's battery life under one set of conditions and your competitor's under another set.

CLASSIFICATION OR PARTITION

Classification is the process of assigning items to categories. For instance, all the students at a university could be classified by sex, age, major, and many other characteristics. You can also create subcategories within categories, such as males and females majoring in business.

Classification is common in technical communication. In a *feasibility study* about building a facility, you classify sites into two categories: domestic or

◢ GUIDELINES Organizing Information by Classification or Partition

These six suggestions can help you write an effective classification or partition passage.

▶ **Choose a basis of classification or partition that fits your audience and purpose.** If you are writing a warning about snakes for hikers in a particular state park, your basis of classification will probably be whether the snakes are poisonous. You will describe all the poisonous snakes, then all the nonpoisonous ones.

▶ **Use only one basis of classification or partition at a time.** If you are classifying graphics programs according to their technology—paint programs and draw programs—do not include another basis of classification, such as cost.

▶ **Avoid overlap.** In classifying, make sure that no single item could logically be placed in more than one category. In partitioning, make sure that no listed component includes another listed component. Overlapping generally occurs when you change the basis of classification or the level at which you are partitioning a unit. In the following classification of bicycles, for instance, the writer introduces a new basis of classification that results in overlapping categories:

— mountain bikes

— racing bikes

— comfort bikes

— ten-speed bikes

The first three items share a basis of classification: the general category of bicycle. The fourth item has a different basis of classification: number of speeds. Adding the fourth item is illogical because a particular ten-speed bike could be a mountain bike, a racing bike, or a comfort bike.

▶ **Be inclusive.** Include all the categories necessary to complete your basis of classification. For example, a partition of an automobile by major systems would be incomplete if it included the electrical, fuel, and drive systems but not the cooling system. If you decide to omit a category, explain why.

▶ **Arrange the categories in a logical sequence.** Use a reasonable plan, such as chronology (first to last), spatial development (top to bottom), or importance (most important to least important).

▶ **Consider using graphics to complement the text.** Organization charts are commonly used in classification passages; drawings and diagrams are often used in partition passages.

foreign. In a *journal article* about ways to treat a medical condition, you classify the treatments as surgical or nonsurgical. In a description of a major in a *college catalog*, you classify courses as required or elective.

Partition is the process of breaking a unit into its components. For example, a home-theater system could be partitioned into the following components:

TV, amplifier, peripheral devices such as DVD players, and speakers. Each component is separate, but together they form a whole system. Each component can, of course, be partitioned further.

Partition is used in descriptions of objects, mechanisms, and processes. In an *equipment catalog*, you use partition to describe the major components of one of your products. In a *proposal*, you use partition to present a detailed description of an instrument you propose to develop. In a *brochure*, you explain how to operate a product by describing each of its features.

In Figure 7.7, the writer uses classification effectively in introducing categories of tornados to a general audience.

Figure 7.8 illustrates partition. For more examples of partition, see Chapter 20, which includes descriptions of objects, mechanisms, and processes.

Explanation of EF-Scale Ratings

Over the course of April 27th, 2011, damage across the entire range of the EF scale was sustained in some portion of the Huntsville County Warning Forecast Area. Below is a chart that explains what type of damage is associated with each ranking on the EF scale, including example photographs from the April 27th event.

EF Rating	Wind Speeds	Expected Damage
EF-0	65-85 mph	'Minor' damage: shingles blown off or parts of a roof peeled off, damage to gutters/siding, branches broken off trees, shallow rooted trees toppled.
EF-1	86-110 mph	'Moderate' damage: more significant roof damage, windows broken, exterior doors damaged or lost, mobile homes overturned or badly damaged.
EF-2	111-135 mph	'Considerable' damage: roofs torn off well constructed homes, homes shifted off their foundation, mobile homes completely destroyed, large trees snapped or uprooted, cars can be tossed.
EF-3	136-165 mph	'Severe' damage: entire stories of well constructed homes destroyed, significant damage done to large buildings, homes with weak foundations can be blown away, trees begin to lose their bark.
EF-4	166-200 mph	'Extreme' damage: Well constructed homes are leveled, cars are thrown significant distances, top story exterior walls of masonry buildings would likely collapse.
EF-5	> 200 mph	'Massive/incredible' damage: Well constructed homes are swept away, steel-reinforced concrete structures are critically damaged, high-rise buildings sustain severe structural damage, trees are usually completely debarked, stripped of branches and snapped.

FIGURE 7.7 Information Organized by Classification

The Enhanced Fujita (EF) rating scale classifies tornados according to their wind speed and destructiveness.

Information from National Oceanic and Atmospheric Administration, 2012. Explanation of EF-scale ratings: www.srh .noaa.gov/hun/?n=efscale_explanation.

FIGURE 7.8   Information Organized by Partition

Information from U.S. Department of Energy, 2019: http://www2.eere.energy .gov/wind/printable_versions/inside_a _wind_turbine.html.

This example of partition begins with a textual overview of the topic.

This interactive graphic enables the reader to see the components of the wind turbine in operation as the equipment generates electricity.

Following this graphic is a description of each of the components shown in the graphic.

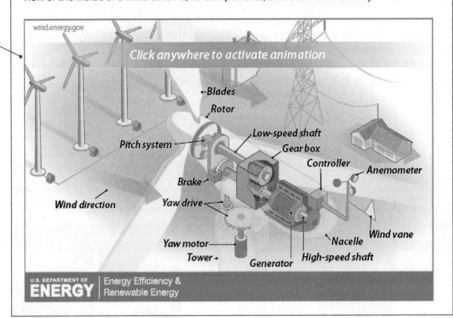

THE INSIDE OF A WIND TURBINE

Wind turbines harness the power of the wind and use it to generate electricity. Simply stated, a wind turbine works the opposite of a fan. Instead of using electricity to make wind, like a fan, wind turbines use wind to make electricity. The energy in the wind turns two or three propeller-like blades around a rotor. The rotor is connected to the main shaft, which spins a generator to create electricity. This illustration provides a detailed view of the inside of a wind turbine, its components, and their functionality.

PROBLEM–METHODS–SOLUTION

The problem–methods–solution pattern reflects the logic used in carrying out a project. The three components of this pattern are simple to identify:

- **Problem.** A description of what was not working (or not working effectively) or what opportunity exists for improving current processes.

- **Methods.** The procedures performed to confirm the analysis of the problem, solve the problem, or exploit the opportunity.

- **Solution.** The statement of whether the analysis of the problem was correct or of what was discovered or devised to solve the problem or capitalize on the opportunity.

The problem–methods–solution pattern is common in technical communication. In a *proposal*, you describe a problem in your business, how you plan to carry out your research, and how your deliverable (an object or a report)

◢

GUIDELINES Organizing Information by
Problem-Methods-Solution

These five suggestions can help you write an effective problem–methods–solution passage.

▶ **In describing the problem, be clear and specific.** Don't write, "Our energy expenditures are getting out of hand." Instead, write, "Our energy usage has increased 7 percent in the last year, while utility rates have risen 11 percent." Then calculate the total increase in energy costs.

▶ **In describing your methods, help your readers understand what you did and why you did it that way.** You might need to justify your choices. Why, for example, did you use a *t*-test in calculating the statistics in an experiment? If you can't defend your choice, you lose credibility.

▶ **In describing the solution, don't overstate.** Avoid overly optimistic claims, such as "This project will increase our market share from 7 percent to 10 percent within 12 months." Instead, be cautious: "This project could increase our market share from 7 percent to 10 percent." This way, you won't be embarrassed if things don't turn out as well as you had hoped.

▶ **Choose a logical sequence.** The most common sequence is to start with the problem and conclude with the solution. However, different sequences work equally well as long as you provide a preliminary summary to give readers an overview and include headings or some other design elements to help readers find the information they want (see Ch. 11). For instance, you might want to put the methods last if you think your readers already know them or are more interested in the solution.

▶ **Consider using graphics to complement the text.** Graphics, such as flow-charts, diagrams, and drawings, can clarify problem–methods–solution passages.

can help solve the problem. In a *completion report* about a project to improve a manufacturing process, you describe the problem that motivated the project, the methods you used to carry out the project, and the findings: the results, conclusions, and recommendations.

Figure 7.9 shows the problem–methods–solution pattern. The passage is from a case study of a police department using TASER equipment to solve two problems.

CAUSE AND EFFECT

Technical communication often involves cause-and-effect discussions. Sometimes you will reason forward, from cause to effect: if we raise the price of a particular product we manufacture (cause), what will happen to our sales (effect)? Sometimes you will reason backward, from effect to cause: productivity went down by 6 percent in the last quarter (effect); what factors

"Challenge" presents the problem at the Rialto, California, police department.

Challenge When facing the public, Rialto PD found two main areas for improvement: Use of Force, and Officer Complaints. These issues cost the department valuable time and resources. Rialto PD believed that improving oversight, gathering more video evidence, and improving trust within the community would decrease the frequency of these issues.

"Solution" begins with a discussion of the methods the police department used to solve the two problems.

Solution Rialto PD invested in TASER's Digital Evidence Ecosystem, AXON flex and EVIDENCE.com. After purchasing 66 cameras and licenses to EVIDENCE.com, the PD began a scientific research study to determine the effects of TASER's AXON flex and EVIDENCE.com solution.

To protect the integrity of data gathered during the experiment, Rialto PD used the "Cambridge Randomizer" and followed a strict scientific process. This strategy shaped a sophisticated, Web-based experiment with data protected from outside influences. . . . Because of Rialto PD's extensive data gathering and controlled study, the data is compelling. Over the course of 1 year, officer complaints fell by 87.5% in the experimental group. The data shows the officers increased interactions with the public compared to the previous year, and still complaints fell dramatically.

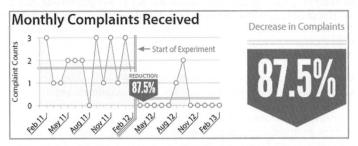

Note that writers do not necessarily use the words *problem*, *methods*, and *solution* in this method of organization. Don't worry about the terminology; the important point is to recognize that this organizational pattern is based on identifying a problem, doing something to respond to it, and thereby reducing or solving it.

Rialto PD also focused on their Officer use-of-force data. During the experiment, individuals wearing an AXON flex reduced use-of-force by 59%. This data indicates that the presence of the camera not only encouraged compliance from the public but it also reduced instances of use of force by officers.

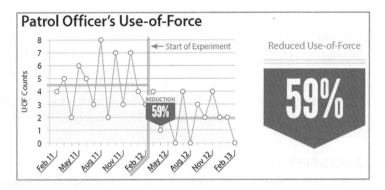

FIGURE 7.9   Information Organized by the Problem–Methods–Solution Pattern
Reprinted by permission of TASER International, Inc.

led to this decrease (causes)? Cause-and-effect reasoning, therefore, provides a way to answer the following two questions:

- What will be the effect(s) of X?
- What caused X?

Arguments organized by cause and effect appear in various types of technical communication. In an *environmental impact statement*, you argue that a proposed construction project would have three important effects on the ecosystem. In the recommendation section of a *report*, you argue that a recommended solution would improve operations in two major ways. In a *memo*, you describe a new policy and then explain the effects you anticipate the policy will have.

Cause-and-effect relationships are difficult to describe because there is no scientific way to determine causes or effects. You draw on your common sense and your knowledge of your subject. When you try to determine, for example, why the product your company introduced last year sold poorly, you start with the obvious possibilities: the market was saturated, the product was of low quality, the product was poorly marketed, and so forth. The more you know about your subject, the more precise and insightful your analysis will be.

But a causal discussion can never be certain. You cannot *prove* why a product failed in the marketplace; you can only explain why the factors you are identifying are the most plausible causes or effects. For instance, to make a plausible case that the main reason for the product's weak performance is that it was poorly marketed, you can show that, in the past, your company's other unsuccessful products were marketed in similar ways and your company's successful products were marketed in other ways.

Figure 7.10 illustrates an effective cause-and-effect argument. The writer is explaining why electric vehicles have not sold well in the United States.

◢|

GUIDELINES Organizing Information by Cause and Effect

These four suggestions can help you write an effective cause-and-effect passage.

▸ **Explain your reasoning.** To support your claim that the product was marketed poorly, use specific facts and figures: the low marketing budget, delays in beginning the marketing campaign, and so forth.

▸ **Avoid overstating your argument.** For instance, if you write that Bill Gates, the co-founder of Microsoft, "created the computer revolution," you are claiming too much. It is better to write that Gates "was one of the central players in creating the computer revolution."

▸ **Avoid logical fallacies.** Logical fallacies, such as hasty generalizations or post hoc reasoning, can also undermine your discussion.

▸ **Consider using graphics to complement the text.** Graphics, such as flowcharts, organization charts, diagrams, and drawings, can clarify and emphasize cause-and-effect passages.

For more about logical fallacies, see "Avoiding Logical Fallacies," Ch. 8, p. 191.

The first paragraph presents the effect in this cause-and-effect argument: electric cars are not popular in the United States.

The bullet list presents four causes.

Electric motors are superior to internal-combustion engines — on paper, at least. They have better torque, they have only one moving part, and they are easy to maintain. But the sales of all-electric cars in the United States have been weak. Four factors are holding back the sales of all-electric cars:

- **Range.** The electric car with the best range can travel about 300 miles, but it is a very expensive two-seater. The best-selling and more affordable electric models claim between 150 and 240 miles. Compared to a gasoline-powered car, with a range of 300–500 miles, the electric car simply isn't practical for someone who doesn't already have a standard car to use for long trips.

- **Charge time.** On a 120-volt outlet, the average electric car takes almost 14 hours to charge. On a 240-volt outlet, it's 7 hours. Few drivers want to plan their trips around downtimes as long as that.

- **Infrastructure.** Even in the most densely populated regions of the country, there are still only about a sixth as many charging stations as there are gas stations. There are around 130,000 gas stations in the nation, but as of 2019 there were only 20,000 electric-car charge points.

- **Cost.** The enormous R&D costs of electric cars are being passed on to consumers. An electric car can cost 40% more than a comparable gasoline-powered car, so even with tax credits, it can take drivers a while to make up the difference in fuel savings depending on how often they drive.

FIGURE 7.10   A Discussion Organized by the Cause-and-Effect Pattern

DOCUMENT ANALYSIS ACTIVITY

Using Multiple Organizational Patterns in an Infographic

This infographic about how job seekers in England use social media presents three sets of data, each of which uses a different organizational pattern. The questions below ask you to think about the organizational patterns.

1. On the left, Facebook and LinkedIn are compared in two pairs of graphics. Is the comparison in each pair clear and easy to understand? Would other types of graphics be easier to understand?

2. In the middle section of the infographic, which organizational pattern is being used? How effective is it in helping readers understand the information?

3. What are the two organizational patterns being used to communicate the data in the map of England?

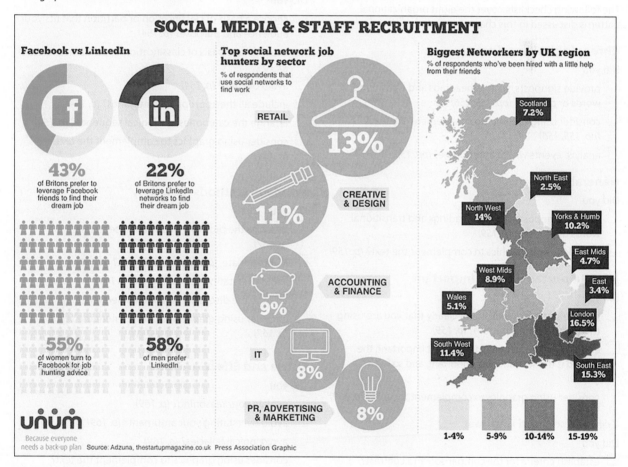

SOCIAL MEDIA & STAFF RECRUITMENT

Facebook vs LinkedIn

43% of Britons prefer to leverage Facebook friends to find their dream job

22% of Britons prefer to leverage LinkedIn networks to find their dream job

55% of women turn to Facebook for job hunting advice

58% of men prefer LinkedIn

unum
Because everyone needs a back-up plan   Source: Adzuna, thestartupmagazine.co.uk Press Association Graphic

Top social network job hunters by sector
% of respondents that use social networks to find work

RETAIL **13%**

CREATIVE & DESIGN **11%**

ACCOUNTING & FINANCE **9%**

IT **8%**

PR, ADVERTISING & MARKETING **8%**

Biggest Networkers by UK region
% of respondents who've been hired with a little help from their friends

Scotland 7.2%
North East 2.5%
North West 14%
Yorks & Humb 10.2%
East Mids 4.7%
West Mids 8.9%
East 3.4%
Wales 5.1%
London 16.5%
South West 11.4%
South East 15.3%

1-4%   5-9%   10-14%   15-19%

Source: Unum, 2013: www.unum.co.uk.
Used by permission of Unum, Ltd.

WRITER'S CHECKLIST

☐ Did you analyze your audience and purpose? *(p. 151)*

☐ Did you consider using a conventional pattern of organization? *(p. 152)*

Did you display your organizational pattern prominently by

☐ creating a detailed table of contents? *(p. 153)*

☐ using headings liberally? *(p. 153)*

☐ using topic sentences at the beginnings of your paragraphs? *(p. 153)*

The following checklists cover the eight organizational patterns discussed in this chapter.

Chronological and Spatial

Did you

☐ provide signposts, such as headings and transitional words or phrases? *(pp. 155, 156)*

☐ consider using graphics to complement the text? *(pp. 155, 156)*

☐ analyze events where appropriate? *(pp. 155, 156)*

General to Specific

Did you

☐ provide signposts, such as headings and transitional words or phrases? *(p. 159)*

☐ consider using graphics to complement the text? *(p. 159)*

More Important to Less Important

Did you

☐ provide signposts, explaining clearly that you are using this organizational pattern? *(p. 159)*

☐ explain why the first point is the most important, the second is the second most important, and so forth? *(p. 159)*

☐ consider using graphics to complement the text? *(p. 159)*

Comparison and Contrast

Did you

☐ establish criteria for the comparison and contrast? *(p. 163)*

☐ evaluate each item according to the criteria you established? *(p. 163)*

☐ organize the discussion by choosing the pattern — whole-by-whole or part-by-part — that is most appropriate for your audience and purpose? *(p. 163)*

☐ consider using graphics to complement the text? *(p. 163)*

Classification or Partition

Did you

☐ choose a basis of classification or partition that fits your audience and purpose? *(p. 164)*

☐ use only one basis of classification or partition at a time? *(p. 164)*

☐ avoid overlap? *(p. 164)*

☐ include all the appropriate categories? *(p. 164)*

☐ arrange the categories in a logical sequence? *(p. 164)*

☐ consider using graphics to complement the text? *(p. 164)*

Problem–Methods–Solution

Did you

☐ describe the problem clearly and specifically? *(p. 167)*

☐ if appropriate, justify your methods? *(p. 167)*

☐ avoid overstating your solution? *(p. 167)*

☐ arrange the discussion in a logical sequence? *(p. 167)*

☐ consider using graphics to complement the text? *(p. 167)*

Cause and Effect

Did you

☐ explain your reasoning? *(p. 169)*

☐ avoid overstating your argument? *(p. 169)*

☐ avoid logical fallacies? *(p. 169)*

☐ consider using graphics to complement the text? *(p. 169)*

EXERCISES

1. Find the website of a company that makes a product used by professionals in your field. (Personal computers are a safe choice.) Locate three discussions on the site that use different organizational patterns. For example, there will probably be a passage devoted to ordering a product from the site (using a chronological pattern), a description of a product (using a partition pattern), and a passage describing why the company's products are superior to those of its competitors (using a comparison-and-contrast argument). Print a copy of the passages you've identified.

2. Identify the best organizational pattern for a discussion of each of the lettered topics that follow. For example, a discussion of distance education and on-campus courses could be organized using the comparison-and-contrast pattern. Write a brief explanation of why the organizational pattern you chose for each topic would be the best one to use. (Use each of the organizational patterns discussed in this chapter at least once.)

    a. how to register for courses at your college or university

    b. how you propose to reduce the time required to register for classes or to change a schedule

    c. your car's dashboard

    d. the current price of gasoline

    e. advances in manufacturing technology

    f. the reasons you chose your college or major

    g. a student organization on your campus

    h. two music-streaming services

    i. tablet computers

    j. how you propose to increase the ties between your college or university and local business and industry

    k. college courses

    l. increased security at airports

    m. the room in which you are sitting

    n. the three most important changes you would like to see at your school

    o. a guitar

    p. cooperative education and internships for college students

    q. how to prepare for a job interview

3. You are researching portable projection systems (projectors and screens) for your company's sales staff to use. You are considering such factors as ease of use, size and weight, resolution, and Wi-Fi connectivity. You conclude that the three leading systems are quite similar in all but one characteristic: price. One model costs about 30 percent less than the other two models. In organizing your discussion of the three systems, should you use the whole-by-whole pattern or the part-by-part pattern? Why?

4. Write a 500-word discussion of one of the lettered topics in Exercise 2. If appropriate, include graphics. Preface your discussion with a few sentences explaining the audience and purpose of the discussion and the organizational pattern or patterns you decided to use.

CASE 7: Organizing a Document for Clarity—and Diplomacy

As part of your participation in a teaching-quality initiative for your school's Department of Civil Engineering, you have been assigned to write a brief report that summarizes student evaluations of the department's introductory course. When your supervisor expresses concerns about the report outline you sent her for review, you decide to revisit the organizational patterns covered in this chapter to see how they can help you develop a more effective structure for the report. If your instructor has assigned it, go to Achieve to read your supervisor's email and start revising the outline.

Part 3

Developing and Testing the Verbal and Visual Information

8

Communicating Persuasively

TECHNICAL COMMUNICATION, like any other kind of communication, calls for making persuasive claims and supporting them effectively. It is a mistake to think that technical communication is only about facts. Certainly, facts are important. But communication is about determining which facts are appropriate, describing the context that helps people understand what those facts mean, and presenting a well-reasoned argument about those facts. Your job as a communicator is to convince a reader of a viewpoint—about what factors caused a situation, for example, or what a company ought to do to solve a problem. If you are lucky, you will be reinforcing a viewpoint the reader already holds. Sometimes, however, you will want to change the reader's mind. Regardless, you are presenting an *argument*: an arrangement of facts and judgments about some aspect of the world.

This chapter explains how to craft a persuasive argument, avoid logical fallacies, present yourself effectively, and use graphics in your arguments.

Considering the Context of Your Argument

An argument can be as short as a sentence or as long as a multivolume report. It can take many forms, including oral communication. And it can discuss almost any kind of issue. Here are some examples:

- *From a description of a construction site:*

    Features A, B, and C characterize the site.

- *From a study of why a competitor is outselling your company:*

    Company X's dominance can be attributed to four major factors: A, B, C, and D.

- *From a feasibility study considering four courses of action:*

    Alternative A is better than alternatives B, C, and D.

- *From a set of instructions for performing a task:*

    The safest way to perform the task is to complete task A, then task B, and so on.

Before you can develop an effective argument, you must understand your audience's broader goals and your own constraints.

UNDERSTANDING YOUR AUDIENCE'S BROADER GOALS

When you analyze your audience, consider the values that motivate them. Most people are concerned about their own welfare and interests within the company, but they also want their company and their colleagues to prosper. If your document is intended for the public, as opposed to the employees in an organization, consider your audience's personal goals—their desire for health and well-being, for example, or their need to feel safe. Your argument is most likely to be effective if it responds to four goals that most people share: security, recognition, growth, and connectedness.

Security People resist controversial actions that might hurt their own interests. Those who might lose their jobs will likely oppose an argument that their division be eliminated, even if there are many valid reasons to support the argument. Another aspect of security is workload; most people resist an argument that calls for them to work more. People also want security outside the workplace—for instance, in their health care, finances, and personal safety. If you are drafting a press release about the addition of bicycle lanes to a town's already-congested streets, you need to assure residents that the town's civil engineers took the proper steps to ensure that the bike lanes were designed safely.

Recognition People like to be praised for their hard work and their successes. Where appropriate, be generous in your praise. Similarly, people hate being humiliated. Therefore, allow people to save face. Avoid criticizing their actions or positions and speculating about their motivations. Instead, present your argument as a response to the company's or other stakeholders' present and future needs. Look ahead, not back, and be diplomatic. A persuasive advertisement for a hospital's weight-loss support group will not criticize potential members for their lack of exercise or poor diet; rather, it will recognize that they have already been working hard to maintain their health.

One type of workplace document that is used to recognize professional success is a newsletter. A newsletter, a short newspaper published by an organization, can help the organization foster a sense of community within its membership, both internal and external, including customers, employees, investors, and the general public. Newsletters often include descriptions of new activities undertaken by the organization; major investments by the organization in new equipment or facilities; announcements of upcoming events and summaries of previous events, such as presentations, performances, or lectures given by organization members; notices of jobs available in the organization; profiles of new members, officers, or administrators; and important changes in relevant laws or regulations. Figure 8.1 shows an excerpt from a U.S. Department of Labor newsletter.

Growth People want to develop and grow. They want to learn new skills and assume new duties. People also want to work for an organization that is developing and growing. Your argument will be more persuasive if you can show how the recommended action will help an organization improve the quality of its products or services, branch out into new areas, or serve new customers and stakeholders. A brochure advertising a CPR certification course might emphasize the sense of empowerment that comes with the ability to assist co-workers in danger.

Connectedness People like to be part of communities, whether at work or at home. In the workplace, connectedness can take many forms, from working with others on project teams to participating in company sports leagues to helping improve the community. Organizations that encourage

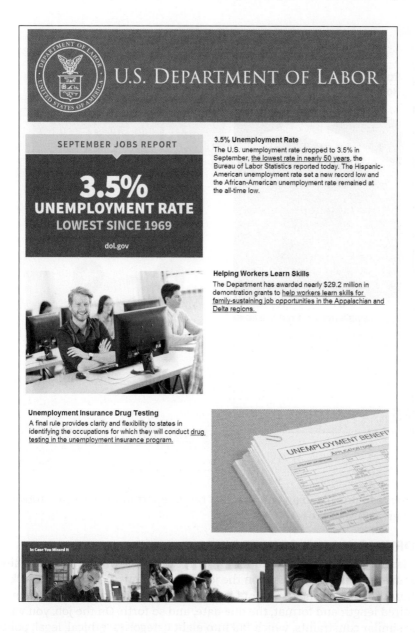

FIGURE 8.1
Recognizing Accomplishments in a Newsletter
Newsletter articles that report on the activities and accomplishments of the organization not only help keep employees informed but also improve employee morale by making them feel that they are making a difference and that their efforts are appreciated.
U.S. Department of Labor.

employees to connect with their peers through social media such as wikis, blogs, and discussion forums help satisfy this human need for community. A new trend in the working world is to encourage employees to spend weeks or even months of company time working on community educational or environmental projects. These projects not only improve the organization's image but also help employees feel connected to the community.

Figure 8.2 shows an example of a program that takes advantage of people's need for connectedness. BOS:311 is a Boston-based initiative that enables city

FIGURE 8.2 Promoting Connectedness

Citizens use a free app on their mobile devices to photograph and report problems. In the first two years after the City of Boston started BOS:311 (then called Citizens Connect), satisfaction with city services rose 22 percent. City of Boston.

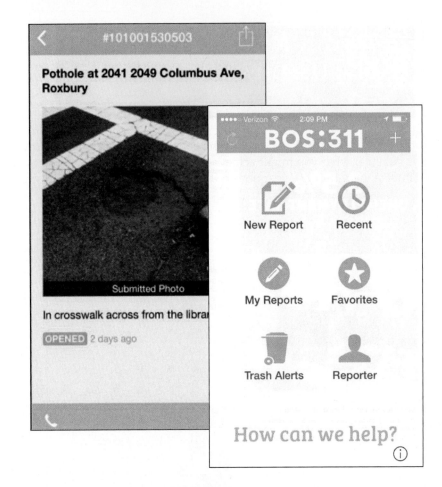

residents to download an app that lets them report infrastructure problems, such as graffiti or broken street lights.

WORKING WITHIN CONSTRAINTS

In planning a persuasive document, you need to work within the constraints that shape your environment on the job. As a student, you routinely work within constraints: the amount of information you can gather for a paper, the required length and format, the due date, and so forth. On the job, you will face similar constraints, which fall into eight categories: ethical, legal, political, informational, personnel, financial, time, and format.

For more about ethical and legal constraints, see Ch. 2.

Ethical Constraints   Your greatest responsibility is to your own sense of what constitutes ethical behavior. Being asked to lie or mislead challenges your ethical standards directly, but in most cases you have options. Some organizations and professional communities have a published code of conduct. In addition, many large companies have ombudspersons: ethics officers who use mediation to help employees resolve ethical conflicts.

Legal Constraints You must abide by all applicable laws on labor practices, environmental issues, fair trade, consumer rights, and so forth. If you think you have been asked to do something that might be illegal, meet with your organization's legal counsel and, if necessary, with attorneys outside the organization.

Political Constraints Don't spend all your energy and credibility on a losing cause. If you know that your proposal would help the company but that management disagrees with you or that the company can't afford to approve it, either consider what you might achieve through some other means or scale back the idea. Two big exceptions to this rule are matters of ethics and matters of safety. As discussed in Chapter 2, ethical and legal constraints might mean compromise is unacceptable.

Informational Constraints The most common informational constraint is the inability to get the information you need. You might want your organization to buy a piece of equipment, for example, but be unable to find unbiased evidence that would convince a skeptical reader.

What do you do? You tell the truth. Explain the situation, weighing the available evidence and carefully noting what is missing. If you unintentionally suggest that your evidence is better than it really is, you will lose your most important credential: your credibility.

Personnel Constraints The personnel constraint you are most likely to face is a lack of access to as many collaborators as you need. In such cases, present a persuasive proposal to hire the personnel you need. However, don't be surprised if you have to make do with fewer people than you want.

For more about collaboration, see Ch. 4.

Financial Constraints Financial constraints are related to personnel constraints: if you had unlimited funds, you could hire all the personnel you needed. But financial constraints can also affect other kinds of resources: you might not be able to print as many copies of a document as you want, or you might need to settle for black and white instead of full color.

Time Constraints Start by determining the document's deadline. (Sometimes a document will have several intermediate deadlines.) Then create a schedule. Keep in mind that tasks almost always take longer than estimated. And when you collaborate, the number of potential problems increases, because when one person is delayed, others may lack the necessary information to proceed, leading to a work slowdown.

For more about scheduling, see "Devising a Schedule and a Budget," Ch. 3, p. 47.

Format Constraints Format constraints are limitations on the size, shape, or style of a document. For example, your reader might want all tables and figures presented at the end of the report. If you are writing to someone in your own organization, follow the format constraints described in the company style guide, if there is one, or check similar documents to see what other writers have done. Also ask more experienced co-workers for their advice. If you are writing to someone in another organization, learn what you can about that organization's preferences.

Crafting a Persuasive Argument

Persuasion is important, whether you wish to affect a reader's attitude or merely present information clearly. To make a persuasive case, you must identify the elements of your argument, consider opposing viewpoints, use the right kinds of evidence, understand the use of visuals as persuasive elements, appeal to emotions responsibly, decide where to state your claim, and understand the role of culture in persuasion.

IDENTIFYING THE ELEMENTS OF YOUR ARGUMENT

A persuasive argument has three main elements:

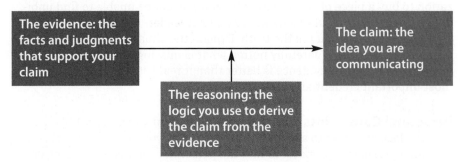

The evidence: the facts and judgments that support your claim

The reasoning: the logic you use to derive the claim from the evidence

The claim: the idea you are communicating

The *claim* is the conclusion you want your readers to accept. For example, your claim might be that your company should institute flextime, a scheduling approach that gives employees some flexibility in when they begin and end their workdays. You want your readers to agree with this idea and to take the next steps toward instituting flextime.

The *evidence* is the information you want your readers to consider. For the argument about flextime, the evidence might include the following:

- The turnover rate of our employees with young children is 50 percent higher than that of our employees without young children. The turnover rate for female employees with young children is double that of all employees without young children.

- At exit interviews, 40 percent of our employees with young children stated that they quit so that they could be home for their school-age children.

- Replacing a staff-level employee costs us about one-half the employee's annual salary; replacing a professional-level employee costs a whole year's salary.

- Other companies have found that flextime significantly decreases turnover among employees with young children.

- Other companies have found that flextime has additional benefits and introduces no significant problems.

The *reasoning* is the logic you use to connect the evidence to your claim. In the discussion of flextime, the reasoning involves three links:

- At other companies, flextime appears to have reduced the turnover problem among employees with young children.

- Our company is similar to these other companies.

- Flextime is therefore likely to prove helpful at our company.

CONSIDERING OPPOSING VIEWPOINTS

When you present an argument, you need to address opposing points of view. If you don't, your opponents will conclude that your proposal is flawed because it doesn't address problems that they think are important. In meeting a skeptical or hostile reader's possible objections to your case, you can use one of three tactics, depending on the situation:

- **The opposing argument is based on illogical reasoning or on inaccurate or incomplete facts.** You can counter the argument that flextime increases utility bills by citing unbiased research studies showing that it does not.

- **The opposing argument is valid but is less powerful than your own.** If you can show that the opposing argument makes sense but is outweighed by your own argument, you will appear to be a fair-minded person who understands that reality is complicated. You can counter the argument that flextime reduces carpooling opportunities by showing that only 3 percent of your employees currently use carpooling and that three-quarters of these employees favor flextime anyway because of its other advantages.

- **The two arguments can be reconciled.** If an opposing argument is not invalid or clearly inferior to your own, you can offer to study the situation thoroughly to find a solution that incorporates the best from each argument. For example, if flextime might cause serious problems for your company's many carpoolers, you could propose a trial period during which you would study several ways to help employees find other carpooling opportunities. If the company cannot solve the problem or if most of the employees prefer the old system, you would switch back to it. This proposal can remove much of the threat posed by your ideas.

When you address an opposing argument, be gracious and understated. Focus on the argument, not on the people who oppose you. If you embarrass or humiliate them, you undermine your own credibility and motivate your opponents to continue opposing you.

There is no one best place in your document to address opposing arguments. In general, however, if you know that important readers hold opposing views, address those views relatively early. Your goal is to show *all* your readers that you are a fair-minded person who has thought carefully about the subject and that your argument is stronger than the opposing arguments.

For advice on evaluating information from the internet, see the Guidelines box "Evaluating Print and Online Sources," Ch. 6, p. 134.

USING THE RIGHT KINDS OF EVIDENCE

People most often react favorably to the following kinds of evidence: numerical data, examples, expert testimony, and visual evidence.

- **Numerical data.** Numerical data—statistics—are generally more persuasive than commonsense arguments.

  > Statistics drawn from the personnel literature (McClellan, 2013) show that, among Fortune 500 companies, flextime decreases turnover by 25 to 35 percent among employees with young children.

  Notice that the writer states that the study covered many companies, not just one or a handful. If the sample size were small, the claim would be much less persuasive. (The discussion of logical fallacies later in this chapter explains such *hasty generalizations*.)

- **Examples.** An example makes an abstract point more concrete and therefore more vivid and memorable.

  > Mary Saunders tried for weeks to arrange for child care for her two preschoolers that would enable her to start work at 7 A.M., as required at her workplace. The best she could manage was having her children stay with a nonlicensed provider. When conditions at that provider led both of her children to develop behavioral problems, Mary decided that she could no longer continue working.

  Examples are often used along with numerical data. The example above gives the problem a human dimension, but the argument also requires numerical data to show that the problem is part of a pattern, not an isolated event.

- **Expert testimony.** A message from an expert is more persuasive than the same message from someone without credentials. A well-researched article on flextime written by a respected business scholar in a reputable business journal is likely to be persuasive. When you make arguments, you will often cite expert testimony from published sources or interviews you have conducted.

  Related to expert testimony are testimonials by peers and members of the general public. Although individually testimonials aren't as strong as expert testimony, a series of strong testimonials from reliable sources can make a convincing case about a product, service, or policy. Figure 8.3, from the website of Skillcrush, shows an effective use of testimonials.

- **Visual evidence.** Images and graphics can help you convey technical information to support your points. Photographs, for example, are often used to document an event. The photographs in Figure 8.4 show the urban growth in Las Vegas, Nevada, over a period of 46 years. Other types of visuals, such as maps and charts, can demonstrate data or ideas graphically, making information easier to understand. For more on the use of graphics, see Chapter 12.

  Figure 8.5, excerpts from a white paper published by McAfee, the computer-security company, shows a portion of an argument that combines several of these types of evidence. A white paper is an argument, typically 10–20 pages

If you work for Skillcrush, which describes itself as "an interactive online learning community for creatives, thinkers, and makers," and wish to make the point that your service is valuable, you explain why. But your argument is more persuasive if you can also show that others think so, too. These three testimonials are enhanced by the use of the companies' logos.

PEOPLE ARE TALKING

What They Say About Skillcrush:

"The beauty of Skillcrush is how it turns a world that outsiders view as either walled off or indecipherable, into simple, relatable language."

FAST COMPANY

"Using Skillcrush is like learning from your friendly, accessible best girl friend (not that it matters — about 25% of Skillcrush users are men)."

Mashable

"Skillcrush is teaching the next generation of programmers and entrepreneurs. [They're] re-shaping the whole discussion about how you learn to code and what you do with it. That's a big deal."

BUSINESS INSIDER

FIGURE 8.3 **Using Testimonials To Make a Persuasive Argument**

Images of the same scene at different times can provide technical information about changes in a physical environment. On the left is a photo of Las Vegas, Nevada in 1972; on the right is the same scene in 2018.

FIGURE 8.4 **A Photograph Used To Provide Technical Information**
NASA.

long, that a company's product or service will solve a technological or business challenge in an industry. The readers of white papers are technical experts who implement technology and managers who make purchasing decisions.

USING VISUALS AS PERSUASIVE ELEMENTS

When used responsibly, visuals that provide nontechnical information can lend powerful support to your argument. The alarming image in Figure 8.6 of tap water catching on fire was used by Greenpeace to illustrate the potential

This white paper was written by Dmitri Alperovitch, McAfee's vice president for threat research. A highly regarded security expert, Alperovitch has won numerous awards, including selection in 2013 as one of *MIT Technology Review's* Top 35 Innovators Under 35. This first paragraph, with its use of "I" and the references to projects with which Alperovitch is associated, presents him as an expert. The logic is that if he thinks these security threats are credible, you should, too.

Paragraph 2 presents a series of **examples** of what the writer calls an "unprecedented transfer of wealth."

The writer presents additional **examples** of the nature and scope of the attacks. In the rest of the 14-page white paper, he presents **statistics** and **examples** describing the 71 attacks that he is calling Operation Shady RAT. The evidence adds up to a compelling argument that the threat is real and serious, and McAfee is the organization you should trust to help you protect yourself from it.

Having investigated intrusions such as Operation Aurora and NightDragon (the systemic long-term compromise of Western oil and gas industry), as well as numerous others that have not been disclosed publicly, I am convinced that every company in every conceivable industry with significant size and valuable intellectual property and trade secrets has been compromised (or will be shortly), with the great majority of the victims rarely discovering the intrusion or its impact. In fact, I divide the entire set of Fortune Global 2,000 firms into two categories: those that *know they've been compromised* and those that *don't yet know.*

…

What we have witnessed over the past five to six years has been nothing short of a historically unprecedented transfer of wealth — closely guarded national secrets (including those from classified government networks), source code, bug databases, email archives, negotiation plans and exploration details for new oil and gas field auctions, document stores, legal contracts, supervisory control and data acquisition (SCADA) configurations, design schematics, and much more has "fallen off the truck" of numerous, mostly Western companies and disappeared in the ever-growing electronic archives of dogged adversaries.

What is happening to all this data — by now reaching petabytes as a whole — is still largely an open question. . . . Yet, the public (and often the industry) understanding of this significant national security threat is largely minimal due to the very limited number of voluntary disclosures by victims of intrusion activity compared to the actual number of compromises that take place. With the goal of raising the level of public awareness today, we are publishing the most comprehensive analysis ever revealed of victim profiles from a five-year targeted operation by one specific actor — "Operation Shady RAT," as I have named it at McAfee (RAT is a common acronym in the industry that stands for remote access tool).

…

McAfee has gained access to one specific command and control (C&C) server used by the intruders. We have collected logs that reveal the full extent of the victim population since mid-2006 when the log collection began. Note that the actual intrusion activity may have begun well before that time, but that is the earliest evidence we have for the start of the compromises. The compromises themselves were standard procedure for these types of targeted intrusions: a spear-phishing email containing an exploit is sent to an individual with the right level of access at the company, and the exploit, when opened, on an unpatched system will trigger a download of the implant malware. That

FIGURE 8.5 **Using Different Types of Evidence in an Argument** *(continued)*

FIGURE 8.5 Using Different Types of Evidence in an Argument (*continued*)
McAfee, Inc.

malware will execute and initiate a backdoor communication channel to the C&C Web server and interpret the instructions encoded in the hidden comments embedded in the Web page code. This will be quickly followed by live intruders jumping on to the Infected machine and proceeding to quickly escalate privileges and move laterally within the organization to establish new persistent footholds via additional compromised machines running implant malware, as well as targeting for quick exfiltration the key data they came for.

After painstaking analysis of the logs, even we were surprised by the enormous diversity of the victim organizations and were taken aback by the audacity of the perpetrators. Although we will refrain from explicitly identifying most of the victims, describing only their general industry, we feel that naming names is warranted in certain cases, not with the goal of attracting attention to a specific victim organization, but to reinforce the fact that virtually everyone is falling prey to these intrusions, regardless of whether they are the United Nations, a multinational Fortune 100 company, a small, non-profit think tank, a national Olympic team, or even an unfortunate computer security firm.

dangers of hydraulic fracturing ("fracking"). The poster in Figure 8.7 combines verbal and visual techniques to convince readers to take precautions to avoid contracting a dangerous virus.

ETHICS NOTE

USING DIGITAL ENHANCEMENT TOOLS RESPONSIBLY

Many tools are available to enhance and otherwise alter digital images, but manipulating photographs or videos in order to strengthen an argument is most likely unethical and possibly illegal. Photo editing, according to the Code of Ethics of the National Press Photographers Association (2016), "should maintain the integrity of the photographic images' content and context. Do not manipulate images or add or alter sound in any way that can mislead viewers or misrepresent subjects."

APPEALING TO EMOTIONS RESPONSIBLY

Writers sometimes appeal to the emotions of their readers. Writers usually combine emotional appeals with appeals to reason. For example, an argument that we ought to increase foreign aid to drought-stricken African countries might describe (and present images of) the human plight of the victims but also include reason-based sections about the extent of the problem, the causes, the possible solutions, and the pragmatic reasons we might want to increase foreign aid.

When you use emotional appeals, do not overstate or overdramatize them, or you will risk alienating readers. Try to think of additional kinds of evidence to present that will also help support your claim. Figure 8.8 (on p. 189) shows a brief argument that relies on an emotional appeal.

FIGURE 8.6 A Persuasive Photograph

A Pennsylvania woman who lives near a fracking site demonstrates that flammable methane gas has contaminated her home's water supply. The photograph of water catching on fire is much more striking than a text description would be.
© Les Stone/Greenpeace.

FIGURE 8.7 **Verbal and Visual Techniques in Persuasion**

Information from U.S. Department of Health and Human Services, Centers for Disease Control and Prevention, 2016: www.cdc.gov/zika/pdfs/fs-outdoors.pdf.

DECIDING WHERE TO PRESENT THE CLAIM

In most cases, the best place to state your claim is at the start of the argument. Then provide the evidence and, if appropriate, the reasoning. Sometimes, however, it is more effective to place the claim *after* the evidence and the reasoning. This indirect structure works best if a large number of readers oppose your claim. If you present your claim right away, these readers might become alienated and stop paying attention. You want a chance to present your evidence and your reasoning without causing this kind of undesirable reaction.

This excerpt from the Army recruitment site, GoArmy.com, describes the Drill Sergeant School.

DRILL SERGEANT SCHOOL

To Become A Drill Sergeant, You Always Have To Be "Squared Away"

A spot in Drill Sergeant School. It's one of the highest honors the U.S. Army can bestow a Non-Commissioned Officer (NCO). Only the most qualified NCOs are chosen to attend Drill Sergeant School, where they are trained to fulfill a role of utmost importance — the role of a Drill Sergeant. After all, Drill Sergeants teach new recruits every aspect of Basic Combat Training — which means they have the great responsibility of shaping recruits into the best Soldiers in the world.

NCOs who attend Drill Sergeant School are called Drill Sergeant Candidates. Their training is strenuous. The School's curriculum mimics Basic Combat Training, week for week, because Candidates must be experts in all facets of BCT to begin training recruits. They receive top-notch training from their Drill Sergeant Instructors because they'll soon be expected to deliver great training.

The "Ultimate Job" For A Sergeant

For many Candidates, becoming a Drill Sergeant is a "military dream." It means they have proven themselves again and again — so much so that they're entrusted with training new recruits. They know that when they receive their Drill Sergeant hat, they'll have the ultimate job — being a role model — and they take it very seriously.

More Than Just A Unique Hat

Earning the Drill Sergeant's hat is not easy. When NCOs are tapped to attend Drill Sergeant School, they know they'll have to be able to teach new recruits the proper way to do absolutely everything in the Army — from making a bed, to wearing a uniform, to firing a rifle. They will have to become the best, because U.S. Army recruits deserve to learn from the best. In the end, Drill Sergeants are instantly recognizable. Not only because of their unique hat, but also because of the way they speak with authority and carry themselves with utmost pride.

The photo and the text present a reasonable mix of information and emotion. The site provides facts about how drill sergeants are chosen and trained and the responsibilities they carry. The lives of drill sergeants are not always heroic and romantic; they have to teach recruits how to make their beds, for instance. But the discussion is clearly meant to appeal to the emotions of people who are considering joining the Army with the goal of becoming drill sergeants. The passage repeatedly refers to drill sergeants as being "the best." Only a select few NCOs can become drill sergeants. They become role models, carrying themselves with pride.

Everyone likes to think of himself or herself as a special person doing an important job. As long as the facts that accompany an emotional appeal are accurate and presented honestly, an emotional appeal is responsible.

FIGURE 8.8 **An Argument Based on an Emotional Appeal**
Goarmy.com.

DOCUMENT ANALYSIS ACTIVITY

Analyzing Evidence in an Argument

In this excerpt from an article on the job service Monster .com, the writer presents an argument about hiring a social-media officer. The questions below ask you to consider the nature of the evidence this writer presents.

1. In the first two paragraphs, the writer tells a story. Which kind of evidence is this, and how effective is it?

2. In paragraph 3, we learn the occupation of the person on that unpleasant flight. How does this new information add to the effectiveness of the argument?

3. Does paragraph 4 present any evidence? If not, what function does it serve?

Social Media Strategy: Is It Time to Hire a Social Media Officer?

① When Ted Rubin (@tedrubin) touched down in Asheville, NC after a particularly unpleasant flight with a carrier he rarely uses, he immediately posted an update to his 54,000 Twitter followers. "Just landed … boy do I miss @JetBlue."

A few minutes later, a representative from Jet Blue responded to say thanks. While Rubin tagged the other airline in his original tweet, he never heard back from them. "Guess who I'll be flying next?" he laughs.

② Rubin, who serves as Chief Social Marketing Officer for the shopping Web site Collective Bias, says this type of personal engagement isn't a novelty anymore — customers have come to expect it. "Social media is way deeper than most companies understand," he says. "It's time to recognize that social isn't just campaign-based, it's an integrated part of your ongoing business strategy."

③ Let's face it — your social media strategy is about more than monitoring social media — it touches customer service, vendor relations, social media recruiting and more. Thus many organizations are bringing in new staff to handle their social media strategy.

Monster Worldwide.

UNDERSTANDING THE ROLE OF CULTURE IN PERSUASION

If you are making a persuasive argument to readers from another culture, keep in mind that cultures differ significantly not only in matters such as business customs but also in their most fundamental values. These differences can affect persuasive writing. Culture determines both what makes an argument persuasive and how arguments are structured:

For more about writing for people from other cultures, see "Considering Cultural Variables as You Write," Ch. 5, p. 105.

- **What makes an argument persuasive.** Statistics and experimental data are fundamental kinds of evidence in the West, but testimony from respected authority figures can be much more persuasive in the East.

- **How to structure an argument.** In a Western culture, the claim is usually presented up front. In an Eastern culture, it is likely to be delayed or to remain unstated but implied.

    When you write for an audience from another culture, use two techniques:

- Study that culture, and adjust the content, structure, and style of your arguments to fit it.

- Include in your budget the cost of having important documents reviewed and edited by a person from the target culture. Few people are experts on cultures other than their own.

Avoiding Logical Fallacies

A logical fallacy—that is, a mistake in reasoning—can undercut the persuasiveness of your writing. An example is "Antidepressants are a scam; I know that because Tom Cruise says so, and he's a world-famous actor." Although Tom Cruise is a world-famous actor, it does not follow that what he thinks about antidepressants is true. Table 8.1 explains some of the most common logical fallacies.

TABLE 8.1   Common Logical Fallacies

FALLACY	EXPLANATION	EXAMPLE AND COMMENT
Ad hominem argument; also called *argument against the speaker*	An argument against the writer, not against the writer's argument	"Of course Matthew wants us to buy more computers—he's a computer geek." The fact that Matthew is a "computer geek" doesn't necessarily mean that his argument for buying more computers is unwise.
Argument from ignorance	An argument that a claim is true because it has never been proven false, or false because it has never been proven true	"Nobody has ever proven that life exists on other planets. Therefore, extraterrestrial life is a myth." The fact that a concept has not yet been proven does not necessarily mean that it is false. Perhaps the measurement techniques are insufficiently precise or not yet available.

(continued)

TABLE 8.1	Common Logical Fallacies *(continued)*	
FALLACY	**EXPLANATION**	**EXAMPLE AND COMMENT**
Appeal to pity	An argument based on emotion, not reason	"We shouldn't sell the Ridgeway division. It's been part of the company for over 40 years."
		The fact that the division has long been a part of the company is not in itself a good reason to retain it.
Argument from authority	An argument that a claim is valid because the person making the claim is an authority	"According to world-renowned physicist Dr. Chiara Michaels, artificial intelligence will be the end of the human race."
		Even if Dr. Michaels is a recognized authority in this field, the claim that artificial intelligence will be the end of the human race is not valid unless you present a valid argument to support it.
Circular argument	An argument that restates its main point without presenting any evidence to support it	"Facebook's stock price keeps falling because the company's value is still going down."
		Because a company's stock price is a measure of the company's value, the argument simply says that Facebook's stock price keeps falling because its stock price keeps falling. Using the word *because* doesn't necessarily mean that the writer has presented a reason. The writer needs to explain *why* the stock price keeps going down.
Either–or argument	An argument that poses only two alternatives when in fact there might be more	"Either we start selling our products online or we're going to be out of business within a year."
		This statement does not explain why these are the only two alternatives. The company might improve its sales by taking measures other than selling online.
Ad populum argument; also called *bandwagon argument*	An argument that a claim is valid because many people think it is or act as if it is	"Our four major competitors have started selling online so we should, too."
		The fact that our competitors are selling online is not in itself an argument that we should sell online, too.
Hasty generalization; sometimes called *inadequate sampling*	An argument that draws conclusions based on an insufficient number of cases	"The new Tata is an unreliable car. Two of my friends own Tatas, and both have had reliability problems."
		To reach any valid conclusions, you would have to study a much larger sample and compare your findings with those for other cars in the Tata's class.
Post hoc reasoning (the complete phrase is *post hoc, ergo propter hoc*)	An argument that claims that because A precedes B, A caused B	"There must be something wrong with the new circuit breaker in the office. Ever since we had it installed, the air conditioners haven't worked right."
		Maybe the air conditioners are malfunctioning because of the circuit breaker, but the malfunction might have other causes.
Oversimplifying	An argument that omits important information in establishing a causal link	"The way to solve the balance-of-trade problem is to improve the quality of the products we produce."
		Although improving quality is important, international trade balances are determined by many factors, including tariffs and currency rates, and therefore cannot be explained by simple cause-and-effect reasoning.

Presenting Yourself Effectively

No matter how strong your arguments, your audience won't read them—or won't read them sympathetically—unless they see you as a professional.

◢| GUIDELINES Creating a Professional Persona

Your *persona* is how you appear to your readers. Demonstrating the following characteristics will help you establish an attractive professional persona.

▶ **Cooperativeness.** Make clear that your goal is to solve a problem, not to advance your own interests.

▶ **Moderation.** Be moderate in your judgments. The problem you are describing will not likely spell doom for your organization, and the solution you propose will not solve all the company's problems.

▶ **Fair-mindedness.** Acknowledge the strengths of opposing points of view, even as you offer counterarguments.

▶ **Modesty.** If you fail to acknowledge that you don't know everything, someone else will be sure to volunteer that insight.

The following paragraph shows how a writer can demonstrate the qualities of cooperativeness, moderation, fair-mindedness, and modesty:

> This plan is certainly not perfect. For one thing, it calls for a greater up-front investment than we had anticipated. And the return on investment through the first three quarters is likely to fall short of our initial goals. However, I think this plan is the best of the three alternatives for the following reasons. . . . Therefore, I recommend that we begin planning immediately to implement the plan. I am confident that this plan will enable us to enter the 3-D market successfully, building on our fine reputation for high-quality advanced electronics.

In the first three sentences, the writer acknowledges the problems with his recommendation.

The use of "I think" adds an attractive modesty; the recommendation might be unwise.

The recommendation itself is moderate; the writer does not claim that the plan will save the world.

In the last two sentences, the writer shows a spirit of cooperativeness by focusing on the company's goals.

Figure 8.9 presents two professional-sounding paragraphs from a student's job-application letter.

> At Western State University, I have earned 87 credits toward a degree in Technical Communication. I have been a full-time student (no fewer than 12 credit hours per semester) while working full-time for the Northwest Watershed Research Center. The four upper-division courses I am taking this semester, including Advanced Technical Communication and Technical Editing, are required for the BA in Technical Communication.
>
> In addition to my formal education, I have completed 34 training courses on the job. These courses have included diverse topics such as financial management, the Fair Labor Standards Act, the Americans with Disabilities Act, career-development opportunities in public affairs, and software applications such as MS Office, Quark XPress, and RoboHelp.

A student writer uses specific examples to persuade a prospective employer.

Without making her claim explicit, the writer presents evidence that she is hardworking and lets the prospective employer draw his or her own conclusions.

In listing some of the training courses she has taken, the writer supports an earlier claim that her broad background might be of use to her next employer.

FIGURE 8.9   **Persuading a Prospective Employer**

ETHICS NOTE

SEEMING HONEST VERSUS *BEING* HONEST IN PERSUASIVE WRITING

The young actor asks the old actor, "What's the key to great acting?" The old actor replies, "Sincerity. Once you learn how to fake sincerity. . . ." Any discussion of image and persuasion has to address the question at the heart of this old joke. Does a writer have to be honest to appear honest?

There are tricks for appearing honest, and they can work for a while. But the easiest way to appear honest is to *be* honest. As suggested in Chapter 2, you need to tell the truth and not mislead your readers. As suggested in Chapter 4, you also need to be cooperative, diplomatic, and constructive. And as suggested in this chapter, you need to remember people's broader goals: to protect their own security, to achieve recognition, to learn and grow in their professional and personal lives, and to connect with others.

WRITER'S CHECKLIST

In analyzing your audience, did you consider their broader goals of

☐ maintaining security? *(p. 178)*

☐ achieving recognition? *(p. 178)*

☐ growing professionally and personally? *(p. 178)*

☐ staying connected? *(p. 178)*

In planning, did you consider the following constraints:

☐ ethical? *(p. 180)*

☐ legal? *(p. 181)*

☐ political? *(p. 181)*

☐ informational? *(p. 181)*

☐ personnel? *(p. 181)*

☐ financial? *(p. 181)*

☐ time? *(p. 181)*

☐ format? *(p. 181)*

In crafting a persuasive argument, did you

☐ use the three-part structure of claim, evidence, and reasoning? *(p. 182)*

☐ consider opposing viewpoints? *(p. 183)*

☐ choose appropriate kinds of evidence? *(p. 184)*

☐ consider using graphics as persuasive elements? *(p. 186)*

☐ appeal to emotions responsibly? *(p. 187)*

☐ carefully consider where to present the claim? *(p. 188)*

☐ consider the role of your readers' culture? *(p. 191)*

In writing the argument, did you avoid the following logical fallacies:

☐ ad hominem argument? *(p. 191)*

☐ argument from ignorance? *(p. 191)*

☐ appeal to pity? *(p. 192)*

☐ argument from authority? *(p. 192)*

☐ circular argument? *(p. 192)*

☐ either–or argument? *(p. 192)*

☐ ad populum argument? *(p. 192)*

☐ hasty generalization? *(p. 192)*

☐ post hoc reasoning? *(p. 192)*

☐ oversimplifying? *(p. 192)*

In drafting your argument, did you create a persona that is

☐ cooperative? *(p. 193)*

☐ moderate? *(p. 193)*

☐ fair-minded? *(p. 193)*

☐ modest? *(p. 193)*

EXERCISES

1. Visit the website of a car manufacturer, such as Ford (ford.com) or Mercedes-Benz (mbusa.com). Identify the major techniques of persuasion used in the words and graphics on the site. For example, what claims are made? What types of evidence are used? Is the reasoning sound?

2. Victory Air has been criticized in the press because of its policy of charging an overweight passenger for a second seat if he or she cannot fit in a single coach seat without his or her body crossing the armrest boundary. In a public letter printed on its website, Victory used the following evidence as part of its defense of its policy:

   a. In 2003, a commuter plane crashed on takeoff from Charlotte, North Carolina, in part due to excess weight. We need to be able to require that a heavier passenger pay for and use two seats in order to keep the plane's total weight within acceptable limits for safe operation of the plane.

   b. Our policy is not an attempt to increase revenues: if there is an available empty seat, we do not charge the heavier passenger for a second seat.

   c. Every passenger pays more for a ticket because heavier passengers increase fuel consumption. It's only fair that heavier passengers pay extra for the increased fuel consumption.

   d. According to a study by the National Transportation Safety Board, an overweight passenger squeezed into a single coach seat might be a safety risk to another passenger or to himself or herself if the plane must be evacuated quickly.

   e. The average weight of a passenger climbed from 180 pounds in 1995 to 190 pounds in 2003. Estimates place the current average weight at almost 195 pounds.

   For each of these five items, write a brief paragraph in which you identify the nature of the evidence (if any) — numerical data, example, or expert testimony — and identify any logical fallacies. If you think the evidence is not as effective as it might be, what is the problem, and how would you make it more effective?

3. For each of the following claims, write one paragraph identifying the logical flaw:

   a. The election couldn't have been fair — I don't know anyone who voted for the winner.

   b. It would be wrong to prosecute Allied for age discrimination; Allied has always been a great corporate neighbor.

   c. The decrease in smoking can be attributed to increased restrictions on smoking in public.

   d. Bill Jensen's proposal to create an on-site day-care center is just the latest of his harebrained ideas.

   e. Since the introduction of cola drinks at the start of the twentieth century, cancer has become the second-greatest killer in the United States. Cola drinks should be outlawed.

   f. If mutual-fund guru Peter Lynch recommends this investment, I think we ought to buy it.

   g. We should not go into the flash-memory market; we have always been a leading manufacturer of DRAM.

   h. The other two hospitals in the city have implemented computerized patient record keeping; I think we need to do so, too.

   i. Our Model X500 didn't succeed because we failed to sell a sufficient number of units.

   j. No research has ever established that UFOs exist. They are fictions of our imaginations.

4. **TEAM EXERCISE** Pair with another student for this research project on multicultural communication styles. Follow these steps:

   a. Working by yourself, enter the name of a country and the word *business* in a search engine. For example, enter "Nicaragua business." Find the website of a business in that country, and then print out the About the Company page or some similar page, such as Mission or Projects. Or enter the name of a country and the word *government*, such as "Nicaragua government." Find a government agency in that country that has published a report available on the internet. Print several pages of the report.

b. On your copy of the pages you have printed, disguise the country of origin by blacking out the name of the company or government agency and any other information that would indicate the country of origin.

c. Exchange pages with your partner. Study your partner's pages. Do the pages show a different strategy of persuasion than you would expect from a U.S. writer? For instance, does the writer support his or her claims with the kinds of evidence you would expect to see in the United States? Is the information organized as you would expect? Does the writer create a persona that you would expect to see?

d. Meet with your partner and explain to him or her what you see in the pages that is similar to or different from what you would expect if the document came from the United States. Ask your partner whether he or she saw the same things. Present your findings in a memo to your instructor. For more about memos, see Ch. 14, p. 386.

CASE 8: Analyzing the Persuasiveness of a Poster

You work in the media department of the U.S. Nuclear Regulatory Commission (U.S. NRC), and your supervisor has asked you to put together a survey to determine what employees at nuclear facilities think about the NRC's poster on safety culture. Before you can draft a questionnaire, you must analyze the education and outreach pages on the NRC's website and then think about effective means of persuasion that might improve the poster. If your instructor has assigned it, go to Achieve to get started on your assignment.

9

Emphasizing Important Information

MOST OF US WOULD AGREE that there is too much information for us to learn—and not nearly enough time for us to learn it. That is why instant messages and tweets are so popular: we can read them quickly and then get on to the next thing.

But much of what needs to be communicated in the workplace cannot be reduced to 280 characters or an 8-second video. For instance, a plan to create a new interactive corporate website that will enable vendors and customers to do business with the company conveniently and securely will require many hallway conversations, emails, and meetings—and a number of lengthy documents.

When you write information longer than a few hundred words, you want to help your readers understand what you are writing about and what your main point is. You want to help them see how you have organized the information. You want to emphasize the most important information. Doing so helps them find that information, understand it, and remember it. Your audience will be able to read your document faster and understand it better. And they will be more likely to agree with your ideas and view your recommendations positively.

This chapter discusses a number of techniques to help you emphasize the most important information in your technical documents: writing clear and informative titles and headings, using lists, and structuring paragraphs effectively.

Writing Clear, Informative Titles

The title of a document is crucial because it is your first chance to define your subject and purpose for your readers, giving them their first clue to whether the document contains the information they need. The title is an implicit promise to readers: "This document is about Subject A, and it was written to achieve Purpose B." Everything that follows has to relate clearly to the subject and purpose defined in the title; if it doesn't, either the title is misleading or the document has failed to make good on the title's promise.

You might want to put off giving a final title to your document until you have completed the document, because you cannot be sure that the subject and purpose you established during the planning stages will not change. However, you should jot down a working title before you start drafting; you can revise it later. To give yourself a strong sense of direction, make sure the working title defines not only the subject of the document but also its purpose. The working title "Snowboarding Injuries" states the subject but not the purpose. "How To Prevent Snowboarding Injuries" is better because it helps keep you focused on your purpose.

An effective title is precise. For example, if you are writing a feasibility study on the subject of offering free cholesterol screening at your company, the title should contain the key terms *free cholesterol screening* and *feasibility*. The following title would be effective:

Offering Free Cholesterol Screening at Thrall Associates: A Feasibility Study

If your document is an internal report discussing company business, you might not need to identify the company. In that case, the following would be clear:

Offering Free Cholesterol Screening: A Feasibility Study

Or you could present the purpose before the subject:

A Feasibility Study of Offering Free Cholesterol Screening

Avoid substituting general terms, such as *health screening* for *cholesterol screening* or *study* for *feasibility study*; the more precise your terms, the more useful your readers will find the title. An added benefit of using precise terms is that your document can be more accurately and effectively indexed in databases and online libraries, increasing the chances that someone researching your subject will be able to find the document.

Before settling on a title, test its effectiveness by asking whether readers will be able to paraphrase it in a clear, meaningful sentence. For instance, "A Feasibility Study of Offering Free Cholesterol Screening to Employees of Thrall Associates" could be paraphrased as follows: "This document reports on a project to determine whether it is feasible to offer free cholesterol screening to employees of Thrall Associates."

But notice what happens when the title is incomplete: "Free Cholesterol Screening." With only those three words to go on, the reader has to guess about the document's purpose. The reader knows that the document has something to do with free cholesterol screening, but is the writer recommending that screening be implemented, modified, or discontinued? Or is the writer reporting on the success of an existing screening program?

Clear, comprehensive titles can be long. If you need eight or ten words to say what you want to say about your subject and purpose, use them.

Writing Clear, Informative Headings

Headings, which are lower-level titles for the sections and subsections in a document, do more than announce the subject that will be discussed in the document. Collectively, they create a *hierarchy of information*, dividing the document into major sections and subdividing those sections into subsections. In this way, coherent headings communicate the relative importance and generality of the information that follows, helping readers recognize major sections as *primary* (likely to contain more important or more general information) and subsections as *secondary* or *subordinate* (likely to contain less important or more specific information).

Clear, informative headings communicate this relationship not only through their content but also through their design. For this reason, make sure that the design of a primary heading (sometimes referred to as a *level 1 heading*, *1 heading*, or *A heading*) clearly distinguishes it from a subordinate heading (a *level 2 heading*, *2 heading*, or *B heading*), and that the design of that subordinate heading clearly distinguishes it from yet a lower level of subordinate heading (a *level 3 heading*, *3 heading*, or *C heading*).

The headings used in this book illustrate this principle, as does the example below. Notice that the example uses both typography and indentation to distinguish one heading from another and to communicate visually how information at one level logically relates to information at other levels.

Level 1 Heading

Level 2 Heading

Level 3 Heading

The best way to make sure you use typefaces and indentation consistently is to use the Styles function. As discussed in Chapter 3, a style is a set of formatting instructions that you can apply to all titles, headings, lists, or other design elements that you want to look alike. Because you create a style only once but then apply it to any number of headings or other design elements, you're far more likely to format these items consistently than if you were to format each one individually.

Styles also speed up the process of changing the appearance of titles, headings, and lists. As you revise, you might notice that two levels of headings are insufficiently distinct. You can easily use the Styles function to change the design of one of those headings so that it is distinct and therefore does a better job of helping readers follow the discussion and understand where they are in the document. In addition, you can create new styles to ensure consistency when, for instance, you further subdivide a subsection of a document or introduce bulleted lists into the discussion.

Because a heading is a type of title, much of the advice about titles in the previous section also applies to headings. For instance, a clear, informative heading is crucial because it announces the subject and purpose of the discussion that follows it, just as a title does for the whole document. Announcing the subject and purpose in a heading helps readers understand what they will be reading or, in some cases, helps them decide whether they need to read the section at all. For the writer, a heading eliminates the need for awkward transitional sentences such as "Let us now turn to the advantages of the mandatory enrollment process" or "The next step in replacing the saw blade is to remove the arbor nut from the drive shaft."

Effective headings help both reader and writer by forecasting not only the subject and purpose of the discussion that follows but also its scope and organization. When readers encounter the heading "Three Health Benefits of Yoga: Improved Muscle Tone, Enhanced Flexibility, Better Posture," they can reasonably assume that the discussion will consist of three parts (not two or four) and that it will begin with a discussion of muscle tone, followed by a discussion of flexibility, and then posture.

Because headings introduce text that discusses or otherwise elaborates on the subject defined by the heading, avoid back-to-back headings. In other words, avoid following one heading directly with another heading:

3. Approaches to Neighborhood Policing

3.1 Community Policing

According to the COPS Agency (a component of the U.S. Department of Justice), "Community policing focuses on crime and social disorder." . . .

What's wrong with back-to-back headings? First, they're illogical. If your document contains a level 1 heading, you have to say something at that level before jumping to the discussion at level 2. Second, back-to-back headings distract and confuse readers. The heading "3. Approaches to Neighborhood Policing" announces to readers that you have something to say about neighborhood policing—but you don't say anything. Instead, another, subordinate heading appears, announcing to readers that you now have something to say about community policing.

To avoid confusing and frustrating readers, separate the headings with text, as in this example:

3. Approaches to Neighborhood Policing

Over the past decade, researchers have concluded that community policing offers significant advantages over the traditional approach based on patrolling in police cars. However, the traditional approach has some distinct strengths. In the following discussion, we define each approach and then explain its advantages and disadvantages. Finally, we profile three departments that have successfully made the transition to community policing while preserving the major strengths of the traditional approach.

3.1 Community Policing

According to the COPS Agency (a component of the U.S. Department of Justice), "Community policing focuses on crime and social disorder." . . .

The text after the heading "3. Approaches to Neighborhood Policing" is called an *advance organizer*. It indicates the background, purpose, scope, and organization of the discussion that follows it. Advance organizers give readers an overview of the discussion's key points before they encounter the details in the discussion itself.

GUIDELINES Revising Headings

Follow these suggestions to make your headings more effective.

▶ **Avoid long noun strings.** The following example is ambiguous and hard to understand:

Proposed Production Enhancement Strategies Analysis Techniques

For more about noun strings, see "Avoid Long Noun Strings," Ch. 10, p. 239.

(continued)

Is the heading introducing a discussion of techniques for analyzing strategies that have been proposed? Or is it introducing a discussion that proposes using certain techniques to analyze strategies? Readers shouldn't have to ask such questions. Adding prepositions makes the heading clearer:

> Techniques for Analyzing the Proposed Strategies for Enhancing Production

This heading announces more clearly that the discussion describes techniques for analyzing strategies, that those strategies have been proposed, and that the strategies are aimed at enhancing production. It's a longer heading than the original, but that's okay. It's also much clearer.

▶ **Be informative.** In the preceding example, you could add information about how many techniques will be described:

> Three Techniques for Analyzing the Proposed Strategies for Enhancing Production

You can go one step further by indicating what you wish to say about the three techniques:

> Advantages and Disadvantages of the Three Techniques for Analyzing the Proposed Strategies for Enhancing Production

Again, don't worry if the heading seems long; clarity is more important than conciseness.

▶ **Use a grammatical form appropriate to your audience.** The question form works well for readers who are not knowledgeable about the subject and for nonnative speakers:

> What Are the Three Techniques for Analyzing the Proposed Strategies for Enhancing Production?

The "how-to" form is best for instructional material, such as manuals:

> How To Analyze the Proposed Strategies for Enhancing Production

The gerund form (*-ing*) works well for discussions and descriptions of processes:

> Analyzing the Proposed Strategies for Enhancing Production

▶ **Avoid back-to-back headings.** Use advance organizers to separate the headings.

For more about how to format headings, see "Titles and Headings," Ch. 11, p. 275.

Writing Clear, Informative Lists

Technical documents often contain lists. Lists are especially effective in conveying information that can be itemized (such as three physical conditions that frequently lead to patients' developing adult-onset diabetes). Lists also work well for presenting information that can be expressed in a sequence (such as the operation of a four-stroke gasoline engine: *intake, compression, ignition, exhaust*).

This section explains how to create effective paragraph lists and sentence lists.

WRITE EFFECTIVE PARAGRAPH LISTS

A paragraph list is a list in which the bulleted or numbered items are paragraphs, not merely phrases or sentences. Figure 9.1 shows the same information presented in traditional paragraphs and in a paragraph list.

For readers, the chief advantage of a paragraph list is that it makes the information easier to read and remember. Readers see the structure of the discussion—often in a single glance—before they read the details. Once they start reading the list, they can more easily follow the discussion because its design mirrors its logic. For example, a paragraph-list discussion of the four stages of mitosis (*prophase, metaphase, anaphase, telophase*) would arrange the stages in the order in which they occur and would use bullets or numbers to distinguish one stage from another. As a result, the paragraph-list format enables readers to navigate the discussion easily and confidently, if only because they can see where the discussion of prophase ends and the discussion of metaphase begins.

For you as a writer, turning paragraphs into lists has four advantages:

- **It forces you to look at the big picture.** While drafting a document, you can easily lose sight of the information outside the paragraph you are writing. Turning traditional paragraphs into paragraph lists expands your

TRADITIONAL PARAGRAPHS	PARAGRAPH LIST	
Although there are several theories of human conformity, Kelman's model (1935) is still popular. Kelman described three main types of conformity.	Although there are several theories of human conformity, Kelman's model (1935) is still popular. Kelman described three main types of conformity:	The author is presenting one model of categories of human conformity. Creating a paragraph list forces the writer to use key words that sharply focus each bulleted entry.
The first type of conformity is called compliance. A person who conforms out of compliance changes his or her behavior but not his or her attitudes, thoughts, and feelings. In effect, the person is simply copying someone else's behavior in order to satisfy some external norm.	• *Compliance.* A person who conforms out of compliance changes his or her behavior but not his or her attitudes, thoughts, and feelings. In effect, the person is simply copying someone else's behavior in order to satisfy some external norm.	Notice that the writer of the paragraph list uses italics to emphasize the key term at the start of each bullet item.
The second type of conformity is called identification. A person who conforms by identification wants to be like that other person, but he or she might not yet have succeeded in changing his or her attitudes, thoughts, and feelings.	• *Identification.* A person who conforms by identification wants to be like that other person, but he or she might not yet have succeeded in changing his or her attitudes, thoughts, and feelings.	Bullet items should be sequenced logically. Here, the sequence for the three types of conformity is from the type in which the person is least committed (compliance) to the type in which the person is most committed (internalization).
The third type of conformity is called internalization. A person who conforms by internalization has undergone a complete change in public behavior and private attitudes, thoughts, and feelings. A member of a cult has conformed by internalizing.	• *Internalization.* A person who conforms by internalization has undergone a complete change in public behavior and private attitudes, thoughts, and feelings. A member of a cult has conformed by internalizing.	By deleting the wordy topic sentences from the traditional paragraphs, the writer saves space. The list version of the passage is about the same length as the paragraph version, despite the indentations.

FIGURE 9.1 **Traditional Paragraphs and a Paragraph List**

perspective beyond a single paragraph, increasing your chances of noticing that an important item is missing or that an item is unclear. It also increases the chances that you'll think more deeply about how items and key ideas are related to one another.

- **It forces you to examine the sequence.** As you write paragraph lists, you get a chance to reconsider whether the sequence of the information is logical. Sometimes, the visual dimension that lists add to the text will reveal an illogical sequence you might have overlooked in traditional paragraphs.

- **It forces you to create a helpful lead-in.** Every list requires a *lead-in*, or introduction to the list; without one, readers are left to guess at how the list relates to the discussion and how the items in the list relate to each other. In the lead-in, you can add a number signal that further forecasts the content and organization of the material that follows:

Auto sales declined last year because of four major factors:

- **It forces you to tighten and clarify your prose.** When you make a list, you look for a word, phrase, or sentence that identifies each item. Your focus shifts from weaving sentences together in a paragraph to highlighting key ideas, giving you an opportunity to critically consider those key ideas and revise accordingly.

WRITE EFFECTIVE SENTENCE LISTS

A sentence list is a list in which the bulleted or numbered items are words, phrases, or single sentences. Figure 9.2 shows a traditional sentence and a list presenting the same information.

If you don't have enough space to list the items vertically or if you are not permitted to do so, number the items within the sentence:

We recommend that more work on heat-exchanger performance be done (1) with a larger variety of different fuels at the same temperature, (2) with similar fuels at different temperatures, and (3) with special fuels such as diesel fuel and shale-oil-derived fuels.

TRADITIONAL SENTENCE	SENTENCE LIST
We recommend that more work on heat-exchanger performance be done with a larger variety of different fuels at the same temperature, with similar fuels at different temperatures, and with special fuels such as diesel fuel and shale-oil-derived fuels.	We recommend that more work on heat-exchanger performance be done • with a larger variety of different fuels at the same temperature • with similar fuels at different temperatures • with special fuels such as diesel fuel and shale-oil-derived fuels

FIGURE 9.2 A Traditional Sentence and a Sentence List

GUIDELINES Creating Effective Lists

These five suggestions will help you write clearer, more effective paragraph lists and sentence lists.

▶ **Set off each listed item with a number, a letter, or a symbol (usually a bullet).**

— Use numbered lists to suggest sequence (as in the steps in a set of instructions) or priority (the first item being the most important). Numbers help readers see the total number of items in a list. For sublists, use lowercase letters:

1. Item
   a. subitem
   b. subitem

2. Item
   a. subitem
   b. subitem

— Use bullets to avoid suggesting either sequence or priority, such as for lists of people (everyone except number 1 gets offended). For sublists, use dashes.

• Item
   — subitem
   — subitem

— Use an open (unshaded) box (☐) for checklists.

▶ **Break up long lists.** Because most people can remember only 5 to 9 items easily, break up lists of 10 or more items.

▶ **Present the items in a parallel structure.** A list is parallel if all the items have the same grammatical form. In the parallel list below, each item is a verb phrase.

▶ **Structure and punctuate the lead-in correctly.** The lead-in tells readers how the list relates to the discussion and how the items in the list relate to each other. Although standards vary from one organization to another, the most common lead-in consists of a grammatically complete clause followed by a colon, as shown in the following examples:

Following are the three main assets:

The three main assets are as follows:

The three main assets are the following:

The committee found that the employee

• did not cause the accident

• acted properly immediately after the accident

• reported the accident according to procedures

▶ **Punctuate the list correctly.** Because rules for punctuating lists vary, you should find out whether people in your organization have a preference. If not, punctuate lists as follows:

— If the items are phrases, use a lowercase letter at the start. Do not use a period or a comma at the end. The white space beneath the last item indicates the end of the list.

For more about designing checklists, see "Checklists," Ch. 12, p. 333.

For more about parallelism, see "Use Parallel Structure," Ch. 10, p. 230.

(continued)

> The new facility will offer three advantages:
> - lower leasing costs
> - shorter commuting distance
> - a larger pool of potential workers
>
> — If the items are complete sentences, use an uppercase letter at the start and a period at the end.
>
> The new facility will offer three advantages:
> - The leasing costs will be lower.
> - The commuting distance for most employees will be shorter.
> - The pool of potential workers will be larger.
>
> — If the items are phrases followed by complete sentences, start each phrase with an uppercase letter and end it with a period. Begin the complete sentences with uppercase letters and end them with periods. Use italics to emphasize the phrases.
>
> The new facility will offer three advantages:
> - *Lower leasing costs.* The lease will cost $1,800 per month; currently we pay $2,300.
> - *Shorter commuting distance.* Our workers' average commute of 18 minutes would drop to 14 minutes.
> - *Larger pool of potential workers.* In the last decade, the population has shifted westward to the area near the new facility. As a result, we would increase our potential workforce in both the semiskilled and the managerial categories by relocating.
>
> — If the list consists of two kinds of items — phrases and complete sentences — capitalize each item and end it with a period.
>
> The new facility will offer three advantages:
> - Lower leasing costs.
> - Shorter commuting distance. Our workers' average commute of 18 minutes would drop to 14 minutes.
> - Larger pool of potential workers. In the last decade, the population has shifted westward to the area near the new facility. As a result, we would increase our potential workforce in both the semiskilled and the managerial categories by relocating.
>
> In most lists, the second and subsequent lines, called turnovers, align under the first letter of the first line, highlighting the bullet or number to the left of the text. This hanging indentation helps the reader see and understand the organization of the passage.

In many other cultures, headings and lists are considered too informal for some documents. Try to find samples written by people from the culture you are addressing to examine their use of headings and lists. Consider the following questions in studying documents from other cultures:

- **How does the writer make the information usable?** That is, how does the writer help readers easily find the information they need, without flipping through pages or clicking links unnecessarily?

- **How does the writer show the relationship among types of information?** Is related information grouped, highlighted, listed, set off by headings, or set in a typeface different from that used for other types of information? When information that can be itemized or sequenced is conveyed, what form does the itemization or sequencing take?

- **How does the writer communicate to readers the organization of the document as a whole and of the parts making up the whole?**

- **How does the writer make transitions from one subject to another?** As noted earlier, a heading eliminates the need for awkward transitional sentences. In some cultures, however, the heading itself would be considered awkward— and possibly brusque, informal, or disrespectful.

Writing Clear, Informative Paragraphs

There are two kinds of paragraphs—body paragraphs and transitional paragraphs—both of which play an important role in helping you emphasize important information.

A *body paragraph*, the basic unit for communicating information, is a group of sentences (or sometimes a single sentence) that is complete and self-sufficient and that contributes to a larger discussion. In an effective paragraph, all the sentences clearly and directly articulate one main point, either by introducing the point or by providing support for it. In addition, the whole paragraph follows logically from the material that precedes it.

A *transitional paragraph* helps readers move from one major point to another. Like a body paragraph, it can consist of a group of sentences or be a single sentence. Usually it summarizes the previous point, introduces the next point, and helps readers understand how the two are related.

The following example of a transitional paragraph appeared in a discussion of how a company plans to use this year's net proceeds.

> Our best estimate of how we will use these net proceeds, then, is to develop a second data center and increase our marketing efforts. We base this estimate on our current plans and on projections of anticipated expenditures. However, at this time we cannot precisely determine the exact cost of these activities. Our actual expenditures may exceed what we've predicted, making it necessary or advisable to reallocate the net proceeds within the two uses (data center and marketing) or to use portions of the net proceeds for other purposes. The most likely uses appear to be reducing short-term debt and addressing salary inequities among software developers; each of these uses is discussed below, including their respective advantages and disadvantages.

The first sentence contains the word "then" to signal that it introduces a summary.

The final sentence clearly indicates the relationship between what precedes it and what follows it.

STRUCTURE PARAGRAPHS CLEARLY

Most paragraphs consist of a topic sentence and supporting information.

The Topic Sentence Because a topic sentence states, summarizes, or forecasts the main point of the paragraph, put it up front. Technical communication should be clear and easy to read, not suspenseful. If a paragraph describes a test you performed, include the result of the test in your first sentence:

> The point-to-point continuity test on Cabinet 3 revealed an intermittent open circuit in the Phase 1 wiring.

Then go on to explain the details. If the paragraph describes a complicated idea, start with an overview. In other words, put the "bottom line" on top:

> Mitosis is the usual method of cell division, occurring in four stages: (1) prophase, (2) metaphase, (3) anaphase, and (4) telophase.

Putting the bottom line on top makes the paragraph much easier to read, as shown in Figure 9.3 below.

Make sure each of your topic sentences relates clearly to the organizational pattern you are using. In a discussion of the physical condition of a building, for example, you might use a spatial pattern and start a paragraph with the following topic sentence:

> On the north side of Building B, water damage to about 75 percent of the roof insulation and insulation in some areas in the north wall indicates that the roof has been leaking for some time. The leaking has contributed to . . .

Your next paragraph should begin with a topic sentence that continues the spatial organizational pattern:

> On the east side of the building, a downspout has eroded the lawn and has caused a small silt deposit to form on the neighboring property directly to the east. Riprap should be placed under the spout to . . .

Note that the phrases "on the north side" and "on the east side" signal that the discussion is following the points of the compass in a clockwise direction, further emphasizing the spatial pattern. Readers can reasonably assume that the next two parts of the discussion will be about the south side of the building and the west side, in that order.

The topic sentences are italicized for emphasis in this figure.

Notice that placing the topic sentence at the start gives a focus to the paragraph, helping readers understand the information in the rest of the paragraph.

TOPIC SENTENCE AT THE END OF THE PARAGRAPH	TOPIC SENTENCE AT THE START OF THE PARAGRAPH
A solar panel affixed to a satellite in distant geosynchronous orbit receives about 1,400 watts of sunlight per square meter. On Earth, cut this number in half, due to the day/night cycle. Cut it in half again because sunlight hits the Earth obliquely (except exactly on the equator). Cut it in half again due to clouds and dust in the atmosphere. *The result: eight times the amount of sunlight falls on a solar panel in sun-synchronous orbit as falls on the same size area on Earth.*	*Eight times the amount of sunlight falls on a solar panel in distant geosynchronous orbit as falls on the same size area on Earth.* A solar panel affixed to a satellite in sun-synchronous orbit receives about 1,400 watts of sunlight per square meter. On Earth, cut this number in half, due to the day/night cycle. Cut it in half again because sunlight hits the Earth obliquely (except exactly on the equator). Cut it in half again due to clouds and dust in the atmosphere.

FIGURE 9.3   A Topic Sentence Works Better at the Start of the Paragraph

Similarly, if your first topic sentence is "First, we need to . . . ," your next topic sentence should refer to the chronological pattern: "Second, we should . . ." (Of course, sometimes well-written headings can make such references to the organizational pattern unnecessary, as when headings are numbered to emphasize that the material is arranged in a chronological pattern.)

ETHICS NOTE

AVOIDING BURYING BAD NEWS IN PARAGRAPHS

The most emphatic location in a paragraph is the topic sentence, usually the first sentence in a paragraph. The second most emphatic location is the end of the paragraph. Do not bury bad news in the middle of the paragraph, hoping readers won't see it. It would be misleading to structure a paragraph like this:

> In our proposal, we stated that the project would be completed by May. In making this projection, we used the same algorithms that we have used successfully for more than 14 years. In this case, however, the projection was not realized, due to several factors beyond our control. . . . We have since completed the project satisfactorily and believe strongly that this missed deadline was an anomaly that is unlikely to be repeated. In fact, we have beaten every other deadline for projects this fiscal year.

The writer has buried the bad news in a paragraph beginning with a topic sentence that appears to suggest good news. The last sentence, too, suggests good news.

A more forthright approach would be as follows:

> We missed our May deadline for completing the project. Although we derived this schedule using the same algorithms that we have used successfully for more than 14 years, several factors, including especially bad weather at the site, delayed the construction. . . .

> However, we have since completed the project satisfactorily and believe strongly that this missed deadline was an anomaly that is unlikely to be repeated. . . . In fact, we have beaten every other deadline for projects this fiscal year.

Here the writer forthrightly presents the bad news in a topic sentence. Then she creates a separate paragraph with the good news.

The Supporting Information The supporting information makes the topic sentence clear and convincing. Sometimes a few explanatory details provide all the support you need. At other times, however, you need a lot of information to clarify a difficult thought or to defend a controversial idea. How much supporting information to provide also depends on your audience and purpose. Readers knowledgeable about your subject may require little supporting information; less knowledgeable readers might require a lot. Likewise, you may need to provide little supporting information if your purpose is merely to *state* a controversial point of view rather than *persuade* your reader to agree with it. In deciding such matters, your best bet is to be generous with your supporting information. Paragraphs with too little support are far more common than paragraphs with too much.

Supporting information, which is most often developed using the basic patterns of organization discussed in Chapter 7, usually fulfills one of these five roles:

1. It defines a key term or idea included in the topic sentence.
2. It provides examples or illustrations of the situation described in the topic sentence.

3. It identifies causes: factors that led to the situation.

4. It defines effects: implications of the situation.

5. It supports the claim made in the topic sentence.

A topic sentence is like a promise to readers. At the very least, when you write a topic sentence that says "Within five years, the City of McCall will need to upgrade its wastewater-treatment facilities because of increased demands from a rapidly rising population," you are implicitly promising readers that the paragraph not only will be about wastewater-treatment facilities but also will explain that the rapidly rising population is the reason the facilities need to be upgraded. If your paragraph fails to discuss these things, it has failed to deliver on the promise you made. If the paragraph discusses these things but also goes on to speculate about the price of concrete over the next five years, it is delivering on promises that the topic sentence never made. In both situations, the paragraph has gone astray.

Paragraph Length How long should a paragraph be? In general, 75 to 125 words are enough for a topic sentence and four or five supporting sentences. Long paragraphs are more difficult to read than short paragraphs because they require more focused concentration. They can also intimidate some readers, who might skip over them.

But don't let arbitrary guidelines about length take precedence over your own analysis of the audience and purpose. You might need only one or two sentences to introduce a graphic, for example. Transitional paragraphs are also likely to be quite short. If a brief paragraph fulfills its function, let it be. Do not combine two ideas in one paragraph simply to achieve a minimum word count.

You may need to break up your discussion of one idea into two or more paragraphs. An idea that requires 200 or 300 words to develop should probably not be squeezed into one paragraph.

A note about one-sentence paragraphs: body paragraphs and transitional paragraphs alike can consist of a single sentence. However, many single-sentence paragraphs are likely to need revision. Sometimes the idea in that sentence belongs with the paragraph immediately before it or immediately after it or in another paragraph elsewhere in the document. Sometimes the idea needs to be developed into a paragraph of its own. And sometimes the idea doesn't belong in the document at all.

When you think about paragraph length, consider how the information will be printed or displayed. If the information will be presented in a narrow column, such as in a newsletter, short paragraphs are much easier to read. If the information will be presented in a wider column, readers will be able to handle a longer paragraph.

◀
GUIDELINES Dividing Long Paragraphs

Here are three techniques for dividing long paragraphs.

▶ **Break the discussion at a logical place.** The most logical place to divide this material is at the introduction of the second factor. Because the paragraphs are still relatively long and cues are minimal, this strategy should be reserved for skilled readers.

> High-tech companies have been moving their operations to the suburbs for two main reasons: cheaper, more modern space and a better labor pool. A new office complex in the suburbs will charge from one-half to two-thirds of the rent charged for the same square footage in the city. And that money goes a lot further, too. The new office complexes are bright and airy; new office space is already wired for computers; and exercise clubs, shopping centers, and even libraries are often on-site.
>
> The second major factor attracting high-tech companies to the suburbs is the availability of experienced labor. Office workers and middle managers are abundant. In addition, the engineers and executives, who tend to live in the suburbs anyway, are happy to forgo the commuting, the city wage taxes, and the noise and stress of city life.

▶ **Make the topic sentence a separate paragraph and break up the supporting information.** This version is easier to understand than the one above because the brief paragraph at the start clearly introduces the information. In addition, each of the two main paragraphs now has a clear topic sentence.

> High-tech companies have been moving their operations to the suburbs for two main reasons: cheaper, more modern space and a better labor pool.
>
> First, office space is a bargain in the suburbs. A new office complex in the suburbs will charge from one-half to two-thirds of the rent charged for the same square footage in the city. And that money goes a lot further, too. The new office complexes are bright and airy; new office space is already wired for computers; and exercise clubs, shopping centers, and even libraries are often on-site.
>
> Second, experienced labor is plentiful. Office workers and middle managers are abundant. In addition, the engineers and executives, who tend to live in the suburbs anyway, are happy to forgo the commuting, the city wage taxes, and the noise and stress of city life.

▶ **Use a list.** This is the easiest of the three versions for all readers because of the extra visual cues provided by the list format.

> High-tech companies have been moving their operations to the suburbs for two main reasons:
>
> • *Cheaper, more modern space.* Office space is a bargain in the suburbs. A new office complex in the suburbs will charge anywhere from one-half to two-thirds of the rent charged for the same square footage in the city. And that money goes a lot further, too. The new office complexes are bright and airy; new office space is already wired for computers; and exercise clubs, shopping centers, and even libraries are often on-site.
>
> • *A better labor pool.* Office workers and middle managers are abundant. In addition, the engineers and executives, who tend to live in the suburbs anyway, are happy to forgo the commuting, the city wage taxes, and the noise and stress of city life.

TABLE 9.1	Transitional Words and Phrases
RELATIONSHIP	**TRANSITION**
addition	also, and, finally, first (second, etc.), furthermore, in addition, likewise, moreover, similarly
comparison	in the same way, likewise, similarly
contrast	although, but, however, in contrast, nevertheless, on the other hand, yet
illustration	for example, for instance, in other words, to illustrate
cause–effect	as a result, because, consequently, hence, so, therefore, thus
time or space	above, around, earlier, later, next, soon, then, to the right (left, west, etc.)
summary or conclusion	at last, finally, in conclusion, to conclude, to summarize

USE COHERENCE DEVICES WITHIN AND BETWEEN PARAGRAPHS

For the main idea in the topic sentence to be clear and memorable, you need to make the support—the rest of the paragraph—coherent. That is, you must link the ideas together clearly and logically, and you must express parallel ideas in parallel grammatical constructions. Even if the paragraph already moves smoothly from sentence to sentence, you can strengthen the coherence by adding transitional words and phrases, repeating key words, and using demonstrative pronouns followed by nouns.

Adding Transitional Words and Phrases Transitional words and phrases help the reader understand a discussion by explicitly stating the logical relationship between two ideas. Table 9.1 lists the most common logical relationships between two ideas and some of the common transitions that express those relationships.

Transitional words and phrases benefit both readers and writers. When a transitional word or phrase explicitly states the logical relationship between two ideas, readers don't have to guess at what that relationship might be. Using transitional words and phrases in your writing forces you to think more deeply about the logical relationships between ideas than you might otherwise.

To better understand how transitional words and phrases benefit both reader and writer, consider the following pairs of examples:

| WEAK | Demand for flash-memory chips is down by 15 percent. We have laid off 12 production-line workers. |
| IMPROVED | Demand for flash-memory chips is down by 15 percent; as a result, we have laid off 12 production-line workers. |

WEAK	The project was originally expected to cost $300,000. The final cost was $450,000.
IMPROVED	The project was originally expected to cost $300,000. However, the final cost was $450,000.

The next sentence pair differs from the others in that the weak example *does* contain a transitional word, but it's a weak transitional word:

WEAK	According to the report from Human Resources, the employee spoke rudely to a group of customers waiting to enter the store, and he repeatedly ignored requests from co-workers to unlock the door so the customers could enter.
IMPROVED	According to the report from Human Resources, the employee spoke rudely to a group of customers waiting to enter the store; moreover, he repeatedly ignored requests from co-workers to unlock the door so the customers could enter.

In the weak version, *and* implies simple addition: the employee did this, and then he did that. The improved version is stronger, conveying not merely simple addition but also the idea that refusing to unlock the door compounded the employee's rude behavior, elevating it to something more serious. By using *moreover*, the writer is saying that speaking rudely to customers was bad enough, but the employee *really* crossed the line when he refused to open the door.

Whichever transitional word or phrase you use, place it as close as possible to the beginning of the second idea. As shown in the examples above, the link between two ideas should be near the start of the second idea, to provide context for it. Consider the following example:

> The vendor assured us that the replacement parts would be delivered in time for the product release. The parts were delivered nearly two weeks after the product release, however.

The idea of Sentence 2 stands in contrast to the idea of Sentence 1, but the reader doesn't see the transition until the end of Sentence 2. Put the transition at the start of the second idea, where it will do the most good.

You should also use transitional words to maintain coherence *between* paragraphs, just as you use them to maintain coherence *within* paragraphs. The link between two paragraphs should be near the start of the second paragraph.

Repeating Key Words Repeating key words—usually nouns—helps readers follow the discussion. In the following example, the first version could be confusing:

UNCLEAR	For months the project leaders carefully planned their research. The cost of the work was estimated to be over $200,000.
	What is *the work:* the planning or the research?
CLEAR	For months the project leaders carefully planned their research. The cost of the research was estimated to be over $200,000.

From a misguided desire to be interesting, some writers keep changing their important terms. *Plankton* becomes *miniature seaweed*, then *the ocean's fast food.* Avoid this kind of word game; it can confuse readers.

Of course, too much repetition can be boring. You can vary nonessential terms as long as you don't sacrifice clarity.

SLUGGISH   The purpose of the new plan is to *reduce* the *problems* we are seeing in our accounting operations. We hope to see a *reduction* in the *problems* by early next quarter.

BETTER   The purpose of the new plan is to *reduce* the *problems* we are seeing in our accounting operations. We hope to see an *improvement* by early next quarter.

Using Demonstrative Pronouns Followed by Nouns   Demonstrative pronouns—*this, that, these,* and *those*—can help you maintain the coherence of a discussion by linking ideas securely. In almost all cases, demonstrative pronouns should be followed by nouns, rather than standing alone in the sentence. In the following examples, notice that a demonstrative pronoun by itself can be vague and confusing.

UNCLEAR   New screening techniques are being developed to combat viral infections. These are the subject of a new research effort in California.

What is being studied in California: *new screening techniques* or *viral infections*?

CLEAR   New screening techniques are being developed to combat viral infections. These techniques are the subject of a new research effort in California.

UNCLEAR   The task force could not complete its study of the mine accident. This was the subject of a scathing editorial in the union newsletter.

What was the subject of the editorial: *the mine accident* or the task force's *inability to complete its study* of the accident?

CLEAR   The task force failed to complete its study of the mine accident. This failure was the subject of a scathing editorial in the union newsletter.

Even when the context is clear, a demonstrative pronoun used without a noun might interrupt readers' progress by forcing them to refer back to an earlier idea.

INTERRUPTIVE   The law firm advised that the company initiate proceedings. This caused the company to search for a second legal opinion.

FLUID   The law firm advised that the company initiate proceedings. This advice caused the company to search for a second legal opinion.

DOCUMENT ANALYSIS ACTIVITY

Identifying the Elements of a Coherent Paragraph

The following paragraph is taken from a report published by a water company. In this paragraph, the writer is describing how he decided on a method for increasing the company's business within his particular branch. (The sentences are numbered.)

The questions on the left ask you to think about the qualities of coherent paragraphs.

(1) We found that the best way to improve the Montana branch would be to add a storage facility to our existing supply sources. (2) Currently, we can handle the average demand on a maximum day; the storage facility will enable us to meet peaking requirements and fire-protection needs. (3) In conducting our investigation, we considered developing new supply sources with sufficient capacity to meet current and future needs. (4) This alternative was rejected, however, when our consultants (Smith and Jones) did groundwater studies that revealed that insufficient groundwater is available and that the new wells would have to be located too far apart if they were not to interfere with each other.

1. In what ways does the topic sentence function as it should?

2. Identify the transitional words or phrases. How are they used effectively?

3. Identify the repeated key words. How effectively does the writer use key words?

4. Identify the demonstrative pronouns followed by nouns. How effectively does the writer use them?

WRITER'S CHECKLIST

Did you craft the title of your document so that it

☐ clearly states the subject and purpose of your document? *(p. 198)*

☐ is precise and informative? *(p. 198)*

Did you write the headings to

☐ avoid long noun strings? *(p. 201)*

☐ be informative? *(p. 201)*

☐ use the question form for readers who are not knowledgeable about the subject? *(p. 202)*

☐ use the "how-to" form in instructional materials? *(p. 202)*

☐ use the gerund form (*-ing*) for the discussion of a process? *(p. 202)*

☐ Did you avoid back-to-back headings by including an advance organizer? *(p. 202)*

Did you develop your paragraphs so that each one

☐ Did you look for opportunities to turn traditional paragraphs into lists? *(p. 203)*

☐ begins with a clear topic sentence? *(p. 207)*

☐ has adequate and appropriate support? *(p. 209)*

☐ is not too long for readers? *(p. 210)*

☐ uses coherence devices such as transitional words and phrases, repetition of key words, and demonstrative pronouns followed by nouns? *(p. 212)*

EXERCISES

1. Write a one-paragraph evaluation of each of the following titles. How clearly does the title indicate the subject and purpose of the document? In what ways does it fall short of incorporating this chapter's advice about titles? On the basis of your analysis, rewrite each title.

   a. Recommended Forecasting Techniques for Haldane Company

   b. A Study of Tablet Computers

   c. Agriculture in the West: A 10-Year View

2. Write a one-paragraph evaluation of each of the following headings. How clearly does the heading indicate the subject and purpose of the text that will follow it? In what ways does it fall short of incorporating this chapter's advice about headings? On the basis of your analysis, rewrite each heading to make it clearer and more informative. Invent any necessary details.

   a. Multigroup Processing Technique Review Board Report Findings

   b. The Great Depression of 1929

   c. Electronic Health Records

3. Revise the following list so that the lead-in is clear, easy to understand, and punctuated correctly. In addition, be sure the bullet items are grammatically parallel with one another and punctuated correctly.

   There are several goals being pursued by the Natural and Accelerated Bioremediation Research office;

   • the development of cost-effective *in situ* bioremediation strategies for subsurface radionuclides and metals;

   • an understanding of intrinsic bioremediation as well as accelerated bioremediation using nutrient amendments to immobilize contaminants;

   • identifying societal issues associated with bioremediation research, and communication of bioremediation research findings to stakeholders.

4. Provide a topic sentence for each of the following paragraphs:

   a. _____. Rising health-insurance premiums make American businesses less competitive and decrease workers' salaries. Health-care costs make up an increasing proportion of state and federal budgets, weakening the nation's financial outlook, diverting resources

from other pressing national priorities. Perhaps the most important outcome is that millions of Americans are priced out of the market, unable to afford the health-care services that they desperately need to become fully productive in the economy.

   b. _____. The reason for this difference is that a larger percentage of engineers working in small firms may be expected to hold high-level positions. In firms with fewer than 20 engineers, for example, the median income was $68,200. In firms of 20 to 200 engineers, the median income was $66,345. For the largest firms, the median was $64,600.

5. In the following paragraph, transitional words and phrases have been removed. Add an appropriate transition in each blank space. Where necessary, add punctuation.

   One formula that appeared foolproof for selling computers was direct sales by the manufacturer to the consumer. Dell, _____, climbed to number two in PC sales by selling customized products directly on its website. _____, the recent success of Acer, now number three in sales, suggests that the older formula of distributing commodity items through retailers might be best for today's PC industry. Acer's success can be attributed to three decisions it made. First, it sold off its division that manufactured components for other PC brands. _____, it correctly concluded that consumers, who generally prefer preconfigured PCs, would outnumber business customers. And _____, it decided to expand its line of inexpensive netbooks (small PCs) just when the economic downturn increased the demand for cheaper PC products. These decisions appear to have paid off for Acer: last year, its market share rose 3 percentage points, from 8 to 11. _____, Dell rose only 0.1 point, from 14.8 to 14.9.

6. In each of the following exercises, the second sentence begins with a demonstrative pronoun. Add a noun after the demonstrative to enhance coherence.

   a. The Zoning Commission has scheduled an open hearing for March 14. This _____ will enable concerned citizens to voice their opinions on the proposed construction.

b. The university has increased the number of parking spaces, instituted a shuttle system, and increased parking fees. These _____ are expected to ease the parking problems.

c. Congress's decision to withdraw support for the supercollider in 1994 was a shock to the U.S. particle-physics community. This _____ is seen as instrumental in the revival of the European research community.

CASE 9: Emphasizing Important Information in a Technical Description

You and two classmates have been asked to write a technical description of a new 3D printer purchased by the engineering college at your school. Your professor, however, has concerns about the draft you have submitted, and he has outlined those concerns in an email. If your instructor has assigned it, go to Achieve to read the email, identify passages that warrant improvement, and begin revising the technical description for emphasis and coherence.

10

Writing Correct and Effective Sentences

10

IN THE WORKPLACE, it's important to choose words carefully and write accurate, clear, concise, correct, and forceful sentences. If a sentence doesn't say what you intended, misunderstandings can occur, and misunderstandings can cost money and time. More important, the ability to write well — word by word and sentence by sentence — reflects positively on you and your organization. If you write well, you sound like a professional; you sound like someone worth reading.

Writing Grammatically Correct Sentences

Grammar is the study of how words can be combined into sentences to make meaning. Why does it matter if you can write grammatically correct sentences? One reason is that many grammar conventions are functional. If you write, "After sitting on a mildewed shelf in the garage for thirty years, my brother decided to throw out the old computer," you've said that your brother spent thirty years sitting on a mildewed shelf in the garage, which gave him plenty of time to decide what to do with the old computer. If you write, "Did Sean tell Liam when he was expected to report to work?" the reader might have a hard time figuring out whether *he* refers to Sean or Liam.

Even if a grammar mistake doesn't make you sound silly or confuse the reader, it can hurt you by making readers doubt your credibility. The logic is that if you are careless about grammar, you might also be careless about the quality of the technical information you communicate. Many readers will assume that documents that are unprofessional because of grammar problems might also be unprofessional in other ways.

This section will review nine principles for using clear, correct grammar:

1. Avoid sentence fragments.

2. Avoid comma splices.

3. Avoid run-on sentences.

4. Avoid ambiguous pronoun references.

219

5. Compare items clearly.
6. Use adjectives clearly.
7. Maintain subject–verb agreement.
8. Maintain pronoun–antecedent agreement.
9. Use tenses correctly.

AVOID SENTENCE FRAGMENTS

A sentence fragment is an incomplete sentence. A sentence fragment occurs when a sentence is missing either a verb or an independent clause. To correct a sentence fragment, use one of the following two strategies:

1. **Introduce a verb.**

   FRAGMENT   The pressure loss caused by a worn gasket.

   This example is a fragment because it lacks a verb. (The word *caused* does not function as a verb here; rather, it introduces a phrase that describes the pressure loss.)

   COMPLETE   The pressure loss was caused by a worn gasket.

   Pressure loss now has a verb: *was caused*.

   COMPLETE   We identified the pressure loss caused by a worn gasket.

   Pressure loss becomes the object in a new main clause: We *identified the pressure loss.*

   FRAGMENT   A plotting program with clipboard plotting, 3D animation, and FFTs.

   COMPLETE   It is a plotting program with clipboard plotting, 3D animation, and FFTs.

   COMPLETE   A plotting program with clipboard plotting, 3D animation, and FFTs will be released today.

2. **Link the fragment (a dependent element) to an independent clause.**

   FRAGMENT   The article was rejected for publication. Because the data could not be verified.

   Because the data could not be verified is a fragment because it lacks an independent clause: a clause that has a subject and a verb and could stand alone as a sentence. To be complete, the clause needs more information.

   COMPLETE   The article was rejected for publication because the data could not be verified.

   The *dependent* element is joined to the independent clause that precedes it.

   COMPLETE   Because the data could not be verified, the article was rejected for publication.

   The *dependent* element is followed by the independent clause.

   FRAGMENT   Delivering over 150 horsepower. The two-passenger coupe will cost over $32,000.

   COMPLETE   Delivering over 150 horsepower, the two-passenger coupe will cost over $32,000.

   COMPLETE   The two-passenger coupe will deliver over 150 horsepower and cost over $32,000.

AVOID COMMA SPLICES

A comma splice is an error that occurs when two independent clauses are joined, or spliced together, by a comma. Independent clauses in a comma splice can be linked correctly in three ways:

1. Use a comma and a coordinating conjunction (*and, or, nor, but, for, so,* or *yet*).

SPLICE The 909 printer is our most popular model, it offers an unequaled blend of power and versatility.

CORRECT The 909 printer is our most popular model, for it offers an unequaled blend of power and versatility.

     The coordinating conjunction *for* explicitly states the relationship between the two clauses.

2. Use a semicolon.

SPLICE The 909 printer is our most popular model, it offers an unequaled blend of power and versatility.

CORRECT The 909 printer is our most popular model; it offers an unequaled blend of power and versatility.

     The semicolon creates a somewhat more distant relationship between the two clauses than the comma and coordinating conjunction do; the link remains implicit.

3. Use a period or another form of terminal punctuation.

SPLICE The 909 printer is our most popular model, it offers an unequaled blend of power and versatility.

CORRECT The 909 printer is our most popular model. It offers an unequaled blend of power and versatility.

     The two independent clauses are separate sentences. Of the three ways to punctuate the two clauses correctly, this one suggests the most distant relationship between them.

AVOID RUN-ON SENTENCES

In a run-on sentence (sometimes called a *fused sentence*), two independent clauses appear together with no punctuation between them. A run-on sentence can be corrected in the same three ways as a comma splice:

1. Use a comma and a coordinating conjunction (*and, or, nor, but, for, so,* or *yet*).

RUN-ON The 909 printer is our most popular model it offers an unequaled blend of power and versatility.

CORRECT The 909 printer is our most popular model, for it offers an unequaled blend of power and versatility.

2. Use a semicolon.

RUN-ON The 909 printer is our most popular model it offers an unequaled blend of power and versatility.

CORRECT The 909 printer is our most popular model; it offers an unequaled blend of power and versatility.

3. Use a period or another form of terminal punctuation.

RUN-ON   The 909 printer is our most popular model it offers an unequaled blend of power and versatility.

CORRECT   The 909 printer is our most popular model. It offers an unequaled blend of power and versatility.

AVOID AMBIGUOUS PRONOUN REFERENCES

Pronouns must refer clearly to their antecedents—the words or phrases they replace. To correct ambiguous pronoun references, use one of these four strategies:

1. Clarify the pronoun's antecedent.

UNCLEAR   Remove the cell cluster from the medium and analyze it.

Analyze what: the cell cluster or the medium?

CLEAR   Analyze the cell cluster after removing it from the medium.

CLEAR   Analyze the medium after removing the cell cluster from it.

CLEAR   Remove the cell cluster from the medium. Then analyze the cell cluster.

CLEAR   Remove the cell cluster from the medium. Then analyze the medium.

2. Clarify the relative pronoun, such as *which*, introducing a dependent clause.

UNCLEAR   She decided to evaluate the program, which would take five months.

What would take five months: the program or the evaluation?

CLEAR   She decided to evaluate the program, a process that would take five months.

By replacing *which* with *a process that*, the writer clearly indicates that it is the evaluation that will take five months.

CLEAR   She decided to evaluate the five-month program.

By using the adjective *five-month*, the writer clearly indicates that it is the program that will take five months.

3. Clarify the subordinating conjunction, such as *where*, introducing a dependent clause.

UNCLEAR   This procedure will increase the handling of toxic materials outside the plant, where adequate safety measures can be taken.

Where can adequate safety measures be taken: inside the plant or outside?

CLEAR   This procedure will increase the handling of toxic materials outside the plant. Because adequate safety measures can be taken only in the plant, the procedure poses risks.

CLEAR   This procedure will increase the handling of toxic materials outside the plant. Because adequate safety measures can be taken only outside the plant, the procedure will decrease safety risks.

Sometimes the best way to clarify an unclear reference is to split the sentence in two, drop the subordinating conjunction, and add clarifying information.

4. Clarify the ambiguous pronoun that begins a sentence.

UNCLEAR   Allophanate linkages are among the most important structural components of polyurethane elastomers. They act as cross-linking sites.

What act as cross-linking sites: allophanate linkages or polyurethane elastomers?

CLEAR   Allophanate linkages, which are among the most important structural components of polyurethane elastomers, act as cross-linking sites.

The writer has rewritten part of the first sentence to add a clear nonrestrictive modifier and has combined the rewritten phrase with the second sentence.

If you begin a sentence with a demonstrative pronoun that might be unclear to the reader, be sure to follow it immediately with a noun that clarifies the reference.

UNCLEAR   The new parking regulations require that all employees pay for parking permits. These are on the agenda for the next senate meeting.

What are on the agenda: the regulations or the permits?

CLEAR   The new parking regulations require that all employees pay for parking permits. These regulations are on the agenda for the next senate meeting.

COMPARE ITEMS CLEARLY

When comparing or contrasting items, make sure your sentence communicates their relationship clearly. A simple comparison between two items usually causes no problems: "The X3000 has more storage than the X2500." Simple comparisons, however, can sometimes result in ambiguous statements:

AMBIGUOUS   Trout eat more than minnows.

Do trout eat minnows in addition to other food, or do trout eat more than minnows eat?

CLEAR   Trout eat more than minnows do.

If you are introducing three items, make sure the reader can tell which two are being compared:

AMBIGUOUS   Trout eat more algae than minnows.

CLEAR   Trout eat more algae than they do minnows.

CLEAR   Trout eat more algae than minnows do.

Beware of comparisons in which different aspects of the two items are compared:

ILLOGICAL   The resistance of the copper wiring is lower than the tin wiring.

LOGICAL   The resistance of the copper wiring is lower than that of the tin wiring.

Resistance cannot be logically compared with *tin wiring*. In the revision, the pronoun *that* substitutes for *resistance* in the second part of the comparison.

USE ADJECTIVES CLEARLY

In general, adjectives are placed before the nouns that they modify: *the plastic washer*. In technical communication, however, writers often need to use clusters of adjectives. To prevent confusion in technical communication, follow two guidelines:

1. **Use commas to separate coordinate adjectives.** Adjectives that describe different aspects of the same noun are known as coordinate adjectives.

   portable, programmable device

   adjustable, removable housings

   The comma is used instead of the word *and*.

   Sometimes an adjective is considered part of the noun it describes: *electric drill*. When one adjective modifies *electric drill*, no comma is required: *a reversible electric drill*. The addition of two or more adjectives, however, creates the traditional coordinate construction: *a two-speed, reversible electric drill*.

2. **Use hyphens to link compound adjectives.** A compound adjective is made up of two or more words. Use hyphens to link these elements when compound adjectives precede nouns.

   a variable-angle accessory

   increased cost-of-living raises

   The hyphens in the second example prevent *increased* from being read as an adjective modifying *cost*.

   A long string of compound adjectives can be confusing even if you use hyphens appropriately. To ensure clarity, turn the adjectives into a clause or a phrase following the noun.

   UNCLEAR   an *operator-initiated default-prevention* technique

   CLEAR   a technique *initiated by the operator to prevent default*

MAINTAIN SUBJECT–VERB AGREEMENT

The subject and verb of a sentence must agree in number, even when a prepositional phrase comes between them. The object of the preposition might be plural in a singular sentence.

INCORRECT   The *result* of the tests *are* promising.

CORRECT   The *result* of the tests *is* promising.

The object of the preposition might be singular in a plural sentence.

INCORRECT   The *results* of the test *is* promising.

CORRECT   The *results* of the test *are* promising.

Don't be misled by the fact that the object of the preposition and the verb don't sound natural together, as in *tests is* or *test are*. Here, the noun *test(s)* precedes the verb, but it is not the subject of the verb. As long as the subject and verb agree, the sentence is correct.

MAINTAIN PRONOUN–ANTECEDENT AGREEMENT

A pronoun and its antecedent (the word or phrase being replaced by the pronoun) must agree in number. Often an error occurs when the antecedent is a collective noun—one that can be interpreted as either singular or plural, depending on its usage.

INCORRECT   The *company* is proud to announce a new stock option plan for *their* employees.

CORRECT   The *company* is proud to announce a new stock option plan for *its* employees.

             Company acts as a single unit; therefore, the singular pronoun is appropriate.

When the individual members of a collective noun are emphasized, however, a plural pronoun is appropriate.

CORRECT   The inspection team have prepared their reports.

CORRECT   The members of the inspection team have prepared their reports.

             The use of *their* emphasizes that the team members have prepared their own reports.

USE TENSES CORRECTLY

Two verb tenses are commonly used in technical communication: the present tense and the past perfect tense. It is important to understand the specific purpose of each.

1. **The present tense is used to describe scientific principles and recurring events.**

   INCORRECT   In 1992, McKay and his coauthors argued that the atmosphere of Mars *was* salmon pink.

   CORRECT   In 1992, McKay and his coauthors argued that the atmosphere of Mars *is* salmon pink.

                   Although the argument was made in the historical past—1992—the point is expressed in the present tense because the atmosphere of Mars continues to be salmon pink.

   When the date of the argument is omitted, some writers express the entire sentence in the present tense.

   CORRECT   McKay and his coauthors *argue* that the atmosphere of Mars *is* salmon pink.

2. **The past perfect tense is used to describe the earlier of two events that occurred in the past.**

   CORRECT   We *had begun* excavation when the foreman *discovered* the burial remains.

                   Had begun is the past perfect tense. The excavation began before the burial remains were discovered.

   CORRECT   The seminar *had concluded* before I *got* a chance to talk with Dr. Tran.

Structuring Effective Sentences

Good technical communication consists of clear, graceful sentences that convey information economically. This section describes six principles for structuring effective sentences:

- Emphasize new and important information.
- Choose an appropriate sentence length.
- Focus on the "real" subject.
- Focus on the "real" verb.
- Use parallel structure.
- Use modifiers effectively.

EMPHASIZE NEW AND IMPORTANT INFORMATION

Sentences are often easier to understand and more emphatic if new information appears at the end. For instance, if your company has labor problems and you want to describe the possible results, structure the sentence like this:

    Because of labor problems, we anticipate a three-week delay.

    In this case, *three-week delay* is the new information.

If your readers already expect a three-week delay but don't know the reason for it, reverse the structure:

> We anticipate the three-week delay in production because of labor problems.

> Here, the new and important information is *labor problems*.

Try not to end the sentence with qualifying information that blunts the impact of the new information.

> WEAK   The joint could fail under special circumstances.

> IMPROVED   Under special circumstances, the joint could fail.

Put references to time and space at the beginning of the sentence, where they can provide context for the main idea that the sentence expresses.

> *Since the last quarter of 2014,* we have experienced an 8 percent turnover rate in personnel assigned to the project.

> *On the north side of the building,* water from the leaking pipes has damaged the exterior siding and the sheetrock on some interior walls.

CHOOSE AN APPROPRIATE SENTENCE LENGTH

Sometimes sentence length affects the quality of the writing. In general, an average of 15 to 20 words per sentence is effective for most technical communication. A series of 10-word sentences would be choppy. A series of 35-word sentences would probably be too demanding. And a succession of sentences of approximately the same length would be monotonous.

In revising a draft, use your software to compute the average sentence length of a representative passage.

Avoid Overly Long Sentences How long is too long? There is no simple answer, because ease of reading depends on the vocabulary, sentence structure, and sentence length; the reader's motivation and knowledge of the topic; the purpose of the communication; and the conventions of the application you are using. For instance, you use shorter sentences in tweets and text messages than in reports.

Often a draft will include sentences such as the following:

> The construction of the new facility is scheduled to begin in March, but it might be delayed by one or even two months by winter weather conditions, which can make it impossible or nearly impossible to begin excavating the foundation.

To avoid creating such long sentences, say one thing clearly and simply before moving on to the next idea. For instance, to make this difficult 40-word sentence easier to read, divide it into two sentences:

> The construction of the new facility is scheduled to begin in March. However, construction might be delayed until April or even May by winter weather conditions, which can make it impossible or nearly impossible to begin excavating the foundation.

Sometimes an overly long sentence can be fixed by creating a list (see the Guidelines box "Creating Effective Lists" in Ch. 9, p. 205).

Avoid Overly Short Sentences Just as sentences can be too long, they can also be too short and choppy, as in the following example:

> Customarily, environmental cleanups are conducted on a "time-and-materials" (T&M) basis. Using the T&M basis, the contractor performs the work. Then the contractor bills for the hours worked and the cost of equipment and materials used during the work. With the T&M approach, spending for environmental cleanups by private and government entities has been difficult to contain. Also, actual contamination reduction has been slow.

The problem here is that some of the sentences are choppy and contain too little information, calling readers' attention to how the sentences are constructed rather than to what the sentences say. In cases like this, the best way to revise is to combine sentences:

> Customarily, environmental cleanups are conducted on a "time-and-materials" (T&M) basis: the contractor performs the work, then bills for the hours worked and the cost of equipment and materials. With the T&M approach, spending for environmental cleanups by private and government entities has been difficult to contain, and contamination reduction has been slow.

Another problem with excessively short sentences is that they needlessly repeat key terms. Again, consider combining sentences:

SLUGGISH	I have experience working with various *microprocessor-based systems*. Some of these *microprocessor-based systems* include the T90, RCA 9600, and AIM 7600.
BETTER	I have experience working with various microprocessor-based systems, including the T90, RCA 9600, and AIM 7600.

FOCUS ON THE "REAL" SUBJECT

The conceptual, or "real," subject of the sentence should also be the grammatical subject. Don't disguise or bury the real subject in a prepositional phrase following a weak grammatical subject. In the following examples, the weak subjects obscure the real subjects. (The grammatical subjects are italicized.)

WEAK	The *use* of this method would eliminate the problem of motor damage.
STRONG	This *method* would eliminate the problem of motor damage.

WEAK	The *presence* of a six-membered lactone ring was detected.
STRONG	A six-membered lactone *ring* was detected.

In revising a draft, look for the real subject (the topic) and ask yourself whether the sentence would be more effective if the real subject was also the grammatical subject. Sometimes all that is necessary is to ask yourself this question: *What is the topic of this sentence?* The author of the first example above wasn't trying to say something about *using* a method; she was trying to say something about the method itself. Likewise, in the second example, it wasn't the *presence* of a lactone ring that was detected; rather, the lactone ring itself was detected.

Another way to make the subject of the sentence prominent is to reduce the number of grammatical expletives. *Expletives* are words that serve a grammatical function in a sentence but have no meaning. The most common expletives are *it* (generally followed by *is*) and *there* (generally followed by *is* or *are*).

| WEAK | There is no alternative for us except to withdraw the product. |
| STRONG | We have no alternative except to withdraw the product. |

| WEAK | It is hoped that testing the evaluation copies of the software will help us make this decision. |
| STRONG | We hope that testing the evaluation copies of the software will help us make this decision. |

The second example uses the expletive *it* with the passive voice. The problem is that the sentence does not make clear who is doing the hoping.

For more about using the passive voice, see "Use Active and Passive Voice Appropriately," p. 235.

Expletives are not errors. Rather, they are conversational expressions that can clarify meaning by emphasizing the information that follows them.

| WITH THE EXPLETIVE | It is hard to say whether the downturn will last more than a few months. |
| WITHOUT THE EXPLETIVE | Whether the downturn will last more than a few months is hard to say. |

The second version is harder to understand because the reader has to remember a long subject (*Whether the downturn will last more than a few months*) before getting to the verb (*is*). Fortunately, you can revise the sentence in other ways to make it easier to understand and to eliminate the expletive.

I don't know whether the downturn will last more than a few months.

Nobody knows whether the downturn will last more than a few months.

Use the search function of your word processor to locate both weak subjects (usually they precede the word *of*) and expletives (search for *it is, there is,* and *there are*).

FOCUS ON THE "REAL" VERB

A "real" verb, like a "real" subject, should stand out in every sentence. A common problem in technical communication is the inappropriate use of a *nominalized* verb—a verb that has been changed into a noun, then coupled with a weaker verb. *To install* becomes *to effect an installation; to analyze* becomes *to conduct an analysis.* Notice how nominalizing the verbs makes the following sentences both awkward and unnecessarily long (the nominalized verbs are italicized).

WEAK	Each *preparation* of the solution is done twice.
STRONG	Each solution is prepared twice.

WEAK	*Consideration* should be given to an acquisition of the properties.
STRONG	We should consider acquiring the properties.

Like expletives, nominalizations are not errors. In fact, many common nouns are nominalizations: *maintenance, requirement,* and *analysis,* for example. In addition, nominalizations often effectively summarize an idea from a previous sentence (in italics below).

> The telephone-service provider decided not to replace the land lines that were damaged in the recent storm. This *decision* could prove a real problem for those residents who used land lines to connect to the internet and for their medical-alert services.

Some software programs search for common nominalizations. With any word processor, however, you can identify most of them by searching for character strings such as *tion, ment, sis, ence, ing,* and *ance,* as well as the word *of.*

USE PARALLEL STRUCTURE

A sentence is parallel if its coordinate elements follow the same grammatical form: for example, all the clauses are either passive or active, all the verbs are either infinitives or participles, and so on. Parallel structure creates a recognizable pattern, making a sentence easier for the reader to follow. Nonparallel structure creates no such pattern, distracting and possibly confusing readers. In the following examples of nonparallel constructions, the verbs are not in the same form (verbs are italicized).

NONPARALLEL	Our present system *is costing* us profits and *reduces* our productivity.
PARALLEL	Our present system *is costing* us profits and *reducing* our productivity.

NONPARALLEL	The compositor *should follow* the printed directions; *do not change* the originator's work.
PARALLEL	The compositor *should follow* the printed directions and *should not change* the originator's work.

When using parallel constructions, make sure that parallel items in a series do not overlap, causing confusion or even changing the meaning of the sentence:

CONFUSING   The speakers will include partners of law firms, businesspeople, and civic leaders.

Partners of appears to apply to *businesspeople* and *civic leaders*, as well as to *law firms*. That is, *partners of* carries over to the other items in the series. The following revision solves the problem by rearranging the items so that *partners* can apply only to *law firms*.

CLEAR   The speakers will include businesspeople, civic leaders, and partners of law firms.

CONFUSING   We need to buy more lumber, hardware, tools, and hire the subcontractors.

The writer has linked two ideas inappropriately. The first idea is that we need to buy three things: lumber, hardware, and tools. The second is that we need to hire the subcontractors. Hiring is not in the same category as the items to be bought. In other words, the writer has structured and punctuated the sentence as if it contained a four-item series, when in fact it should contain a three-item series followed by a second verb phrase.

CLEAR   We need to buy more lumber, hardware, and tools, and we need to hire the subcontractors.

USE MODIFIERS EFFECTIVELY

Modifiers are words, phrases, and clauses that describe other elements in the sentence. To make your meaning clear, you must indicate whether a modifier provides necessary information about the word or phrase it refers to (its *antecedent*) or whether it simply provides additional information. You must also clearly identify the antecedent—the element in the sentence that the modifier is describing or otherwise referring to.

Distinguish Between Restrictive and Nonrestrictive Modifiers   As the term implies, a *restrictive modifier* restricts the meaning of its antecedent; it provides information that the reader needs to identify the antecedent and is, therefore, crucial to understanding the sentence. Notice that restrictive modifiers—italicized in the following examples—are not set off by commas:

The airplanes *used in the exhibitions* are slightly modified.

The modifying phrase *used in the exhibitions* identifies which airplanes the writer is referring to. Presumably, there are at least two groups of airplanes: those that are used in the exhibitions and those that are not. The restrictive modifier tells readers which of the two groups is being discussed.

> Please disregard the notice *you recently received from us.*
>
> The modifying phrase *you recently received from us* identifies which notice. Without it, the sentence could be referring to one of any number of notices.

In most cases, the restrictive modifier doesn't require a relative pronoun, such as *that*, but you can choose to use the pronoun *that* (or *who*, for people):

> Please disregard the notice *that* you recently received from us.

A *nonrestrictive modifier* does not restrict the meaning of its antecedent: the reader does not need the information to identify what the modifier is describing or referring to. If you omit the nonrestrictive modifier, the basic sentence retains its primary meaning.

> The Hubble telescope, *intended to answer fundamental questions about the origin of the universe,* was last repaired in 2009.
>
> Here, the basic sentence is *The Hubble telescope was last repaired in 2009.* Removing the modifier doesn't change the meaning of the basic sentence.

If you use a relative pronoun with a nonrestrictive modifier, choose *which* (or *who* or *whom* for a person).

> Go to the Registration Area, *which is located on the second floor.*

Use commas to separate a nonrestrictive modifier from the rest of the sentence. In the example about the Hubble telescope, a pair of commas encloses the nonrestrictive modifier and separates it from the rest of the sentence. In that respect, the commas function much like parentheses, indicating that the modifying information is parenthetical. In the example about the Registration Area, the comma indicates that the modifying information is tacked on at the end of the sentence as additional information.

Avoid Misplaced Modifiers The placement of the modifier often determines the meaning of the sentence, as the placement of *only* in the following sentences illustrates:

> *Only* Turner received a cost-of-living increase last year.
> Meaning: Nobody else received one.
>
> Turner received *only* a cost-of-living increase last year.
> Meaning: He didn't receive a merit increase.
>
> Turner received a cost-of-living increase *only* last year.
> Meaning: He received a cost-of-living increase as recently as last year.
>
> Turner received a cost-of-living increase last year *only*.
> Meaning: He received a cost-of-living increase in no other year.

Misplaced modifiers—those that appear to modify the wrong antecedent—are a common problem. Usually, the best solution is to place the modifier as close as possible to its intended antecedent.

MISPLACED   The subject of the meeting is the future of geothermal energy *in the downtown Webster Hotel*.

CORRECT   The subject of the meeting *in the downtown Webster Hotel* is the future of geothermal energy.

A *squinting modifier* falls ambiguously between two possible antecedents, so the reader cannot tell which one is being modified:

UNCLEAR   We decided *immediately* to purchase the new system.

Did we decide immediately, or did we decide to make the purchase immediately?

CLEAR   We *immediately* decided to purchase the new system.

CLEAR   We decided to purchase the new system *immediately*.

A subtle form of misplaced modification can also occur with *correlative constructions*, such as *either . . . or, neither . . . nor,* and *not only . . . but also*:

MISPLACED   The new refrigerant *not only decreases* energy costs *but also* spoilage losses.

Here, the writer is implying that the refrigerant does at least two things to energy costs: it decreases them and then does something else to them. Unfortunately, that's not how the sentence unfolds. The second thing the refrigerant does to energy costs never appears.

CORRECT   The new refrigerant *decreases not only* energy costs *but also* spoilage losses.

In the revised sentence, the phrase *decreases not only* implies that at least two things will be decreased, and as the sentence develops that turns out to be the case. *Decreases* applies to both *energy costs* and *spoilage losses*. Therefore, the first half of the correlative construction (*not only*) follows the verb (*decreases*). Note that if the sentence contains two different verbs, each half of the correlative construction precedes a verb:

The new refrigerant *not only decreases* energy costs *but also reduces* spoilage losses.

Avoid Dangling Modifiers   A *dangling modifier* has no antecedent in the sentence and can therefore be unclear:

DANGLING   Trying to solve the problem, the instructions seemed unclear.

This sentence says that the instructions are trying to solve the problem. To correct the sentence, rewrite it, adding the clarifying information either within the modifier or next to it:

CORRECT   As I was trying to solve the problem, the instructions seemed unclear.

CORRECT   Trying to solve the problem, I thought the instructions seemed unclear.

Sometimes you can correct a dangling modifier by switching from the *indicative mood* (a statement of fact) to the *imperative mood* (a request or command):

DANGLING   To initiate the procedure, the BEGIN button should be pushed. (indicative mood)

CORRECT   To initiate the procedure, push the BEGIN button. (imperative mood)

Choosing the Right Words and Phrases

This section discusses four principles that will help you use the right words and phrases in the right places: select an appropriate level of formality, be clear and specific, be concise, and use inoffensive language.

SELECT AN APPROPRIATE LEVEL OF FORMALITY

Although no standard definition of levels of formality exists, most experts would agree that there are three levels:

INFORMAL   The Acorn 560 is a real screamer. With 5.5 GHz of pure computing power, it slashes through even the thickest spreadsheets before you can say $2 + 2 = 4$.

MODERATELY   With its 5.5-GHz microprocessor, the Acorn 560 can handle even

FORMAL   the most complicated spreadsheets quickly.

HIGHLY FORMAL   With a 5.5-GHz microprocessor, the Acorn 560 is a high-speed personal computer appropriate for computation-intensive applications such as large, complex spreadsheets.

Technical communication usually requires a moderately formal or highly formal style.

To achieve the appropriate level and tone, think about your audience, your subject, and your purpose:

For more about writing to a multicultural audience, see the Guidelines box "Writing for Readers from Other Cultures," Ch. 5, p. 107.

- **Audience.** You would probably write more formally to a group of retired executives than to a group of college students. You would likewise write more formally to the company vice president than to your co-workers, and you would probably write more formally to people from most other cultures than to people from your own.

- **Subject.** You would write more formally about a serious subject—safety regulations or important projects—than about plans for an office party.
- **Purpose.** You would write more formally in presenting quarterly economic results to shareholders than in responding to an email requesting sales figures on one of the company's products.

In general, it is better to err on the side of formality. Avoid an informal style in any writing you do at the office, for two reasons:

- **Informal writing tends to be imprecise.** In the example "The Acorn 560 is a real screamer," what exactly is a *screamer?*
- **Informal writing can be embarrassing.** If your boss spots your email to a colleague, you might wish it didn't begin, " 'Sup, dawg?"

BE CLEAR

Follow these seven guidelines to make your writing clear:

- Use active and passive voice appropriately.
- Be specific.
- Avoid unnecessary jargon.
- Use positive constructions.
- Avoid long noun strings.
- Avoid clichés.
- Avoid euphemisms.

USE ACTIVE AND PASSIVE VOICE APPROPRIATELY

In a sentence using the active voice, the subject performs the action expressed by the verb: the "doer" of the action is the grammatical subject. By contrast, in a sentence using the passive voice, the recipient of the action is the grammatical subject. Compare the following examples (the subjects are italicized):

ACTIVE   *Dave Brushaw* drove the launch vehicle.

The doer of the action is the subject of the sentence.

PASSIVE   The launch *vehicle* was driven by Dave Brushaw.

The recipient of the action is the subject of the sentence.

In most cases, the active voice works better than the passive voice because it emphasizes the *agent* (the doer of the action). An active-voice sentence also is shorter because it does not require a form of the verb *to be* and the past participle, as a passive-voice sentence does. In the active version of the example sentence, the verb is *drove* rather than *was driven*, and the word *by* does not appear.

The passive voice, however, is generally better in these four cases:

1. When the agent is clear from the context:

   Students are required to take both writing courses.

   Here, the context makes it clear that the college sets the requirements.

2. When the agent is unknown:

   The comet was first referred to in an ancient Egyptian text.

   We don't know who wrote this text.

3. When the agent is less important than the action:

   The blueprints were hand-delivered this morning.

   It doesn't matter who the messenger was.

For more about ethics, see Ch. 2.

4. When a reference to the agent is embarrassing, dangerous, or in some other way inappropriate:

   Incorrect figures were recorded for the flow rate.

   It might be unwise or tactless to specify who recorded the incorrect figures. Perhaps it was your boss. However, it is unethical to use the passive voice to avoid responsibility for an action.

The passive voice can also help you maintain the focus of your paragraph.

Cloud computing offers three major advantages. First, the need for server space is reduced. Second, security updates are installed automatically . . .

Some people believe that the active voice is inappropriate in technical communication because it emphasizes the person who does the work rather than the work itself, making the writing less objective. In many cases, this objection is valid. Why write "I analyzed the sample for traces of iodine" if there is no ambiguity about who did the analysis or no need to identify who did it? The passive focuses on the action, not the actor: "The samples were analyzed for traces of iodine." But if in doubt, use the active voice.

For more about the use of the passive voice in lab reports, see "Materials and Methods," Ch. 19, p. 536.

Other people argue that the passive voice produces a double ambiguity. In the sentence "The samples were analyzed for traces of iodine," the reader is not quite sure who did the analysis (the writer or someone else) or when it was done (during the project or some time previously). Identifying the actor can often clarify both ambiguities.

The best approach is to recognize that the two voices differ and to use each one where it is most effective.

Many grammar-checkers can help you locate the passive voice. Some of them will advise you that the passive is undesirable, almost an error, but this advice is misleading. Use the passive voice when it works better than the active voice for your purposes.

Any word processor allows you to search for the forms of *to be* used most commonly in passive-voice expressions: *is, are, was,* and *were.* You can also search for *ed* to isolate past participles (for example, *purchased*, *implemented*, and *delivered*); such past participles appear in most passive-voice constructions.

Be Specific Being specific involves using precise words, providing adequate detail, and avoiding ambiguity.

- **Use precise words.** A Ford Focus is an automobile, but it is also a vehicle, a machine, and a thing. In describing the Focus, *automobile* is better than the less specific *vehicle*, because *vehicle* can also refer to pickup trucks, trains, hot-air balloons, and other means of transport. As words become more abstract—from *machine* to *thing*, for instance—chances for misunderstanding increase.

- **Provide adequate detail.** Readers probably know less about your subject than you do. What might be perfectly clear to you might be too vague for them.

VAGUE	An engine on the plane experienced some difficulties.
	Which engine? What plane? What kinds of difficulties?
CLEAR	The left engine on the Cessna 310 temporarily lost power during flight.

- **Avoid ambiguity.** Don't let readers wonder which of two meanings you are trying to convey.

AMBIGUOUS	After stirring by hand for 10 seconds, add three drops of the iodine mixture to the solution.
	After stirring the iodine mixture or the solution?
CLEAR	Stir the iodine mixture by hand for 10 seconds. Then add three drops to the solution.
CLEAR	Stir the solution by hand for 10 seconds. Then add three drops of the iodine mixture.

If you don't have the specific data, you should approximate—and clearly tell readers you are doing so—or explain why the specific data are unavailable and indicate when they will be available:

The fuel leakage is much greater than we had anticipated; we estimate it to be at least 5 gallons per minute, not 2.

The fuel leakage is much greater than we had anticipated; we expect to have specific data by 4 P.M. today.

Avoid Unnecessary Jargon Jargon is shoptalk. To an audiophile, *LP* is a long-playing record; to an engineer, it is liquid propane; to a guitarist, it is a Gibson Les Paul model; to a physician, it is a lumbar puncture; to a drummer, it is Latin Percussion, a drum maker.

Jargon is often ridiculed; many dictionaries define it as "writing that one does not understand" or "nonsensical, incoherent, or meaningless talk." However, jargon is useful in its proper sphere. For one thing, jargon enables members of a particular profession to communicate clearly and economically with one another.

If you are addressing a technically knowledgeable audience, use jargon recognized in that field. However, keep in mind that technical documents often have many audiences in addition to the primary audience. When in doubt, avoid jargon; use more common expressions or simpler terms.

Using jargon inappropriately is inadvisable for four reasons:

- **It can be imprecise.** If you ask a co-worker to review a document and provide *feedback*, are you asking for a facial expression, body language, a phone call, or a written evaluation?

- **It can be confusing.** If you ask a computer novice to *cold swap the drive*, he or she might have no idea what you're talking about.

- **It is often seen as condescending.** Many readers will react as if you were showing off—displaying a level of expertise that excludes them. If readers feel alienated, they will likely miss your message.

- **It is often intimidating.** People might feel inadequate or stupid because they do not know what you are talking about. Obviously, this reaction undermines communication.

Use Positive Constructions   The term *positive construction* has nothing to do with being cheerful. It indicates that the writer is describing what something is instead of what it is not. In the sentence "I was sad to see this project completed," "sad" is a positive construction. The negative construction would be "not happy."

Here are a few more examples of positive and negative constructions:

Positive construction	Negative construction
most	not all
few	not many
on time	not late, not delayed
positive	not negative
inefficient	not efficient
reject	cannot accept
impossible	not possible

Readers understand positive constructions more quickly and more easily than negative constructions. Consider the following examples:

DIFFICULT   Because the team did not have sufficient time to complete the project, it was unable to produce a satisfactory report.

SIMPLER   Because the team had too little time to complete the project, it produced an unsatisfactory report.

Avoid Long Noun Strings A noun string contains a series of nouns (or nouns, adjectives, and adverbs), all of which together modify the last noun. For example, in the phrase *parking-garage regulations*, the first pair of words modifies *regulations*. Noun strings save time, and if your readers understand them, they are fine. It is easier to write *passive-restraint system* than *a system that uses passive restraints*.

Hyphens can clarify noun strings by linking words that go together. For example, in the phrase *flat-panel monitor*, the hyphen links *flat* and *panel*. Together they modify *monitor*. In other words, it is not a *flat panel* or a *panel monitor*, but a *flat-panel monitor*. However, noun strings are sometimes so long or so complex that hyphens can't ensure clarity. To clarify a long noun string, untangle the phrases and restore prepositions, as in the following example:

For more about hyphens, see Appendix, Part C, p. 676.

UNCLEAR   preregistration procedures instruction sheet update

CLEAR   an update of the instruction sheet for preregistration procedures

Noun strings can sometimes be ambiguous—they can have two or more plausible meanings, leaving readers to guess at which meaning you're trying to convey.

AMBIGUOUS   The building contains a special incoming materials storage area.

What's special? Are the incoming materials special? Or is the area they're stored in special?

UNAMBIGUOUS   The building contains a special area for storing incoming materials.

UNAMBIGUOUS   The building contains an area for storing special incoming materials.

An additional danger is that noun strings can sometimes sound pompous. If you are writing about a simple smoke detector, there is no reason to call it a *smoke-detection device* or, worse, a *smoke-detection system*.

Avoid Clichés Good writing is original and fresh. Rather than use a cliché, say what you want to say in plain English. Current clichés include *pushing the envelope*; *synergy*; *mission critical*; *bleeding edge*; *paradigm shift*; and *been there, done that*. The best advice is to avoid clichés: if you are used to hearing or reading a phrase, don't use it. Jimi Hendrix was a rock star; the Employee of the Month sitting in the next cubicle isn't. Don't think outside the box, pick low-hanging fruit, leverage your assets, bring your "A" game, be a change agent, raise the bar, throw anyone under a bus, be proactive, put lipstick on a pig, or give 110 percent. And you can assume that everyone already knows that it is what it is.

Avoid Euphemisms A euphemism is a polite way of saying something that makes people uncomfortable. For instance, a near miss between two airplanes is officially an "air proximity incident." The more uncomfortable the subject, the more often people resort to euphemisms. Dozens of euphemisms deal with drinking, bathrooms, sex, and death. Here are several euphemisms for firing someone:

personnel-surplus reduction	dehiring
workforce-imbalance correction	decruiting
rightsizing	redundancy elimination
indefinite idling	career-change-opportunity creation
downsizing	permanent furloughing
administrative streamlining	personnel realignment
synergy-related headcount restructuring	

ETHICS NOTE

EUPHEMISMS AND TRUTH TELLING

There is nothing wrong with using the euphemism *restroom*, even though few people visit one to rest. The British use the phrase *go to the toilet* in polite company, and nobody seems to mind. In this case, if you want to use a euphemism, no harm done.

But it is unethical to use a euphemism to gloss over an issue that has important implications for people or the environment. People get uncomfortable when discussing layoffs — and they should. It's an uncomfortable issue. But calling a layoff a *redundancy elimination initiative* ought to make you even more uncomfortable. Don't use language to cloud reality. It's an ethical issue.

BE CONCISE

The following five principles can help you write concise technical documents:

- Avoid obvious statements.
- Avoid filler.
- Avoid unnecessary prepositional phrases.
- Avoid wordy phrases.
- Avoid fancy words.

Avoid Obvious Statements Writing can become sluggish if it overexplains. The italicized words in the following example are sluggish:

SLUGGISH   The market for *the sale of* flash memory chips is dominated by *two chip manufacturers*: Intel and Advanced Micro Systems. These two *chip manufacturers* are responsible for 76 percent of the $1.3 billion market *in flash memory chips* last year.

IMPROVED   The market for flash memory chips is dominated by Intel and Advanced Micro Systems, two companies that claimed 76 percent of the $1.3 billion industry last year.

Avoid Filler In our writing, we sometimes use filler, much of which is more suited to speech. Consider the following examples:

basically	kind of
certain	rather
essentially	sort of

Such words are common in oral communication, when we need to think fast, but they are meaningless in writing.

> BLOATED   *I think that, basically,* the board felt *sort of* betrayed, *in a sense,* by the *kind of* behavior the president displayed.
>
> BETTER   The board felt betrayed by the president's behavior.

But modifiers are not always meaningless. For instance, it might be wise to use *I think* or *it seems to me* to show that you are aware of other views.

> BLUNT   Next year we will face unprecedented challenges to our market dominance.
>
> LESS BLUNT   In my view, next year we will face unprecedented challenges to our market dominance.

Of course, a sentence that sounds blunt to one reader can sound self-confident to another. As you write, keep your audience's preferences and expectations in mind.

Other fillers include redundant expressions, such as *collaborate together, past history, end result, any and all, still remain, completely eliminate,* and *very unique.* Say it once.

> REDUNDANT   This project would not have succeeded if not for the *hard work and considerable effort* of *each and every one* of the auditors assigned to the project.
>
> BETTER   This project would not have succeeded if not for the *hard work* of *every one* of the auditors assigned to the project.

Avoid Unnecessary Prepositional Phrases A prepositional phrase consists of a preposition followed by a noun or a noun equivalent, such as *in the summary, on the engine,* and *under the heading.* Unnecessary prepositional phrases, often used along with abstract nouns and nominalizations, can make your writing long and boring.

> LONG   The increase *in* the number *of* students enrolled *in* the materials-engineering program *at* Lehigh University is suggestive *of* the regard *in* which that program is held *by* the university's new students.
>
> SHORTER   The increased enrollment in Lehigh University's materials-engineering program suggests that the university's new students consider it a good program.

Avoid Wordy Phrases Wordy phrases also make writing long and boring. For example, some people write *on a daily basis* rather than *daily*. The long phrase may sound more important, but *daily* says the same thing more concisely.

Table 10.1 lists common wordy phrases and their more concise equivalents.

TABLE 10.1	**Wordy Phrases and Their Concise Equivalents**		
WORDY PHRASE	**CONCISE PHRASE**	**WORDY PHRASE**	**CONCISE PHRASE**
a majority of	most	in the event that	if
a number of	some, many	in view of the fact that	because
at an early date	soon	it is often the case that	often
at the conclusion of	after, following	it is our opinion that	we think that
at the present time	now	it is our recommendation that	we recommend that
at this point in time	now	it is our understanding that	we understand that
based on the fact that	because	make reference to	refer to
check out	check	of the opinion that	think that
despite the fact that	although	on a daily basis	daily
due to the fact that	because	on the grounds that	because
during the course of	during	prior to	before
during the time that	during, while	relative to	regarding, about
have the capability to	can	so as to	to
in connection with	about, concerning	subsequent to	after
in order to	to	take into consideration	consider
in regard to	regarding, about	until such time as	until

Compare the following wordy sentence and its concise translation:

WORDY   I am of the opinion that, in regard to profit achievement, the statistics pertaining to this month will appear to indicate an upward tendency.

CONCISE   I think this month's statistics will show an increase in profits.

Avoid Fancy Words   Writers sometimes think they will impress their readers by using fancy words—*utilize* for *use*, *initiate* for *begin*, *perform* for *do*, *due to* for *because of*, and *prioritize* for *rank*. In technical communication, plain talk is best. Compare the following fancy sentence with its plain-English version:

FANCY   The purchase of a database program will enhance our record-maintenance capabilities.

PLAIN   Buying a database program will help us maintain our records.

Table 10.2 lists commonly used fancy words and their plain equivalents.

TABLE 10.2   Fancy Words and their Plain Equivalents

FANCY WORD	PLAIN WORD	FANCY WORD	PLAIN WORD
advise	tell	herein	here
ascertain	learn, find out	impact (verb)	affect
attempt (verb)	try	initiate	begin
commence	start, begin	manifest (verb)	show
demonstrate	show	parameters	variables, conditions
due to	because of	perform	do
employ (verb)	use	prioritize	rank
endeavor (verb)	try	procure	get, buy
eventuate	happen	quantify	measure
evidence (verb)	show	terminate	end, stop
finalize	end, settle, agree, finish	utilize	use
furnish	provide, give		

DOCUMENT ANALYSIS ACTIVITY

Revising for Conciseness and Simplicity

The following passage is from a request for proposals published by the National Science Foundation. (Sentence numbers have been added here.) The questions below ask you to think about word choice (as discussed on pp. 234–43).

1. This passage contains many prepositional phrases. Identify two of them. For each one, determine whether its use is justified or whether the sentence would be easier to understand if it were eliminated.

2. Part of this passage is written in the passive voice. Select one sentence in the passive voice that would be clearer in the active voice, and rewrite it in the active voice.

3. This passage contains a number of examples of fancy words. Identify two of them. How can they be translated into plain English?

1. Grants.gov, part of the President's Management Agenda to improve government services to the public, provides a single Government-wide portal for finding and applying for Federal grants online.

2. Proposals submitted via Grants.gov must be prepared and submitted in accordance with the *NSF Grants.gov Application Guide*, available through Grants.gov as well as on the NSF website at: http://www.nsf.gov/bfa/dias /policy/docs/grantsgovguide.pdf.

3. The Grants.gov Application Guide contains important information on:

   • general instructions for submission via Grants.gov, including the Grants.gov registration process and Grants.gov software requirements;

   • NSF-specific instructions for submission via Grants.gov, including creation of PDF files;

   • grant application package instructions;

   • required SF 424 (R&R) forms and instructions; and

   • NSF-specific forms and instructions.

4. Upon successful insertion of the Grants.gov submitted proposal in the NSF FastLane system, no further interaction with Grants.gov is required.

5. All further interaction is conducted via the NSF FastLane system.

Information from National Science Foundation, 2008: www.nsf.gov/pubs/policydocs/pappguide/nsf08_1/gpg_1.jsp#IA1.

USE INOFFENSIVE LANGUAGE

Writing to avoid offense is not merely a matter of politeness; it is a matter of perception. Language reflects attitudes, but it also helps to form attitudes. Writing inoffensively is one way to break down stereotypes. After writing, consider inviting a classmate or colleague to review your work for unintentional language that may have racist, sexist, ableist, or other negative overtones. It is the responsibility of business and technical communicators to ensure that their writing is free of harmful language.

Gender-Neutral Language Sexist language can include writing that relies only on male pronouns (*he, him, his*) as well as attributing specific professions to specific genders, such as only referring to doctors as men and nurses as women. In addition, using exclusively male or female pronouns can be exclusionary to those who do not identify as a binary gender. Solutions can include using the singular *they* if you are writing for a publication or audience that allows you to do so. Alternately, you might rewrite sentences to avoid the use of pronouns that do not refer to specific individuals.

For books about nonsexist writing, see the Selected Bibliography, p. 710. Many of the books in the "Usage and General Writing" section also address nonsexist writing.

◢|
GUIDELINES Avoiding Sexist Language

Follow these four suggestions for writing gender-neutral text.

▸ **Replace male-gender words with non-gender-specific words.** *Chairman,* for instance, can become *chairperson* or *chair*. *Firemen* are *firefighters; policemen* are *police officers.*

▸ **Switch to a different form of the verb.**

SEXIST   The operator must pass rigorous tests before he is promoted.

NONSEXIST   The operator must pass rigorous tests before being promoted.

▸ **Switch to the plural.**

NONSEXIST   Operators must pass rigorous tests before they are promoted.

Many organizations accept the use of plural pronouns with singular nouns, particularly in memos and other informal documents:

  If an employee wishes to apply for tuition reimbursement, they should consult Section 14.5 of the Employee Manual.

▸ **Address the reader directly**. Use *you* and *your* or the understood *you*.

  [You] Enter the serial number in the first text box.

People-First Language for Referring to People with Disabilities
Almost one in five Americans—some 41 million people—has a physical, sensory, emotional, or mental impairment that interferes with daily life (Institute on Disability, 2017). In writing about people with disabilities, use the "people-first" approach: treat the person as someone with a disability, not as someone defined by that disability. The disability is a condition the person has, not what the person is.

▶TECH TIP

Why To Customize Grammar-Checker Features

By customizing the rules that your word processor's grammar-checker uses to check your writing, you can get help with the problems you find most difficult to detect on your own, such as run-on sentences or wordiness. You can also set the feature to look for specific issues in a particular type of document. For example, in a lab report, you may want to allow passive-voice sentences, which you would typically avoid in most writing. Although Word's grammar-checker isn't foolproof, it can provide a basic review and uncover some important errors. If you are unsure about any suggestions made by the grammar-checker, do an online search to see if you can confirm its advice.

How To Customize Grammar-Checker Features

From Word's **File** menu, choose **Options**, then **Proofing**.

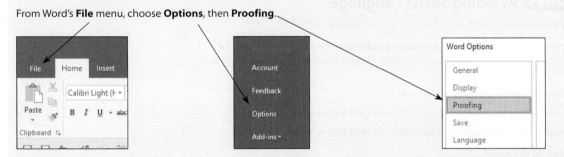

Under the section **When correcting spelling and grammar in Word**, the **Writing Style** drop-down menu allows you to choose **Grammar** (called **Grammar Only** in some versions of Word) or **Grammar & More** (called **Grammar & Style** in some versions of Word). The **Settings** box provides a long list of options that can be customized by selecting the issues you want Word to check for you.

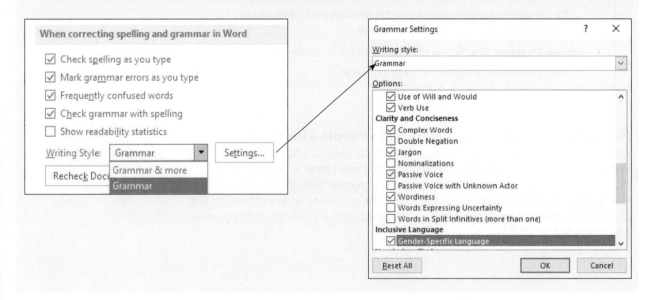

◢|

GUIDELINES Using the People-First Approach

When writing about people with disabilities, follow these five guidelines, which are based on Snow (2009).

▶ **Refer to the person first, the disability second.** Write *people with intellectual disability*, not *intellectually disabled people*.

▶ **Don't confuse *handicap* with *disability*.** *Disability* refers to the impairment or condition; *handicap* refers to the interaction between the person and his or her environment. A person can have a disability without being handicapped.

▶ **Don't refer to victimization.** Write *a person with AIDS*, not *an AIDS victim* or *an AIDS sufferer*.

▶ **Don't refer to a person as *wheelchair bound* or *confined to a wheelchair*.** People who use wheelchairs to get around are not confined.

▶ **Don't refer to people with disabilities as abnormal.** They are atypical, not abnormal.

Understanding Simplified English for Nonnative Speakers

Because English is the language of more than half of the world's scientific and technical communication, millions of nonnative speakers of English read technical documents in English. To address the information needs of such readers, many companies and professional associations have created versions of Simplified English. Each version consists of a basic set of grammar rules and a vocabulary of about 1,000 words, each of which has only one meaning: for example, *right* is the opposite of *left*; it does not mean "correct." Each version of Simplified English is made for a specific discipline. For example, ASD Simplified Technical English is intended for aerospace workers.

Here is a sample of text and its Simplified English version.

ORIGINAL VERSION   Before filling the gas tank, it is necessary to turn off the propane line to the refrigerator. Failure to do so significantly increases the risk of explosion.

SIMPLIFIED ENGLISH VERSION   Before you pump gasoline into the gas tank, turn off the propane line to the refrigerator. If you do not turn off the propane line, it could explode.

For more on Simplified English, see ASD (2010).

Preparing Text for Translation

As discussed in Chapter 5, more and more organizations prepare their documents and websites not only in English but also in other languages. Although you won't have to do the translating yourself, you should be aware of some simple steps you can take to make it easier for someone else to translate your writing. Luckily, most of the steps are the same ones you use to make your writing clear and easy to read in English.

- **Use short sentences.** Try for an average of no more than 20 words per sentence.

- **Use the active voice.** The active voice ("You should do this procedure after the engine has run for 100 hours") is easier to translate than the passive voice ("This procedure should be done after the engine has run for 100 hours").

- **Use simple words.** Translators will find *do* easier to translate than *perform*.

- **Include a glossary.** If you need to use technical terms, define them in a glossary.

For more on glossaries, see "Glossary and List of Symbols," Ch. 18, p. 500.

- **Use words that have only one meaning.** Write "This is the correct valve," not "This is the right valve," because *right* could also mean "the one on the right side."

- **Use pronouns carefully.** Don't write "Matthews phoned Hawkins to ask if he was scheduled to speak at the meeting." The translator might not know which person *he* refers to. Instead, write "Matthews phoned Hawkins to ask if Hawkins was scheduled to speak at the meeting."

- **Avoid jokes, puns, and culture-bound references.** Humor doesn't translate well. If you refer to a box of computer pointing devices as "a box of mice," the translator might translate the words literally because the device (a mouse) is not known by that name everywhere. Also avoid other culture-bound references, such as sports metaphors (*hat trick* or *grand slam*) or references to national heroes or holidays (*George Washington* or *Fourth of July*).

WRITER'S CHECKLIST

Grammar

Did you

- [ ] avoid sentence fragments? *(p. 220)*
- [ ] avoid comma splices? *(p. 221)*
- [ ] avoid run-on sentences? *(p. 221)*
- [ ] avoid ambiguous pronoun references? *(p. 222)*
- [ ] compare items clearly? *(p. 223)*
- [ ] use adjectives clearly? *(p. 224)*
- [ ] maintain subject–verb agreement? *(p. 225)*
- [ ] maintain pronoun–antecedent agreement? *(p. 225)*
- [ ] use tenses correctly? *(p. 225)*

Sentences

☐ Are the sentences structured with the new or important information near the end? *(p. 226)*

☐ Are the sentences of the appropriate length: neither long and difficult to understand nor short and choppy? *(p. 227)*

☐ Does each sentence focus on the "real" subject? *(p. 228)*

☐ Have you limited the number of expletives used as sentence openers? *(p. 229)*

☐ Does each sentence focus on the "real" verb, without weak nominalizations? *(p. 229)*

☐ Have you used parallel structure in your sentences? *(p. 230)*

☐ Have you used restrictive and nonrestrictive modifiers appropriately? *(p. 231)*

☐ Have you eliminated misplaced modifiers, squinting modifiers, and dangling modifiers? *(p. 232)*

Words and Phrases

Did you

☐ select an appropriate level of formality? *(p. 234)*

☐ use active and passive voice appropriately? *(p. 235)*

☐ use precise words? *(p. 237)*

☐ provide adequate detail? *(p. 237)*

☐ avoid ambiguity? *(p. 237)*

☐ avoid unnecessary jargon? *(p. 237)*

☐ use positive rather than negative constructions? *(p. 238)*

☐ avoid long noun strings? *(p. 239)*

☐ avoid clichés? *(p. 239)*

☐ avoid euphemisms? *(p. 239)*

☐ avoid stating the obvious? *(p. 240)*

☐ avoid filler? *(p. 241)*

☐ avoid unnecessary prepositional phrases? *(p. 241)*

☐ use the most concise phrases? *(p. 241)*

☐ avoid fancy words? *(p. 243)*

☐ use nonsexist language? *(p. 245)*

☐ use the people-first approach in referring to people with disabilities? *(p. 245)*

☐ make your document easy to translate? *(p. 248)*

EXERCISES

NOTE: Pay close attention to what you are being asked to do in each exercise, and do only as much revising as is necessary. Take special care to preserve the meaning of the original material. If necessary, invent reasonable details.

1. Referring to the advice on p. 220, rewrite each of the following sentence fragments to form a complete sentence.

   a. Nine bones from a Pacific walrus that were found in a coffin beneath St. Pancras Railway Station in London.

   b. The physical impossibility of knowing both the position and the momentum of a particle at the same time.

2. Referring to the advice on p. 221, rewrite each of the following sentences to eliminate comma splices.

   a. Porsche has won the J. D. Power new-model satisfaction award more than any other car maker, the German company is expected to win next year, too.

   b. The federal Bureau of Safety and Environmental Enforcement is developing new regulations for offshore oil and gas operations in the Arctic, these regulations are expected to be ready for review later this year.

3. Referring to the advice on pp. 221–22, rewrite each of the following sentences to eliminate run-ons.

   a. A group of US scientists has encoded a 53,000-word book entirely in DNA this means DNA could become a future means of storing large amounts of data.

   b. Now you can burn your digital music library to DVDs burning to DVDs gives you a significant increase in storage space (4.7 Gb for a standard DVD v. 700 Mb for a CD).

4. Referring to the advice on pp. 222–23, rewrite each of the following sentences to eliminate ambiguous pronoun references.

   a. Kathleen Norris is in charge of analyzing the summer-semester orientation session, which is expected to last five days.

   b. The football program and the basketball programs are the highest grossing of the seventeen sports at the university. They posted revenues of $1.9 million last year.

5. Referring to the advice on pp. 223–24, rewrite each of the following sentences to eliminate unclear comparisons.

    a. The experiences of children with disabilities differ from adults with disabilities.

    b. Universities enter into contracts with food-service providers more than hospitals.

6. Referring to the advice on p. 224, rewrite each of the following sentences to eliminate unclear adjectives.

    a. More Latinos in the United States than ever are watching news on English-language television programs.

    b. There are four parking spots on campus that may be used only by Nobel Prize winning faculty.

7. Referring to the advice on p. 225, rewrite each of the following sentences so that it maintains subject–verb agreement.

    a. Samples from the survey is subject to sampling and nonsampling errors.

    b. The typical question received at our call centers are not answered in any of the user guides.

8. Referring to the advice on p. 225, rewrite each of the following sentences so that it maintains pronoun–antecedent agreement.

    a. A researcher who has submitted all the IRB forms is still required to submit their proposal to the Research Committee.

    b. The team were assembled to carry out the study and report its findings to management.

9. Referring to the advice on pp. 225–26, rewrite each of the following sentences to eliminate incorrect use of tenses.

    a. Galileo paid dearly for his belief that the Earth revolved around the Sun.

    b. All the seminars finished by the time I arrived at 3:00 on Thursday afternoon.

10. The following sentences might be too long for some readers. Referring to the advice on pp. 227–28, break each sentence into two or more sentences.

    a. If we get the contract, we must be ready by June 1 with the necessary personnel and equipment, so with this in mind a staff meeting, which all group managers are expected to attend, is scheduled for February 12.

    b. Although we had a frank discussion with Backer's legal staff, we were unable to get them to specify what they would be looking for in an out-of-court settlement, but they gave us a strong impression that they would rather settle out of court.

11. The following examples contain choppy, abrupt sentences. Referring to the advice on p. 228, combine sentences to create a smoother style.

    a. I need a figure on the surrender value of a policy. The number of the policy is A4399827. Can you get me this figure by tomorrow?

    b. The supervisor is responsible for processing the outgoing mail. He is also responsible for maintaining and operating the equipment.

12. In the following sentences, the real subjects are buried in prepositional phrases or obscured by expletives. Referring to the advice on pp. 228–29, revise the sentences so that the real subjects appear prominently.

    a. There has been a decrease in the number of students enrolled in our training sessions.

    b. The use of in-store demonstrations has resulted in a dramatic increase in business.

13. In the following sentences, unnecessary nominalization obscures the real verb. Referring to the advice on pp. 229–30, revise the sentences to focus on the real verb.

    a. Pollution constitutes a threat to the Matthews Wildlife Preserve.

    b. Evaluation of the gumming tendency of the four tire types will be accomplished by comparing the amount of rubber that can be scraped from the tires.

14. Referring to the advice on pp. 230–31, revise the following sentences to eliminate nonparallelism.

    a. The next two sections of the manual discuss how to analyze the data, the conclusions that can be drawn from your analysis, and how to decide what further steps are needed before establishing a journal list.

    b. In the box, we should include a copy of the documentation, the cables, and the docking station.

15. Referring to the advice on pp. 230–31, revise the following sentences to correct punctuation or pronoun errors related to modifiers.

    a. This problem that has been traced to manufacturing delays, has resulted in our losing four major contracts.

    b. Please get in touch with Tom Harvey who is updating the instructions.

16. Referring to the advice on pp. 231–33, revise the following sentences to eliminate the misplaced modifiers.

    a. Over the past three years we have estimated that eight hours per week are spent on this problem.

    b. Information provided by this program is displayed at the close of the business day on the information board.

17. Referring to the advice on pp. 251–52, revise the following sentences to eliminate the dangling modifiers.

    a. To examine the chemical homogeneity of the plaque sample, one plaque was cut into nine sections.

    b. The boats in production could be modified in time for the February debut by choosing this method.

18. Referring to the advice on p. 234–35, revise the following informal sentences to make them moderately formal.

    a. The biggest problem faced by multimedia designers is that users freak if they don't see a button — or, heaven forbid, if they have to make up their own buttons!

    b. If the University of Arizona can't figure out where to dump its low-level radioactive waste, Uncle Sam could pull the plug on millions of dollars of research grants.

19. Referring to the advice on pp. 235–37, rewrite the following sentences to remove inappropriate use of the passive voice.

    a. Mistakes were made.

    b. Come to the reception desk when you arrive. A packet with your name on it can be picked up there.

20. Referring to the advice on p. 237, revise the following sentences by replacing the vague elements with specific information. Make up any reasonable details.

    a. The chemical spill in the lab caused extensive damage.

    b. Analysis of the soil beneath the new stadium revealed an interesting fact.

21. Referring to the advice on pp. 237–38, revise the following sentences to remove unnecessary jargon.

    a. We need to be prepared for blowback from the announcement.

    b. Police apprehended the perpetrator and placed her under arrest directly adjacent to the scene of the incident.

22. Referring to the advice on p. 238, revise the following sentences to convert the negative constructions to positive constructions.

    a. Management accused Williams of filing trip reports that were not accurate.

    b. We must make sure that all our representatives do not act unprofessionally to potential clients.

23. General readers might find the following sentences awkward or difficult to understand. Referring to the advice on p. 239, rewrite the following sentences to eliminate the long noun strings.

    a. The research team discovered a glycerin-initiated, alkylene-oxide-based, long-chain polyether.

    b. We are considering purchasing a digital-imaging capable, diffusion-pump equipped, tungsten-gun SEM.

24. Referring to the advice on p. 239, revise the following sentences to eliminate clichés.

    a. If we are to survive this difficult period, we are going to have to keep our ears to the ground and our noses to the grindstone.

    b. At the end of the day, if everyone is on the same page and it turns out to be the wrong page, you're really up a creek without a paddle.

25. Referring to the advice on pp. 239–40, revise the following sentences to eliminate euphemisms.

    a. Downsizing our workforce will enable our division to achieve a more favorable cash-flow profile.

    b. Of course, accident statistics can be expected to show a moderate increase in response to a streamlining of the training schedule.

26. Referring to the advice on p. 240, revise the following sentences to eliminate the obvious material.

    a. To register to take a course offered by the university, you must first determine whether the university will be offering that course that semester.

    b. The starting date of the project had to be postponed for a certain period of time due to a delay in obtaining the necessary authorization from the Project Oversight Committee.

27. Referring to the advice on p. 241, revise the following sentences to remove meaningless filler.

    a. For all intents and purposes, our company's long-term success depends to a certain degree on various factors that are in general difficult to foresee.

b. The presentation was generally well received for the most part, despite the fact that we received a rather small number of questionnaire responses.

28. Referring to the advice on p. 241, revise the following sentences to remove the redundancies.

   a. In grateful appreciation of your patronage, we are pleased to offer you this free gift as a small token gesture of our gratitude.

   b. An anticipated major breakthrough in storage technology will allow us to proceed ahead in the continuing evolution of our products.

29. Referring to the advice on p. 241, revise the following sentences to eliminate unnecessary prepositional phrases.

   a. The complexity of the module will hamper the ability of the operator in the diagnosis of problems in equipment configuration.

   b. The purpose of this test of your aptitudes is to help you with the question of the decision of which major to enroll in.

30. Referring to the advice on pp. 242–43, revise the following sentences to make them more concise.

   a. The instruction manual for the new copier is lacking in clarity and completeness.

   b. We remain in communication with our sales staff on a weekly basis.

31. Referring to the advice on p. 243, revise the following sentences to eliminate fancy words.

   a. This state-of-the-art soda-dispensing module is to be utilized by Marketing Department personnel.

   b. We have failed to furnish the proposal to the proper agency by the mandated date by which such proposals must be in receipt.

32. Referring to the advice on p. 245, revise the following sentences to eliminate sexist language.

   a. Each doctor is asked to make sure he follows the standard procedure for handling Medicare forms.

   b. Policemen are required to live in the city in which they work.

33. Referring to the advice on pp. 245–47, revise the following sentences to eliminate the offensive language.

   a. This year, the number of female lung-cancer victims is expected to rise because of increased smoking.

   b. Mentally retarded people are finding greater opportunities in the service sector of the economy.

34. **TEAM EXERCISE** Form small teams. Have one person on the team distribute a multipage document he or she has written recently, either in this class or in another. Have each member annotate a copy of the document according to the principles of sentence effectiveness discussed in this chapter. For advice on how to critique a draft effectively, see Ch. 4, p. 72. Then have each team member write a summary statement about the document, highlighting its effective techniques of sentence construction and possible improvements. Meet as a team, study these annotated documents, and write a memo to your instructor describing the sentence features cited by more than one team member, as well as those features cited by only one member. Overall, what are the basic differences between the team members' annotations and the summary statements? Do you think that, as a general practice, it would be worthwhile to have a draft reviewed and annotated by more than one person? What have you learned about the usefulness of peer review?

CASE 10: Revising a Document for Nonnative Speakers and for Translation

As an assistant in the U.S. Transportation Security Administration (TSA) Office of Traveler Information, you've been asked to revise a policy statement on airport screening into a consumer guide for travelers. Your department intends to translate the guide into a dozen languages, and your manager emphasizes that the writing must be as clear and as concise as possible. If your instructor has assigned it, go to Achieve to access the policy statement and get to work.

Designing Print and Online Documents

THE DESIGN OF a print or online document can help a writer achieve many goals: to entertain, to amaze, to intrigue, to sell. In technical communication, the goal is typically to help the reader learn something, perform a task, or accept a point of view. When you look at a well-designed page or screen, you intuitively understand how to use it.

Design refers to the physical appearance of print and online documents. For print documents, design features include binding, page size, typography, and use of color. For online documents, many of the same design elements apply, but there are unique elements, too. On a web page, for instance, there are navigation bars, headers and footers, and (sometimes) tables of contents and site maps.

The effectiveness of a document depends largely on how well it is designed, because readers see the document before they actually read it. In less than a second, the document makes an impression on them, one that might determine how well they read it — or even whether they decide to read it at all.

Goals of Document Design

In designing a document, you have five major goals:

1. **To make a good impression on readers.** Your document should reflect your own professional standards and those of your company.

2. **To help readers understand the structure and organization of the information.** As they navigate a document, readers should know where they are and how to get where they are headed. They should also be able to see the relationship, hierarchical and otherwise, between one piece of information and another.

3. **To help readers locate and access the information they need.** Usually, people don't read every word in a print document, and they don't study every screen of an online document. In print documents, design elements (such as tabs, icons, and color), page design, and typography help readers find the information they need quickly and easily. In online documents, design elements are critically important because readers can see only what is displayed on the screen; without design elements to help them navigate, they are stranded.

4. **To help readers understand the information.** Effective design can clarify information. For instance, designing a set of instructions so that the text describing each step is next to the accompanying graphic makes the instructions easier to understand. An online document with a navigation bar displaying the main sections is easier to understand than an online document without one.

5. **To help readers remember the information.** An effective design helps readers create a visual image of the information, making it easier to remember. Text boxes, pull quotes, and similar design elements help readers remember important explanations and passages.

Understanding Design Principles

One of your biggest challenges in thinking about how to design a document is that, more than ever, readers control how the document appears. When they view documents online, through websites, apps, and other kinds of programs, readers can control many aspects of the design, including color and the size, shape, and location of objects on the screen. A significant variable that you have to consider is screen size. Some devices on which your readers will use your document will be as large as big-screen TVs, whereas others will be as small as wrist watches.

In this chapter, the term *print document* will be used to refer to documents that are designed to be printed on paper, such as letters, memos, and reports, regardless of whether readers hold pieces of paper in their hands or view the documents online. The term *online document* will be used to refer to documents that are designed to be used online, through websites, apps, and other software.

Because there are so many different types of print and online documents used in so many different environments by so many different people for so many different purposes, it is impossible to provide detailed advice about "how to design" a technical document. Still, there are some powerful and durable principles that can help you design any kind of print or online document. The following list is based on Robin Williams's *The Non-designer's Design Book* (2015), which describes four principles of design: proximity, alignment, repetition, and contrast. All of these principles are illustrated in Figure 11.1 on pages 257–58.

- **Proximity.** The principle of proximity is simple: if two items appear close to each other, the reader will interpret them as related to each other. If they are far apart, the reader will interpret them as unrelated. Text describing a graphic should be positioned close to the graphic.

- **Alignment.** The principle of alignment says that you should consciously line up text and graphics along a real or imaginary vertical axis so that the reader can understand the relationships among elements.

- **Repetition.** The principle of repetition says that you should format the same kind of information in the same way so that readers can recognize consistent patterns. For example, all first-level headings should have the same typeface, type size, spacing above and below, and so forth. This repetition signals a connection between headings, making the content easier to understand. Other elements that are used to create consistent visual patterns are colors, icons, rules (straight lines), and screens (shaded backgrounds).

- **Contrast.** The principle of contrast says that the human eye is drawn to—and the brain interprets—differences in appearance between two items. For example, the principle of contrast explains why black print is easier to read against a white background than against a dark gray background; why 16-point type stands out more clearly against 8-point type than against 12-point type; and why information printed in a color, such as red, grabs readers' attention when the information around it is printed in black.

Planning Your Design

In a typical day at work, you might produce a number of documents without having to worry about design at all. Blog posts, text messages, presentation slides, and memos that use standard company templates—these applications and others present no design challenges either because you *cannot* design them or because you don't have the *authority* to design them.

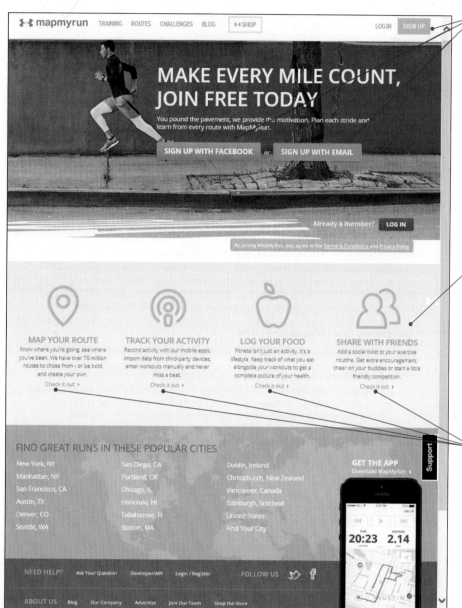

Contrast: Brightly colored buttons highlight the places the web designer wants users to click.

Proximity: Text and graphics are clearly related by their position. The textual descriptions are placed directly below the icons to which they refer.

Repetition: Repeated type styles, sizes, and colors indicate headings, descriptions, and links.

FIGURE 11.1   Effective Use of Design Principles   *(continued)*
MapMyRun.

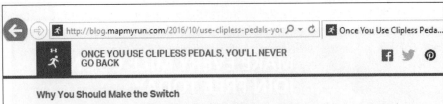

http://blog.mapmyrun.com/2016/10/use-clipless-pedals-you ☆ ▾ C | Once You Use Clipless Peda...

ONCE YOU USE CLIPLESS PEDALS, YOU'LL NEVER GO BACK

Why You Should Make the Switch

Securing your foot to a pedal in a fixed position is the most efficient way to turn the energy you create into forward motion. When you're clipped in, you can maintain more consistent force throughout the circular motion of pedaling — instead of a less effective pushing down motion in a flat pedal.

See, clipless pedals allow you to pull up on the pedals on the upstroke (6 o'clock to 12 o'clock) and incorporate additional, bigger muscle groups such as the hamstrings and glutes. This not only improves efficiency, but it also helps to keep you from fatiguing as quickly, as you can produce more power on the bike.

On top of increased efficiency, a clipless pedal system is easier on the joints. When your cleat is lined up properly, your foot will be in the correct position over the pedal axle, which helps lessen strain on the knee joint. This makes it much easier to pedal at a higher cadence of around 90–100 revolutions per minute without losing contact with the pedal, and it also helps ease strain on the knee that comes from pedaling at lower rpms in larger gear ratios.

The Different Types of Pedals and Cleats

In terms of which cleat-pedal system you need, there are three main options:

1. **Two-bolt cleats:** Used most often by mountain bikers, off-road cyclists and commuters (as well as spin class attendees), two-bolt cleats are much smaller and can be used with a shoe that's more flexible and easier to walk in. They're also commonly used with pedal systems that allow for dual-sided entry, which can be slightly easier for beginners. Shimano SPD and Crankbrothers are two major manufacturers.
2. **Three-bolt cleats:** This is the most common design for road cyclists. The cleat is fairly large and triangular in shape, and it screw into a stiff carbon or fiberglass sole on a dedicated road cycling shoe. Entry on most road cycling pedal designs is one-sided. Examples of major pedal manufacturers include Shimano SPD-SL, Look and Time.
3. **Four-bolt cleats:** As of right now, Speedplay is the only manufacturer using a four-bolt cleat design. Unlike the three-bolt design, Speedplay's offering has a locking mechanism on the cleat instead of the pedal. The rectangular cleat is placed over a smaller, circular pedal that allows more side-to-side float of the foot during the pedaling motion. This design also allows for dual-sided entry, which can make clipping in a bit easier. In terms of performance, the choice between this design and the generally more secure three-bolt design will likely come down to personal preference.

Keep in mind that cleats are usually only compatible with the type of pedal you choose. For instance, if you decide to buy Look Keo Classic pedals, you will also need the Look three-bolt cleats that work with that pedal. Likewise, Shimano three-bolt cleats will have a slightly different design and will work exclusively with Shimano pedals.

Alignment: The writer uses two levels of headings, each reinforced by a different alignment.

FIGURE 11.1 **Effective Use of Design Principles** *(continued)*

Source: MapMyRun, 2017: http://mapymyrun.com.
MapMyRun.

You will, however, have a say in the design of many documents you produce or to which you contribute. In such a case, the first step in designing the document is to plan. Analyze your audience and purpose, and then determine your resources.

ANALYZE YOUR AUDIENCE AND PURPOSE

Consider factors such as your readers' knowledge of the subject, their attitudes, their reasons for reading, the way they will be using the document, and the kinds of tasks they will perform. For instance, if you are writing a benefits manual for employees, you know that few people will read it from start to finish but that many people will refer to it. Therefore, you should include navigational tools: a table of contents, an index, tabs, and so forth.

Think too about your audience's expectations. Readers expect to see certain kinds of information presented in certain ways. Try to fulfill those expectations. For example, hyperlinks in websites are often emphasized in some fashion and presented in an alternative color.

For more about analyzing your audience, see Ch. 5. For more about tables of contents, see "Table of Contents," Ch. 18, p. 496.

If you are writing for multicultural readers, keep in mind that many aspects of design vary from one culture to another. In memos, letters, reports, and manuals, you may see significant differences in design practice. The best advice, therefore, is to study documents from the culture you are addressing. Here are a few design elements to look for:

- **Paper size.** Paper size will dictate some aspects of your page design. If your document will be printed in another country, find out about standard paper sizes in that country.

- **Typeface preferences.** One survey found that Korean readers were more likely to find highly stylized typefaces illegible in comparison to non-Korean readers (Peterson, 2017).

Typography is discussed in "Typography" on pp. 269–75.

- **Color preferences.** In China, for example, red suggests happiness, whereas in Japan it suggests danger.

- **Text direction.** If some members of your audience read from right to left but others read from left to right, you might arrange your graphics vertically, from top to bottom; everybody reads from top to bottom. Or you might use Arabic numerals to indicate the order in which items are to be read (Horton, 1993).

Another important consideration is accessibility. Up to one-fifth of your online audience may have visual, hearing, mobility, or cognitive impairments that could make it difficult for them to use your online document (WebAIM, 2019). For more details about legal and ethical recommendations for designing accessible websites, see Consider Matters of Accessibility on pages 287–90.

Think, too, about your purpose or purposes. For example, imagine that you are opening a dental office and you want to create a website. The first question is *What is the purpose of the site?* It's one thing to provide information on your hours and directions to the office. But do you also want to direct

For more about analyzing your purpose, see "Understanding Audience and Purpose," Ch. 5, p. 90.

patients to high-quality dental information? To enable them to set up or change appointments or ask you a question? Each of these purposes affects the design, whether the document is going to be printed or online.

DETERMINE YOUR RESOURCES

Think about your resources of time, money, and equipment. Short, informal documents are usually produced in-house; more ambitious projects are often subcontracted to specialists. If your organization has a technical-publications department, consult the people there about scheduling and budgeting.

- **Time.** What is your schedule? To come up with a sophisticated design you might need professionals at service bureaus or print shops or specialists in online production. These professionals can require weeks or months.

- **Money.** Can you afford professional designers, print shops, and online-content developers? Most managers would budget thousands of dollars to design an annual report but not an in-house newsletter.

- **Equipment.** Complex designs require graphics and web software, as well as layout programs. A basic laser printer can produce attractive documents in black and white, but you need a more expensive printer for high-resolution color.

For information on designing online documents, see "Designing Online Documents," p. 280, and "Designing Online Pages," p. 290.

Designing Print Documents

Before you design the individual pages of a printed document, design the overall document. Decide whether to use paper of standard size (8.5 × 11 inches) or another size, choose a grade of paper, and decide how you will bind the pages together. Decide on the navigational elements you will include, such as a table of contents, index, and tabs. You want the different elements to work together to accomplish your objectives, and you want to stay within your budget for producing and (perhaps) shipping. Then think about how to design the document pages.

SIZE

Size refers to two aspects of print-document design: page size and page count.

- **Page size.** Think about the best page size for your information and about how the document will be used. For a procedures manual that will sit on a shelf most of the time, three-hole 8.5 × 11-inch paper is a good choice. For a software tutorial that must fit easily on a desk while the reader works at the keyboard, consider a 5.5 × 8.5-inch size. Paper comes precut in a number of sizes, including 4.5 × 6 inches and 6 × 9 inches. Although paper can be cut to any size, nonstandard sizes are more expensive.

- **Page count.** Because paper is expensive and heavy, you want as few pages as possible, especially if you are printing and mailing many copies. And there is a psychological factor, too: people don't want to spend a lot of time reading technical documents. Therefore, if you can design a document so that it is 15 pages long rather than 30—but still attractive and easy to read—your readers will appreciate it.

PAPER

Paper is made not only in different standard sizes but also in different weights and with different coatings. Heavier paper costs more than lighter paper but provides better resolution for text and graphics. Coated paper is stronger and more durable than noncoated paper and provides the best resolution, but some coatings can produce a glare. To deal with this problem, designers often choose paper with a slight tint.

Work closely with printing professionals. They know, for example, about UV-coated paper, which greatly reduces fading, and about recycled paper, which is continually improving in quality and decreasing in price.

BINDINGS

Although the pages of a very short document can be attached with a paper clip or a staple, longer documents require more sophisticated binding techniques. Table 11.1 illustrates and describes the four types of bindings commonly used in technical communication.

TABLE 11.1   Common Types of Binding

Loose-leaf binders. Loose-leaf binders are convenient when pages must be added and removed frequently. A high-quality binder can cost as much as several dollars.

Ring or spiral binders. The wire or plastic coils or combs that hold the pages together enable you to open the document flat on a desk or even fold it over so that it takes up the space of only one page. Print shops can bind documents of almost any size in plastic coils or combs.

© Macmillan. Photo by Regina Tavani.

Saddle binding. The document is opened to its middle pages, and large staples are inserted from the outside. Saddle binding is impractical for large documents.

© Macmillan. Photo by Regina Tavani.

Perfect binding. Pages are glued together along the spine edge, and a cover is attached. Perfect binding, used in book publishing, produces the most formal appearance, but it is relatively fragile, and the open document usually does not lie flat.

▶TECH TIP

Why To Set Up Pages

An important key to meeting your audience's needs and expectations is effective page layout. Microsoft Word and other programs provide default page-layout settings, which you can easily adjust for any document you create in order to meet the needs of your audience and accomplish your purpose.

How To Set Up Pages

In the **Page Setup** group, use the **Page Setup** dialog box launcher to display the **Page Setup** dialog box.

Use the **Margins**, **Paper**, and **Layout** tabs to specify such design elements as page margins, paper orientation, paper size, starting locations for new sections, and header and footer placement.

You can also use the drop-down menus on the **Page Setup** group to control many of the same design elements.

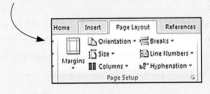

NAVIGATIONAL AIDS

In a well-designed document, readers can easily find the information they seek. Most navigational aids use the design principles of repetition and contrast to help readers navigate the document. Table 11.2 explains six common kinds of navigational aids.

TABLE 11.2	Typical Navigational Aids	
IF YOU WANT TO...	**NAVIGATION AID**	**EXAMPLE**
Symbolize actions or ideas	**Media** ▶ YouTube — Watch, upload and share videos 📖 Books — Search the full text of books 📰 News — Search thousands of news stories 🌀 Picasa — Find, edit and share your photos	**Icons.** Icons are pictures that symbolize actions or ideas. Perhaps the most important icon is the stop sign, which alerts you to a warning. Icons depend on repetition: every time you see the warning icon, you know what kind of information the writer is presenting. Don't be too clever in thinking up icons. One computer manual uses a cocktail glass about to fall over to symbolize "tip." This is a bad idea, because the pun is not functional: when you think of a cocktail glass, you don't think of a tip for using computers. Don't use too many different icons, or your readers will forget what each one represents.

(continued)

TABLE 11.2   Typical Navigational Aids *(continued)*

IF YOU WANT TO...	NAVIGATION AID	EXAMPLE
Draw attention to important features or sections of the document *For more about using color, see "Using Color Effectively," Ch. 12, p. 309.*	 Here green is used to emphasize the titles of the sections, the box at the top left, and the bar along the edge of the page.	**Color.** A strong visual attribute is color. Use color to draw attention to important features of the document, such as warnings, hints, major headings, and section tabs. But use it sparingly, or it will overpower everything else in the document. Color exploits the principles of repetition (every item in a particular color is logically linked) and contrast (items in one color contrast with items in another color). Use color logically. Third-level headings should not be in color, for example, if first- and second-level headings are printed in black. Using paper of a different color for each section of a document is another way to simplify access.
Enable readers to identify and flip to sections		**Dividers and tabs.** You are already familiar with dividers and tabs from loose-leaf notebooks. A tab provides a place for a label, which enables readers to identify and flip to a particular section. Sometimes dividers and tabs are color-coded. Tabs work according to the design principle of contrast: the tabs literally stick out.
Refer readers to related information within the document	*Read...* *To learn to...* Ch. 1 connect to the router Ch. 2 set up a firewall	**Cross-reference tables.** These tables, which exploit the principle of alignment, refer readers to related discussions.
Help readers see where they are in the document	[image of handbook page with heading CARS] General Services Administration	**Headers and footers.** Headers and footers help readers see where they are in the document. In a book, for example, the headers on the left-hand pages might repeat the chapter number and title; those on the right-hand pages might contain the most recent first-level heading. Sometimes writers build other identifying information into the headers. For example, your instructor might ask you to identify your assignments with a header like the following: "Smith, Progress Report, English 302, page 6." Headers and footers work according to the principle of repetition: readers learn where to look on the page to see where they are in the document.

(continued)

TABLE 11.2 Typical Navigational Aids (*continued*)		
IF YOU WANT TO...	**NAVIGATION AID**	**EXAMPLE**
Help readers find specific material in the document	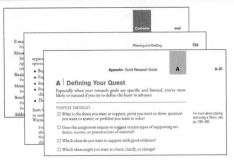	**Page numbering.** For one-sided documents, use Arabic numerals in the upper right corner, although the first page of most documents does not have a number on it. For two-sided documents, put the page numbers near the outside margins.

Complex documents often use two number sequences: lowercase Roman numerals (i, ii, and so on) for front matter and Arabic numerals for the body. There is no number on the title page, but the page following it is ii.

Appendixes are often paginated with a letter and number combination: Appendix A begins with page A-1, followed by A-2, and so on; Appendix B starts with page B-1.

Sometimes documents list the total number of pages in the document (so recipients can be sure they have all of them). The second page is "2 of 17," and the third page is "3 of 17."

Documents that will be updated are sometimes numbered by section: Section 3 begins with page 3-1, followed by 3-2; Section 4 begins with 4-1. This way, a complete revision of one section does not affect the page numbering of subsequent sections.

Designing Print Pages

In a well-designed printed page of technical communication, the reader can recognize patterns, such as where to look for certain kinds of information.

PAGE LAYOUT

Every page has two kinds of space: white space and space devoted to text and graphics. The best way to design a page is to make a grid: a drawing of what the page will look like. In making a grid, you decide how to use white space and determine how many columns to have on the page.

◢ **GUIDELINES** Understanding Learning Theory and Page Design

In designing the page, create visual patterns that help readers find, understand, and remember information. Three principles of learning theory, the result of research into how people learn, can help you design effective pages: chunking, queuing, and filtering.

▶ **Chunking.** People understand information best if it is delivered to them in chunks — small units — rather than all at once. For single-spaced type, chunking involves double-spacing between paragraphs, as shown in Figure 11.2.

a. Without chunking

An unmanned aircraft system (UAS), sometimes called a drone, is an aircraft without a human pilot onboard — instead, the UAS is controlled from an operator on the ground. When you fly a drone in the United States, it is your responsibility to understand and abide by the rules.

Recreational or hobby UAS use is defined as flying for enjoyment and not for work, business purposes, or for compensation or hire. There are two ways for recreational or hobby UAS fliers to operate in the National Airspace System in accordance with the law and/or FAA regulations. Each of the two options has specific requirements that the UAS operator must follow. The decision as to which option to follow is up to the individual operator.

The first option is to fly in accordance with the Special Rule for Model Aircraft (Public Law 112-95 Section 336). Under this rule, operators must fly for hobby or recreational purposes only; follow a community-based set of safety guidelines; fly the UAS within visual line-of-sight; give way to manned aircraft; provide prior notification to the airport and air traffic control tower, if one is present, when flying within 5 miles of an airport; fly UAS that weigh no more than 55 lb unless certified by a community-based organization; and register the aircraft (UAS over 0.55 lb and less than 55 lb can be registered online at registermyuas .faa.gov; UAS 55 lb or greater must be registered through the FAA's paper-based process).

The second option is to fly in accordance with the FAA's Small UAS Rule (Part 107). This requires operators to obtain a remote pilot certificate or be under the direct supervision of someone who holds such a certificate; register the aircraft as a non-modeler at register-myuas.faa.gov; and follow all the operating rules in accordance with the regulation.

b. With chunking

An unmanned aircraft system (UAS), sometimes called a drone, is an aircraft without a human pilot onboard — instead, the UAS is controlled from an operator on the ground. When you fly a drone in the United States, it is your responsibility to understand and abide by the rules.

Recreational Use of Unmanned Aircraft Systems

Recreational or hobby UAS use is defined as flying for enjoyment and not for work, business purposes, or for compensation or hire. There are two ways for recreational or hobby UAS fliers to operate in the National Airspace System in accordance with the law and FAA regulations. Each of the two options has specific requirements that the UAS operator must follow. The decision as to which option to follow is up to the individual operator.

Option 1

The first option is to fly in accordance with the Special Rule for Model Aircraft (Public Law 112-95 Section 336). Under this rule, operators must do all of the following:

- Fly for hobby or recreational purposes only.
- Follow a community-based set of safety guidelines.
- Fly the UAS within visual line-of-sight.
- Give way to manned aircraft.
- Provide prior notification to the airport and air traffic control tower, if one is present, when flying within 5 miles of an airport.
- Fly UAS that weigh no more than 55 lb unless certified by a community-based organization.
- Register the aircraft with the FAA.

Option 2

The second option is to fly in accordance with the FAA's Small UAS Rule (Part 107). This requires operators to obtain a remote pilot certificate or be under the direct supervision of someone who holds such a certificate; register the aircraft as a non-modeler at registermyuas .faa.gov; and follow all the operating rules in accordance with the regulation.

FIGURE 11.2   Chunking

Chunking emphasizes units of related information. Note how the use of headings and lists creates clear chunks of information.
Text adapted from Federal Aviation Administration, 2016: www.faa.gov.

▶ **Queuing.** Queuing refers to creating visual distinctions to indicate levels of importance. More emphatic elements — those with bigger type or boldface type — are more important than less emphatic ones. Another visual element of queuing is alignment. Designers start more important information closer to the left margin and indent less important information. (An exception is titles, which are often centered in reports in the United States.) Figure 11.3 shows queuing.

▶ **Filtering.** Filtering is the use of visual patterns to distinguish various types of information. Introductory material might be displayed in larger type, and notes might appear in italics, another typeface, and a smaller size. Figure 11.4 shows filtering.

(continued)

STRATEGIC GOALS AND RESULTS

To assess FY 2012 results, program managers examined quantitative and qualitative indicators to determine whether indicators met previously established annual targets. Managers also considered how the results impact the achievement of the Department and USAID's strategic goals. A rating was then assigned to each indicator based on the analysis. In the Strategic Goals and Results sections that follows, 16 illustrative indicators are highlighted to provide the reader with timely data and analysis of key achievements reported during FY 2012.

STRATEGIC GOAL 1:
ACHIEVING PEACE AND SECURITY

Preserve international peace by preventing regional conflicts and transnational crime, combating terrorism and weapons of mass destruction, and supporting homeland security and security cooperation.

PUBLIC BENEFIT

U.S. policy states that the security of U.S. citizens at home and abroad is best guaranteed when countries and societies are secure, free, prosperous, and at peace. The Department, USAID, and their partners seek to strengthen their diplomatic and development capabilities, as well as those of international partners and allies, to prevent or mitigate conflict, stabilize countries in crisis, promote regional stability, and protect civilians. In 2012, a profound and dramatic wave of change continued to sweep across the Middle East as people courageously stood up to their governments to express their legitimate aspirations for greater political participation and economic opportunity. Our close relationship with our inter-agency partners has enabled the United States to strengthen our national security and provide leadership in conflict areas, such as the Middle East, to promote democratic and political reforms and ensure a voice for all peoples, including women, in building stable and peaceful societies.

Secretary of State Clinton delivers remarks at the Global Counterterrorism Forum in Istanbul, Turkey, June 7, 2012. Department of State

SUMMARY OF PERFORMANCE AND RESOURCES

The Department and USAID allocated $16.928 billion toward this Strategic Goal in FY 2012, which is 32 percent of the total State-USAID budget supporting all strategic goals. The performance of the illustrative indicator is provided in the following section.

FY 2012 Resources Invested: $16.928 Billion

State Operations: $4.427 billion — State Operations
Foreign Operations: $10.101 billion — Foreign Operations

DEPARTMENT OF STATE USAID JOINT SUMMARY OF PERFORMANCE AND FINANCIAL INFORMATION • FISCAL YEAR 2012 | 11

The size of the type used for the various headings indicates their importance.

The largest type suggests that *Strategic Goals and Results* is a chapter heading.

The next largest type indicates that *Strategic Goal 1: Achieving Peace and Security* is an A head (the highest level within a chapter).

Public Benefit and *Summary of Performance and Resources* are B heads (the next highest level).

FIGURE 11.3   Queuing

Information from U.S. Department of State, 2013: www.state.gov.
U.S. Department of State

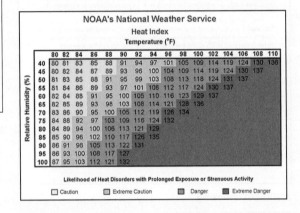

NOAA's National Weather Service
Heat Index
Temperature (°F)

	80	82	84	86	88	90	92	94	96	98	100	102	104	106	108	110
40	80	81	83	85	88	91	94	97	101	105	109	114	119	124	130	136
45	80	82	84	87	89	93	96	100	104	109	114	119	124	130	137	
50	81	83	85	88	91	95	99	103	108	113	118	124	131	137		
55	81	84	86	89	93	97	101	106	112	117	124	130	137			
60	82	84	88	91	95	100	105	110	116	123	129	137				
65	82	85	89	93	98	103	108	114	121	128	136					
70	83	86	90	95	100	105	112	119	126	134						
75	84	88	92	97	103	109	116	124	132							
80	84	89	94	100	106	113	121	129								
85	85	90	96	102	110	117	126	135								
90	86	91	98	105	113	122	131									
95	86	93	100	108	117	127										
100	87	95	103	112	121	132										

Relative Humidity (%)

Likelihood of Heat Disorders with Prolonged Exposure or Strenuous Activity

☐ Caution   ☐ Extreme Caution   ☐ Danger   ☐ Extreme Danger

FIGURE 11.4   Filtering

Effective technical communication presents data and explains what the data mean. In this table about the heat index, the writer uses color as a filtering device. In Western cultures, red signals danger.
Data from National Weather Service, 2019: https://www.weather.gov/safety/heat-index.

Page Grids As the phrase suggests, a *page grid* is like a map on which you plan where the text, the graphics, and the white space will go. Many writers like to begin with a *thumbnail sketch*, a rough drawing that shows how the text and graphics will look on the page. Figure 11.5 shows thumbnail sketches of several options for a page from the body of a manual.

Experiment by sketching the different kinds of pages of your document: body pages, front matter, and so on. When you are satisfied, make page grids.

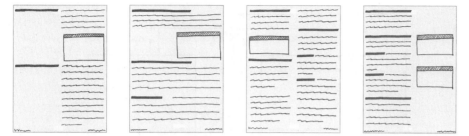

FIGURE 11.5   Thumbnail Sketches

You can use either a computer or a pencil and paper, or you can combine the two techniques.

Figure 11.6 shows two simple grids: one using *picas* (the unit that printing professionals use, which equals one-sixth of an inch) and one using inches. On the right is an example of a page laid out using the grid in the figure.

White Space   Sometimes called *negative space*, white space is the area of the paper with no writing or graphics: the space between two columns of text, the space between text and graphics, and, most obviously, the margins.

Margins, which make up close to half the area on a typical page, serve four main purposes:

- They reduce the amount of information on the page, making the document easier to read and use.
- They provide space for binding and allow readers to hold the page without covering up the text.
- They provide a neat frame around the type.
- They provide space for marginal glosses.

For more about marginal glosses, see Table 11.3, p. 278.

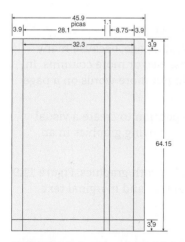

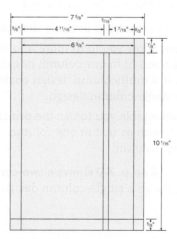

FIGURE 11.6   Sample Grids Using Picas and Inches

Increase the size of the margins if the subject is difficult or if your readers are not knowledgeable about it.

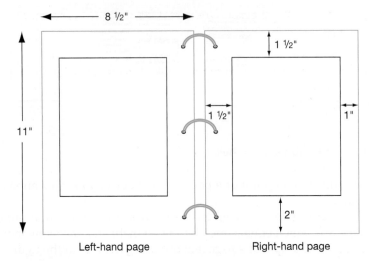

FIGURE 11.7 **Typical Margins for a Document That Is Bound Like a Book**

Figure 11.7 shows common margin widths for an 8.5 × 11-inch document.

White space can also set off and emphasize an element on the page. For instance, white space around a graphic separates it from the text and draws readers' eyes to it. White space between columns helps readers read the text easily. And white space between sections of text helps readers see that one section is ending and another is beginning.

Columns Many workplace documents have multiple columns. A multicolumn design offers three major advantages:

- Text is easier to read because the lines are shorter.
- Columns allow you to fit more information on the page, because many graphics can fit in one column or extend across two or more columns. In addition, a multicolumn design enables you to put more words on a page than a single-column design.
- Columns enable you to use the principle of repetition to create a visual pattern, such as text in one column and accompanying graphics in an adjacent column.

Figure 11.8 on p. 270 shows a two-column design with graphics. Figure 11.9 on p. 271 shows a single-column design with graphics and marginal text boxes.

Why To Format Columns

A multicolumn format allows you to fit more text on the page, create easier-to-read and more visually interesting pages, and have more options when sizing and placing graphics.

How To Format Columns

To divide your document into multiple columns, select the **Page Layout** tab in Word to access the **Page Setup** group.

In the **Page Setup** group, select **Columns** and use the **Columns** drop-down menu to view **preset** layouts.

You can also select **More Columns** to launch the **Columns** dialog box. You can control the **number of columns** and specify the **width** and **spacing** yourself.

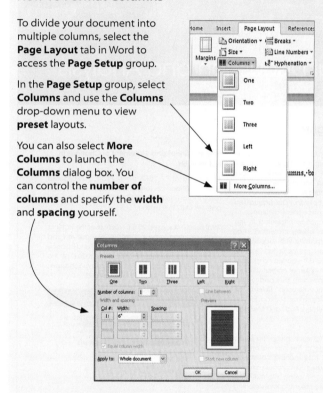

When you divide your document into columns, text flows from the bottom of one column to the top of the next column. Columns enable you to use the principle of repetition to create a visual pattern, such as text in one column and accompanying graphics in an adjacent column.

If you want to end a column of text in a specific location or create columns of equal length, use the **Breaks** drop-down menu to insert a **column break**. This action will move the text following the break to the next column.

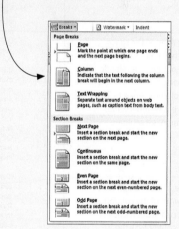

TYPOGRAPHY

Typography, the study of type and the way people read it, encompasses typefaces, type families, case, and type size, as well as factors that affect the white space of a document: line length, line spacing, and justification.

Typefaces A typeface is a set of letters, numbers, punctuation marks, and other symbols, all bearing a characteristic design. There are thousands of typefaces, and more are designed every year. Figure 11.10 on page 272 shows three contrasting typefaces.

A multicolumn design enables you to present a lot of text and graphics of different sizes.

Notice how the designer has used the whole width of the page for one graphic and a single column for a smaller graphic.

Note that the alley — the space between the two columns of text — need not be wide. Nor do you need to include a vertical rule to keep the columns separate. The human brain easily understands that each column is a separate space.

In this sample, the bar graph is exactly the width of the column in which it appears. But it doesn't have to be. It could break the shape of the column and extend into the other column or even into the margin. Or it could be narrower than its column, with the text wrapping around it. The design you see here looks neat and professional. If the graph were wider or narrower than the column, the design might appear somewhat more creative.

Financial Discussion and Analysis

Financial Highlights

The USPTO received an unqualified (clean) audit opinion from the independent public accounting firm of KPMG LLP on its FY 2012 financial statements, provided in the Financial Section of this report. This is the 20th consecutive year that the USPTO received a clean opinion. Our unqualified audit opinion provides independent assurance to the public that the information presented in the USPTO financial statements is fairly presented, in all material respects, in conformity with accounting principles generally accepted in the United States of America. In addition, KPMG LLP reported no material weaknesses in the USPTO's internal control, and no instances of non-compliance with laws and regulations affecting the financial statements. Refer to the Other Accompanying Information section for the Summary of Financial Statement Audit and Management Assurances.

The summary financial highlights presented in this section provide an analysis of the information that appears in the USPTO's FY 2012 financial statements. The USPTO financial management process ensures that management decision-making information is dependable, internal controls over financial reporting are effective, and that compliance with laws and regulations is maintained. The issuance of these financial statements is a component of the USPTO's objective to continually improve the accuracy and usefulness of its financial management information.

Balance Sheet and Statement of Changes in Net Position

At the end of FY 2012, the USPTO's consolidated Balance Sheet presents total assets of $1,982.1 million, total liabilities of $1,255.2 million, and a net position of $726.9 million.

Total assets increased 20.3 percent over the last four years, resulting largely from the increase in Fund Balance with Treasury. The decrease in Fund Balance with Treasury during FY 2009 is a result of the decrease in fee income. The following graph shows the changes in assets during this period.

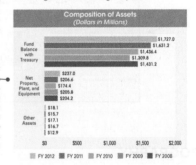

68

PERFORMANCE AND ACCOUNTABILITY REPORT: FISCAL YEAR 2012

FIGURE 11.8   A Multicolumn Design
Information from U.S. Patent and Trademark Office, 2013: www.uspto.gov/about/stratplan/ar/USPTOFY2012PAR.pdf.

This page from a software company's white paper — a marketing document usually distributed on the web — shows one approach to a one-column design.

PDF PAGE CONTENT

Page Description Language

PDF is a page description language, i.e. it describes how a page looks so that it can be reproduced for viewing and printing. The language resembles Postscript, but is much simpler to allow for more efficient processing. For example, it does not contain control structures like loops and „if" statements.

PDF Page Content Elements

Basically PDF recognizes three types of page content elements:

- Text (fonts programs)
- Graphic paths (lines and curves)
- Images (raster samples)

Content Objects

PDF uses objects and object types to describe the content. Every string of text and all graphics and images are defined by one or several objects, created from one or more object types.

- **Text Objects** – Text objects are defined by a number of attributes including font family, style and size, a string of characters, and a position on a page. PDF does not recognize nor store objects for line breaks, headers, paragraphs, indentation etc. (i.e. paragraph formatting operators used in word processing applications like Microsoft Word). Text is broken down into fragments as small as single characters but not more than one line. The fragments can be randomly stored and are like pieces of a puzzle that all have to be placed in their correct location on the page to complete its appearance.

- **Graphic Path Objects** – A graphic path object is an arbitrary shape made up of straight lines, rectangles, and cubic Bézier curves. A graphic path object ends with one or more painting operators that specify whether the path is stroked, filled, used as a clipping boundary or some combination of these operations.

- **PDF Image Objects** – A PDF-specific image format is used for embedding images in a PDF file. This format is independent of the input image format. For example, scanned pages in TIFF format or GIF images that are converted to PDF are newly packaged into PDF image format. Once an image has been converted to PDF image format, it is usually not possible to determine what the original image format was. It is however possible to export PDF images into raster image formats, provided the raster image format supports all features of the image (e.g. transparency).

© PDF Tools AG – Premium PDF Technology

A one-column design allows greater flexibility for a variety of elements, such as a bulleted list with paragraphs of text, which would be dense and difficult to read in a two-column design.

There is more white space in the right margin than the left, an asymmetric design that focuses attention of the main headings running on the left. One goal of document design is to reduce the number of pages needed — but when you design a page, you want to make the text inviting and easy to read. Figuring out how to balance these two priorities is one of the major challenges of designing a page.

FIGURE 11.9   A One-Column Design
PDF Tools AG.

**FIGURE 11.10   Three
Contrasting Typefaces**

This paragraph is typed in French Script typeface. You are unlikely to see this style of font in a technical document because it is too ornate and too hard to read. It is better suited to wedding invitations and other formal announcements.

This paragraph is Times Roman. It looks like the kind of type used by the *New York Times* and other newspapers in the nineteenth century. It is an effective typeface for text in the body of technical documents.

This paragraph is Univers, which has a modern, high-tech look. It is best suited for headings and titles in technical documents.

As Figure 11.11 illustrates, typefaces are generally classified into two categories: *serif* and *sans serif*.

Although scholars used to think that serif typefaces were easier to read because the serifs encourage readers' eyes to move along the line, most now believe that there is no difference in readability between serif and sans-serif typefaces, either in print or online. Readers are most comfortable with the style they see most often.

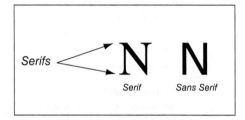

**FIGURE 11.11   Serif and Sans-Serif
Typefaces**

Most of the time you will use a handful of standard typefaces such as Times New Roman, Cambria, Calibri, and Arial, which are included in your word-processing software and which your printer can reproduce.

Type Families   Each typeface belongs to a family of typefaces, which consists of variations on the basic style, such as italic and boldface. Figure 11.12, for example, shows the Helvetica family.

Helvetica Light	*Helvetica Bold Italic*
Helvetica Light Italic	**Helvetica Heavy**
Helvetica Regular	*Helvetica Heavy Italic*
Helvetica Regular Italic	Helvetica Regular Condensed
Helvetica Bold	*Helvetica Regular Condensed Italic*

FIGURE 11.12   Helvetica Family of Type

Be careful not to overload your document with too many different members of the same family. Used sparingly and consistently, these variations can help you with filtering: calling attention to various kinds of text, such as warnings and notes. Use italics for book titles and other elements, and use bold type for emphasis and headings. Stay away from outlined and shadowed variations. You can live a full, rewarding life without ever using them.

Case To make your document easy to read, use uppercase and lowercase letters as you would in any other kind of writing (see Figure 11.13). Most people require 10 to 25 percent more time to read text using all uppercase letters than to read text using both uppercase and lowercase. In addition, uppercase letters take up as much as 35 percent more space than lowercase letters (Haley, 1991). If the text includes both cases, readers will find it easier to see where new sentences begin (Poulton, 1968).

Type Size Type size is measured with a unit called a *point*. There are 12 points in a pica and 72 points in an inch. In most technical documents 10-, 11-, or 12-point type is used for the body of the text:

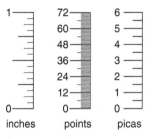

This paragraph is printed in 10-point type. This size is easy to read, provided it is reproduced on a high-quality ink-jet printer or laser printer.

This paragraph is printed in 12-point type. If the document will be read by people over age 40, 12-point type is a good size because it is more legible than a smaller size.

This paragraph is printed in 14-point type. This size is appropriate for headings.

Type sizes used for other parts of a document include the following:

footnotes	8- or 9-point type
indexes	2 points smaller than body text
slides or transparencies	24- to 36-point type

In general, aim for at least a 2- to 4-point difference between the headings and the body. Too many size variations, however, suggest a sweepstakes advertisement rather than a serious text.

Individual variations are greater in lowercase words

THAN THEY ARE IN UPPERCASE WORDS.

FIGURE 11.13 Individual Variations in Lowercase and Uppercase Type
Lowercase letters are easier to read than uppercase because the individual variations from one letter to another are greater.

ETHICS NOTE

USING TYPE SIZES RESPONSIBLY

Text set in large type contrasts with text set in small type. It makes sense to use large type to emphasize headings and other important information. But be careful with small type. It is unethical (and, according to some court rulings, illegal) to use excessively small type (such as 6-point or smaller type) to disguise information that you don't want to stand out. When you read the fine print in an ad for cell-phone service, you get annoyed if you discover that the low rates are guaranteed for only three months or that you are committing to a long-term contract. You *should* get annoyed. Hiding information in tiny type is unethical. Don't do it.

Line Length The line length most often used on an 8.5 × 11-inch page—about 80 characters—is somewhat difficult to read. A shorter line of 50 to 60 characters is easier, especially in a long document.

Line Spacing Sometimes called *leading* (pronounced "ledding"), *line spacing* refers to the amount of white space between lines or between a line of text and a graphic. If lines are too far apart, the page looks diffuse, the text loses coherence, and readers tire quickly. If lines are too close together, the page looks crowded and becomes difficult to read. Some research suggests that documents that have small type, long lines, and/or sans-serif typefaces benefit from extra line spacing. Figure 11.14 shows three variations in line spacing.

a. **Excessive line spacing**

Aronomink Systems has been contracted by Cecil Electric Cooperative, Inc.

(CECI) to design a solid waste management system for the Cecil County plant,

Units 1 and 2, to be built in Cranston, Maryland. The system will consist of two

600 MW pulverized coal-burning units fitted with high-efficiency electrostatic

precipitators and limestone reagent FGD systems.

b. **Appropriate line spacing**

Aronomink Systems has been contracted by Cecil Electric Cooperative, Inc. (CECI) to design a solid waste management system for the Cecil County plant, Units 1 and 2, to be built in Cranston, Maryland. The system will consist of two 600 MW pulverized coal-burning units fitted with high-efficiency electrostatic precipitators and limestone reagent FGD systems.

c. **Inadequate line spacing**

Aronomink Systems has been contracted by Cecil Electric Cooperative, Inc. (CECI) to design a solid waste management system for the Cecil County plant, Units 1 and 2, to be built in Cranston, Maryland. The system will consist of two 600 MW pulverized coal-burning units fitted with high-efficiency electrostatic precipitators and limestone reagent FGD systems.

FIGURE 11.14 Line Spacing

Line spacing is usually determined by the kind of document you are writing. Memos and letters are single-spaced; reports, proposals, and similar documents are often double-spaced or one-and-a-half-spaced.

Figure 11.15 on page 276 shows how line spacing can be used to distinguish one section of text from another and to separate text from graphics.

Justification Justification refers to the alignment of words along the left and right margins. In technical communication, text is often *left-justified* (also called *ragged right*). Except for the first line in each paragraph, which is sometimes indented, the lines begin along a uniform left margin but end on an irregular right margin. Ragged right is most common in word-processed text (even though word processors can justify the right margin).

In *justified* text, also called *full-justified text*, both the left and the right margin are justified. Justified text is seen most often in formal documents, such as books. The following passage from a Department of Agriculture publication is presented first in left-justified form and then in justified form:

We recruited participants to reflect the racial diversity of the area in which the focus groups were conducted. Participants had to meet the following eligibility criteria: have primary responsibility or share responsibility for cooking in their household; prepare food and cook in the home at least three times a week; eat meat and/or poultry; prepare meat and/or poultry in the home at least twice a week; and not regularly use a digital food thermometer when cooking at home.

Notice that the space between words is uniform in left-justified text.

We recruited participants to reflect the racial diversity of the area in which the focus groups were conducted. Participants had to meet the following eligibility criteria: have primary responsibility or share responsibility for cooking in their household; prepare food and cook in the home at least three times a week; eat meat and/or poultry; prepare meat and/or poultry in the home at least twice a week; and not regularly use a digital food thermometer when cooking at home.

In justified text, the spacing between words is irregular, slowing down the reader. Because a big space suggests a break between sentences, not a break between words, readers can become confused, frustrated, and fatigued.

Notice that the irregular spacing not only slows down reading but also can create "rivers" of white space. Readers are tempted to concentrate on the rivers running south rather than on the information itself.

Full justification can make the text harder to read in one more way. Some word processors and typesetting systems automatically hyphenate words that do not fit on the line. Hyphenation slows down and distracts the reader. Left-justified text does not require as much hyphenation as full-justified text.

TITLES AND HEADINGS

Titles and headings should stand out visually on the page because they introduce new ideas.

Titles Because the title is the most important heading in a document, it should be displayed clearly and prominently. On a cover page or a title page, use boldface type in a large size, such as 18 or 24 points. If the title also

For more about titling your document, see "Writing Clear, Informative Headings," Ch. 9, p. 199.

FIGURE 11.15   Line Spacing Used To Distinguish One Section from Another

Information from U.S. Patent and Trademark Office, 2010: www.uspto.gov/.

The line spacing between two sections is greater than the line spacing within a section.

Line spacing is also used to separate the text from the graphics.

Net (Cost)/Income *(Dollars in Millions)*	FY 2005	FY 2006	FY 2007	FY 2008	FY 2009
Earned Revenue	$ 1,372.8	$ 1,594.4	$ 1,735.7	$ 1,862.2	$ 1,927.1
Program Cost	(1,424.0)	(1,514.2)	(1,769.6)	(1,892.6)	(1,981.9)
Net (Cost)/Income	$ (51.2)	$ 80.2	$ (33.9)	$ (30.4)	$ (54.8)

STATEMENT OF NET COST

The Statement of Net Cost presents the USPTO's results of operations by the following responsibility segments – Patent, Trademark, and Intellectual Property Protection and Enforcement Domestically and Abroad. The above table presents the total USPTO's results of operations for the past five fiscal years. In FY 2005, the USPTO's operations resulted in a net cost. In FY 2006, the USPTO generated a net income due to the increased maintenance fees received and revenue recognition of previously deferred revenue collected subsequent to the fee increase on December 8, 2004. During FY 2007, FY 2008, and FY 2009 the USPTO's operations resulted in a net cost of $33.9 million, $30.4 million, and $54.8 million, respectively.

The Statement of Net Cost compares fees earned to costs incurred during a specific period of time. It is not necessarily an indicator of net income or net cost over the life of a patent or trademark. Net income or net cost for the fiscal year is dependent upon work that has been completed over the various phases of the production life cycle. The net income calculation is based on fees earned during the fiscal year being reported, regardless of when those fees were collected. Maintenance fees also play a large part in whether a total net income or net cost is recognized. Maintenance fees collected in FY 2009 are a reflection of patent issue levels 3.5, 7.5, and 11.5 years ago, rather than a reflection of patents issued in FY 2009. Therefore, maintenance fees can have a significant impact on matching costs and revenue.

During FY 2009, with the number of patent filings decreasing by 2.3 percent over the prior year, the backlog for patent applica-

tions likewise decreased, decreasing deferred revenue and increasing earned revenue. This was evidenced by the Patent organization disposing of 22.9 percent more applications than were disposed of during FY 2008.

During FY 2009, with the number of trademark applications decreasing by 12.3 percent over the prior year, the Trademark organization was able to continue to address the existing inventory and reduce pendency by 0.3 months from FY 2008. The Trademark organization was able to do this while recognizing a slight decrease in revenue earned.

EARNED REVENUE

The USPTO's earned revenue is derived from the fees collected for patent and trademark products and services. Fee collections are recognized as earned revenue when the activities to complete the work associated with the fee are completed. The table below presents the earned revenue for the past five years.

Earned revenue totaled $1,927.1 million for FY 2009, an increase of $64.9 million, or 3.5 percent, over FY 2008 earned revenue of $1,862.2 million. Of revenue earned during FY 2009, $454.3 million related to fee collections that were deferred for revenue recognition in prior fiscal years, $546.7 million related to maintenance fees collected during FY 2009, which were considered earned immediately, $920.7 million related to work performed for fees collected during FY 2009, and $5.4 million were not fee-related.

Earned Revenue *(Dollars in Millions)*	FY 2005	FY 2006	FY 2007	FY 2008	FY 2009
Patent	$ 1,197.8	$ 1,384.2	$ 1,507.0	$ 1,625.0	$ 1,697.4
Percentage Change in Patent Earned Revenue	*9.6%*	*15.6%*	*8.9%*	*7.8%*	*4.5%*
Trademark	175.0	210.2	228.7	237.2	229.7
Percentage Change in Trademark Earned Revenue	*19.5%*	*20.1%*	*8.8%*	*3.7%*	*(3.2)%*
Total Earned Revenue	$ 1,372.8	$ 1,594.4	$ 1,735.7	$ 1,862.2	$ 1,927.1
Percentage Change in Earned Revenue	*10.8%*	*16.1%*	*8.9%*	*7.3%*	*3.5%*

48   PERFORMANCE AND ACCOUNTABILITY REPORT: FISCAL YEAR 2009

U.S. Patent and Trademark Office

appears at the top of the first page, make it slightly larger than the rest of the text—perhaps 16 or 18 points for a document printed in 12 point—but smaller than it is on the cover or title page. Many designers center titles on the page between the right and left margins.

Headings   Readers should be able to tell when you are beginning a new topic. The most effective way to distinguish one level of heading from another is to use size variations (Williams & Spyridakis, 1992). Most readers will notice a 20-percent size difference between an A head (a first-level heading) and a B head (a second-level heading). Boldface also sets off headings effectively. The *least* effective way to set off headings is underlining, because the underline obscures the *descenders*, the portions of some letters that extend below the body of the letters, such as in *p* and *y*.

In general, the more important the heading, the closer it is to the left margin: A heads usually begin at the left margin, B heads are often indented a half inch, and C heads are often indented an inch. Indented C heads can also be run into the text.

In designing headings, use line spacing carefully. A perceivable distance between a heading and the following text increases the impact of the heading. Consider these three examples:

For more about using headings, see "Writing Clear, Informative Headings," Ch. 9, p. 199.

Summary

In this example, the writer has skipped a line between the heading and the text that follows it. The heading stands out clearly.

Summary
In this example, the writer has not skipped a line between the heading and the text that follows it. The heading stands out, but not as emphatically.

Summary. In this example, the writer has begun the text on the same line as the heading. This run-in style makes the heading stand out the least.

OTHER DESIGN FEATURES

Table 11.3 shows five other design features that are used frequently in technical communication: rules, boxes, screens, marginal glosses, and pull quotes.

TABLE 11.3 Additional Design Features for Technical Communication

Two types of rules are used here: vertical rules to separate the columns and horizontal rules to separate the items. Rules enable you to fit a lot of information on a page, but when overused they make the page look cluttered.

Rules. *Rule* is a design term for a straight line. You can add rules to your document using the drawing tools in a word processor. Horizontal rules can separate headers and footers from the body of the page or divide two sections of text. Vertical rules can separate columns on a multicolumn page or identify revised text in a manual. Rules exploit the principles of alignment and proximity.

(continued)

TABLE 11.3 Additional Design Features for Technical Communication (*continued*)

Boxes. Adding rules on all four sides of an item creates a box. Boxes can enclose graphics or special sections of text or can form a border for the whole page. Boxed text is often positioned to extend into the margin, giving it further emphasis. Boxes exploit the principles of contrast and repetition.

The different-colored screens clearly distinguish the three sets of equations.

Screens. The background shading used behind text or graphics for emphasis is called a screen. The density of a screen can range from 1 percent to 100 percent; 5 to 10 percent is usually enough to provide emphasis without making the text illegible. You can use screens with or without boxes. Screens exploit the principles of contrast and repetition.

The marginal glosses present definitions of key words.

Marginal glosses. A marginal gloss is a brief comment on the main discussion. Marginal glosses are usually set in a different typeface — and sometimes in a different color — from the main discussion. Although marginal glosses can be helpful in providing a quick overview of the main discussion, they can also compete with the text for readers' attention. Marginal glosses exploit the principles of contrast and repetition.

(continued)

TABLE 11.3	Additional Design Features for Technical Communication (*continued*)

This pull quote extends into the margin, but a pull quote can go anywhere on the page, even spanning two or more columns or the whole page.

Pull quotes. A pull quote is a brief quotation (usually just a sentence or two) that is pulled from the text, displayed in a larger type size and usually in a different typeface, and sometimes enclosed in a box. Newspapers and magazines use pull quotes to attract readers' attention. Pull quotes are inappropriate for reports and similar documents because they look too informal. They are increasingly popular, however, in newsletters. Pull quotes exploit the principles of contrast and repetition.

▶ TECH TIP

Why To Create Borders and Screens

You can use background borders and screens (or shading) in Microsoft Word to emphasize page elements such as text and graphics. By emphasizing certain elements, you are letting your readers know what is important.

How To Create Borders and Screens

Start with the **Borders and Shading** dialog box.

To create a **border** around a page element or an entire page, select the area you want to format. Select the **Page Layout** tab, and then select **Page Borders** in the **Page Background** group.

To create **shading**, also called a screen, select the area you want to format, and then select **Page Borders** in the **Page Background** group. Select the **Shading** tab.

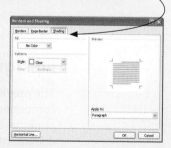

Select the **Borders** or **Page Border** tab. You can specify the type of border, line style, color, and line width.

You can specify the color within the box as well as the style of the pattern.

> **TECH TIP**

Why To Create Text Boxes

In Microsoft Word, text boxes allow you to position words independently of the margins and other settings on the page. You can place a quotation in a text box, for example, and then position the box in the middle of a column of text to draw attention to the quote.

How To Create Text Boxes

Start with the **Text Box** feature in the **Text** group on the **Insert** tab.

To **create** a text box, select **Draw Text Box** from the **Text Box** drop-down menu.

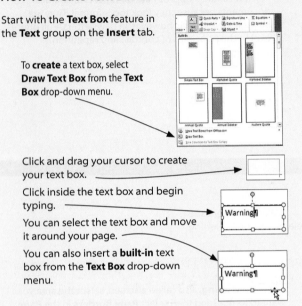

Click and drag your cursor to create your text box.

Click inside the text box and begin typing.

You can select the text box and move it around your page.

You can also insert a **built-in** text box from the **Text Box** drop-down menu.

To **format** your text box, select the box and then select the **Format Shape** dialog-box launcher from the **Shape Styles** group on the **Format** tab.

The **Arrange** group allows you to specify design elements such as the text box's position in relation to other objects and the wrapping style of the surrounding text.

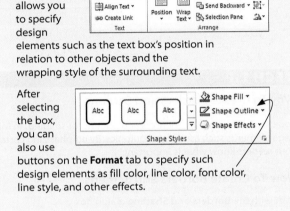

After selecting the box, you can also use buttons on the **Format** tab to specify such design elements as fill color, line color, font color, line style, and other effects.

Designing Online Documents

The previous discussion of designing printed documents focused on four components: size, paper, bindings, and navigational aids. Of these four components, size and navigational aids are relevant to websites and other online documents.

Size is important in that you can control—to some extent, at least—how much information (text, graphics, animation) you present on the screen. On all but the smallest screens, you can use multiple columns and vary column width, and you can fill screens with content (and thereby use fewer screens) or leave a lot of white space (and thereby use more screens). As people are increasingly turning to smaller screens for reading online content, you want to pay even more attention to designing your information so that it is clear and attractive. You also want to be sure that you design online documents so that key information is emphasized and easily accessible to users. In addition, you want to consider audience characteristics such as age (use bigger type for older people) and disabilities (for example, include alternative text for images so that people with vision disabilities can use software that "reads" your descriptions of the images). For more on accessibility for people with disabilities, see pages 287–90.

Navigational tools are vitally important for online documents, because if your audience can't figure out how to find the information they want, they're out of luck. With a print document, they can at least flip through the pages.

The following discussion focuses on seven principles that can help you make it easy for readers to find and understand the information they seek:

- Use design to emphasize important information.
- Create informative headers and footers.
- Help readers navigate the document.
- Include extra features your readers might need.
- Help readers connect with others.
- Design for accessibility.
- Design for multicultural readers.

Although some of these principles do not apply to every type of online document, they provide a useful starting point as you think about designing your document.

USE DESIGN TO EMPHASIZE IMPORTANT INFORMATION

The smaller the screen, the more cluttered it can become, making it difficult for readers to see what is truly important. No matter what size screen they are using, you want readers to be able to find what they want quickly and easily. As you begin planning an online document, decide what types of information are most essential for your audience, and ensure that that content in particular is clearly findable from the home screen. Give your buttons, tabs, and other navigational features clear, informative headings. For more guidance on emphasizing important information, see Chapter 9.

Once you have determined the information you want to emphasize, adhere to design principles rigorously so that users can easily identify key content. Use logical patterns of organization and the principles of proximity, alignment, repetition, and contrast so that readers know where they are and how to carry out the tasks they want to accomplish. Figure 11.16 on page 284 shows a well-designed screen for a mobile phone.

DOCUMENT ANALYSIS ACTIVITY

Analyzing Page Designs

The two pages shown here come from different government reports. Both are printed on 8½ × 11-inch paper. The questions next to each ask you to think about page design as discussed in this chapter.

1. How many columns are used in this document? How does the column design affect the readability of the page?

2. What type of justification has been used for the text? Was this a wise choice for this page size? Why or why not?

3. What alignment features, if any, have been used? What problems with alignment, if any, do you see?

(f) *Drug Purity - DEA Form 7*

(1) The presentence report will normally provide drug weight/purity information from DEA Form 7. This is a complicated form. "Total net weight" [normally in Item 31] refers to the amount of the pure drug. This is the weight used in calculation of the Commission's severity rating. For your information, "gross weight" is the weight of the drug plus adulterants plus the container (normally found in Item 24). Also normally found in Item 24 is "net weight" (the weight of the drug plus adulterants). "Strength" (the percent purity of the drug) is normally found in Item 28. Multiplying "net weight" x "strength" is how DEA arrives at the "total net weight". Remember, "total net weight" is the weight of the pure drug to be used in assessing the Commission's severity rating.

(2) If a presentence report does not specify "total net weight", the probation officer should be contacted for clarification (please be specific as to the clarification necessary; this will enhance feedback/training). Note: DEA lab reports (DEA Form 7), if necessary, also may be obtained directly from the DEA field office for the geographic area in which the offense occurred. If a request to the DEA field office is required, provide the subject's name, date of birth, place of offense, and dates of offense.

(g) If neither weight nor purity is available, but only a money value, DEA may be requested to provide an estimate of the amount of pure drug associated with that money value. In the absence of a specific estimate from DEA pertaining to the particular case, DEA publishes a report (Domestic Drug Prices) providing estimates of average drug prices by year and region from which an estimate may be obtained.

(h) *Determining Offense Severity Relative to Simple Possession of Drugs.* In certain cases, the Commission must determine whether the offense behavior should be considered as "simple possession" of a controlled substance or "possession with intent to distribute." In making this determination, the Commission shall examine a variety of factors (if available). These factors are shown below. The presence of any of the following factors may be considered as a presumption of possession with intent to distribute. However, this presumption may be rebutted if there are circumstances in the individual case which indicate that there was no intention to distribute.

(1) *Weight/amount/purity of the substance:* Possession of the following amounts of controlled substances are presumed to indicate possession with intent to distribute:

Heroin   1 gm. at 100% purity, or equivalent amount; or more
Cocaine   5 gms. at 100% purity, or equivalent amount; or more
Marijuana   10 lbs. or more
Hashish   3 lbs. or more
Hash Oil   .3 lbs. or more
Drugs (other than above) 1,000 doses or more.

(2) *Other Factors:* The presence of any of the following factors may be considered indicative of intent to distribute: (A) the substance has been separated into multiple, individual packets; (B) the offender is a non-user of the substance in question; (C) the presence of instruments used in preparing

---

*Terms marked by an asterisk are defined in Chapter Thirteen.

11/15/07   Page 60 of 337

U.S. Department of Justice

Analyzing Page Designs (*continued*)

Figure 1-2.

Total Revenues and Outlays

(Percentage of gross domestic product)

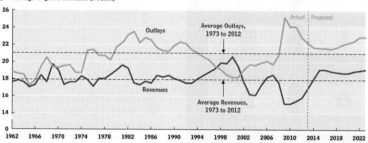

Source: Congressional Budget Office.

4. How many levels of headings appear on this page? Are the different levels designed effectively so that they are easy to distinguish? If not, what changes would you make to the design?

5. How are rules used on this page? Are they effective? Would you change any of them?

6. Describe the design of the body text on this page, focusing on columns and alignment. Is the design of the body text effective? Would you change it in any way?

health care costs, and a significant expansion in eligibility for federal subsidies for health insurance, outlays for Social Security and the federal government's major health care programs are projected to rise substantially relative to the size of the economy over the next 10 years. In addition, growing debt and rising interest rates will boost net interest payments. Spending on all other programs—in the aggregate—is projected to decline relative to GDP between 2014 and 2023, primarily because of improving economic conditions and the spending limits in current law.

Revenues

CBO projects that, if current tax laws remain unchanged, revenues will rise relative to GDP over the next two years and then remain at about 19 percent of GDP through 2023. After 2015, increases in individual income tax receipts relative to GDP will roughly offset projected declines in corporate income tax receipts and declines in remittances from the Federal Reserve as a share of GDP.

Individual Income Taxes. CBO projects that, under current law, individual income tax receipts will rise from $1.3 trillion this year to $2.5 trillion in 2023—or from 7.9 percent to 9.8 percent of GDP. The projected increase in receipts relative to the economy in CBO's baseline reflects real (inflation-adjusted) bracket creep, the economic expansion, recent and scheduled changes in tax provisions, and other factors. In previous baselines,

CBO had projected that those receipts would increase to a much higher percentage of GDP by the early part of the next decade, but the American Taxpayer Relief Act's permanent extension of most of the expiring income tax reductions has significantly reduced the amount of revenues anticipated under current law.

Real Bracket Creep. Increases in real income will push more income into higher tax brackets, which boosts revenues relative to GDP in CBO's projections by 0.9 percentage points over the next decade.[11]

Economic Recovery. CBO expects that the economic expansion and related factors will cause taxable incomes to rise faster than GDP, boosting individual income tax revenues as a share of GDP by about 0.4 percentage points over the next decade; most of that effect will occur by 2017. Certain components of taxable income—including wages and salaries, capital gains realizations, interest income, and proprietors' income—declined as a share of GDP over the past several years. CBO expects that, as the economy recovers, such income will rebound more quickly than the economy as a whole, increasing

---

11. Roughly three-quarters of that amount is a longer-term effect that results from increases in the potential output of the economy (that is, the maximum sustainable level of economic output), and the rest results from the return of output to its potential level over the next several years.

FIGURE 11.16 Screen for a Mobile Application

Sepsis Clinical Guide mobile app, Escavo, Inc. (www.escavo.com). Used by permission.

This app helps physicians diagnose sepsis quickly and effectively. The information most crucial to evaluating the condition is easily accessible on the home screen. At the top of the screen, where the reader's eyes will initially fall, is an overview of the condition and, most importantly, the diagnostic tool. Less essential items, such as resources and references, are located at the bottom of the screen. Supplementary information, such as a call for authors and a feedback form, is deeper on the site, behind the "More" tab.

This simple screen uses the principle of contrast effectively to highlight key content. Each of the eight main content areas has its own color and its own icon to distinguish it from the seven other areas. In addition, the four navigation items at the bottom of the screen use contrast in that the icon for the screen the reader is now viewing — in this case, the home page — is presented against a blue background, whereas the other three icons are presented against a black background.

CREATE INFORMATIVE HEADERS AND FOOTERS

Headers and footers help readers understand and navigate your document, and they help establish your credibility. You want readers to know that they are reading an official document from your organization and that it was created by professionals. Figure 11.17 shows a typical website header, and Figure 11.18 shows a typical footer.

FIGURE 11.17 Website Header

Notice that a header in a website provides much more accessing information than a header in a printed document. This header enables readers to search the site, as the header on almost every site does, but it also includes other elements that are particularly important to the American Red Cross. For instance, there is a link to information about becoming a volunteer, and there is a link for helping people find their local chapter.

Courtesy of the American Red Cross.
© 2020 The American National Red Cross ALL RIGHTS RESERVED.

FIGURE 11.18   Website Footer

This simply designed footer presents all the links as text. Readers with impaired vision who use text-to-speech devices will be able to understand these textual links; they would not be able to understand graphical links.
Courtesy of the American Red Cross.
© 2020 The American National Red Cross ALL RIGHTS RESERVED.

The footer contains the copyright notice, as well as links to the terms and conditions for using the site, the privacy policy, contact information, a page with frequently asked questions (FAQ), and social media.

There are also links to content pages the American Red Cross wants to spotlight. These pages provide information on using mobile apps and donating blood.

HELP READERS NAVIGATE THE DOCUMENT

One important way to help readers navigate is to create and sustain a consistent visual design on every page or screen. Make the header, footer, background color or pattern, typography (typeface, type size, and color), and placement of the navigational links the same on every page. That way, readers will know where to look for these items.

GUIDELINES Making Your Document Easy To Navigate

Follow these five suggestions to make it easy for readers to find what they want in your document.

▸ **Include a site map or index.** A site map, which lists the pages on the site, can be a graphic or a textual list of the pages, classified according to logical categories. An index is an alphabetized list of the pages. Figure 11.19 shows a portion of a site map.

FIGURE 11.19   Site Map

For large websites, help your readers by organizing the site map rather than just presenting an alphabetical list of the pages. In this portion of a site map, Micron Technology classifies the pages in logical categories to help visitors find the pages they seek.
© 2017 Micron Technology, Inc. All rights reserved. Used with permission.

(continued)

▶ **Use a table of contents at the top of long pages.** If your page extends for more than a couple of screens, include a table of contents — a set of links to the items on that page — so that readers do not have to scroll down to find the topic they want. Tables of contents can link to information farther down on the same page or to information on separate pages. Figure 11.20 shows an excerpt from the table of contents at the top of a frequently asked questions (FAQ) page.

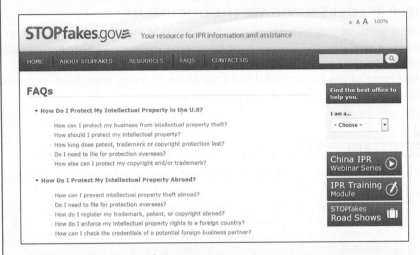

FIGURE 11.20   Table of Contents

The table of contents is classified by topic (first all the topics about protecting your intellectual property in the United States, then all the topics about protecting it outside the United States). For any online document, large or small, use the principles of organizing information presented in Chapter 7.

Information from U.S. Department of Commerce, 2013: www.stopfakes.gov/faqs.

▶ **Help readers get back to the top of long pages.** If a page is long enough to justify a table of contents, include a "Back to top" link (a textual link or a button or icon) before the start of each new chunk of information.

▶ **Include a link to the home page on every page.** This link can be a simple "Back to home page" textual link, a button, or an icon.

▶ **Include textual navigational links at the bottom of the page.** If you use buttons or icons for links, include textual versions of those links at the bottom of the page. Readers with impaired vision might use special software that reads the information on the screen. This software interprets text only, not graphics.

INCLUDE EXTRA FEATURES YOUR READERS MIGHT NEED

Because readers with a range of interests and needs will visit your site, consider adding some or all of the following five features:

- **An FAQ page.** A list of frequently asked questions helps new readers by providing basic information, explaining how to use the site, and directing them to more detailed discussions.

- **A search page or engine.** A search page or search engine enables readers to enter a keyword or phrase and find all the pages in the document that contain it.

- **Resource links.** If one of the purposes of your document is to educate readers, provide links to other sites.

- **A printable version of your site.** Online documents are designed for a screen, not a page. A printable version of your document, with black text on a white background and all the text and graphics consolidated into one big file, will save readers paper and toner.

- **A text-only version of your document.** Many readers with impaired vision rely on text because their specialized software cannot interpret graphics. Consider creating a text-only version on your document for these readers, and include a link to it on your home page.

HELP READERS CONNECT WITH OTHERS

Organizations use their online documents, in particular their websites, to promote interaction with clients, customers, suppliers, journalists, government agencies, and the general public. For this reason, most organizations use their sites to encourage their various stakeholders to connect with them through social media such as discussion forums and blogs.

Use your online document to direct readers to interactive features of your own website, as well as to your pages on social-media sites such as Facebook or Twitter. Figure 11.21 on page 288 shows a portion of NASA's community page.

CONSIDER MATTERS OF ACCESSIBILITY

According to Web Accessibility in Mind (WebAIM, 2016), an estimated 20 percent of the population has some form of visual, hearing, motor, or cognitive disability. Impairments vary widely in type and severity, but a significant number of people will be denied access to online material unless that material includes adaptations such as closed captioning of videos, links to audio for text files, and magnification of visuals. It's worth noting that such adaptions are also beneficial to people without disabilities who are in situations in which they need alternative accessibility—for example, when audio is unavailable or when they are using a very small screen.

Laws in the United States and throughout the world require that websites be accessible to people with disabilities. In addition to being a matter of ethics, accessibility also makes good business sense: why exclude any

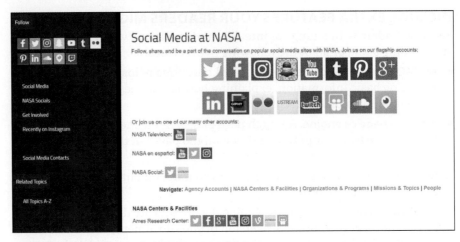

FIGURE 11.21 Maintaining Communities

As a federal agency with a mission that includes public education, NASA has a robust social-media presence. NASA has dozens of accounts on Facebook and the other popular social-media platforms, and it offers many opportunities for scientists and the general public alike to stay connected through blogs, podcasts, chat rooms, and educational programs and activities on such topics as how to view the International Space Station. Information from National Aeronautics and Space Administration, 2019: www.nasa.gov/socialmedia/. NASA.

members of the population? Moreover, principles of accessible design generally coincide with principles of good design in general. The Worldwide Web Consortium (W3C), the governing body of the web, has produced a list of international guidelines for good web design. WebAIM summarizes these guidelines as the "POUR" principles: documents should be perceivable, operable, understandable, and robust.

- **Perceivable.** Content is available to the senses (vision and hearing primarily) either through the browser or through assistive technologies (e.g., screen readers, screen enlargers).

- **Operable.** Users can interact with all controls and interactive elements using either a mouse, a keyboard, or an assistive device.

- **Understandable.** Content is clear and limits confusion and ambiguity.

- **Robust.** A wide range of technologies (including old and new user agents and assistive technologies) can access the content.

When designing for web and mobile devices, it's helpful to consider matters of accessibility in the planning stages of your design. For example, keep in mind the space that may be needed for closed captioning to run at the bottom of the screen. Or think about the placement of labels on graphics that may be magnified to 200 percent of their original size. A more detailed list of design principles is included in the Guidelines box on page 289.

GUIDELINES Designing Accessible Websites

The following key principles of accessible design have been adapted from WebAIM (2016). Most accessibility principles can be implemented very easily and will not affect the overall look or "feel" of your website. This list does not cover all accessibility issues, but by addressing these eleven basic principles, you can ensure that your web content is more accessible to everyone.

▶ **Provide appropriate alternative text.** Alternative text is a textual alternative to nontext content, such as the graphics in web pages. It is especially helpful for people who are blind and rely on a screen reader to read the content of the website to them.

▶ **Provide appropriate document structure.** Headings, lists, and other structural elements lend meaning and structure to web pages. They can also facilitate keyboard navigation within the page.

▶ **Provide headers for data tables.** Tables are used online for layout and to organize data. Tables that are used to organize data should have appropriate column headers. Data cells should be associated with their appropriate headers, making it easier for users of screen readers to navigate and understand the data table.

▶ **Ensure that users can complete and submit all forms.** Ensure that every element of a form (text field, checkbox, dropdown list, etc.) has a label. Also make sure the user can submit the form and recover from any errors, such as the failure to fill in all required fields.

▶ **Ensure that links make sense out of context.** Every link should make sense if the link text is read by itself. Users of screen readers may choose to read only the links on a web page. Certain phrases like "click here" and "more" should be avoided.

▶ **Caption and provide transcripts for media.** Videos and live audio must have captions and a transcript. With archived audio, a transcript may be sufficient.

▶ **Ensure accessibility of non-HTML content.** PDF documents and other non-HTML content must be as accessible as possible. If you cannot make such content accessible, consider using HTML formatting instead or, at the very least, provide an accessible alternative. A PDF document should also include a series of tags to make it more accessible. A tagged PDF file looks the same as an untagged file, but it is almost always more accessible to a person using a screen reader.

▶ **Allow users to skip repetitive elements on the page.** You should provide a method that allows users to skip navigation or other elements that repeat on every page. This is usually accomplished by providing a "Skip to Main Content" or "Skip Navigation" link at the top of the page; such a link allows the user to jump to the main content of the page.

▶ **Do not rely on color alone to convey meaning.** The use of color can enhance comprehension, but do not use color alone to convey information. That information may not be available to a person who is colorblind and will be unavailable to users of screen readers.

(continued)

▶ **Make sure content is clearly written and easy to read.** There are many ways to make your content easier to understand. Write clearly, use clear fonts, and use headings and lists appropriately.

▶ **Design to standards.** HTML-compliant and accessible pages are more robust and provide better search engine optimization. Cascading Style Sheets (CSS) allow you to separate content from presentation, providing more flexibility and making your content more accessible.

DESIGN FOR MULTICULTURAL AUDIENCES

Only about 8 percent of the people using the internet are from North America (Internet World Stats, 2019). Therefore, it makes sense in planning your online documents to assume that many of your readers will not be proficient in English.

Planning for a multicultural website is similar to planning for a multicultural printed document:

- **Use common words and short sentences and paragraphs.**
- **Avoid idioms, both verbal and visual, that might be confusing.** For instance, don't use sports metaphors, such as *full-court press*, or a graphic of an American-style mailbox to suggest an email link.
- **If a large percentage of your readers speak a language other than English, consider creating a version of your site in that language.** The expense can be considerable, but so can the benefits.

ETHICS NOTE

DESIGNING LEGAL AND HONEST ONLINE DOCUMENTS

You know that the words and images that you see on the internet are covered by copyright, even if you do not see a copyright symbol. The only exception is information that is in the public domain either because it is not covered by copyright (such as information created by entities of the U.S. federal government), because copyright has expired (the author has been dead over 70 years), or because the creator of the information has explicitly stated that the information is in the public domain and you are free to copy it.

For more about copyright law, see "Copyright Law," Ch. 2, p. 24.

But what about the design of a site? Almost all web designers readily admit to spending a lot of time looking at other sites and pages for inspiration. And they admit to looking at the computer code to see how that design was achieved. This is perfectly ethical. So is copying the code for routine elements such as tables. But is it ethical to download the code for a whole page, including the layout and the design, and then plug in your own data? No. Your responsibility is to create your own information, then display it with your own design.

Designing Online Pages

Well-designed online pages are simple, with only a few colors and nothing extraneous. The text is easy to read and chunked effectively, and the links are written carefully so readers know where they are being directed.

AIM FOR SIMPLICITY

When you create an online document, remember that readers are increasingly likely to use it on a device with a small screen. In addition, they will likely read in noisy, distracting environments with too much light or not enough light. For these reasons, keep the design as simple as you can. A good example of an app designed for a small screen can be seen in Figure 11.22.

GUIDELINES Designing a Simple Site

Follow these four suggestions to make your design attractive and easy to use.

▶ **Use simple backgrounds.** A plain background is best. Avoid busy patterns that distract the reader from the words and graphics of the text.

▶ **Use conservative color combinations to increase text legibility.** The greater the contrast between the text color and the background color, the more legible the text. The most legible color combination is black text against a white background. Bad idea: black on purple.

▶ **Avoid decorative graphics.** Don't waste space using graphics that convey no useful information. Think twice before you use clip art.

▶ **Use thumbnail graphics.** Instead of a large graphic, which takes up space, requires a long time to download, and uses up your reader's data-download allotment, use a thumbnail that readers can click on if they wish to open a larger version.

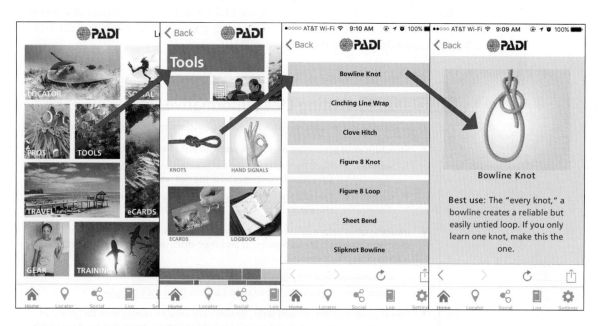

FIGURE 11.22 Simply Designed Smartphone App

The PADI (Professional Association of Dive Instructors) smartphone app for scuba divers uses bright, colorful, and simple thumbnail images to link its homepage to more detailed information. For example, within the "Knots" tool, users can choose from several types of knots, then view an animation demonstrating how to make each knot and read about best uses.

MAKE THE TEXT EASY TO READ AND UNDERSTAND

Online pages are harder to read than paper documents because screen resolution is less sharp. Figure 11.23 on page 293 is a good illustration of a website design that makes the small print easy to read and understand.

◢
GUIDELINES Designing Easy-To-Read Text

Follow these suggestions to make the text on your sites easy to read.

▶ **Keep the text short.** Poor screen resolution makes reading long stretches of text difficult. In general, pages should contain no more than two or three screens of information.

For more about chunking, see the Guidelines box "Understanding Learning Theory and Page Design," p. 265.

▶ **Chunk information.** When you write for the screen, chunk information to make it easier to understand. Use frequent headings, brief paragraphs, and lists.

▶ **Make the text as simple as possible.** Use common words and short sentences to make the information as simple as the subject allows.

CREATE CLEAR, INFORMATIVE LINKS

Well-phrased links are easy to read and understand. By clearly indicating what kind of information the linked site provides, links can help readers decide whether to follow them. Figure 11.24 is a good illustration of a website with clear, informative links. The following guidelines box is based on *Web Style Guide Online* (Lynch & Horton, 2011).

◢
GUIDELINES Writing Clear, Informative Links

Links are critically important. Follow these suggestions to make them easy to use.

▶ **Structure your sentences as if there were no links in your text.**

AWKWARD   Click here to go to the Rehabilitation Center page, which links to research centers across the nation.

SMOOTH   The Rehabilitation Center page links to research centers across the nation.

▶ **Indicate what information the linked page contains.** Readers get frustrated if they wait for a web file to download and then discover that it doesn't contain the information they expected.

UNINFORMATIVE   See the Rehabilitation Center.

INFORMATIVE   See the Rehabilitation Center's hours of operation.

▶ **Use standard colors for text links.** Readers are used to seeing blue for links that have not yet been clicked and purple for links that have been clicked. If you have no good reason to use other colors, stick with the ones most readers expect.

4. Our Rights & Obligations

We may change or discontinue Services, and in such case, we do not promise to keep showing or storing your information and materials.

A. Services Availability

For as long as LinkedIn continues to offer the Services, LinkedIn shall provide and seek to update, improve and expand the Services. As a result, we allow you to access LinkedIn as it may exist and be available on any given day and we have no other obligations, except as expressly stated in this Agreement. We may modify, replace, refuse access to, suspend or discontinue LinkedIn, partially or entirely, or change and modify prices prospectively for all or part of the Services for you or for all our Members in our sole discretion. All of these changes shall be effective upon their posting on LinkedIn or by direct communication to you unless otherwise noted. LinkedIn further reserves the right to withhold, remove or discard any content available as part of your account, with or without notice if deemed by LinkedIn to be contrary to this Agreement. For avoidance of doubt, LinkedIn has no obligation to store, maintain or provide you a copy of any content that you or other Members provide when using the Services.

Third parties may offer their own products and services through LinkedIn, and we are not responsible for these third-party activities.

B. Third Party Sites and Developers

LinkedIn may include links to third party web sites ("Third Party Sites") on www.linkedin.com, developer.linkedin.com, and elsewhere. LinkedIn also enables third party developers ("Platform Developers") to create applications ("Platform Applications") that provide features and functionality using data and developer tools made available by LinkedIn through its developer platform. You are responsible for evaluating whether you want to access or use a Third Party Site or Platform Application. You should review any applicable terms or privacy policy of a Third Party Site or Platform Application before using it or sharing any information with it, because you may give the third-party permission to use your information in ways we would not. LinkedIn is not

Nobody likes user agreements, and few people read them carefully. LinkedIn, the online professional network, uses a simple table design to make its user agreement a little easier to read.

In this excerpt, the right column presents a simple overview of a portion of the agreement. The left column presents the "small print": the specific provision, including links to even more detailed information.

FIGURE 11.23   Making the Small Print a Little Larger
Information from: LinkedIn, 2013; www.linkedin.com/legal/user-agreement.

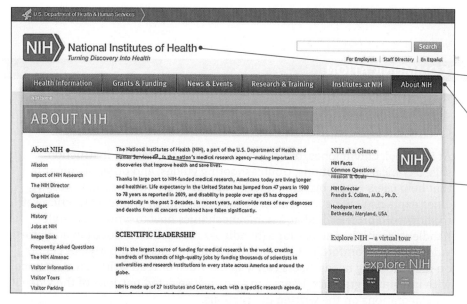

The About NIH page on the National Institutes of Health website conveys its message simply but effectively.

The top row is reserved for the name of this government agency.

Below the agency's name is the main navigation pane, beginning with "Health Information."

Below the main navigation pane is the navigation pane for the section in which this page appears: "About NIH." The About NIH page has 18 sections, beginning with "Mission."

FIGURE 11.24   An About Us Page with Clear, Informative Links
Information from: National Institutes of Health: www.nih.gov.

Combining Print and Online Documents

If understanding learning theory helps technical communicators design pages and screens, it also helps them recognize that users receive and process data and information in different ways. For example, some people may be visual learners, preferring graphics and other types of spatial representations, while others may do best with kinesthetic or physical activities. Still others may be verbal or linguistic learners, wanting written and spoken words. Technical communicators can draw on a variety of modalities—verbal, visual, aural, physical, and more—in which to present data and information, and technical communicators can integrate several modalities in a single context to support multiple learning styles.

If your analysis of audience and purpose suggests that users would benefit from support for multiple learning styles, you have the option of providing both print and online documents. In the example in Figure 11.25, technical communicators at Park Tool provide written and video-based instructions for the same task. The written instructions include graphics, some of which overlay spatial-cueing devices; the video can be watched but also listened to while working. Users have access to a variety of learning options.

STRATEGIES FOR ONLINE COMMUNICATION

Calvin Jones on Using Multiple Modalities

Courtesy Park Tool

CALVIN JONES

At Park Tool, Calvin Jones, director of education, creates the instruction sets, technical descriptions, troubleshooting guides, and other documents that help users repair bicycles. In this example from the Park Tool website, Jones explains how he uses multiple modalities in an online instruction set to show both professional and home mechanics how to wrap drop-style handlebars with handlebar tape (handlebar tape reduces vibration and provides grip and comfort, but can unwind if not installed properly). Depending on their learning needs, users can watch a video or read written instructions with integrated graphics. Users can also view selected portions of the video for elaborations on the written instructions.

The instructions provide users with different options for learning how to do the task. Providing options gives users the opportunity to learn in the method that works best for their experience level and learning style. This strategy increases the likelihood that users will be successful in following the instructions and benefiting from Park Tool's products and assistance.

The options for learning involve both telling (verbal instructions) and showing (video-based instructions). The video-based instructions also support customers with vision impairments because they can hear the instructions spoken out loud. In addition, the talking modality allows people to listen to the instructions while wrapping the handlebars, keeping their attention focused on the bike rather than dividing their attention between the bike and the screen.

The video (at over 16 minutes in length) is an elaborated version of the verbal instructions, providing added support for novices.

PREPARATION

WHAT TOOLS DO I NEED?

Wrapping drop handlebars is a skill that requires practice and patience. The finished job should look tidy and clean for the user. Wrapping also provides a good time to replacing cables and housing. Additionally, with the bar tape off, it is an opportune time to move the levers up or down the bars as desired. If you are using white or light colored tape, wash hands thoroughly or wear MG-2 gloves to keep the tape clean.

When re-wrapping bars, begin with an inspection. Adhesive padded tapes may leave lumps as they are removed, and these should be cleaned off. Housing and cables are often routed under the tape. Use thin adhesive tape such as electrical tape or narrow pieces of fiber tape to hold the housing in place.

FIGURE 11.25 Excerpt from Online Instructions Incorporating Multiple Modalities
Courtesy Park Tool.

Park Tool

2 WRAPPING PROCEDURE

During stressful riding, the rider's hands tend to apply a torque to the bars. Matching the direction of wrap helps minimize loosening of the tape. As seen from the back (the rider's point of view), the stress is outward on each side of the drops. Consequently, the right side should be wrapped in a clockwise direction while the left side should be counter-clockwise.

THE STRESS APPLIED TO THE TAPE WHILE ON THE DROPS

FIGURE 11.25   Excerpt from Online Instructions Incorporating Multiple Modalities (*continued*)
Courtesy Park Tool.

Hosting instructions on the company website allows Park Tool to provide their customers with support in a variety of modalities.

The visuals in the verbal instructions incorporate spatial modalities — in this example, directional arrows — to help users with the task at hand (handlebar tape is wrapped in different directions on a handlebar, depending on how stress is applied by riders).

WRITER'S CHECKLIST

Did you

☐ analyze your audience: their knowledge of the subject, their attitudes, their reasons for reading, and the kinds of tasks they will be carrying out? *(p. 259)*

☐ consider the purpose or purposes you are trying to achieve? *(p. 259)*

☐ determine your resources in time, money, and equipment? *(p. 260)*

Designing Print Documents and Pages

Did you

☐ consider the best size for the document? *(p. 260)*

☐ consider the best paper? *(p. 261)*

☐ consider the best binding? *(p. 261)*

☐ think about which navigational aids would be most appropriate, such as icons, color, dividers and tabs, and cross-reference tables? *(p. 262)*

☐ use color, if available, to highlight certain items, such as warnings? *(p. 263)*

☐ devise a style for headers and footers? *(p. 263)*

☐ devise a style for page numbers? *(p. 264)*

☐ employ learning theory principles of chunking, queuing, and filtering? *(p. 265)*

☐ draw thumbnail sketches and page grids that define columns and white space? *(p. 266)*

☐ choose typefaces that are appropriate for your subject? *(p. 269)*

☐ use appropriate styles from the type families? *(p. 272)*

☐ use type sizes that are appropriate for your subject and audience? *(p. 273)*

☐ choose a line length that is suitable for your subject and audience? *(p. 274)*

☐ choose line spacing that is suitable for your line length, subject, and audience? *(p. 274)*

☐ consider whether to use left-justified text or full-justified text? *(p. 275)*

☐ design your title for clarity and emphasis? *(p. 275)*

☐ devise a logical, consistent style for each heading level? *(p. 276)*

☐ use rules, boxes, screens, marginal glosses, and pull quotes where appropriate? *(p. 277)*

Designing Online Documents and Pages

Did you

☐ create informative headers and footers? *(p. 284)*

☐ help readers navigate the site by including a site map, a table of contents, "Back to top" links, and textual navigation buttons? *(p. 285)*

☐ include extra features your readers might need, such as an FAQ page, a search page or engine, resource links, or a printable version of your site? *(p. 287)*

☐ help readers connect with others through links to interactive portions of your site and to social-media sites? *(p. 287)*

☐ consider matters of accessibility? *(p. 287)*

☐ design for multicultural audiences? *(p. 290)*

☐ aim for simplicity in web page design by using simple backgrounds and conservative color combinations and by avoiding decorative graphics? *(p. 291)*

☐ make the text easy to read and understand by keeping it short, chunking information, and writing simply? *(p. 292)*

☐ create clear, informative links? *(p. 292)*

EXERCISES

For more about memos, see Ch. 14, p. 386.

1. Study the first and second pages of an article in a journal in your field. Describe ten design features on these two pages. Which design features are most effective for the audience and purpose? Which are least effective?

2. **TEAM EXERCISE** Form small groups for this collaborative exercise in analyzing design. Photocopy or scan a page from a book or a magazine. Choose a page that does not contain advertisements. Each person works independently for the first part of this project:

   • One person describes the design elements.

- One person evaluates the design. Which aspects of the design are effective, and which could be improved?

- One person creates a new design using thumbnail sketches.

Then meet as a group and compare notes. Do all members of the group agree with the first member's description of the design? With the second member's evaluation of the design? Do all members like the third member's redesign? What have your discussions taught you about design? Write a memo to your instructor presenting your findings, and include the photocopy or scan of the page with your memo.

3. Study the following excerpt from a Micron data flyer (2012, p. 1). Describe the designer's use of the design principle of alignment. How effective is it? How would you modify it? Present your analysis and recommendations in a brief memo to your instructor.

 CSN 33: Micron BGA Manufacturer's User Guide
Introduction

Customer Service Note
BGA Manufacturer's User Guide for Micron BGA Parts

Introduction

This customer service note provides information that will enable customers to easily integrate both leading-edge and legacy Micron® ball grid array (BGA) packages into their manufacturing processes. It is intended as a set of high-level guidelines and a reference manual describing typical package-related and manufacturing process-flow practices. The recommendations and suggestions provided in this customer service note serve as a guideline to help the end user to develop user-specific solutions. It is the responsibility of the end user to optimize the process to obtain the desired results.

Because the package landscape changes rapidly and information can become outdated very quickly, refer to the latest product specifications. Contact your sales representative for any additional questions not covered within this guide.

An overview of a typical BGA package and its components are shown in Figure 1.

Figure 1:   Ball Grid Array Package (Dual Die, Wire Bonded)

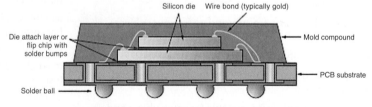

JEDEC Terminology

This document uses JEDEC terminology. JEDEC-based BGA devices in the semiconductor industry are identified by two key attributes:
- Maximum package height (profile)
- Ball pitch

For example: TFBGA - 1.2mm package height and less than 1.0mm ball pitch.

Package descriptors F1 through F6 have been added to provide more detailed ball pitch information for devices with a ball pitch of less than 0.8mm. Within the industry, many memory manufacturers continue to use only the "F" descriptor for any ball pitch of 1.0mm or less (see JEDEC JESD30E for additional information). Maximum package height profile and ball pitch codes based on the JEDEC standard are shown in Tables 1

PDF: 09005aef847l9001fSource: 09005aef847l927fe
csn33_bga_user_guide.fm-Rev. A 12/12 EN1   1   Micron Technology, Inc., reserves the right to change products or specifications without notice.
                                                                          ©2011 Micron Technology, Inc. All rights reserved.

Products and specifications discussed herein are for evaluation and reference purposes only and are subject to change by Micron without notice. Products are only warranted by Micron to meet Micron's production data sheet specifications. All information discussed herein is provided on an "as is" basis, without warranties of any kind.

4. Find the websites of three manufacturers within a single industry, such as personal watercraft, cars, computers, or medical equipment. Study the three sites, focusing on one of these aspects of site design:

   - use of color
   - quality of the writing
   - quality of the site map or index
   - navigation, including the clarity and placement of links to other pages in the site
   - accommodation of multicultural readers

   - accommodation of people with disabilities
   - phrasing of the links

   Which of the three sites is most effective? Which is least effective? Why? Compare and contrast the three sites in terms of their effectiveness.

5. Find a website that serves the needs of people with a physical disability (for example, the Glaucoma Foundation, www.glaucomafoundation.org). What attempts have the designers made to accommodate the needs of visitors to the site? How effective do you think those attempts have been?

CASE 11: Designing a Flyer

As an employee in the educational information office in the U.S. Department of Education, you have been asked by your supervisor to design a flyer for international students hoping to complete graduate school in the United States. She's given you a text document with all of the relevant information; it's your job to turn that information into a visually appealing flyer that will catch students' attention. Your supervisor has asked you to write her a memo before you begin, describing and defending the design you have in mind. If your instructor has assigned it, go to Achieve to get started on your memo.

12

Creating Graphics

➡

12

GRAPHICS ARE THE "PICTURES" in technical communication: drawings, maps, photographs, diagrams, charts, graphs, and tables. Graphics range from realistic, such as photographs, to highly abstract, such as organization charts. They range from decorative, such as clip art and stock photos that show people seated at a conference table, to highly informative, such as a schematic diagram of an electronic device.

Graphics are important in technical communication because they do the following:

- catch readers' attention and interest
- help writers communicate information that is difficult to communicate with words
- help writers clarify and emphasize information
- help nonnative speakers understand information
- help writers communicate information to multiple audiences with different interests, aptitudes, and reading habits

The Functions of Graphics

We have known for decades that graphics motivate people to study documents more closely. Some 83 percent of what we learn derives from what we see, whereas only 11 percent derives from what we hear (Gatlin, 1988). Because we are good at acquiring information through sight, a document that includes a visual element in addition to the words is more effective than one that doesn't. People studying a document with graphics learn about one-third more than people studying a document without graphics (Levie & Lentz, 1982). And people remember 43 percent more when a document includes graphics (Morrison & Jimmerson, 1989). In addition, readers like graphics. According to one survey, readers of computer documentation consistently want more graphics and fewer words (Brockmann, 1990, p. 203).

Graphics offer five benefits that words alone cannot:

1. **Graphics are indispensable in demonstrating logical and numerical relationships.** For example, an organization chart effectively represents the lines of authority in an organization. And if you want to communicate the number of power plants built in each of the last 10 years, a bar graph works better than a paragraph.

2. **Graphics can communicate spatial information more effectively than words alone.** If you want to show the details of a bicycle derailleur, a diagram of the bicycle with a close-up of the derailleur is more effective than a verbal description.

3. **Graphics can communicate steps in a process more effectively than words alone.** A troubleshooter's guide, a common kind of table, explains what might be causing a problem in a process and how you might fix it. And a diagram can show clearly how acid rain forms.

4. **Graphics can save space.** Consider the following paragraph:

   In the Wilmington area, some 80 percent of the population aged 18 to 24 have watched streamed movies on their computers. They watch an average of 1.86 movies a week. Among 25- to 34-year-olds, the percentage is 72, and the average number of movies is 1.62. Among 35- to 49-year-olds, the percentage is 62, and the average number of movies is 1.19. Among the 50 to 64 age group, the percentage is 47, and the number of movies watched averages 0.50. Finally, among those people 65 years old or older, the percentage is 28, and the average number of movies watched weekly is 0.31.

   Presenting this information in a paragraph is uneconomical and makes the information hard to remember. Presented as a table, however, the information is more concise and more memorable.

AGE	PERCENTAGE WATCHING STREAMED MOVIES	NUMBER OF MOVIES WATCHED PER WEEK
18–24	80	1.86
25–34	72	1.62
35–49	62	1.19
50–64	47	0.50
65+	28	0.31

5. **Graphics can reduce the cost of documents intended for international readers.** Translation costs an average of nearly 15 cents per word (Straker Translations, 2019). Used effectively, graphics can reduce the number of words you have to translate.

As you plan and draft your document, look for opportunities to use graphics to clarify, emphasize, summarize, and organize information.

The Characteristics of an Effective Graphic

To be effective, graphics must be clear, understandable, and meaningfully related to the larger discussion. Follow these five principles:

- **A graphic should serve a purpose.** Don't include a graphic unless it will help readers understand or remember information. Avoid content-free photographs and clip art, such as drawings of businesspeople shaking hands.

- **A graphic should be simple and uncluttered.** Three-dimensional bar graphs are easy to make, but they are harder to understand than two-dimensional ones, as shown in Figure 12.1.

- **A graphic should present a manageable amount of information.** Presenting too much information can confuse readers. Consider audience and purpose: what kinds of graphics are your readers familiar with, how much do they already know about the subject, and what do you want the document to do? Because readers learn best if you present information in small chunks, create several simple graphics rather than a single complicated one.

- **A graphic should meet readers' format expectations.** Through experience, readers learn how to read different kinds of graphics. Follow the conventions—for instance, use diamonds to represent decision points in a flowchart—unless you have a good reason not to.

- **A graphic should be clearly labeled.** Give every graphic (except a brief, informal one) a unique, clear, informative title. Fully label the columns of a table and the axes and lines of a graph. Don't make readers guess whether you are using meters or yards, or whether you are also including statistics from the previous year.

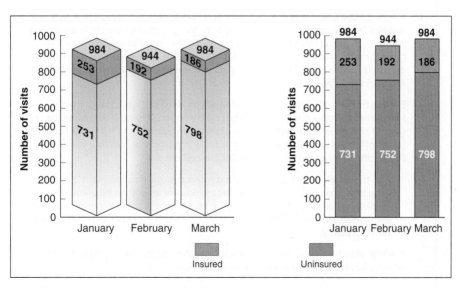

Unnecessary 3D is one example of chartjunk, a term used by Tufte (1983) to describe the ornamentation that clutters up a graphic, distracting readers from the message.

The two-dimensional bar graph is clean and uncluttered; the three-dimensional graph is more difficult to understand because the additional dimension obscures the main data points. The number of uninsured emergency-room visits in February, for example, is very difficult to see in the three-dimensional graph.

FIGURE 12.1   Chartjunk and Clear Art

ETHICS NOTE

CREATING HONEST GRAPHICS

Follow these six suggestions to ensure that you represent data honestly in your graphics.

- If you did not create the graphic or generate the data, cite your source. If you want to publish a graphic that you did not create, obtain permission. For more on citing graphics, see page 309.

- Include all relevant data. For example, if you have a data point that you cannot explain, do not change the scale to eliminate it.

- Begin the axes in your graphs at zero — or mark them clearly — so that you represent quantities honestly.

- Do not use a table to hide a data point that would be obvious in a graph.

- Show items as they really are. Do not manipulate a photograph of a computer monitor to make the screen look bigger than it is, for example.

- Do not use color or shading to misrepresent an item's importance. A light-shaded bar in a bar graph, for example, appears larger and nearer than a dark-shaded bar of the same size.

Common problem areas are pointed out in the discussions of various kinds of graphics throughout this chapter.

◢
GUIDELINES Integrating Graphics and Text

It is not enough to add graphics to your text; you have to integrate the two.

▶ **Place the graphic in an appropriate location.** If readers need the graphic in order to understand the discussion, put it directly after the relevant point in the discussion or as soon after it as possible. If the graphic merely supports or elaborates a point, include it as an appendix.

▶ **Introduce the graphic in the text.** Whenever possible, refer to a graphic before it appears (ideally, on the same page). Refer to the graphic by number (such as "see Figure 7"). Do not refer to "the figure above" or "the figure below," because the graphic might move during the production process. If the graphic is in an appendix, cross-reference it: "For complete details of the operating characteristics, see Appendix B, page 17."

▶ **Explain the graphic in the text.** State what you want readers to learn from it. Sometimes a simple paraphrase of the title is enough: "Figure 2 compares the costs of the three major types of coal gasification plants." At other times, however, you might need to explain why the graphic is important or how to interpret it. If the graphic is intended to make a point, be explicit:

> As Figure 2 shows, a high-sulfur bituminous coal gasification plant is more expensive than either a low-sulfur bituminous or an anthracite plant, but more than half of its cost is for cleanup equipment. If these expenses could be eliminated, high-sulfur bituminous would be the least expensive of the three types of plants.

In addition to text explanations, graphics are often accompanied by captions, ranging from a sentence to several paragraphs.

(continued)

For more about white space, screens, boxes, and rules, see Ch. 11, "White Space," p. 267, and "Other Design Features," pp. 277–80. For more about lists of illustrations, see "List of Illustrations," Ch. 18, p. 497.

▶ **Make the graphic clearly visible.** Distinguish the graphic from the surrounding text by adding white space around it, placing rules (lines) above and below it, putting a screen behind it, or enclosing it in a box.

▶ **Make the graphic easy to find.** If the document is more than a few pages long and contains more than four or five graphics, consider including a list of illustrations so that readers can find them easily.

Understanding the Process of Creating Graphics

Creating graphics involves planning, producing, revising, and citing.

PLANNING GRAPHICS

Whether you focus first on the text or the graphics, consider the following four issues as you plan your graphics.

- **Audience.** Will readers understand the kinds of graphics you want to use? Will they know the standard icons in your field? Are they motivated to read your document, or do you need to enliven the text—for example, by adding color for emphasis—to hold their attention? General audiences know how to read common types of graphics, such as those that appear frequently in newspapers or on popular websites. A general audience, for example, could use this bar graph to compare two bottles of wine:

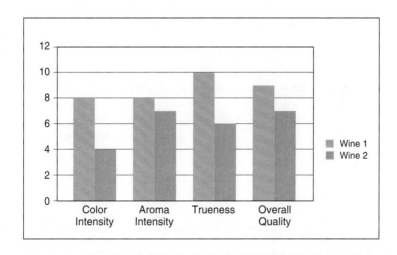

However, they would probably have trouble with the following radar graph:

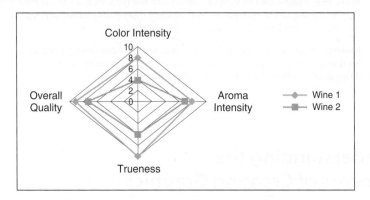

- **Purpose.** What point are you trying to make with the graphic? Imagine what you want your readers to know and do with the information. For example, if you want readers to know the exact dollar amounts spent on athletics by a college, use a table:

YEAR	MEN'S ATHLETICS ($)	WOMEN'S ATHLETICS ($)
2017	38,990	29,305
2018	42,400	30,080
2019	44,567	44,213

If you want readers to know how spending on athletics is changing over time, use a line graph:

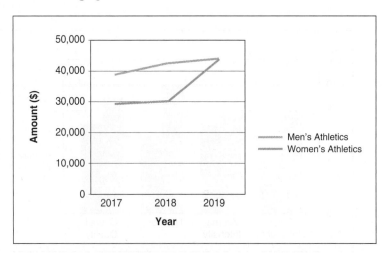

- **The kind of information you want to communicate.** Your subject will help you decide what type of graphic to include. For example, in writing about languages spoken by your state's citizens, you might use a table for the statistical data, a map for the patterns of language use, and a graph for statistical trends over time.

- **Physical conditions.** The physical conditions in which readers will use the document—amount of lighting, amount of surface space available, the size of the screen on which the information will be displayed, and so forth—will influence the type of graphic as well as its size and shape, the thickness of lines, the size of type, and the color.

As you plan how you are going to create the graphics, consider four important factors:

- **Time.** Because making a complicated graphic can take a lot of time, you need to establish a schedule.

- **Money.** Creating a high-quality graphic can be expensive. How big is the project budget? How can you use that money effectively?

- **Equipment.** Determine what tools and software you will require, such as spreadsheets for tables and graphs or graphics software for diagrams.

- **Expertise.** How much do you know about creating graphics? Do you have access to the expertise of others?

For more about planning and budgeting, see "Devising a Schedule and a Budget," Ch. 3, p. 47.

PRODUCING GRAPHICS

Usually, you won't have all the resources you would like. You will have to choose one of the following four approaches:

- **Use existing graphics.** For a student paper that *will not be published*, some instructors allow the use of copied and pasted existing graphics; other instructors do not. For a document that *will be published*, whether written by a student or a professional, using an existing graphic is permissible if the graphic is in the public domain (that is, not under copyright), if it is the property of the writer's organization, or if the organization has obtained permission to use it. Be particularly careful about graphics you find on the web. Many people mistakenly think that anything on the web can be used without permission. The same copyright laws that apply to printed material apply to web-based material, whether words or graphics. For more on citing graphics, see "Citing Sources of Graphics," page 309.

  Aside from the issue of copyright, think carefully before you use existing graphics. The style of the graphic might not match that of the others you want to use; the graphic might lack some features you want or include some you don't. If you use an existing graphic, assign it your own number and title.

- **Modify existing graphics.** You can redraw an existing graphic or use a scanner to digitize the graphic and then modify it electronically with graphics software. The same copyright laws that apply to existing graphics also apply to modified graphics. See "Citing Sources of Graphics," page 309, for more on citing graphics.

- **Create graphics on a computer.** You can create many kinds of graphics using your spreadsheet software and the drawing tools in your word processor.

Why To Insert and Modify Graphics

You can insert graphics into your document in order to highlight, clarify, summarize, and/or organize information. You may have access to graphics, from online stock photo agencies or your company's graphics library, that could benefit from some modification.

How To Insert and Modify Graphics

To **insert a graphic**—such as a photograph, drawing, chart, or graph—into your document, place your cursor where you want to make the insertion. From the **Insert** tab in either Microsoft Word or Google Docs, choose the type of item you wish to insert.

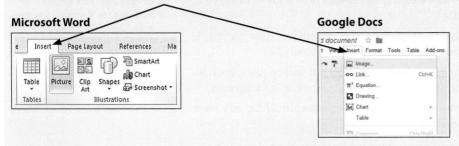

Microsoft Word

Google Docs

To **modify a graphic**, select it and then work with the range of tools available in your program, which can usually be seen by right-clicking on the graphic. Typical commands relate to cropping, resizing, and making adjustments to color, brightness, and contrast.

Microsoft Word

Google Docs

Consult the Selected Bibliography, page 710, for a list of books about computers and technical communication.

For more about work made for hire, see "Copyright Law," Ch. 2, p. 24.

• **Have someone else create the graphics.** Professional-level graphics software can cost hundreds of dollars and require hundreds of hours of practice. Some companies have technical-publications departments with graphics experts, but others subcontract this work. Many print shops and service bureaus have graphics experts on staff or can direct you to them.

Note that even if you create a graphic yourself or hire someone to create one for you, you need to cite the source of any copyright-protected information used to create it.

REVISING GRAPHICS

As with any other aspect of technical communication, build in enough time and budget enough money to revise the graphics you want to use. Create a checklist and evaluate each graphic for effectiveness. The Writer's Checklist at the end of this chapter is a good starting point. Show your graphics to people whose backgrounds are similar to those of your intended readers and ask them for suggestions. Revise the graphics and solicit more reactions.

CITING SOURCES OF GRAPHICS

If you wish to publish a graphic that is protected by copyright (even if you have revised it), you need to obtain written permission from the copyright holder. The same goes for any copyright-protected information you use to create a graphic. Related to the issue of permission is the issue of citation. Of course, you do not have to cite the source of a graphic if you created it yourself, if it is not protected by copyright, or if your organization owns the copyright.

For more information about copyright, see "Copyright Law," Ch. 2, p. 24.

In all other cases, however, you should include a source citation, even if your document is a course assignment and will not be published. Citing the sources of graphics, even those you have revised substantially, shows your instructor that you understand professional conventions and your ethical responsibilities.

If you are following a style manual, check to see whether it presents a format for citing sources of graphics. In addition to citing a graphic's source in the reference list, most style manuals call for a source statement in the caption:

For more about style manuals, see Appendix, Part B, p. 632.

PRINT SOURCE

Source: Verduijn, 2015, p. 14. Copyright 2015 by Tedopres International B.V. Reprinted with permission.

ONLINE SOURCE

Source: Johnson Space Center Digital Image Collection. Copyright 2019 by NASA. Reprinted with permission.

If your graphic is based on an existing graphic or based on copyright-protected information from another source, the source statement should state that your graphic is "based on" or "adapted from" your source:

Source: Adapted from Jonklaas et al., 2011, p. 771. Copyright 2008 by American Medical Association. Reprinted with permission.

Using Color Effectively

Color draws attention to information you want to emphasize, establishes visual patterns to promote understanding, and adds interest. But it is also easy to misuse. The following discussion is based on Jan V. White's still-excellent text *Color for the Electronic Age* (1990).

In using color in graphics and page design, keep these six principles in mind:

- **Don't overdo it.** Readers can interpret only two or three colors at a time. Use colors for small items, such as portions of graphics and important words. And don't use colors where black and white will work better.

- **Use color to emphasize particular items.** People interpret color before they interpret shape, size, or placement on the page. Color effectively draws readers' attention to a particular item or group of items on a page. In Figure 12.2, for example, color adds emphasis to different kinds of information.

For more about designing your document, see Ch. 11.

- **Use color to create patterns.** The principle of repetition—readers learn to recognize patterns—applies in graphics as well as in document design. In creating patterns, also consider shape. For instance, use red for safety comments but place them in octagons resembling a stop sign. This way, you give your readers two visual cues to help them recognize the pattern. Figure 12.3 (on p. 311) shows the use of color to establish patterns. Color is also an effective way to emphasize design features such as text boxes, rules, screens, and headers and footers.

For more about presentation graphics, see "Preparing Presentation Graphics," Ch. 21, p. 599.

- **Use contrast effectively.** The visibility of a color is a function of the background against which it appears (see Figure 12.4 on p. 311). The strongest contrasts are between black and white and between black and yellow. The need for effective contrast also applies to graphics used in presentations, as shown in Figure 12.5 on page 311.

For more about cultural patterns, see "Communicating Across Cultures," Ch. 5, p. 101.

- **Take advantage of any symbolic meanings colors may already have.** In American culture, for example, red signals danger, heat, or electricity; yellow signals caution; and orange signals warning. Using these warm colors

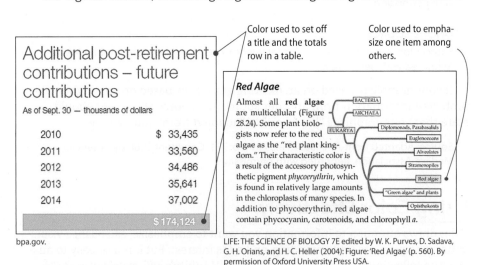

Color used to set off a title and the totals row in a table.

Color used to emphasize one item among others.

Additional post-retirement contributions – future contributions

As of Sept. 30 — thousands of dollars

2010	$ 33,435
2011	33,560
2012	34,486
2013	35,641
2014	37,002
	$ 174,124

bpa.gov.

Red Algae

Almost all **red algae** are multicellular (Figure 28.24). Some plant biologists now refer to the red algae as the "red plant kingdom." Their characteristic color is a result of the accessory photosynthetic pigment *phycoerythrin*, which is found in relatively large amounts in the chloroplasts of many species. In addition to phycoerythrin, red algae contain phycocyanin, carotenoids, and chlorophyll *a*.

BACTERIA
ARCHAEA
EUKARYA
Diplomonads, Parabasalids
Euglenozoans
Alveolates
Stramenopiles
Red algae
"Green algae" and plants
Opisthokonts

LIFE: THE SCIENCE OF BIOLOGY 7E edited by W. K. Purves, D. Sadava, G. H. Orians, and H. C. Heller (2004): Figure: 'Red Algae' (p. 560). By permission of Oxford University Press USA.

FIGURE 12.2   Color Used for Emphasis

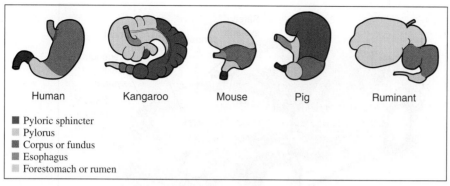

FIGURE 12.3   **Color Used to Establish Patterns**

in ways that depart from these familiar meanings could be confusing. The cooler colors—blues and greens—are more conservative and subtle. (Figure 12.6 illustrates these principles.) Keep in mind, however, that people in different cultures interpret colors differently.

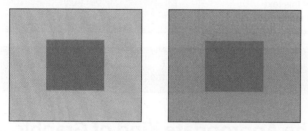

Notice that a color washes out if the background color is too similar.

FIGURE 12.4   **The Effect of Background in Creating Contrast**

a. Insufficient contrast   **b.** Effective contrast

In graphic (a), the text is hard to read because of insufficient contrast. The greater contrast in graphic (b) makes the text easier to read.

FIGURE 12.5   **Effective Contrast Used in a Presentation Slide**

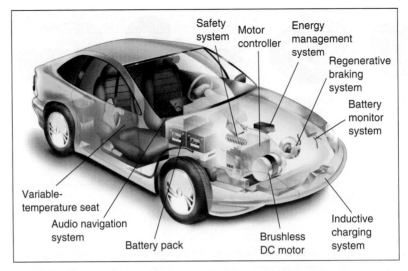

The batteries are red. The warm red contrasts effectively with the cool green of the car body.

Safety system
Motor controller
Energy management system
Regenerative braking system
Battery monitor system
Variable-temperature seat
Audio navigation system
Battery pack
Brushless DC motor
Inductive charging system

FIGURE 12.6 Colors Have Clear Associations for Readers

- Be aware that color can obscure or swallow up text.

If you are using print against a colored background, you might need to make the type a little bigger, because color makes text look smaller.

Text printed against a white background looks bigger than the same-size text printed against a colored background. White letters counteract this effect.

Is this text the same size?

Is this text the same size?

This line of type appears to reach out to the reader.
This line of type appears to recede into the background.

Choosing the Appropriate Kind of Graphic

As Figure 12.7 (on p. 313) shows, even a few simple facts can yield a number of different points. Your responsibility when creating a graphic is to determine what point you want to make and how best to make it. Don't rely on your software to do your thinking; it can't.

Graphics used in technical documents are classified as tables or figures. Tables are lists of data, usually numbers, arranged in columns. Figures are everything else: graphs, charts, diagrams, photographs, and the like. Typically, tables and figures are numbered separately: the first table in a document is Table 1; the first figure is Figure 1. In documents of more than one chapter (like this book), the graphics are usually numbered within each chapter. That is, Figure 3.2 is the second figure in Chapter 3.

The discussion that follows is based on the classification system in William Horton's "Pictures Please—Presenting Information Visually," in *Techniques for Technical Communicators* (Horton, 1992). Table 12.1 on pages 314–15 presents an overview of the discussion that begins on p. 316.

Rail Line	November		December		January	
	Disabled by electrical problems (%)	Total disabled	Disabled by electrical problems (%)	Total disabled	Disabled by electrical problems (%)	Total disabled
Bryn Mawr	19 (70)	27	17 (60)	28	20 (76)	26
Swarthmore	12 (75)	16	9 (52)	17	13 (81)	16
Manayunk	22 (64)	34	26 (83)	31	24 (72)	33

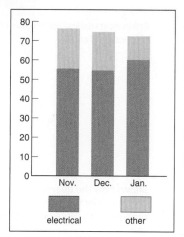

a. Number of railcars disabled, November–January

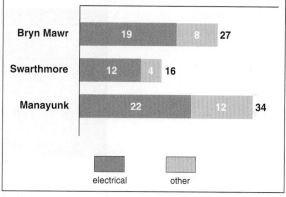

b. Number of railcars disabled in November

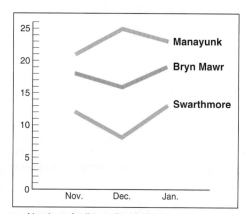

c. Number of railcars disabled by electrical problems, November–January

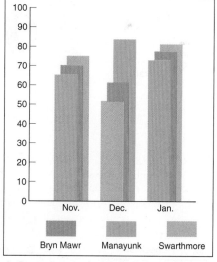

d. Range in percentage of railcars, disabled by electrical problems, November–January

FIGURE 12.7   Different Graphics Emphasizing Different Points

Each of these four graphs emphasizes a different point derived from the data in the table. Graph (a) focuses on the total number of railcars disabled each month, classified by cause, graph (b) focuses on the three rail lines during one month, and so forth. For information on bar graphs, see pages 318–23; for information on line graphs, see pages 325–28.

TABLE 12.1   Choosing the Appropriate Kind of Graphic

PURPOSE	TYPE OF GRAPHIC		WHAT THE GRAPHIC DOES BEST
Illustrating numerical information	Table		Shows large amounts of numerical data, especially when there are several variables for a number of items.
	Bar graph		Shows the relative values of two or more items.
	Infographic		Enlivens statistical information for the general reader.
	Line graph		Shows how the quantity of an item changes over time. A line graph can present much more data than a bar graph can.
	Pie chart		Shows the relative sizes of the parts of a whole. Pie charts are instantly familiar to most readers.
Illustrating logical relationships	Diagram		Represents relationships among items or properties of items.
	Organization chart		Shows the lines of authority and responsibility in an organization or hierarchical relationships among items.
Illustrating process descriptions and instructions	Checklist		Lists or shows what equipment or materials to gather or describes an action.

(continued)

TABLE 12.1 Choosing the Appropriate Kind of Graphic (*continued*)		
PURPOSE	**TYPE OF GRAPHIC**	**WHAT THE GRAPHIC DOES BEST**
Illustrating process descriptions and instructions (*continued*)	Table	Shows numbers of items or indicates the state (on/off) of an item.
	Flowchart	Shows the stages of a procedure or a process.
	Logic tree	Shows which of two or more paths to follow.
Illustrating visual and spatial characteristics	Photograph	Shows precisely the external surface of objects.
	Screen shot	Shows what appears on a computer screen.
	Line drawing	Shows simplified representations of objects.
	Map	Shows geographic areas.

Information from W. Horton, "The Almost Universal Language: Graphics for International Documentation" from TECHNICAL COMMUNICATION 40 (1993): 682–693.

ILLUSTRATING NUMERICAL INFORMATION

The kinds of graphics used most often to display numerical values are tables, bar graphs, infographics, line graphs, and pie charts.

Tables *Tables* convey large amounts of numerical data easily, and they are often the only way to present several variables for a number of items. For example, if you wanted to show how many people are employed in 6 industries in 10 states, a table would probably be most effective. Although tables lack the visual appeal of other kinds of graphics, they can present much more information.

In addition to having a number ("Table 1"), tables are identified by an informative title that includes the items being compared and the basis (or bases) of comparison:

Table 3. Mallard Population in Rangeley, 2009–2016
Table 4.7. The Growth of the Robotics Industry in Japan and the United States, 2016

Figure 12.8 illustrates the standard parts of a table.

Tables are usually titled at the top because readers scan them from top to bottom.

The data in this table consist of numbers, but tables can also present textual information or a combination of numbers and text.

Some tables include a stub head. The stub — the left-hand column — lists the items for which data are displayed. Note that indentation in the stub helps show relationships. The heading "Natural Gas Liquids" is left-aligned. This row functions as a Totals row. Indented beneath this heading are the two categories that make up the totals: pentanes and liquefied petroleum gases. Beneath the category heading are rows for the four kinds of liquefied petroleum gases.

Note that the numbers are right-aligned.

Note that tables often contain one or more source statements and footnotes.

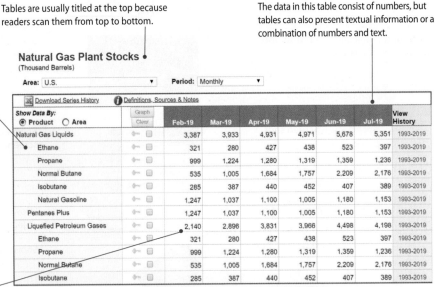

Natural Gas Plant Stocks
(Thousand Barrels)

Area: U.S. ▼   Period: Monthly ▼

		Feb-19	Mar-19	Apr-19	May-19	Jun-19	Jul-19	View History
Natural Gas Liquids		3,387	3,933	4,931	4,971	5,678	5,351	1993-2019
Ethane		321	280	427	438	523	397	1993-2019
Propane		999	1,224	1,280	1,319	1,359	1,236	1993-2019
Normal Butane		535	1,005	1,684	1,757	2.209	2,176	1993-2019
Isobutane		285	387	440	452	407	389	1993-2019
Natural Gasoline		1,247	1,037	1,100	1,005	1,180	1,153	1993-2019
Pentanes Plus		1,247	1,037	1,100	1,005	1,180	1,153	1993-2019
Liquefied Petroleum Gases		2,140	2.896	3,831	3,966	4,498	4,198	1993-2019
Ethane		321	280	427	438	523	397	1993-2019
Propane		999	1,224	1,280	1,319	1,359	1,236	1993-2019
Normal Butane		535	1,005	1,684	1,757	2.209	2,176	1993-2019
Isobutane		285	387	440	452	407		1993-2019

Download Series History   Definitions, Sources & Notes
Show Data By: ⦿ Product ○ Area   Graph / Clear

◆= Click on the source key icon to learn how to download series into Excel, or to embed a chart or map on your website.
• = No Data Reported; -- = Not Applicable; **NA** = Not Available; **W** = Withheld to avoid disclosure of individual company data.
Notes: See Definitions, Sources, and Notes link above for more information on this table.
Release Date: 9/30/2019
Next Release Date: 10/31/2019

FIGURE 12.8   Parts of a Table

This is an interactive table from the Energy Information Administration showing the amount of natural gas stocks in the United States over a six-month period. Note that you can use the radio buttons to show the data by location or product, and you can use the pull-down menu to specify a time frame. Even though this table is interactive, it functions much the way any table does.

U.S. Energy Information Administration.

◢
GUIDELINES **Creating Effective Tables**

Follow these nine suggestions to make sure your tables are clear and professional.

▶ **Indicate the units of measure.** If all the data are expressed in the same unit, indicate that unit in the title:

> Farm Size in the Midwestern States (in Hectares)

If the data in different columns are expressed in different units, indicate the units in the column heads:

| Population (in Millions) | Per Capita Income (in Thousands of U.S. Dollars) |

You can express data in both real numbers and percentages. A column head and the first data cell under it might read as follows:

> <u>Number of Students (Percentage)</u>
>
> 53 (83)

▶ **In the stub—the left-hand column—list the items being compared.** Arrange the items in a logical order: big to small, more important to less important, alphabetical, chronological, geographical, and so forth. If the items fall into several categories, include the names of the categories in the stub:

> *Snowbelt States* . . . .
> > Connecticut . . . .
> > New York . . . .
> > Vermont . . . .
> *Sunbelt States* . . . .
> > Arizona . . . .
> > California . . . .
> > New Mexico . . . .

If you cannot group the items in the stub in logical categories, skip a line after every five rows to help the reader follow the rows across the table. Or use a screen (a colored background) for every other set of five rows. Also useful is linking the stub and the next column with a row of dots called *dot leaders*.

▶ **In the columns, arrange the data clearly and logically.** Use the decimal-tab feature to line up the decimal points:

> 3,147.4
> 365.7
> 46,803.5

In general, don't vary the units used in a column unless the quantities are so dissimilar that your readers would have a difficult time understanding them if expressed in the same units.

For more about screens, see Table 11.3, Ch. 11, p. 277.

(continued)

3.4 hr
12.7 min
4.3 sec

This list would probably be easier for most readers to understand than one in which all quantities were expressed in the same unit.

▶ **Do the math.** If your readers will need to know the totals for the columns or the rows, provide them. If your readers will need to know percentage changes from one column to the next, present them:

Number of Students (Percentage Change from Previous Year)

2017	2018	2019
619	644 (+4.0)	614 (–4.7)

▶ **Use dot leaders if a column contains a "blank" spot**—a place where there are no appropriate data:

3,147

. . .

46,803

But don't substitute dot leaders for a quantity of zero.

▶ **Don't make the table wider than it needs to be.** The reader should be able to scan across a row easily. As White (1984) points out, there is no reason to make a table as wide as the text column in the document. If a column head is long—more than five or six words—stack the words:

Computers Sold Without
a Memory-Card Reader

▶ **Minimize the use of rules.** Grimstead (1987) recommends using rules only when necessary: to separate the title and the heads, the heads and the body, and the body and the notes. When you use rules, make them thin rather than thick.

▶ **Provide footnotes where necessary.** All the information your readers need in order to understand the table should accompany it.

▶ **If you did not generate the information yourself, indicate your source.** See the discussion of citing sources of graphics on page 309.

Bar Graphs Like tables, *bar graphs* can communicate numerical values, but they are better at showing the relative values of two or more items. Figure 12.9 on page 319 shows typical horizontal and vertical bar graphs that you can make easily using your spreadsheet software. Figure 12.10 on page 319 shows an effective bar graph that uses grid lines.

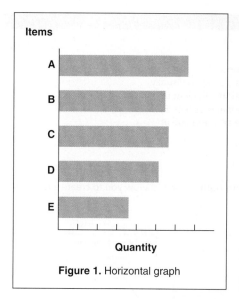

Figure 1. Horizontal graph

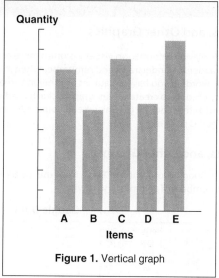

Figure 1. Vertical graph

Horizontal bars are best for showing quantities such as speed and distance. Vertical bars are best for showing quantities such as height, size, and amount. However, these distinctions are not ironclad; as long as the axes are clearly labeled, readers should have no trouble understanding the graph.

FIGURE 12.9   Structures of Horizontal and Vertical Bar Graphs

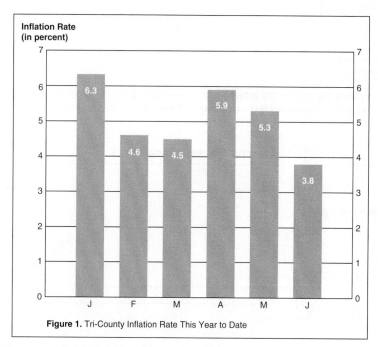

Figure 1. Tri-County Inflation Rate This Year to Date

FIGURE 12.10   Effective Bar Graph with Grid Lines

▶TECH TIP

Why To Create Tables, Charts, and Other Graphics

As noted throughout this chapter, displaying information visually is often more economical than writing it out, and material is easier for readers to understand and remember when it is displayed visually than when it is presented using only words. If you have a data set or other information you want to display visually, you can use a variety of tools to create tables, graphs, charts, and other graphics. Be careful, however, not to go overboard with elaborate graphics. Keep your audience and purpose in mind, and make your message as clear as possible.

How To Create Tables, Charts, and Other Graphics

To create tables in Microsoft Word or Google Docs, choose **Table** from the **Insert** tab. Both programs allow you to create a table by dragging your cursor to specify the numbers of columns and rows.

Microsoft Word

Word offers additional options, such as using the **Insert Table** dialog box to specify the numbers of columns and rows, converting text into a table, importing data from Excel, or selecting a **Quick Tables** template and replacing the data with your own.

Google Docs

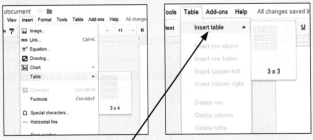

Another way to insert a table in Google Docs is to choose the **Insert Table** feature from the **Table** tab.

Both Google Docs and Microsoft Word include **Drawing** tools in the **Insert** tab that allow you to insert shapes into your document, many of which can incorporate text. In addition, Word's **Smart Art** feature provides an elaborate array of customizable graphics that are organized by category, such as List, Process, and Cycle.

Smart Art in Microsoft Word

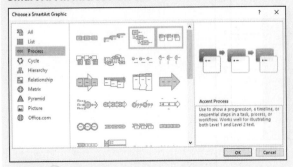

Drawing Shapes in Google Docs

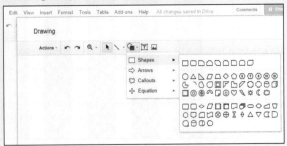

(continued)

To create charts in Microsoft Excel or Google Spreadsheets, first enter the data into the spreadsheet and select the cells you want to include in your graphic. In Excel, use the drop-down menus in the **Charts** group on the **Insert** tab, or select **See All Charts** in the lower right to open the **Chart** dialog box. In Google, select **Chart** from the **Insert** tab to launch the chart selection dialog box. Both programs allow you to choose from a wide range of graphics, but simpler is usually better.

Microsoft Excel

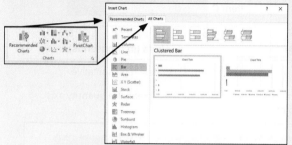

Google Spreadsheets

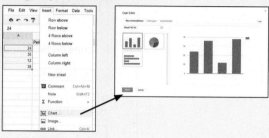

 GUIDELINES Creating Effective Bar Graphs

▶ **Make the proportions fair.** Make your vertical axis about 25 percent shorter than your horizontal axis. An excessively long vertical axis exaggerates the differences in quantities; an excessively long horizontal axis minimizes the differences. Make all the bars the same width, and make the space between them about half as wide as a bar. Here are two poorly proportioned graphs:

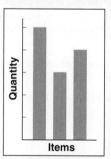

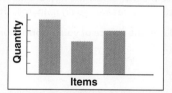

a. Excessively long vertical axis   b. Excessively long horizontal axis

▶ **If possible, begin the quantity scale at zero.** Doing so ensures that the bars accurately represent the quantities. Notice how misleading a graph can be if the scale doesn't begin at zero.

(continued)

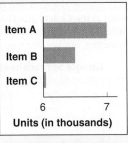
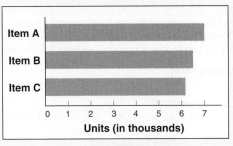

c. Misleading   **d.** Accurately representative

If it is not practical to start the quantity scale at zero, break the quantity axis clearly at a common point on all the bars.

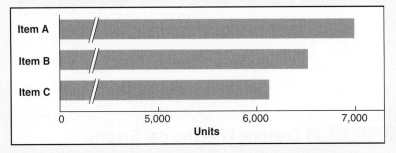

▸ **Use tick marks—marks along the axis—to signal the amounts.** Use grid lines—tick marks that extend across the entire graph—if the graph has several bars, some of which are too far away from the tick marks to enable readers to gauge the quantities easily. (See Figure 12.10 on p. 319.)

▸ **Arrange the bars in a logical sequence.** For a vertical bar graph, use chronology if possible. For a horizontal bar graph, arrange the bars in order of descending size, beginning at the top of the graph, unless some other logical sequence seems more appropriate.

▸ **Place the title below the figure.** Unlike tables, which are usually read from top to bottom, figures are usually read from the bottom up.

▸ **Indicate the source of your information if you did not generate it yourself.**

The five variations on the basic bar graph shown in Table 12.2 can help you accommodate different communication needs. You can make all these types using your spreadsheet software.

TABLE 12.2   Variations on the Basic Bar Graph

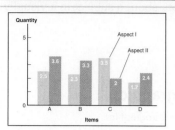

Grouped bar graph. The *grouped bar graph* lets you compare two or three aspects for each item. Grouped bar graphs would be useful, for example, for showing the numbers of full-time and part-time students at several universities. One bar could represent full-time students; the other, part-time students. To distinguish between the bars, use hatching (striping), shading, or color, and either label one set of bars or provide a key.

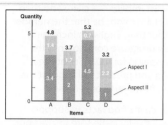

Subdivided bar graph. In the *subdivided bar graph*, Aspect I and Aspect II are stacked like wooden blocks placed on top of each other. Although totals are easy to compare in a subdivided bar graph, individual quantities are not.

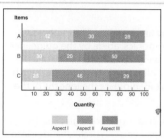

100-percent bar graph. The *100-percent bar graph*, which shows the relative proportions of the aspects that make up several items, is useful in portraying, for example, the proportion of full-scholarship, partial-scholarship, and nonscholarship students at a number of colleges.

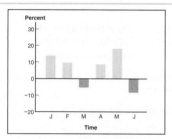

Deviation bar graph. The *deviation bar graph* shows how various quantities deviate from a norm. Deviation bar graphs are often used when the information contains both positive and negative values, such as profits and losses. Bars on the positive side of the norm line (above it) represent profits; bars on the negative side (below it), losses.

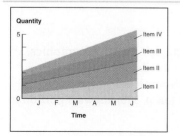

Stratum graph. The *stratum graph*, also called an *area graph*, shows the change in quantities of several items over time. Although stratum graphs are used frequently in business and scientific fields, general readers sometimes have trouble understanding how to read them.

Infographics An *infographic*—short for *information graphic*—is a combination of words and graphics used to present factual data about a subject in a visually interesting way.

◢ **GUIDELINES** Creating Effective Infographics

Follow these seven suggestions for making effective infographics.

For more about claims and support, see "Using the Right Kinds of Evidence," Ch. 8, p. 184.

▶ **Make a claim.** A good infographic states—or at least implies—a claim and then presents evidence to support it. For instance, the claim might be that the number of people accessing the internet in a language other than English is increasing at an accelerating rate, that the pace at which new drugs are coming onto the market is slowing, or that the cost of waging a campaign for a U.S. Senate seat has increased tenfold in the last 20 years. The claim you present will suggest the theme of your graphics: you might consider maps, flowcharts, or statistics.

For more about research techniques, see Ch. 6.

▶ **Use accurate data.** Once you have settled on your claim, find facts to support it. Use reputable sources, and then check and recheck the facts. Be sure to cite your sources on the infographic itself.

▶ **Follow the guidelines for the type of graphic you are creating.** Although you want to express your creativity when you create graphics, abide by the guidelines for that type of graphic. For instance, if you use a bar graph to present data on the number of zebras born in captivity, your first obligation is to make the length of each bar reflect the quantity it represents; don't manipulate the lengths of the bars to make the graph look like a zebra.

▶ **Write concisely.** If you need more than a paragraph to introduce a graphic, try revising the text to get the word count down or see if you can break the idea into several smaller ones.

▶ **Don't present too much information.** It's natural to want to include all the data you have found, but if the infographic is too tightly packed with text and graphics, readers will be intimidated. Use white space to let the graphics breathe.

▶ **Don't go on forever.** Your readers will want to spend a minute—maybe two—on the infographic. They won't want to spend 15 minutes.

For more about evaluating and testing, see Ch. 13.

▶ **Test the infographic.** As with any kind of technical document, the more you evaluate and test the infographic, the better it will be.

Figure 12.11 (on p. 325), a portion of an infographic about infographics, shows many of the techniques used in this type of display.

Infographics are also an effective way to communicate information through a visual/verbal argument. Figure 12.12 (on p. 326) shows a portion of

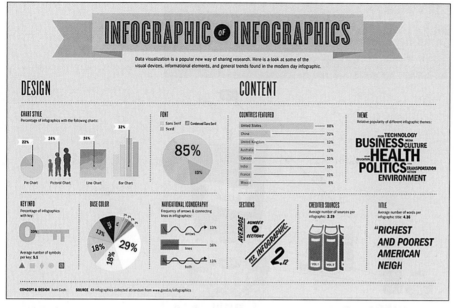

FIGURE 12.11 **An Infographic About Infographics**
Used by permission of Ivan Cash/Cash Studios.

Designer Ivan Cash created this infographic by collecting data about infographics and then creating graphics to make the data interesting and visually appealing.

Infographics are built around basic types of graphical display: pie charts, line graphs, bar graphs, and diagrams. In an effective infographic, each visual display adheres to the conventions of the graphic on which it is based. For instance, in the "Countries Featured" bar graph, the length of each bar accurately reflects the quantity of the item it represents.

The art makes the data visually interesting, but the most important characteristic of an infographic is accuracy: the data must be accurate and presented fairly.

an infographic that makes a very clear argument about the rising size of food portions.

Infographics are very popular, but many of them are of low quality. Before you create an infographic to communicate technical information, be sure you are not skewing your data or oversimplifying to promote an agenda. Doing so is unethical. In Figure 12.13 (on p. 326), digital strategist Hervé Peitrequin offers a clever commentary on infographics.

Line Graphs *Line graphs* are used almost exclusively to show changes in quantity over time: for example, the month-by-month production figures for a product. A line graph focuses readers' attention on the change in quantity, whereas a bar graph emphasizes the quantities themselves.

You can plot three or four lines on a line graph. If the lines intersect, use different colors or patterns to distinguish them. If the lines intersect too often, however, the graph will be unclear; in this case, draw separate graphs. Figure 12.14 (on p. 327) shows a line graph.

Many organizations use infographics to present arguments. Here, the Centers for Disease Control and Prevention compares fast-food portion sizes from the 1950s and today to make the case that, as the text at the top states, "Portion sizes have been growing. So have we." The text goes on to suggest steps people can take to reduce their portion sizes.

Several sites on the web, such as infogr.am, offer free templates for making infographics.

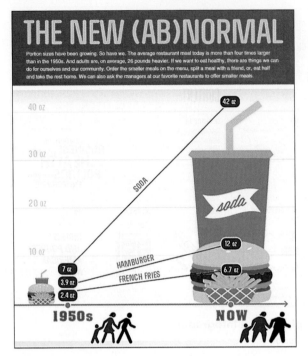

FIGURE 12.12   A Persuasive Infographic
Centers for Disease Control, 2012: http://makinghealtheasier.org
/newabnormal/.

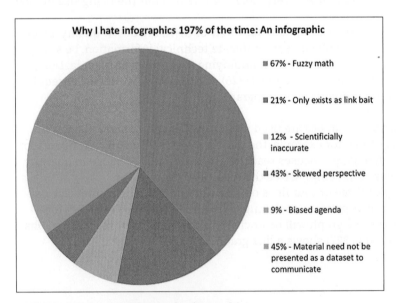

FIGURE 12.13   A Critique of Infographics

Figure 3. U.S. Greenhouse Gas Emissions per Capita and per Dollar of GDP, 1990–2014

This figure shows trends in greenhouse gas emissions from 1990 to 2014 per capita (heavy orange line), based on the total U.S. population (thin orange line). It also shows trends in emissions per dollar of real GDP (heavy blue line). Real GDP (thin blue line) is the value of all goods and services produced in the country during a given year, adjusted for inflation. All data are indexed to 1990 as the base year, which is assigned a value of 100. For instance, a real GDP value of 178 in the year 2014 would represent a 78 percent increase since 1990.

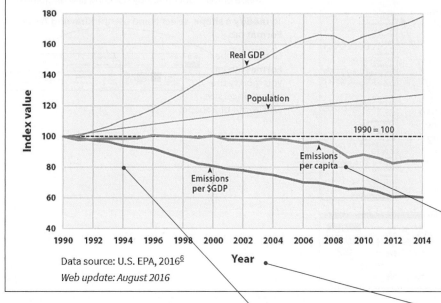

Data source: U.S. EPA, 2016[6]
Web update: August 2016

Note that the title is lengthy because it specifically names the main variables presented in the graph. Name all the important data in the title; it is better for a title to be lengthy than to be imprecise or unclear.

The designer has included a caption that explains how to read the graph. Because this graph is illustrating several items that are measured in different units and therefore cannot be plotted on the same scale (including population and greenhouse gases), the designer chose to have the y-axis express variations from a norm. In this case, the norm is represented by the quantity of each item in the year 1990. If this graph illustrated several items that were measured in the same units, such as the sales figures, in dollars, of several salespersons, the designer would start the y-axis at zero.

Because the four data lines are sufficiently far apart, the designer placed the appropriate data label next to each line. Alternatively, the designer could have used a separate color-coded legend.

Using different colors and thicknesses for the lines helps readers distinguish them.

The grid lines — both vertical and horizontal — help readers see the specific quantity for any data point on the graph.

Each axis is labeled clearly.

FIGURE 12.14 Line Graph
U.S. Environmental Protection Agency.

> **TECH TIP**

Why To Use Drawing Tools

Although you can make many types of graphics using a spreadsheet, some types, such as pictograms, call for drawing tools. Your word processor includes basic drawing tools. Use them to create and edit graphics.

How To Use Drawing Tools

To **create shapes** and **SmartArt**, use the **illustrations** group on the **Insert** tab.

Use the **Shapes** drop-down menu to select a simple shape, such as a line, arrow, rectangle, or oval. Then drag your cursor to create the shape.

You can select complex shapes from the **SmartArt** drop-down menu in the **Illustrations** group.

Once you have created a shape, you can position the shape on your document by selecting and dragging it.

To **modify a shape**, select it and use the **Drawing Tools Format** tab.

Groups on the **Format** tab let you modify the appearance, size, and layout of a shape.

◢ **GUIDELINES** Creating Effective Line Graphs

Follow these three suggestions to create line graphs that are clear and easy to read.

▶ **If possible, begin the quantity scale at zero.** Doing so is the best way to portray the information honestly. If you cannot begin at zero, clearly indicate a break in the axis, if appropriate.

▶ **Use reasonable proportions for the vertical and horizontal axes.** As with bar graphs, make the vertical axis about 25 percent shorter than the horizontal axis.

▶ **Use grid lines — horizontal, vertical, or both — rather than tick marks when your readers need to read the quantities precisely.**

Pie Charts The *pie chart* is a simple but limited design used for showing the relative sizes of the parts of a whole. You can make pie charts with your spreadsheet software. Figure 12.15 shows typical examples.

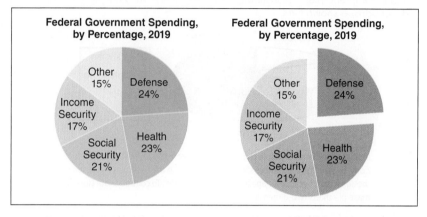

FIGURE 12.15   Pie Charts

You can set your software so that the slices use different saturations of the same color. This approach makes the slices easy to distinguish from each other — without any distractions or misrepresentations caused by a rainbow of colors.

You can set your software to emphasize one slice by separating it from the rest of the pie.

GUIDELINES Creating Effective Pie Charts

Follow these eight suggestions to ensure that your pie charts are easy to understand and professional looking.

▶ **Restrict the number of slices to no more than seven.** As the slices get smaller, judging their relative sizes becomes more difficult.

▶ **Begin with the largest slice at the top and work clockwise in order of decreasing size, unless you have a good reason to arrange the slices otherwise.**

▶ **If you have several very small quantities, put them together in one slice to maintain clarity.** Explain its contents in a footnote. This slice, sometimes called "other," follows the other slices.

▶ **Place a label (horizontally, not radially) inside the slice, if space permits.** Include the percentage that each slice represents and, if appropriate, the raw number.

(continued)

▶ **To emphasize one slice, use a bright, contrasting color or separate the slice from the pie.** Do this, for example, when you introduce a discussion of the item represented by that slice.

▶ **Check to see that your software follows the appropriate guidelines for pie charts.** Some spreadsheet programs add fancy visual effects that can impair comprehension. For instance, many programs portray the pie in three dimensions, as shown here.

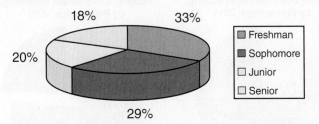

In this three-dimensional pie chart about the percentages of a college's student body, by year, the sophomore slice looks bigger than the freshman slice, even though it isn't, because it appears closer to the reader. To communicate clearly, make pie charts two-dimensional.

▶ **Don't overdo fill patterns.** Fill patterns are patterns, shades, or colors that distinguish one slice from another. In general, use simple, understated patterns or none at all.

▶ **Check that your percentages add up to 100.** If you are doing the calculations yourself, check your math.

ILLUSTRATING LOGICAL RELATIONSHIPS

Graphics can help you present logical relationships among items. For instance, in describing a piece of hardware, you might want to show its major components. The two kinds of graphics that best show logical relationships are diagrams and organization charts.

Diagrams A *diagram* is a visual metaphor that uses symbols to represent relationships among items or their properties. In technical communication, common kinds of diagrams are blueprints, wiring diagrams, and schematics. Figure 12.16 is a diagram.

Organization Charts A popular form of diagram is the *organization chart*, in which simple geometric shapes, usually rectangles, suggest logical relationships, as shown in Figure 12.17. You can create organization charts with your word processor.

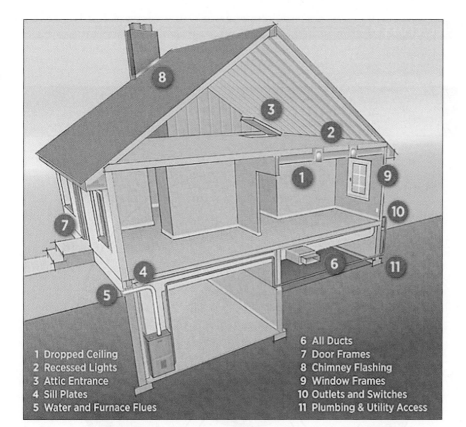

FIGURE 12.16   Diagram
U.S. Department of Energy.

1 Dropped Ceiling
2 Recessed Lights
3 Attic Entrance
4 Sill Plates
5 Water and Furnace Flues

6 All Ducts
7 Door Frames
8 Chimney Flashing
9 Window Frames
10 Outlets and Switches
11 Plumbing & Utility Access

The purpose of this diagram is to help people understand the different areas in their home that need to be insulated. In diagrams, items do not necessarily look realistic. Here the designer is trying to represent logical relationships, not the physical appearances of items.

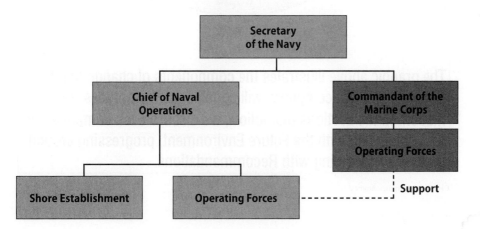

Secretary of the Navy

Chief of Naval Operations

Commandant of the Marine Corps

Operating Forces

Shore Establishment

Operating Forces

Support

**FIGURE 12.17
Organization Chart**
United States Department of the Navy.

An organization chart is often used to show the hierarchy in an organization, with the most senior person in the organization in the box at the top.

Alternatively, an organization chart can show the functional divisions of a system, such as the human nervous system.

Analyzing a Graphic

This diagram is from a government report. The questions below ask you to think about diagrams, as discussed on page 330.

1. This design resembles a pie chart, but it does not have the same function as a pie chart. What message does this design communicate? Is it effective?

2. Do the colors communicate any information, or are they merely decorative? If you think they are decorative, would you revise the design to change them in any way?

3. What does the phrase "Future Environment," above the graphic, mean? Is it meant to refer only to the "Technology" and "Process" shapes?

4. Is the explanation below the graphic clear? Would you change it in any way?

Context for Change

Future Environment

Technology

Process

Strategy

Structure

People

The graphic above illustrates the components of change that the Defense Intelligence Agency will consider as it embraces transformation. In the sections that follow, we discuss each component in turn, beginning with the Future Environment, progressing around the circle and ending with Recommendations.

Defense Intelligence Agency.

ILLUSTRATING PROCESS DESCRIPTIONS AND INSTRUCTIONS

Graphics often accompany process descriptions and instructions (see Ch. 20). The following discussion looks at some of the graphics used in writing about actions: checklists, flowcharts, and logic trees. It also discusses techniques for showing motion in graphics.

Checklists In explaining how to carry out a task, you often need to show the reader what equipment or materials to gather, or describe an action or a series of actions to take. A *checklist* is a list of items, each preceded by a check box. If readers might be unfamiliar with the items you are listing, include drawings of the items, as shown in Figure 12.18. You can use the list function in your word processor to create checklists.

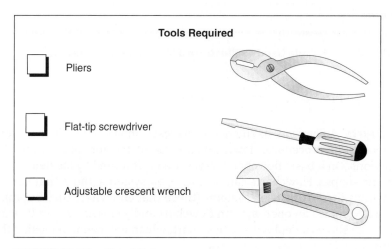

FIGURE 12.18   Checklist

Often you need to indicate that readers are to carry out certain tasks at certain intervals. A table is a useful graphic for this kind of information, as shown in Figure 12.19.

Regular Maintenance, First 40,000 Miles

	Mileage							
	5,000	10,000	15,000	20,000	25,000	30,000	35,000	40,000
Change oil, replace filter	✓	✓	✓	✓	✓	✓	✓	✓
Rotate tires	✓	✓	✓	✓	✓	✓	✓	✓
Replace air filter				✓				✓
Replace spark plugs				✓				✓
Replace coolant fluid								✓
Replace ignition cables								✓
Replace timing belt								✓

FIGURE 12.19   A Table Used To Illustrate a Maintenance Schedule

Flowcharts A *flowchart*, as the name suggests, shows the various stages of a process or a procedure. Flowcharts are useful, too, for summarizing instructions. On a basic flowchart, stages are represented by labeled geometric shapes. Flowcharts can portray open systems (those that have a start and a finish) or closed systems (those that end where they began). Figure 12.20 shows an open-system flowchart and a closed-system flowchart. Figure 12.21 shows a deployment flowchart, which you can make using the drawing tools in your word processor.

Logic Trees *Logic trees* use a branching metaphor. The logic tree shown in Figure 12.22 (on p. 336) helps students think through the process of registering for a course.

Techniques for Showing Action or Motion In some types of process descriptions and instructions, you will want to show action or motion. For instance, in an instruction manual for helicopter technicians, you might want to illustrate the process of removing an oil dipstick or tightening a bolt, or you might want to show a warning light flashing. Although animation and video are frequently used to illustrate action or motion in online documents, such processes still need to be communicated in static graphics for print documents.

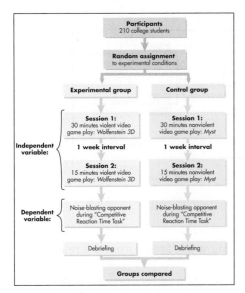

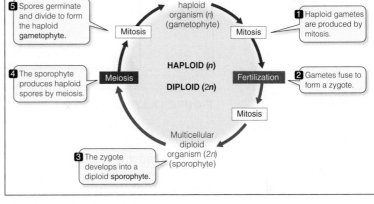

a. Open-system flowchart

From Don Hockenbury and Sandra E. Hockenbury, DISCOVERING PSYCHOLOGY, Sixth Edition, Figure 1.3. Copyright © 2014 by Worth Publishers. Used by permission of the publisher.

b. Closed-system flowchart

Studyguide for Life the Science of Biology by Purves (2004) Fig. 27.14, p. 594. By permission of Oxford University Press, USA.

FIGURE 12.20   Flowcharts

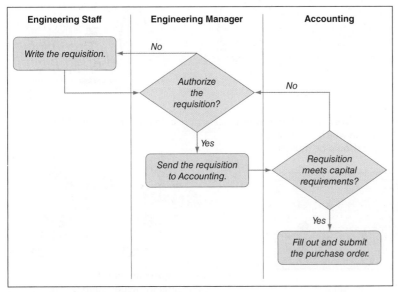

A deployment flowchart shows who is responsible for carrying out which tasks. Here the engineering staff writes the requisition, then sends it to the engineering manager.

FIGURE 12.21   Deployment Flowchart

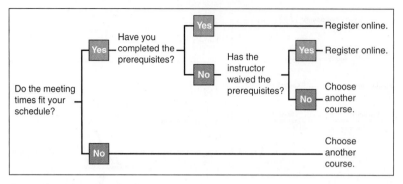

FIGURE 12.22 Logic Tree

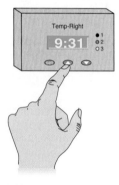

FIGURE 12.23 Showing Action from the Reader's Perspective

In many cases, you need to show only the person's hands, not the whole body.

If the reader is to perform the action, show the action from the reader's point of view, as in Figure 12.23.

Figure 12.24 illustrates four additional techniques for showing action. These techniques are conventional but not universal. If you are addressing readers from another culture, consult a qualified person from that culture to make sure your symbols are clear and inoffensive.

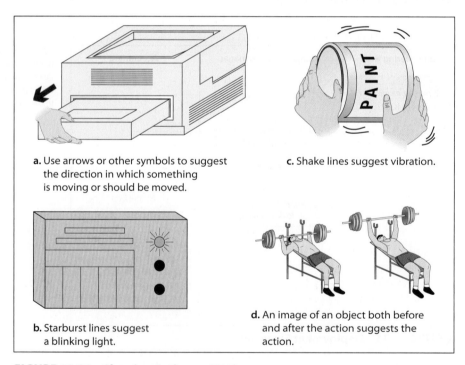

a. Use arrows or other symbols to suggest the direction in which something is moving or should be moved.

c. Shake lines suggest vibration.

b. Starburst lines suggest a blinking light.

d. An image of an object both before and after the action suggests the action.

FIGURE 12.24 Showing Action or Motion

ILLUSTRATING VISUAL AND SPATIAL CHARACTERISTICS

To illustrate visual and spatial characteristics, use photographs, screen shots, line drawings, and maps.

Photographs *Photographs* are unmatched for reproducing visual detail. Sometimes, however, a photograph can provide too much information. In a sales brochure for an automobile, a glossy photograph of the dashboard might be very effective. But in an owner's manual, if you want to show how to use the trip odometer, use a diagram that focuses on that one item.

Sometimes a photograph can provide too little information. The item you want to highlight might be located inside the mechanism or obscured by another component.

◢|
GUIDELINES Presenting Photographs Effectively

Follow these five suggestions to make sure your photographs are clear, honest, and easy to understand.

▶ **Eliminate extraneous background clutter that can distract readers.** Crop the photograph to delete unnecessary detail. Figure 12.25 (on p. 338) shows examples of cropped and uncropped photographs.

▶ **Do not electronically manipulate the photograph.** There is nothing unethical about removing blemishes or cropping a digital photograph. However, manipulating a photograph—for example, enlarging the size of the monitor that comes with a computer system—*is* unethical.

▶ **Help readers understand the perspective.** Most objects in magazines and journals are photographed at an angle to show the object's depth as well as its height and width.

▶ **If appropriate, include some common object, such as a coin or a ruler, in the photograph to give readers a sense of scale.**

▶ **If appropriate, label components or important features.**

Screen Shots *Screen shots*—images of what appears on a computer monitor or some other screen—are often used in manuals to show users what the screen will look like as they perform tasks with the device. Readers who see that the screen shot accurately portrays what appears on their own devices are reassured and therefore better able to concentrate on the task they are trying to perform. Figure 12.26 (on p. 338) is an example of how screen shots are used.

FIGURE 12.25   Cropping a Photograph

Sometimes, writers and designers crop photographs to save space. Ideally, you should crop a photo because it helps you make your point. If you want to show how vulnerable to natural forces the structure in the photograph is, the left-hand version is better because it emphasizes the vastness of the sea. But if you want to discuss the ways the structure has been designed and built to resist natural forces, the right-hand version is better.

KenWiedemann/Getty Images.

This screen shot, from a user guide on NASA's website, shows users how to select a ringtone.

FIGURE 12.26   Screen Shot

NASA, 2013: http://www.nasa.gov/connect/sounds
/iphone_install_directions.html.

▶TECH TIP

Why To Create and Insert Screen Shots

You may find that you need to share an image of your computer screen with an instructor, a colleague, or a tech-support worker. To show your reader what appears in a window on your monitor, you can create a screen shot by using a program such as Microsoft Word or simply by using your Windows or Mac operating system. If you plan to create many screen shots or if you want more sophisticated functionality, including video capture, search the internet for "screen capture apps" such as TechSmith's SnagIt.

How To Create and Insert Screen Shots

On Windows computers, press the **Print Screen** or **PrtScn** key on your keyboard to capture the entire screen, or **Alt + Print Screen** to capture only the active window. The screen shot will automatically be saved on your clipboard and can be inserted into a document using the **Paste** (or **Ctrl + V**) command. On Mac computers, press **Cmd + Shift + 3** to capture the entire screen, or **Cmd + Shift + 4** to define a screen selection to capture using your cursor. You can also use Microsoft Word and Adobe Acrobat to capture screen shots and then modify them by cropping or resizing.

Microsoft Word

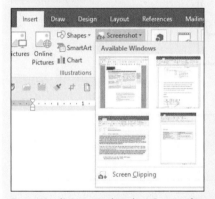

From Word's **Insert** tab, select **Screenshot** to see a small version of each window you have open on your desktop. Click on the screen you want to show your readers, and Word will insert the picture into your document. To define your own screen selection, select **Screen Clipping** and use your cursor to select the portion of your screen you want to capture. To modify a screen shot, select it and use the **Format** tab tools as you would for any image.

Adobe Acrobat Reader

In Adobe Acrobat Reader, from the **Edit** menu, select **Take a Snapshot** and then use your cursor to select the portion of the screen you want to capture. The selection will automatically be saved to your clipboard. To select the entire page, simply click on the screen without dragging the mouse.

Line Drawings *Line drawings* are simplified visual representations of objects. Line drawings offer three possible advantages over photographs:

- Line drawings can focus readers' attention on desired information better than a photograph can.

- Line drawings can highlight information that might be obscured by bad lighting or a bad angle in a photograph.

- Line drawings are sometimes easier for readers to understand than photographs are.

Figure 12.27 shows the effectiveness of line drawings.

You have probably seen the three variations on the basic line drawing shown in Figure 12.28.

This drawing, which accompanies a manual about the Americans with Disabilities Act, illustrates the idea that "wheelchair seating locations must provide lines of sight comparable to those provided to other spectators." A photograph could not show this concept as clearly as this drawing does.

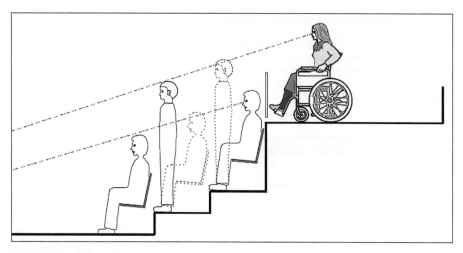

FIGURE 12.27   Line Drawing
U.S. Department of Justice.

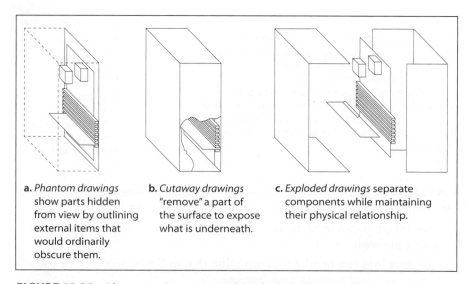

a. *Phantom drawings* show parts hidden from view by outlining external items that would ordinarily obscure them.

b. *Cutaway drawings* "remove" a part of the surface to expose what is underneath.

c. *Exploded drawings* separate components while maintaining their physical relationship.

FIGURE 12.28   Phantom, Cutaway, and Exploded Views

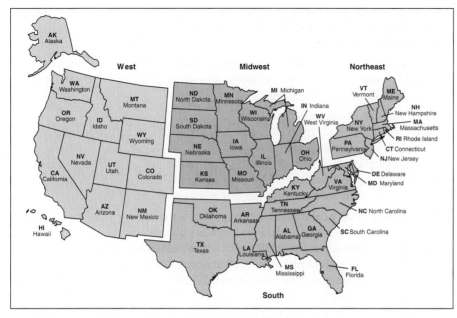

FIGURE 12.29   Map

Include a scale and a legend if the map is one that is not thoroughly familiar to your readers. Also, use conventional colors, such as blue for water.

Maps Maps are readily available as clip art that can be modified with a graphics program. Figure 12.29 shows a map derived from clip art.

Creating Effective Graphics for Multicultural Readers

Whether you are writing for people within your organization or outside it, consider the needs of readers whose first language is different from your own. Like words, graphics have cultural meanings. If you are unaware of these meanings, you could communicate something very different from what you intend. The following guidelines are based on William Horton's article "The Almost Universal Language: Graphics for International Documents" (1993).

- **Be aware that reading patterns differ.** In some countries, people read from right to left or from top to bottom. In some cultures, direction signifies value: the right-hand side is superior to the left, or the reverse. You need to think about how to sequence graphics that show action or where to put "before" and "after" graphics. If you want to show a direction, as in an informal flowchart, consider using arrows to indicate how to read the chart.

- **Be aware of varying cultural attitudes toward giving instruction.** Instructions for products made in Japan are highly polite and deferential: "Please attach the cable at this time." Some cultures favor spelling out general principles but leaving the reader to supply the details. To people in these cultures, instructions containing a detailed close-up of how to carry out a task might appear insulting.

- **Deemphasize trivial details.** Because common objects, such as plugs on the ends of power cords, come in different shapes around the world, draw them to look generic rather than specific to one country.

- **Avoid culture-specific language, symbols, and references.** Don't use a picture of a mouse (the furry rodent) to symbolize a computer mouse because the device is not known by that name everywhere. Avoid the casual use of national symbols (such as the maple leaf or national flags); any error in a detail might offend your readers. Use colors carefully: red means danger to most people from Western cultures, but it is a celebratory color to the Chinese.

- **Portray people very carefully.** Every aspect of a person's appearance, from clothing to hairstyle to physical features, is culture- or race-specific. A photograph of a woman in casual Western attire seated at a workstation would be ineffective in an Islamic culture where only a woman's hands and eyes may be shown. Horton (1993) recommends using stick figures or silhouettes that do not suggest any one culture, race, or sex.

- **Be particularly careful in portraying hand gestures.** Many Western hand gestures, such as the "okay" sign, are considered obscene in other cultures, and some people consider long red fingernails inappropriate. Use hands in graphics only when necessary—for example, to illustrate carrying out a task—and obscure the person's sex and race.

Cultural differences are many and subtle. Learn as much as possible about your readers and about their culture and outlook, and have your graphics reviewed by a native of the culture.

WRITER'S CHECKLIST

☐ Does the graphic have a purpose? *(p. 303)*

☐ Is the graphic simple and uncluttered? *(p. 303)*

☐ Does the graphic present a manageable amount of information? *(p. 303)*

☐ Does the graphic meet readers' format expectations? *(p. 303)*

☐ Is the graphic clearly labeled? *(p. 303)*

☐ Is the graphic honest? *(p. 304)*

☐ Does the graphic appear in a logical location in the document? *(p. 304)*

☐ Is the graphic introduced clearly in the text? *(p. 304)*

☐ Is the graphic explained in the text? *(p. 304)*

☐ Is the graphic clearly visible in the text? *(p. 305)*

☐ Is the graphic easily accessible to readers? *(p. 305)*

☐ If you want to use an existing graphic, do you have the legal right to do so? If so, have you cited its source appropriately? *(p. 309)*

☐ Is the graphic inoffensive to your readers? *(p. 341)*

EXERCISES

For more about memos, see Ch. 14, p. 386.

1. Find out from the admissions office at your college or university the number of students enrolled from the different states or from the different counties in your state. Present this information in four different kinds of graphics:

   a. map

   b. table

   c. bar graph

   d. pie chart

   In three or four paragraphs, explain why each graphic is appropriate for a particular audience and purpose and how each emphasizes different aspects of the information.

2. Design a flowchart for a process you are familiar with, such as applying for a summer job, studying for a test, preparing a paper, or performing some task at work. Your audience is someone who will be carrying out the process for the first time.

3. The following table provides statistics on federal research and development expenditures (Congressional Research Service, 2019, Table 3). Study the table, and then perform the following tasks:

   a. Create two different graphics, each of which compares federal R&D funding in 2011 and 2012.

   b. Create two different graphics, each of which compares defense and nondefense R&D funding in either 2011 or 2012.

Table 3. Selected R&D Funding Agencies by Character of Work, Facilities, and Equipment, FY2018 Actual and FY2020 Request

(budget authority, dollar amounts in millions)

Character of Work/Agency	FY2018 Actual	FY2020 Request	Change, FY2018-FY2020	
			Dollars	Percent
Basic Research				
Health and Human Services	18,278	16,785	-1,493	-8.2%
Energy	5,005	4,647	-358	-7.2%
National Science Foundation	5,066	4,568	-498	-9.8%
Applied Research				
Health and Human Services	18,414	16,624	-1,790	-9.7%
Energy	7,998	6,410	-1,588	-19.9%
Defense	5,690	5,440	-250	-4.4%
Experimental Development				
Defense	44,363	51,686	7,323	16.5%
NASA	5,872	3,791	-2,081	-35.4%
Energy	2,549	1,952	-597	-23.4%
Facilities and Equipment				
Energy	1,930	1,709	-221	-11.5%
Commerce	633	566	-67	-10.6%
National Science Foundation	503	505	2	0.4%

Source: CRS analysis of data from EOP, OMB, *Analytical Perspectives, Budget of the United States Government, Fiscal Year 2020, Research and Development,* March 18, 2019, pp. 271-272, https://www.whitehouse.gov/wp-content/uploads/2019/03/ap_21_research-fy2020.pdf.

Note: This table shows only the top three funding agencies in each category, based on the FY2020 request.

Congressional Research Service.

4. For each of the following four graphics, write a paragraph evaluating its effectiveness and describing how you would revise it.

a. Majors

	2017	2018	2019
Civil Engineering	236	231	253
Chemical Engineering	126	134	142
Comparative Literature	97	86	74
Electrical Engineering	317	326	401
English	714	623	592
Fine Arts	112	96	72
Foreign Languages	608	584	566
Materials Engineering	213	227	241
Mechanical Engineering	196	203	201
Other	46	42	51
Philosophy	211	142	151
Religion	86	91	72

b. Number of Members of the U.S. Armed Forces in 2012 (in Thousands)

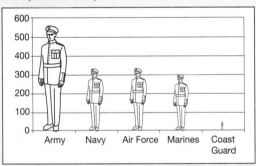

c. Expenses at Hillway Corporation

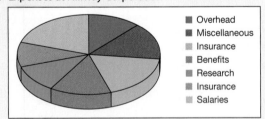

d. Costs of the Components of a PC

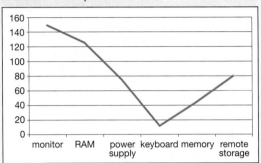

5. The following three graphs illustrate the sales of two products — Series 1 and Series 2 — for each quarter of 2019. Which is the most effective in conveying the information? Which is the least effective? What additional information would make the most effective graph better?

a.

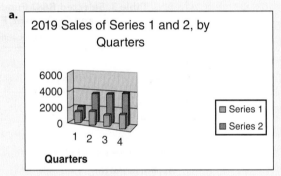

b.

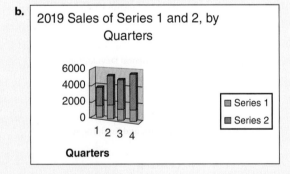

c.

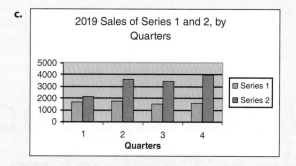

6. Using a search engine, search for "infographics college tuition." Find two infographics that present information on similar topics, such as tuition costs for public and private colleges and universities, average tuition costs in each of the 50 states, or the relationship between tuition costs and future earnings potential. Write a 1,000-word memo to your instructor in which you identify the audience and purpose of the infographics and compare and contrast them using such criteria as audience, purpose, clarity, visual appeal, use of different types of graphics, and citation of the data sources. Which infographic do you think is better? Why?

7. Locate a graphic on the web that you consider inappropriate for an international audience because it might be offensive or unclear to readers in some cultures. Imagine an intended audience for the graphic, such as people from a certain region in the Middle East, and write a brief statement explaining the potential problem. Finally, revise the graphic so that it would be appropriate for its intended audience.

CASE 12: Creating Appropriate Graphics To Accompany a Report

Following a series of texting-related driving accidents, a representative in your state legislature has decided to introduce legislation restricting the use of cell phones while driving. As an assistant to the state's insurance commissioner, you have been asked to collect data on how cell-phone use affects driving. The representative hopes to use these data to make his case for the legislation. When you present your findings to your supervisor, she asks that you pare them down to the facts most relevant to the representative. She also asks that you consider presenting some of the data graphically. If your instructor assigned it, got to Achieve to get to work improving your research.

13

Evaluating and Testing Technical Documents

THIS CHAPTER FOCUSES on techniques for evaluating and improving the usability of technical documents, including websites and mobile applications. In technical communication, *usability* is a measure of how successfully a document achieves its purposes and meets its audience's needs. In one popular formulation, *usability* refers to factors related to a person's use of the item, or document (Nielsen, 2012):

- **Ease of learning:** The time it takes a person to learn to use the item
- **Efficiency of use:** The time it takes a person to carry out the task after learning how to do it
- **Memorability:** How well a person can remember how to carry out the task
- **Error frequency, severity, and recovery:** The number and severity of errors a person makes in carrying out the task, and the ease with which a person recovers from these errors
- **Subjective satisfaction:** How much a person likes (or dislikes) carrying out the task

Understanding Usability Studies

As a writer, you can improve the usability of documents by evaluating and testing them. Usability studies take many forms, depending on the type of document, the stage in the document's development, and the goals of the study. Your needs and contexts will determine whether you should conduct a usability study and, if you do, which methods you should use.

ASSESSING THE NEED FOR A USABILITY STUDY

To be successful, usability studies require careful planning and effective test methods, and they must be followed up with analysis and reporting of findings. How do you know whether you need to have a document evaluated and tested for usability? Typically, you consider three factors:

- **Importance.** If a document or site is important, it should be carefully studied. For instance, an annual report is so important that you want to make it as good as possible. Your company's website is also crucial. You keep testing it and monitoring its effectiveness even after it is launched. A routine memo describing a workaround for a technical problem is not as important. Review it yourself, and then send it out.
- **Time.** Almost every document has a deadline, and almost every deadline comes too quickly. If the document is even moderately important and you have the time to conduct evaluations and tests, do so.
- **Money.** It costs money to evaluate and test documents, whether that money takes the form of the indirect costs of employee time or the direct fees for evaluators and test participants. Consider your project's budget when you weigh whether to conduct a usability study.

DETERMINING THE GOALS OF THE STUDY

If you decide that a usability study is necessary for your document, you will next want to determine the goals of the study. In general, the purpose of the technical document itself—what the document is supposed to do—will inform the goals of the usability study. That is, studies are usually performed to make sure a document is doing what it is supposed to do. But writers of technical documents may also have more specific goals in mind, perhaps for particular features or design elements. For example, creators of a wiki might want to be sure that the "Edit" function is easy to find and use.

When the National Air and Space Museum (NASM) decided to create a giant interactive welcome wall for visitors, it identified the key goals for the project before developing a prototype that it would eventually test with users (Bloom, 2016):

- give an overall impression of the museum and its underlying curatorial theme ("aviation and human spaceflight transform the world")
- orient visitors to the collection and help them find items on display
- promote and connect to the GO FLIGHT app
- be a short experience that keeps people moving and doesn't impede traffic flow

A photograph of a visitor participating in the NASM usability study is shown in Figure 13.1.

FIGURE 13.1   Usability Study of a Prototype

In a usability study at the Smithsonian's National Air and Space Museum, visitors were encouraged to tap the paper prototype of an interactive wall panel that was being developed. Staff members would put up a new "screen" with each user's tap, simulating the interactive experience.

National Air and Space Museum.

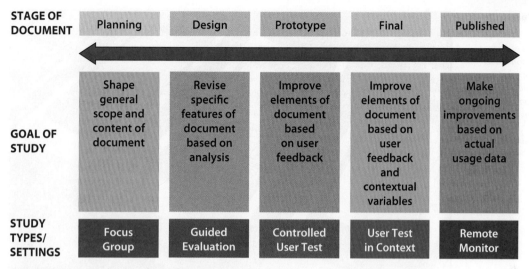

STAGE OF DOCUMENT	Planning	Design	Prototype	Final	Published
GOAL OF STUDY	Shape general scope and content of document	Revise specific features of document based on analysis	Improve elements of document based on user feedback	Improve elements of document based on user feedback and contextual variables	Make ongoing improvements based on actual usage data
STUDY TYPES/ SETTINGS	Focus Group	Guided Evaluation	Controlled User Test	User Test in Context	Remote Monitor

FIGURE 13.2 Relationship of Study Goals and Types to Document Stages

As you think about whether you need to conduct a usability study and what its goal will be, you should also reflect on how the study will be conducted. For example, your study may be an informal evaluation of an early design of your document, conducted by your colleagues in a few hours. Or you may hire experts to conduct a formal test of an existing document. You may even conduct an extended study in an actual user's context over a period of days or weeks.

As shown in Figure 13.2, the specific goal of the study, as well as the type of study and its setting, is likely to depend on what stage of development the document is in. And all of these factors, not surprisingly, affect the cost of the study.

As with any document, the stages in drafting a technical document are recursive rather than linear. Particularly after conducting a usability study, you will likely want to return to an earlier stage, such as planning or design, in order to make adjustments to the document. The next section discusses the different stages of documents, both prototypes and published documents. Study settings are the focus of the remainder of the chapter.

For more on planning, see Chs. 5–7; for more on design, see Ch. 11.

STUDYING EXISTING DOCUMENTS VERSUS PROTOTYPES

A usability study can be performed on an existing document or on a prototype. A *prototype* is a model that is built to try out ideas and drafts of an item before it becomes final. In technical communication, a prototype is typically an early draft of a document, website, or software program. Prototypes can range in *fidelity*—that is, in how closely they resemble an actual product or document. A prototype may be a simple drawing on paper, a computer screen mock-up, or a fully functioning system that looks exactly like a commercial product. Figure 13.3 (on p. 350) shows an example of a paper prototype.

FIGURE 13.3   Paper Prototype

These paper prototypes of screens from a mobile application model the way the app will function once the program is built. With a usability study, evaluators can assess how effective the program is likely to be.

The Mobile Frontier: A Guide for Designing Mobile Experiences. Rachel Hinman; Rosenfeld Media, 2012.

FIGURE 13.4   Wireframe Prototype

Unlike a hand-drawn paper proto-type, this wireframe, with minimal design and limited functionality, is displayed on a computer screen so that test participants can explore it.

DigitalGov, 2016: www.digitalgov.gov /2014/08/08/design-sketching-the-easiest -prototype-method-ever/.

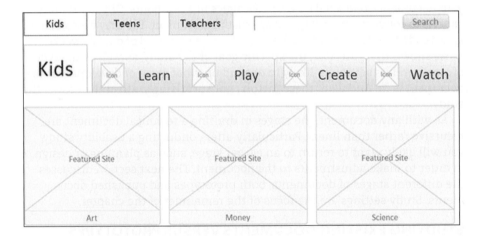

Figure 13.4 shows an example of a wireframe, a mock-up with limited func-tionality, displayed on a screen.

Usability studies are also conducted on existing documents to assess their effectiveness and see how they can be improved. Figure 13.5 illustrates how feedback from a usability study led to improvements being made to a pub-lished website.

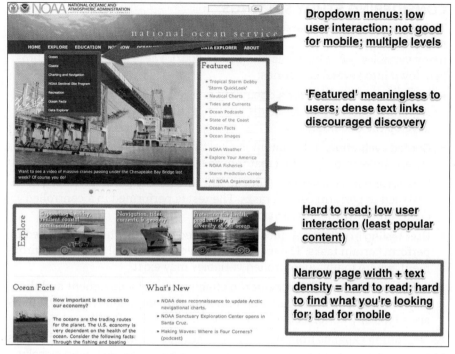

Dropdown menus: low user interaction; not good for mobile; multiple levels

'Featured' meaningless to users; dense text links discouraged discovery

Hard to read; low user interaction (least popular content)

Narrow page width + text density = hard to read; hard to find what you're looking for; bad for mobile

a. Home page with usability problems

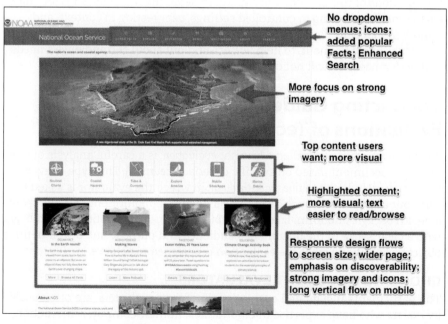

No dropdown menus; icons; added popular Facts; Enhanced Search

More focus on strong imagery

Top content users want; more visual

Highlighted content; more visual; text easier to read/browse

Responsive design flows to screen size; wider page; emphasis on discoverability; strong imagery and icons; long vertical flow on mobile

b. Home page after improvements

FIGURE 13.5

Improvements Based on a Usability Study

The staff at the National Oceanographic and Atmospheric Administration (NOAA) improved the usability of the home page of the organization's website based on informal tests and other data. DigitalGov, 2016: www.digitalgov.gov/2014/04/14/noaa-national-ocean-service-usability-case-study/.

CONSIDERING STUDY SETTINGS

The usability of a technical document can be examined in a variety of settings, ranging from specific, confined environments to broad contexts with many variables (Johnson-Eilola and Selber, 2007). These settings can be broken down into several categories.

- **Focus groups.** An idea for a document is discussed by a group of people. A group moderator leads the discussion, gathering insights about how to develop the document.
- **Guided evaluation.** A document is directly evaluated by reviewers based on criteria determined by the creator of the document.
- **User testing in a lab setting.** A document is tested by participants who are assigned to perform certain tasks. The test is performed in a controlled environment with limited variables.
- **User testing in context.** A document is tested by users who are assigned to perform certain tasks. The test is performed in an actual working environment, where many uncontrolled variables may exist.
- **Remote monitoring.** Data about the effectiveness of a document and the way it is being used are gathered remotely and often anonymously. Analysis is typically performed without test participants or facilitators.

As the setting expands from the controlled environments of direct evaluations to the broader environments of actual workplaces, the context more closely matches the real world and the variables of the study grow more complex. The next sections of this chapter will explain in detail the major settings for guided evaluation, user testing in controlled settings, user testing in context, and remote monitoring. (Because focus groups tend to be used mostly in the planning stage of a document, to help writers find out about the audience's needs and preferences, we will not discuss focus groups further.)

Conducting Guided Evaluations of Technical Documents

A *guided evaluation*, also called a *heuristic evaluation*, is a careful analysis of a technical document based on specific criteria (a *heuristic*). This type of evaluation may include a *cognitive walk-through*, in which the evaluator is asked to carry out a set of tasks, such as making a doctor's appointment and filling out a health background form. Like any usability study, an evaluation should begin with a clear sense of the document's audience and purpose and a well-defined objective specifying what the evaluation is designed to achieve.

CHOOSING DOCUMENT EVALUATORS

The participants in a guided evaluation, known as *evaluators*, are often *usability experts* who have expertise in ergonomics, human-computer interaction, usability engineering, or cognitive psychology. They can also be experts in technical communication.

A *subject-matter expert (SME)*—an expert in the subject of the document, website, or software—can also be very useful in evaluating a draft. For instance, a database engineer is presumably an SME in database software programs.

This person probably could see more—and different—potential problems in a new database program than a typical user could. He or she might also be the person in charge of carrying out the usability evaluation.

According to Jakob Nielsen (1995), the ideal number of evaluators is roughly three to five. Although this number may seem small, Nielsen has shown that even a small number of people can recognize more than half the problems in a product; hire more than five and you are likely wasting money.

If you don't have access to usability experts because of budget or time constraints, you can still have nonexperts conduct evaluations based on criteria you establish.

ESTABLISHING EVALUATION GUIDELINES

Whether or not you are working with an expert, you need to establish guidelines that spell out for your evaluators the criteria you want them to consider during their analysis. Your evaluation guidelines should match the goal of your document. For example, if the goal of your website is to allow company employees to submit their weekly hours quickly and accurately, your guidelines should specifically ask evaluators to examine the speed and accuracy of the submission process.

Your guidelines should also explain the kinds of problems you want your evaluators to look for as they evaluate your document. In technical communication, usability problems often fall into one of the following categories (based on Selber, Johnson-Eilola, & Mehlenbacher, 1997). You might want your evaluators to pay special attention to one or more of these aspects of your document:

- **Organization.** Is information presented in a logical order that makes sense to users? Is the organization of the document clearly visible? Is information chunked appropriately with devices such as sections, pages, headings, and lists?

- **Navigation.** Can users easily find the information they need? If they can't find what they're looking for, can they easily backtrack or return to a starting point? Are the methods of navigation—such as scrolling, linking, browsing, or turning pages—appropriate for the users' needs? Can users see more than one piece of the document at the same time if necessary?

- **Visual design.** Does the document make good use of basic design principles such as proximity, alignment, repetition, and contrast? (See Chapter 11.) Is it aesthetically pleasing? Is the text legible? Are the graphics well designed and well integrated? (See Chapter 12.) Are icons familiar and easy to understand? Are design elements and functions consistent throughout the site?

- **Language.** Is the document written in language that users will understand? Is it free of jargon? Does it explain terms that may be unfamiliar to users? Does it use correct grammar, and is it free of typographical errors?

- **Conventions.** Does the document follow standard conventions? Does it meet user expectations for this type of document?

- **Accessibility.** Can the document be used by people with varying physical abilities? (See Chapter 11.)

- **Maintainability.** Is the document easy to update? Can users edit portions of the document if necessary?

- **Support.** Is additional help or documentation provided for users who need assistance?

Develop questions that will help evaluators consider the kinds of problems that would have the most impact on your document—that is, the problems that are most likely to prevent your document from achieving its purpose and goals. For example, if you have created a website whose primary purpose is to attract new business for your company, an attractive visual design will be especially important. By contrast, in a document such as an instruction manual, organization and consistency of the design are likely to be paramount.

PREPARING MATERIALS FOR THE EVALUATION

Your evaluators will need something to evaluate. Will you provide them with a paper prototype, screen shots, or a close-to-final product?

You will also need to create a way for evaluators to record their findings. Evaluators performing a cognitive walk-through should be provided with forms on which to record any problems they encounter with your document. Figure 13.6 shows an example of a form used by Oracle.

Nielsen (1994, p. 47) proposes including a "severity rating" scale that considers a problem's frequency, impact, and persistence. Ranking the severity of problems using numbers allows usability experts to prioritize their findings. Nielsen's scale is shown in Figure 13.7.

If your users include people from other cultures, be sure to include people from these cultures among your evaluators. Also, if your users include people with disabilities, be sure your evaluation considers their needs.

After completing any usability evaluation, you need to gather the important information that you learned and report it. See "Interpreting and Reporting Your Findings" on pages 366–67.

Testing Documents in a Controlled Setting

At some point in a document's development, the writer of the document may choose to have it tested in a controlled setting to determine its effectiveness. Like guided evaluations, usability tests may be conducted on an early version of a document, to see if it will be easy to use, or on an existing document, to see if it needs any improvements.

ORACLE°   ux.direct

**FIGURE 13.6 Guided
Evaluation Form**

Appendix B: Heuristic Evaluation
Evaluator's Form, p. 20 from Oracle's
"User Experience Direct, FAQ: How to
Conduct Heuristic Evaluation"
http://www.oracle.com/webfolder/ux
/applications/uxd/assets/faq/how-to
-conduct-heuristic-evaluation.pdf. Used
with permission.

**Appendix B: Heuristic Evaluation
Evaluator's Form**

Name: _____

Date: _____

Describe the usability problem:

_____

_____

_____

_____

What task and step was being attempted when the problem occurred?

_____

_____

_____

_____

Where in the product did the problem arise?

_____

_____

_____

What solution will solve the problem?

_____

_____

_____

_____

20

Unlike the evaluators in a guided evaluation, participants in a controlled-setting test are representative users of the document. Participants are not asked to evaluate the document based on a set of predetermined guidelines; rather, participants' behavior is observed as they use the document. Users can provide important information by making mistakes that someone more familiar with the document wouldn't make.

FIGURE 13.7 Nielsen's Five-Point Rating Scale

0   I don't agree that this is a usability problem at all

1   Cosmetic problem only — need not be fixed unless extra time is available on project

2   Minor usability problem — fixing this should be given low priority

3   Major usability problem — important to fix, so should be given high priority

4   Usability catastrophe — imperative to fix this before product can be released

Controlled settings, such as specialized usability labs, are designed to limit the number of variables that users encounter as they test a document. Figure 13.8 shows a usability test taking place in a controlled setting. An advantage of such settings is that they minimize distractions and keep the users focused on the document. They also allow for more formal analysis and more standardized testing methods than field testing would permit. For example, creators of an online sizing chart for a footwear company might carry out a laboratory test to observe users working with the chart. All participants would use the same computer, chair, desk, and measuring tools in order to test the sizing chart. The results might show that the chart worked better for women than for men, or that a certain part of the website was difficult for all users to access.

On the other hand, because they test documents in isolation, controlled tests may fail to uncover important problems. For example, if the document being tested was a mobile application that assists users in making bicycle repairs, the controlled setting of a laboratory would take out some important

FIGURE 13.8 Usability Test in a Controlled Setting

This tester in Microsoft's usability lab observes how a test participant on the other side of the window works with one of Microsoft's operating systems.
AP Images/Ted S. Warren.

variables. Rather than using the app in a relatively clean, quiet environment, bicyclists might need to use it on the side of a busy city street or on a muddy trail in the woods. Or it might need to be used in a loud factory or garage with low lighting, by technicians with greasy hands.

PREPARING FOR THE TEST

When you conduct a usability test with users, you take some of the same steps as you would for a guided evaluation: you prepare the materials and select the participants for the test. You also need to make some additional preparations related to the test team and the test environment.

CONDUCTING THE TEST

The testing team must plan the test carefully and then stay organized. Typically, the team creates a checklist and a schedule for the test day, specifying every task that every person, including the test participant, is to carry out. Conducting the test usually includes interacting with the test participant both during the formal test and later, during a follow-up interview.

◢|
GUIDELINES **Preparing for a Usability Test**

Follow these five steps to prepare to conduct a usability test.

▶ **Staff the test team.** The test team for an extensive usability-testing program involves multiple specialists, each doing one job. Smaller programs involve only a handful of people, each doing several jobs. For instance, a testing team might include a subject-matter expert on the product, who can suggest workarounds if necessary; a test administrator, who administers the test to participants; a note taker, who fills out the evaluation forms and records important comments users make; and a videographer, who operates the recording equipment.

▶ **Set up the test environment.** Controlled tests often take place in a lab-type setting so that all test participants undergo a similar experience. Necessary equipment includes any devices that the participants will be working with, as well as recording instruments. Seating should be provided for both participants and observers.

▶ **Select participants.** Choose participants who match the profiles of the intended users—the people who use or will be using the document, site, app, or program, usually as part of their jobs. Participants can be current or future users; they can be novice, experienced, or expert users. Generally, it is best not to use company employees, who might have specialized knowledge that would make them atypical.

▶ **Prepare the test materials.** For most tests, you will need to prepare legal forms for the participants to complete, a checklist and schedule for the test day, a script for the test administrator, instructions for the participants to follow, a log on which administrators can record data during the test, and a post-test questionnaire for participants. Figure 13.9 (on pp. 358–59) shows a sample script for a test administrator.

▶ **Consider conducting a pilot test.** A *pilot test* is a usability test for the usability test. A pilot test can uncover problems with the equipment; the document, site, or software being tested; the test materials; or the test design.

BEFORE THE TEST

- *Introduce yourself.*

- *Explain the permission form.*

- *Be sure the participant has signed the permission form before you begin the test.*

BEGIN TEST

The test administrator provides a clear overview of what is expected.

Today you'll be helping us test a portion of the college's website to find out whether it's working as intended. During the session, I'll ask you to complete a few tasks using the site. Don't worry if you're not able to do everything I ask — that just tells us there's a problem with the site that we need to fix.

Throughout the session, it'll be really helpful to me if you think aloud as much as possible. Talk to me about what you're doing, what you're thinking, and anything about the site that's confusing. And if you need to take a break at any point, just let me know.

Do you have any questions before we start?

[Answer questions as needed.]

BEGIN TASKS

Okay, let's begin.

The script includes instructions for the test administrator and time limits for the tasks.

[Show the home page of the college registrar, but don't say what it is. Allow up to 10 minutes total for the first three tasks and discussion.]

1) Tell me what you think is the purpose of this page. What kinds of information would you expect to find here?

2) What kinds of things would you expect to be able to do on this page?

3) Look over the page a little more, and feel free to scroll around. Think out loud about what you see. Do you see all the information you expected to find? Does anything seem to be missing?

The administrator reminds participants to think aloud.

Okay, now let's try doing a few things on the site. Remember to keep thinking aloud as we go through these tasks.

The script reminds the administrator to ask neutral questions.

[If participant gets stuck on any of the tasks, ask questions such as "What were you expecting when you clicked there?" or "What do you think you should do next?"]

4) Imagine that you want to register for a class. How would you do that?

FIGURE 13.9   Usability Test Script

[Allow 3 minutes for participant to find and click either the "Register for a course" button or the "Class registration" option on the dropdown menu.]

5) Does this page look like what you expected to see?

[Allow 2 minutes for discussion.]

6) Now imagine that you want to register for a class in the Machinist Certificate Program. How would you do that? This is a test environment, so you won't really be registering, but go ahead and go through the process you think you would follow.

[Allow up to 10 minutes for participant to finish the registration process.]

7) How was that experience of registering for a class?

[Allow 2 minutes for discussion.]

8) OK, please navigate back to the registrar home page.

[Wait until participant has returned to home page.]

9) Now, imagine that you need information about how to drop a class. What would you do?

[Wait until participant has navigated to the "Add/Drop a Class" page.]

10) Now that you've completed these tasks, what is your overall impression of the site? Do you have any recommendations about what we could change? Or any questions about it?

[Allow 10 minutes for discussion.]

END TEST

Okay, we're finished with today's test! Thank you so much for your help in improving this website.

The administrator ends by thanking the participant.

FIGURE 13.9   Usability Test Script (*continued*)

Interacting with the Test Participant Among the most popular techniques for eliciting information from a test participant is the *think-aloud protocol*, in which the participant says aloud what he or she is thinking while using a document or a website. The test administrator might demonstrate how to think aloud at the beginning of the session in order to set expectations and put the participant at ease.

In a typical usability test, at least one observer takes notes on the test participant's words and actions (both on screen and off) and is available to intervene if necessary. While the test participant thinks aloud, the observer records anything that is confusing and any point at which the test participant is not sure about what to do. If the test participant gets stuck, the administrator asks a leading question, such as "Where do you think that function might be located?" or "What did you expect to see when you clicked that link?" Questions should not take the user's knowledge for granted or embarrass the test participant for failing a task. For example, "Why didn't you click the Calculate button?" assumes that the user should have seen the button and should have known how to use it.

In addition, questions should not bias the test participant. When testers ask a participant a question, they should try not to reveal the answer they want. They should not say, "Well, that part of the test was pretty easy, wasn't it?" Regardless of whether the participant thought it was simple or difficult, his or her impulse will be to answer yes. Usability specialists Joseph S. Dumas and Janice Redish (1999) recommend using neutral phrasing, such as "How was it performing that procedure?" or "Did you find that procedure easy or difficult?" In responding to questions, testers should be indirect. If the participant asks, "Should I press 'Enter' now?" the tester might respond, "Do you think you should?" or "I'd like to see you decide."

To ensure that the test stays on schedule and is completed on time, the test administrator should set a time limit for each task. If the test participant cannot complete a task in the allotted time, the administrator should move on to the next task.

ETHICS NOTE

UNDERSTANDING THE ETHICS OF INFORMED CONSENT

For legal and ethical reasons, organizations that conduct usability testing — especially tests that involve recording the test participant's behavior — abide by the principle of informed consent. *Informed consent* means that the organization fully informs the participant of the conditions under which the test will be held, as well as how the results of the test will be used. Only if the participant gives his or her consent, in writing, will the test occur. When you obtain informed consent for tests that involve recording, be sure to do the following five things:

- Explain that the test participant can leave at any time and can report any discomfort to the testing team at any time, at which point the team will stop the test.

- Explain that the participant's face, voice, and on-screen activity will be recorded. Ask for permission to record the test participant *before* you begin recording.

(continued)

- Explain the purpose of the recording and the uses to which it will be put. If, for example, the recording will be used later to show others how to participate in a usability study, the test participant must be informed of this.

- Explain who will have access to the recording and where it might be shown. A participant might object to having the recording shown at a professional conference, for example.

- Explain how the test participant's identity will be disguised — if at all — if the recording is shown publicly.

Following Up After a usability study, test administrators usually have questions about the test participant's actions, which they ask in a post-test interview. This interview is critically important, for once the participant walks out the door, it is difficult and expensive to ask any further questions, and the participant likely will have forgotten the details of the test experience. Consequently, the interview can take as long as the test itself did.

Usability specialists Jeffrey Rubin and Dana Chisnell (2008) suggest beginning the interview with a neutral and open-ended question, such as "So, what did you think?" This kind of question encourages the participant to start off with an important suggestion or impression. During the interview session, testers should probe overall concerns before getting to the smaller details. They should try not to get sidetracked by minor problems. Figure 13.10 shows a list of sample interview questions.

As a final step, test administrators ask the participants to fill out a post-test questionnaire. The questionnaire differs from the post-test interview in that it provides a direct written record of the participants' opinions about specific issues such as navigation and design. Figure 13.11 (on p. 363) shows a list of sample questions from a post-test questionnaire.

---

1. What are your overall impressions of the Web site?
2. If you had to give the site a grade from A to F, where A was exemplary and F was failing, what grade would you give it, and why?
3. Name three words or characteristics that describe this Web site.
4. What are the three things you like best about the Web site?
5. What are the three things you like least about the Web site?
6. If you could make one significant change to this Web site, what change would you make?
7. Would you return to this Web site on your own in the future? Why/why not?
8. What would entice you to return?
9. Are there materials you would like to see added to the Web site? Which ones?
10. Would you recommend this Web site to a colleague? To a friend?
11. Do you have any other questions or comments about the Web site or your experiences with it?

FIGURE 13.10   Sample of Post-Test Interview Questions
World Wide Web Consortium (W3C).

Obtaining Informed Consent

NASA, the U.S. space agency, uses this consent form in its usability testing. The questions below ask you to examine this document in light of the guidelines for informed consent (see p. 360).

1. Which features of an effective informed-consent form, as described in the Ethics Note on page 360, does this form include?

2. Are any provisions in this form potentially unclear?

Understanding Your Participation
Please read this page carefully.

You have agreed to participate in a usability study that will evaluate [system]. By participating in this study, you will help NASA to improve [system] in future redesigns. Our team will observe you and record information about how you work with the [system]. We will also ask you to fill out questionnaires about your experience and follow-up questions. We will record your comments and actions using written notes and video cameras.

Our team will use the data from your study session, including videotapes, solely for the purposes of evaluating the [system] and sharing results of these evaluations with [the study sponsor]. Your full name will not be used during any presentation or in the results of this study.

By signing this form, you give permission for NASA to use:

- Your recorded voice: ☐ Yes ☐ No
- Your verbal statements: ☐ Yes ☐ No
- The videotape of your session: ☐ Yes ☐ No

If you need a break at any time, please inform the study facilitator immediately. If you have questions about how the session will proceed, you may ask them at any time. You may withdraw from your study session at any time.

Receipt for [Incentive]

Please acknowledge that you have received from [NASA, or study sponsor] [the exact amount of money, or describe the nonmonetary incentive, if it is merchandise] for your participation by signing below. Your acceptance of this [incentive] does not constitute employment by [NASA, or study sponsor].

☐ I have received my [incentive].

If you agree with these terms, please indicate your agreement by signing below:

Signature: _____

Print Name: _____

Date: _____

NASA.

Please read each of the statements below and rate your agreement using the following scale:

1   Disagree strongly
2   Disagree somewhat
3   Neither agree nor disagree
4   Agree somewhat
5   Agree strongly

1.   The website has an attractive design. _____
2.   The website is easy to navigate. _____
3.   The website is easy to read. _____
4.   The website is relevant to me. _____
5.   The website addresses my needs. _____
6.   It is easy to backtrack or fix my errors when I use the website. _____
7.   I know what I can do on the website. _____
8.   I am likely to visit the website again. _____

FIGURE 13.11   Post-Test Questionnaire

While the participant fills out the post-test questionnaire, the test team quickly looks through the data log and notes the most important areas to investigate. Their purpose is to obtain as much information as possible about what occurred during the test as well as to uncover any additional questions they want to ask participants before they leave.

As with guided evaluations, you need to follow up a usability test by gathering the important information that you learned and reporting it. See "Interpreting and Reporting Your Findings" on pages 366–67.

Testing Documents in Context

The most complex usability studies are conducted in the real world, with actual users working with technical documents in context (Johnson-Eilola and Selber, 2007). Tests conducted in context are far more complicated than tests conducted in labs: they require more planning time and labor, and they involve many more variables, such as different kinds of computer equipment, interruptions, background noise, and lighting. These usability tests are also called *contextual inquiries* because the participants are asked questions as they use the document in a work context.

The benefit of testing documents in working contexts is that doing so provides "a much richer body of feedback" than can be gathered when documents are tested in isolation (Johnson-Eilola and Selber, 2007). For example, testing software for a patient-monitoring system would be much more effective in a hospital setting than it would be in the closed environment of a usability lab. Viewing the true user–document interaction in context allows authors to get a much fuller understanding of how their document is used and how it can be made better. Figure 13.12 (on p. 364) shows a usability test in context.

PREPARING FOR A SITE VISIT

To determine the site for an in-context test, talk with several users or potential users of your document. Find out whether a site visit at their location is possible and identify a contact person at the site. Ideally, you will visit multiple sites to gather different perspectives.

Visit the site ahead of time, before conducting the test. Meet with users or potential users about how they use or might use your document. Tour the site, if possible, and find out where your document is or might be used. During your tour, take these steps in order to develop an effective test tailored to the needs of your users:

- **Take notes about the workspace.** Note any important details, such as distractions that may interfere with effective use of the document.

- **Take notes about timing.** Consider how time of day may affect the use of the document: are there busy times of day during which users might react differently than at other times?

- **Take pictures of the site.** Photographs will help you remember details about the space as you plan the test.

CONDUCTING A TEST IN CONTEXT

When you conduct a usability test in a working context, take the same steps as you would for a test in a laboratory setting: staff your team and prepare your materials. Consider staging a pilot test before conducting the actual on-site study to work out any potential problems.

During the test, ask the participants relevant questions—not only the ones that you've prepared, but also ones that come up as you observe their interaction with your document. These studies are context-dependent, so your list of questions will vary depending on your situation. You typically want the user to think about the use of your document within his or her broader work context. For example, if you were studying the effectiveness of a quick-start guide for a laptop, you might ask users what they find most difficult when starting up a new computer in their office. You might also ask what types of problems they want to be able to address on their own, without consulting their office's information technology professional. In general, you'll want to ask users about the kinds of tasks they perform, the problems or difficulties involved in performing those tasks, and how the document helps them perform those tasks.

Monitoring Documents Remotely

After a document "goes live" or gets published, it can—and, in many cases, should—continue to evolve. In addition to the usability testing methods discussed above, a variety of tools exist to help you determine what is working and what can be improved, especially with respect to online documents. These tools, which typically involve only anonymous users and capture limited data, are not technically usability tests, but they can provide you with information to improve the usability of your documents. And the tools can be customized to focus on your needs and goals.

Heat Mapping Heat mapping tools track the places on a website or app that gain the most attention from users and then use colors to present that information. In Figure 13.13, the "white hot" areas are the places clicked on the most by site visitors. Such information can help document owners to understand what information is most (and least) important to their users, and to see areas being clicked on that are not actually links.

Web Analytics Tools such as Google Analytics provide subscribers with marketing data about how their website is being used and how it can be improved to increase traffic, sales, and customer satisfaction. These tools also allow website owners to test multiple versions of a page simultaneously to determine the most effective layout.

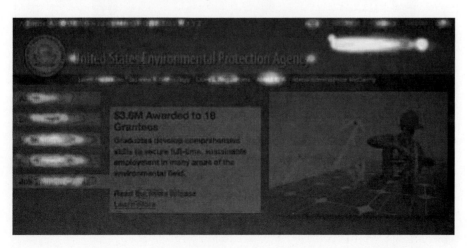

FIGURE 13.13 Heat Map of an EPA Web Page

White areas indicate links on the site that received the most clicks from visitors. Blue areas received fewer clicks. This information could help the site's designers make decisions about which links to make more prominent or which to remove.

DigitalGov, 2016: https://www.digitalgov .gov/2014/08/12/heat-mapping-case -study-epa-gov-homepage/.

Online Feedback Forms By providing users with feedback forms, document owners can solicit information about documents directly from users. Although this process is neither a guided evaluation nor a user test, it does share elements of both types of studies.

Interpreting and Reporting Your Findings

After a usability study, testers have a large collection of data, including notes, questionnaire responses, and videos. Turning the data into useful information involves three steps:

For more on creating graphics, see Ch. 12.

- **Tabulate the data.** Gather all the information from the study, which may include both quantitative data (such as statistics) and qualitative data (such as opinions). Figure 13.14 shows an example of a graphic that presents quantitative data from a usability study. Qualitative data include *impressions* and *attitudes*, such as how easy the participant found a task. Qualitative feedback may be turned into quantitative data using a system such as Nielsen's five-point rating scale, shown in Figure 13.7 on page 356. Qualitative data also include *discursive* information, such as responses to open-ended interview questions.

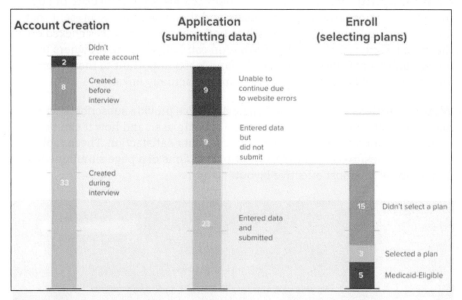

FIGURE 13.14
Quantitative Data

This graphic illustrates how many users could perform basic tasks using the California Health Exchange website in 2013. Although 33 users were able to create an account during the interview, only 23 submitted applications, and only 3 enrolled in a plan. Other, qualitative details derived from the usability study may uncover why users chose to quit at different points in the process.
User Experience Magazine.

- **Analyze the information.** Analyze the data, concentrating on the most important problems revealed in the study and trying to determine the severity and the frequency of each one. Keep your analysis focused by remembering the goals of the study.

- **Report your findings.** Writing a clear, comprehensive report based on your study's findings will often lead to insights you might not have achieved otherwise. For more information on writing informational reports, see Chapter 17; for details on writing recommendation reports, see Chapter 18. Figure 13.15 shows the recommendations section from a report prepared for Maryland's State Board of Elections about a new voting system.

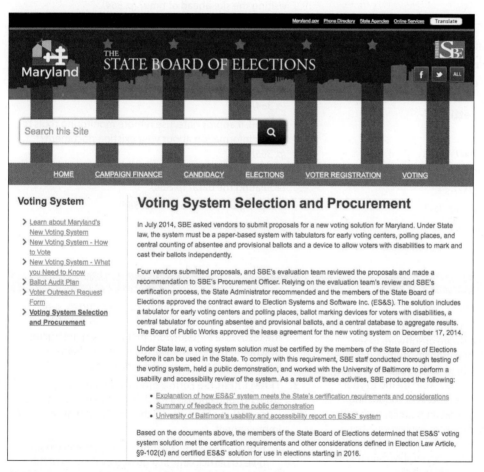

FIGURE 13.15   Recommendations from a Usability Study

After conducting a usability test of a new voting system, a team from the University of Baltimore compiled this list of recommendations for improving the system.

Maryland State Board of Elections.

WRITER'S CHECKLIST

☐ Did you assess the need for a usability study, considering the importance of the document and the time and money available? *(p. 347)*

☐ Did you determine the goals of the study, which may be affected by the stage of development the document is in? *(p. 348)*

☐ Did you determine whether you will work with an existing document or a prototype? *(p. 349)*

☐ Did you consider the study setting? *(p. 352)*

Guided Evaluations

Did you

☐ choose document evaluators? *(p. 352)*

☐ establish evaluation guidelines? *(p. 353)*

☐ prepare materials for the evaluation? *(p. 354)*

Testing in a Controlled Setting

Did you prepare for the test by

☐ staffing the test team? *(p. 357)*

☐ setting up the test environment? *(p. 357)*

☐ selecting participants? *(p. 357)*

☐ preparing the test materials? *(p. 357)*

☐ conducting a pilot test? *(p. 357)*

Did you conduct the test effectively by

☐ interacting appropriately with the participant? *(p. 360)*

☐ obtaining informed consent? *(p. 360)*

☐ following up with the participant? *(p. 360)*

Testing in Context

Did you prepare for the site visit by

☐ talking with several users or potential users? *(p. 363)*

☐ identifying a contact person? *(p. 364)*

☐ visiting the site ahead of time? *(p. 364)*

☐ taking notes about the workspace and variations in the workday? *(p. 364)*

☐ taking pictures? *(p. 364)*

☐ Did you come up with a list of questions specific to your document and the context in which it is or will be used? *(p. 364)*

☐ Did you, if appropriate, use remote monitoring tools to gather information about your existing document? *(p. 365)*

Did you interpret and report your findings by

☐ tabulating the data? *(p. 366)*

☐ analyzing the information? *(p. 366)*

☐ generating a report? *(p. 366)*

EXERCISES

For more about memos, see Ch. 14, p. 386.

1. Contact local manufacturing companies or companies that produce computer hardware or software to see whether any of them perform usability studies. Interview a person who performs usability testing at one of these organizations. Then write a 1,000-word memo to your instructor describing how the process of conducting usability testing at this organization is similar to the processes described in this chapter. Explain whether the organization conducts guided evaluations, tests in controlled settings, tests in context, remote monitoring, or some combination of these types of tests.

2. If a local company conducts usability studies, see whether you can become a test participant. After the test, write a 1,000-word memo to your instructor describing the experience, focusing on what you learned about this particular type of study.

3. **TEAM EXERCISE** Form a group of four or five students, and choose a local government website (such as that of a town or school district) that could use improvement.

   a. Prepare a set of evaluation guidelines you would give to participants in a guided evaluation of the website.

b. Come up with three tasks you would want test participants to perform on the website in a controlled-setting test.

c. Identify a workplace setting where you could conduct a worthwhile in-context test of the website.

d. Prepare a list of 5 post-test interview questions and 10 post-test questionnaire questions for participants in either the controlled-setting test or the in-context test.

e. Propose a plan for using a remote monitoring tool to gather data about the website.

Submit a memo to your instructor explaining which method (or combination of methods) you think would be most worthwhile.

CASE 13: Evaluating a Technical Document

You work in Albuquerque's water-conservation office, where your supervisor is looking for ways to provide homeowners with more information on xeriscaping in order to cut down on residential water usage. She gives you a booklet that was developed as a print document but now exists only on the city's website. Your supervisor would like you to come up with a list of evaluators and evaluation criteria to make sure the document is doing what it is supposed to do. If your instructor has assigned it, go to Achieve to get started on your assignment.

Part 4

Learning Important Applications

Corresponding in Print and Online

➡

14

REGARDLESS OF THE APPLICATION you use, you will communicate in writing every day on the job. This chapter discusses the four major formats used for producing workplace correspondence: letters, memos, emails, and microblog posts. Throughout this chapter, the word *correspondence* refers to all these forms.

Understanding the Process of Writing Correspondence

The process of writing correspondence is essentially like that of writing any other kind of workplace document. The Focus on Process box presents an overview of this process, focusing on letters, memos, and emails. The more formal the correspondence, the more time you are likely to spend on each of these steps.

FOCUS ON PROCESS: Correspondence

When writing correspondence, pay special attention to these steps of the writing process.

PLANNING	You will need to choose the appropriate type of correspondence for your writing situation.
DRAFTING	For letters, memos, and emails, clearly state your purpose, use headings to help your readers, summarize your message, provide adequate background, organize the discussion, and highlight action items. For microblogs, state your message or question early and clearly.
REVISING	You might need to write correspondence quickly, but you still need to write carefully. Review the section of the Writer's Checklist at the end of this chapter that applies to your document.
EDITING	See Chapter 10 for advice on writing correct and effective sentences.
PROOFREADING	See Appendix, Part C, for proofreading tips.

Selecting a Type of Correspondence

When you need to correspond with others in the workplace, your first task is to decide on the appropriate type of document. Here are the main characteristics of each major type:

- **Letters.** Because letters still use centuries-old conventions such as the salutation and complimentary close, they are the most formal of the four types of correspondence and are therefore most appropriate for communicating with people outside your organization or, in some formal situations, with people within your organization. Letters are typically sent through the postal service or a shipping company, though they can also be attached to emails.

- **Memos.** This type of correspondence is moderately formal and therefore appropriate for people in your own organization. Memos can be distributed via interoffice mail or through emails (as attachments).

- **Email.** This type of correspondence is best for quick, relatively informal communication with one or many recipients. Recipients can store and forward email easily, as well as capture the text and reuse it in other documents. In addition, the writer can attach other files to an email message.

- **Microblog posts.** Microblog posts such as Twitter tweets or Facebook status updates can be useful to address quick questions to a group. This is the most informal type of correspondence.

Presenting Yourself Effectively in Correspondence

When you write business correspondence, follow these five suggestions for presenting yourself as a professional:

- Use the appropriate level of formality.
- Communicate correctly.
- Project the "you attitude."
- Avoid correspondence clichés.
- Communicate honestly.

USE THE APPROPRIATE LEVEL OF FORMALITY

People are sometimes tempted to use very informal writing in informal digital applications such as email and microblogs. Don't. Everything you write on the job is legally the property of the organization for which you work, and messages are almost always archived digitally, even after senders and recipients have deleted them. Your documents might be read by the company president, or they might appear in a newspaper or in a court of law. Therefore, use a moderately formal tone to avoid potential embarrassment.

| TOO INFORMAL | Our meeting with United went south right away when they threw a hissy fit, saying that we blew off the deadline for the progress report. |
| MODERATELY FORMAL | In our meeting, the United representative expressed concern that we had missed the deadline for the progress report. |

However, you don't want to sound like a dictionary.

| TOO FORMAL | It was indubitably the case that our team was successful in presenting a proposal that was characterized by quality of the highest order. My appreciation for your industriousness is herewith extended. |
| MODERATELY FORMAL | I think we put together an excellent proposal. Thank you very much for your hard work. |

COMMUNICATE CORRECTLY

One issue closely related to formality is correctness. As discussed in Chapter 1, correct writing is free of errors in grammar, punctuation, style, usage, and spelling. Correctness problems occur most often in email and microblogs.

Some writers mistakenly think that they do not need to worry about correctness because these digital applications are meant for quick communication. They are wrong. You have to plan your digital correspondence just as you plan any other written communication, and you should revise, edit, and proofread it. Sending correspondence that contains language errors is unprofessional because it suggests a lack of respect for your reader—and for yourself. It also causes your reader to think that you are careless about your job.

For more about editing, see "Editing" in Ch. 3, pp. 59–60; for more about proofreading, see "Proofreading" in Ch. 3, p. 60.

PROJECT THE "YOU ATTITUDE"

Correspondence should convey a courteous, positive tone. The key to accomplishing this task is using the "you attitude"—looking at the situation from the reader's point of view and adjusting the content, structure, and tone to meet his or her needs. For example, if you are writing to a supplier who has failed to deliver some merchandise by the agreed-on date, the "you attitude" dictates that you not discuss problems you are having with other suppliers; those problems don't concern your reader. Instead, concentrate on explaining clearly and politely that the reader has violated your agreement and that not having the merchandise is costing you money. Then propose ways to expedite the shipment.

Following are two examples of thoughtless sentences, each followed by an improved version that shows the "you attitude."

ACCUSING	You must have dropped the engine. The housing is badly cracked.
BETTER	The badly cracked housing suggests that the engine must have fallen onto a hard surface from some height.
SARCASTIC	You'll need two months to deliver these parts? Who do you think you are, the post office?
BETTER	Surely you would find a two-month delay for the delivery of parts unacceptable in your business. That's how I feel, too.

A calm, respectful tone makes the best impression and increases the chances that you will achieve your goal.

AVOID CORRESPONDENCE CLICHÉS

Over the centuries, a group of words and phrases have come to be associated with business correspondence; one common example is *as per your request.* These phrases sound stilted and insincere. Don't use them.

For more on language, see "Choosing the Right Words and Phrases" in Ch. 10 on p. 234.

Table 14.1 is a list of common clichés and their plain-language equivalents. Figure 14.1 shows two versions of the same email: one written in clichés, the other in plain language.

TABLE 14.1 Clichés and Plain-Language Equivalents

CLICHÉ	PLAIN-LANGUAGE EQUIVALENT
attached please find	attached is
enclosed please find	enclosed is
pursuant to our agreement	as we agreed
referring to your ("Referring to your letter of March 19, the shipment of pianos . . .")	"As you wrote in your letter of March 19, the . . ." (or subordinate the reference at the end of your sentence)
wish to advise ("We wish to advise that . . .")	(The phrase doesn't say anything. Just say what you want to say.)
the writer ("The writer believes that . . .")	"I believe . . ."

COMMUNICATE HONESTLY

You should communicate honestly when you write any kind of document, and business correspondence is no exception. Communicating honestly shows respect for your reader and for yourself.

ETHICS NOTE

WRITING HONEST BUSINESS CORRESPONDENCE

Why is dishonesty a big problem in correspondence? Perhaps because the topics discussed in business correspondence often relate to the writer's professionalism and the quality of his or her work. For instance, when a salesperson working for a supplier writes to a customer explaining why a product did not arrive on time, he is tempted to make it seem as if his company—and he personally—were blameless. Similarly, when a manager has to announce a new policy that employees will dislike, she might be tempted to distance herself from the policy.

The professional approach is to tell the truth. If you mislead a reader in explaining why the shipment didn't arrive on time, the reader will likely double-check the facts, conclude that you are trying to avoid responsibility, and end your business relationship. If you try to convince readers that you had nothing to do with a new, unpopular policy, some of them will know you are being misleading, and you will lose your most important credential: your credibility.

EMAIL CONTAINING CLICHÉS	EMAIL IN PLAIN LANGUAGE
Dear Mr. Smith:	Dear Mr. Smith:
Referring to your complaint regarding the problem encountered with your new Trailrider Snowmobile, our Customer Service Department has just submitted its report.	Thank you for letting us know about the problem with your new Trailrider Snowmobile.
It is their conclusion that the malfunction is caused by water being present in the fuel line. It is our conclusion that you must have purchased some bad gasoline. We trust you are cognizant of the fact that while we guarantee our snowmobiles for a period of not less than one year against defects in workmanship and materials, responsibility cannot be assumed for inadequate care. We wish to advise, for the reason mentioned hereinabove, that we cannot grant your request to repair the snowmobile free of charge.	Our Customer Service Department has found water in the fuel line. Apparently some of the gasoline was bad. While we guarantee our snowmobiles for one year against defects in workmanship and materials, we cannot assume responsibility for problems caused by bad gasoline. We cannot, therefore, grant your request to repair the snowmobile free of charge.
Permit me to say, however, that the writer would be pleased to see that the fuel line is flushed at cost, $30. Your Trailrider would then give you many years of trouble-free service.	However, no serious harm was done to the snowmobile. We would be happy to flush the fuel line at cost, $30. Your Trailrider would then give you many years of trouble-free service. If you will authorize us to do this work, we will have your snowmobile back to you within four working days. Just fill out the attached authorization statement and return it as an attachment in a reply to this email or fax it to the number shown on the form.
Attached please find an authorization statement. Should we receive it, we shall perform the above-mentioned repair and deliver your snowmobile forthwith.	Sincerely yours,
Sincerely yours,	

The email on the right avoids clichés and shows an understanding of the "you attitude." Instead of focusing on the violation of the warranty, it presents the conclusion as good news: the snowmobile is not ruined, and it can be repaired and returned in less than a week for a small charge.

FIGURE 14.1   Sample Emails With and Without Clichés

Writing Letters

Letters are still a basic means of communication between organizations, with millions written each day. To write effective letters, you need to understand the elements of a letter, its format, and the types of letters commonly sent in the business world.

ELEMENTS OF A LETTER

Most letters include a heading, inside address, salutation, body, complimentary close, and signature. Some letters also include one or more of the following: attention line, subject line, enclosure line, and copy line. Figure 14.2 shows the elements of a letter.

Heading. Most organizations use letterhead stationery with their heading printed at the top. This preprinted information and the date the letter is sent make up the heading. If you are using blank paper rather than letterhead, your address (without your name) and the date form the heading. Whether you use letterhead or blank paper for the first page, do not number it. Use blank paper for the second and all subsequent pages.

Inside Address. If you are writing to an individual who has a professional title — such as Professor, Dr., or, for public officials, Honorable — use it. If not, use Mr. or Ms. (unless you know the recipient prefers Mrs. or Miss). If the reader's position fits on the same line as the name, add it after a comma; otherwise, drop it to the line below. Spell the name of the organization the way the organization itself does: for example, International Business Machines calls itself IBM. Include the complete mailing address: street number and name, city, state, and zip code.

Attention Line. Sometimes you will be unable to address a letter to a particular person because you don't know (and cannot easily find out) the name of the individual who holds that position in the company.

DAVIS TREE CARE
1300 Lancaster Avenue
Berwyn, PA 19092
www.davisfortrees.com

May 11, 2020

Fairlawn Industrial Park
1910 Ridgeway Drive
Berwyn, PA 19092

Attention: Director of Maintenance

Subject: Fall pruning

Dear Director of Maintenance:

Do you know how much your trees are worth? That's right — your trees. As a maintenance director, you know how much of an investment your organization has in its physical plant. And the landscaping is a big part of your total investment.

Most people don't know that even the hardiest trees need periodic care. Like shrubs, trees should be fertilized and pruned. And they should be protected against the many kinds of diseases and pests that are common in this area.

At Davis Tree Care, we have the skills and experience to keep your trees healthy and beautiful. Our diagnostic staff is made up of graduates of major agricultural and forestry universities, and all of our crews attend special workshops to keep current with the latest information on tree maintenance. Add to this our proven record of 43 years of continuous service in the Berwyn area, and you have a company you can trust.

Subject Line. The subject line is an optional element in a letter. Use either a project number (for example, "Subject: Project 31402") or a brief phrase defining the subject (for example, "Subject: Price quotation for the R13 submersible pump").

Salutation. If you decide not to use an attention line or a subject line, put the salutation, or greeting, two lines below the inside address. The traditional salutation is "Dear," followed by the reader's courtesy title and last name and then a colon (not a comma):

Dear Ms. Hawkins:

FIGURE 14.2 Elements of a Letter (*continued*)

Image: Sapik/Shutterstock.com.

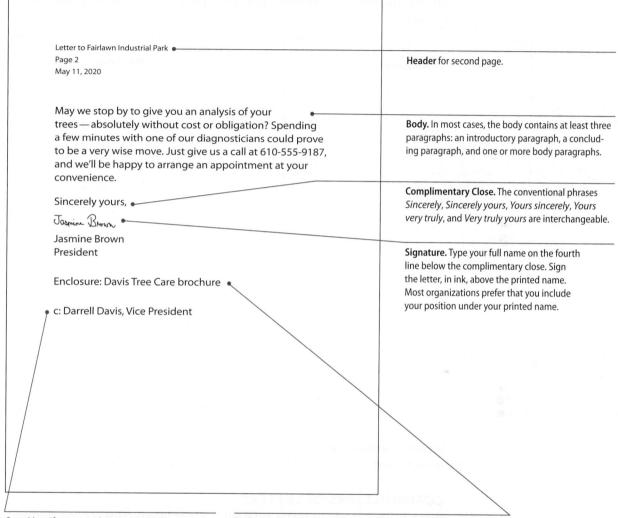

Letter to Fairlawn Industrial Park
Page 2
May 11, 2020

Header for second page.

May we stop by to give you an analysis of your trees — absolutely without cost or obligation? Spending a few minutes with one of our diagnosticians could prove to be a very wise move. Just give us a call at 610-555-9187, and we'll be happy to arrange an appointment at your convenience.

Body. In most cases, the body contains at least three paragraphs: an introductory paragraph, a concluding paragraph, and one or more body paragraphs.

Sincerely yours,

Jasmine Brown

Jasmine Brown
President

Complimentary Close. The conventional phrases *Sincerely, Sincerely yours, Yours sincerely, Yours very truly,* and *Very truly yours* are interchangeable.

Enclosure: Davis Tree Care brochure

c: Darrell Davis, Vice President

Signature. Type your full name on the fourth line below the complimentary close. Sign the letter, in ink, above the printed name. Most organizations prefer that you include your position under your printed name.

Copy Line. If you want the primary recipient to know that other people are receiving a copy of the letter, include a copy line. Use the symbol "c" (for "copy") followed by the names of the other recipients (listed either alphabetically or according to organizational rank). If appropriate, use the symbol "cc" (for "courtesy copy") followed by the names of recipients who are less directly affected by the letter.

Enclosure Line. If the envelope contains documents other than the letter, include an enclosure line that indicates the number of enclosures. For more than one enclosure, add the number: "Enclosures (2)." In determining the number of enclosures, count only separate items, not pages. A three-page memo and a ten-page report constitute only two enclosures. Some writers like to identify the enclosures:

Enclosure: 2019 Placement Bulletin
Enclosures (2): "This Year at Ammex"
2019 Annual Report

FIGURE 14.2 Elements of a Letter (*continued*)

Letters follow one of two typical formats: modified block or full block. Figure 14.3 illustrates these two formats. When sending a letter as an email attachment, you can save it as a PDF file to preserve the formatting for the recipient.

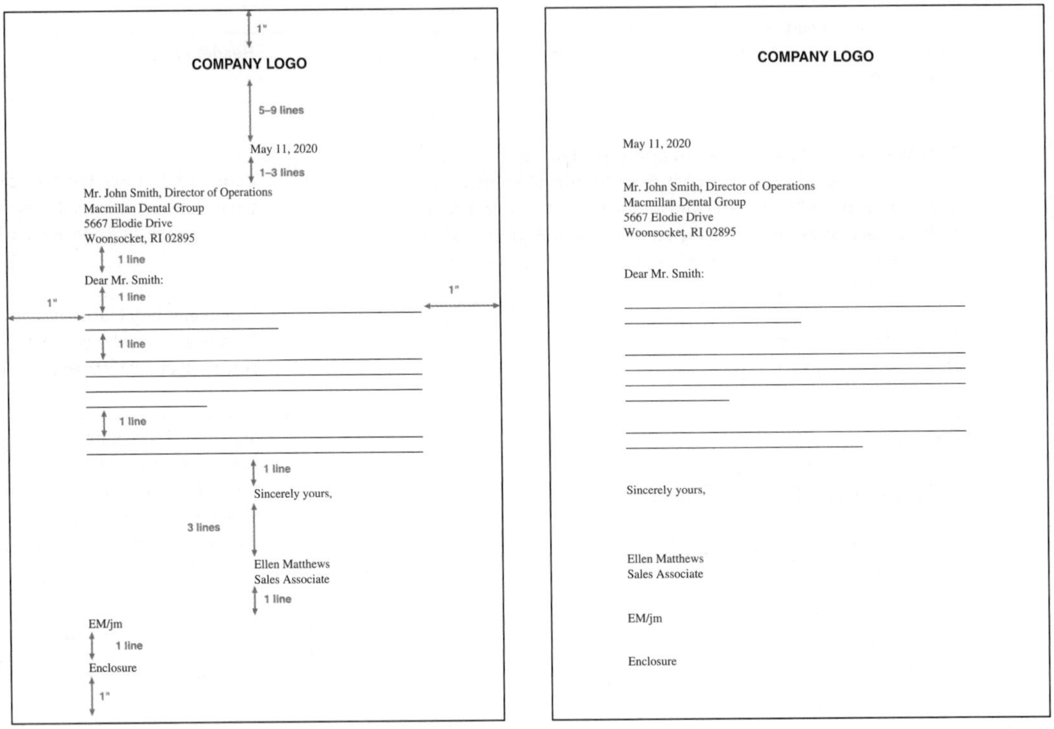

a. Modified block format

b. Full block format — everything aligned along the left margin

FIGURE 14.3   Typical Letter Formats
The dimensions and spacing shown for the modified block format also apply to the full block format.

COMMON TYPES OF LETTERS

Two other types of letters are discussed in this book: "Letter of Transmittal" in Ch. 18, p. 495, and "Writing Job-Application Letters" in Ch. 15, p. 427.

Organizations send out many different kinds of letters. This section focuses on four types of letters written frequently in the workplace: inquiry, response to an inquiry, claim, and adjustment.

Inquiry Letter   Figure 14.4 shows an inquiry letter, in which you ask questions.

Response to an Inquiry   Figure 14.5 (on page 382) shows a response to the inquiry letter in Figure 14.4.

Claim Letter   Figure 14.6 (on page 383) is an example of a claim letter that the writer scanned and attached to an email to the reader. The writer's decision to present his message in a letter rather than an email suggests that he wishes to convey the more formal tone associated with letters—and yet he wants the letter to arrive quickly.

14 Hawthorne Ave.
Belleview, TX 75234

November 2, 2020

Dr. Andrea Shakir
Director of Technical Services
Orion Corporation
721 West Douglas Avenue
Maryville, TN 31409

Dear Dr. Shakir:

I am writing to you because of Orion's reputation as a leader in the manufacture of adjustable x-ray tables. I am a graduate student in biomedical engineering at the University of Texas, and I am working on an analysis of diagnostic equipment for a seminar paper. Would you be able to answer a few questions about your Microspot 311?

1. Can the Microspot 311 be used with lead oxide cassettes, or does it accept only lead-free cassettes?
2. Are standard generators compatible with the Microspot 311?
3. What would you say is the greatest advantage, for the operator, of using the Microspot 311? For the patient?

Because my project is due on January 15, I would greatly appreciate your assistance in answering these questions by January 10. Of course, I would be happy to send you a copy of my report when it is completed.

Yours very truly,

Albert K. Stern

Albert K. Stern

You write an inquiry letter to acquire information. Explain who you are and why you are writing. Make your questions precise and clear, and therefore easy to answer. Explain what you plan to do with the information and how you can compensate the reader for answering your questions.

This writer's task is to motivate the reader to provide some information. That information is not likely to lead to a sale because the writer is a graduate student doing research, not a potential customer.

Notice the flattery in the first sentence.

The writer presents specific questions in a list format, making the questions easy to read and understand.

In the final paragraph, the writer politely indicates his schedule and requests the reader's response. Note that he offers to send the reader a copy of his report.

If the reader provides information, the writer should send a thank-you letter.

FIGURE 14.4   **Inquiry Letter**

In responding to an inquiry letter, answer the questions if you can. If you cannot, either because you don't know the answers or because you cannot divulge proprietary information, explain the reasons and offer to assist with other requests.

ORION

721 WEST DOUGLAS AVE.
MARYVILLE, TN 31409

(615) 619-8132
www.orioninstruments.com

November 9, 2020

Mr. Albert K. Stern
14 Hawthorne Ave.
Belleview, TX 75234

Dear Mr. Stern:

The writer responds graciously.

I would be pleased to answer your questions about the Microspot 311. We think it is the best unit of its type on the market today.

The writer answers the three questions posed in the inquiry letter.

1. The 311 can handle lead oxide or lead-free cassettes.
2. At the moment, the 311 is fully compatible only with our Duramatic generator. However, special wiring kits are available to make the 311 compatible with our earlier generator models—the Olympus and the Saturn. We are currently working on other wiring kits.
3. For the operator, the 311 increases the effectiveness of the radiological procedure while at the same time cutting down the amount of film used. For the patient, it reduces the number of repeat exposures and therefore reduces the total dose.

The writer encloses other information to give the reader a fuller understanding of the product.

I am enclosing a copy of our brochure on the Microspot 311. If you would like additional information, please visit our website at www.orioninstruments.com/products/microspot311. I would be happy to receive a copy of your analysis when it is complete. Good luck!

Sincerely yours,

Andrea Shakir, M.D.

Andrea Shakir, M.D.
Director of Technical Services

The writer uses the enclosure notation to signal that she is attaching an item to the letter.

Enclosure

The writer indicates that she is forwarding a copy to her supervisor.

c: Robert Anderson, Executive Vice President

FIGURE 14.5 **Response to an Inquiry**

ROBBINS CONSTRUCTION, INC.

255 Robbins Place, Centerville, MO 65101 | [417] 555-1850 | robbinsconstruction.com

August 17, 2020

Mr. David Larsyn
Larsyn Supply Company
311 Elmerine Avenue
Anderson, MO 63501

Dear Mr. Larsyn:

As steady customers of yours for over 15 years, we came to you first when
we needed a quiet pile driver for a job near a residential area. On your
recommendation, we bought your Vista 500 Quiet Driver, at $14,900. We have
since found, much to our embarrassment, that it is not substantially quieter
than a regular pile driver.

We received the contract to do the bridge repair here in Centerville after
promising to keep the noise to under 90 dB during the day. The Vista 500 (see
enclosed copy of bill of sale for particulars) is rated at 85 dB, maximum. We
began our work and, although one of our workers said the driver didn't seem
sufficiently quiet to him, assured the people living near the job site that we
were well within the agreed sound limit. One of them, an acoustical engineer,
marched out the next day and demonstrated that we were putting out 104 dB.
Obviously, something is wrong with the pile driver.

I think you will agree that we have a problem. We were able to secure other
equipment, at considerable inconvenience, to finish the job on schedule. When
I telephoned your company that humiliating day, however, a Mr. Meredith
informed me that I should have done an acoustical reading on the driver before
I accepted delivery.

I would like you to send out a technician—as soon as possible—either to
repair the driver so that it performs according to specifications or to take it
back for a full refund.

Yours truly,

Jack Robbins

Jack Robbins, President

Enclosure

A claim letter is a polite, reasonable complaint. If you purchase a defective or falsely advertised product or receive inadequate service, you write a claim letter. If the letter is convincing, your chances of receiving a satisfactory settlement are good because most organizations realize that unhappy customers are bad for business. In addition, claim letters help companies identify weaknesses in their products or services.

The writer indicates clearly in the first paragraph that he is writing about an unsatisfactory product. Note that he identifies the product by model name.

The writer presents the background, filling in specific details about the problem. Notice how he supports his earlier claim that the problem embarrassed him professionally.

The writer states that he thinks the reader will agree that there was a problem with the equipment.

Then the writer suggests that the reader's colleague did not respond satisfactorily.

The writer proposes a solution: that the reader take appropriate action. The writer's clear, specific account of the problem and his professional tone increase his chances of receiving the solution he proposes.

FIGURE 14.6   Claim Letter

Adjustment Letter Figures 14.7 and 14.8 show "good news" and "bad news" adjustment letters. The first is a reply to the claim letter shown in Figure 14.6 on page 383.

An adjustment letter, a response to a claim letter, tells the customer how you plan to handle the situation. Your purpose is to show that your organization is fair and reasonable and that you value the customer's business.

If you can grant the request, the letter is easy to write. Express your regret, state the adjustment you are going to make, and end on a positive note by encouraging the customer to continue doing business with you.

The writer wisely expresses regret about the two problems cited in the claim letter.

The writer describes the actions he has already taken and formally states that he will do whatever the reader wishes.

The writer expresses empathy in making the offer of adjustment. Doing so helps to create a bond: you and I are both professionals who rely on our good reputations.

This polite conclusion appeals to the reader's sense of fairness and good business practice.

Larsyn Supply Company

311 Elmerine Avenue
Anderson, MO 63501
(417) 555-2484
larsynsupply.com

August 24, 2020

Mr. Jack Robbins, President
Robbins Construction, Inc.
255 Robbins Place
Centerville, MO 65101

Dear Mr. Robbins:

I was very unhappy to read your letter of August 17 telling me about the failure of the Vista 500. I regretted most the treatment you received from one of my employees when you called us.

Harry Rivers, our best technician, has already been in touch with you to arrange a convenient time to come out to Centerville to talk with you about the driver. We will of course repair it, replace it, or refund the price. Just let us know your wish.

I realize that I cannot undo the damage that was done on the day that a piece of our equipment failed. To make up for some of the extra trouble and expense you incurred, let me offer you a 10 percent discount on your next purchase or service order with us, up to a $1,000 total discount.

You have indeed been a good customer for many years, and I would hate to have this unfortunate incident spoil that relationship. Won't you give us another chance? Just bring in this letter when you visit us next, and we'll give you that 10 percent discount.

Sincerely,

Dave Larsyn

Dave Larsyn, President

FIGURE 14.7   "Good News" Adjustment Letter

Quality Storage Media

2077 Highland, Burley, ID 84765
208 555 1613
qualstorage.com

February 3, 2020

Ms. Dale Devlin
1903 Highland Avenue
Glenn Mills, NE 69032

Dear Ms. Devlin:

Thank you for writing us about the external hard drive you purchased on January 11, 2020. I know from personal experience how frustrating it is when a drive fails.

According to your letter, you used the drive to store the business plan for your new consulting business. When you attempted to copy that file to your internal hard drive, the external drive failed, and the business plan was lost. You have no other copy of that file. You are asking us to reimburse you $1,500 for the cost of re-creating that business plan from notes and rough drafts.

As you know, our drives carry a lifetime guarantee covering parts and workmanship. We will gladly replace the defective external drive. However, the guarantee states that the manufacturer and the retailer will not assume any incidental liability. Thus we are responsible only for the retail value of the external drive, not for the cost of duplicating the work that went into making the files stored on the drive.

However, your file might still be recoverable. A reputable data-recovery firm might be able to restore the data from the file at a very reasonable cost. To prevent such problems in the future, we always recommend that you back up all valuable files periodically.

We have already sent out your new external drive by overnight delivery. It should arrive within the next two days.

Please contact us if we can be of any further assistance.

Sincerely yours,

Paul R. Blackwood

Paul R. Blackwood, Manager
Customer Relations

If you are writing a "bad news" adjustment letter, salvage as much goodwill as you can by showing that you have acted reasonably. In denying a request, explain your side of the matter, thus educating the customer about how the problem occurred and how to prevent it in the future.

The writer does not begin by stating that he is denying the reader's request. Instead, he begins politely by trying to form a bond with the reader. In trying to meet the customer on neutral ground, be careful about admitting that the customer is right. If you say "We are sorry that the engine you purchased from us is defective," it will bolster the customer's claim if the dispute ends up in court.

The writer summarizes the facts of the incident, as he sees them.

The writer explains that he is unable to fulfill the reader's request. Notice that the writer never explicitly denies the request. It is more effective to explain why granting the request is not appropriate. Also notice that the writer does not explicitly say that the reader failed to make a backup copy of the plan and therefore the problem is her fault.

The writer shifts from the bad news to the good news. The writer explains that he has already responded appropriately to the reader's request.

The writer ends with a polite conclusion. A common technique is to offer the reader a special discount on a future purchase.

FIGURE 14.8 "Bad News" Adjustment Letter

Writing Memos

Like letters, memos have a characteristic format, which consists of the elements shown in Figure 14.9.

```
AMRO       MEMO

   To:     B. Pabst
 From:     J. Alonso  JA
Subject:   MIXER RECOMMENDATION FOR PHILLIPS
  Date:    12 June 2020
```

```
INTEROFFICE

      To:     C. Cleveland              c:   B. Aaron
    From:     H. Rainbow  H. R.              K. Lau
 Subject:     Shipment Date of Blueprints     J. Manuputra
              to Collier                      W. Williams
    Date:     2 October 2020
```

```
NORTHERN PETROLEUM COMPANY
INTERNAL CORRESPONDENCE

  Date:     January 3, 2020
    To:     William Weeks, Director of Operations
  From:     Helen Cho, Chemical Engineering Dept.  H. C.
Subject:    Trip Report—Conference on Improved Procedures
            for Chemical Analysis Laboratory
```

FIGURE 14.9   Identifying Information in a Memo

Some organizations prefer the full names of the writer and reader; others want only the first initials and last names. Some prefer job titles; others do not. If your organization does not object, include your job title and your reader's. The memo will then be informative for anyone who refers to it after either of you has moved on to a new position, as well as for others in the organization who do not know you.

As with letters, you can attach memos to emails and deliver them electronically. To preserve the memo format for the email recipient, save the memo as a PDF before sending.

If you prefer to distribute hard copies, print the second and all subsequent pages of a memo on plain paper rather than on letterhead. Include three items in the upper right-hand or left-hand corner of each subsequent page: the name of the recipient, the date of the memo, and the page number. See the header in Figure 14.2 on page 378.

Figure 14.10, a sample memo, is a trip report, a record of a business trip written after the employee returned to the office. Readers are less interested

Dynacol Corporation

INTEROFFICE COMMUNICATION

To: G. Granby, R&D
From: P. Rabin, Technical Services *P. R.*
Subject: Trip Report — Computer Dynamics, Inc.
Date: September 21, 2020

The purpose of this memo is to present my impressions of the Computer Dynamics technical seminar of September 19. The goal of the seminar was to introduce the company's new PQ-500 line of high-capacity storage drives.

Summary
In general, I was impressed with the technical capabilities and interface of the drives. Of the two models in the 500 series, I think we ought to consider the external drives, not the internal ones. I'd like to talk to you about this issue when you have a chance.

Discussion of Product Options
Computer Dynamics offers two models in its 500 series: an internal drive and an external drive. Both models have the same capacity (2T of storage), and they both work the same way: they extend the storage capacity of a server by integrating an optical disk library into the file system. The concept is that they move files between the server's faster, but limited-capacity, storage devices (hard disks) and its slower, high-capacity storage devices (magneto-optical disks). This process, which they call data migration and demigration, is transparent to the user.

For the system administrator, integrating either of the models would require no more than one hour. The external model would be truly portable; the user would not need to install any drivers, as long as his or her device is docked on our network. The system administrator would push the necessary drivers onto all the networked devices without the user having to do anything.

Although the internal drive is convenient — it is already configured for the computer — I think we should consider only the external drive. Because so many of our employees do teleconferencing, the advantage of portability outweighs the disadvantage of inconvenience. The tech rep from Computer Dynamics walked me through the process of configuring both models. A second advantage of the external drive is that it can be salvaged easily when we take a computer out of service.

Recommendation
I'd like to talk to you, when you get a chance, about negotiating with Computer Dynamics for a quantity discount. I think we should ask McKinley and Rossiter to participate in the discussion. Give me a call (x3442) and we'll talk.

FIGURE 14.10 Sample Memo
Image: Bumbim/Shutterstock.com.

The subject line is specific: the reader can tell at a glance that the memo reports on a trip to Computer Dynamics, Inc. If the subject line read only "Computer Dynamics, Inc.," the reader would not know what the writer was going to discuss about that company.

The memo begins with a clear statement of purpose, as discussed in Chapter 5.

Note that the writer has provided a summary, even though the memo is less than a page. The summary gives the writer an opportunity to convey his main request: he would like to meet with the reader.

The main section of the memo is the discussion, which conveys the detailed version of the writer's message. Often the discussion begins with the background: the facts that readers will need to know to understand the memo. In this case, the background consists of a two-paragraph discussion of the two models in the company's 500 series. Presumably, the reader already knows why the writer went on the trip.

Note that the writer ends this discussion with a conclusion, or statement of the meaning of the facts. In this case, the writer's conclusion is that the company should consider only the external drive.

A recommendation is the writer's statement of what he would like the reader to do next. In this case, the writer would like to sit down with the reader to discuss how to proceed.

in an hour-by-hour narrative of what happened than in a carefully structured discussion of what was important. Although writer and reader appear to be relatively equal in rank, the writer goes to the trouble of organizing the memo to make it easy to read and refer to later.

◢|
GUIDELINES Organizing a Memo

When you write a memo, organize it so that it is easy to follow. Consider these five organizational elements.

▶ **A specific subject line.** "Breast Cancer Walk" is too general. "Breast Cancer Walk Rescheduled to May 14" is better.

▶ **A clear statement of purpose.** As discussed in Chapter 5, Determining Your Purpose (p. 87), the purpose statement is built around a verb that clearly states what you want the readers to know, believe, or do.

▶ **A brief summary.** Even if a memo fits on one page, consider including a summary. For readers who want to read the whole memo, the summary is an advance organizer; for readers in a hurry, reading the summary substitutes for reading the whole memo.

▶ **Informative headings.** Headings make the memo easier to read by enabling readers to skip sections they don't need and by helping them understand what each section is about. In addition, headings make the memo easier to write because they prompt the writer to provide the kind of information readers need.

▶ **A prominent recommendation.** Many memos end with one or more recommendations. Sometimes these recommendations take the form of action steps: bulleted or numbered lists of what the writer will do or what the writer would like others to do. Here is an example:

> **Action items:**
> I would appreciate it if you would work on the following tasks and have your results ready for the meeting on Monday, June 9.
> - Henderson: recalculate the flow rate.
> - Smith: set up meeting with the regional EPA representative for some time during the week of May 13.
> - Falvey: ask Armitra in Houston for his advice.

Writing Emails

Before you write an email in the workplace, find out your organization's email policies. Most companies have written policies that discuss circumstances under which you may and may not use email, principles you should use in writing emails, and the monitoring of employee email. The Tech Tip box shows the basic elements of an email.

❯TECH TIP

Why To Use Email for Business Correspondence

Email allows for quick, direct correspondence with one or more recipients. It also provides a time- and date-stamped record of your communication, and users can create a "thread" or "string" to keep track of questions, comments, and responses. Although email itself is some-what informal, it is a convenient time- and cost-saving option, especially for correspondence being sent internationally, and formal documents can easily be attached.

How To Use Email for Business Correspondence

When using an email as a substitute for a memo or letter, keep in mind the points illustrated below, as well as the Guidelines box "Following Netiquette" on page 390.

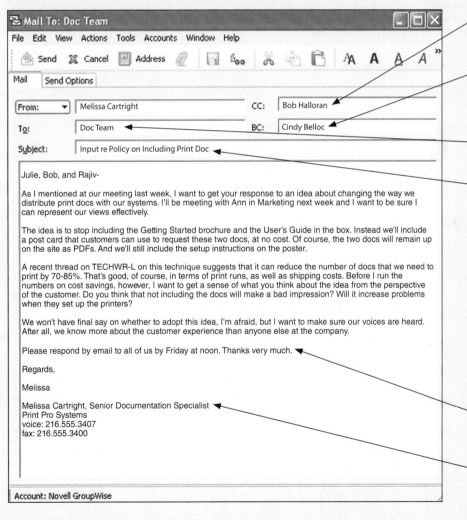

"CC" stands for courtesy copy. All of your recipients will know that you are sending a copy to this person or group.

"BC" or "Bcc" stands for blind copy or blind courtesy copy. None of your readers will know that you are sending a copy to this person or group.

You can create a "group" for people whom you email frequently.

Like a memo, an email should have a specific subject line.

By naming her readers at the start, the writer is showing respect for them.

The first paragraph of the email clarifies the writer's purpose.

The second paragraph describes the idea. You want to be sure your readers understand the context.

Notice that paragraphs are relatively brief and that the writer skips a line between paragraphs.

The writer explains what she would like her readers to do, and she states a deadline. Then she ends politely.

The writer has created a signature, which includes her contact information. This signature is attached automatically to her emails.

(continued)

The writer has attached a PDF version of her memo, avoiding any formatting problems for her readers.

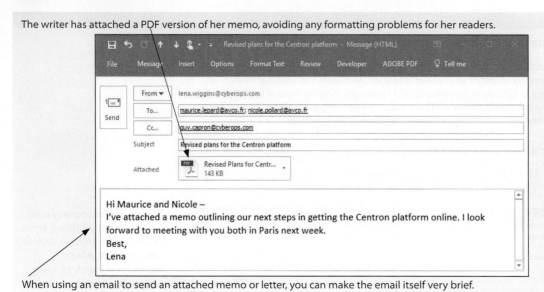

When using an email to send an attached memo or letter, you can make the email itself very brief.

GUIDELINES Following Netiquette

When you write email in the workplace, adhere to the following netiquette guidelines. *Netiquette* refers to etiquette on a network.

▶ **Stick to business.** Don't send jokes or other nonbusiness messages.

▶ **Use the appropriate level of formality.** As discussed earlier in the chapter, avoid informal writing.

▶ **Write correctly.** Remember to revise, edit, and proofread your emails before sending them.

▶ **Don't flame.** To *flame* is to scorch a reader with scathing criticism, usually in response to something that person wrote in a previous message. When you are angry, keep your hands away from the keyboard.

▶ **Make your message easy on the eyes.** Use uppercase and lowercase letters, and skip lines between paragraphs. Use uppercase letters or boldface (sparingly) for emphasis.

▶ **Don't forward a message to an online discussion forum without the writer's permission.** Doing so is unethical and illegal; the email is the intellectual property of the writer or (if it was written as part of the writer's work responsibilities) the writer's company.

▶ **Don't send a message unless you have something to say.** If you can add something new, do so, but don't send a message just to be part of the conversation.

Figure 14.11a shows an email that violates netiquette guidelines. The writer is a technical professional working for a microchip manufacturer. Figure 14.11b shows a revised version of this email message.

FIGURE 14.11 Netiquette

To: Supers and Leads
Subject:

LATELY, WE HAVE BEEN MISSING LASER REPAIR FILES FOR OUR 16MEG WAFERS. AFTER BRIEF INVESTIGATION, I HAVE FOUND THE MAIN REASON FOR THE MISSING DATA.
OCCASIONALLY, SOME OF YOU HAVE WRONGLY PROBED THE WAFERS UNDER THE CORRELATE STEP AND THE DATA IS THEN COPIED INTO THE NONPROD STEP USING THE QTR PROGRAM. THIS IS REALLY STUPID. WHEN DATE IS COPIED THIS WAY THE REPAIR DATA IS NOT COPIED. IT REMAINS UNDER THE CORRELATE STEP.
TO AVOID THIS PROBLEM, FIRST PROBE THE WAFERS THE RIGHT WAY. IF A WAFER MUST BE PROBED UNDER A DIFFERENT STEP, THE WAFER IN THE CHANGE FILE MUST BE RENAMED TO THE ** FORMAT.
EDITING THE WAFER DATA FILE SHOULD BE USED ONLY AS A LAST RESORT. IF THIS BECOMES A COMMON PROBLEM, WE COULD HAVE MORE PROBLEMS WITH INVALID DATA THAT THERE ARE NOW.
SUPERS AND LEADS: PLEASE PASS THIS INFORMATION ALONG TO THOSE WHO NEED TO KNOW.

ROGER VANDENHEUVAL

a. Email that violates netiquette guidelines

The writer does not clearly state his purpose in the subject line and the first paragraph.

Using all uppercase letters gives the impression that the writer is yelling at his readers.

The writer has not proofread.

The writer's tone is hostile.

With long lines and no spaces between paragraphs, this email is difficult to read.

To: Supers and Leads
Subject: Fix for Missing Laser Repair Files for 16MB Wafers

Supers and Leads:

Lately, we have been missing laser repair files for our 16MB wafers. In this email I want to briefly describe the problem and recommend a method for solving it.

Here is what I think is happening. Some of the wafers have been probed under the correlate step; this method copies the data into the nonprod step and leaves the repair data uncopied. It remains under the correlate step.

To prevent this problem, please use the probing method outlined in Spec 344-012. If a wafer must be probed using a different method, rename the wafer in the CHANGE file to the *.* format. Edit the wafer data file only as a last resort.

I'm sending along copies of Spec 344-012. Would you please pass along this email and the spec to all of your operators.

Thanks. Please get in touch with me if you have any questions.

Roger Vandenheuval

b. Email that adheres to netiquette guidelines

The writer has edited and proofread the email.

The subject line and first paragraph clearly state the writer's purpose.

Double-spacing between paragraphs and using short lines make the email easier to read.

The writer concludes politely.

Writing Microblogs

As discussed earlier in this chapter, microblog posts are different from letters, memos, and email in that they are often extremely brief and quite informal in tone. However, the fact that microblog posts are fast and informal does not mean that anything goes. When you write microblog posts, you are creating communication that will be archived and that will reflect on you and your organization. In addition, anything you write is subject to the same laws and regulations that pertain to all other kinds of documents. Many of the guidelines laid out in "Following Netiquette" (see below) apply to microblog posts as well as email. Take care, especially, not to flame. Become familiar with your microblog's privacy settings, and be aware of which groups of readers may view and share your posts.

The best way to understand your responsibilities when you write a microblog post at work is to study your organization's guidelines. Sometimes, these guidelines are part of the organization's guidelines for all business practices or all digital communication. Sometimes, they are treated separately. Figure 14.12 shows one organization's microblogging guidelines.

DOCUMENT ANALYSIS ACTIVITY

Following Netiquette in an Email Message

This message was written in response to a question emailed to several colleagues by a technical communicator seeking advice on how to write meeting minutes effectively. A response to an email message should adhere to the principles of effective emails and proper netiquette. The questions below ask you to think about these principles (explained in "Writing Emails" on pp. 388–91).

1. How effectively has the writer stated her purpose?

2. How effectively has the writer projected a "you attitude"?

3. How effectively has the writer made her message easy to read?

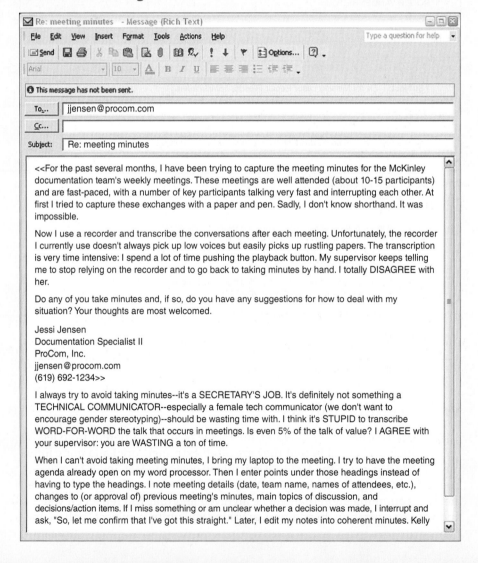

Re: meeting minutes - Message (Rich Text)

File   Edit   View   Insert   Format   Tools   Actions   Help   Type a question for help

Send

Arial   10   **B** *I* U

This message has not been sent.

To... | jjensen@procom.com

Cc... |

Subject: | Re: meeting minutes

<<For the past several months, I have been trying to capture the meeting minutes for the McKinley documentation team's weekly meetings. These meetings are well attended (about 10-15 participants) and are fast-paced, with a number of key participants talking very fast and interrupting each other. At first I tried to capture these exchanges with a paper and pen. Sadly, I don't know shorthand. It was impossible.

Now I use a recorder and transcribe the conversations after each meeting. Unfortunately, the recorder I currently use doesn't always pick up low voices but easily picks up rustling papers. The transcription is very time intensive: I spend a lot of time pushing the playback button. My supervisor keeps telling me to stop relying on the recorder and to go back to taking minutes by hand. I totally DISAGREE with her.

Do any of you take minutes and, if so, do you have any suggestions for how to deal with my situation? Your thoughts are most welcomed.

Jessi Jensen
Documentation Specialist II
ProCom, Inc.
jjensen@procom.com
(619) 692-1234>>

I always try to avoid taking minutes--it's a SECRETARY'S JOB. It's definitely not something a TECHNICAL COMMUNICATOR--especially a female tech communicator (we don't want to encourage gender stereotyping)--should be wasting time with. I think it's STUPID to transcribe WORD-FOR-WORD the talk that occurs in meetings. Is even 5% of the talk of value? I AGREE with your supervisor: you are WASTING a ton of time.

When I can't avoid taking meeting minutes, I bring my laptop to the meeting. I try to have the meeting agenda already open on my word processor. Then I enter points under those headings instead of having to type the headings. I note meeting details (date, team name, names of attendees, etc.), changes to (or approval of) previous meeting's minutes, main topics of discussion, and decisions/action items. If I miss something or am unclear whether a decision was made, I interrupt and ask, "So, let me confirm that I've got this straight." Later, I edit my notes into coherent minutes. Kelly

These guidelines walk personnel through the steps of responding to (or not responding to) a post related to their organization.

AIR FORCE WEB POSTING RESPONSE ASSESSMENT
AIR FORCE PUBLIC AFFAIRS AGENCY – EMERGING TECHNOLOGY DIVISION

DISCOVER

(YES)

WEB POSTING
Has someone discovered a post about the organization?
Is it positive or balanced?

"Produced by Air Force Public Affairs Agency. This product is public domain and may be used freely."

(NO)

EVALUATE

"TROLLS"
Is this a site dedicated to bashing and degrading others?

CONCURRENCE
A factual and well-cited response, which may agree or disagree with the post, yet is not factually erroneous, a rant or rage, bashing or negative in nature.
You can concur with the post, let stand or provide a positive review.
Do you want to respond?

(NO)

(YES)

MONITOR ONLY
Avoid responding to specific posts, monitor site for relevant information and comments. Notify HQ.

"RAGER"
Is the posting a rant, rage, joke or satirical in nature?

(NO)

FIX THE FACTS
Do you wish to respond with factual information directly on the comment board?

(NO)

"MISGUIDED"
Are there erroneous facts in the posting?

(YES)

LET STAND
Let the post stand— no response.

(YES)

(NO)

(YES)

"UNHAPPY CUSTOMER"
Is the posting a result of a negative experience?

(YES)

RESTORATION
Do you wish to rectify the situation and act upon a reasonable solution?

RESPOND

(NO)

SHARE SUCCESS
Do you wish to proactively share your story and your mission?

FINAL EVALUATON
Write response for current circumstances only. Will you respond?

(YES)

RESPONSE CONSIDERATIONS

TRANSPARENCY
Disclose your Air Force connection.

SOURCING
Cite your sources by including hyperlinks, images, video or other references.

TIMELINESS
Take time to create good responses.
Don't rush.

TONE
Respond in a tone that reflects highly on the rich heritage of the Air Force.

INFLUENCE
Focus on the most used sites related to the Air Force.

FIGURE 14.12 Guidelines for Microblogging
United States Air Force, 2016: www.publicaffairs.af.mil/Portals/1/documents/AF_web_Posting_Response_Assessment.pdf.

◢ GUIDELINES Representing Your Organization on a Microblog

If you use a microblog at work to communicate with people outside your own organization, such as vendors and customers, you want to use it in such a way that people are encouraged to like, respect, and trust you. These suggestions can help.

▶ **Decide on your audience and your purpose.** Are you connecting with clients, providing customer service, or helping people understand your company's goals and vision? You might want to have different accounts if you have several different audiences and purposes.

▶ **Learn the technology.** Know how to use hashtags, how to mention other users in your tweets, how to reply publicly and privately, how to integrate images and videos, and how to cross-post to your other social media accounts should you need to.

▶ **Learn the culture of the community.** Listen and learn before you post. Most communities have a distinct culture, which influences how and when people post, link, and reply. For instance, in some communities, people stick close to the technical topic; in others, they roam more freely and include personal comments.

▶ **Share, don't sell.** Post about incidents and developments that reinforce your organization's core principles, such as environmental awareness or making technology available around the world. Talk about leadership, teamwork, and cooperation. Don't try to sell products.

▶ **Help educate readers and solve their problems.** Regardless of whether you're responding to individual questions and complaints or helping people understand your company's culture or goals, focus on helping people learn and solve problems.

▶ **Sound like a person.** Use an informal tone. Readers are especially pleased when high-ranking employees show their human side, such as when the Zappos CEO posted, "Dropped my laptop on floor this morning. I usually drop my phone, so good to know I'm moving on to bigger and better things" (Hall, 2009).

▶ **Apologize when you make a mistake.** At the start of a basketball game against their rivals the Dallas Mavericks, the Houston Rockets sent out a tweet with a gun emoji pointed at a horse. Within two hours, after receiving heavy criticism, the Rockets apologized and removed the tweet (Meyer, 2016).

▶ **Link generously.** When you want to talk about something you've learned online, don't paraphrase. Rather, link back to the original source. Use a URL shortener such as Bitly or TinyURL so that the link won't take up too many of your 280 characters on Twitter.

▶ **Get your facts right.** Like anything online, your post is permanent. Double-check your facts before you post. Otherwise, you could embarrass yourself and erode people's trust in your organization.

▶ **Edit and proofread before you post.** You should be informal, but you shouldn't be sloppy. It sends the wrong message.

Writing Correspondence to Multicultural Readers

The four types of business correspondence discussed in this chapter are used in countries around the world. The ways they are used, however, can differ significantly from the ways they are used in the United States. These differences fall into three categories:

For more about cultural variables, see "Understanding the Cultural Variables 'On the Surface'" in Ch. 5, p. 101.

- **Cultural practices.** As discussed in Chapter 5, cultures differ in a number of ways, such as whether they focus on individuals or groups, the distance between power ranks, and attitudes toward uncertainty. Typically, a culture's attitudes are reflected in its business communication. For example, in Japan, which has a high power distance—that is, people in top positions are treated with great respect by their subordinates—a reader might be addressed as "Most Esteemed Mr. Director." Some cultural practices, however, are not intuitively obvious even if you understand the culture. For example, in Japanese business culture, it is considered rude to reply to an email by using the reply function in the email software; it is polite to begin a new email (Sasaki, 2010).

- **Language use and tone.** In the United States, writers tend to use contractions, the first names of their readers, and other instances of informal language. In many other countries, this informality is potentially offensive. Also potentially offensive is U.S. directness. A writer from the United States might write, for example, that "14 percent of the products we received from you failed to meet the specifications." A Korean would more likely write, "We were pleased to note that 86 percent of the products we received met the specifications." The writer either would not refer to the other 14 percent (assuming that the reader would get the point and replace the defective products quickly) or would write, "We would appreciate replacement of the remaining products." Many other aspects of business correspondence differ from culture to culture, such as preferred length, specificity, and the use of seasonal references in the correspondence.

- **Application choice and use.** In cultures in which documents tend to be formal, letters might be preferred to memos, or face-to-face meetings to phone calls or email. In Asia, for instance, a person is more likely to walk down the hall to deliver a brief message in person because doing so shows more respect. In addition, the formal characteristics of letters, memos, and emails are different in different cultures. The French, for instance, use indented paragraphs in their letters, whereas in the United States, paragraphs are typically left-justified. The ordering of the information in the inside address and complimentary close of letters varies widely. In many countries, emails are structured like memos, with the "to," "from," "subject," and "date" information added at the top, even though this information is already present in the routing information.

Try to study business correspondence written by people from the culture you will be addressing. When possible, have important documents reviewed by a person from that culture before you send them.

Letter Format

- ☐ Is the first page printed on letterhead stationery? *(p. 378)*
- ☐ Is the date included? *(p. 378)*
- ☐ Is the inside address complete and correct? *(p. 378)*
- ☐ Is the appropriate courtesy title used? *(p. 378)*
- ☐ If appropriate, is an attention line included? *(p. 378)*
- ☐ If appropriate, is a subject line included? *(p. 378)*
- ☐ Is the salutation appropriate? *(p. 378)*
- ☐ Is the complimentary close typed with only the first word capitalized? *(p. 379)*
- ☐ Is the signature legible, and is the writer's name typed beneath the signature? *(p. 379)*
- ☐ If appropriate, is an enclosure line included? *(p. 379)*
- ☐ If appropriate, is a copy and/or courtesy-copy line included? *(p. 379)*
- ☐ Is the letter typed in one of the standard formats? *(p. 380)*
- ☐ If the letter is to be sent by email, did you consider saving it as a PDF? *(p. 380)*

Types of Letters

Does the inquiry letter

- ☐ explain why you chose the reader to receive the inquiry? *(p. 381)*
- ☐ explain why you are requesting the information and how you will use it? *(p. 381)*
- ☐ specify the date when you need the information? *(p. 381)*
- ☐ list the questions clearly? *(p. 381)*
- ☐ offer, if appropriate, the product of your research? *(p. 381)*

Does the response to an inquiry letter

- ☐ answer the reader's questions? *(p. 382)*
- ☐ explain why, if any of the reader's questions cannot be answered? *(p. 382)*

Does the claim letter

- ☐ identify specifically the unsatisfactory product or service? *(p. 383)*
- ☐ explain the problem(s) clearly? *(p. 383)*
- ☐ propose an adjustment? *(p. 383)*
- ☐ conclude courteously? *(p. 383)*

Does the "good news" adjustment letter

- ☐ express your regret? *(p. 384)*
- ☐ explain the adjustment you will make? *(p. 384)*
- ☐ conclude on a positive note? *(p. 384)*

Does the "bad news" adjustment letter

- ☐ meet the reader on neutral ground, expressing regret but not apologizing? *(p. 385)*
- ☐ explain why the company is not at fault? *(p. 385)*
- ☐ clearly imply that the reader's request is denied? *(p. 385)*
- ☐ attempt to create goodwill? *(p. 385)*

Memos

- ☐ Does the identifying information adhere to your organization's standards? *(p. 386)*
- ☐ If the memo is to be sent by email, did you consider saving it as a PDF? *(p. 386)*
- ☐ Did you include a specific subject line? *(p. 387)*
- ☐ Did you clearly state your purpose at the start of the memo? *(p. 387)*
- ☐ If appropriate, did you summarize your message? *(p. 387)*
- ☐ Did you provide appropriate background for the discussion? *(p. 387)*
- ☐ Did you organize the discussion clearly? *(p. 388)*
- ☐ Did you include informative headings to help your readers? *(p. 388)*
- ☐ Did you highlight items requiring action? *(p. 388)*

Email

- ☐ Did you refrain from sending jokes or other nonbusiness messages? *(p. 390)*
- ☐ Did you keep the email as brief as possible and send it only to appropriate people? *(p. 390)*
- ☐ Did you use the appropriate level of formality? *(p. 390)*
- ☐ Did you write correctly? *(p. 390)*
- ☐ Did you avoid flaming? *(p. 390)*
- ☐ Did you check with the writer before forwarding his or her message? *(p. 390)*

☐ Did you write a specific, accurate subject line? *(p. 391)*

☐ Did you use uppercase and lowercase letters? *(p. 391)*

☐ Did you skip lines between paragraphs? *(p. 391)*

Microblogs

☐ Did you study your organization's policy on which microblog sites you may use and how you should use them? *(p. 392)*

☐ Did you exercise care in representing your organization on a microblog? *(p. 394)*

Multicultural Readers

☐ Did you consider varying cultural practices? *(p. 395)*

☐ Were you careful with language use and tone? *(p. 395)*

☐ Did you take into account your readers' preferences in application choice and use? *(p. 395)*

EXERCISES

1. You are the head of research for a biological research organization. Six months ago, you purchased a $2,000 commercial refrigerator for storing research samples. Recently, you suffered a loss of more than $600 in samples when the thermostat failed and the temperature in the refrigerator rose to more than 48 degrees over the weekend. Inventing any reasonable details, write a claim letter to the manufacturer of the refrigerator.

2. As the recipient of the claim letter described in Exercise 1, write an adjustment letter granting the customer's request.

3. As the manager of a retail electronics store, you guarantee that the store will not be undersold. If a customer finds another retailer selling the same equipment at a lower price within one month of his or her purchase, you will refund the difference. A customer has written to you and enclosed an ad from another store showing that it is selling a router for $26.50 less than he paid at your store. The advertised price at the other store was a one-week sale that began five weeks after the date of his purchase. He wants a $26.50 refund. Inventing any reasonable details, write an adjustment letter denying his request. You are willing, however, to offer him a 16-GB USB drive worth $9.95 if he would like to come pick it up.

4. **TEAM EXERCISE** Form small groups for this exercise on claim and adjustment letters. Have each member of your group study the following social-media post and the response, which function as a claim and an adjustment. Then meet and discuss your reactions to the two posts. How effectively does the writer of the claim present her case? How effective is the response from the company? Does its writer succeed in showing that the company's procedures for ensuring safety are effective? Does its writer succeed in projecting a professional tone? In both posts, how might the context of social media be affecting the tone? Write an email to

your instructor discussing the two posts, and attach to your email a revised version of the company's response.

Melissa Jackson

Star-Tel, your new Corona ME smartphone is the worst I've ever purchased! Two days into using it, I saw the back of the phone starting to smoke and the battery caught fire. The guy at the store said the battery must have been defective and replaced the phone. But three days later the same thing happened and sparks started coming out of it! Clearly it is not just the battery but something to do with the phone. It is too dangerous to keep using it, but I don't want to keep returning this phone and getting yet another defective product! I have lost hours of work this week because of this. I think you owe me — and everyone who's bought your defective phone — a refund!

Star-Tel Communications

Melissa, we're sorry to hear you weren't happy with your Corona ME. Problems like this are usually due to a defect in the battery or user error, such as exposing the phone to extreme heat. All of our products go through rigorous testing and safety checks before they're shipped, so we really don't see how this could be a problem with the Corona ME model. If you purchased the phone from one of our authorized dealers, they should provide you with a replacement at no charge or offer you store credit.

Sincerely,

The Customer Service Team

5. Louise and Paul work for the same manufacturing company. Louise, a senior engineer, is chairing a committee to investigate ways to improve the hiring process at the company. Paul, a technical editor, also serves on the committee. The excerpts quoted in Louise's email are from Paul's email to all members of the committee in response to Louise's request that members describe their approach to evaluating job-application materials. How would you revise Louise's email to make it more effective?

6. Because students use email to communicate with other group members when they write collaboratively, your college or university would like to create a one-page handout on how to use email responsibly. Find three or four netiquette guides on the internet that focus on email. Study these guides and write a one-page student guide to using email to communicate with other students. Somewhere in the guide, be sure to list the sites you studied, so that students can visit them for further information about netiquette.

To: Paul
From: Louise

Sometimes I just have to wonder what you're thinking, Paul.

>Of course, it's not possible to expect perfect resumes. But I
>have to screen them, and last year I had to read over 200. I'm
>not looking for perfection, but as soon as I spot an error I
>make a mental note of it and, when I hit a second and
>then a third error I can't really concentrate on the writer's
>credentials.

Listen, Paul, you might be a sharp editor, but the rest of us have a different responsibility: to make the products and move them out as soon as possible. We don't have the luxury of studying documents to see if we can find errors. I suggest you concentrate on what you were hired to do, without imposing your "standards" on the rest of us.

>From my point of view, an error can include a
>misused tradmark.

Misusing a "tradmark," Paul? Is that Error Number 1?

CASE 14: Writing a Memo

As the editor-in-chief of your college newspaper, you have recently been granted permission to create a Twitter account. The newspaper's faculty advisor has requested that, before you set up the account, you develop a memo to her outlining the audience and purpose as well as outlining your plan for the account based on the school's social media policy. If your instructor has assigned it, go to Achieve to begin drafting your memo.

Applying for a Job

GETTING HIRED has always involved writing. Whether you apply online through a company's website, reply to a post on LinkedIn, or send a formal letter and résumé through the mail, you will use words to make the case that the organization should offer you a position.

You will probably make that case quite a few times. According to the U.S. Department of Labor (2019), the typical American worker holds more than 11 different jobs while he or she is between the ages of 18 and 48. Obviously, most of those jobs don't last long. Even among American workers who begin a new job between the ages of 40 and 48, a third will no longer be with that company at the end of one year, and two-thirds will no longer be there in five years.

For most of you, looking for professional work is the first nonacademic test of your technical-communication skills. And it's an important test. Kyle Wiens, CEO of two tech companies, iFixit and Dozuki, requires all new employees to pass a writing test. His reason? "If it takes someone more than 20 years to notice how to properly use 'it's,' then that's not a learning curve I'm comfortable with" (Bowers, 2013).

Understanding the Job-Application Process

Preparing job-application materials requires weeks and months, not days, and there is no way to cut corners. The Focus on Process box on page 401 presents an overview of the process.

Establishing Your Professional Brand

One way to look at the process of looking for work is to keep in mind that, except for those times when you don't want to be in the workforce, you are *always* looking for work. That doesn't literally mean you're always applying for jobs; it means you're always open to the possibility that a job that interests you will come along. In other words, you are a *passive* applicant. When employers have an opening, they seek out the best candidates—regardless of whether those candidates are looking actively or passively (Cohen, 2013).

FOCUS ON PROCESS: Job-Application Materials

In writing job-application materials, pay special attention to these steps in the writing process.

PLANNING	Learn as much as you can about the organizations to which you will apply. See Chapter 6 for help with research.
DRAFTING	Decide whether to write a chronological or skills résumé, and use traditional sections and headings. You also have the option of preparing a nontraditional résumé. In your job-application letter, elaborate on key points from your résumé.
REVISING	You want these documents to be perfect. Ask several people to review them for you, and go over the section of the Writer's Checklist at the end of this chapter that applies to your document.
EDITING	See Chapter 10 for advice on writing correct and effective sentences.
PROOFREADING	See Appendix, Part C, for proofreading tips.

Being a successful job seeker requires a particular frame of mind. Think of yourself not as a student at this college or an employee of that company but rather as a professional with a brand to establish and maintain. For instance, say your name is Amber Cunningham, and you work as a human-resources officer for Apple. Don't think of yourself as an Apple human-resources officer. Instead, think of yourself as Amber Cunningham, a human-resources specialist who has worked for several companies (including Apple) and who has a number of marketable skills and a substantial record of accomplishments. Your *professional brand* (sometimes referred to as a "personal brand") is Amber Cunningham. Your challenge is to attract employers successfully—even if you're happy with your current position at Apple and are not looking to change jobs.

To present your professional brand successfully, you need to understand what employers are looking for, and then you need to craft the materials that will present that brand to the world.

UNDERSTANDING WHAT EMPLOYERS WANT

There is really no mystery about what employers want in an employee. Across all fields, employers want a person who is honest, hard-working, technically competent, skilled at solving problems, able to work effectively alone and in teams, willing to share information with others, and eager to keep learning.

You need to find evidence that you can use to display these qualities. Begin by thinking about everything you have done throughout your college career (courses, projects, service-learning experiences, organizations, leadership roles) and your professional career (job responsibilities, supervision of others, accomplishments, awards). And don't forget your volunteer activities; through these activities, many people acquire what are called *transferable skills*—skills that are useful or even necessary in seemingly unrelated jobs. For instance, volunteering for Habitat for Humanity says something important not only about your character but also about your ability to work effectively on a team and to solve problems. Even if you will never swing a hammer on the job, you will want to refer to this experience. Make a list—a long list—of your experiences, characteristics, skills, and accomplishments that will furnish the kinds of evidence that you can use in establishing your professional brand.

◢|
GUIDELINES Building the Foundation of
Your Professional Brand

Follow these five guidelines in developing your professional brand.

▸ **Research what others have done.** What kinds of information do they present about themselves online? On which social-media sites are they active? What kinds of comments and questions do they post? How do they reply to what others have posted?

▸ **Tell the truth.** Statistics about how many people lie and exaggerate in describing themselves in the job search vary, but it is probably between a third and a half. Companies search online themselves or hire investigators to verify the information you provide about yourself, to see if you are honest.

▸ **Communicate professionally.** Show that you can write clearly and correctly, and remember that it is inappropriate (and in some cases illegal) to divulge trade secrets or personal information about colleagues.

▸ **Describe your job skills.** Employers want to see that you have the technical skills that the job requires. They look for degrees, certifications, speeches and publications, and descriptions of what you do in your present position and have done in previous positions.

▸ **Focus on problem-solving and accomplishments.** The most compelling evidence that you would be a good hire is a solid record of identifying problems and devising solutions that met customers' needs, reduced costs, increased revenues, improved safety, and reduced environmental impact. Numbers tell the story: try to present your accomplishments as quantifiable data.

CRAFTING YOUR PROFESSIONAL BRAND

With your long list of characteristics, experiences, skills, and accomplishments in hand, it's time to start creating the materials—primarily online materials—that will display your professional brand.

▲
GUIDELINES Presenting Your Professional Brand

The following six guidelines can help you display your professional brand.

▶ **Create a strong online presence.** The best online presence is your own website, which functions as your online headquarters. All your other online activities will link back to this one site, the only site on the internet that is all about you. Register a site and try to name it *yourname.com* (you will be required to pay a small fee to secure the domain name). If you aren't experienced designing and creating sites, try a drag-and-drop site builder like Weebly or Squarespace, or use a template from a free blogging site such as WordPress. Upload to your site everything you want potential employers to see: contact information, a professional history, work samples, documents, and links to your accounts on social-media sites. If you don't have a website, take advantage of all the features on LinkedIn.

▶ **Participate on LinkedIn.** LinkedIn is the major social-media site used by employers to find employees. Set up a LinkedIn account and create a profile that includes the keywords that will attract potential employers. Rather than calling yourself a "programmer at ADP," which describes your current situation, call yourself "an experienced programmer in various programming languages (Java, C, C++, and PHP) and scripting languages (JavaScript, Perl, WSH, and UNIX shells) who understands interactive web pages and web-based applications, including JavaServer Pages (JSP), Java servlets, Active Server Pages (ASP), and ActiveX controls." Including keywords makes it easier for potential employers to find you when they search for employees. In addition, remember to list specific skills in the "Skills and Abilities" section of your profile. Potential employers searching for specific skills can then locate you more easily, and colleagues who know your work can endorse you for various skills. And don't merely set up an account—participate actively on LinkedIn. When you read a good article or see a useful video, link to it so others can find it. Participate in forum discussions. Make connections and endorse people who you know have good qualifications.

▶ **Participate on Facebook.** You probably already have a Facebook account and use Facebook's Timeline feature. Within your account, you also have the option of creating separate Pages for specific interests. Create a public Facebook Page and use it only for professional activities. Share information that will be interesting and useful to other professionals.

▶ **Participate on Twitter.** Follow influential people in your industry on Twitter to see the kinds of activities, conferences, and publications that interest them. Comment on and retweet useful tweets, link to the best items you see in the media, and reply when others send you messages.

▶ **Create a business card.** Having a business card if you're a student might seem odd, but a card is the best way to direct people to your website when you meet them in person. Your card should have your contact information, a few phrases

(continued)

highlighting your skills, and the URL of your website. Some people add a QR code (a Quick Response code, the square barcode that smartphones can read) to allow others to link to their websites instantly. (Search for "QR code generator" to find free sites that will help you generate a QR code.)

▶ **Practice an "elevator pitch."** An elevator pitch is a brief oral summary of your credentials. At less than 20 seconds long, it's brief enough that you can say it if you find yourself in an elevator with a potential employer. After the pitch, you hand the person your business card, which contains all the information he or she needs to get to your website, which links to everything else you want that person to see about you.

In making job offers, employers often rely on information they learn about potential new employees on the internet. According to a 2015 study commissioned by CareerBuilder, 52 percent of companies research job applicants on social media (Tarpey, 2015). The good news: 32 percent of those companies were motivated to seek out an applicant because of the positive information they found online, including the following:

- background information that supported job qualifications
- personality that fit with company culture
- professional-looking site
- great communication skills
- creativity

The bad news: 48 percent found information that made them reject an applicant. The employers who rejected applicants most often cited the following five problems:

- provocative or inappropriate photos
- suggestion of drug or alcohol use
- negative comments about a former employer or co-worker
- poor communication skills
- discriminatory comments about race, gender, or religion

Search online for your own name. Look at what potential employers will see and ask yourself whether your online personal brand is what you want to display. If it isn't, start to change it.

ETHICS NOTE

WRITING HONEST JOB-APPLICATION MATERIALS

Many résumés contain lies or exaggerations. Job applicants say they attended colleges they didn't and were awarded degrees they weren't, give themselves inflated job titles, say they were laid off when they were really fired for poor performance, and inflate their accomplishments. A CareerBuilder survey found that 38 percent of employees have embellished their job responsibilities at some point, and 18 percent have lied about their skills (Lorenz, 2012).

(continued)

Economist Steven D. Levitt, co-author of *Freakonomics,* concludes that more than 50 percent of job applicants lie on their résumés (Isaacs, 2012).

Companies take this problem seriously. They hire agencies that verify an applicant's education and employment history and check for a criminal record. They do their own research online. They phone people whose names the candidate has provided. If they find any discrepancies, they do not offer the candidate a position. If the person is already working for the company when discrepancies arise, they fire the employee.

Finding the Right Position

Once you have constructed your personal brand online—a process that can take weeks or even months—you can embark on finding the job that is right for you.

PLANNING THE JOB SEARCH

Planning requires thinking about the type of work you want, learning about employers, and preparing the materials you will need.

- **Do a self-inventory.** Before you can start thinking about where you want to work, you need to answer some questions about yourself:

  — **What are your strengths and weaknesses?** Are your skills primarily technical? Do you work best with others or on your own?

  — **What subjects do you like?** Think about what you have liked or disliked about your jobs and college courses.

  — **What kind of organization would you like to work for?** For-profit or nonprofit? Government or private industry? Small or large? Startup or established?

  — **What are your geographical preferences?** If you are free to relocate, where would you like to live? How do you feel about commuting? About telecommuting (working from home or from another remote location)?

- **Learn about potential employers.** Once you've identified a company of interest—maybe because you have seen an ad for a position, know someone who works there, or have always thought about working there—start learning about the company by studying its website. But don't stop there. Conduct informational interviews with people who have worked there or who know people who have; ask your professors if they can help you identify people to interview. Search the company's name; the results will point you to articles in newspapers and magazines, as well as to blogs, discussion forums, and podcasts. Search for the company on LinkedIn and Glassdoor. Many companies use sites like these as hiring portals. On Glassdoor, you can browse company ratings, salaries, and interviewing strategies as well as job opportunities. Figure 15.1 (on page 406) shows a portion of the LinkedIn portal for the Centers for Disease Control and Prevention. Learn about the organization through other means as well:

  — **Attend job fairs.** Your college and your community probably hold job fairs, where employers provide information about their organizations.

For more about interviewing, see "Interviews" in Ch. 6, p. 140.

FIGURE 15.1 One
Agency's Portal
on LinkedIn
Centers for Disease Control and Prevention,
2014: www.linkedin.com/company
/157336.

Many companies and other organizations use LinkedIn as a hiring
portal. A typical portal includes
descriptions and videos about
the organization, lists of all open
positions (and links to the organization website, where you can apply
online), and profiles of employees.
Because organizations want to
attract the best candidates, they
put real effort into presenting the
information you will need to decide
whether to apply.

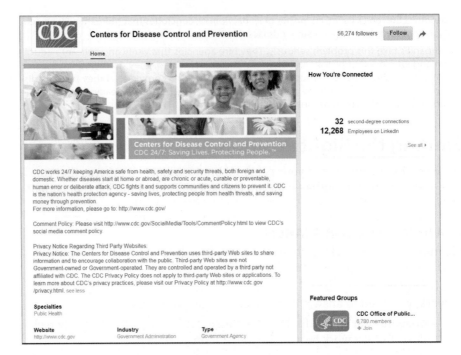

Sometimes, a single organization will hold a job fair to find qualified
candidates for a wide variety of jobs.

— **Find out about trends in your field.** Read the *Occupational Outlook Handbook*, published by the U.S. Department of Labor, for information about
your field and related fields. Read industry-related publications to find
out about highly (and poorly) regarded companies, job openings, and
the latest business news in your field. Talk with professors and with the
staff at your job-placement office.

• **Prepare a résumé and (perhaps) a job-application letter (a cover letter).** You
will need a résumé, a one- or two-page document that describes your most
important credentials. In most cases, you will upload a résumé to a job
board such as Monster or to a company's website; in some cases, you enter
the information on a company's web-based form. Some companies also
request a job-application letter. Start planning early by obtaining materials from the career-placement office at your college. Talk with friends who
have gone through the process successfully; study their application materials. Read books and visit websites about different aspects of the job search.

• **Put your portfolio items online.** A *portfolio* is a collection of your best work,
including your résumé, letters of recommendation, transcripts and professional
certifications, and reports, papers, websites, slides of oral presentations,

and other types of documents you have written or created as a student or an employee. You should put your portfolio on your website and other online locations, such as your LinkedIn account. The more items you have online, the more likely it is your name will appear when a potential employer searches for applicants.

If you wish to apply for a position in another country, keep in mind that the conventions of the process vary—sometimes quite a bit. You will need to adapt your résumé and letter to the expectations of employers in the country in which you would like to work. For instance, résumés in the United States do not include information such as the writer's height, weight, date of birth, and marital status; federal legislation prohibits organizations from asking for this information. In some other countries, however, personal information is expected on a résumé. Consult a book or online resource that offers specific guidance on the region where you wish to apply.

UNDERSTANDING JOB-SEARCH STRATEGIES

Once you have done your planning, you can start to look for a position. There are four major ways to find a job.

- **Through an organization's website.** Most organizations list their job offerings in a careers section on their websites and explain how to apply. If you are interested in a particular organization, start with its own site.

- **Through a job board on the internet.** Job boards are sites sponsored by federal agencies, internet service providers, and private organizations. Some sites merely list positions; you respond to such listings by email. Other sites let you upload your résumé electronically, so that employers can get in touch with you. Some job boards offer resources on how to prepare job-application materials; others do not. Among the biggest job boards are the following:

  — AfterCollege

  — Beyond

  — CareerBuilder

  — CareerOneStop (sponsored by the U.S. Department of Labor)

  — Glassdoor

  — Indeed (a metasearch engine for job seekers)

  — Monster

- One caution about using job boards: once you upload your résumé to an internet site, you probably have lost control of it. Here are four questions to consider before you post to a job board:

  — Who has access to your résumé? You might want to remove your home address and phone number from it if anyone can view it.

— How will you know if an employer requests your résumé? Will you be notified by the job board?

— Can your current employer see your résumé? If your employer discovers that you are looking for a new job, your current position could be in jeopardy.

— Can you update your résumé at no cost? Some job boards charge you each time you update your résumé.

- **Through your network.** A relative or an acquaintance can exert influence to help you get a job, or at least point out a new position. Other good contacts include past employers and professors. Also consider becoming active in the student chapter of a professional organization in your field, through which you can meet professionals in your local area. Many people use Twitter, Facebook, and—in particular—LinkedIn to connect with their contacts, as well as to try to identify hiring officers and other professionals who can help them apply. Figure 15.2 shows excerpts from one professional's LinkedIn profile.

Everything in this excerpt from Charlotte Robidoux's LinkedIn profile makes the argument that she is talented, hard-working, and successful.

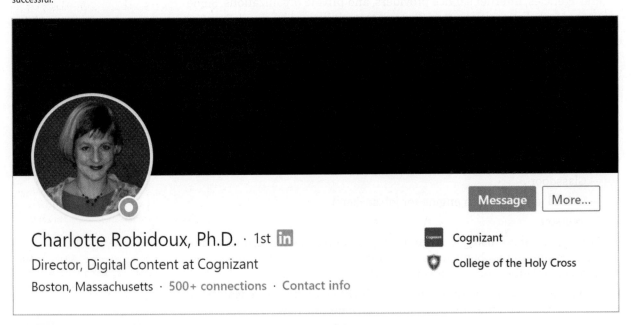

FIGURE 15.2   Excerpts from a Professional's LinkedIn Profile   *(continued)*
Charlotte Robidoux.

Experience

Director, Digital Content
Cognizant
Nov 2016 – Present · 3 yrs 3 mos

Professional Summary
• Deep experience leading global strategic content development teams
• Collaboration expert – co-editor and author
• Proven ability directing content strategy
• Skilled managing content workflow in CMS tools
• Expertise creating standard-leading web content
• Proficient reusing content for multi-channel output
• Ability to tailor storylines to specific audience needs
• Refined skill collaborating across industries / practices
• Proficient driving brand, style, content strategy
see less

Hewlett Packard Enterprise
16 yrs 1 mo

Senior Content Strategy Manager
Sep 2010 – Nov 2016 · 6 yrs 3 mos

Standardized Collateral Program
• Led a global initiative to standardize external and internal collateral for Enterprise Services, an $18B business, improving content usability, improving site traffic, and increasing win rates by 8%.
• Managed and contributed to the creation of 700+ pieces of collateral across 100+ serv ...see more

Content Strategist, Publications Manager, Managing Editor
Nov 2000 – Sep 2010 · 9 yrs 11 mos

Hired by Compaq Computer Corporation to serve as managing editor for publications related to data storage and networking prior to the merger with HP. Promoted to manager at HP to oversee writing and editing team and to develop and strategy for implementing a content management system for storage, server, and networking products. ...see more

| Human Genome Project discoveries: Dialectics... | MANAGEMENT Best Practices | Streamlining Your Path to Metadata Charlotte... |

Skills & Endorsements

(+) **Content Management** · 74

Endorsed by **Andrya F. and 11 others** who are highly skilled at this

Endorsed by **4 of Charlotte's colleagues at Cognizant**

(+) **Software Documentation** · 52

Endorsed by **Ray Dixon and 15 others** who are highly skilled at this

Endorsed by **27 of Charlotte's colleagues at Hewlett Packard Enterprise**

(+) **Management** · 40

Endorsed by **23 of Charlotte's colleagues at Hewlett Packard Enterprise**

Endorsed by **7 people who know Management**

Show more ⌄

Accomplishments

7 Publications
Theorizing a Practical Rhetoric for Virtual Collaboration amongWriters in Academia and Industry • Virtual Collaborative Writing in the Workplace: Computer-Mediated Communication Technologies and Processes • Streamlining your path to metadata: Develop a metadata strategy in eight steps • Is There a Write Way to Collaborate? • Human Genome Project discoveries: Dialectics and rhetoric in the science of genetics • Rhetorically Structured Content: Developing a Collaborative Single-Sourcing Curriculum • The Human Genome Project: Novel Approaches, Probable Reasoning, and the Advancement of Science

2 Honors & Awards
The Rhetoric Society of America Dissertation Award • CIDM Rare Bird Award

2 Languages
English • French

1 Organization
ITSMA

FIGURE 15.2 Excerpts from a Professional's LinkedIn Profile (*continued*)

Charlotte includes a full description of her experience, with details about her responsibilities, specific types of projects she's completed, and leadership roles she has taken. All of this detail increases her chances of attracting potential employers.

Charlotte also lists a number of specific skills in the "Skills & Endorsements" section of her profile. Other LinkedIn users have endorsed her skills, not only affirming her abilities but also suggesting that she is an active LinkedIn user who probably endorses her colleagues, as is appropriate, in return.

The "Accomplishments" section lists additional information that will be attractive to employers. Charlotte has included relevant publications and awards, demonstrating that her experience and capabilities are recognized outside of the companies where she has worked. Employers will note that she contributes to her field by being active in a professional organization and publishing articles on topics related to her work.

- **Through a college or university placement office or professional placement bureau.** College and university placement offices bring companies and students together. Student résumés are made available to representatives of business, government, and industry, who arrange on-campus interviews. Students who do well in the campus interviews are then invited by the representatives to visit the organization for a tour and another interview. A professional placement bureau offers essentially the same service but charges a fee (payable by either the employer or the person who is hired for a job). Placement bureaus cater primarily to more advanced professionals who are changing jobs.

GUIDELINES Using LinkedIn's Employment Features

In 2015, 84 percent of employers used social media to recruit. Among those employers, 96 percent said they used LinkedIn (Society for Human Resource Management, 2016). The following five guidelines can help you take advantage of the employment features on the world's most influential networking site for professionals.

▶ **Use the profile section fully.** The profile section includes information from your résumé, but unlike a résumé, which needs to be concise and contains only words, the profile section can include any kind of digital file, such as presentation slides or videos. Describe your education and professional jobs in detail; remember that the keywords in your descriptions will enable potential employers to find you as they search for employees. If you add "skills" to your profile, others have an opportunity to "endorse" those skills, adding credibility to your profile.

▶ **Include a picture.** A picture increases by sevenfold the chances that a reader will read your profile (Halzack, 2013).

▶ **Post updates.** Post information about interesting articles you have read, conferences you are attending, and other professional activities. Be generous in praising co-workers and others you follow on the internet. Mention your volunteer activities. Nicole Williams, a career expert at LinkedIn, writes that posting an update once a week makes you 10 times more likely to have your profile viewed by a hiring manager (Halzack, 2013).

▶ **Write unique invitation requests.** You can ask one of your connections to introduce you to someone who is not one of your connections. In doing so, explain why you want to be introduced ("I plan to relocate to Bill's city later this year and want to describe the services I offer"), give your connection the opportunity to say no gracefully ("Would you be willing to help me make this introduction? If not, I understand"), and thank your connection ("I really appreciate your taking the time to consider my request").

▶ **Write unique invitations to connect.** When you want to connect with another LinkedIn member, especially one whom you do not know well in person, avoid the template invitation, "I'd like to add you to my professional network." Explain how you know the other person: "As a fellow Aggie who's admired your company's strategy for some time, I'd like to connect."

Writing Résumés

Although you will present your credentials on LinkedIn and other sites, you will also need to create a résumé, which you will upload to a job board or a company's website, email to the company, or paste into a web-based form.

Many of the job boards listed on p. 407 include samples of résumés.

Many students wonder whether to write their résumés themselves or use a résumé-preparation agency. It is best to write your own résumé, for three reasons:

- **You know yourself better than anyone else does.** No matter how professional the work of a résumé-preparation agency is, you can do a better job communicating important information about yourself.

- **Employment officers know the style of the local agencies.** Readers who recognize that you did not write your own résumé might wonder whether you are hiding any deficiencies.

- **If you write your own résumé, you will be more likely to adapt it to different situations.** You are unlikely to return to a résumé-preparation agency and pay an additional fee to make a minor revision.

Because most companies use résumé-application software to scan résumés into databases and search for keywords, a good résumé includes the right keywords. Only after a résumé has made it through that initial electronic pass will it be read by a person. Résumé consultant Ramsey Penegar puts it this way: "If your résumé doesn't have the keywords that match their job requirements, your résumé may hit the 'no' pile early in the process" (Auerbach, 2012).

The best way to be sure you have the appropriate keywords in your résumé is to study the job description in the actual job posting you want to respond to. Then find 10 other ads for similar positions and identify the terms that come up frequently. Think in terms of job titles, names of products, companies, technologies, and professional organizations. For instance, if the job is to develop web pages, you will likely see many references to "web page," "internet," "XHTML," "HTML5," "Java," "W3C," and "CSS." Also include keywords that refer to your communication skills, such as "public speaking," "oral communication," and "communication skills."

But don't just list the keywords. Instead, integrate them into sentences about your skills and accomplishments. For instance, a computer-science student might write, "Wrote applications for migrating data between systems/databases using C#, XML, and Excel Macros." A chemical engineer might write, "Worked with polymers, mixing and de-gassing polydimethylsiloxane."

How long should a résumé be? It should be long enough to include all pertinent information but not so long that it bores or irritates the reader. Although some hiring consultants have guidelines (such as that a student's résumé should be no longer than one page, or that applicants who are vice presidents at companies can write two-page résumés), the consensus is that length is unimportant. If an applicant has more experience, the résumé will be longer; if an applicant has less experience, it will be shorter. If all the information in the résumé helps make the case that the applicant is an excellent fit for the position, it's the right length.

The information that goes into a résumé is commonly ordered either chronologically or by skills. In a *chronological résumé*, you use time as the organizing pattern for each section, including education and experience, and discuss your responsibilities for each job you have held. In a *skills résumé* (sometimes called a *functional résumé*), you merely list your previous jobs but include a skills section in which you describe your talents, skills, and achievements.

A chronological résumé focuses on the record of employment, giving an applicant the opportunity to describe the duties and accomplishments related to each job. The skills résumé highlights the skills that the candidate demonstrated at several different companies, such as supervising others, managing a large department, or reducing production costs. The skills résumé is a popular choice for applicants who have a gap in their employment history, who are re-entering the workforce, or who have changed jobs frequently.

In both types of résumé, you use reverse chronology; that is, you present the most recent jobs and degrees first, to emphasize them.

ELEMENTS OF THE CHRONOLOGICAL RÉSUMÉ

Most chronological résumés have five basic elements: identifying information, summary of qualifications, education, employment history, and interests and activities. Sometimes writers include a sixth section: references. In filling in these basic sections, remember that you want to include the keywords that will attract employers. For a sample chronological résumé, see Figure 15.3.

Identifying Information If you are submitting your résumé directly to a company, include your full name, address, phone number, and email address. Use your complete address, including the zip code. If your address during the academic year differs from your home address, list both and identify them clearly. An employer might call during an academic holiday to arrange an interview.

However, if you are posting your résumé to an internet job board, where it can be seen by anyone, you will be more vulnerable to scammers, spammers, and identity thieves. Don't include a mailing address or phone number, and use an email address that does not identify you.

Summary Statement After the identifying information, add a summary statement, a brief paragraph that highlights three or four important skills or accomplishments. For example:

Summary
Six years' experience creating testing documentation to qualify production programs that run on Automated Test and Handling Equipment. Four years' experience running QA tests on software, hardware, and semiconductor products. Bilingual English and Italian. Secret security clearance.

CARL OPPENHEIMER
3109 Vista Street
Philadelphia, PA 19136
(215) 555-3880
coppen@dragon.du.edu

The writer provides his contact information, including his email address.

SUMMARY

Recent BSEE graduate with experience as an electrical engineer intern for RCA Advanced Technology Laboratory. Analytical, technical, and communication skills for laboratory and customer-facing applications. Strong understanding of large-scale integrated systems and CMOS applications.

The writer presents a summary statement. Some applicants find it awkward to praise themselves, describing their skills, but it is important to have keywords such as "analytical skills" in the résumé, particularly if the job ad mentioned them.

EDUCATION

BS in Electrical Engineering   **6/2019**
Drexel University, Philadelphia, PA
GPA: 3.67 (on a scale of 4.0)
Senior Design Project: "Enhanced Path-Planning Software for Robotics"
Advanced Engineering Courses
- Digital Signal Processing
- Computer Hardware
- Introduction to Operating Systems I, II
- Systems Design
- Digital Filters
- Computer Logic Circuits I, II

The writer chooses to emphasize his advanced engineering courses. For another job, he might emphasize other courses.

EMPLOYMENT

Electrical Engineering Intern II   **6/2016–1/2017**
RCA Advanced Technology Laboratory, Moorestown, NJ
Designed ultra-large-scale integrated circuits using VERILOG and VHDL hardware description languages. Assisted senior engineer in CMOS IC layout, modeling, parasitic capacitance extraction, and PSPICE simulation operations.

Electrical Engineering Intern I   **6/2015–1/2016**
RCA Advanced Technology Laboratory, Moorestown, NJ
Verified and documented several integrated circuit designs. Used CAD software and hardware to simulate, check, and evaluate these designs. Gained experience with Mathcad.

The writer wisely creates a category that calls attention to his academic awards and his membership in his field's major professional organization.

The writer does not include his references or write "References available upon request." If the reader invites him to proceed to the next step in the process, Carl will send a list of references, with their contact information.

HONORS AND ORGANIZATIONS

Eta Kappa Nu (Electrical Engineering Honor Society)
Tau Beta Pi (General Engineering Honor Society)
IEEE

FIGURE 15.3   **Chronological Résumé of a Traditional Student**

Education If you are a student or a recent graduate, place the education section next. If you have substantial professional experience, place the employment-history section before the education section.

Include at least the following information in the education section:

- **Your degree.** After the degree abbreviation (such as BS, BA, AA, or MS), list your academic major (and, if you have one, your minor)—for example, "BS in Materials Engineering, minor in General Business."
- **The institution.** Identify the institution by its full name: "Louisiana State University," not "LSU."
- **The location of the institution.** Include the city and state.
- **The date of graduation.** If your degree has not yet been granted, add "Anticipated date of graduation" or a similar phrase.
- **Information about other schools you attended.** List any other institutions you attended beyond high school, even those from which you did not earn a degree. The description for other institutions should include the same information as in the main listing. Arrange entries in reverse chronological order: that is, list first the school you attended most recently.

GUIDELINES Elaborating on Your Education

The following four guidelines can help you develop the education section of your résumé.

▶ **List your grade-point average.** If your average is significantly above the median for the graduating class, list it. Or list your average in your major courses, or all your courses in the last two years. Calculate it however you wish, but be honest and clear.

▶ **Compile a list of courses.** Include courses that will interest an employer, such as advanced courses in your major or courses in technical communication, public speaking, or organizational communication. For example, a list of business courses on an engineer's résumé might show special knowledge and skills. But don't bother listing required courses; everyone else in your major took the same courses. Include the substantive titles of listed courses. Employers won't know what "Chemistry 450" is; call it by its official title: "Chemistry 450. Organic Chemistry."

▶ **Describe a special accomplishment.** If you completed a special senior design or research project, present the title and objective of the project, any special or advanced techniques or equipment you used, and, if you know them, the major results: "A Study of Shape Memory Alloys in Fabricating Actuators for Underwater Biomimetic Applications—a senior design project to simulate the swimming styles and anatomy of fish." A project description makes you seem more like a professional: someone who designs and carries out projects.

▶ **List honors and awards you received.** Scholarships, internships, and academic awards suggest exceptional ability. If you have received a number of such honors, or some that were not exclusively academic, you might list them separately (in a section called "Honors" or "Awards") rather than in the education section. Decide where this information will make the best impression.

The education section is the easiest part of the résumé to adapt in applying for different positions. For example, a student majoring in electrical engineering who is applying for a position requiring strong communication skills can emphasize communication courses in one version of the résumé and advanced electrical engineering courses in another version. As you compose the education section, emphasize those aspects of your background that meet the requirements for the particular job.

Employment History Present at least the basic information about each job you have held: the dates of employment, the organization's name and location, and your position or title. Then add carefully selected details. Readers want to know what you did and accomplished. Provide at least a two- to three-line description for each position. For particularly important or relevant jobs, write more, focusing on one or more of the following factors:

- **Skills.** What technical skills did you use on the job?
- **Equipment.** What equipment did you operate or oversee? In particular, mention computer equipment or software with which you are familiar.
- **Money.** How much money were you responsible for? Even if you considered your data-entry position fairly easy, the fact that the organization grossed, say, $2 million a year shows that the position involved real responsibility.
- **Documents.** What important documents did you write or assist in writing, such as brochures, reports, manuals, proposals, or websites?
- **Personnel.** How many people did you supervise?
- **Clients.** What kinds of clients, and how many, did you do business with in representing your organization?

Whenever possible, emphasize *accomplishments*. If you reorganized the shifts of the weekend employees you supervised, state the results:

> Reorganized the weekend shift, resulting in a cost savings of more than $3,000 per year.

> Wrote and produced (with Adobe InDesign) a 56-page parts catalog that is still used by the company and that increased our phone inquiries by more than 25 percent.

When you describe positions, functions, or responsibilities, use the active voice ("supervised three workers") rather than the passive voice ("three workers were supervised by me"). The active voice highlights action. Note that writers often omit the *I* at the start of sentences: "Prepared bids," rather than "I prepared bids." Whichever style you use, be consistent. Table 15.1 (on page 416) lists some strong verbs to use in describing your experience.

For more about using strong verbs, see "Structuring Effective Sentences" in Ch. 10 on p. 226.

TABLE 15.1   Strong Action Verbs Used In Résumés

administered	coordinated	evaluated	maintained	provided
advised	corresponded	examined	managed	purchased
analyzed	created	expanded	monitored	recorded
assembled	delivered	hired	obtained	reported
built	developed	identified	operated	researched
collected	devised	implemented	organized	solved
completed	directed	improved	performed	supervised
conducted	discovered	increased	prepared	trained
constructed	edited	instituted	produced	wrote

Here is a sample listing of employment history:

June–September 2019: Student Dietitian

Millersville General Hospital, Millersville, TX

Gathered dietary histories and assisted in preparing menus for a 300-bed hospital.

Received "excellent" on all seven items in evaluation by head dietitian.

In just a few lines, you can show that you sought and accepted responsibility and that you acted professionally. Do not write, "I accepted responsibility"; instead, present facts that lead the reader to that conclusion.

Naturally, not all jobs entail professional skills and responsibilities. Many students find summer work as laborers, sales clerks, and so forth. If you have not held a professional position, list the jobs you have held, even if they were unrelated to your career plans. If the job title is self-explanatory, such as restaurant server or service-station attendant, don't elaborate. If you can write that you contributed to your tuition or expenses, such as by earning 50 percent of your annual expenses through a job, employers will be impressed by your self-reliance.

If you have held a number of nonprofessional as well as several professional positions, group the nonprofessional ones:

Other Employment: cashier (summer 2016), salesperson (part-time, 2017), clerk (summer 2018)

This strategy prevents the nonprofessional positions from drawing the reader's attention away from the more important positions.

If you have gaps in your employment history—because you were raising children, attending school, recovering from an accident, or for other reasons—consider using a skills résumé, which focuses more on your skills and less on your job history. You can explain the gaps in the job-application letter (if you write one) or in an interview. For instance, you could say, "I spent 2017 and part of 2018 caring for my elderly parent, but during that time I was able to do some substitute teaching and study at home to prepare for my A+ and

Network+ certification, which I earned in late 2018." Do not lie or mislead about your dates of employment.

If you have had several positions with the same employer, you can present one description that encompasses all the positions or present a separate description for each position.

PRESENTING ONE DESCRIPTION

Blue Cross of Iowa, Ames, Iowa (January 2012–present)
- *Internal Auditor II (2016–present)*
- *Member Service Representative/Claims Examiner II (2014–2016)*
- *Claims Examiner II (2012–2014)*

As Claims Examiner II, processed national account inquiries and claims in accordance with . . . After promotion to Member Service Representative/Claims Examiner II position, planned policies and procedures . . . As Internal Auditor II, audit claims, enrollment, and inquiries; run dataset population and sample reports . . .

This format enables you to mention your promotions and to create a clear narrative that emphasizes your progress within the company.

PRESENTING SEPARATE DESCRIPTIONS

Blue Cross of Iowa, Ames, Iowa (January 2012–present)
- *Internal Auditor II (2016–present)*
  Audit claims, enrollment, and inquiries . . .
- *Member Service Representative/Claims Examiner II (2014–2016)*
  Planned policies and procedures . . .
- *Claims Examiner II (2012–2014)*
  Processed national account inquiries and claims in accordance with . . .

This format, which enables you to create a fuller description of each position, is effective if you are trying to show that each position is distinct and you wish to describe the more recent positions more fully.

Interests and Activities The interests-and-activities section of the résumé is the appropriate place for several kinds of information about you:
- participation in community-service organizations, such as Big Brothers/Big Sisters or volunteer work in a hospital
- hobbies related to your career (for example, electronics for an engineer)
- sports, especially those that might be socially useful in your professional career, such as tennis, racquetball, and golf
- university-sanctioned activities, such as membership on a team, work on the college newspaper, or election to a responsible position in an academic organization or a residence hall

Do not include activities that might create a negative impression, such as gambling or performing in a death-metal rock band. And always omit such activities as meeting people and reading. Everybody does these things.

References Potential employers will want to learn more about you from your professors and previous employers. These people who are willing to speak or write on your behalf are called *references*.

Some applicants list their references on their résumé. The advantage of this strategy is that the potential employer can contact the references without having to contact the applicant. Other applicants prefer to wait until the potential employer has asked for the list. The advantage of this strategy is that the applicant can assemble a different set of references for each position without having to create different résumés. Although applicants in the past added a note stating "References available upon request" at the end of their résumés, many applicants today do not do so because they think the comment is unnecessary: employers assume that applicants can provide a list of references—and that they would love to do so.

Regardless of whether you list your references on your résumé, choose your references carefully. Solicit references only from those who know your work best and for whom you have done your best work—for instance, a previous employer with whom you worked closely or a professor from whom you received A's. Don't ask prominent professors who do not know your work well; they will be unable to write informative letters.

Do not simply assume that someone is willing to serve as a reference for you. Give the potential reference writer an opportunity to decline gracefully. The person might not have been as impressed with your work as you think. If you simply ask the person to serve as a reference, he or she might accept and then write a lukewarm letter. It is better to ask, "Would you be able to write an enthusiastic letter for me?" or "Do you feel you know me well enough to write a strong recommendation?" If the person shows any signs of hesitation or reluctance, withdraw the request. It may be a little embarrassing, but it is better than receiving a weak recommendation.

In listing their references, some applicants add, for each reference, a sentence or two describing their relationship with the person, as shown in this sample listing for a reference.

Dr. Dale Cletis
Professor of English
Boise State University
Boise, ID 83725
208.555.2637
dcletis@boisestate.edu

Dr. Cletis was my instructor in three literature courses, as well as my adviser.

Other Elements The sections discussed so far appear on almost every-one's résumé. Other sections are either optional or appropriate for only some job seekers.

- **Computer skills.** Classify your skills in categories such as hardware, soft-ware, languages, and operating systems. List any professional certifica-tions you have earned.

- **Military experience.** If you are a veteran, describe your military service as if it were a job, citing dates, locations, positions, ranks, and tasks. List posi-tive job-performance evaluations.

- **Language ability.** A working knowledge of another language can be very valu-able, particularly if the potential employer has international interests and you could be useful in translation or foreign service. List your proficiency, using terms such as *beginner*, *intermediate*, or *advanced*. Some applicants dis-tinguish among reading, writing, and speaking abilities. Don't overstate your abilities; you could be embarrassed—and without a job—when the potential employer hands you a business letter written in the language you say you know, or invites a native speaker of that language to sit in on the interview.

- **Willingness to relocate.** If you are willing to relocate, say so. Many organiza-tions will find this flexibility attractive.

ELEMENTS OF THE SKILLS RÉSUMÉ

A skills résumé differs from a chronological résumé in that it includes a sepa-rate section, usually called "Skills" or "Skills and Abilities," that emphasizes job skills and knowledge. In a skills résumé, the employment section becomes a brief list of information about your employment history: companies, dates of employment, and positions. Here is an example of a skills section.

Skills and Abilities

Management
Served as weekend manager of six employees in a retail clothing business. Also trained three summer interns at a health-maintenance organization.

Writing and Editing
Wrote status reports, edited performance appraisals, participated in assembling and producing an environmental impact statement using desktop publishing.

Teaching and Tutoring
Tutored in the university writing center. Taught a two-week course in electronics for teenagers. Coached youth basketball.

In a skills section, you choose the headings, the arrangement, and the level of detail. Your goal, of course, is to highlight the skills an employer is seeking. See Figure 15.4 (on page 420) for an example of a skills résumé.

In a skills résumé, you present the skills section at the start. This organization lets you emphasize your professional attributes. Notice that the writer uses specific details, including names of software, number of credits, types of documents, and kinds of activities.

The employment section contains a list of positions rather than descriptions of what the writer did in each position.

This writer has used a two-column table to organize the information. The left column presents the headings; the right column presents the data. The advantage of using a table rather than moving text using tabs is that you can use different text attributes (for instance, the headings can be boldfaced, set in a different typeface, or set in a different size) without having to worry about whether the different attributes will alter the line spacing. In addition, if you use a table, you can easily revise and edit; with tabs, your editing will create awkward line breaks and alignment.

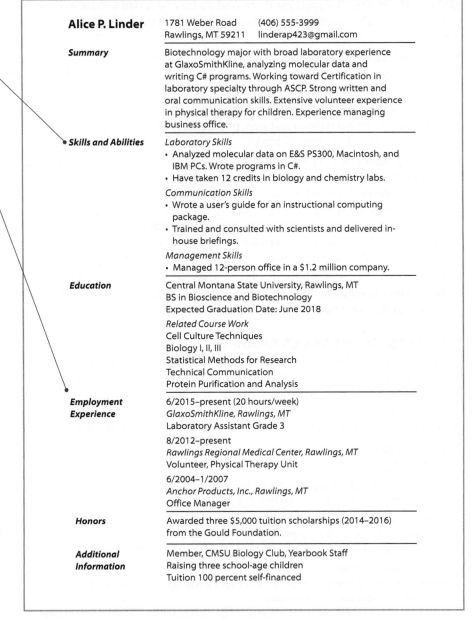

Alice P. Linder 1781 Weber Road   (406) 555-3999
Rawlings, MT 59211   linderap423@gmail.com

Summary
Biotechnology major with broad laboratory experience at GlaxoSmithKline, analyzing molecular data and writing C# programs. Working toward Certification in laboratory specialty through ASCP. Strong written and oral communication skills. Extensive volunteer experience in physical therapy for children. Experience managing business office.

Skills and Abilities
Laboratory Skills
- Analyzed molecular data on E&S PS300, Macintosh, and IBM PCs. Wrote programs in C#.
- Have taken 12 credits in biology and chemistry labs.

Communication Skills
- Wrote a user's guide for an instructional computing package.
- Trained and consulted with scientists and delivered in-house briefings.

Management Skills
- Managed 12-person office in a $1.2 million company.

Education
Central Montana State University, Rawlings, MT
BS in Bioscience and Biotechnology
Expected Graduation Date: June 2018

Related Course Work
Cell Culture Techniques
Biology I, II, III
Statistical Methods for Research
Technical Communication
Protein Purification and Analysis

Employment Experience
6/2015–present (20 hours/week)
GlaxoSmithKline, Rawlings, MT
Laboratory Assistant Grade 3

8/2012–present
Rawlings Regional Medical Center, Rawlings, MT
Volunteer, Physical Therapy Unit

6/2004–1/2007
Anchor Products, Inc., Rawlings, MT
Office Manager

Honors
Awarded three $5,000 tuition scholarships (2014–2016) from the Gould Foundation.

Additional Information
Member, CMSU Biology Club, Yearbook Staff
Raising three school-age children
Tuition 100 percent self-financed

FIGURE 15.4   **Skills Résumé of a Nontraditional Student**

PREPARING A PLAIN-TEXT RÉSUMÉ

Most companies use computerized *applicant-tracking systems*, such as RESUMate, Bullhorn, or HRsmart, to evaluate the dozens, hundreds, or even thousands of job applications they receive every day. The information from these applications is stored in databases, which can be searched electronically for keywords to generate a pool of applicants for specific positions. Once a pool of candidates has been generated, someone at the company reads their résumés. Prepare a plain-text résumé so that you can survive this two-stage process.

A *plain-text résumé*, also called a *text résumé*, *ASCII résumé*, or *electronic résumé*, is a résumé that uses a very limited character set and has little formatting so that it can be stored in any database and read by any software. It will not be as attractive as a fully formatted document created with a word processor, but if you prepare it carefully it will say what you want it to say and be easy to read.

GUIDELINES Formatting a Plain-Text Résumé

Start with the résumé that you prepared in Word or with some other word-processing software. Save it as "Plain text" and then paste it into Notepad or another text editor. Revise the Notepad version so that it has these five characteristics:

▶ **It has no special characters.** It uses only the letters, numbers, and basic punctuation marks visible on your keyboard. That is, it *does not* use boldface, italics, bullets, or tabs.

▶ **It has a line length of 65 or fewer characters.** Use the space bar to break longer lines or, in Notepad, set the left and right margins (in File/Page Setup) to 1.5 inches.

▶ **It uses a nonproportional typeface such as Courier.** (A nonproportional typeface is one in which each letter takes up the same amount of space on the line; narrow letters are surrounded by a lot of space, whereas wider letters are surrounded by a smaller space.) Using a nonproportional typeface makes it easier to keep the line length to 65 characters.

▶ **Most of the information is left justified.** If you want, you can use the space bar (not the Tab key) to move text to the right. For instance, you might want to center the main headings.

▶ **It uses ALL UPPERCASE or repeated characters for emphasis.** For example, a series of equal signs or hyphens might signal a new heading.

You might want to create two versions of your plain-text résumé: a version using word wrap (in Notepad's Format tab) to be attached to an email, and a version *not* using word wrap to be pasted into the body of an email.

Check each new version to be sure the information has converted properly. Copy and paste the version not using word wrap into an email and send it to yourself, and then review it. Attach the new file using word wrap to an email, open it in your text editor, and review it.

Figure 15.5 (on p. 422) shows a plain-text skills résumé.

This plain-text résumé uses only a row of commas to signal a break in sections.

Headings are in all capital letters, but there is no special type formatting such as boldface or italic

```
Alice P. Linder
1781 Weber Road
Rawlings, MT 59211
(406) 555-3999
linderap423@gmail.com
,,,,,,,,,,,,,,,,,,,,,,,,,,,,,,,,,,,,,,,,,,,,,,,,,,,,,,,,,,,,,
SUMMARY
Biotechnology major with broad laboratory experience at
GlaxoSmithKline, analyzing molecular data and writing C#
programs. Working toward Certification in laboratory specialty
through ASCP. Strong written and oral communication skills.
Extensive volunteer experience in physical therapy for children.
Experience managing business office.
,,,,,,,,,,,,,,,,,,,,,,,,,,,,,,,,,,,,,,,,,,,,,,,,,,,,,,,,,,,,,
SKILLS AND ABILITIES
Laboratory Skills
-Analyzed molecular data on E&S PS300, Macintosh, and IBM PCs.
Wrote programs in C#.
-Have taken 12 credits in biology and chemistry labs.
Communication Skills
-Wrote a user's guide for an instructional computing package.
-Trained and consulted with scientists and delivered in-house
briefings.
Management Skills
-Managed 12-person office in $1.2 million company.
,,,,,,,,,,,,,,,,,,,,,,,,,,,,,,,,,,,,,,,,,,,,,,,,,,,,,,,,,,,,,
EDUCATION
Central Montana State University, Rawlings, MT
BS in Bioscience and Biotechnology
Expected Graduation Date: 6/2018
Related Course Work
Cell Culture Techniques
Statistical Methods for Research
Technical Communication
Protein Purification and Analysis
,,,,,,,,,,,,,,,,,,,,,,,,,,,,,,,,,,,,,,,,,,,,,,,,,,,,,,,,,,,,,
EMPLOYMENT EXPERIENCE
6/2015-present (20 hours per week): Laboratory Assistant Grade 3
GlaxoSmithKline, Rawlings, MT
8/2012-present: Volunteer, Physical Therapy Unit
Rawlings Regional Medical Center, Rawlings, MT
6/2004-1/2007: Office Manager
Anchor Products, Inc., Rawlings, MT
,,,,,,,,,,,,,,,,,,,,,,,,,,,,,,,,,,,,,,,,,,,,,,,,,,,,,,,,,,,,,
HONORS
Awarded three $5,000 tuition scholarships (2014-2016) from the
Gould Foundation.
,,,,,,,,,,,,,,,,,,,,,,,,,,,,,,,,,,,,,,,,,,,,,,,,,,,,,,,,,,,,,
ADDITIONAL INFORMATION
Member, CMSU Biology Club, Yearbook Staff
Raising three school-age children
Tuition 100% self-financed
```

FIGURE 15.5 Plain-Text Version of a Skills Résumé

Preparing a Résumé

BURTON L. KREBS

34456 West Jewell St.   208-555-9627

Boise, ID 83704   burtonkrebs@mail.com

Objective

Lead crew position on rappel crew.

Career History

- Senior Firefighter, Moyer Rappel Crew, 05/17-present
- Senior Firefighter, Boise Helitack, 05/16-10/16
- Hotshot Crew Member, Boise Interagency Hotshot Crew, 07/15-09/15
- Helirappel Crew Member, Moyer Rappel Crew, 06/11-09/14

Fire and Aviation Qualifications

Crew Boss (T)

Helicopter Manager

Helicopter Rappeller

Helirappel Spotter

Helispot Manager

Type 2 Helibase Manager (T)

Incident Commander Type 4 (T)

Education

Bachelor of Arts in Communication Training and Development, Boise State University, Boise, Idaho, GPA 3.57, May 2018

Skills

- Excellent oral and written communication skills
- Proficient in Word, Excel, and PowerPoint
- Knowledgeable of helicopter contract administration
- Perform daily and cumulative flight invoice cost summaries

Awards

"Outstanding Performance" Recognition, U.S. Bureau of Land Management, 2016

"Outstanding Performance" Recognition, U.S. Forest Service, 2013, 2014, 2015

This résumé was written by a graduating college senior who wanted to work for a wildland firefighting agency such as the U.S. Bureau of Land Management or U.S. Forest Service. The writer plans to save the résumé as a .txt file and enter it directly into these agencies' employment databases. The questions below ask you to think about electronic résumés.

1. How effectively has the writer formatted this résumé?

2. What elements are likely to be problematic when the writer saves this résumé as a .txt file?

3. What is the function of the industry-specific jargon in this résumé?

4. Why does the writer place the education section below the sections on career history and fire and aviation qualifications?

CONSIDERING NONTRADITIONAL RÉSUMÉS

In applying for a job, you have the option of submitting a nontraditional résumé. Nontraditional résumés include elements of chronological and skills résumés, but draw on a broader range of characteristics from print and digital media. Some approaches expand the use of visual design techniques to organize and emphasize résumé content. Others use video to present résumé content or a professional introduction. You will need to think carefully about your job-search contexts and if nontraditional résumés are an appropriate option. Figures 15.6, 15.7 (on pages 425–426), and 15.8 (on page 427) show a visually enhanced résumé, an infographic résumé, and a video résumé.

◢ GUIDELINES Planning a Nontraditional Résumé

The following five planning tasks will help you prepare a nontraditional résumé.

▸ **Analyze the job-search context.** Determine whether a nontraditional résumé is appropriate to the workplace culture for the job. Does the job posting invite applicants to submit a nontraditional résumé? If not, what is your reasoning for submitting one?

▸ **Consider your résumé content.** Think about which aspects of your content lend themselves to being redesigned for a nontraditional résumé, especially whether there are words and numbers that can be represented visually. Ask yourself what content might be well-suited to a video, and why.

▸ **Research software programs.** What software programs will you need to access in order to produce a nontraditional résumé? Will your current programs work, or will you need to learn new programs? Keep in mind that if you are using free programs, there may be limits to what you can do with them.

▸ **Research delivery options.** Consider whether you will host a video résumé on your own website, through a streaming service such as YouTube or Vimeo, or by using a job-search portal that allows candidates to upload videos. What are the advantages and disadvantages of the different options?

▸ **Draft an element.** Test your ideas by drafting an element of a nontraditional résumé. What's a good starting point? Why? You may need to change your plans depending on the results of your draft.

The writer uses a geometric design to add visual interest.

ASTRID CLARK

PROFESSIONAL EXPERIENCE

The logo on the résumé also appears on the writer's cover letter and professional website, helping to communicate a professional brand.

SOCIAL MEDIA INTERN
August 2016 - June 2017

The Undergraduate Admissions Office | University Park, PA

- Produced and created original videos, editorial content, and photos for the social media pages, specifically Facebook, Twitter and Instagram.
- Managed and scheduled publication of content on the student blog section of the Admissions website.
- Coordinated and performed interviews with various students and faculty about their Penn State experience.
- Co-lead meetings with the department to discuss new content.

In the PDF version, the left column functions as a navigation column, linking to contact information and social media sites.

DIRECTOR OF COMMUNICATIONS
August 2016 - May 2017

State College Communications | University Park, PA

- Created and coordinated posts for State College Communications's social media accounts, including Facebook, Instagram, Twitter and LinkedIn.
- Copyedited and proofread all final content, including blog posts, social media posts, and client assets.
- Assisted in hiring account associates and account executives. Lead monthly firm-wide meetings.

The left column uses both icons and text to represent links.

ADVERTISING INTERN
June 2016 - August 2016

D.C. Relations Inc. | Washington, D.C.

- Designed flyers, newsletters, email campaigns, and online promotions.
- Helped the Marketing and Advertising departments target new media audiences.
- Researched and analyzed competitor marketing and communication strategies.
- Collaborated on team presentations and pitches for management and clients.

The main content area emphasizes professional experience and includes elements typical to chronological and skills résumés, such as headings, bulleted lists, and action verbs.

DIGITAL WEB INTERN
May 2015 - August 2015

Delicious Dining Magazine | Los Angeles, CA

- Wrote two to three 500-1000 word articles per week.
- Fact-checked and transcribed publication-wide interviews, recipes, and stories.
- Assisted in designing and producing how-to recipe videos.

WEB WRITER
December 2014 - May 2016

The Collegiate Lion Magazine | University Park, PA

- Pitched, researched, and wrote one 400-600 word article per week.
- Conducted interviews with students, faculty, visitors, and locals in the Penn State community.
- Covered timely events both on and off campus.

PROFESSIONAL SKILLS

- Technical Writing
- Technical Editing
- Graphic Design
- Video Production
- Photography
- Media Management

SOFTWARE SKILLS

- Microsoft Office
- Adobe Creative Cloud
- WordPress
- Google Analytics
- Hootsuite
- MediaWiki

EDUCATION

The Pennsylvania State University
August 2013 - May 2017
B.A. Advertising, minor in Digital Media Trends and Analytics
GPA 3.56

CONTACT

📞 (202) 555-0172
✉ astridclark@imail.com
🔗 www.astridclark.web

SOCIAL MEDIA

⬛ fb.me/astridxc23
⭕ @astridclark23
🐦 @astridclark23
in linkedin.com/in/astridxc

HONORS

Advertising Award of Excellence | Awarded to graduates who achieve academic distinction | May 2017

Alpha Delta Sigma Honor Society, Member | National Honor Society sponsored by the American Advertising Federation, recognizing scholastic achievement in advertising studies | Fall 2017 - Present

Dean's List | GPA of 3.5 or higher each semester | Spring 2013 - Spring 2017

FIGURE 15.6   Visually Enhanced Résumé

The overall visual design, which is oriented vertically, encourages audiences to read from top to bottom, left to right.

The approach blends elements from traditional and visually enhanced résumés, but also emphasizes icons and includes graphics to enliven statistical information.

The horizontal dots create a visual rating system for self-evaluation, replacing phrases like "skilled in" or "experienced with."

The line graph supports the job description by illustrating the impact of the work.

Captions help audiences interpret the graphics.

The pie chart supports the job description by illustrating where online work time is spent.

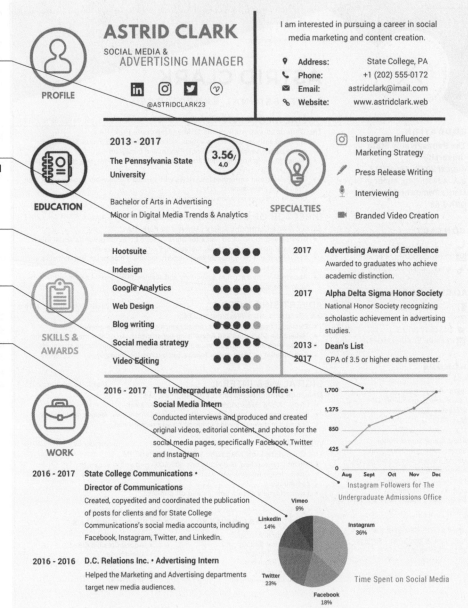

ASTRID CLARK

SOCIAL MEDIA & ADVERTISING MANAGER

@ASTRIDCLARK23

I am interested in pursuing a career in social media marketing and content creation.

- Address: State College, PA
- Phone: +1 (202) 555-0172
- Email: astridclark@imail.com
- Website: www.astridclark.web

PROFILE

EDUCATION

2013 - 2017

The Pennsylvania State University

Bachelor of Arts in Advertising
Minor in Digital Media Trends & Analytics

3.56/4.0

SPECIALTIES

- Instagram Influencer Marketing Strategy
- Press Release Writing
- Interviewing
- Branded Video Creation

SKILLS & AWARDS

Hootsuite	●●●●●
Indesign	●●●●○
Google Analytics	●●●●●
Web Design	●●●○○
Blog writing	●●●●○
Social media strategy	●●●●●
Video Editing	●●●●○

2017 **Advertising Award of Excellence**
Awarded to graduates who achieve academic distinction.

2017 **Alpha Delta Sigma Honor Society**
National Honor Society recognizing scholastic achievement in advertising studies.

2013 - 2017 **Dean's List**
GPA of 3.5 or higher each semester.

WORK

2016 - 2017 **The Undergraduate Admissions Office •**
Social Media Intern
Conducted interviews and produced and created original videos, editorial content, and photos for the social media pages, specifically Facebook, Twitter and Instagram

Instagram Followers for The Undergraduate Admissions Office

2016 - 2017 **State College Communications •**
Director of Communications
Created, copyedited and coordinated the publication of posts for clients and for State College Communications's social media accounts, including Facebook, Instagram, Twitter, and LinkedIn.

Vimeo 9%
LinkedIn 14%
Instagram 36%

2016 - 2016 **D.C. Relations Inc. • Advertising Intern**
Helped the Marketing and Advertising departments target new media audiences.

Twitter 23%
Facebook 18%

Time Spent on Social Media

FIGURE 15.7 Infographic Résumé

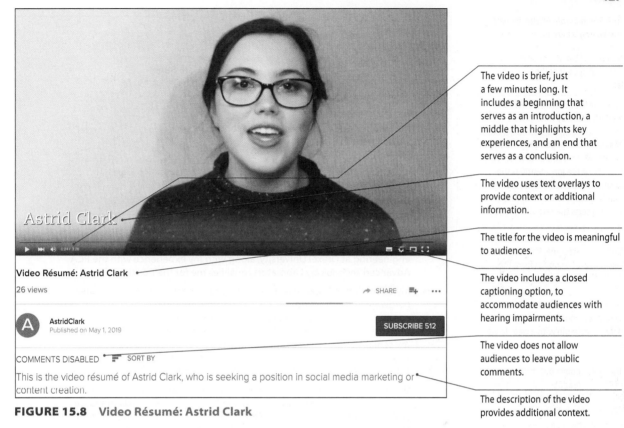

The video is brief, just a few minutes long. It includes a beginning that serves as an introduction, a middle that highlights key experiences, and an end that serves as a conclusion.

The video uses text overlays to provide context or additional information.

The title for the video is meaningful to audiences.

The video includes a closed captioning option, to accommodate audiences with hearing impairments.

The video does not allow audiences to leave public comments.

The description of the video provides additional context.

FIGURE 15.8   Video Résumé: Astrid Clark

Writing Job-Application Letters

Although the job-application letter (sometimes called a *cover letter*) may seem obsolete, many experts agree that it is still important. Applicants can explain more clearly in a letter than in a résumé how their qualifications match the employer's requirements. They can explain their professional relationship with someone in the employer's organization or gaps in their employment history. Perhaps most important, applicants can show that they can write well.

At a minimum, the cover letter serves as the applicant's introduction to the hiring manager, identifying the position being applied for and providing an overview of qualifications. The letter can't include as many details as the résumé, but it can emphasize a few key points. It can also include a specific request for an interview.

Figure 15.9 shows a job-application letter that can be printed and mailed, uploaded to a job-application website, or attached to a brief email. In all three cases, a résumé would be included along with the cover letter.

Many of the job boards listed on p. 407 in "Understanding Job-Search Strategies" include samples of job-application letters.

For information about letter formatting, see "Writing Letters" in Ch. 14 on p. 377.

Notice that the writer's own name does not appear at the top of his letter.

In the inside address, he uses the reader's courtesy title, "Mr."

The introductory paragraph identifies the writer's source of information about the job, identifies the position he is applying for, states that he wishes to be considered, and forecasts the rest of the letter.

In a letter, you can't discuss everything in the résumé. Rather, you select a few key points from the résumé to emphasize.

Note that both the education paragraph and the employment paragraph begin with a clear topic sentence.

The writer points out that he has taken two graduate courses, and he discusses his senior design project, which makes him look more like an engineer solving a problem than a recent graduate.

Notice how the writer makes a smooth transition from the discussion of his college education to the discussion of his internship experience.

A concluding paragraph usually includes a reference to the résumé, a polite but confident request for an interview, and the writer's contact information.

The enclosure notation refers to the writer's résumé. Do not use an enclosure notation unless you are literally enclosing something along with the letter in the envelope.

3109 Vista Street
Philadelphia, PA 19136

January 20, 2018

Mr. Stephen Spencer, Director of Personnel
Department 411
Boeing Naval Systems
103 Industrial Drive
Wilmington, DE 20093

Dear Mr. Spencer:

I am writing in response to your advertisement in the January 16 *Philadelphia Inquirer.* Would you please consider me for the position in Signal Processing? I believe that my academic training in electrical engineering at Drexel University, along with my experience with the RCA Advanced Technology Laboratory, qualifies me for the position.

My education at Drexel has given me a strong background in computer hardware and system design. I have concentrated on digital and computer applications, developing and designing computer and signal-processing hardware in two graduate-level engineering courses. For my senior design project, I am working with four other undergraduates in using OO programming techniques to enhance the path-planning software for an infrared night-vision robotics application.

While working at the RCA Advanced Technology Laboratory, I was able to apply my computer experience to the field of DSP. I designed ultra-large-scale integrated circuits using VERILOG and VHDL hardware description languages. In addition, I assisted a senior engineer in CMOS IC layout, modeling, parasitic capacitance extraction, and PSPICE simulation operations.

The enclosed résumé provides an overview of my education and experience. Could I meet with you at your convenience to discuss my qualifications for this position? Please leave a message any time at (215) 555-3880 or email me at coppen@dragon.du.edu.

Yours truly,

Carl Oppenheimer

Carl Oppenheimer

Enclosure (1)

FIGURE 15.9 **Job-Application Letter**

Preparing for a Job Interview

If your résumé is successful, you will be invited to a job interview, where both you and the organization can start to see whether you would be a good fit there. Job boards on the internet can help you prepare for a job interview. They discuss questions such as the following:

- When should you arrive for the interview?
- What should you wear?
- How might interviewers interpret your body language?
- What questions are you likely to be asked?
- How long should your answers be?
- How do you know when the interviewer wishes to end the interview?
- How can you get the interviewer's contact information so you can write a follow-up letter?

GUIDELINES **Preparing for a Job Interview**

For every hour you spend in a job interview, you need to spend many hours in preparation.

▶ **Study job interviews.** The hundreds of books and websites devoted to job interviews cover everything from how to do your initial research to common interview questions to how to dress. Although you can't prepare for everything that will happen, you can prepare for a lot of things.

▶ **Study the organization to which you applied.** If you show that you haven't done your homework, the interviewer might conclude that you're always unprepared. Learn what products or services the organization provides, how well it has done in recent years, what its plans are, and so forth. Start with the organization's own website, especially corporate blogs, and then proceed to other online and print resources. Search for the organization's name on the internet.

For more about research techniques, see Ch. 6.

▶ **Think about what you can offer the organization.** Your goal during the interview is to show how you can help the organization accomplish its goals. Think about how your academic career, your work experience, and your personal characteristics and experiences have prepared you to solve problems and carry out projects to help the organization succeed. Make notes about projects you carried out in courses, experiences on the job, and experiences in your personal life that can serve as persuasive evidence to support claims about your qualifications.

For more about communicating persuasively, see Ch. 8.

▶ **Study lists of common interview questions.** Interviewers study these lists; you should, too. You're probably familiar with some of the favorites:
 — Can you tell me about yourself?
 — Where do you see yourself in five years?
 — Why did you apply to our company?
 — What do you see as your greatest strengths and weaknesses?
 — Tell me about an incident that taught you something important about yourself.
 — What was your best course in college? Why?

(continued)

▶ **Compile a list of questions you wish to ask.** Near the end of the interview, the interviewer will probably ask if you have any questions. The interviewer expects you to have compiled a brief list of questions about working for the organization. Do not focus on salary, vacation days, or sick leave. Instead, ask about ways you can continue to develop as a professional, improving your ability to contribute to the organization.

▶ **Rehearse for the interview.** It's one thing to think about how you might answer an interview question. It's another to have to answer it. Rehearse for the interview by asking friends or colleagues to play the role of the interviewer, making up questions that you haven't thought about. Then ask these people for constructive criticism.

◢ **GUIDELINES** Preparing for an Online Job Interview

Some employers now hold interviews online using video-based software such as Skype or Zoom, especially if the position attracts applicants from around the country, or even the world. Although online interviews involve some of the same preparation activities as face-to-face interviews, they also require applicants to consider a range of additional issues.

▶ **Prepare your physical environment.** The environment for your interview should be business-like and tidy. Remove any embarrassing personal effects. The space should be well lit but free of light sources that can cast a shadow on your face. The space should also be as quiet as possible, and you should make arrangements to ensure that people or pets will not interrupt the interview. Of course, be sure to silence your cell phone. Set out paper and a writing utensil for any necessary note taking, and have a copy of your resume on hand for easy reference.

▶ **Test your computer setup.** It is important to become familiar with how the software and hardware works. The best way to do this is to ask a friend to conduct a mock online interview with you. Then evaluate how well the session went. Be sure to resolve any technical issues with your video and audio equipment. Also, be sure that your internet connection is fast and stable enough to support a smooth video-based interview.

▶ **Rehearse how you deliver nonverbal feedback.** Good eye contact and body language are essential to a successful online interview. If you position your webcam so that it is around eye level, you will be centered on the screen. And practice looking at your webcam while answering questions instead of at the interviewer on the screen. This approach will simulate good eye contact. Answers to interview questions should be accompanied by appropriate nonverbal gestures. Nod and smile when appropriate to indicate you are listening, and avoid fidgeting. Hand gestures should be kept to a minimum and close to the body to stay within the frame of the webcam. Be sure to ask your practice partners to assess your nonverbal feedback.

Following Up After an Interview

After an interview, you should write a letter of appreciation, typically in the form of an email for speed of delivery. If you are offered the job, you also may have to write a letter accepting or rejecting the position.

- **Letter of appreciation after an interview.** Thank the interviewer for taking the time to see you, and emphasize your particular qualifications. You can also restate your interest in the position and mention a specific topic of conversation you found particularly interesting or a fact about the position you found exciting. A follow-up letter can do more good with less effort than any other step in the job-application procedure because so few candidates take the time to write one.

  Dear Mr. Weaver:

  Thank you for taking the time yesterday to show me your facilities and to introduce me to your colleagues.

  Your company's advances in piping design were particularly impressive. As a person with hands-on experience in piping design, I can appreciate the advantages your design will have.

  The vitality of your projects and the good fellowship among your employees further confirm my initial belief that Cynergo would be a fine place to work. I would look forward to joining your staff.

  Sincerely yours,

  Harriet Bommarito

- **Letter accepting a job offer.** This one is easy: express appreciation, show enthusiasm, and repeat the major terms of your employment.

  Dear Mr. Weaver:

  Thank you very much for the offer to join your staff. I accept.

  I look forward to joining your design team on Monday, July 19. The salary, as you indicate in your letter, is $48,250.

  As you have recommended, I will get in touch with Mr. Matthews in Personnel to get a start on the paperwork.

  I appreciate the trust you have placed in me, and I assure you that I will do what I can to be a productive team member at Cynergo.

  Sincerely yours,

  Mark Greenberg

- **Letter rejecting a job offer.** If you decide not to accept a job offer, express your appreciation for the offer and, if appropriate, explain why you are declining it. Remember, you might want to work for this company at some time in the future.

Dear Mr. Weaver:

I appreciate very much the offer to join your staff.

Although I am certain that I would benefit greatly from working at Cynergo, I have decided to take a job with a firm in Baltimore, where I have been accepted at Johns Hopkins to pursue my master's degree at night.

Again, thank you for your generous offer.

Sincerely yours,

Cynthia O'Malley

- **Letter acknowledging a rejection.** Why write back after you have been rejected for a job? To maintain good relations. You might get a phone call the next week explaining that the person who accepted the job has had a change of plans and offering you the position.

Dear Mr. Weaver:

I was disappointed to learn that I will not have a chance to join your staff, because I feel that I could make a substantial contribution. However, I realize that job decisions are complex, involving many candidates and many factors.

Thank you very much for the courtesy you have shown me.

Sincerely yours,

Paul Goicochea

WRITER'S CHECKLIST

Your Professional Brand

- ☐ Have you researched how others in your field present themselves online? *(p. 402)*
- ☐ Is the information you present about yourself online truthful, well written, and appropriate? *(p. 402)*
- ☐ Does your online information describe your job skills and focus on problem-solving and accomplishments? *(p. 402)*
- ☐ Have you created a strong online presence, perhaps by creating your own website? *(p. 403)*
- ☐ Do you participate actively and professionally online through sites such as LinkedIn, Facebook, and Twitter? *(p. 403)*
- ☐ Do you have a business card? *(p. 403)*
- ☐ Have you practiced an "elevator pitch"? *(p. 404)*

When presenting yourself online, have you avoided

- ☐ provocative or inappropriate photos? *(p. 404)*
- ☐ suggestion of drug or alcohol use? *(p. 404)*
- ☐ negative comments about a former employer or co-worker? *(p. 404)*
- ☐ showing poor communication skills? *(p. 404)*
- ☐ discriminatory comments about others? *(p. 404)*

Finding a Job

- ☐ Have you done a self-inventory, considering your strengths and weaknesses, favorite subjects, preferred type of organization, and ideal location? *(p. 405)*
- ☐ Have you researched potential employers? *(p. 405)*
- ☐ Have you attended job fairs? *(p. 405)*
- ☐ Have you read about the trends in your field? *(p. 406)*
- ☐ Have you begun researching the process of writing a résumé and cover letter? *(p. 406)*
- ☐ Have you put portfolio items online? *(p. 406)*
- ☐ Have you tried searching on organizations' websites? *(p. 407)*
- ☐ Have you tried searching on internet job boards? *(p. 407)*
- ☐ Have you tried networking in person and online? *(p. 408)*

☐ Have you tried using university or professional placement services? *(p. 410)*

☐ Have you made the most of LinkedIn's employment features? *(p. 410)*

Résumé

☐ Does the résumé include appropriate keywords? *(p. 411)*

☐ Does the identifying information contain your name, address(es), phone number(s), and email address(es)? *(p. 412)*

☐ Does the résumé include a clear summary of your qualifications? *(p. 412)*

☐ Does the education section include your degree, your institution and its location, and your (anticipated) date of graduation, as well as any other information that will help a reader appreciate your qualifications? *(p. 414)*

☐ Does the employment section include, for each job, the dates of employment, the organization's name and location, and (if you are writing a chronological résumé) your position or title, as well as a description of your duties and accomplishments? *(p. 415)*

☐ Have you used strong action verbs? *(p. 416)*

☐ Does the interests-and-activities section include relevant hobbies or activities, including extracurricular interests? *(p. 417)*

☐ Have you omitted any personal information that might reflect poorly on you? *(p. 418)*

☐ Does the résumé include any other appropriate sections, such as skills and abilities, military service, language abilities, or willingness to relocate? *(p. 419)*

Job-Application Letter

☐ Does the introductory paragraph identify the position you are applying for, state that you wish to be considered, and forecast the rest of the letter? *(p. 428)*

☐ Does the education paragraph respond to your reader's needs with a unified idea introduced by a topic sentence? *(p. 428)*

☐ Does the employment paragraph respond to your reader's needs with a unified idea introduced by a topic sentence? *(p. 428)*

☐ Does the concluding paragraph include a reference to your résumé, a request for an interview, your phone number, and your email address? *(p. 428)*

☐ Does the letter include an enclosure notation? *(p. 428)*

Preparing for a Job Interview

Did you

☐ study job interviews? *(p. 429)*

☐ study the organization to which you applied? *(p. 429)*

☐ think about what you can offer the organization? *(p. 429)*

☐ study lists of common interview questions? *(p. 429)*

☐ compile a list of questions you wish to ask? *(p. 430)*

☐ rehearse for the interview? *(p. 430)*

Following Up

☐ Does your letter of appreciation for a job interview thank the interviewer and briefly restate your qualifications? *(p. 431)*

☐ Does your letter accepting a job offer show enthusiasm and repeat the major terms of your employment? *(p. 431)*

☐ Does your letter rejecting a job offer express your appreciation for the offer and, if appropriate, explain why you are declining it? *(p. 431)*

☐ Does your letter acknowledging a rejection have a positive tone that will help you maintain good relations? *(p. 432)*

EXERCISES

1. Browse a job-search website such as Indeed.com. Then, list and briefly describe five positions being offered in a field that interests you. What skills, experience, and background does each position require? What is the salary range for each position?

2. Locate three job websites that provide interactive forms for creating a résumé automatically. In a brief memo to your instructor, note the three URLs and describe the strengths and weaknesses of each site. Which job board appears to be the easiest to use? Why?

3. The following résumé was submitted in response to this ad: "CAM Technician to work with other technicians and manage some GIS and mapping projects. Also perform updating of the GIS database. Experience required." In a brief memo to your instructor, analyze the effectiveness of the résumé. What are some of its problems?

Kenneth Bradley

530 Maplegrove   Bozeman, Mont. 59715 (406)-484-2916

Objective	Entry level position as a CAM Technician. I am also interested in staying with the company until after graduation, possibly moving into a position as a Mechanical Engineer.
Education	Enrolled at Montana State University August 2017- Present
Employment	Fred Meyer 65520 Chinden Garden City, MT (208)-323-7030

Janitor- 7/16-6/17
Responsible for cleaning entire store, as well as equipment maintenance and floor maintenance and repair.

Assistant Janitorial Manager- 6/17-9/17
Responsible for cleaning entire store, equipment maintenance, floor maintenance and repair, scheduling, and managing personnel

Head of Freight- 9/17-Present
In charge of braking down all new freight, stocking shelves, cleaning the stock room, and managing personnel

Montana State University
Bozeman, MT
Teachers Aide ME 120- 1/16-5/16
Teachers Aide ME 120
In charge of keeping students in line and answering any questions related to drafting.

References	Timothy Rayburn Janitorial Manager (406)-555-8571
	Eduardo Perez Co-worker (406)-555-2032

4. The following job-application letter responds to this ad: "CAM Technician to work with other technicians and manage some GIS and mapping projects. Also perform updating of the GIS database. Experience required." In a brief memo to your instructor, analyze the effectiveness of the letter and suggest how it could be improved. For more about memos, see Ch. 14, p. 386.

530 Maplegrove
Bozeman, Mont. 59715
November 11, 2020

Mr. Bruce Hedley
Adecco Technical
Bozeman, Mont. 59715

Dear Mr. Hedley,

I am writing you in response to your ad on Monsterjobs.com. Would you please consider me for the position of CAM technician? I believe that my academic schooling at Montana State University, along with my work experience would make me an excellent candidate for the position.

While at Montana State University, I took one class in particular that applies well to this job. It was a CAD drafting class, which I received a 97% in. The next semester I was a Teachers Aid for that same class, where I was responsible for answering questions about drafting from my peers. This gave me a much stronger grasp on all aspects of CAD work than I could have ever gotten from simply taking the class.

My employment at Fred Meyer is also a notable experience. While there is no technical aspects of either positions I have held, I believe that my experience there will shed light on my work ethic and interpersonal skills. I started out as a graveyard shift janitor, with no previous experience. All of my coworkers were at least thirty years older than me, and had a minimum of five years of janitorial experience. However after working there for only one year I was promoted to assistant manager. Three months after I received this position, I was informed that Fred Meyer was going to contract out the janitorial work and that all of us would be losing our jobs. I decided that I wanted to stay within the company, and I was able to receive a position as head of freight.

The enclosed resumé provides an overview of my education and work experience. I would appreciate an opportunity to meet with you at your convenience to discuss my qualifications for this position. Please write me at the above address or leave a message any time. If you would like to contact me by email, my email address is kbradley@montanastate.edu.

Yours truly,
Ken Bradley

5. How effective is the following letter of appreciation? How could it be improved? Present your findings in a brief memo to your instructor.

914 Imperial Boulevard
Durham, NC 27708

November 13, 2020

Mr. Ronald O'Shea
Division Engineering
Safeway Electronics, Inc.
Holland, MI 49423

Dear Mr. O'Shea:

Thanks very much for showing me around your plant. I hope I was able to convince you that I'm the best person for the job.

Sincerely yours,
Rania Harad

6. In a newspaper or journal or on the internet, find an ad for a position in your field for which you might be qualified. Write a résumé and a job-application letter in response to the ad; include the job ad or a photocopy. You will be evaluated not only on the content and appearance of the materials, but also on how well you have targeted them to the job ad.

CASE 15: Writing a Cover Letter

After the director of the Career Center at your school visits one of your classes, you decide to visit the Career Center's website. You study the available resources, but you find that they don't offer as much support as you and your fellow classmates need to create effective job applications or cover letters. You decide to write the director with your concerns. She agrees with your critique and asks you to put together a model resource for seniors at your college. If your instructor has assigned it, go to Achieve to get started with your project.

Writing Proposals

→

16

A PROPOSAL IS an offer to carry out research or to provide a product or service. For instance, a physical therapist might write a proposal to her supervisor for funding to attend a convention to learn about current rehabilitation practices. A defense contractor might submit a proposal to design and build a fleet of drones for the Air Force. A homeless shelter might submit a proposal to a philanthropic organization for funding to provide more services to the homeless community. Whether a project is small or big, within your own company or outside it, it is likely to call for a proposal.

Understanding the Process of Writing Proposals

Writing a proposal calls for the same process of planning, drafting, revising, editing, and proofreading that you use for other kinds of documents. The Focus on Process box that follows presents an overview of this process.

The Logistics of Proposals

Proposals can be classified as either internal or external; external proposals are either solicited or unsolicited. Figure 16.1 shows the relationships among these four terms.

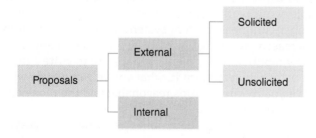

FIGURE 16.1   The Logistics of Proposals

437

FOCUS ON PROCESS: Writing Proposals

When writing a proposal, pay special attention to these steps in the writing process.

PLANNING	Consider your readers' knowledge about and attitudes toward what you are proposing. Use the techniques discussed in Chapters 5 and 6 to learn as much as you can about your readers' needs and about the subject. Also consider whether you have the personnel, facilities, and equipment to do what you propose to do.
DRAFTING	Collaboration is critical for large proposals because no one person has the time and expertise to do all the work. See Chapter 4 for more about collaboration. In writing the proposal, follow the instructions in any request for proposal (RFP) or information for bid (IFB) from the prospective customer. If there are no instructions, follow the structure for proposals outlined in this chapter.
REVISING	External proposals usually have a firm deadline. Build in time to revise, edit, and proofread the proposal thoroughly and still get it to readers on time. See the Writer's Checklist at the end of this chapter.
EDITING	See Chapter 10 for advice on writing correct and effective sentences.
PROOFREADING	See Appendix, Part C, for proofreading tips.

INTERNAL AND EXTERNAL PROPOSALS

Internal proposals are submitted to the writer's own organization; external proposals are submitted to another organization.

Internal Proposals An internal proposal is an argument, submitted within an organization, for carrying out an activity that will benefit the organization. An internal proposal might recommend that the organization conduct research, purchase a product, or change some aspect of its policies or procedures.

For example, while working on a project in the laboratory, you realize that if you had a fiber-curl measurement system, you could do your job better and faster. The increased productivity would save your company the cost of the system in a few months. Your supervisor asks you to write a memo describing what you want, why you want it, what you're going to do with it, and what it costs; if your request seems reasonable and the money is available, you'll likely get the new system.

Often, the scope of a proposal determines its format. A request for a small amount of money might be conveyed orally or by email or a brief memo. A request for a large amount, however, is likely to be presented in a formal report.

External Proposals No organization produces all the products or provides all the services it needs. Websites need to be designed, written, and maintained; inventory databases need to be created; facilities need to be constructed.

Sometimes projects require unusual expertise, such as sophisticated market analyses. Because many companies supply such products and services, most organizations require a prospective supplier to compete for the business by submitting a proposal, a document arguing that it deserves the business.

SOLICITED AND UNSOLICITED PROPOSALS

External proposals are either solicited or unsolicited. A *solicited proposal* is submitted in response to a request from the prospective customer. An *unsolicited proposal* is submitted by a supplier who believes that the prospective customer has a need for goods or services.

Solicited Proposals When an organization wants to purchase a product or service, it publishes one of two basic kinds of statements:

- An *information for bid (IFB)* is used for standard products. When a state agency needs desktop computers, for instance, it informs computer manufacturers of the configuration it needs. All other things being equal, the supplier that offers the lowest bid for a product with that configuration wins the contract. When an agency solicits bids for a specific brand and model, the solicitation is sometimes called a *request for quotation (RFQ)*.

- A *request for proposal (RFP)* is used for more customized products or services. For example, if the Air Force needs an "identification, friend or foe" system, the RFP it publishes might be a long and detailed set of technical specifications. The supplier that can design, produce, and deliver the device most closely resembling the specifications—at a reasonable price—will probably win the contract.

Most organizations issue IFBs and RFPs in print and online. Government solicitations are published on the beta.SAM.gov website. Figure 16.2 (on page 440) shows a portion of an RFQ for the National Institutes of Health that originally appeared on that site.

Unsolicited Proposals An unsolicited proposal is like a solicited proposal except that it does not refer to an RFP. In most cases, even though the potential customer did not formally request the proposal, the supplier was invited to submit the proposal after people from the two organizations met and discussed the project. Because proposals are expensive to write, suppliers are reluctant to submit them without assurances that they will be considered carefully. Thus, the word *unsolicited* is only partially accurate.

The "Deliverables" of Proposals

A *deliverable* is what a supplier will deliver at the end of a project. Deliverables can be classified into two major categories: research or goods and services.

RESEARCH PROPOSALS

In a research proposal, you are promising to perform research and then provide a report about it. For example, a biologist for a state bureau of land

FIGURE 16.2 Excerpt from an RFQ
FedBixOpps.Gov.

This is an excerpt from an RFQ from the National Institutes of Health (NIH). The NIH is seeking to hire up to four call-center personnel. The specific details of the skills and experience required for the four persons are provided in a separate file.

This RFQ spells out the evaluation criteria by which the "offerors" will be judged.

Solicitation Number: NIHCCOPC13014476

The Clinical Center at the National Institutes of Health (NIH) in Bethesda, Maryland, is one of the 27 institutes and centers that comprise NIH. The NIH Clinical Center is the nation's largest hospital devoted entirely to clinical research. With patients from all over the United States and some from abroad, the Clinical Center provides medical care and research services to support patients participating in over 1,500 active protocol sponsored by the NIH Institutes. The Office of Patient Recruitment (OPR) reports to the Clinical Center Office of the Director. OPR is responsible for supporting the NIH intramural program by providing patient recruitment services for institutes, staffing a call center to receive public inquiries, providing services to support the clinical research volunteer program, and serving as the NIH Intramural Liaison for Research Match (RM), an online recruitment tool.

The NIH has a requirement for call center services. Please see the attached Statement of Work. This is anticipated for up to four (4) full time positions onsite at the NIH Clinical Center. Offerors are to submit resumes with documentation for medical terminology training. Offerors may submit multiple resumes for positions.

Evaluation Criteria

Approach 30%: Proposal meets requirements and indicates an exceptional approach and understanding of the requirements. Risk of unsuccessful performance is very low. Adequacy of ability to meet the volume of contacts. Ability to provide consistent staffing and standards of staff performance.

Staffing 30%: Evidence of a broad pool of applicants that have been placed in the metropolitan DC area with the skill set desired within the last 2 years. Proposed staff meets the requirements (experience and credentialing) as stated in the Statement of Work. Staff has relevant experience with volume of contacts. Staff are recruited and retained. Ability to meet the 48 hours replacement time.

Corporate Experience 25%: Adequacy of the contractor's prior experience in providing support. The information shall include sufficient information to demonstrate previous effectiveness of staffing and oversight on performance.

Past Performance 15%: The quotation will be evaluated on 3 recent references (within the last 5 years.)

Price Best Value

The government will evaluate the total price contained in the contractor's proposal. With the understanding and ability to project costs which are reasonable and indicates that the contractor understands the nature and extent of the work to be performed.

Period of Performance is one year September, 2019 to September, 2020 with up to 4 successive options.

The RFQ states that the solicitation is for "price best value." In other words, the contract will not necessarily be awarded to the lowest bidder. It will be awarded to the bidder that offers what the evaluators consider to be the best value, regardless of price.

management writes a proposal to the National Science Foundation requesting resources to build a window-lined tunnel in the forest to study tree and plant roots and the growth of fungi. The biologist also wishes to investigate the relationship between plant growth and the activity of insects and worms. The deliverable will be a report submitted to the National Science Foundation and, perhaps, an article published in a professional journal.

Research proposals often lead to two other applications: progress reports and recommendation reports.

After a proposal has been approved and the researchers have begun work, they often submit one or more *progress reports*, which tell the sponsor of the project how the work is proceeding. Is it following the plan of work outlined in the proposal? Is it going according to schedule? Is it staying within budget?

At the end of the project, researchers prepare a *recommendation report*, often called a *final report*, a *project report*, a *completion report*, or simply a *report*. A recommendation report tells the whole story of a research project, beginning with the problem or opportunity that motivated it and continuing with the methods used in carrying it out, the results, and the researchers' conclusions and recommendations.

For more about progress reports and recommendation reports, see Ch. 17 and Ch. 18.

People carry out research projects to satisfy their curiosity and to advance professionally. Organizations often require that their professional employees carry out research and publish in appropriate journals or books. Government researchers and university professors, for instance, are expected to remain active in their fields. Writing proposals is one way to get the resources—time and money for travel, equipment, and assistants—to carry out research.

GOODS AND SERVICES PROPOSALS

A *goods and services proposal* is an offer to supply a tangible product (a fleet of automobiles), a service (building maintenance), or some combination of the two (the construction of a building).

A vast network of goods and services contracts spans the working world. The U.S. government, the world's biggest customer, spent over $375 billion in 2019 buying military equipment from organizations that submitted proposals (USAspending.gov, 2019). But goods and services contracts are by no means limited to government contractors. An auto manufacturer might buy its engines from another manufacturer; a company that makes spark plugs might buy its steel and other raw materials from another company.

Another kind of goods and services proposal requests funding to support a local organization. For example, a women's shelter might receive some of its funding from a city or county but might rely on grants from private philanthropies. Typically, an organization such as a shelter would apply for a grant to fund increased demand for its services because of a natural disaster or an economic slowdown in the community. Or it might apply for a grant to fund a pilot program to offer job training at the shelter. Most large corporations have philanthropic programs offering grants to help local colleges and universities, arts organizations, and social-service agencies.

Persuasion and Proposals

For more about persuasion, see Ch. 8.

A proposal is an argument. You must convince readers that the future benefits will outweigh the immediate and projected costs. Basically, you must persuade your readers of three things:

1. that you understand the context: what your readers need

2. that you have already determined what you plan to do and that you are able to do it

3. that you are a professional and are committed to fulfilling your promises

UNDERSTANDING CONTEXTS

For more about analyzing your audience, see Ch. 5.

The most crucial element of the proposal is the definition of the problem or opportunity to which the proposed project responds. Although this point seems obvious, people who evaluate proposals agree that the most common weakness they see is an inadequate or inaccurate understanding of the problem or opportunity.

Internal Contexts Writing an internal proposal is both simpler and more complicated than writing an external one. It is simpler because you have greater access to internal readers than you do to external readers and you can get information more easily. However, it is more complicated because you might find it hard to understand the situation in your organization. Some colleagues will not tell you that your proposal is a long shot or that your ideas might threaten someone in the organization. Before you write an internal proposal, discuss your ideas with as many potential readers as you can to learn what those in the organization really think of them.

External Contexts When you receive an RFP, study it thoroughly. If you don't understand something in it, contact the organization. People there will be happy to clarify it: a proposal based on misunderstood needs wastes everyone's time.

When you write an unsolicited proposal, analyze your audience carefully. How can you define the problem or opportunity so that readers will understand it? Keep in mind readers' needs and, if possible, their backgrounds. Concentrate on how the problem has decreased productivity or quality or how your ideas would create new opportunities. When you submit an unsolicited proposal, your task in many cases is to convince readers that a need exists. Even if you have reached an understanding with some of your potential customer's representatives, your proposal will still have to persuade other officials in the company. Most readers will reject a proposal as soon as they realize that it doesn't address their needs.

When you are preparing a proposal to be submitted to an organization in another culture, keep in mind the following six suggestions (Newman, 2011):

- **Understand that what makes an argument persuasive can differ from one culture to another.** Paying attention to the welfare of the company or the community might be more persuasive than offering a low bottom-line price. Representatives of an American company were surprised to learn that the Venezuelan readers of their proposal had selected a French company whose staff "had been making personal visits for years, bringing their families, and engaging in social activities long before there was any question of a contract" (Thrush, 2000).

- **Budget enough time for translating.** If your proposal has to be translated into another language, build in plenty of time. Translating long technical documents is a lengthy process because, even though some of the work can be done by computer software, the machine translation needs to be reviewed by native speakers of the target language.

- **Use simple graphics, with captions.** To reduce the chances of misunderstanding, use a lot of simple graphics, such as pie charts and bar graphs. Include captions so that readers can understand the graphics easily, without having to look through the text to see what each graphic means.

For more about graphics, see Ch. 12.

- **Write short sentences, using common vocabulary.** Short sentences are easier to understand than long sentences. Choose words that have few meanings. For example, use the word *right* as the opposite of *left*; use *correct* as the opposite of *incorrect*.

- **Use local conventions regarding punctuation, spelling, and mechanics.** Be aware that these conventions differ from place to place, even in the English-speaking world.

- **Ask if the prospective customer will do a read-through.** A *read-through* is the process of reading a draft of a proposal to look for any misunderstandings due to language or cultural differences. Why do prospective customers do this? Because it's in everyone's interest for the proposal to respond clearly to the customer's needs.

DESCRIBING WHAT YOU PLAN TO DO

Once you have shown that you understand what needs to be done and why, describe what you plan to do. Convince your readers that you can respond effectively to the situation you have just described. Discuss procedures and equipment you would use. If appropriate, justify your choices. For example, if you say you want to do ultrasonic testing on a structure, explain why, unless the reason is obvious.

Present a complete picture of what you would do from the first day of the project to the last. You need more than enthusiasm and good faith; you need a detailed plan showing that you have already started to do the work. Although no proposal can anticipate every question about what you plan to do, the more planning you have done before you submit the proposal, the greater the chances you will be able to do the work successfully if it is approved.

DEMONSTRATING YOUR PROFESSIONALISM

Once you have shown that you understand readers' needs and can offer a well-conceived plan, demonstrate that you are the kind of person (or that yours is the kind of organization) that is committed to delivering what you promise. Convince readers that you have the pride, ingenuity, and perseverance to solve the problems that are likely to occur. In short, show that you are a professional.

◢│
GUIDELINES Demonstrating Your Professionalism in a Proposal

In your proposal, demonstrate your ability to carry out the project by providing four kinds of information:

▶ **Credentials and work history.** Show that you know how to do this project because you have done similar ones. Who are the people in your organization with the qualifications to carry out the project? What equipment and facilities do you have that will enable you to do the work? What management structure will you use to coordinate the activities and keep the project running smoothly?

▶ **Work schedule.** Sometimes called a *task schedule*, a work schedule is a graph or chart that shows when the various phases of the project will be carried out. The work schedule reveals more about your attitudes toward your work than about what you will be doing on any given day. A detailed work schedule shows that you have tried to foresee problems that might threaten the project.

▶ **Quality-control measures.** Describe how you will evaluate the effectiveness and efficiency of your work. Quality-control procedures might consist of technical evaluations carried out periodically by the project staff, on-site evaluations by recognized authorities or by the prospective customer, or progress reports.

▶ **Budget.** Most proposals conclude with a detailed budget, a statement of how much the project will cost. Including a budget is another way of showing that you have done your homework on a project.

ETHICS NOTE

WRITING HONEST PROPOSALS

When an organization approves a proposal, it needs to trust that the people who will carry out the project will do it professionally. Dishonest proposal writers, however, have perfected a number of ways to trick prospective customers into thinking the project will go smoothly:

- saying that certain qualified people will participate in the project, even though they will not
- saying that the project will be finished by a certain date, even though it will not
- saying that the deliverable will have certain characteristics, even though it will not
- saying that the project will be completed under budget, even though it will not

Copying from another company's proposal is another common dishonest tactic. Proposals are protected by copyright law. An employee may not copy from a proposal he or she wrote while working for a different company.

There are three reasons to be honest in writing a proposal:

- to avoid serious legal trouble stemming from breach-of-contract suits
- to avoid acquiring a bad reputation, thus ruining your business
- to do the right thing

Writing a Proposal

Although writing a proposal requires the same writing process that you use for most other kinds of technical documents, a proposal can be so large that two aspects of the writing process—resource planning and collaboration—are even more important than they are for smaller documents.

Like planning a writing project, discussed in Chapter 5, planning a proposal requires a lot of work. You need to see whether your organization can devote the needed resources to writing the proposal and then to carrying out the project if the proposal is approved. Sometimes an organization writes a proposal, wins the contract, and then loses money because it lacks the resources to do the project and must subcontract major portions of it. The resources you need fall into three basic categories:

- **Personnel.** Will you have the technical personnel, managers, and support people you will need?

- **Facilities.** Will you have the facilities, or can you lease them? Can you profitably subcontract tasks to companies that have the necessary facilities?

- **Equipment.** Do you have the right equipment? If not, can you buy it or lease it or subcontract the work? Some contracts provide for the purchase of equipment, but others don't.

Don't write the proposal unless you are confident that you can carry out the project if you get the go-ahead.

Collaboration is critical in preparing large proposals because no one person has the time and expertise to do all the work. Writing major proposals requires the expertise of technical personnel, writers, editors, graphic artists, managers, lawyers, and document-production specialists. Often, proposal writers use shared document workspaces and wikis. Usually, a project manager coordinates the process.

For more about collaboration, see Ch. 4.

Proposal writers almost always reuse existing information, including *boilerplate* such as descriptions of other projects the company has done, histories and descriptions of the company, and résumés of the primary personnel who will work on the project. This reuse of information is legal and ethical as long as the information is the intellectual property of the company.

For more about boilerplate, see Ch. 2, p. 26.

The Structure of the Proposal

Proposal structures vary greatly from one organization to another. A long, complex proposal might have 10 or more sections, including introduction, problem, objectives, solution, methods and resources, and management. If the authorizing agency provides an IFB, an RFP, an RFQ, or a set of guidelines, follow it closely. If you have no guidelines, or if you are writing an unsolicited proposal, use the structure shown here as a starting point. Then modify it according to your subject, your purpose, and the needs of your audience. An example of a proposal is presented at the end of this chapter, in Figure 16.6 (pp. 453–59).

For more about summaries, see "Executive Summary" in Ch. 18 on p. 499.

SUMMARY

For a proposal of more than a few pages, provide a summary. Many organizations impose a length limit—such as 250 words—and ask the writer to present the summary, single-spaced, on the title page. The summary is crucial, because it might be the only item that readers study in their initial review of the proposal.

The summary covers the major elements of the proposal but devotes only a few sentences to each. Define the problem in a sentence or two. Next, describe the proposed program and provide a brief statement of your qualifications and experience. Some organizations wish to see the completion date and the final budget figure in the summary; others prefer that this information be presented separately on the title page along with other identifying information about the supplier and the proposed project.

INTRODUCTION

The purpose of the introduction is to help readers understand the context, scope, and organization of the proposal.

GUIDELINES Introducing a Proposal

The introduction to a proposal should answer the following seven questions:

▶ **What is the problem or opportunity?** Describe the problem or opportunity in specific monetary terms because the proposal itself will include a budget, and you want to convince your readers that spending money on what you propose is smart. Don't say that a design problem is slowing down production; say that it is costing $4,500 a day in lost productivity.

▶ **What is the purpose of the proposal?** The purpose of the proposal is to describe a solution to a problem or an approach to an opportunity and propose activities that will culminate in a deliverable. Be specific in explaining what you want to do.

▶ **What is the background of the problem or opportunity?** Although you probably will not be telling your readers anything they don't already know, show them that you understand the problem or opportunity, the circumstances that led to its discovery, the relationships or events that will affect the problem and its solution, and so on.

▶ **What are your sources of information?** Review the relevant literature, ranging from internal reports and memos to published articles or even books, so that readers will understand the context of your work.

▶ **What is the scope of the proposal?** If appropriate, indicate not only what you are proposing to do but also what you are not proposing to do.

▶ **What is the organization of the proposal?** Explain the organizational pattern you will use.

▶ **What are the key terms that you will use in the proposal?** If you will use any specialized or unusual terms, define them in the introduction.

PROPOSED PROGRAM

In the section on the proposed program, sometimes called the *plan of work*, explain what you want to do. Be specific. You won't persuade anyone by saying that you plan to "gather the data and analyze it." *How* will you gather and analyze the data? Justify your claims. Every word you say—or don't say—will give your readers evidence on which to base their decision.

If your project concerns a subject written about in the professional literature, show your familiarity with the scholarship by referring to the pertinent studies. However, don't just string together a bunch of citations. For example, don't write, "Carruthers (2015), Harding (2016), and Vega (2016) have all researched the relationship between global warming and groundwater contamination." Rather, use the recent literature to sketch the necessary background and provide the justification for your proposed program. For instance:

> Carruthers (2015), Harding (2016), and Vega (2016) have demonstrated the relationship between global warming and groundwater contamination. None of these studies, however, included an analysis of the long-term contamination of the aquifer. The current study will consist of . . .

You might include only a few references to recent research. However, if your topic is complex, you might devote several paragraphs or even several pages to recent scholarship.

For more about researching a subject, see Ch. 6.

Whether your project calls for primary research, secondary research, or both, the proposal will be unpersuasive if you haven't already done a substantial amount of research. For instance, say you are writing a proposal to do research on purchasing new industrial-grade lawn mowers for your company. Simply stating that you will visit Walmart, Lowe's, and Home Depot to see what kinds of lawn mowers they carry would be unpersuasive for two reasons:

- You need to justify why you are going to visit those three retailers rather than others. Anticipate your readers' questions: Why did you choose these three retailers? Why didn't you choose specialized dealers?

- You should already have determined what stores carry what kinds of lawn mowers and completed any other preliminary research. If you haven't done the homework, readers have no assurance that you will in fact do it or that it will pay off. If your supervisor authorizes the project and then you learn that none of the lawn mowers in these stores meets your organization's needs, you will have to go back and submit a different proposal—an embarrassing move.

Unless you can show in your proposed program that you have done the research—and that the research indicates that the project is likely to succeed—the reader has no reason to authorize the project.

QUALIFICATIONS AND EXPERIENCE

After you have described how you would carry out the project, show that you can do it. The more elaborate the proposal, the more substantial the discussion of your qualifications and experience has to be. For a small project,

DOCUMENT ANALYSIS ACTIVITY

Writing the Proposed Program

The following project description is excerpted from a sample grant proposal seeking funding to begin a project to help police officers stay healthy. The questions in the margin ask you to think about how to describe the project in a proposal.

1. The writer has used a lettering system to describe the four main tasks that will be undertaken if the project receives funding. Is the lettering system effective?

2. How effective is the description of Task A? What factors contribute to the description's effectiveness or lack of effectiveness?

3. The descriptions of the tasks do not include cost estimates. Where would those estimates be presented in the proposal? Why would they be presented there?

4. How effective is the description of Task D? What additional information would improve its effectiveness?

PROJECT DESCRIPTION

The proposed project is comprised of several different but related activities:

A. Physical Evaluation of the Officers

The first component of this project is the physical examination of all Summerville P.D. sworn employees. Of special interest for purposes of the project are resting pulse rate, target pulse rate, blood pressure, and percentage of body fat of the program participants. Dr. Feinberg will perform the physical examinations of all participating officers. The measurement of body fat will be conducted at the University of Summerville's Health Center under the direction of Dr. Farron Updike.

B. Renovation of Basement

Another phase of this project involves the renovation of the basement of police headquarters. The space is currently being used for storing Christmas decorations for City Hall.

The main storage room will be converted into a gym. This room will accommodate the Universal weight machine, the stationary bike, the treadmill, and the rowing machine. Renovation will consist of first transferring all the Christmas decorations to the basement of the new City Hall. Once that is accomplished, it will be necessary to paint the walls, install indoor/outdoor carpeting, and set up the equipment.

A second, smaller room will be converted into a locker room. Renovation will include painting the floors and the installation of lockers and benches.

To complete the fitness center, a third basement room will be equipped as a shower room. A local plumber will tap into existing plumbing to install several showerheads.

C. Purchase of Fitness Equipment

The Department of Public Safety has identified five vendors of exercise equipment in the greater Summerville area. Each of these vendors submitted bids for the following equipment:
- Universal Weight Machine
- Atlas Stationary Bike
- Yale Rowing Machine
- Speedster Treadmill

D. Training of Officers

Participating officers must be trained in the safe, responsible use of the exercise equipment. Dr. Updike of the University of Summerville will hold periodic training sessions at the Department's facility.

Ohio Office of Criminal Justice Services.

include a few paragraphs describing your credentials and those of your co-workers. For larger projects, include the résumés of the project leader, often called the *principal investigator*, and the other primary participants.

External proposals should also discuss the qualifications of the supplier's organization, describing similar projects the supplier has completed successfully. For example, a company bidding on a contract to build a large suspension bridge should describe other suspension bridges it has built. It should also focus on the equipment and facilities the company already has and on the management structure that will ensure the project will go smoothly.

BUDGET

Good ideas aren't good unless they're affordable. The budget section of a proposal specifies how much the proposed program will cost.

Budgets vary greatly in scope and format. For simple internal proposals, add the budget request to the statement of the proposed program: "This study will take me two days, at a cost of about $400" or "The variable-speed recorder currently costs $225, with a 10 percent discount on orders of five or more." For more complicated internal proposals and for all external proposals, include a more explicit and complete budget.

Many budgets are divided into two parts: direct costs and indirect costs. *Direct costs* include such expenses as salaries and fringe benefits of program personnel, travel costs, and costs of necessary equipment, materials, and supplies. *Indirect costs* cover expenses that are sometimes called *overhead*: general secretarial and clerical expenses not devoted exclusively to any one project, as well as operating expenses such as costs of utilities and maintenance. Indirect costs are usually expressed as a percentage—ranging from less than 20 percent to more than 100 percent—of the direct expenses.

APPENDIXES

Many types of appendixes might accompany a proposal. Most organizations have boilerplate descriptions of the organization and of the projects it has completed. Another item commonly included in an appendix is a supporting letter: a testimonial to the supplier's skill and integrity, written by a reputable and well-known person in the field.

Two other sections commonly found in proposals can be positioned either in the appendix or in the main body of the document: the task schedule and the description of evaluation techniques.

TASK SCHEDULE

A *task schedule* is almost always presented in one of three graphical formats: as a table, a bar chart, or a network diagram.

Tables The simplest but least informative way to present a schedule is in a table, as shown in Figure 16.3. As with all graphics, provide a textual reference that introduces and, if necessary, explains the table.

TASK SCHEDULE

Activity	Start date	Finish date
Design the security system	4 Oct. 17	19 Oct. 17
Research available systems	4 Oct. 17	3 Jan. 18
Etc.		

FIGURE 16.3   Task Schedule Presented as a Table

Although displaying information in a table is better than writing it out in sentences, readers still cannot "see" the information. They have to read the table to figure out how long each activity will last, and they cannot tell whether any of the activities are interdependent. They have no way of determining what would happen to the overall project schedule if one of the activities faced delays.

Bar Charts Bar charts, also called *Gantt charts* after the early twentieth-century civil engineer who first used them, are more informative than tables. The basic bar chart shown in Figure 16.4 allows readers to see how long each task will take and whether different tasks will occur simultaneously. Like tables, however, bar charts do not indicate the interdependence of tasks.

Schedule for Parking Analysis Project

Number	Task	1/14	1/21	1/28	2/4	2/11
1	Perform research	▬				
2	Identify options		▬			
3	Analyze options		▬			
4	Test options			▬		
5	Collect and analyze data				▬	
6	Formulate recommendations					▬
7	Prepare report					▬

FIGURE 16.4   Task Schedule Presented as a Bar Chart

▶ TECH TIP

Why To Create a Gantt Chart

A Gantt chart is useful for showing how activities occur over time. Although they do not indicate the interdependence of tasks, Gantt charts can show overlaps in a schedule. In addition, color coding can visually indicate task priorities, task completion, task responsibilities, and so on.

How To Create a Gantt Chart

Using a program such as Word, Excel, or Google Spreadsheets, create a table or worksheet with enough cells to include all your tasks and dates.

Use the Fill command to color-code cells.

Word and Excel

Google Spreadsheets

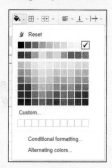

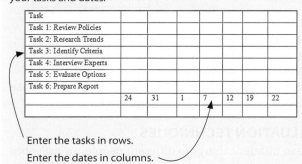

Task							
Task 1: Review Policies							
Task 2: Research Trends							
Task 3: Identify Criteria							
Task 4: Interview Experts							
Task 5: Evaluate Options							
Task 6: Prepare Report							
	24	31	1	7	12	19	22

Enter the tasks in rows.

Enter the dates in columns.

To create cells that span several columns, use the **Merge Cells** function. In Word and Excel, select the cells you wish to merge and right-click, then choose Merge Cells from the pop-up menu. In Google Spreadsheets, choose from the Merge Cells options in the Format tab.

Word

Excel

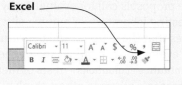

Google Spreadsheets

Sample Gantt chart with merged cells and color coding:

#	Task	7	15	22	29	5	12	19	26	3	10	17	24
		\multicolumn{4}{March}				\multicolumn{4}{April}				\multicolumn{4}{May}			
1	Conceptualization												
2	Engineering Phase												
3	Pre-Production												
4	Product Testing												
5	Production												
6	Release												

FIGURE 16.5 Task Schedule Presented as a Network Diagram

A network diagram provides more useful information than either a table or a bar chart.

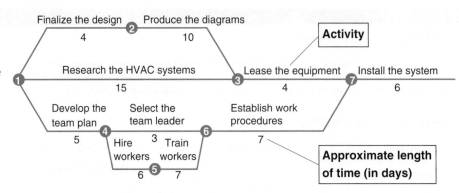

Network Diagrams Network diagrams show interdependence among various activities, clearly indicating which must be completed before others can begin. However, even a relatively simple network diagram, such as the one shown in Figure 16.5, can be difficult to read. You would probably not use this type of diagram in a document intended for general readers.

DESCRIPTION OF EVALUATION TECHNIQUES

Although *evaluation* can mean different things to different people, an *evaluation technique* typically refers to any procedure used to determine whether the proposed program is both effective and efficient. Evaluation techniques can range from writing simple progress reports to conducting sophisticated statistical analyses. Some proposals call for evaluation by an outside agent, such as a consultant, a testing laboratory, or a university. Other proposals describe evaluation techniques that the supplier will perform, such as cost–benefit analyses.

The issue of evaluation is complicated by the fact that some people think in terms of *quantitative evaluations*—tests of measurable quantities, such as production increases—whereas others think in terms of *qualitative evaluations*—tests of whether a proposed program is improving, say, the workmanship on a product. And some people include both qualitative and quantitative testing when they refer to evaluation. An additional complication is that projects can be tested while they are being carried out (*formative evaluations*) as well as after they have been completed (*summative evaluations*).

When an RFP calls for "evaluation," experienced proposal writers contact the prospective customer's representatives to determine precisely what the word means.

Sample Internal Proposal

The following example of an internal proposal has been formatted as a memo rather than as a formal proposal. (See Chapter 17, Figure 17.4, on pp. 471–78, for the progress report written after this project was under way and Chapter 18, Figure 18.8, on pp. 503–27, for the recommendation report.)

Rawlings Regional Medical Center
7500 Bannock Avenue
Rawlings, MT 59211

Date: October 6, 2020
To: Jill Bremerton, M.D.
            Chief Executive Officer
            Rawlings Regional Medical Center
From: Jeremy Elkins, Director of Information Technology
            Eloise Carruthers, Director of Nursing
            Rawlings Regional Medical Center
Subject: Proposal for the Tablet Study at RRMC

Purpose

The purpose of our proposal is to request authorization to conduct
a study to determine the best course of action for integrating tablet
computers into the RRMC clinical setting.

Summary

On September 16, 2020, Dr. Jill Bremerton, RRMC Chief Executive
Officer, asked us to develop a plan to study national trends on tablet
use, determine clinical-staff knowledge of and attitudes toward tablets,
examine administrative models for tablet use, devise criteria for assessing
tablets, and present our findings, including a recommendation.

Currently, RRMC has no formal policy on tablet usage by clinical staff. By
default, we are following a bring-your-own-device (BYOD) approach. More
than half of our clinical staff use their personal tablets in their work. This
situation is not ideal because not all clinical staff are taking advantage of
the enormous potential for improving patient care and reducing costs
by using tablets, and IT is struggling to keep up with the work needed
to ensure that all the different tablets are working properly and that
information-security protocols required by HIPAA and current health care
laws are not being violated.

FIGURE 16.6   Sample Internal Proposal   *(continued)*

In most professional settings,
writers use letterhead stationery
for memos.

Proposals can be presented as
memos or as reports. Memos are
more popular for brief documents
(fewer than five pages), whereas
reports are more popular for longer
documents.

The writers include their titles and
that of their primary reader. This
way, future readers will be able
to readily identify the reader and
writers.

The subject heading indicates the
subject of the memo (the tablet
study at Rawlings).

As discussed in Ch. 14, memos of
more than one page should begin
with a clear statement of purpose.
Here, the writers communicate the
primary purpose of the document
in one sentence.

Memos of more than one page
should contain a summary to serve
as an advance organizer or to help
readers who want only an overview
of the document.

Although the writers are writing to
Dr. Bremerton, they refer to her in
the third person to suggest the formality of their relationship.

The background of the problem.
Don't assume that your reader
knows what you are discussing,
even if it was the reader who suggested the project in the first place.

The problem at the heart of the
project.

Memo to Jill Bremerton, M.D.   October 6, 2020   Page 2

Therefore, Dr. Bremerton wanted us to determine the best approach to making tablets available to all our clinical staff. Specifically, Dr. Bremerton asked that we develop a plan to determine how tablets are being used by clinical staff across the nation, determine the RRMC clinical staff's current knowledge of and attitudes toward tablet use, determine how hospitals administer the use of tablets in a clinical setting, establish criteria by which we might evaluate tablets for RRMC, and assess available tablets based on our criteria.

We propose to research tablet use in clinical settings and present our findings to Dr. Bremerton. To perform these tasks, we would carry out secondary and primary research. We would study the literature on tablet use, distribute a questionnaire to RRMC clinical staff, and interview Dr. Bremerton. Then, we would collect and analyze our data and write the report.

To perform this research and present a recommendation report, we estimate that we would each require approximately 40 hours over the next two months, at a cost of $2,680. Jeremy Elkins, Director of Information Technology, has been with RRMC for 9 years and has overseen numerous IT feasibility studies. Eloise Carruthers has been with RRMC for 13 years, the last 8 of which have been as Director of Nursing.

If this proposal is authorized, we would begin our research immediately, submitting to Dr. Bremerton a progress report on November 14, 2018, and a recommendation report on December 14, 2018. The recommendation report would include the details of our research and recommendations regarding how to proceed with the feasibility study.

Introduction

On September 16, 2018, Dr. Jill Bremerton, RRMC Chief Executive Officer, asked us to develop a plan to determine the best course of action for integrating tablet computers into the RRMC clinical setting.

Currently, RRMC has no formal policy on tablet usage by clinical staff. By default, we are following a bring-your-own-device (BYOD) approach. More than half of our clinical staff use their personal tablets in their work. This situation is not ideal because not all clinical staff are taking advantage of the enormous potential for improving patient care and reducing costs

---

The proposal. The writers have already begun to plan what they will do if the proposal is accepted, but they use the conditional tense ("would") because they cannot assume that their proposal will be approved.

A summary of the schedule and the credentials of the writers. Because the reader will likely want to read this entire proposal, the summary functions as an advance organizer.

A brief statement of the context for the proposal.

An explanation of the problem: the current situation is inadequate because the medical center is not taking full advantage of tablets and because IT is spending a lot of time ensuring that the tablets in use are in compliance with federal requirements.

This same paragraph appeared in the "Summary" section of the proposal. In technical communication, writers often present the same information several times because some readers will read only selected portions of the document.

FIGURE 16.6   Sample Internal Proposal (*continued*)

by using tablets, and IT is struggling to keep up with the work needed to ensure that all the different tablets are working properly and that information-security protocols required by HIPAA and current health care laws are not being violated.

Therefore, Dr. Bremerton wanted us to determine the best approach to making tablets available to all our clinical staff. Specifically, Dr. Bremerton asked that we develop a plan to perform five tasks:

- Determine how tablets are being used by clinical staff across the nation.
- Determine the RRMC clinical staff's current knowledge of and attitudes toward tablet use.
- Determine how hospitals administer the use of tablets in a clinical setting.
- Establish criteria by which we might evaluate tablets for RRMC.
- Assess available tablets based on our criteria.

In the following sections, we provide additional details about the proposed tasks, schedule, and budget, as well as our credentials and references.

Proposed Tasks

With Dr. Bremerton's approval, we would perform the following six tasks to help determine the best course of action for integrating tablet computers into the RRMC clinical setting.

Task 1. Acquire a basic understanding of tablet use by clinical staff across the nation

We have already begun our research by interviewing Dr. Bremerton, who emphasized that we need to maintain our focus on our priorities — patient care and service to the community — and not let technical questions about the tablets distract us from the needs of our clinical staff. "We're not going to do anything without the approval of the doctors and nurses," she said.

We also discovered an article that corroborated what Dr. Bremerton had told us (Narisi, 2013). Two keys to doing the research were to focus on security features — data-privacy issues mandated in HIPAA and in current health care laws — and to get the clinical staff's input.

The writers paraphrase text from a memo Dr. Bremerton had written to them. Often in technical communication, you will quote or paraphrase your reader's words to remind him or her of the context and to show that you are carrying out your tasks professionally — and to give the reader the opportunity to change the direction of the study before it officially begins.

The introduction concludes with an advance organizer for the rest of the proposal.

By presenting the project as a set of tasks, the writers show that they are well organized. This organization by tasks will be used in the progress report (see Ch. 17, Figure 17.4, on pp. 471–78) and the recommendation report (see Ch. 18, Figure 18.8, on pp. 503–27).

FIGURE 16.6   Sample Internal Proposal (*continued*)

The proposal sounds credible because the writers have already begun their secondary research. Readers are reluctant to approve proposals unless they are sure that the writers have at least begun their research.

Dr. Bremerton pointed us to a number of resources on tablet use in clinical settings. In addition, we have begun to conduct our own literature review. Most of the research we studied falls into one of four categories:

- general introductions to tablet use in trade magazines and general-interest periodicals
- more focused articles about tablets used in health care
- technical specifications of tablets provided in trade magazines and on manufacturers' websites
- trade-magazine articles about best practices for managing the use of tablets in clinical settings

Following the recommendation from Dr. Bremerton, the writers start by outlining the secondary research they plan to do. The logic is obvious: if they are to present sensible recommendations, they need to understand their subject.

As we expected, the information we acquired is a mix of user opinions, benchmark-test results, and marketing. We would rely most heavily on case studies from hospital administrators and technical specialists in health IT. Because of the unreliability of information on manufacturers' websites, we are hesitant to rely on claims about product performance.

By stating that they know that their sources are a mixture of different kinds of information, not all of which are equally useful for every kind of question that needs to be answered, the writers suggest that they are careful analysts.

Task 2: Determine the RRMC clinical staff's knowledge of and attitudes toward tablet use

Next week, we propose to send all clinical staff members an email linking to a four-question Qualtrix survey. The email would explain that we were seeking opinions about tablet use by clinical-staff members who already own tablets and would make clear that the survey would take less than two minutes to complete.

The writers show that they have applied the insights they gathered from their secondary research. Now they propose doing primary research to determine whether the RRMC clinical staff share the attitudes of clinical staff across the country. The logic is clear: if they do, the hospital administrators will know that they can rely on the national data.

Task 3. Assess the BYOD and hospital-owned tablet models

Our research has already revealed that hospitals currently use one of two models for giving clinical staff access to tablets: the bring-your-own-device (BYOD) approach and purchasing tablets to distribute to staff. We have found literature that assesses the advantages and disadvantages of each of these models (Jackson, 2011a, 2011b).

For statistics on the popularity of each of these administrative models, we would rely on a survey (Terry, 2011).

The writers cite their sources throughout the proposal.

FIGURE 16.6   Sample Internal Proposal (*continued*)

Task 4: Establish criteria for evaluating tablets

We (Jeremy Elkins and Eloise Carruthers) have both begun to study the voluminous literature on tablets. Jeremy Elkins has met informally with his five IT colleagues to discuss the data, and Eloise Carruthers has met informally with her nursing staff and with selected physicians, including several who already own tablets and use them in the clinic.

We would begin with the first criterion: cost. Dr. Bremerton told us in our interview that the budget for the project (assuming that RRMC would supply a tablet to each member of the clinical staff) would be $800 per device, fully configured with any commercial software needed to operate it. For this reason, we would not thoroughly examine any tablets that do not meet this criterion.

Often you will begin your project with a cost criterion: your recommended solution must not cost more than a certain amount.

In addition, we would pay particular attention to the complexities of the current tablet market, focusing on whether the various devices would work seamlessly with our health-records system and other security features ("Top Five," 2013), on the need to be able to disinfect the tablets (Carr, 2011), and on durability (Narisi, 2013). Furthermore, we know from experience with all kinds of portable information technology that the question of battery life would be problematic because it can vary so much depending on load and other factors.

We anticipate that two factors might be critically important: operating system and availability of relevant apps.

Task 5. Assess available tablets based on our criteria

We would begin our study of the tablets by examining trade magazines. We realize, however, that several of our likely criteria — namely, the ability to disinfect the tablet, as well as durability and battery life — might not be addressed adequately in the literature because each hospital has its own specific needs. If the literature cannot help us complete our assessments, we would need to carry out on-site evaluations at RRMC.

Task 6. Analyze our data and prepare a recommendation report

We would draft our recommendation report and upload it to a wiki to make it convenient for the other IT staff members and interested clinical staff members to help us revise it. We would then incorporate our

Preparing the recommendation report is part of the project because the report is the deliverable.

FIGURE 16.6   **Sample Internal Proposal** (*continued*)

Organizing the project by tasks makes it easy for the writers to present a Gantt chart. In addition, the task organization will help the writers stay on track if the proposal is approved and they continue their research.

Each task is presented with parallel grammar, which shows that the writers are careful and professional.

Some tasks overlap in time: researchers often work on several tasks simultaneously.

The Tech Tip on p. 451 explains how to create a Gantt chart.

Memo to Jill Bremerton, M.D.   October 6, 2020   Page 6

colleagues' suggestions and present a final draft of the report on the wiki to gather any final editing suggestions.

Schedule

Figure 1 is a schedule of the tasks we would complete for this project.

Tasks	Date of Tasks (by Weeks)									
Task 1: Research tablet use	■	■								
Task 2: Determine staff knowledge and attitudes			■	■	■					
Task 3: Research management models						■	■			
Task 4: Establish criteria						■	■			
Task 5: Assess tablets based on criteria							■	■		
Task 6: Prepare report									■	■
	10	17	24	31	7	14	21	28	5	12
	Oct.				Nov.				Dec.	

Figure 1.   Schedule of Project Tasks

Budget

Following is an itemized budget for our proposed research.

Name	Hours	Hourly rate ($)	Cost ($)
Jeremy Elkins	40	28	1,120
Eloise Carruthers	40	39	1,560
			Total: $2,680

FIGURE 16.6   Sample Internal Proposal (*continued*)

Experience

We are experienced professionals who have participated in numerous studies both here at RRMC and elsewhere.

- Jeremy Elkins, Director of Information Technology, has chaired the Technology Infrastructure Committee and served as *ad hoc* member of the Steering Committee at RRMC for 9 years. He has designed the current IT infrastructure at RRMC, oversees the purchase of all IT equipment, and is currently implementing RRMC's electronic health records software.
- Eloise Carruthers, Director of Nursing at RRMC, holds bachelor's and master's degrees in nursing and has earned over 100 CEUs in virtually every aspect of the profession, including budgeting and management. She has administrative responsibility for all the registered and licensed nurses, as well as all nursing assistants. She has provided leadership in every aspect of patient care at RRMC for the last 13 years.

The writers summarize their credentials. Strong credentials help reinforce the writers' professionalism.

References

Carr, D. F. (2011, May 21). Healthcare puts tablets to the test. *InformationWeek Healthcare.* Retrieved October 12, 2018, from http://www.informationweek.com/healthcare/mobile-wireless/healthcare-puts-tablets-to-the-test/229503387

Jackson, S. (2011a, August 15). Five reasons hospitals should buy tablets for physicians. *FierceMobileHealthcare.* Retrieved October 14, 2018, from http://www.fiercemobilehealthcare.com/story/5-reasons-why-hospitals-should-buy-tablets-physicians/2011-08-15

Jackson, S. (2011b, August 3). Why physicians should buy their own mobile devices. *FierceMobileHealthcare.* Retrieved October 16, 2018, from http://www.fiercemobilehealthcare.com/story/why-physicians-should-buy-their-own-mobile-devices/2011-08-03

Narisi, S. (2013, April 24). Choosing the best tablets for doctors: 3 keys. *Healthcare Business & Technology.* Retrieved October 15, 2018, from http://www.healthcarebusinesstech.com/best-tablets-for-doctors

Terry, K. (2011, Dec. 9). Apple capitalizes on doctors' iPad romance. *InformationWeek Healthcare.* Retrieved October 14, 2018, from http://www.informationweek.com/healthcare/mobile-wireless/apple-capitalizes-on-doctors-ipad-roman/232300218

Top Five Tablet Security Features. (2013). *Healthcare Data Solutions.* Retrieved October 14, 2018, from http://www.healthcaredatasolutions.com/top-five-tablet-security-features.html

This list of references follows the APA documentation style, which is discussed in Appendix, Part B, p. 632, although the APA documentation system calls for References to begin on a new page. Check with your instructor.

FIGURE 16.6   **Sample Internal Proposal** *(continued)*

WRITER'S CHECKLIST

The following checklist covers the basic elements of a proposal. Guidelines established by the recipient of the proposal should take precedence over these general suggestions.

☐ Did you consider the context of your proposal and make it clear to your readers? *(p. 442)*

☐ Did you describe to your reader what you plan to do? *(p. 443)*

☐ Did you demonstrate your professionalism? *(p. 443)*

☐ Did you write an honest proposal? *(p. 444)*

Does the summary provide an overview of

☐ the problem or the opportunity? *(p. 446)*

☐ the proposed program? *(p. 446)*

☐ your qualifications and experience? *(p. 446)*

Does the introduction indicate

☐ the problem or opportunity? *(p. 446)*

☐ the purpose of the proposal? *(p. 446)*

☐ the background of the problem or opportunity? *(p. 446)*

☐ your sources of information? *(p. 446)*

☐ the scope of the proposal? *(p. 446)*

☐ the organization of the proposal? *(p. 446)*

☐ the key terms that you will use in the proposal? *(p. 446)*

☐ Does the description of the proposed program provide a clear, specific plan of action and justify the tasks you propose performing? *(p. 447)*

Does the description of qualifications and experience clearly outline

☐ your relevant skills and past work? *(p. 447)*

☐ the skills and background of the other participants? *(p. 449)*

☐ your department's (or organization's) relevant equipment, facilities, and experience? *(p. 449)*

Is the budget

☐ complete? *(p. 449)*

☐ correct? *(p. 449)*

☐ Do the appendixes include the relevant supporting materials? *(p. 449)*

☐ Did you include other relevant sections, such as a task schedule or a description of evaluation techniques? *(p. 449)*

EXERCISES

For more about memos, see Ch. 14, p. 386.

1. Study the National Science Foundation's (NSF) Proposal & Award Policies & Procedures Guide (www.nsf.gov /publications/pub_summ.jsp?ods_key=papp). In what important ways does the NSF's guide differ from the advice provided in this chapter? What accounts for these differences? Present your findings in a 500-word memo to your instructor.

2. **TEAM EXERCISE** Form groups according to major. Using the government contracting website (beta.sam .gov/), find and study an RFP for a project related to your academic field. What can you learn about the needs of the organization that issued the RFP? How effectively does the RFP describe what the issuing organization expects to see in the proposal? Is it relatively general or specific? What sorts of evaluation techniques does it call for? In your response, include a list of questions that you would ask the issuing organization if you were considering responding to the RFP. Present your results in a memo to your instructor.

3. Write a proposal for a research project that will constitute a major assignment in this course. Your instructor will tell you whether the proposal is to be written individually or collaboratively. Start by defining a technical subject that interests you. (This subject could be one that is relevant to your job or that you have encountered in another course.) Using abstract services and other bibliographic tools, compile a bibliography of articles and books on the subject. (See Chapter 6 for a discussion of finding information.) Create a reasonable real-world context. Here are three common scenarios from the business world:

   1. Our company uses Technology X to perform Task A. Should we instead be using Technology Y to perform Task A? For instance, our company uses standard surveying tools in its contracting business. Should we be using 3D-equipped stations instead?

2. Our company has decided to purchase a tool to perform Task A. Which make and model of the tool should we purchase, and from which supplier should we buy it? For instance, our company has decided to purchase 10 laptop computers. Which brand and model should we buy, and from whom should we buy them? Is leasing the tool a better option than purchasing?

3. Our company does not currently perform Function X. Is it feasible to perform Function X? For instance, we do not currently offer day care for our employees. Should we? What are the advantages and disadvantages of doing so? What forms can day care take? How is it paid for?

Following are some additional ideas for topics:

- the value of using social media to form ties with students in a technical-communication class on another campus

- the need for expanded opportunities for internships or service learning in your major

- the need to create an advisory board of industry professionals to provide expertise about your major

- the need to raise money to keep the college's computer labs up to date

- the need to evaluate the course of study offered by your university in your major to ensure that it is responsive to students' needs

- the advisability of starting a campus branch of a professional organization in your field

- the need to improve parking facilities on campus

- the need to create or improve organizations for minorities or women on campus

---

CASE 16: Writing an Introduction for a Proposal

You work for a company that provides web-development services to external clients. Your job is to seek out requests for proposals (RFPs) posted by organizations looking for companies like yours. You have found an RFP posted by the borough council of a small town, seeking help in updating and enhancing the town's website. You know that your company is capable of providing these services. Your supervisor agrees and asks you to draft an introduction to the proposal while other team members work on incorporating boilerplate language and handle the scheduling and budgeting details. If your instructor has assigned it, go to Achieve to get started drafting the introduction.

Writing Informational Reports

COMPLEX, EXPENSIVE PROJECTS call for a lot of documents. Before a project begins, a vendor might write a *proposal* to interest prospective clients in its work. After a project is completed, an organization might write a *completion report* to document the project or a *recommendation report* to argue for a future course of action. In between, many people will write various *informational reports*.

Whether they are presented as memos, emails, reports, or web pages, informational reports share one goal: to describe something that has happened or is happening now. Their main purpose is to provide clear, accurate, specific information to an audience. Sometimes, informational reports also analyze the situation. An *analysis* is an explanation of why something happened or how it happened. For instance, in an incident report about an accident on the job, the writer might speculate about how and why the accident occurred.

This chapter discusses five kinds of informational reports:

- A supervisor writes a *directive* explaining a company's new policy on recycling and describing informational sessions that the company will offer to help employees understand how to implement the policy.

- An insurance adjuster writes a *field report* presenting the results of his inspection of a building after a storm caused extensive damage.

- A research team writes a *progress report* explaining what the team has accomplished in the first half of the project, speculating on whether it will finish on time and within budget, and describing how it has responded to unexpected problems.

- A worker at a manufacturing company writes an *incident report* after a toxic chemical spill.

- A recording secretary writes a set of *meeting minutes* that will become the official record of what occurred at a meeting of the management team of a government agency.

Other types of informational reports are *recommendation reports* (see Chapter 18) and *lab reports* (see Chapter 19).

Understanding the Process of Writing Informational Reports

Writing informational reports involves the same writing process used in most other kinds of technical communication. The Focus on Process box on page 464 outlines this process.

Much informational report writing involves synthesizing material from other sources. For an explanation of how to incorporate outside sources into your document without plagiarizing, see Appendix, Part A. For details on documenting your sources, see Appendix, Part B.

FOCUS ON PROCESS: Informational Reports

In writing informational reports, pay special attention to these steps in the writing process.

PLANNING

In some cases, determining your audience and to whom to address the report is difficult. Choosing the appropriate format for your report can also be difficult. Consider whether your organization has a preferred format for reports and whether your report will be read by readers from other cultures who might expect a formal style and application. See Chapter 5 for more about analyzing your audience.

DRAFTING

Some informational reports are drafted on site. For instance, an engineer might use a tablet computer to "draft" a report as she walks around a site. For routine reports, you can sometimes use sections of previous reports or boilerplate. In a status report, for instance, you can copy the description of your current project from the previous report and then update it as necessary. See the Ethics Notes in Chapter 2 on page 26 for more about boilerplate.

REVISING

Because reports are often complex and have multiple audiences and purposes, revising carefully to ensure you have included all of the necessary information in a clear and consistent format is particularly important. See the Writer's Checklist at the end of this chapter for detailed advice.

EDITING

See Chapter 10 for advice on writing correct and effective sentences.

PROOFREADING

Even brief or informal reports sent by email should be free of errors. Revise, edit, and proofread the report thoroughly. See Appendix, Part C, for proofreading tips.

For more about analyzing your audience, see Ch. 5.

As with any type of writing, you should begin by analyzing your audience. If your informational report is being written for a nontechnical audience, you will want to take care to use terminology that a general audience will understand and to define any important terms they may be unfamiliar with. If your report will be addressed to people from another culture, think about how your readers will react to your choice of application and your writing style. If your readers expect a formal style, you will want to select a formal application (such as a report) rather than a memo. And consider adjusting your writing style, perhaps by adding parenthetical definitions and graphics or by using shorter sentences or more headings, to help readers whose first language is not English.

Writing Directives

In a *directive*, you explain a policy or a procedure you want your readers to follow. Even though you have the authority to require your readers to follow the policy, you want to explain why the policy is desirable or at least necessary. As discussed in Chapter 8, you are most persuasive when you present clear, compelling evidence (in the form of commonsense arguments, numerical data, and examples); when you consider opposing arguments effectively; and when you present yourself as cooperative, moderate, fair-minded, and modest. If appropriate, include arguments that appeal to your readers' broader goals of security, recognition, personal and professional growth, and connectedness. Figure 17.1 is an example of a directive.

For more about understanding your audience's goals, see "Considering the Context of Your Argument" in Ch. 8 on p. 177.

NOTICE TO EMPLOYEES

Research has shown that minors find it easy to buy tobacco products even though state law prohibits sales to anyone under 18. To stop the sale of tobacco to minors and to comply with state law, we are implementing the following policy immediately:

THIS COMPANY WILL NOT SELL CIGARETTES, CHEWING TOBACCO, SMOKELESS TOBACCO, OR SMOKING PARAPHERNALIA TO ANYONE UNDER THE AGE OF 18.

YOU CAN BE FINED $100 PLUS COURT COSTS AND FEES FOR SELLING ANY OF THESE PRODUCTS TO ANYONE UNDER THE AGE OF 18.

Under this new policy, you are required to request valid photo identification for anyone attempting to purchase tobacco products *who appears to be under the age of 27.*

If a customer questions this policy, please explain that state law prohibits the sale of tobacco products to those under the age of 18, and therefore we refuse to sell to minors.

A copy of the law is posted near the cash register. Please read the law carefully and, if you have questions, confer with your supervisor.

Any employee who does not follow this policy will be subject to disciplinary action. Thank you for your cooperation.

The writer, the owner of a convenience store, begins with a clear explanation of the problem the directive addresses. Presenting the reasons for the new policy shows respect for the readers and therefore makes the directive more persuasive.

The writer uses a polite but official tone because the new policy is a policy, not a request. Notice that the directive specifies a penalty for not adhering to the policy and directs readers to their supervisors if they have questions.

FIGURE 17.1   A Directive

DOCUMENT ANALYSIS ACTIVITY

Writing a Persuasive Directive

This directive was sent to the members of a Montana government department. The questions below ask you to think about the process of writing persuasive directives.

1. How would you describe the tone used by the writer? Provide an example to support your claim.

2. The writer presents examples of what he calls violations of the state travel policy. Do these examples provide solid evidence that violations of the policy have, in fact, occurred?

3. How effectively has the writer encouraged his staff to abide by the travel policy? How might he improve the persuasiveness of the directive?

To: Members, Budget Allocation Office
From: Harold J. Jefferson, Director
Subject: Travel Policy
Date: January 23, 2020

It has come to my attention that certain members of this office are not abiding by the travel policies approved by the state. Let me offer a few examples.

The Montana Revised Code includes this statement in its introduction:

> Persons who travel on State business are encouraged to incur the lowest practical and reasonable expense while still traveling in an efficient and timely manner. Those traveling on State business are expected to avoid impropriety, or the appearance of impropriety, in any travel expense. They must conduct State business with integrity, in compliance with applicable laws, and in a manner that excludes consideration of personal advantage.

Yet I have learned from official sources that on four occasions in the last fiscal year, employees of this office have acted in flagrant violation of this policy. Two occasions involved choosing a flight that left at a more convenient time in the morning but that cost almost $160 more. One involved selecting a cab, rather than a shuttle bus, for a trip from the airport to downtown (a $24 difference), and one involved using room service when the motel has a café (a $14 difference).

Another provision of the travel policy that has been violated on more than one occasion is the following:

> Travel expenses are not paid in advance except for airfare charged to the State air travel card, for online (internet) air or train ticket purchases, and for conference registrations.

Two employees have on more than three occasions each received reimbursements for air and/or train reservations made using their personal credit cards. As you know, using personal credit cards leaves the State without official documentation of the expense and gives the traveler bonus miles and/or cash back that properly belongs to the State.

These are just two of the kinds of irregularities that have been brought to my attention. I do not need to tell you that these violations constitute serious breaches of public ethics. If they recur, they will be dealt with harshly. I sincerely hope that I do not have to address this issue again.

Writing Field Reports

A common kind of informational report describes inspections, maintenance, and site studies. Such reports, often known as *field reports*, explain problems, methods, results, and conclusions, but they deemphasize methods and can include recommendations. The report in Figure 17.2 illustrates a possible variation on this standard report structure.

FIGURE 17.2
A Field Report
Image: Kamil Abbasov/Shutterstock.

Because the writer and the reader work for different companies, a letter is the appropriate format for this brief informational report.

The word *visual* describes the method.

The writer states the purpose of the inspection.

The writer has chosen to incorporate the words *summary* and *conclusion* in the body of the letter rather than use headings as a method of organization.

LOBATE CONSTRUCTION
3311 Industrial Parkway
Speonk, NY 13508
Quality Construction Since 1957

April 11, 2020

Ms. Christine Amalli, Head
Civil Engineering
New York Power
Smithtown, NY 13507

Dear Ms. Amalli:

We are pleased to report the results of our visual inspection of the Chemopump after Run #9, a 30-day trial on Kentucky #10 coal.

The inspection was designed to determine if the new Chemopump is compatible with Kentucky #10, the lowest-grade coal that you anticipate using. In preparation for the 30-day test run, the following three modifications were made by your technicians:

- New front-bearing housing buffer plates of tungsten carbide were installed.
- The pump-casting volute liner was coated with tungsten carbide.
- New bearings were installed.

Our summary is as follows. A number of small problems with the pump were observed, but nothing serious and nothing surprising. Normal break-in accounts for the wear. The pump accepted the Kentucky #10 well.

The following four minor problems were observed:

- The outer lip of the front-end bell was chipped along two-thirds of its circumference.
- Opposite the pump discharge, the volute liner received a slight wear groove along one-third of its circumference.
- The impeller was not free-rotating.
- The holes in the front-end bell were filled with insulating mud.

The following three components showed no wear:

- 5½" impeller
- suction neck liner
- discharge neck liner

Our conclusion is that the problems can be attributed to normal break-in for a new Chemopump. The Kentucky #10 coal does not appear to have caused any extraordinary problems. In general, the new Chemopump seems to be operating well.

(continued)

page 2

Informational reports sometimes include recommendations.

• We would recommend, however, that the pump be modified as follows:

1. Replace the front-end bell with a tungsten carbide-coated front-end bell.
2. Replace the bearings on the impeller.
3. Install insulation plugs in the holes in the front-end bell.

Further, we recommend that the pump be reinspected after another 30-day run on Kentucky #10.

The writer concludes politely.

• If you have any questions or would like to authorize these modifications, please call me at 555-321-1241. As always, we appreciate the trust you have placed in us.

Sincerely,

Marvin Littridge

Marvin Littridge
Director of Testing and Evaluation

FIGURE 17.2   A Field Report (*continued*)

◢
GUIDELINES Responding to Readers'
Questions in a Field Report

When you write a field report, be sure to answer the following six questions:

▶ What is the purpose of the report?

▶ What are the main points covered in the report?

▶ What were the problems leading to the decision to perform the procedure?

▶ What methods were used?

▶ What were the results?

▶ What do the results mean?

If appropriate, also discuss what you think should be done next.

Writing Progress and Status Reports

A *progress report* describes an ongoing project. A *status report*, sometimes called an *activity report*, describes the entire range of operations of a department or division. For example, the director of marketing for a manufacturing company might submit a monthly status report.

A progress report is an intermediate communication between a proposal (the argument that a project be undertaken) and a completion report (the comprehensive record of a completed project) or a recommendation report (an argument to take further action). Progress reports let you check in with your audience.

For more about proposals, see Ch. 16. For more about completion reports and recommendation reports, see Ch. 18.

Regardless of how well the project is proceeding, explain clearly and fully what has happened and how those activities or events will affect the overall project. Your tone should be objective, neither defensive nor casual. Unless your own ineptitude or negligence caused a problem, you're not to blame. Regardless of the news you are delivering—good, bad, or mixed—your job is the same: to provide a clear and complete account of your activities and to forecast the next stage of the project.

When things go wrong, you might be tempted to cover up problems and hope that you can solve them before the next progress report. This course of action is unwise and unethical. Chances are that problems will multiply, and you will have a harder time explaining why you didn't alert your readers earlier.

ETHICS NOTE

REPORTING YOUR PROGRESS HONESTLY

Withholding bad news is unethical because it can mislead readers. As sponsors or supervisors of the project, readers have a right to know how it is going. If you find yourself faced with any of the following three common problems, consider responding in these ways:

- **The deliverable—the document or product you will submit at the end of the project— won't be what you thought it would be.** Without being defensive, describe the events that led to the situation and explain how the deliverable will differ from what you described in the proposal.

- **You won't meet your schedule.** Explain why you are going to be late, and state when the project will be complete.

- **You won't meet the budget.** Explain why you need more money, and state how much more you will need.

ORGANIZING PROGRESS AND STATUS REPORTS

The time pattern and the task pattern, two organizational patterns frequently used in progress and status reports, are illustrated in Figure 17.3.

In the time pattern, you describe all the work that you have completed in the present reporting period and then sketch in the work that remains. Some writers include a section on present work, which enables them to focus on a long or complex task still in progress.

THE TIME PATTERN	THE TASK PATTERN
Discussion	Discussion
A. Past Work	A. Task 1
B. Future Work	1. Past work
	2. Future work
	B. Task 2
	1. Past work
	2. Future work

The task pattern enables you to describe, in order, what has been accomplished on each task. Often a task-oriented structure incorporates the chronological structure.

FIGURE 17.3 **Organizational Patterns in Reports**

A status report is usually organized according to task; by its nature, this type of report covers a specified time period.

CONCLUDING PROGRESS AND STATUS REPORTS

In the conclusion of a progress or status report, evaluate how the project is proceeding. In the broadest sense, there are two possible messages: things are going well, or things are not going as well as anticipated.

If appropriate, use appendixes for supporting materials, such as computations, schematics, diagrams, tables, or a revised task schedule. Be sure to cross-reference these appendixes in the body of the report, so that readers can find them easily.

GUIDELINES Projecting an Appropriate Tone in a Progress or Status Report

Whether the news is positive or negative, these two suggestions will help you sound like a professional.

▶ **If the news is good, convey your optimism but avoid overstatement.**

OVERSTATED   We are sure the device will do all that we ask of it, and more.

REALISTIC   We expect that the device will perform well and that, in addition, it might offer some unanticipated advantages.

▶ **Beware of promising early completion.** Such optimistic forecasts rarely prove accurate, and it is embarrassing to have to report a failure to meet an optimistic deadline.

▶ **Don't panic if the preliminary results are not as promising as you had planned or if the project is behind schedule.** Even the best-prepared proposal writers cannot anticipate all problems. As long as the original proposal was well planned and contained no wildly inaccurate computations, don't feel responsible. Just do your best to explain unanticipated problems and the status of the project. If your news is bad, at least give the reader as much time as possible to deal with it effectively.

Sample Progress Report

The progress report in Figure 17.4 (pp. 471–78) was written for the project proposed in Figure 16.6 (pp. 453–59) in Chapter 16. [The recommendation report for this study is in Figure 18.8 (pp. 504–527) in Chapter 18.]

Rawlings Regional Medical Center
7500 Bannock Avenue
Rawlings, MT 59211

Date: November 14, 2018
To: Jill Bremerton, M.D.
           Chief Executive Officer
           Rawlings Regional Medical Center
From: Jeremy Elkins, Director of Information Technology
           Eloise Carruthers, Director of Nursing
           Rawlings Regional Medical Center
Subject: Progress Report for the Tablet Study at RRMC

Purpose

This is a progress report on our study to recommend the best course of action for integrating tablet computers into the RRMC clinical setting.

Summary

On October 8, 2018, Dr. Jill Bremerton, RRMC Chief Executive Officer, approved our proposal to study national trends in tablet use, determine clinical-staff knowledge of and attitudes toward tablets, examine administrative models for tablet use, devise criteria for assessing tablets, and present our findings, including a recommendation.

We have completed Tasks 1 and 2 (understanding tablet use in a clinical setting and determining the clinical staff's knowledge of and attitudes toward tablet use), as well as part of Task 3 (assessing the bring-your-own-device and hospital-owned tablet models).

Our study is currently on schedule, and we expect to submit a recommendation report on December 14, 2018, as indicated in our proposal dated October 6, 2018.

In most professional settings, writers use letterhead stationery for memos.

Progress reports can be presented as memos or as reports.

The writers include their titles and that of their primary reader. This way, future readers will be able to readily identify the reader and writers.

The subject heading indicates the subject of the memo (the tablet study at Rawlings Regional Medical Center) and the purpose of the memo (progress report).

Memos of more than one page should begin with a clear statement of purpose. Here, the writers communicate the primary purpose of the document in one sentence.

Memos of more than one page should contain a summary to serve as an advance organizer or to help readers who want only an overview of the document.

Readers of progress reports want to know whether the project is proceeding according to schedule and (if applicable) on budget.

FIGURE 17.4   Sample Progress Report (*continued*)

A brief statement of the context for the proposal. Note that the writers refer to the reader's having authorized the proposal.

An explanation of the problem: the current situation is inadequate because the medical center is not taking full advantage of tablets and because IT is spending a lot of time ensuring that the tablets in use are in compliance with federal requirements.

A formal statement of the task that Dr. Bremerton asked the writers to perform.

Most of the information in the introduction is taken directly from the proposal. This reuse of text is ethical because the writers created it for that earlier document.

The introduction concludes with an advance organizer for the rest of the proposal.

The writers begin by describing the organization of the results section. For a progress report, a chronological organization — completed work, then future work — makes good sense.

The writers follow the task structure that they used in the proposal.

Memo to Jill Bremerton, M.D.   November 14, 2018   Page 2

Introduction

On October 8, 2018, Dr. Jill Bremerton, RRMC Chief Executive Officer, approved our proposal to determine the best course of action for integrating tablet computers into the RRMC clinical setting.

Currently, RRMC has no formal policy on tablet usage by clinical staff. By default, we are following a bring-your-own-device (BYOD) approach. More than half of our clinical staff use their personal tablets in their work. This situation is not ideal because not all clinical staff are taking advantage of the enormous potential for improving patient care and reducing costs by using tablets, and IT is struggling to keep up with the work needed to ensure that all the different tablets are working properly and that information-security protocols required by HIPAA and current health care laws are not being violated.

Dr. Bremerton approved our proposal to determine the best approach to take in making tablets available to all our clinical staff. Specifically, Dr. Bremerton asked us to perform five tasks:
- Determine how tablets are being used by clinical staff across the nation.
- Determine the RRMC clinical staff's knowledge of and attitudes toward tablet use.
- Determine how hospitals administer the use of tablets in a clinical setting.
- Establish criteria by which we might evaluate tablets for RRMC.
- Assess available tablets based on our criteria.

In the following sections, we present the results of our research to date, followed by an updated task schedule and references.

Results of Research

In this progress report, we present our completed work on Tasks 1–2 and our status on Task 3. Then we discuss our future work: Tasks 4–6.

Task 1. Acquire a basic understanding of tablet use by clinical staff across the nation
Since the introduction of the Apple iPad in 2010, the use of tablets by clinical staff in hospitals across the country has been growing steadily. Although there are no precise statistics on how many hospitals either distribute tablets to clinical staff or let them use their own devices in

---

FIGURE 17.4   **Sample Progress Report** (*continued*)

their work, the number of articles in trade magazines, exhibits at medical conferences, and discussions on discussion forums suggests that tablets are quickly becoming established in the clinical setting. And many hundreds of apps have already been written to enable users to carry out health-care-related tasks on tablets.

The most extensive set of data on tablets in hospitals relates to the use of the iPad, the first tablet on the market. Ottawa Hospital has distributed more than 1,000 iPads to clinical staff; California Hospital is piloting a program with more than 100 iPads for hospital use; Kaiser Permanente is testing the iPad for hospital and clinical workflow; and Cedars-Sinai Medical Center is testing the iPad in its hospital. The University of Chicago's Internal Medicine Residency Program uses the iPad; the iPad is also being distributed to first-year medical students at Stanford, University of California–Irvine, and University of San Francisco. In addition, there are reports of Windows-based and Android-based tablets being distributed at numerous other hospitals and medical schools (Husain, 2011).

> The writers skillfully integrate their secondary research into their discussion of the task. By doing so, they enhance their credibility.

Today, tablets have five main clinical applications (Carr, 2011):

- *Monitoring patients and collecting data.* Clinical staff connect tablets to the hospital's monitoring instruments to collect patient information and transfer it to patients' health records without significant human intervention. In addition, staff access patient information on their tablets.
- *Ordering prescriptions, authorizations, and refills.* Clinical staff use tablets to communicate instantly with the hospital pharmacy and off-site pharmacies, as well as with other departments within the hospital, such as the Imaging Department.
- *Scheduling appointments.* Clinical staff use tablets to schedule doctor and nurse visits and laboratory tests, to send reminders, and to handle re-scheduling and cancellations.
- *Conducting research on the fly.* Clinical staff use tablets to access medication databases and numerous reference works.
- *Educating patients.* Clinical staff use videos and animations to educate patients on their conditions and treatment options.

Tablets provide clinical staff with significant advantages. Staff do not need to go back to their offices to connect to the internet or to the hospital's own medical-record system. Staff save time, reduce paper usage, and reduce transcription errors by not having to enter nearly as much data by hand.

FIGURE 17.4　Sample Progress Report (*continued*)

Task 2: Determine the RRMC clinical staff's knowledge of and attitudes toward tablet use

On October 14, 2018, we sent all 147 clinical staff members an email linking to a four-question Qualtrix survey. In the email, we said that we were seeking opinions about tablet use by clinical-staff members who already own tablets and made clear that the survey would take less than two minutes to complete. (The questionnaire, including the responses, appears in the Appendix, page 9.)

We received 96 responses, which represents 65 percent of the 147 staff members. We cannot be certain that all 96 respondents who indicated that they are tablet owners in fact own tablets. We also do not know whether all those staff members who own a tablet responded. However, given that some 75 percent of physicians in a 2013 poll own tablets, we suspect that the 96 respondents accurately represent the proportion of our clinical staff who own tablets (Drinkwater, 2013).

Here are the four main findings from the survey of tablet owners:

- Some 47 percent of respondents own an Apple iPad, and 47 percent own either a Samsung Galaxy or another tablet that uses the Android operating system. Only 6 percent use the Microsoft Surface, one of the several Windows-based tablets.
- Some 58 percent of the respondents strongly agree with the statement that they are expert users of their tablets. Overall, 90 percent agree more than they disagree with the statement.
- Some 63 percent of respondents use their tablets for at least one clinical application. They have either loaded apps on their tablets themselves or had IT do so for them.
- Some 27 percent of the respondents would prefer to continue to use their own tablets for clinical applications, whereas 38 percent would prefer to use a tablet supplied by RRMC. Some 35 percent had no strong feelings either way. None of the respondents indicated that they would prefer not to use a tablet at all for clinical applications.

Task 3. Assess the BYOD and hospital-owned tablet models

Currently, hospitals use one of two models for giving clinical staff access to tablets: the bring-your-own-device (BYOD) model and the purchase model, whereby the hospital purchases tablets to distribute to staff. In this section, we will present our findings on the relative advantages of each model.

FIGURE 17.4   Sample Progress Report (*continued*)

Memo to Jill Bremerton, M.D.   November 14, 2018   Page 5

The BYOD model is based on the fact that, nationally, some three-quarters of physicians already own tablets (with the Apple iPad the single most popular model) (Drinkwater, 2013). We could find no data on how many nurses own tablets.

The main advantage of the BYOD model is that clinical staff already know and like their tablets; therefore, they are motivated to use them and less likely to need extensive training. In addition, the hardware costs are eliminated (or almost eliminated, since some hospitals choose to purchase some tablets for staff who do not have their own). Todd Richardson, CIO with Deaconess Health System, Evansville, Indiana (Jackson, 2011), argues that staff members who own their own tablets use and maintain them carefully: they know how to charge, clean, store, and protect them. In addition, the hospital doesn't have to worry about the question of liability if staff members lose them during personal use. And if the staff member moves on to a new position at a different hospital, there is no dispute about who owns the information on the tablet. All the hospital has to do is disable the staff member's account.

However, there are three main disadvantages to the BYOD model:
- Some clinical staff do not have their own tablets, and some who do don't want to use them at work; to make the advantages of tablet use available to all the clinical staff, therefore, the hospital needs to decide whether to purchase tablets and distribute them to these staff members.
- Labor costs are high because each tablet needs to be examined carefully by the hospital IT department to ensure that it contains no software that might interfere with or be incompatible with the health-care software that needs to be loaded onto it. This labor-intensive assessment by IT can seriously erode the cost savings from not having to buy the tablet itself.
- Chances of loss increase because the staff member is more likely to use the tablet at home as well as in the hospital.

Currently, we are studying the advantages and disadvantages of the other model for making tablets available to clinical staff: for the hospital to purchase the same tablet for each staff member.

We are now completing Task 3 and beginning work on Task 4.

The writers explain that they are in the process of completing Task 3.

FIGURE 17.4 Sample Progress Report (*continued*)

The Gantt chart shows the progress toward completing each of the project tasks. See the Tech Tip *"How To Create a Gantt Chart"* in Ch. 16 on p. 451 for advice on how to create Gantt charts.

Memo to Jill Bremerton, M.D.   November 14, 2018   Page 6

Task 4: Establish criteria for evaluating tablets
We will study the voluminous literature on tablets. We have already determined our first criterion: a cost of no more than $800 per device, fully configured with any commercial software needed to operate it. We will then determine the additional criteria to use in our study.

Task 5. Assess available tablets based on our criteria
We will study reviews in trade magazines and, if necessary, carry out on-site evaluations at RRMC.

Task 6. Analyze our data and prepare a recommendation report
We will draft our recommendation report and edit it in response to suggestions from interested readers among the clinical staff. Then, we will solicit one more round of edits and revise the report. Finally, we will present the report to you on December 14, 2018.

Updated Schedule

Figure 1 is an updated task schedule. The light blue bars represent tasks yet to be completed.

Tasks	Date of Tasks (by Weeks)									
Task 1: Research tablet use										
Task 2: Determine staff knowledge and attitudes										
Task 3: Research management models										
Task 4: Establish criteria										
Task 5: Assess tablets based on criteria										
Task 6: Prepare report										
	10	17	24	31	7	14	21	28	5	12
	Oct.				Nov.				Dec.	

Figure 1.   **Schedule of Project Tasks**

FIGURE 17.4   **Sample Progress Report** (*continued*)

Conclusion

We have successfully completed Tasks 1–2 (and part of 3) and begun Tasks 4 and 5. We are on schedule to complete all tasks by the December 14 deadline. We have a good understanding of how tablets are used nationwide, and we have completed our survey of tablet users among the RRMC clinical staff, as well as half of our study of the two administrative models used by hospitals. We are currently completing that task and are about to begin to establish criteria and analyze tablets based on them. In the report we will present on December 14, we will include our recommendation on how we think RRMC should proceed to take better advantage of the potential for clinical use of tablets.

Please contact Jeremy Elkins, at jelkins@rrmc.org or at 555-444-3967, or Eloise Carruthers, at ecarruthers@rrmc.org or at 555-444-3982, if you have questions or comments or would like to discuss this project further.

The conclusion summarizes the status of the project.

The writers end with a polite offer to provide additional information.

References

Carr, D. F. (2011, May 21). Healthcare puts tablets to the test. *InformationWeek Healthcare*. Retrieved October 1, 2018, from http://www.informationweek.com/healthcare/mobile-wireless/healthcare-puts-tablets-to-the-test/229503387

Drinkwater, D. (2013, April 19). Three in 4 physicians are using tablets; some are even prescribing apps. *TabTimes*. Retrieved October 12, 2018, from http://tabtimes.com/news/ittech-stats-research/2013/04/19/3-4-physicians-are-using-tablets-some-are-even-prescribing

Husain, I. (2011, March 10). Why Apple's iPad will beat Android tablets for hospital use. *iMedicalApps*. Retrieved October 15, 2018, from http://www.imedicalapps.com/2011/03/ipad-beat-android-tablets-hospital-medical-use/

Jackson, S. (2011, August 3). Why physicians should buy their own mobile devices. *FierceMobileHealthcare*. Retrieved October 16, 2018, from http://www.fiercemobilehealthcare.com/story/why-physicians-should-buy-their-own-mobile-devices/2011-08-03

This list of references follows the APA documentation style, which is discussed in Appendix, Part B, p. 632. The APA documentation system calls for References to begin on a new page. Check with your instructor.

FIGURE 17.4   **Sample Progress Report** (*continued*)

Presenting the percentage data in boldface after each question is a clear way to communicate how the respondents replied. Although most readers will not be interested in the raw data, some will.

Memo to Jill Bremerton, M.D. November 14, 2018 Page 9

Appendix: Clinical-Staff Questionnaire

This is the questionnaire we distributed to the 147 RRMC clinical staff members. We received 96 responses. The numbers in boldface below represent the percentage of respondents who chose each response.

Questionnaire on Tablet Use at RRMC

Directions: As you may know, Dr. Bremerton is conducting a study to determine whether to institute a formal policy on tablet use by clinical staff.

If you own a tablet device, please respond to the following four questions. Your opinions can help us decide whether and how to develop a policy for tablet use at RRMC. We greatly appreciate your answering the following four questions.

1. Which brand of tablet do you own?
   47% Apple iPad
   28% Samsung Galaxy
   9% Amazon Kindle Fire
   6% Microsoft Surface
   10% Other (please name the brand) **(Respondents named the Asus, Google Nexus, and a Toshiba model.)**

2. "I consider myself an expert user of my tablet."
   Strongly disagree ____ **8%** **2%** **13%** **19%** **58%** Strongly agree

3. Do you currently use your tablet for a clinical application, such as monitoring patients or ordering procedures?
   63% Yes
   37% No

4. If RRMC were to adopt a policy of using tablets for clinical applications (and to supply the appropriate software and training), which response best describes your attitude?
   27% I would prefer to use my own tablet.
   38% I would prefer to use a hospital-supplied tablet.
   35% I don't have strong feelings either way about using my own or a hospital-supplied tablet.
   0% I would prefer not to use any tablet at all for clinical applications.

Thank you!

FIGURE 17.4 Sample Progress Report (*continued*)

Writing Incident Reports

An incident report describes an event such as a workplace accident, a health or safety emergency, or an equipment problem. (Specialized kinds of incident reports go by other names, such as *accident reports* or *trouble reports*.) The purpose of an incident report is to explain what happened, why it happened, and what the organization did (or is going to do) to follow up on the incident. Incident reports often contain a variety of graphics, including tables, drawings, diagrams, and photographs, as well as videos.

Incident reports can range from single-page forms that are filled out on paper or online to reports hundreds of pages long. Figure 17.5 shows an accident form used at a university.

UNC – Chapel Hill – Facilities Services – Safety Plan

APPENDIX A

Employee's Accident Report Form
University of North Carolina at Chapel Hill

This form is to be completed by the employee and forwarded to the Health and Safety office as soon as practicable after the injury. (See Human Resources Manual)

Accident Date:

1. Name of employee:

2. Date and time of injury:

3. Describe how the injury occurred:

4. Describe what job duty you were doing at the time of your injury:

5. Describe what part of your body was injured:

6. Describe what you would recommend to prevent a reoccurrence:

7. Further information you would like to include regarding your injury:

Employee signature   Date

http://www.fac.unc.edu

FIGURE 17.5   An Accident Report Form
Source: University of North Carolina–Chapel Hill Environment, Health, and Safety.

Figure 17.6 is the executive summary of a National Transportation Safety Board accident report on a 2012 head-on collision between two freight trains in Oklahoma. Investigators spent many months researching and writing the full report.

FIGURE 17.6 **Executive Summary of a Complex Accident Report**

Information from National Transportation Safety Board, 2013: www.ntsb.gov /investigations/AccidentReports/Pages /RAR1302.aspx.

The summary—two pages near the beginning of a 65-page report—begins with the basic facts about the accident.

On Sunday, June 24, 2012, at 10:02 a.m. central daylight time, eastbound Union Pacific Railroad (UP) freight train ZLAAH-22 and westbound UP freight train AAMMLX-22 collided head-on while operating on straight track on the UP Pratt subdivision near Goodwell, Oklahoma. Skies were clear, the temperature was 89°F, and visibility was 10 miles.

The collision derailed 3 locomotives and 24 cars of the eastbound train and 2 locomotives and 8 cars of the westbound train. The engineer and the conductor of the eastbound train and the engineer of the westbound train were killed. The conductor of the westbound train jumped to safety. During the collision and derailment, several fuel tanks from the derailed locomotives ruptured, releasing diesel fuel that ignited and burned. Damage was estimated at $14.8 million.

The writers discuss the probable cause of the accident and the result- ing damage to the trains.

The National Transportation Safety Board determines that the probable cause of this accident was the eastbound Union Pacific Railroad train crew's lack of response to wayside signals because of the engineer's inability to see and correctly interpret the signals; the conductor's disengagement from his duties; and the lack of positive train control, which would have stopped the train and prevented the collision regardless of the crew's inaction. Contributing to the accident was a medical examination process that failed to decertify the engineer before his deteriorating vision adversely affected his ability to operate a train safely.

The writers explain the issues raised by this fatal accident.

The accident investigation focused on the following safety issues:
- The actions and responsibilities of the train crews: Crew conversations in the locomotive cab concerning signal aspects, radio transmissions, or any condition that can affect the safe operation of the train are important crew activities. In this accident, as the train passed signals for advance approach, approach, and stop, the engineer actively adjusted the throttle and dynamic brake as if all three signals were clear. The fact that the conductor was disengaged from his duties and did not appropriately intervene as the train proceeded through the signals demonstrates . . .
- The medical examination process for railroad engineer certification: The UP's medical records for the engineer of the eastbound train indicated that the engineer had passed his required vision test in 2009. However, the medical records from the engineer's personal physician, his ophthalmologist, and his optometrist documented . . .
- The survivability of event recorder data: The lead and trailing locomotives of both trains in this accident had event recorders to capture and preserve operational data that is important to accident investigation. However, most of the data could not be retrieved after the severe damage to the lead locomotives from the postaccident fire. . .

(continued)

FIGURE 17.6 Executive Summary of a Complex Accident Report (*continued*)

- The need for implementation of positive train control: Before reaching the Goodwell siding, the eastbound train crew had passed three signals without appropriately responding by slowing and then stopping their train. Regardless of the reason for the crew's nonresponse, had a positive train control system been in place in the area of the accident, it would have slowed and stopped the train, avoiding the collision.

As a result of this investigation, the National Transportation Safety Board makes safety recommendations to the Federal Railroad Administration, the Brotherhood of Locomotive Engineers and Trainmen, . . . The National Transportation Safety Board also reiterates recommendations to the Federal Railroad Administration and the Association of American Railroads and reclassifies three recommendations to the Federal Railroad Administration.

Finally, the writers list the results of the investigation.

Writing Meeting Minutes

Minutes, an organization's official record of a meeting, are distributed to all those who belong to the committee or group represented at the meeting. Sometimes, minutes are written by administrative assistants; other times they are written by technical professionals or technical communicators.

For more about conducting meetings, see Ch. 4.

In writing minutes, be clear, comprehensive, objective, and diplomatic. Do not interpret what happened; simply report it. Because meetings rarely follow the agenda perfectly, you might find it challenging to provide an accurate record of the meeting. If necessary, interrupt the discussion to request a clarification.

Do not record emotional exchanges between participants. Because minutes are the official record of the meeting, you want them to reflect positively on the participants and the organization. For example, in a meeting a person might say, undiplomatically, that another person's idea is stupid, a comment that might lead to an argument. Don't record the argument. Instead, describe the outcome: "After a discussion of the merits of the two approaches, the chair asked the Facilities Committee to consider the approaches and report back to membership at the next meeting."

Figure 17.7 (on p. 482), an example of an effective set of minutes, was written using a Microsoft template. (For more on templates, see Chapter 3.) Many organizations today use templates like this one, which has three advantages:

1. Because it is a word-processing template, the note taker can enter information on his or her computer or tablet during the meeting, reducing the time it takes to publish the minutes.

2. Because the template is a form, it prompts the note taker to fill in the appropriate information, thus reducing the chances that he or she will overlook something important.

3. Because the template is a table, readers quickly become accustomed to reading it and thereby learn where to look for the information they seek.

The first section of this template calls for information about the logistics of the meeting. You can modify the template to make it appropriate for your organization.

Weekly Planning Committee Meeting

MINUTES   February 14, 2020   3:40 p.m.   conference room

meeting called by	Principal Robert Barson
type of meeting	regular weekly
note taker	Zenda Hill
attendees	William Sipe, Patty Leahy, George Zaerr, Herbert Simon, Robert Barson, Zenda Hill. Absent: Heather Evett

The second section of this template is devoted to the agenda items for the meeting.

Agenda topics

2 minutes   approval of minutes   Zenda Hill

discussion	The minutes of the February 7, 2020, meeting were read.	
action items	**person responsible**	**deadline**
One correction was made: In paragraph 2, "800 hours" was replaced with "80 hours." The minutes were then unanimously approved.	Zenda Hill	N/A

Note that for each agenda item, the note taker is prompted to state how long the discussion took, the subject of the discussion, and the name of the person leading the discussion.

30 minutes   authorization for antidrug presentation by Alan Winston   Principal Barson

discussion	Principal Barson reported on his discussion with Peggy Giles of the School District, who offered positive comments about Winston's presentations at other schools in the district last year.
	Mr. Zaerr expressed concern about the effect of the visit on the teaching schedule. Principal Barson acknowledged that the visit would disrupt one whole day but said that the chairs unanimously approved of the visit. Student participation would be voluntary, and the chairs offered to give review sessions to those students who elected not to attend.
	Ms. Hill asked if there was any new business. There was none.

For each agenda item, the note taker records the main points of the discussion and the action items. Because the template calls for the action item (such as a vote or a task to be done), the name of the person responsible for doing the task, and the deadline for the task, there should be no confusion about who is to do which task and when it is due.

action items	person responsible	deadline
Ms. Hill called for a vote on the motion. The motion carried 5–0, with one abstention.	Ms. Hill will arrange the Winston visit.	February 23, 2020
There being no new business, Ms. Hill moved that the committee adjourn. Motion passed. The committee adjourned at 4:15 p.m.	N/A	N/A

FIGURE 17.7   A Set of Meeting Minutes

WRITER'S CHECKLIST

☐ Did you choose an appropriate application for the informational report? *(p. 463)*

Does the directive

☐ clearly and politely explain your message? *(p. 465)*

☐ explain your reasoning, if appropriate? *(p. 465)*

Does the field report

☐ clearly explain the important information? *(p. 467)*

☐ use, if appropriate, a problem–methods–results–conclusion–recommendations organization? *(p. 467)*

Does the progress or status report

☐ clearly announce that it is a progress or status report? *(p. 469)*

☐ use an appropriate organization? *(p. 469)*

☐ clearly and honestly report on the subject and forecast the problems and possibilities of the future work? *(p. 469)*

☐ include, if appropriate, an appendix containing supporting materials that substantiate the discussion? *(p. 470)*

Does the incident report

☐ explain what happened? *(p. 479)*

☐ explain why it happened? *(p. 479)*

☐ explain what the organization did about it or will do about it? *(p. 479)*

Do the minutes

☐ provide the necessary housekeeping details about the meeting? *(p. 481)*

☐ explain the events of the meeting accurately? *(p. 481)*

☐ reflect positively on the participants and the organization? *(p. 481)*

EXERCISES

1. As the manager of Lewis, Lewis, and Wollensky Law, LLC, you have been informed by some clients that tattoos on the arms and necks of your employees are creating a negative impression. Write a directive in the form of a memo defining a new policy: employees are required to wear clothing that covers any tattoos on their arms and necks. For more about memos, see Ch. 14, p. 386.

2. Write a progress report about the research project you are working on in response to Exercise 3 on p. 460 in Chapter 16. If the proposal was a collaborative effort, collaborate with the same group members on the progress report.

3. **TEAM EXERCISE** You are one of three members of the administrative council of your college's student association. Recently, the three of you have concluded that your weekly meetings, which are open to all students, have become chaotic. There are two main reasons for this: you do not use parliamentary procedure (rules for conducting meetings so that they are efficient and fair), and controversial issues have arisen that have attracted an increasing number of students. You have decided that it is time to consider adopting parliamentary procedures. Look on the web for models of parliamentary procedure. Is there one that you can adopt? Could you combine elements of several models to create an effective process? Find or write a brief set of procedures, being sure to cite your sources. In a memo to your instructor, discuss the advantages and disadvantages of the model you propose, and submit it along with the procedures.

CASE 17: Writing a Directive

You work for a company that is implementing a new waste-reduction initiative, with the goal of saving money and benefiting the environment. Your supervisor has given you an outline of the new policy and asked you to draft a directive that she will distribute to department heads. The directive should explain the purpose and importance of the policy and outline ways department heads and their employees will be expected to participate. If your instructor has assigned it, go to Achieve to get started drafting the directive.

18

Writing Recommendation Reports

➡

CHAPTER 17 DISCUSSED informational reports: those in which the writer's main purpose is to present information. This chapter discusses recommendation reports. A recommendation report also presents information but goes one step further by offering suggestions about what the readers ought to do next.

Here are examples of the kinds of questions a recommendation report might address:

- **What should we do about Problem X?** What should we do about the increased cost of copper, which we use in manufacturing our line of electronic components?

- **Should we do Function X?** Although we cannot afford to pay tuition for all college courses our employees wish to take, can we reimburse them for classes directly related to their work?

- **Should we use Technology A or Technology B to do Function X?** Should we continue to supply our employees with laptops, or should we switch to tablets?

- **We currently use Method A to do Function X. Should we be using Method B?** We sort our bar-coded mail by hand; should we buy an automatic sorter?

Each of these questions can lead to a wide variety of recommendations, ranging from "do nothing" to "study this some more" to "take the following actions immediately."

Understanding the Role of Recommendation Reports

A recommendation report can be the final link in a chain of documents that begins with a proposal and continues with one or more progress reports. This last, formal report is often called a *final report*, a *project report*, a *recommendation report*, a *completion report*, or simply a *report*. The sample report shown in Figure 18.8 (pp. 504–27) is the recommendation report in the series about tablet computers at Rawlings Regional Medical Center presented in Figure 16.6 (pp. 453–59) in Chapter 16 and Figure 17.4 (pp. 471–78) in Chapter 17.

A recommendation report can also be a freestanding document, one that was not preceded by a proposal or by progress reports. For instance, you might be asked for a recommendation on whether your company should offer employees comp time (compensating those who work overtime with time off) instead of overtime pay. This task would call for you to research the subject and write a single recommendation report.

Most recommendation reports discuss questions of feasibility. *Feasibility* is a measure of the practicality of a course of action. For instance, a company might conduct a *feasibility study* of whether it should acquire a competing company. In this case, the two courses of action are to acquire the competing

For more about proposals and progress reports, see Ch. 16 and Ch. 17.

company or not to acquire it. Or a company might do a study to determine which make and model of truck to buy for its fleet.

A feasibility report is a report that answers three kinds of questions:

- **Questions of possibility.** We would like to build a new rail line to link our warehouse and our retail outlet, but if we cannot raise the money, the project is not possible. Even if we can find the money, do we have government authorization? If we do, are the soil conditions appropriate for the rail link?

- **Questions of economic wisdom.** Even if we can afford to build the rail link, should we do so? If we use all our resources on this project, what other projects will have to be postponed or canceled? Is there a less expensive or a less financially risky way to achieve the same goals?

- **Questions of perception.** Because our company's workers have recently accepted a temporary wage freeze, they might view the rail link as an inappropriate use of funds. The truckers' union might see it as a threat to truckers' job security. Some members of the public might also be interested parties, because any large-scale construction might affect the environment.

Using a Problem-Solving Model for Preparing Recommendation Reports

The writing process for a recommendation report is similar to that for any other technical document. The Focus on Process box that follows outlines this process.

In addition to this model of the writing process, you need a problem-solving model for conducting the analysis that will enable you to write the recommendation report. The following discussion explains in more detail the problem-solving model shown in Figure 18.1 on page 488.

IDENTIFY THE PROBLEM OR OPPORTUNITY

What is not working or is not working as well as it might? What situation presents an opportunity to decrease costs or improve the quality of a product or service? Without a clear statement of your problem or opportunity, you cannot plan your research.

For example, your company has found that employees who smoke are absent and ill more often than those who don't smoke. Your supervisor has asked you to investigate whether the company should offer a free smoking-cessation program. The company can offer the program only if the company's insurance carrier will pay for it. The first thing you need to do is talk with the insurance agent; if the insurance carrier will pay for the program, you can proceed with your investigation. If the agent says no, you have to determine whether another insurance carrier offers better coverage or whether there is some other way to encourage employees to stop smoking.

FOCUS ON PROCESS: Recommendation Reports

In writing recommendation reports, pay special attention to these steps in the writing process.

PLANNING	Analyze your audience, determine your purpose, and visualize the deliverable: the report you will submit. Conduct appropriate secondary and primary research. See Chapter 5 for more about analyzing your audience and purpose; see Chapter 6 for more on research.
DRAFTING	Write a draft of the report. Large projects often call for many writers and therefore benefit from shared document spaces. Review the writing advice in Chapter 3 and the collaboration advice in Chapter 4; see Chapter 8 for tips on writing persuasively.
REVISING	Think again about your audience and purpose, and then make appropriate changes to your draft. See the Writer's Checklist at the end of this chapter.
EDITING	Improve the writing in the report, starting with the largest issues of development and emphasis and working down to the sections, paragraphs, sentences, and individual words. See Chapter 9 for help with emphasis and Chapter 10 for advice on writing correct and effective sentences.
PROOFREADING	Go through the draft slowly, making sure you have written what you wanted to write. Get help from others. See Appendix, Part C, for proofreading tips.

ESTABLISH CRITERIA FOR RESPONDING TO THE PROBLEM OR OPPORTUNITY

Criteria are standards against which you measure your options. Criteria can be classified into two categories: *necessary* and *desirable*. For example, if you want to buy a photocopier for your business, necessary criteria might be that each copy cost less than two cents to produce and that the photocopier be able to handle oversized documents. If the photocopier doesn't fulfill those two criteria, you will not consider it further. By contrast, desirable criteria might include that the photocopier be capable of double-sided copying and stapling. Desirable criteria let you make distinctions among a variety of similar objects, objectives, actions, or effects. If a photocopier does not fulfill a desirable criterion, you will still consider it, although it will be less attractive.

Until you establish your criteria, you don't know what your options are. Sometimes you are given your criteria: your supervisor tells you how much money you can spend, for instance, and that figure becomes one of your necessary criteria. Other times, you derive your criteria from your research.

**FIGURE 18.1
A Problem-Solving
Model for
Recommendation
Reports**

As you work through this process, you might find that you need to go back to a previous step — or even to the first step — as you think more about your subject, audience, and purpose.

Identify the Problem or Opportunity

What is not working as well as it might, or what situation can we exploit?

Establish Criteria for Responding to the Problem or Opportunity

For example, any solution to our problem must reduce the number of manufacturing defects by 50 percent and cannot cost more than $75,000.

Determine the Options

List the possible courses of action, from doing nothing to taking immediate action.

Study Each Option According to the Criteria

Analyze each option by studying the data on how well it satisfies each criterion.

Draw Conclusions About Each Option

For each option, determine whether (or how well) it satisfies each criterion.

Formulate Recommendations Based on the Conclusions

Present your suggestions about how to proceed.

DETERMINE THE OPTIONS

After you establish your criteria, you determine your options. *Options* are potential courses of action you can take in responding to a problem or opportunity. Determining your options might be simple or complicated.

Sometimes your options are presented to you. For instance, your supervisor asks you to study two vendors for accounting services and recommend one of them. The options are Vendor A or Vendor B. That's simple.

In other cases, you have to consider a series of options. For example, your department's photocopier is old and breaking down. Your first decision is whether to repair it or replace it. Once you have answered that question, you might have to make more decisions. If you are going to replace it, what features should you look for in a new one? Each time you make a decision, you have to answer more questions until, eventually, you arrive at a recommendation. For a complicated scenario like this, you might find it helpful to use logic boxes or flowcharts to sketch the logic of your options, as shown in Figure 18.2.

As you research your topic, your understanding of your options will likely change. At this point, however, it is useful to understand the basic logic of your options or series of options.

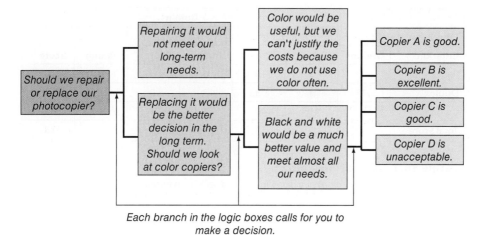

Each branch in the logic boxes calls for you to
make a decision.

FIGURE 18.2 Using Logic Boxes To Plot a Series of Options

STUDY EACH OPTION ACCORDING TO THE CRITERIA

Once you have identified your options (or series of options), study each one according to the criteria. For the photocopier project, secondary research would include studying articles about photocopiers in technical magazines or reputable websites and specification sheets from the different manufacturers. Primary research might include observing product demonstrations as well as interviewing representatives from different manufacturers and managers who have purchased different brands.

For more about research techniques, see Ch. 6.

To make the analysis of the options as objective as possible, professionals sometimes create a *decision matrix*, a tool for systematically evaluating each option according to each criterion. A decision matrix is a table (or a spreadsheet), as shown in Figure 18.3 (on p. 490). Here the writer is nearly at the end of his series of options: he is evaluating three similar photocopiers according to three criteria. Each criterion has its own weight, which suggests how important it is. The greater the weight, the more important the criterion.

As shown in Figure 18.3, the criterion of pages per minute is relatively unimportant: it receives a weight of 1. For this reason, the Ricoh copier, even though it receives a high rating for pages per minute (9), receives only a modest score of 9 ($1 \times 9 = 9$) on this criterion. However, the criterion of color copying is quite important, with a weight of 4. On this criterion, the Ricoh, with its rating of 10, achieves a very high score ($4 \times 10 = 40$).

But a decision matrix cannot stand on its own. You need to explain your methods. That is, in the discussion or in footnotes to the matrix, you need to explain the following three decisions:

1. **Why you chose each criterion—or didn't choose a criterion the reader might have expected to see included.** For instance, why did you choose duplexing (double-sided printing) but not image scanning?

Criteria and Weight		Options					
		Ricoh		Xerox		Sharp	
Criterion	Weight	Rating	Score[1]	Rating	Score[1]	Rating	Score[1]
Pages/min.	1	9	9	6	6	3	3
Duplex	3	1	3	3	9	10	30
Color	4	10	40	1	4	10	40
Total Score			52		19		73

[1]Score = weight × rating.

FIGURE 18.3   A Decision Matrix
Spreadsheet programs often contain templates for creating decision matrices.

2. **Why you assigned a particular weight to each criterion.** For example, why is the copier's ability to make color copies four times more important than its speed?

3. **Why you assigned a particular rating to each option.** For example, why does one copier receive a rating of only 1 on duplexing, whereas another receives a 3 and a third receives a 10?

A decision matrix is helpful only if your readers understand your methods and agree with the logic you used in choosing the criteria and assigning the weight and ratings for each option.

Although a decision matrix has its limitations, it is useful for both you and your readers. For you as the writer, the main advantage is that it helps you do a methodical analysis. For your readers, it makes your analysis easier to follow because it clearly presents your methods and results.

DRAW CONCLUSIONS ABOUT EACH OPTION

Whether you use a decision matrix or a less formal means of recording your evaluations, the next step is to draw conclusions about the options you studied—by interpreting your results and writing evaluative statements about the options.

For the study of photocopiers, your conclusion might be that the Sharp model is the best copier: it meets all your necessary criteria and the greatest number of desirable criteria, or it scores highest on your matrix. Depending on your readers' preferences, you can present your conclusions in any one of three ways.

- **Rank all the options:** the Sharp copier is the best option, the Ricoh copier is second best, and so forth.

- **Classify all the options in one of two categories:** acceptable and unacceptable.

- **Present a compound conclusion:** the Sharp offers the most technical capabilities; the Ricoh is the best value.

FORMULATE RECOMMENDATIONS BASED ON THE CONCLUSIONS

If you conclude that Option A is better than Option B—and you see no obvious problems with Option A—recommend Option A. But if the problem has changed or your company's priorities or resources have changed, you might decide to recommend a course of action that is inconsistent with the conclusions you derived. Your responsibility is to use your judgment and recommend the best course of action.

ETHICS NOTE

PRESENTING HONEST RECOMMENDATIONS

As you formulate your recommendations, you might know what your readers want you to say. For example, they might want you to recommend the cheapest option, or one that uses a certain kind of technology, or one that is supplied by a certain vendor. Naturally, you want to be able to recommend what they want, but sometimes the facts won't let you. Your responsibility is to tell the truth—to do the research honestly and competently and then present the findings honestly. Your name goes on the report. You want to be able to defend your recommendations based on the evidence and your reasoning.

One worrisome situation that arises frequently is that none of the options would be a complete success or none would work at all. What should you do? You should tell the truth about the options, warts and all. Give the best advice you can, even if that advice is to do nothing.

Writing Recommendation Reports

The following discussion presents a basic structure for a recommendation report. Remember that every document you write should reflect its audience, purpose, and subject. Therefore, you might need to modify, add to, or delete some of the elements discussed here.

Reports that are lengthy and complex are often written collaboratively. As you begin the project that will culminate in the report, consider whether it would make sense to set up a shared writing space, a wiki, or some other method for you and your team members to write and edit the report collaboratively.

For more on collaboration, see Ch. 4.

The easiest way to draft a report is to think of it as consisting of three sections: the front matter, the body, and the back matter. Table 18.1 on page 492 shows the purposes of and typical elements in these three sections.

You will probably draft the body before the front and the back matter. This sequence is easiest because you think through what you want to say in the body and then draft the front and back matter based on it.

If you are writing your recommendation report for readers from other cultures, keep in mind that conventions differ from one culture to another. In the United States, reports are commonly organized from general to specific. That is, the most general information (the abstract and the executive summary) appears early in the report. In many cultures, however, reports

TABLE 18.1   Elements of a Typical Report

SECTION OF THE REPORT	PURPOSES OF THE SECTION	TYPICAL ELEMENTS IN THE SECTION
Front matter	• to orient the reader to the subject • to provide summaries for technical and managerial readers • to help readers navigate the report • to help readers decide whether to read the document	• letter of transmittal (p. 495) • cover (p. 495) • title page (p. 495) • abstract (p. 495) • table of contents (p. 496) • list of illustrations (p. 497) • executive summary (p. 499)
Body	• to provide the most comprehensive account of the project, from the problem or opportunity that motivated it to the methods and the most important findings	• introduction (p. 493) • methods (p. 493) • results (p. 493) • conclusions (p. 494) • recommendations (p. 494)
Back matter	• to present supplementary information, such as more detailed explanations than are provided in the body • to enable readers to consult the secondary sources the writers used	• glossary (p. 500) • list of symbols (p. 500) • references (p. 502) • appendixes (p. 503)

are organized from specific to general. Detailed discussions of methods and results precede discussions of the important findings.

Similarly, elements of the front and back matter are rooted in culture. For instance, in some cultures—or in some organizations—writers do not create executive summaries, or their executive summaries differ in length or organization from those discussed here. According to interface designer Pia Honold (1999), German users of high-tech products rely on the table of contents in a manual because they like to understand the scope and organization of the manual. Therefore, writers of manuals for German readers should include comprehensive, detailed tables of contents.

Study samples of writing produced by people from the culture you are addressing to see how they organize their reports and use front and back matter.

WRITING THE BODY OF THE REPORT

The elements that make up the body of a report are discussed here in the order in which they usually appear in a report. However, you should draft the elements in whatever order you prefer. The sample recommendation report shown in Figure 18.8 (pp. 504–27) includes these elements.

Introduction The introduction helps readers understand the discussion that follows. Start by analyzing who your readers are. Then consider these questions:

- **What is the subject of the report?** If the report follows a proposal and a progress report, you can probably copy this information from one of those documents, modifying it as necessary. Reusing this information is efficient and ethical.

- **What is the purpose of the report?** The purpose of the report is not the purpose of the project. The purpose of the report is to explain a project from beginning (identifying a problem or an opportunity) to end (presenting recommendations).

- **What is the background of the report?** Include this information, even if you have presented it before; some of your readers might not have read your previous documents or might have forgotten them.

- **What are your sources of information?** Briefly describe your primary and secondary research, to prepare your readers for a more detailed discussion of your sources in subsequent sections of the report.

- **What is the scope of the report?** Indicate the topics you are including, as well as those you are not.

- **What are the most significant findings?** Summarize the most significant findings of the project.

- **What are your recommendations?** In a short report containing a few simple recommendations, include those recommendations in the introduction. In a lengthy report containing many complex recommendations, briefly summarize them in the introduction, then refer readers to the more detailed discussion in the recommendations section.

- **What is the organization of the report?** Indicate your organizational pattern so that readers can understand where you are going and why.

- **What key terms are you using in the report?** The introduction is an appropriate place to define new terms. If you need to define many terms, place the definitions in a glossary and refer readers to it in the introduction.

Methods The methods section answers the question, "What did you do?" In drafting the methods section, consider your readers' knowledge of the field, their perception of you, and the uniqueness of the project, as well as their reasons for reading the report and their attitudes toward the project. Provide enough information to enable readers to understand what you did and why you did it that way. If others will be using the report to duplicate your methods, include sufficient detail.

Results Whereas the methods section answers the question, "What did you do?" the results section answers the question, "What did you see or determine?"

Results are the data you discovered or compiled. Present the results objectively, without comment. Save the interpretation of the results—your conclusions—for later. If you combine results and conclusions, your readers might be unable to follow your reasoning and might not be able to tell whether the evidence justifies your conclusions.

Your audience's needs will help you decide how to structure the results. How much they know about the subject, what they plan to do with the report, what they expect your recommendation(s) to be—these and many other factors will affect how you present the results. For instance, suppose that your company is considering installing a VoIP phone system that will enable employees to make telephone calls over the internet, and you conducted the research on the available systems. In the introduction, you explain the disadvantages of the company's current phone system. In the methods section, you describe how you established the criteria you applied to the available phone systems, as well as your research procedures. In the results section, you provide the details of each phone system you are considering, as well as the results of your evaluation of each system.

For more about evaluating evidence and drawing conclusions, see Ch. 6.

Conclusions Conclusions answer the question, "What does it mean?" They are the implications of the results. To draw conclusions, you need to think carefully about your results, weighing whether they point clearly to a single meaning.

Recommendations Recommendations answer the question, "What should we do?" As discussed earlier in this chapter, recommendations do not always flow directly from conclusions. Always consider recommending that the organization take no action or no action at this time.

| Methods
What did you do? | → | Results
What did you see or determine? | → | Conclusions
What does it mean? | → | Recommendations
What should we do? |

GUIDELINES Writing Recommendations

As you draft your recommendations, consider the following four factors:

▶ **Content.** Be clear and specific. If the project has been unsuccessful, don't simply recommend that your readers "try some other alternatives." What alternatives do you recommend and why?

▶ **Tone.** When you recommend a new course of action, be careful not to offend whoever formulated the earlier course. Do not write that following your recommendations will "correct the mistakes" that have been made. Instead, your recommendations should "offer great promise for success." A restrained, understated tone is more persuasive because it shows that you are interested only in the good of your organization, not personal rivalries.

▶ **Form.** If the report leads to only one recommendation, use traditional paragraphs. If the report leads to more than one recommendation, consider a numbered list.

▶ **Location.** Consider including a summary of the recommendations—or, if they are brief, the full list—after the executive summary or in the introduction as well as at the end of the body of the report.

WRITING THE FRONT MATTER

Front matter is common in reports, proposals, and manuals. As indicated in Table 18.1 on page 492, front matter helps readers understand the whole report and find the information they seek. Most organizations have established formats for front matter. Study the style guide used in your company or, if there isn't one, examples from the files to see how other writers have assembled their reports.

Letter of Transmittal In the letter of transmittal, which can take the form of a letter, a memo, or even an email, the writer introduces the primary reader to the purpose and content of the report. In addition, the writer often states who authorized or commissioned the report and acknowledges any assistance he or she received in carrying out the project. The letter of transmittal is attached to the report, bound in with it, or simply placed on top of it. Even though the letter likely contains little information that is not included elsewhere in the report, it is important because it is the first thing the reader sees. It establishes a courteous and professional tone. Letters of transmittal are customary even when the writer and the reader both work for the same organization. See the beginning of the sample recommendation report shown in Figure 18.8 (pp. 504–27) for an example of a transmittal letter in the form of a memo.

For more about formatting a letter, see "Writing Letters" in Ch. 14 on p. 377.

Cover Although some reports do not have covers, reports that will be handled a lot or that will be exposed to harsh environmental conditions, such as water or grease, often do. The cover usually contains the title of the report, the name and position of the writer, the date of submission, and the name or logo of the writer's company. Sometimes the cover also includes a security notice or a statement of proprietary information.

Title Page A title page includes at least the title of the report, the name of the writer, and the date of submission. A more complex title page might also include a project number, a list of additional personnel who contributed to the report, and a distribution list. See the third page of the sample recommendation report shown in Figure 18.8 for an example of a title page.

Abstract An abstract is a brief technical summary of the report, usually no more than 200 words. It addresses readers who are familiar with the technical subject and who need to decide whether they want to read the full report. In an abstract, you can use technical terminology and refer to advanced concepts in the field. Abstracts are sometimes published by abstract services, which are useful resources for researchers.

Abstracts often contain a list of half a dozen or so keywords, which are entered into electronic databases. As the writer, one of your tasks is to think of the various keywords that should lead people to the information in your report.

There are two types of abstracts: descriptive and informative. A *descriptive abstract*—sometimes called a *topical, indicative,* or *table-of-contents abstract*—describes the kinds of information contained in the report. It does not provide the major findings (important results, conclusions, or recommendations). It simply lists the topics covered, giving equal emphasis to each. Figure 18.4 is a descriptive abstract from a report by a utility company about its pilot program for measuring how much electricity its customers are using. A descriptive abstract is used most often when space is at a premium. Some government proposals, for example, call for a descriptive abstract to be placed at the bottom of the title page.

An *informative abstract* presents the major findings. If you don't know which kind of abstract the reader wants, write an informative one.

The distinction between descriptive and informative abstracts is not clear-cut. Sometimes you might have to combine elements of both in a single abstract. For instance, if there are 15 recommendations—far too many to list—you might simply note that the report includes numerous recommendations.

See page ii of the sample recommendation report shown in Figure 18.8 for an example of an informative abstract.

Table of Contents The table of contents, the most important guide to navigating the report, has two main functions: to help readers find the information they want and to help them understand the scope and organization of the report.

A table of contents uses the same headings as the report itself. Therefore, to create an effective table of contents, you must first make sure that the headings are clear and that you have provided enough of them. If the

This abstract is descriptive rather than informative because it does not present any of the major data from the survey or present the recommendations that are mentioned in the final sentence.

> **Abstract**
> **"Design of a Radio-Based System for Distribution Automation"**
> **by Brian D. Raven**
> A new survey by the Maryland Public Utilities Commission suggests that utilities have not effectively explained to consumers the benefits of smart meters. The two-year study of 86,000 consumers concludes that the long-term benefits of smart meters will not be realized until consumers understand the benefits of shifting some of their power usage to off-peak hours in response to the data they receive from their meters. The study presents recommendations for utilities and municipal governments to improve customer understanding of how to use the smart meters effectively.
>
> Keywords: smart meters, distribution systems, load, customer attitudes, power consumption, utilities, Maryland Public Utilities Commission

FIGURE 18.4 Descriptive Abstract

table of contents shows no entry for five or six pages, you probably need to partition that section of the report into additional subsections. In fact, some tables of contents have one entry, or even several, for every report page.

The following table of contents, which relies exclusively on generic headings (those that describe an entire class of items), is too general to be useful.

Table of Contents

This methods section, which goes from page 4 to page 18, should have subentries to break up the text and to help readers find the information they seek.

For more informative headings, combine the generic and the specific:

Recommendations: Five Ways to Improve Information-Retrieval Materials Used in the Calcification Study

Results of the Commuting-Time Analysis

Then build more subheadings into the report itself. For instance, for the "Recommendations" example above, you could create a subheading for each of the five recommendations. Once you have established a clear system of headings within the report, use the same text attributes—capitalization, boldface, italics, and outline style (traditional or decimal)—in the table of contents.

For more about text attributes, see Ch. 11.

When adding page numbers to your report, remember two points:

• The table of contents page does not contain an entry for itself.

• Front matter is numbered using lowercase Roman numerals (i, ii, and so forth), often centered at the bottom of the page. The title page of a report is not numbered, although it represents page i. The abstract is usually numbered page ii. The table of contents is usually not numbered, although it represents page iii. The body of the report is numbered with Arabic numerals (1, 2, and so on), typically in the upper outside corner of the page.

See page iii of the sample recommendation report shown in Figure 18.8 for an example of a table of contents.

List of Illustrations A *list of illustrations* is a table of contents for the figures and tables. List the figures first, then the tables. (If the report contains only figures, call it a *list of figures*. If it contains only tables, call it a *list of*

Why To Make a Long Report Navigable

Whether your report is being read in print or online, your readers will appreciate page navigation guides to help them find the information they need. Headers, footers, and page numbers are useful, especially in print documents and PDFs, to help readers know where they are in a document. A table of contents can direct or link readers to the right location as well as provide them with a sense of the scope and organization of the report.

How To Make a Long Report Navigable

With programs such as Microsoft Word or Google Docs, you can easily format a report to include page navigation tools. To insert headers, footers, and page numbers, choose the function you want from the **Insert** tab. Both Word and Google Docs allow you to set up the header differently on the first page of the document. Word offers additional design options, allowing you to insert **section breaks** (in the **Layout tab**) so that you can have different headers and footers in different sections of a long report.

Microsoft Word   **Google Docs**

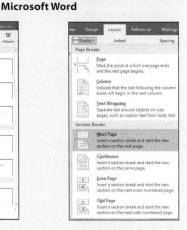

To create a preformatted table of contents, use Word's Table of Contents drop-down menu in the Reference tab; in Google Docs, choose the Table of Contents feature from the Insert tab. For online documents, you can choose to use hyperlinks instead of page numbers in your table of contents. As with headers, footers, and page numbers, Word offers additional customization tools for the table of contents.

Microsoft Word   **Google Docs**

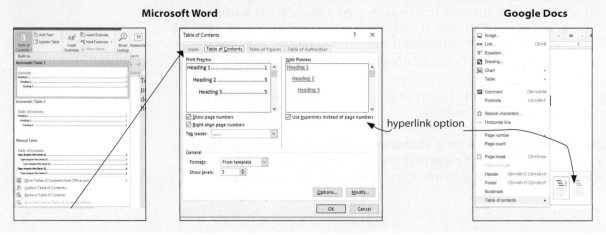

hyperlink option

FIGURE 18.5   List of Illustrations

tables.) You may begin the list of illustrations on the same page as the table of contents, or you may begin the list on a separate page and include it in the table of contents. Figure 18.5 shows a list of illustrations.

Executive Summary   The executive summary (sometimes called the *epitome*, *executive overview*, *management summary*, or *management overview*) is a brief condensation of the report addressed to managers. Most managers need only a broad understanding of the projects that an organization undertakes and how they fit together into a coherent whole.

An executive summary for a report of under 20 pages is typically one page (double-spaced). For longer reports, the maximum length is often calculated as a percentage of the report, such as 5 percent.

The executive summary presents information to managers in two parts:

- **Background.** This section explains the problem or opportunity: what was not working or was not working effectively or efficiently, or what potential modification of a procedure or product had to be analyzed.

- **Major findings and implications.** This section might include a brief description—only one or two sentences—of the methods, followed by a full paragraph about the conclusions and recommendations.

An executive summary differs from an informative abstract. Whereas an abstract focuses on the technical subject (such as whether the public is taking advantage of the data from smart electric meters), an executive summary concentrates on the managerial implications of the subject for a particular company (such as whether PECO, the Philadelphia utility company, should carry out a public-information campaign to educate customers about how to use their smart meters).

◢
GUIDELINES Writing an Executive Summary

Follow these five suggestions in writing executive summaries.

▶ **Use specific evidence in describing the background.** For most managers, the best evidence is in the form of costs and savings. Instead of writing that the equipment you are now using to cut metal foil is ineffective, write that the equipment jams once every 72 hours on average, costing $400 in materials and $2,000 in productivity each time. Then add up these figures for a monthly or an annual total.

▶ **Be specific in describing research.** For instance, research suggests that a computerized energy-management system could cut your company's energy costs by 20 to 25 percent. If the company's energy costs last year were $300,000, it could save $60,000 to $75,000.

▶ **Describe the methods briefly.** If you think your readers are interested, include a brief description of your methods—no more than a sentence or two.

▶ **Describe the findings according to your readers' needs.** If your readers want to know your results, provide them. If your readers are unable to understand the technical data or are uninterested, go directly to the conclusions and recommendations.

▶ **Ask an outside reader to review your draft.** Give the summary to someone who has no connection to the project. That person should be able to read your summary and understand what the project means to the organization.

See page 1 of the sample recommendation report shown in Figure 18.8 for an example of an executive summary.

WRITING THE BACK MATTER

The back matter of a recommendation report might include the following items: glossary, list of symbols, references, and appendixes.

Glossary and List of Symbols A *glossary*, an alphabetical list of definitions, is particularly useful if some of your readers are unfamiliar with the technical vocabulary in your report. Instead of slowing down your discussion by defining technical terms as they appear, you can use boldface, or some similar method of highlighting words, to indicate that the term is defined

DOCUMENT ANALYSIS ACTIVITY

Analyzing an Executive Summary

Executive Summary

On May 11, we received approval to study whether Android tablets could help our 20 engineers receive email, monitor their schedules, take notes, and access reference sources they need in the field. In our study, we addressed these problems experienced by many of our engineers:

- They have missed deadlines and meetings and lost client information.
- They have been unable to access important files and reference materials from the field.
- They have complained about the weight — sometimes more than 40 pounds — of the binders and other materials that they have to carry.
- They have to spend time keyboarding notes that they take in the field.

In 2019, missed meetings and other schedule problems cost the company over $400,000 in lost business. And our insurance carrier settled a claim for $50,000 from an engineer who experienced back and shoulder problems due to the weight of his pack.

We researched the capabilities of Android tablets then established these criteria for our analysis:

- The device must weigh less than 18 ounces.
- It must run on Android 8.0 or higher.
- It must have at least 4GB RAM.
- It must have at least a 2-GHz Quad Core.
- It must have Wi-Fi and LTE 4G connectivity.
- It must have at least a 10-inch screen.
- It must have a camera with a resolution of 8.1MP or better.
- It must be Microsoft Office compatible.
- It must cost $700 or less.

On the basis of our analysis, we recommend that the company purchase Galaxy Tab S4 tablets, for a total cost of $10,950. These devices best meet all our technical and cost criteria.

This executive summary comes from a corporate report on purchasing Android tablets for employees. The questions below ask you to think about the discussion of executive summaries (beginning on p. 499).

1. How clearly do the writers explain the background? Identify the problem or opportunity they describe in this executive summary.

2. Do the writers discuss the methods? If so, identify the discussion.

3. Identify the findings: the results, conclusions, and recommendations. How clearly have the writers explained the benefits to the company?

in the glossary. The first time a boldfaced term appears, explain this system in a footnote. For example, the body of the report might say, "Thus the **positron***acts as the . . . ," while a note at the bottom of the page explains:

*This and all subsequent terms in boldface are defined in the Glossary, page 97.

Although a glossary is usually placed near the end of the report, before the appendixes, it can also be placed immediately after the table of contents if the glossary is brief (less than a page) and if it defines essential terms. Figure 18.6 shows an excerpt from a glossary.

A list of symbols is formatted like a glossary, but it defines symbols and abbreviations rather than terms. It, too, may be placed before the appendixes or after the table of contents. Figure 18.7 shows a list of symbols.

References Many reports contain a list of references (sometimes called a *bibliography* or *list of works cited*) as part of the back matter. References and the accompanying textual citations throughout the report are called *documentation*. Documentation acknowledges your debt to your sources, establishes your

---

Glossary

Applicant: A state agency, local government, or eligible private nonprofit organization that submits a request to the Grantee for disaster assistance under the state's grant.

Case Management: A systems approach to providing equitable and fast service to applicants for disaster assistance. Organized around the needs of the applicant, the system consists of a single point of coordination, a team of on-site specialists, and a centralized, automated filing system.

Cost Estimating Format (CEF): A method for estimating the total cost of repair for large, permanent projects by use of construction industry standards. The format uses a base cost estimate and design and construction contingency factors, applied as a percentage of the base cost.

Declaration: The President's decision that a major disaster qualifies for federal assistance under the Stafford Act.

Hazard Mitigation: Any cost-effective measure that will reduce the potential for damage to a facility from a disaster event.

FIGURE 18.6 Glossary

credibility as a writer, and helps readers locate and review your sources. See Appendix, Part B, for a detailed discussion of documentation. See page 18 of the sample recommendation report shown in Figure 18.8 for an example of a reference list.

Appendixes An *appendix* is any section that follows the body of the report (and the glossary, list of symbols, or reference list). Appendixes (or *appendices*) convey information that is too bulky for the body of the report or that will interest only a few readers. Appendixes might include maps, large technical diagrams or charts, computations, test data, and texts of supporting documents.

Appendixes, usually labeled with letters rather than numbers (Appendix A, Appendix B, and so on), are listed in the table of contents and are referred to at appropriate points in the body of the report. Therefore, they are accessible to any reader who wants to consult them. See page 19 of the sample recommendation report shown in Figure 18.8 for an example of an appendix.

List of Symbols	
β	beta
CRT	cathode-ray tube
γ	gamma
Hz	hertz
rcvr	receiver
SNR	signal-to-noise ratio
uhf	ultra high frequency
vhf	very high frequency

FIGURE 18.7 List of Symbols

Sample Recommendation Report

Figure 18.8 (pp. 504–27) is the recommendation report on the tablet project proposed in Figure 16.6 (pp. 453–59) in Chapter 16. The progress report for this project appears in Figure 17.4 (pp. 471–78) in Chapter 17.

Transmittal "letters" can be presented as memos.

The writers include their titles and that of their primary reader. This way, future readers will be able to readily identify the reader and writers.

The subject heading indicates the subject of the report (the tablet study at RRMC) and the purpose of the report (recommendation report).

The purpose of the study. Notice that the writers link the recommendation report to the proposal, giving them an opportunity to state the main tasks they carried out in the study.

The methods the writers used to carry out the research.

The principal findings: the results and conclusions of the study. Notice that the writers state that they cannot be sure whether the technical information they have found is accurate. Is it okay to state that you are unsure about something? Yes, as long as you then propose a way to become sure about it.

Rawlings Regional Medical Center
7500 Bannock Avenue
Rawlings, MT 59211

Date: December 14, 2018
To: Jill Bremerton, M.D.
    Chief Executive Officer
    Rawlings Regional Medical Center
From: Jeremy Elkins, Director of Information Technology
    Eloise Carruthers, Director of Nursing
    Rawlings Regional Medical Center
Subject: Recommendation Report for the Tablet Study at RRMC

Attached is the report for our study, "Selecting a Tablet Computer for the Clinical Staff at Rawlings Regional Medical Center: A Recommendation Report." We completed the tasks described in our proposal of October 6, 2018: familiarizing ourselves with tablet use by clinical staff in hospitals across the country, assessing RRMC clinical staff's knowledge of and attitudes toward tablet use, studying different models for administering tablet use, determining the criteria by which we might evaluate tablets, and performing the evaluations.

To carry out these tasks, we performed secondary and primary research. We studied the literature on tablet use, distributed a questionnaire to RRMC clinical staff who own tablets, and interviewed Dr. Bremerton. Then, we collected and analyzed our data and wrote the report.

Our main findings are that the clinical staff who already own tablets are very receptive to the idea of using tablets in a clinical setting and slightly prefer having the hospital supply the tablets. We, too, think the hospital-supplied model is preferable to the bring-your-own-device (BYOD) model. Although the best tablets for our needs would be those designed and built for health-care applications, those are too expensive for our budget. Because reports on the technical characteristics of computer products are notoriously unreliable, we cannot be sure whether the many

FIGURE 18.8   **Sample Recommendation Report** *(continued)*

Letter to Jill Bremerton, M.D.
page 2
December 14, 2018

general-purpose tablets can meet our standards for ease of disinfection or durability, and we are not sure whether they have sufficient battery life.

We recommend one of two courses of action: reconsidering the cost criterion or testing a representative sample of general-purpose tablets for disinfection and the other technical characteristics and letting the clinical staff try them out.

We appreciate the trust you have shown in inviting us to participate in this phase of the feasibility study, and we would look forward to working with you on any follow-up activities. If you have any questions or comments, please contact Jeremy Elkins, at jelkins@rrmc.org or at 555-444-3967, or Eloise Carruthers, at ecarruthers@rrmc.org or at 555-444-3982.

The major recommendation. The writers ask their supervisor if she will reconsider whether the hospital can afford tablets specifically designed for health-care environments. That's not insubordination. Just be polite about it.

A polite offer to participate further or to provide more information.

FIGURE 18.8   Sample Recommendation Report (*continued*)

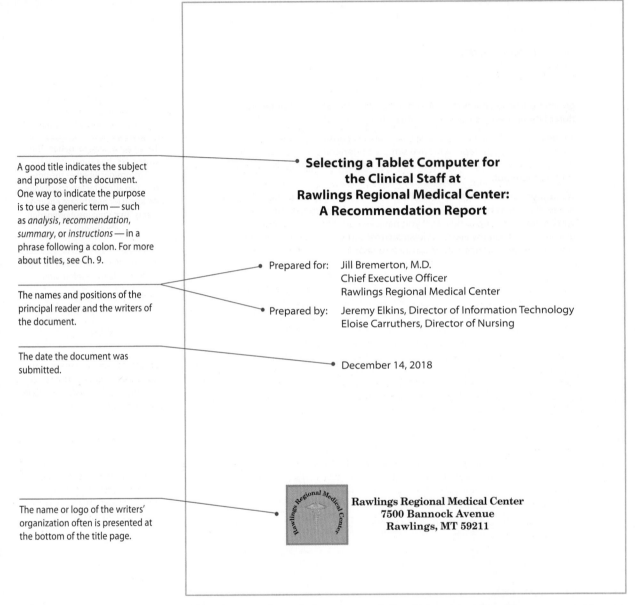

A good title indicates the subject and purpose of the document. One way to indicate the purpose is to use a generic term — such as *analysis*, *recommendation*, *summary*, or *instructions* — in a phrase following a colon. For more about titles, see Ch. 9.

The names and positions of the principal reader and the writers of the document.

The date the document was submitted.

The name or logo of the writers' organization often is presented at the bottom of the title page.

**Selecting a Tablet Computer for
the Clinical Staff at
Rawlings Regional Medical Center:
A Recommendation Report**

Prepared for: Jill Bremerton, M.D.
Chief Executive Officer
Rawlings Regional Medical Center

Prepared by: Jeremy Elkins, Director of Information Technology
Eloise Carruthers, Director of Nursing

December 14, 2018

**Rawlings Regional Medical Center
7500 Bannock Avenue
Rawlings, MT 59211**

FIGURE 18.8   **Sample Recommendation Report** (*continued*)

Abstract

"Selecting a Tablet Computer for the Clinical Staff
at Rawlings Regional Medical Center:
A Recommendation Report"

Prepared by: Jeremy Elkins, Director of Information Technology
Eloise Carruthers, Director of Nursing

On October 8, 2018, Dr. Jill Bremerton, Chief Executive Officer of Rawlings Regional Medical Center (RRMC), approved a proposal by Jeremy Elkins (Director of Information Technology) and Eloise Carruthers (Director of Nursing) to carry out a feasibility study on integrating tablet computers into the RRMC clinical setting and to report their findings. The authors began by performing research to better understand how tablets are being used by clinical staff in hospitals across the country. Then, they assessed RRMC clinical staff attitudes toward tablet use, studied two models for administering use of tablets in hospitals, determined the criteria by which tablets might be evaluated, and performed the evaluations. RRMC clinical staff who already own tablets are very receptive to the idea of using tablets in a clinical setting and slightly prefer having the hospital supply the tablets. The best tablets for RRMC needs are those designed and built for health-care applications because they meet hospital standards for disinfection, are durable, and offer numerous hardware and software options, such as barcode scanners, RFID readers, speech input, and smart-card readers. Unfortunately, they are too expensive for our budget. Because there are numerous health-care apps available for not only the iPad but also the many Android tablets and Windows-based tablets, any of these that meet our other needs would be acceptable. However, we are not sure whether the many general-purpose tablets can meet our standards for ease of disinfection or ruggedness, and we are not sure whether they have sufficient battery life. We recommend that, if we cannot reconsider the cost criterion, we test a representative sample of general-purpose tablets for disinfection and the other technical characteristics that would affect their usefulness in the clinical setting.

Keywords: tablets, health care, HIPAA, disinfection, iPad, Android, Windows, rugged, durability

ii

In the abstract, the title of the report is often enclosed in quotation marks because the abstract might be reproduced in another context (such as in a database), in which case the report title would be the title of a separate document.

Abstracts are often formatted as a single paragraph.

The background and purpose of the report.

The methods.

The major findings.

Note that the writers provide some technical information about tablet use, clinical staff attitudes, and technical characteristics of tablets.

The major recommendations.

A keywords list ensures that the report will appear in the list of results of an electronic search on any of the terms listed.

FIGURE 18.8   Sample Recommendation Report (*continued*)

Note that the typeface and design of the headings in the table of contents mirror the typeface and design of the headings in the report itself.

In this table of contents, the two levels of headings are distinguished by type style (boldface versus italic) and indentation.

Table of Contents

FIGURE 18.8 **Sample Recommendation Report** (*continued*)

1

Executive Summary

To determine the best way to integrate tablet computers into the RRMC clinical setting, Dr. Jill Bremerton, Chief Executive Officer, asked us to study national trends, determine clinical-staff attitudes, examine management models, devise criteria for assessing tablets, and present our findings and recommendations.

Currently, RRMC has no formal policy on tablet usage by clinical staff. By default, we are following a bring-your-own-device (BYOD) approach. More than half of our clinical staff already use their personal tablets in their work. Dr. Bremerton wanted us to determine the best way to make tablets available to all our clinical staff. This charge included assessing the available tablets and recommending which tablet we should make available to our clinical staff.

To carry out this study, we completed the tasks described in our proposal of October 6, 2018: we studied the literature on tablet use; distributed a questionnaire to every member of the RRMC clinical staff, requesting responses from those who own tablets; and interviewed Dr. Bremerton. Then, we collected and analyzed our data and wrote the report.

Our main finding is that the clinical staff who already own tablets are very receptive to the idea of using tablets in a clinical setting. Not one of these staff members thought we should not use tablets in the clinical setting. By a slight margin, these staff members prefer having the hospital supply the tablets. We, too, think the hospital-supplied model is preferable to the BYOD model because it will reduce the chances of privacy violations and streamline the work of the IT department. We concluded, too, that the best tablets for our needs are those designed and built for health-care applications. Unfortunately, they are too expensive for our budget. And we cannot be sure, simply from reading the literature, whether the many general-purpose tablets can meet our standards for ease of disinfection or durability. Nor can we be sure whether they have sufficient battery life. Any of the general-purpose tablets, regardless of operating system or brand, would be adequate if it met these standards.

We recommend one of two courses of action: reconsidering our cost criterion or testing a representative sample of general-purpose tablets for disinfection and the other technical characteristics and making suitable tablets available for clinical staff to try out. We believe reconsidering the cost criterion is the better approach for our needs because the health-care-specific tablets offer significant advantages over the general-purpose tablets.

FIGURE 18.8 Sample Recommendation Report (*continued*)

The executive summary describes the project with a focus on the managerial aspects, particularly the recommendation. Note the writers' emphasis on the problem at RRMC.

Here the writers present a brief statement of the subject of their report.

The background of the feasibility study that Dr. Bremerton is funding.

A brief statement of the methods the writers used to carry out their research. Note that throughout this report the writers use the active voice ("We studied the literature . . ."). See Ch. 10 for more on the active voice. Note, too, that the discussion of the methods is brief: most managers are less interested in the details of the methods you used than in your findings.

Findings are the important results and conclusions of a study.

Note that the writers use the word *recommend*. Using key generic terms such as *problem*, *methods*, *results*, *conclusions*, and *recommendations* helps readers understand the role that each section plays in the document.

Because the executive summary is the report element addressed most directly to management, the writers make clear why they prefer looking again at whether the hospital can afford to purchase health-care-specific tablets.

2

Some organizations require that each first-level heading begin on a new page.

A brief statement of the context for the report.

Note that the word *currently* is used to introduce the background of the study: the current situation is unsatisfactory for several reasons.

A formal statement of the task the committee was asked to perform. The writers paraphrase from the memo Dr. Bremerton gave them. Often in technical communication, you will quote or paraphrase words your reader wrote to you. This practice reminds the reader of the context and shows that you are carrying out your tasks professionally.

The writers incorporate a brief overview of their methods into the list of tasks.

The writers devote two paragraphs to their principal findings. The introduction can present the major findings of a report; technical communication is not about drama and suspense.

Introduction

To determine the best course of action for integrating tablet computers into the RRMC clinical setting, Dr. Jill Bremerton, RRMC Chief Executive Officer, asked us to study national trends, determine clinical-staff knowledge of and attitudes toward tablets, examine administrative models for tablet use, devise criteria for assessing tablets, and present our findings and recommendations.

Currently, RRMC has no formal policy on tablet usage by clinical staff. By default, we are following a bring-your-own-device (BYOD) approach. More than half of our clinical staff use their personal tablets in their work. This situation is not ideal because not all clinical staff are taking advantage of the enormous potential for improving patient care and reducing costs by using tablets, and IT is struggling to keep up with the work needed to ensure that all the different tablets are working properly and that any information-security protocols required by HIPAA and current health care laws are not being violated.

Therefore, Dr. Bremerton wanted us to determine the best way to make tablets available to all our clinical staff. Specifically, Dr. Bremerton asked us to perform five tasks:

- Determine how tablets are being used by clinical staff across the nation. We performed secondary research to complete this task.
- Determine the RRMC clinical staff's current knowledge of and attitudes toward tablet use. To complete this task, we wrote and distributed a survey to clinical staff who already own tablets.
- Determine how hospitals administer the use of tablets in a clinical setting. We performed secondary research to complete this task.
- Establish criteria by which we might evaluate tablets for RRMC. We performed secondary research to complete this task. In addition, we interviewed Dr. Bremerton for her suggestions about the most important criterion.
- Assess available tablets based on our criteria. We performed secondary research to complete this task.

We found that tablet use in clinical settings is increasing quickly, and that clinical staff are finding many ways to use tablets to improve care and save time and money. Among the clinical staff at RRMC who already own

FIGURE 18.8 **Sample Recommendation Report** (*continued*)

3

tablets, nearly half own an iPad and nearly half an Android tablet, most consider themselves expert users of their tablets, and more than two-thirds already use them in the clinical setting; by a slim margin, they would prefer a hospital-supplied model for tablet use to a BYOD model. Our research on the two models for making tablets available also found more advantages and fewer disadvantages to the hospital-supplied model.

Our principal finding regarding tablets themselves is that the best tablets for our use would be those designed and built for health-care applications. These tablets are rugged and easy to disinfect, and they offer a wealth of hardware and software options that would streamline our daily tasks without introducing any risks either to patient care or to data privacy. Unfortunately, purchasing enough of these tablets for all clinical staff would exceed our budget. To determine whether any of the general-purpose tablets meet all our needs, we would need to conduct hands-on testing regarding disinfection, battery life, durability, and several other technical criteria.

We recommend, first, that we reassess whether the budget will permit consideration of any of the health-care-specific tablets. If that is not possible, we recommend that we ask manufacturers of a small set of general-purpose tablets to let us test their products and invite our clinical staff to try them. This option would yield data that would help us decide how to proceed.

In the following sections, we provide additional details about our research methods, the results we obtained, the conclusions we drew from those results, and our recommendation.

> Notice the writers' use of the phrase "we recommend." Repeating key terms in this way helps readers understand the logic of a report and concentrate on the technical information it contains.

> An advance organizer for the rest of the report.

FIGURE 18.8   Sample Recommendation Report (*continued*)

4

Research Methods

We began our research by interviewing Dr. Bremerton, who emphasized that we need to maintain our focus on our priorities—patient care and service to the community—and not let technical questions about the tablets distract us from the needs of our clinical staff. "We're not going to do anything without the approval of the doctors and nurses," she said.

Early on in our research, we discovered an article that corroborated what Dr. Bremerton had told us (Narisi, 2013). Two keys to doing the research were to focus on security features—data-privacy issues mandated in HIPAA and current health care laws—and to get the clinical staff's input.

To perform the analysis requested by Dr. Bremerton, we broke the project into six tasks:
1. acquire a basic understanding of tablet use by clinical staff across the nation
2. determine the RRMC clinical staff's knowledge of and attitudes toward tablet use
3. assess the BYOD and hospital-owned tablet models
4. establish criteria for evaluating tablets
5. assess available tablets based on our criteria
6. analyze our data and prepare this recommendation report

In the following discussion of how we performed each task, we explain the reasoning that guided our research.

Task 1: Acquire a basic understanding of tablet use by clinical staff across the nation

Dr. Bremerton pointed us to a number of resources on tablet use in clinical settings. In addition, we conducted our own literature review. Most of the research we studied fell into one of four categories:
• general introductions to tablet use in trade magazines and general-interest periodicals
• more focused articles about tablets used in health care
• technical specifications of tablets provided in trade magazines and on manufacturers' websites
• trade-magazine articles about best practices for managing the use of tablets in clinical settings

The writers use the same task organization as in the proposal and the progress report.

FIGURE 18.8 Sample Recommendation Report (*continued*)

5

As we expected, the information we acquired was a mix of user opinions, benchmark-test results, and marketing. We relied most heavily on case studies from hospital administrators and technical specialists in health IT. Because of the unreliability of information on manufacturers' websites, we were hesitant to rely on claims about product performance.

By stating that they know that their sources are a mixture of different kinds of information, not all of which is equally useful for every kind of question that needs to be answered, the writers suggest that they are careful analysts.

Task 2: Determine the RRMC clinical staff's knowledge of and attitudes toward tablet use

On October 14, 2018, we sent all 147 clinical staff members an email linking to a four-question Qualtrics survey. The email indicated that we were seeking opinions about tablet use by clinical-staff members who already own tablets and made clear that the survey would take less than two minutes to complete.

Initially, we considered collecting data from all 147 clinical staff members. However, as we constructed that survey, we realized that it would be cumbersome to gather and track information from three different populations: those who didn't own a tablet, those who owned one but didn't use it in the clinic, and those who owned one and did use it in the clinic. Eliciting information from these different groups would require a long, complex questionnaire and some statistical analysis to separate out the attitudes.

The writers carefully explain the logic of their methods. Do not assume that your readers will automatically understand why you did what you did. Sometimes it is best to explain your thinking. Although technical communication contains a lot of facts and figures, like other kinds of writing it relies on clear, logical arguments.

For this reason, we decided to address only the tablet owners, since we assumed that this group would constitute approximately two-thirds of the clinical staff (Drinkwater, 2013). With this streamlined focus, we were able to create a very brief survey, one that would likely yield a high return rate. We assumed, too, that the opinions expressed by current tablet owners would likely be of more value in helping us plan a formal program of tablet use than those of clinicians who were less likely to be experienced tablet users.

We field-tested the questionnaire with six clinical staff members, revised one of the questions, and then, with the authorization of Dr. Bremerton, uploaded the questionnaire to Qualtrics and sent an email to the clinical staff.

As discussed in Ch. 6, some questions will misfire. Therefore, it is smart to field-test a questionnaire before you distribute it.

The questionnaire (including the responses) appears in the Appendix, page 19.

Including a page number in the cross reference to the appendix is a convenience to the reader. When you do so, remember to add the correct page number after you determine where the appendix (or the several appendixes) will appear in the report.

FIGURE 18.8   Sample Recommendation Report (*continued*)

6

Task 3: Assess the BYOD and hospital-owned tablet models

Our research revealed that hospitals use one of two administrative models for giving clinical staff access to tablets: the bring-your-own-device (BYOD) model and purchasing tablets to distribute to staff. To present the advantages and disadvantages of each of these models, we relied on reports from hospital administrators who pioneered these models (Jackson, 2011a, 2011b). For statistics on the popularity of each of these administrative models, we relied on a survey (Terry, 2011).

Task 4: Establish criteria for evaluating tablets

We both studied the voluminous literature on tablets. Jeremy Elkins met informally with his five IT colleagues to discuss the data, and Eloise Carruthers met informally with her nursing staff and with selected physicians, including several who had responded to the survey.

We began with the first criterion: cost. Dr. Bremerton had told us in our interview that the budget for the project (assuming that RRMC would supply a tablet to each of the 147 members of the clinical staff) would be $800 per device, fully configured with any commercial software needed to operate it. For this reason, we did not conduct a thorough examination of the health-care-specific tablets, each of which costs $2,500–3,000.

In addition, we paid particular attention to the complexities of the current tablet market, focusing on whether the various devices would work seamlessly with our health-records system and other security features ("Top Five," 2013), on the need to be able to disinfect the tablets (Carr, 2011), and on durability (Narisi, 2013). We knew from experience with all kinds of portable information technology that the question of battery life would be problematic because it can vary so much depending on load and other factors.

We concluded that two factors that might seem critically important were not: operating system and availability of relevant apps. Although the Apple iPad is the single most popular tablet, the Samsung Galaxy and other Android tablets are currently outselling iPads. As a result, all the important apps are being created for the Apple operating system (iOS), for Android, and for Windows (the OS used by the Microsoft Surface and the major health-care-specific tablets).

Note that the writers present their references to their sources throughout the report.

Here, again, the writers explain the logic of their methods. They decided to rely on the experiences of hospital administrators. This approach will likely appeal to Dr. Bremerton.

Often you will begin your project with a cost criterion; your recommended solution must not cost more than a certain amount.

The writers present just enough information about the technologies to help the reader understand their logic. Writers sometimes present too much information; include only as much as your readers need to be able to follow your report.

FIGURE 18.8 **Sample Recommendation Report** (*continued*)

7

Task 5: Assess available tablets based on our criteria

Because our budget did not permit us to recommend the tablets designed for the health-care industry, we decided not to study them in detail.

To study the general-purpose tablets, we relied on trade magazines. We soon realized, however, that several of our necessary criteria — namely, the ability to disinfect the tablet, as well as durability and battery life — were not adequately addressed in the literature because our needs as a hospital are so specific.

For instance, battery life is typically reported as the mean number of hours the battery will last. But that figure varies significantly, depending on the applications the device is running. In addition, there is the question of whether the device is hot-swappable (that is, whether the battery can be replaced without shutting down the device). However, some tablets boot very quickly, making this characteristic less important. Finally, there is an administrative question: will the clinical staff member use the same tablet every day or check one out at the start of each shift (or perhaps check out a second or even a third one during a 14-hour shift)? Will fresh batteries be available only in one location, or can they be checked out at several locations? Can a staff member grab a handful of fresh batteries at the start of a shift? All these questions bear on how we would need to think about the importance of battery life.

For this reason, we recommend that a representative sample of general-purpose tablets be evaluated for disinfection, durability, and battery life and that this study include a substantial on-site evaluation period at RRMC.

Task 6: Analyze our data and prepare this recommendation report •——————

We drafted this report and uploaded it to a wiki that we created to make it convenient for the other IT staff members and interested clinical staff members to help us revise it. We incorporated most of our colleagues' suggestions and then presented a final draft of this report on the wiki to gather any final editing suggestions.

Because analyzing their data and writing this report is part of the study, it is appropriate to include it as one of the steps. In some organizations, however, this task is assumed to be part of the study and is therefore not presented in the report.

FIGURE 18.8   **Sample Recommendation Report** *(continued)*

8

The writers present an advance organizer for the results section.

Results

In this section, we present the results of our research. For each of the tasks we carried out, we present the most important data we acquired.

Task 1: Acquire a basic understanding of tablet use by clinical staff across the nation

Since the introduction of the Apple iPad in 2010, the use of tablets by clinical staff in hospitals across the country has been growing steadily. Although there are no precise statistics on how many hospitals either distribute tablets to clinical staff or let them use their own devices in their work, the number of articles in trade magazines, exhibits at medical conferences, and discussions on discussion forums suggests that tablets are quickly becoming established in the clinical setting. And many hundreds of apps have already been written to enable users to carry out health-care-related tasks on tablets.

The most extensive set of data on tablets in hospitals relates to the use of the iPad, the first tablet on the market. Ottawa Hospital has distributed more than 1,000 iPads to clinical staff; California Hospital is piloting a program with more than 100 iPads for hospital use; Kaiser Permanente is testing the iPad for hospital and clinical workflow; and Cedars-Sinai Medical Center is testing the iPad in its hospital. The University of Chicago's Internal Medicine Residency Program uses the iPad; the iPad is also being distributed to first-year medical students at Stanford, University of California–Irvine, and University of San Francisco. In addition, there are reports of Windows-based and Android-based tablets being distributed at numerous other hospitals and medical schools (Husain, 2011).

Today, tablets have five main clinical applications (Carr, 2011):
- *Monitoring patients and collecting data.* Clinical staff connect tablets to the hospital's monitoring instruments to collect patient information and transfer it to patients' health records without significant human intervention. In addition, staff access patient information on their tablets.
- *Ordering prescriptions, authorizations, and refills.* Clinical staff use tablets to communicate instantly with the hospital pharmacy and off-site pharmacies, as well as with other departments within the hospital, such as the Imaging Department.

FIGURE 18.8   Sample Recommendation Report (*continued*)

9

- *Scheduling appointments.* Clinical staff use tablets to schedule doctor and nurse visits and laboratory tests, to send reminders, and to handle re-scheduling and cancellations.
- *Conducting research on the fly.* Clinical staff use tablets to access medication databases and numerous reference works.
- *Educating patients.* Clinical staff use videos and animations to educate patients on their conditions and treatment options.

Tablets provide clinical staff with significant advantages. Staff do not need to go back to their offices to connect to the internet or to the hospital's own medical-record system. Staff save time, reduce paper usage, and reduce transcription errors by not having to enter nearly as much data by hand.

Task 2: Determine the RRMC clinical staff's knowledge of and attitudes toward tablet use

On October 14, 2018, we sent all 147 clinical staff members an email linking to a four-question Qualtrics survey. In the email, we said that we were seeking opinions about tablet use by clinical-staff members who already own tablets and made clear that the survey would take less than two minutes to complete.

We received 96 responses, which represents 65 percent of the 147 staff members. We cannot be certain that all 96 respondents who indicated that they are tablet owners in fact own tablets. We also do not know whether all those staff members who own a tablet responded. However, given that some 75 percent of physicians in a 2013 poll own tablets, we suspect that the 96 respondents reasonably accurately represent the proportion of our clinical staff who own tablets (Drinkwater, 2013).

Here are the four main findings from the survey of tablet owners:
- Some 47 percent of respondents own an Apple iPad, and 47 percent own either a Samsung Galaxy or another tablet that uses the Android operating system. Only 6 percent use the Microsoft Surface, one of the several Windows-based tablets.
- Some 58 percent of the respondents strongly agree with the statement that they are expert users of their tablets. Overall, 90 percent agree more than they disagree with the statement.

The writers continue to use the task structure that they used in the methods section.

FIGURE 18.8   Sample Recommendation Report (*continued*)

10

- Some 63 percent of respondents use their tablets for at least one clinical application. They have either loaded apps on their tablets themselves or had IT do so for them.
- Some 27 percent of the respondents would prefer to continue to use their own tablets for clinical applications, whereas 38 percent would prefer to use a tablet supplied by RRMC. Some 35 percent had no strong feelings either way. None of the respondents indicated that they would prefer not to use a tablet at all.

Task 3: Assess the BYOD and hospital-owned tablet models

Currently, hospitals use one of two models for giving clinical staff access to tablets: the bring-your-own-device (BYOD) model and the purchase model, whereby the hospital purchases tablets to distribute to staff. In this section, we will present our findings on the relative advantages of each model.

The BYOD model is based on the fact that, nationally, some three-quarters of physicians already own tablets (with the Apple iPad the single most popular model) (Drinkwater, 2013). We could find no data on how many nurses own tablets.

The main advantage of the BYOD model is that clinical staff already know and like their tablets; therefore, they are motivated to use them and less likely to need extensive training. In addition, the hardware costs are eliminated (or almost eliminated, since some hospitals choose to purchase some tablets for staff who do not own their own). Todd Richardson, CIO with Deaconess Health System, Evansville, Indiana (Jackson, 2011b), argues that staff members who own their own tablets use and maintain them carefully: they know how to charge, clean, store, and protect them. In addition, the hospital doesn't have to worry about the question of liability if staff members lose them during personal use. And if the staff member moves on to a new position at a different hospital, there is no dispute about who owns the information on the tablet. All the hospital has to do is disable the staff member's account.

However, there are three main disadvantages to the BYOD model:
- Some clinical staff do not have their own tablets, and some who do don't want to use them at work; to make the advantages of tablet use

FIGURE 18.8   **Sample Recommendation Report** (*continued*)

11

available to all the clinical staff, therefore, the hospital needs to decide whether to purchase tablets and distribute them to these staff members.

• Labor costs are high because each tablet needs to be examined carefully by the hospital IT department to ensure that it contains no software that might interfere with or be incompatible with the health-care software that needs to be loaded onto it. This labor-intensive assessment by IT can seriously erode the cost savings from not having to buy the tablet itself.

• Chances of loss increase because the staff member is more likely to use the tablet at home as well as in the hospital.

The other model for making tablets available to clinical staff is for the hospital to purchase the same tablet for each staff member.

The purchase model offers two distinct advantages, as described by Dale Potter, CIO of 1,300-bed Ottawa Hospital in Ontario, Canada. Potter has purchased more than 2,000 iPads for his staff (Jackson, 2011a):

• The hospital controls the software and apps loaded on the tablets and can even create its own apps. For instance, Potter hired 120 developers to create apps.

• The hospital reduces labor costs because IT can load exactly the same set of apps and other software on each machine. Updates and upgrades also are far simpler to manage when all the devices are the same.

The main disadvantages of the purchase model are the following:

• Staff members might not like the tablet that the hospital chooses.

• Staff members might need to be trained to use the tablet.

• Liability issues related to loss of the tablets must be addressed officially in the employment contract between the hospital and the staff member.

Beginning in 2010 with the introduction of the iPad, most hospitals used the BYOD model; clinical staff brought their own tablets to work and started to think about ways to use them in a clinical setting. As time passed, however, and more people began to acquire tablets from different manufacturers, hospitals began to see the advantages of standardizing tablet use. A 2011 survey (Terry, 2011) showed that 40 percent of hospitals use the BYOD model, whereas 55 percent of hospitals support only devices provided or owned by the institution.

FIGURE 18.8   **Sample Recommendation Report** (*continued*)

12

Task 4: Establish criteria for evaluating tablets

Our interview with Dr. Bremerton, as well as our research in the available literature, yielded four *necessary* criteria and two *desirable* criteria for tablet use at RRMC.

A tablet that does not meet a necessary criterion would be eliminated from consideration. The four necessary criteria are the following:

- *Cost.* Each device must cost less than $800, fully configured for use.
- *HIPAA compliance.* We cannot use any device or technology that would jeopardize our compliance with the HIPAA and current health care privacy standards for medical information. What this means, in essence, is that a tablet must operate seamlessly with our electronic health-records system, Cerner, which we access through our current utility, Citrix. The tablet must duplicate our current desktop and remote-access capabilities.
- *Other security features.* The tablet must support basic security features, including encryption, remote wipe (IT's ability to remove data on a lost tablet), auto-lock (that cannot be turned off except by IT), and perimeter settings (IT's ability to prevent use of a tablet that has strayed a certain distance from the server) ("Top Five," 2013).
- *Ease of disinfection.* Because the tablets would be used in a clinical setting, they would be subject to the same standards of disinfection as any other equipment or device. A tablet that cannot be disinfected effectively and easily would not be an appropriate choice (Carr, 2011).

In addition, we have established two other criteria against which to evaluate tablets. We have deemed these criteria desirable; a tablet that does not meet a desirable criterion would not be eliminated from consideration.

- *Durability.* Because the tablet would be carried around within the hospital and sometimes would be used in close quarters, it likely would be dropped or bumped. The more durable, the more desirable the tablet would be.
- *Long battery life.* Our clinical staff routinely work shifts as long as 14 hours. The longer the battery life, the better. Related to battery life is the hot-swap feature. In a hot-swappable device, the battery can be removed and replaced with a fresh one without having to shut down the tablet.

FIGURE 18.8   Sample Recommendation Report (*continued*)

13

Task 5: Assess available tablets based on our criteria

One challenge we faced is that it was impractical to do a comprehensive assessment of all of the approximately 100 tablets available on the market. A second challenge is that tablets fall into a dizzying variety of sometimes overlapping categories. For example, the single most popular tablet is the Apple iPad, which runs on Apple's proprietary operating system. Many other tablets run on the Android system. Some, like the Amazon Kindle Fire, run on specialized configurations of Android. And Microsoft's Surface runs on Windows. There are general-purpose tablets, like the Samsung, made for the consumer market, and there are specialized tablets, like the Motion, designed for the health-care industry (Phillips, 2013). There are rugged tablets designed to meet military specifications for durability. Some tablets have USB ports for easy connection to existing clinical instruments and devices, as well as specialized features such as barcode-reading and RFID capabilities. Some tablets come with dozens of native (pre-installed) apps related to health care.

In short, although many brands of tablet are similar, no two are identical. As a result, we decided to review a small set of tablets that are mentioned frequently in health-care magazines and journals. We were sure to include the iPad, the Microsoft Surface, and several Android tablets. We also looked briefly at several tablets specially designed and marketed for health-care applications.

We present our basic findings by returning to our set of necessary and desired criteria.

The four necessary criteria are the following:

- *Cost.* Unfortunately, our cost criterion of $800 per unit eliminates all the tablets designed for health-care applications. These tablets, which cost between $2,500 and $3,000, are easy to disinfect and highly durable and include many desirable features such as barcode scanners, RFID readers, speech, and smart-card readers. The leading tablets in this category are the ProScribe Medical Tablet PC, the Sahara Slate PC, the MediSlate MCA, the Motion C5v Medical Tablet PC, the Teguar TA-10 Medical Tablet PC, the Advantech Medical PC, and the Arbor Antibacterial Medical Tablet.
- *HIPAA compliance.* All of the tablets we reviewed would enable us to remain in compliance with HIPAA and the current health care laws, and all would enable us to use our current record system, Cerner, through our Citrix utility. Some of the tablets have native apps to support this access, whereas others use virtual private networks.

FIGURE 18.8   Sample Recommendation Report (*continued*)

14

- *Other security features.* All of the tablets we reviewed would support the basic security features we identified, although some tablets would be easier than others for IT to configure.
- *Ease of disinfection.* This proved to be a very challenging criterion to assess. On the one hand, all of the so-called ruggedized tablets, as well as all those designed for health care, met this criterion because all the surfaces are sealed. On the other hand, the general-purpose tablets were not designed to withstand medical-grade disinfectants. However, this does not necessarily mean that they would not withstand clinical disinfection. According to John Curin, head of the health-care practice at Burwood, an IT consulting firm, "I couldn't disinfect [an iPad] if I wanted to." By contrast, Dr. John Halamka, the CIO of Beth Israel Deaconess Medical Center in Boston, argues that the iPad is "completely disinfectable." Even though Apple advises against using a disinfecting solution on the iPad, Halamka says he does so and has experienced no problems (Carr, 2011).

On the basis of the cost criterion, we must eliminate all the health-care-specific tablets and study only the general-purpose tablets. We need to devise a method to determine whether any of the general-purpose tablets can be adequately disinfected. For the purposes of this study, however, we decided to assess a representative subset of the general-purpose tablets based on our desirable criteria.

We will now present our major findings regarding the desirable criteria: durability and long battery life. We have decided against presenting a decision matrix because some of the technical characteristics are either imprecise or unknowable. For instance, battery life is a notoriously difficult characteristic to measure, because it can be affected greatly by so many factors.

Our tentative findings are that the Apple iPad, the Samsung Galaxy and the many other Android tablets, and the Microsoft Surface *appear* to meet our two desirable criteria. We would need to carry out our own tests of these tablets, configured with our software and appropriate apps, to determine their battery life. And we would need to determine whether any of the aftermarket protective cases would provide adequate durability. Rugged and waterproof iPad cases are available from Hard Candy Cases, OtterBox, and others. There are also waterproof solutions that are said to sterilize the iPad. In addition, there are some protective cases said to be designed specifically for clinical environments.

FIGURE 18.8 **Sample Recommendation Report** (*continued*)

15

Conclusions •————————————————

In this section, we present our conclusions based on our research related •
to the four questions we were asked to answer.

Tablet use by clinical staff

On the basis of our research, we conclude that increasing numbers of our
clinical staff will begin to use tablets for more applications in a clinical
setting. This increase will spur the creation of more health-care apps for all
tablets.

The RRMC clinical staff's knowledge of and attitudes toward tablet use •

On the basis of our survey of clinical staff who already own tablets, we
conclude that they consider themselves proficient in using the tablets,
and most already use them for at least one clinical application. Because
they prefer the hospital-supplied model for tablet use, we conclude that
they would welcome a formal plan to supply tablets.

The BYOD and hospital-owned tablet models

We conclude that the hospital-owned tablet model offers more
advantages and fewer disadvantages than the BYOD model. Having all
clinical staff use the same model of tablet saves money by streamlining
the process of loading software and installing updates and upgrades.
The medical center IT department can even create hospital-specific
apps.

Criteria for evaluating tablets

Our first necessary criterion, cost, eliminated all the health-care-specific
tablets from consideration, leaving us with only the general-purpose
tablets. All the general-purpose tablets we evaluated met our HIPAA and
health care law compliance and other security criteria. Unfortunately,
because the general-purpose tablets are not designed for clinical settings,
we could not determine from our research whether any of them are easy to
disinfect. We would need to conduct our own tests to answer that question.

We would need to conduct our own testing to determine whether
battery life and durability of any of the general-purpose tablets are
acceptable.

The function of a conclusion is to
explain what the data mean. Here
the writers explain how their results
can help their readers determine
how to proceed with the tablet
study. Notice that a conclusion is
not the same as a recommendation
(which explains what writers think
should be done next).

The writers present an advance
organizer for the conclusions
section.

At this point in the report, the writers have decided to abandon the
"task" labels. Their thinking is that
they are focusing less on what they
did and more on the meaning of the
information they gathered. However, they retain the headings that
help readers understand the topic
they are discussing.

FIGURE 18.8 **Sample Recommendation Report** (*continued*)

16

Assessing available tablets based on our criteria

We drew two main conclusions from our study of available tablets:

- The best tablets for our use — the ones designed and intended for health-care settings — are out of our price range. Because they meet all our criteria, we should reassess whether our budget will permit us to assess them more carefully.
- Any one of the available general-purpose tablets is potentially acceptable (provided it meets the disinfection criterion). We see no compelling reason to favor one operating system over another. Apple iPads, Android tablets, and Windows tablets all come with acceptable power, and there are plenty of health-care apps available for each type. As Android machines establish their dominance over the iPad, health-care apps for Android devices will surpass those for the iPad in variety and number.

FIGURE 18.8 **Sample Recommendation Report** (*continued*)

17

Recommendation

We recommend that the RRMC administration pursue one of two options:

Option 1: Reconsider the cost criterion

Although a health-care-specific tablet, at $2,500–3,000, is some three times the cost of a general-purpose tablet, it offers distinct advantages in terms of disinfection properties, ruggedness, and availability of specialized hardware and software for better integration with our other devices and equipment.

If it is not possible to provide health-care-specific tablets to all clinical staff, we might consider a two-tiered system (some staff members receive a health-care-specific tablet, others a general-purpose one) or a phased-implementation system.

Option 2: Test a representative sample of general-purpose tablets

If RRMC wishes to continue to assess the general-purpose tablets, we recommend that we contact manufacturers of the Apple iPad, the Samsung Galaxy, the Microsoft Surface, and several other Android tablets. We could request that they supply their most powerful products, equipped with the best set of medical apps, for our internal testing and evaluation.

We would then have IT test each tablet in a controlled environment for such technical characteristics as battery life and durability. We would also test each tablet for disinfection. Next, we would invite the manufacturers' representatives to attend a one- or two-day tablet fair, where we would make the products available to our clinical staff to try and offer hands-on assessment. On the basis of these tests and follow-up questionnaires submitted by clinical staff, we would be in a good position to know how to proceed.

This recommendation states explicitly what the writers think the reader should do next. Note that they are sketching in ideas that they have not discussed in detail but that might interest their readers.

FIGURE 18.8 **Sample Recommendation Report** *(continued)*

18

References

Carr, D. F. (2011, May 21). Healthcare puts tablets to the test. *InformationWeek Healthcare.* Retrieved October 1, 2018, from http://www.informationweek.com/healthcare/mobile-wireless/healthcare-puts-tablets-to-the-test/229503387

Drinkwater, D. (2013, April 19). Three in 4 physicians are using tablets; some are even prescribing apps. *TabTimes.* Retrieved October 12, 2018, from http://tabtimes.com/news/ittech-stats-research/2013/04/19/3-4-physicians-are-using-tablets-some-are-even-prescribing

Husain, I. (2011, March 10). Why Apple's iPad will beat Android tablets for hospital use. *iMedicalApps.* Retrieved October 15, 2018, from http://www.imedicalapps.com/2011/03/ipad-beat-android-tablets-hospital-medical-use/

Jackson, S. (2011a, August 15). Five reasons hospitals should buy tablets for physicians. *FierceMobileHealthcare.* Retrieved October 14, 2018, from http://www.fiercemobilehealthcare.com/story/5-reasons-why-hospitals-should-buy-tablets-physicians/2011-08-15

Jackson, S. (2011b, August 3). Why physicians should buy their own mobile devices. *FierceMobileHealthcare.* Retrieved October 16, 2018, from http://www.fiercemobilehealthcare.com/story/why-physicians-should-buy-their-own-mobile-devices/2011-08-03

Narisi, S. (2013, April 24). Choosing the best tablets for doctors: 3 keys. *Healthcare Business & Technology.* Retrieved October 3, 2018, from http://www.healthcarebusinesstech.com/best-tablets-for-doctors

Phillips, A. (2013, 10 April). Top 10 mobile tablets for healthcare professionals. *Healthcare Global.* Retrieved October 13, 2018, from http://www.healthcareglobal.com/top_ten/top-10-business/top-10-mobile-tablets-for-healthcare-professionals

Terry, K. (2011, Dec. 9). Apple capitalizes on doctors' iPad romance. *InformationWeek Healthcare.* Retrieved October 2, 2018, from http://www.informationweek.com/healthcare/mobile-wireless/apple-capitalizes-on-doctors-ipad-roman/232300218

Top Five Tablet Security Features. (2013). *Healthcare Data Solutions.* Retrieved October 2, 2018, from http://www.healthcaredatasolutions.com/top-five-tablet-security-features.html

This list of references is written according to the APA documentation style, which is discussed in Appendix, Part B, page 632.

FIGURE 18.8 **Sample Recommendation Report** (*continued*)

19

Appendix: Clinical-Staff Questionnaire

This is the questionnaire we distributed to the 147 RRMC clinical staff members. We received 96 responses. The numbers in boldface below represent the percentage of respondents who chose each response.

Questionnaire on Tablet Use at RRMC

Directions: As you may know, Dr. Bremerton is conducting a study to determine whether to institute a formal policy on tablet use by clinical staff.

If you own a tablet device, please respond to the following four questions. Your opinions can help us decide whether and how to develop a policy for tablet use at RRMC. We greatly appreciate your answering the following four questions.

1. Which brand of tablet do you own?
   47%   Apple iPad
   28%   Samsung Galaxy
   9%   Amazon Kindle Fire
   6%   Microsoft Surface
   10%   Other (please name the brand) **(Respondents named the Asus, Google Nexus, and a Toshiba model.)**

2. "I consider myself an expert user of my tablet."
   Strongly disagree_____ **8%** **2%** **13%** **19%** **58%** Strongly agree

3. Do you currently use your tablet for a clinical application, such as monitoring patients or ordering procedures?
   63%   Yes
   37%   No

4. If RRMC were to adopt a policy of using tablets for clinical applications (and to supply the appropriate software and training), which response best describes your attitude?
   27%   I would prefer to use my own tablet.
   38%   I would prefer to use a hospital-supplied tablet.
   35%   I don't have strong feelings either way about using my own or a hospital-supplied tablet.
   0%   I would prefer not to use any tablet at all for clinical applications.

Thank you!

Presenting the percentage data in boldface after each question is a clear way to communicate how the respondents replied. Although most readers will not be interested in the raw data, some will.

FIGURE 18.8   Sample Recommendation Report (*continued*)

WRITER'S CHECKLIST

In planning your recommendation report, did you

☐ consider feasibility? *(p. 485)*

☐ identify the questions that need to be answered (considering the problem or the opportunity)? *(p. 486)*

☐ analyze your audience? *(p. 487)*

☐ determine your purpose? *(p. 487)*

☐ establish criteria for the solution? *(p. 487)*

☐ carry out necessary research to determine the options and study them? *(p. 488)*

☐ draw valid conclusions about the results (if appropriate)? *(p. 490)*

☐ formulate recommendations based on the conclusions (if appropriate)? *(p. 491)*

Does the transmittal letter

☐ clearly state the title and, if necessary, the subject and purpose of the report? *(p. 495)*

☐ clearly state who authorized or commissioned the report? *(p. 495)*

☐ acknowledge any assistance you received? *(p. 495)*

☐ establish a courteous and professional tone? *(p. 495)*

Does the cover include

☐ the title of the report? *(p. 495)*

☐ your name and position? *(p. 495)*

☐ the date of submission? *(p. 495)*

☐ the company name or logo? *(p. 495)*

Does the title page

☐ include a title that clearly states the subject and purpose of the report? *(p. 495)*

☐ list your name and position and those of your principal reader(s)? *(p. 495)*

☐ include the date of submission of the report and any other identifying information? *(p. 495)*

Does the abstract

☐ list the report title, your name, and any other identifying information? *(p. 495)*

☐ clearly define the problem or opportunity that led to the project? *(p. 496)*

☐ briefly describe (if appropriate) the research methods? *(p. 496)*

☐ summarize the major results, conclusions, and recommendations? *(p. 496)*

Does the table of contents

☐ contain a sufficiently detailed breakdown of the major sections of the body of the report? *(p. 496)*

☐ reproduce the headings as they appear in your report? *(p. 496)*

☐ include page numbers or hyperlinks? *(p. 497)*

☐ Does the list of illustrations (or list of tables or list of figures) include all the graphics found in the body of the report? *(p. 497)*

Does the executive summary

☐ clearly state the problem or opportunity that led to the project? *(p. 499)*

☐ explain the major results, conclusions, recommendations, and managerial implications of your report? *(p. 499)*

☐ avoid technical vocabulary and concepts that a managerial audience is not likely to be interested in? *(p. 499)*

Does the introduction

☐ explain the subject of the report? *(p. 493)*

☐ explain the purpose of the report? *(p. 493)*

☐ explain the background of the report? *(p. 493)*

☐ describe your sources of information? *(p. 493)*

☐ indicate the scope of the report? *(p. 493)*

☐ briefly summarize the most significant findings of the project? *(p. 493)*

☐ briefly summarize your recommendations? *(p. 493)*

☐ explain the organization of the report? *(p. 493)*

☐ define key terms used in the report? *(p. 493)*

Does the methods section

☐ describe your methods in sufficient detail? *(p. 493)*

☐ justify your methods where necessary, explaining, for instance, why you chose one method over another? *(p. 493)*

Are the results presented
- [ ] clearly? *(p. 493)*
- [ ] objectively? *(p. 493)*
- [ ] without interpretation? *(p. 493)*

Are the conclusions
- [ ] presented clearly? *(p. 494)*
- [ ] drawn logically from the results? *(p. 494)*

Are the recommendations
- [ ] clear? *(p. 494)*
- [ ] specific? *(p. 494)*
- [ ] stated politely? *(p. 494)*

- [ ] in an appropriate form (list or paragraph)? *(p. 494)*
- [ ] in an appropriate location? *(p. 494)*
- [ ] Does the glossary include definitions of all the technical terms your readers might not know? *(p. 500)*
- [ ] Does the list of symbols include all the symbols and abbreviations your readers might not know? *(p. 502)*
- [ ] Does the list of references include all your sources and adhere to an appropriate documentation system? *(p. 502)*
- [ ] Do the appendixes include supporting materials that are too bulky to present in the report body or that are of interest to only a small number of your readers? *(p. 503)*

EXERCISES

1. An important element in carrying out a feasibility study is determining the criteria by which to judge each option. For each of the following topics, list five necessary criteria and five desirable criteria you might apply in assessing the options.
   a. buying a smartphone
   b. selecting a major
   c. choosing a company to work for
   d. buying a car
   e. choosing a place to live while you attend college

2. Go to www.usa.gov and select the "Government Agencies and Elected Officials" tab. Choose an agency and navigate to its website. Then find a recommendation report on a subject that interests you. In what ways does the structure of the report differ from the structure described in this chapter? In other words, does the report lack some of the elements described in this chapter, or does it have additional elements? Are the elements arranged in the order in which they are described in this chapter? In what ways do the differences reflect the audience, purpose, and subject of the report?

3. **TEAM EXERCISE** Write the recommendation report for the research project you proposed in response to Exercise 3 on page 460 in Chapter 16. Your instructor will tell you whether the report is to be written individually or collaboratively, but either way, work closely with a partner to review and revise your report. A partner can be very helpful during the planning phase, too, as you choose a topic, refine it, and plan your research.

4. Secure a recommendation report for a project subsidized by a city or federal agency, a private organization, or a university committee or task force. (Be sure to check your university's website; universities routinely publish strategic planning reports and other sorts of self-study reports. Also check www.nas.edu, which is the site for the National Academy of Sciences, the National Academy of Engineering, the Institute of Medicine, and the National Research Council, all of which publish reports on the web.) In a memo to your instructor, analyze the report. Overall, how effective is the report? How could the writers have improved the report? Submit a copy of the report along with your memo.

CASE 18: Writing a Recommendation

As president of a music-instruction company, you are exploring the possibility of purchasing an electric guitar that can be used for digital recording. You ask your director of guitar instruction to investigate options for you, but you find some problems with her methodology. To get started helping her research the matter more successfully and provide helpful recommendations, go to Achieve.

Writing Lab Reports

EXPERIMENTAL RESEARCH CAN TAKE PLACE in a lab or at a field site. Lab reports play an important role in the process of understanding a scientific problem and solving it in the real world.

Because communicating ideas in writing is central to the process of creating and publicizing knowledge, scientists and engineers spend a significant portion of their professional lives writing. Lab reports are one important way they communicate the results of their work. Adding new knowledge to a field is the collective effort of many people, each contributing information and ideas and building on the work of others. Although scientists and engineers might work alone or in small groups in a lab, if they want to contribute to their fields, they must convince readers that their findings are valid. For this reason, the ability to write clearly and persuasively is both necessary and valued in the sciences and engineering.

Persuasion and Lab Reports

Early in your science or engineering course work, you will likely be required to write lab reports presenting routine findings. That is, you will be asked to replicate studies and test hypotheses that have already been replicated and tested. The reason your instructor asks you to do such labs is to introduce you to the scientific method and teach you important lab skills you will need later when you *do* conduct original research.

Your written lab report is the primary evidence on which your audience will judge your credibility and skills as a researcher. If your writing is poor, your readers might conclude that you are also a sloppy researcher. And if you fail to convince your audience that your work is professional and valuable, you might lose funding to continue.

At first glance, a lab report might appear to be an unadorned presentation of methods, data, and formulas. It isn't. It is a carefully crafted argument meant to persuade an audience to accept your findings and conclusions. You need to justify virtually everything you did in the lab or in the field. To be persuasive, you need to answer these questions:

- Why is this topic important?
- What have others already learned about the subject?
- What remains to be learned about the subject?
- Why are you using this methodology, as opposed to other methodologies, in carrying out the work?
- Why do you draw these inferences, as opposed to others, from the data you generated?
- What should be done next? Why?

These questions do not have only one correct answer. You have to make the case that you have done your work professionally and used good judgment at every point—from choosing what to read in preparation, to designing and conducting the research in the field or the lab, to writing the report.

In other words, you have to be persuasive. In each section of your lab report, you must persuade your readers that you are a competent researcher who is familiar with the subject area and that you are presenting important information.

Because of the way people read lab reports, each section of the report must be persuasive. Although the report is organized as a single argument, most readers will not read it in a linear fashion, from start to finish. In fact, many readers will not read the whole report. They might begin with the title and abstract. If these two elements suggest that the report might be useful, they might skip to the end and read the conclusions. If the conclusions are persuasive, they might next read your introduction. If your introduction makes it clear that you are familiar with the field and know what you are doing, readers might then read the other sections of your report.

Understanding the Process of Writing Lab Reports

Many scientists and engineers record their laboratory work in notebooks with numbered pages or use specialized software. These notebooks contain enough information for other researchers or colleagues to understand how the procedures were conducted, why the procedures were conducted, and what the writer discovered. Your instructor might ask you to keep a lab notebook.

Although lab notebooks can be useful in legal disputes over who was first to conduct an experiment or make a discovery, their main purpose is to serve as researchers' personal records. When researchers are ready to communicate their findings by writing their lab reports, they turn to their notebooks. If you understand what information goes where in a lab report, you can plan ahead during your research.

The sections of a lab report do not need to be written in sequence. Some sections can be written early in the process; other sections must wait until you have finished your analysis of data. For example, although the title and abstract are often the first items to be read, they are usually the last items to be written. Likewise, it's easier to write your introduction after you have written your methods, results, and discussion. Only then will you have a clear idea of how you wish to introduce your argument.

Understanding the Structure of the Lab Report

Most lab reports have eight basic elements: title, abstract, introduction, materials and methods, results, discussion, conclusion, and references. Some lab reports have additional elements, such as acknowledgments and appendixes.

Although each researcher or instructor might prefer a slightly different format and style for organizing and presenting information, most lab reports follow a common structure reflecting the scientific method valued by scientists and engineers for centuries. This structure is typically used in lab reports that describe attempts to test a hypothesis or answer a question. It might also be used in lab reports that merely describe following a procedure and report the results of that procedure.

If you are a student, be sure to follow your instructor's guidelines for the structure of your report. For example, some instructors prefer that you combine the results and discussion sections. For studies involving multiple procedures and generating large amounts of data, your instructor might prefer that you present one set of data and analyze it before you introduce the next set of data.

The following discussion focuses on writing lab reports for undergraduate science and engineering courses.

TITLE

The title should be informative enough to enable readers to decide whether the report interests them. An informative title helps scientists and engineers save time by using abstracting and indexing services to locate the research most relevant for their needs.

Write your title with your readers in mind. Use only words and abbreviations that are familiar to them. The keywords in your title should be the terms commonly used by readers searching for information in your subject area. Keep in mind that because effective titles are specific, they tend to be long.

WEAK	Babbler Behavior
IMPROVED	Endocrine Correlates of Social and Reproductive Behaviors in a Group-Living Australian Passerine, the White-Browed Babbler
WEAK	New Technologies for Power Plants
IMPROVED	Evaluating New Instrumentation and Control Technologies for Safety-Related Applications in Nuclear Power Plants

ABSTRACT

The abstract summarizes the entire report, mirroring its structure: introduction, methods, results, discussion, and conclusion. However, because of space limitations, each section is addressed in only a sentence or two. Because your abstract might be distributed more widely than your entire report, it should contain enough information so that your readers can quickly decide whether to locate and read the whole report. Readers of abstracts are most interested in what questions motivated your study (introduction), what answers you discovered (results), and what implications your findings have (conclusions). A well-written abstract can also meet readers' need to stay up to date on research findings without spending a lot of time doing so.

Most readers prefer *informative abstracts*, which present the major findings. Less popular is the *descriptive abstract*, a shorter form that simply states the topics covered in the report without presenting the important results or conclusions.

For more about informative and descriptive abstracts, see Ch. 18.

INTRODUCTION

The introduction is the section of the report in which you begin to establish that your work is important. Here, you place your work in the broader context of your field by describing the hypothesis or question your study attempted to address and why this question is significant. The introduction should include a concise review of previous research relevant to your study and should describe how your study extends the knowledge in your field or overcomes a weakness in previous studies. By placing your study in the context of previous research, you establish its significance. Provide just enough detail to help readers understand how your study contributes new information to the field and to communicate the purpose of your study.

If you think readers will need specialized knowledge or theoretical background to understand your study, define important terms and present theoretical concepts in this section. Use your understanding of your audience to help you determine how much theoretical background to include. Often, instructors will ask you to write for an audience of classmates who are familiar with the general subject area but not familiar with the specific lab work you are reporting.

For more about definitions, see Ch. 20.

Your introduction should also briefly describe your methods: what you did to find an answer to your research question. Although your methods section provides a detailed account of your approach, your introduction should persuade your readers that your methods are appropriate given what has been done in previous studies.

If you include equations in the introduction, adhere to the conventions presented in the Guidelines box.

GUIDELINES Writing Equations

When you write equations, follow these four suggestions.

▶ **Use an equation editor, or write equations by hand.** Some word processors include equation editors that allow you to insert mathematical symbols, Greek letters, integrals, and fractions. Unless your word processor includes an equation editor or you have access to a commercially available equation editor, do not try to approximate an equation with standard text and punctuation. Many instructors allow students to handwrite equations on lab reports after they have been printed. Check with your instructor.

▶ **Place each equation on a separate line.** Because equations often involve characters positioned above or below the main line of type as well as odd-shaped symbols, equations written in the body of your text can create awkward line spacing,

(continued)

making your text difficult to read. Start each equation on a new line, with extra white space surrounding the equation.

▶ **Number each equation.** Number equations consecutively throughout your report, beginning with equation 1. Refer to the equation by number in your text: "The line represents the theoretical curve based on equation 1."

▶ **If appropriate, omit basic equations.** If your instructor's guidelines permit it, omit equations with which your readers are familiar, especially in advanced lab reports. Starting at too basic a level will make your report too long and will interrupt your readers' train of thought.

MATERIALS AND METHODS

Your purpose in writing the materials and methods section (sometimes called *equipment and methods*) is to convince your readers that your approach was appropriate for the question you hoped to answer, that you conducted your research or experiment carefully, and that your results are credible. Describe your methods in enough detail that another researcher could perform the same experiment using the same materials and methods. This characteristic, called *replicability*, is one of the foundations of the scientific method.

Most researchers begin the materials and methods section with a description or list of materials. Include any human subjects, organisms, chemicals, tools, and measuring devices used. Your description of materials might also include sketches, diagrams, schematics, or photographs of equipment, as well as explanations of how you set it up.

Next, describe your procedures. Include relevant conditions such as temperatures, observation dates and times, instrument settings and calibration, and site locations for field studies. Also indicate whether you encountered any difficulties with standard procedures and, if so, how you modified your approach to address those difficulties. Finally, if you had to make subjective decisions in collecting data, explain your choices. Although your audience might want to repeat your experiment, some instructors prefer that you avoid numbered, step-by-step instructions, presenting instead an organized description of what you did in sufficient detail that readers can understand your process. Organize this section chronologically, in the order in which you conducted your research or experiment. Include only those procedures that led to results that you present in the report.

When providing details, assume your readers are unfamiliar with the particulars of your experiment but know enough about lab procedures to evaluate your efforts. Your credibility rests on your ability to explain clearly what you did and why.

For more about active and passive voice, see Ch. 10.

Although writing in the active voice ("I collected three soil samples") is generally more concise, clearer, and more interesting than writing in the passive voice ("Three soil samples were collected"), the sciences and engineering have a long tradition of using the passive voice. The passive voice emphasizes the material studied and the actions taken, deemphasizing the role of the researcher. However, more and more scientific and engineering publications are accepting use of the active voice. Check with your instructor to learn which style is preferred.

RESULTS

Think of the results section as an opportunity to present the evidence you will use to support the claims you will make in your discussion. How persuasive this evidence is depends on how successfully you present it to your readers.

Your research will likely produce raw data in the form of numbers. In the results section, your task is to summarize the data relevant to the question or hypothesis you discussed in your introduction. Omit irrelevant data, but explain why you are doing so. When summarizing your data, help readers understand your findings by emphasizing major trends, magnitudes of values, associations, patterns of statistical significance, and exceptions. Typically, you present results in the same order used in describing the steps in the methods section, but you can change the order if you have a good reason to do so. For instance, you might use the more-important-to-less-important organizational pattern by beginning with the set of data that most clearly supports or negates your hypothesis.

For more about organizational patterns, see Ch. 7.

Be sure your data are complete and organized. For each major trend or pattern, begin with a statement of your findings and then support your statement with data. Depending on the type of data, you might present your supporting evidence with a combination of text and graphics (such as tables, graphs, and diagrams). If you include graphics, refer to them in the text with a statement explaining their significance.

For more about explaining the significance of graphics, see Ch. 12.

WEAK   Results of bacteria sampling are shown in Table 1.

IMPROVED   As Table 1 shows, the rate of bacteria growth increased as groundwater temperature increased.

In the results section, do not interpret or explain your data and do not speculate about problematic or atypical data. Save those explanations for the next section, the discussion.

ETHICS NOTE

PRESENTING DATA HONESTLY

The hallmark of good science is the honest and complete presentation of results, even if some of those results undercut the hypothesis. It is unethical to omit from your results section data that do not support your hypothesis. For instance, your hypothesis might be that as temperature increases, the growth rate of the organism you are studying increases. However, some of your data show that, above a certain temperature, the growth rate remains steady. You have replicated the procedure several times and gotten the same results, but you can't explain them. What do you do? You present the data and offer your best explanation, but you also state clearly that you can't fully explain the data. In other words, you tell the truth.

Likewise, it is unethical to choose a type of graphic that obscures negative findings or to design a graphic so that data points are omitted. For example, if you used a spreadsheet to record your data about temperature and growth rate, in order to present these data in a graphic, such as a line graph, you must select the cells you want to be represented in the

(continued)

graph. It would be easy to omit cells that included negative or inexplicable findings. However, doing so would be dishonest and therefore unethical—an obvious violation of scientific norms. Inconsistent data or contradictory results often lead researchers to examine their approach and assumptions more carefully, which can lead to breakthroughs in a field of study.

Remember that inconsistent data or contradictory results do not necessarily mean that you performed the research or experiment unprofessionally. They simply mean that reality is complicated. Readers will accept that. What they won't accept is a misleading or dishonest lab report.

DISCUSSION

Sometimes called *analysis*, the discussion section is where you interpret your results; that is, you answer the question or support (or argue against) the hypothesis you discussed in your introduction.

In organizing the discussion section, start by presenting the most important findings, which might include major trends, magnitudes of values, associations, patterns of statistical significance, and exceptions. Focus on offering explanations for your findings. Support your argument with data from your results, and do not hesitate to discuss problematic data or "failed" experiments. Remember that sometimes a negative result or a failure to find a significant difference helps researchers create new knowledge in their field. If your results do not support your hypothesis, argue for rejecting your hypothesis. If appropriate, support your argument with references to the work of other researchers, describing the degree to which your results match the results of previous studies. If your findings do not match the results of previous studies, suggest possible explanations for the differences.

CONCLUSION

Summarize the main points covered by your report in one or two concise paragraphs. Begin by reviewing the purpose of your research or experiment and the hypothesis (or hypotheses) you tested. Next, summarize the most important implications of your findings. The conclusion is your final opportunity to persuade your audience of the significance of your work. Do not introduce any new information or analysis in this section.

ACKNOWLEDGMENTS

If you received assistance from colleagues during the study or while preparing the lab report, identify and thank these people in an acknowledgments section. If your study was supported by funding, list the source of financial support in this section as well. Figure 19.1 shows a concise acknowledgments section. Typically, scientists and engineers ask permission of the people they wish to thank before including them in the acknowledgments.

REFERENCES

List all the references you cited in your lab report. (Do not list any sources that you consulted but did not cite.) Most of your citations will appear in the introduction, materials and methods, and discussion sections. However, check the other sections as well to make sure you include *all* sources cited in

Use *we* if the report was written by more than one author. Use *I* if you were the sole author.

Acknowledgments

We wish to express our appreciation to the Robert Wood Johnson Foundation for their generous support of this study. We also thank Dr. Mark Greenberg, Dr. David Jones, and Dr. Eileen Whitney for their valuable comments about an early draft of this report.

FIGURE 19.1   Acknowledgments Section

your report. Most scientists and engineers follow a particular documentation system for their discipline (see Appendix, Part B, p. 632). Check your instructor's preferences before selecting a documentation system.

APPENDIXES

An appendix, which follows the references, is the appropriate place for information that readers do not need to understand the body of your lab report. For example, an appendix might include long tables of measurements, specialized data, logs, analyses, or calculations.

By following the basic structure of a lab report discussed here, you will help your readers manage the large quantities of information produced in science and engineering. The title and abstract will help readers quickly decide if a report is relevant. The introduction and conclusion will provide the context for the study and describe the most important results of the study. If readers are persuaded to read further, the methods, results, and discussion will provide the detailed information they seek.

Understanding the Role of Science and Engineering Articles

If you are a science or engineering student, you will have many opportunities to write about your field once you enter the working world. Rather than writing for an audience of teachers, you will write for a professional audience of supervisors, members of professional boards, government officials, clients, other scientists or engineers, and potential funding sources. Your reports might be read only by people in your organization, or you might have a global audience.

Both researchers and practitioners sometimes develop their lab reports into articles for publication in professional journals. Some companies offer a monetary bonus to employees who publish articles in scholarly journals. These articles help the companies gain recognition as leaders in innovation and help the researchers demonstrate their ability to contribute new ideas to the field.

DOCUMENT ANALYSIS ACTIVITY

Evaluating Lab Reports

The grading sheet included here is used by an engineering professor to evaluate the lab reports written by students in his Principles of Environmental Engineering lab course. One of the labs in that course requires students to evaluate the efficiencies of several wastewater-treatment strategies and then determine whether the strategies can meet or exceed proposed discharge-effluent limits. The questions that follow ask you to consider the grading sheet based on the discussion of lab reports in this chapter.

SOLIDS REPORT GRADING SHEET

Total: /100		Student Names:
Points Earned	**Points Possible**	**Report Section**
	2	Cover (1) and title page (1)
	10	Abstract, including the following:
		Problem statement (3)
		Methods used (2)
		Results (2)
		Conclusions/Recommendations (3)
	6	Indexes (generated by the software), including the following:
		Table of Contents (2)
		List of Figures (2)
		List of Tables (2)
	12	Summary, including the following:
		Evaluation of results (6)
		Answers to questions that management would be concerned with (6)
	10	Introduction, including the following:
		Background information (2)
		Problem/purpose statement (2)
		Plan/procedures for testing; outline for selection/ solution (2)
		Description of rest of report (2)
		Definition of terms/limitations/assumptions (2)
	5	Procedures correctly name the tests and reference the procedures.
	10	Results summarize final results in paragraph form and include tables or graphs as appropriate. Results reference raw data and all example calculations.
	10	Discussion correctly interprets results and discusses their meanings; correctly discusses acceptable/ typical/reasonable ranges; and explains unexpected results.

(continued)

Evaluating Lab Reports *(continued)*

Total: /100		Student Names:
Points Earned	**Points Possible**	**Report Section**
	5	References (complete and correctly using CSE style)
	10	Appendixes
	10	Sample calculations presented accurately (5 each)
	10	Writing skill and format:
		Correct spelling and grammar (4)
		Consistency of headings, capitalization, bolding, italicization, table and graph appearance, etc. (2)
		Correct numbering and titling of tables (2)
		Correct numbering, titling, and design of graphs (axes labeled correctly, clear legends) (2)
	100	**TOTAL POINTS**

1. In what ways does this grading sheet follow the basic format of a lab report discussed in this chapter? In what ways does it not follow the basic format?

2. Do you agree or disagree with the relative importance placed on report elements in this grading sheet? Would you change the point allocation, and if so, how?

3. If the instructor distributed this grading sheet at the start of a lab assignment, how might students in the lab use it to help them write their lab reports?

Articles in the sciences and engineering are often organized like lab reports. However, rather than following an instructor's preferences, researchers in the workplace follow the *author guidelines* of the journal to which they will submit their article. Figure 19.2 shows one organization's author guidelines for preparing a manuscript.

This page provides prospective authors with information on how to prepare a manuscript for submission to IEEE journals. IEEE (which originally stood for Institute of Electrical and Electronics Engineers, Inc.) is the world's leading professional association for the advancement of technology. With 425,000 members (including 116,000 student members), IEEE publishes almost 150 journals and magazines.

in the subjects being treated. The papers are of long-range interest and broad significance. Applications and technological issues, as well as theory, are emphasized. The topics include all aspects of electrical and computer engineering and science. From time to time, papers on managerial, historical, economic, and ethical aspects of technology are published. Papers are authored by recognized authorities and reviewed by experts. They include extensive introductions written at a level suitable for the nonspecialist, with ample references for those who wish to probe further. Several issues a year are devoted to a single subject of special importance.

Prospective authors, before preparing a full-length manuscript, are urged to submit a proposal containing a description of the topic and its importance to PROCEEDINGS readers, a detailed outline of the proposed paper and its type of coverage, and a brief biography showing the authors' qualifications for writing the paper. A proposal can be reviewed most efficiently if it is sent electronically to the Managing Editor at j.calder@ieee.org. If the proposal receives a favorable review, the author will be encouraged to prepare the paper for publication consideration through the normal review process.

PROCEEDINGS OF THE IEEE
445 Hoes Lane
P.O. Box 1331
Piscataway, NJ 08855-1331 USA
Fax: +1 732 562 5456

IV. GENERAL MANUSCRIPT PREPARATION

A. Consecutive Numbering of Parts

All manuscript pages, footnotes, equations, and references should be labeled in consecutive numerical order. Illustrations and tables should be cited in text in numerical order. See Section IV-G of this guide.

B. Manuscript Formats

See copies of the publications for examples of proper paper formats and requirements for the types of papers accepted for each publication (i.e., Full Papers, Letters, Short Papers, etc.).

Full length papers generally consist of the title, byline, author affiliation, footnote (including any financial support acknowledgment), index terms, abstract, nomenclature if present, introduction, body, conclusions, reference list, list of figures and table captions, and original figures and tables for reproduction. A paper may also include appendices, a glossary of symbols, and an acknowledgment of nonfinancial support.

C. Abstract

The abstract should be limited to 50–200 words and should concisely state what was done, how it was done, principal results, and their significance. The abstract will appear later in various abstracts journals and should contain the most critical information of the paper.

Instructions explain how to number manuscript pages and graphics, how to format papers, what to include in an abstract, and how to document references.

IEEE publications require a unique documentation style and format. Sample formats for common types of references in this field are shown.

The more closely an article follows a journal's author guidelines, the more likely it is to be accepted for publication and the more quickly it will be available to readers.

D. References

A numbered list of references must be provided at the end of the paper. The list should be arranged in the order of citation in text, not in alphabetical order. List only one reference per reference number.

In text, each reference number should be enclosed by square brackets. Citations of references may be given simply as "in [1] ...", rather than as "in reference [1] ...". Similarly, it is not necessary to mention the authors of a reference unless the mention is relevant to the text. It is almost never useful to give dates of references in text. These will usually be deleted by Staff Editors if included.

Footnotes or other words and phrases that are not part of the reference format do not belong on the reference list. Phrases such as "For example," should not introduce references in the list, but should instead be given in parentheses in text, followed by the reference number, i.e., "For example, see [5]."

Sample correct formats for various types of references are as follows.

Books:

[1] G. O. Young, "Synthetic structure of industrial plastics," in *Plastics*, 2nd ed., vol. 3, J. Peters, Ed. New York: McGraw-Hill, 1964, pp. 15–64.
[2] W.-K. Chen, *Linear Networks and Systems*. Belmont, CA: Wadsworth, 1993, pp. 123–135.

Periodicals:

[3] J. U. Duncombe, "Infrared navigation—Part I: An assessment of feasibility," *IEEE Trans. Electron Devices*, vol. ED-11, pp. 34–39, Jan. 1959.
[4] E. P. Wigner, "Theory of traveling-wave optical laser," *Phys. Rev.*, vol. 134, pp. A635–A646, Dec. 1965.
[5] E. H. Miller, "A note on reflector arrays," *IEEE Trans. Antennas Propagat.*, to be published.

Articles from Conference Proceedings (published):

[6] D. B. Payne and J. R. Stern, "Wavelength-switched passively coupled single-mode optical network," in *Proc. IOOC-ECOC*, 1985, pp. 585–590.

Papers Presented at Conferences (unpublished):

[7] D. Ebehard and E. Voges, "Digital single sideband detection for interferometric sensors," presented at the 2nd Int. Conf. Optical Fiber Sensors, Stuttgart, Germany, Jan. 2-5, 1984.

Standards/Patents:

[8] G. Brandli and M. Dick, "Alternating current fed power supply," U.S. Patent 4 084 217, Nov. 4, 1978.

Technical Reports:

[9] E. E. Reber, R. L. Mitchell, and C. J. Carter, "Oxygen absorption in the Earth's atmosphere," Aerospace Corp., Los Angeles, CA, Tech. Rep. TR-0200 (4230-46)-3, Nov. 1968.

4

FIGURE 19.2   **Excerpt from IEEE Author Guidelines**
Excerpt from IEEE, "Information for IEEE Transactions, Journals, and Letters Author," p. 4.

When a scientist or engineer submits an article for publication, the argument and its supporting evidence are carefully evaluated by other professionals in the field. This type of evaluation is called *peer review*. Peer reviewers make suggestions for revision and, ultimately, recommend whether the editor of the journal should accept the article for publication. The review process can involve extensive revisions, multiple drafts, and even disagreements. When the peer reviewers agree that an article represents a persuasive scientific argument and offers significant new insights, the article is ready for copyediting and eventual publication in the journal. The entire process, from initial submission to publication, can last several months to well over a year.

An increasing number of journals now allow prepublication. That is, they permit an author to post a draft of an article either on the journal's own website or on some other site, enabling other researchers to read the draft and offer comments or suggest revisions. Then, the author can revise the article and submit it for publication by the journal. This practice is meant to take advantage of the expertise of a broad community of readers while maintaining the rigor of refereed publication.

Sample Lab Report

Figure 19.3 shows a lab report (adapted from Thomford, 2008) written for an undergraduate human-physiology lab experiment.

BILE SALTS ENHANCE LIPASE DIGESTION OF FATS

Abstract

Bile salts, which are secreted by the gall bladder into the small intestine, play an important role in the digestion of dietary fats by pancreatic lipase. The digestion of milk fat by pancreatic lipase in the presence and absence of bile salts was tested to demonstrate whether bile salts help pancreatic lipase digest fat more efficiently. Based on pH measurements at four time intervals, the production of fatty acids occurred most quickly in the test group containing bile salts and pancreatic lipase. In the test group containing only bile salts, no fat digestion occurred. Bile salts enhanced the rate of lipase-fat digestion but did not digest fats alone. This lab shows that bile salts act only to emulsify fats, enabling pancreatic lipase to digest fats more efficiently.

Keywords in the title reflect the major focus of the lab.

The abstract concisely communicates the purpose of the lab, the approach, the results, and the significance of the findings. Some instructors require an abstract, and some do not.

FIGURE 19.3 Sample Lab Report *(continued)*

Headings reflect common elements in a lab report and help communicate the organization of the report.

Because the discussion moves from general to specific, readers are introduced to background concepts necessary to understand the rest of the report.

Statements are supported by references to research relevant to the lab.

The purpose of the lab is clearly stated.

1

Introduction

The pancreas secretes various enzymes into the small intestine. One of these enzymes, pancreatic lipase, digests dietary fats into products such as glycerol and fatty acids (Mader, 2007). However, fat is insoluble in water-based chyme (the liquefied food processed by the stomach), and in the intestines the fats cling together, providing little surface area for attachment of the enzymes. This prolongs the time it takes the lipase to digest the fat.

In order to speed up the fat digestion process, bile salts, secreted by the gall bladder into the small intestine, act as a detergent that breaks up the fat droplets in the watery chyme, thus increasing the surface area for enzymatic digestion by lipase (Martini & Timmons, 2005). In other words, bile is an emulsifying agent. Emulsification of fats is achieved upon exposure to bile salts, which allows pancreatic lipase to digest the fat more efficiently. To demonstrate that bile salts enhance the digestion of fats, the digestion of milk fat by pancreatic lipase in the presence and absence of bile salts was tested.

Methods are detailed enough that another researcher could perform the same experiment using the same methods.

Methods include relevant procedures, such as the type of pH paper used, incubation temperature, and testing intervals. Note that the entire materials and methods section is written in the past tense.

2

Materials and Methods

Three groups of test tubes were set up; three replicates were set up in each group in order to provide an adequate sample size. To each group of three test tubes, the following were added:

Group 1: 3.0 ml of whole milk + 5.0 ml of water + 3 grains of bile salts
Group 2: 3.0 ml of whole milk + 5.0 ml of pancreatin solution (see below for concentration)
Group 3: 3.0 ml of whole milk + 5.0 ml of pancreatin solution + 3 grains of bile salts

Dehydrated pancreatin, derived from pig pancreas, was reconstituted in water (@ 1g/100ml) immediately before use. This solution contained the pancreatic lipase enzyme that was used to digest the milk fats. Dried grains of bile salts, derived from the pig gall bladder, were dissolved directly in each test tube.

To determine the increase in fatty acid end-products during the digestion of fats, the pH of the incubated solutions (as fatty acid concentration increases, pH decreases) was tested. The pH of each test tube was determined at time zero (beginning of the experiment) using "short range" pH paper (reads pH 6–10). The test tubes were incubated at 37°C for 1 hour. During that hour, the pH was tested every 20 minutes.

FIGURE 19.3   **Sample Lab Report** (*continued*)

3

Results

The pH did not decrease during the 60-minute incubation period in the negative control group 1, which contained only milk and bile salts (Table 1). In groups 2 and 3, the pH did decrease as the digestion of fats progressed, and fatty acids built up in the test tubes. After 20 minutes, the pH decreased in group 2 from 8.5 to 7.5, while there was a greater change in tube 3 (from pH 8.5 to 7.0). At 40 minutes incubation, the pH of the solutions in both groups 2 and 3 had dropped to 6.5 and did not decrease further at 60 minutes.

Table 1. Mean* pH of whole milk during incubation with bile salts and/or pancreatin

Time (minutes)	Group 1 (+ B.S.[1])	Group 2 (+ pancreatin)	Group 3 (+ B.S. + pancreatin)
0	8.3	8.5	8.5
20	8.4	7.5	7.0
40	8.3	6.5	6.5
60	8.3	6.5	6.5

*Mean pH of three sample tubes per group
[1]Bile salts

The data for all three groups are visually plotted in Figure 1.

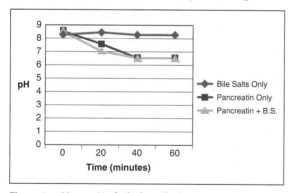

Figure 1.   Mean pH of whole milk during incubation with bile salts and/or pancreatin

---

Data are presented not only in a table but also in the text. Both the table and the figure are referred to in the text. Note that the results are not interpreted in this section of the lab report.

Note that the entire results section is written in the past tense.

The table and figure are labeled with informative titles. Each graphic clearly presents a manageable amount of information.

FIGURE 19.3   Sample Lab Report (*continued*)

4

Discussion

The discussion explains the purpose of the lab: to demonstrate that bile salts enhance the digestion of fats.

The negative control tube containing only bile salts and milk did not exhibit a pH change. Therefore, it was concluded that bile salts alone did not digest milk fats. Digestion of milk fats occurred in tubes 2 and 3, based on the observation of fatty acid by-product accumulation, as measured by a decrease in pH. However, the production of fatty acids occurred faster in group 3, as evidenced by the data at 20 minutes. This finding suggests that something present in the solution of group 3 aided in the digestion of the fats. Since the concentration of pancreatin was identical in groups 2 and 3, the addition of bile salts must have contributed to the digestion of the fats by breaking up those fat droplets into smaller particles, which increased the availability of substrate in group 3. The action of bile salts enhanced the rate of the lipase-fat digestion. The data from group 1, as a negative control, demonstrates that bile salts do not digest fats; therefore, bile salts must act only to emulsify the fats, thus enabling pancreatic lipase to act more efficiently. This conclusion is also supported by work done by Patton and Carey (1979) and reported by Bowen (2007).

The discussion also explains why the experiment yielded the results that it did. Relevant research findings are referenced to support the writer's explanations.

The final paragraph discusses the ambiguity of some of the results and suggests further experiments to address new questions raised by the current experiment.

It was also determined that either the enzymatic activity of pancreatic lipase is inhibited below pH 6.5, or the fat substrates were depleted by 40 minutes in tubes 2 and 3, since there was no change in pH between 40 and 60 minutes. Further experimentation will reveal which of these two possibilities occurred. Fox (2008) reported that the optimal activity of pancreatic lipase occurs at a pH of 8. Therefore, it is most likely that the lack of change in pH between 40 and 60 minutes in tubes 2 and 3 was due to the fact that the accumulation of fatty acid end-products produced an excessively acidic environment (pH 6.5 at 40 minutes), thereby inhibiting further enzyme activity. This may suggest that pancreatic lipase is denatured in weakly acidic conditions between pH 7.0 and 6.5. However, if this is not the case, an alternative conclusion may be that depletion of substrate occurred during the experimental period. This experiment should be re-run using cream or vegetable oil, both of which contain significantly more fat than whole milk.

5

References

The references contain all the works cited in the body of the report. References are a mix of up-to-date sources and older but still relevant research. References follow American Psychological Association (APA) format.

Bowen, R. (2007, August 8). *Absorption of lipids.* www.vivo.colostate.edu/hbooks /pathphys/digestion/smallgut/absorb_lipids.html

Fox, S. (2008). *A laboratory guide to human physiology, concepts and clinical applications.* McGraw-Hill Science/Engineering/Math.

Mader, S. (2007). *Human biology* (10th ed.). McGraw-Hill Science/Engineering/ Math.

Martini, F., & Timmons, M. (2005). *Human anatomy* (5th ed.). Benjamin Cummings.

Patton, J., & Carey, M. (1979). Watching fat digestion. *Science, 204,* 145–148.

FIGURE 19.3   Sample Lab Report (*continued*)

WRITER'S CHECKLIST

Does the title

☐ convey the major focus of your study? *(p. 534)*

☐ use only words and abbreviations familiar to your readers? *(p. 534)*

☐ use keywords that readers would likely use to search for research in your subject area? *(p. 534)*

Does the abstract

☐ state the problem or question addressed by your study? *(p. 534)*

☐ summarize your approach? *(p. 534)*

☐ summarize key results and conclusions? *(p. 534)*

☐ briefly discuss the implications of your study? *(p. 534)*

☐ make sense to readers who have not read your entire report? *(p. 534)*

Does the introduction

☐ concisely review research relevant to your study? *(p. 535)*

☐ explain how your study contributes to the field? *(p. 535)*

☐ state the purpose of your study? *(p. 535)*

☐ briefly describe your methods? *(p. 535)*

Does the materials and methods section

☐ describe the materials and equipment used (if appropriate)? *(p. 536)*

☐ describe your procedures with enough detail for readers to understand what you did? *(p. 536)*

☐ address any problems encountered and describe your solutions? *(p. 536)*

☐ include a description and rationale for any subjective measurements? *(p. 536)*

☐ present information in a logical order? *(p. 536)*

Does the results section

☐ summarize all the data relevant to the question or hypothesis you discussed in your introduction? *(p. 537)*

☐ exclude data not applicable to your argument? *(p. 537)*

☐ emphasize important trends and patterns? *(p. 537)*

☐ use text and graphics to present data concisely? *(p. 537)*

☐ introduce and explain (if appropriate) each graphic in your text? *(p. 537)*

☐ avoid interpreting, analyzing, and speculating about data? *(p. 537)*

Does the discussion section

☐ address the question or hypothesis discussed in your introduction? *(p. 538)*

☐ address the major trends, magnitudes of values, associations, patterns of statistical significance, and exceptions that emerged from your study? *(p. 538)*

☐ present plausible explanations for your results? *(p. 538)*

☐ support your argument with data from your results? *(p. 538)*

☐ compare your work to and comment on relevant work of other researchers? *(p. 538)*

☐ comment on problematic or "negative" results (if appropriate)? *(p. 538)*

Does the conclusion section

☐ briefly review the purpose of the research or experiment? *(p. 538)*

☐ summarize important implications of the findings? *(p. 538)*

☐ avoid introducing new information? *(p. 538)*

Does the acknowledgments section

☐ thank the people who helped you conduct the lab or write the lab report? *(p. 538)*

☐ identify any sources of financial support for the study? *(p. 538)*

☐ identify only people and organizations that have specifically given permission to be listed? *(p. 538)*

Does the references section

☐ identify each source cited in your lab report? *(p. 538)*

☐ contain complete and accurate information for each citation? *(p. 538)*

☐ follow your instructor's preferred format for references? *(p. 538)*

☐ Do the appendixes contain information not needed to understand the body of your report? *(p. 539)*

EXERCISES

1. Using a search engine, locate three or four sample lab reports. In a brief memo to your instructor, compare and contrast the basic elements of the reports. In what ways do they follow a similar format? If the reports differ in format, why do you think the authors chose to present information in the manner they did? For more about memos, see Ch. 14, p. 386.

2. Locate a word-processing program with an equation editor, or download a free equation editor from the internet. Practice creating four to six equations you might use in your field. If you do not regularly use equations, copy a few equations from science or math textbooks. In a brief memo to your instructor, evaluate how easy it is to use the equation editor.

3. **TEAM EXERCISE** Form groups of students from different majors. Each group member should locate author guidelines for a journal in his or her field. Often, author guidelines can be found on the website of a journal or in the back of journal issues. As a group, compare the guidelines. How are the guidelines similar? How are they different? Present your results in a memo to your instructor.

CASE 19: Understanding a Lab Report

You've been asked to assist a professor who is teaching an introductory-level anatomy and physiology course that includes a lab component. Because many students either have not prepared lab reports at all or prepared them much differently in high school, the professor finds it helpful to distribute a sample lab report. The sample, however, is not comprehensive, so you have been asked to create a handout explaining what this particular lab report does and doesn't do, with the main goal of helping students understand the objective of a lab report. If your instructor has assigned it, go to Achieve to get started writing your handout.

Writing Definitions, Descriptions, and Instructions

THIS CHAPTER DISCUSSES definitions, descriptions, and instructions. The first step is to define these three terms:

- A *definition* is typically a brief explanation, using words and sometimes graphics, of what an item is or what a concept means. You could write a definition of *file format* or of *regenerative braking*.

- A *description* is typically a longer explanation — usually accompanied by graphics — of the physical or operational features of an object, mechanism, or process. You could write a description of a wind turbine, of global warming, or of shale-oil extraction.

- A set of *instructions* is a kind of process description, almost always accompanied by graphics, intended to enable a person to carry out a task. You could write a set of instructions for installing a new roof or for using an app on your tablet.

Although each can appear independently, definitions, descriptions, and instructions are often presented together in a set of product information. For instance, a store that sells building materials for homeowners might create a product-information set about how to lay a brick patio. In this set might be definitions of tools (such as a mason's line), descriptions of objects (such as different types of edging materials, including plastic, metal, masonry, and wood), and step-by-step instructions for planning, laying, and maintaining the patio.

Regardless of your field, you will write definitions, descriptions, and instructions frequently. Whether you are communicating with other technical professionals, managers, or the public, you must be able to define key concepts, describe processes, and explain how to carry out tasks.

Writing Definitions

The world of business and industry depends on clear definitions. Suppose you learn at a job interview that the prospective employer pays tuition and expenses for employees' job-related education. You would need to study the employee-benefits manual to understand just what the company would pay for. Who, for instance, is an *employee*? Is it anyone who works for the company, or is it someone who has worked for the company full-time (40 hours per week) for at least six uninterrupted months? What is *tuition*? Does it include incidental laboratory or student fees? What is *job-related education*? Does a course about time management qualify? What, in fact, constitutes *education*?

Definitions are common in communicating policies and standards "for the record." Definitions also have many uses outside legal or contractual contexts. Two such uses occur frequently:

- **Definitions clarify a description of a new development or a new technology in a technical field.** For instance, a zoologist who has discovered a new animal species names and defines it.

- **Definitions help specialists communicate with less knowledgeable readers.** A manual explaining how to tune up a car includes definitions of parts and tools.

Definitions, then, are crucial in many kinds of technical communication, from brief letters and memos to technical reports, manuals, and journal articles. All readers, from the general reader to the expert, need effective definitions to carry out their jobs.

The writing process for a definition is similar to that for any other technical communication. The Focus on Process box that follows outlines this process.

ANALYZING THE WRITING SITUATION FOR DEFINITIONS

The first step in writing effective definitions is to analyze the writing situation: the audience and the purpose of the document.

Unless you know who your readers will be and how much they know about the subject, you cannot determine which terms to define or what kind of definition to write. Physicists wouldn't need a definition of *entropy*, but lawyers might. Builders know what a molly bolt is, but many insurance agents don't.

For more about audience and purpose, see Ch. 5.

When you write for people whose first language is not English, definitions are particularly important. Consider the following suggestions:

1. **For longer documents, create a glossary (a list of definitions).** For more on glossaries, see Chapter 18.

2. **Use Simplified English and easily recognizable terms in definitions.** For more on Simplified English, see Chapter 10.

FOCUS ON PROCESS: Definitions

When writing definitions, pay special attention to these steps in the writing process.

PLANNING

Analyze your audience and determine your purpose to decide how much information to provide and what kind of definition to write.

DRAFTING

Draft your definition with your audience and purpose in mind. To create extended definitions, consider using tools such as graphics, examples, and analogy, as explained in "Determining the Kind of Definition to Write" on pp. 555–58. Also review the writing advice in Chapter 3.

REVISING

Think again about your audience and purpose, and then make appropriate changes to your draft. See the section on "Parenthetical, Sentence, and Extended Definitions" in the Writer's Checklist at the end of this chapter.

EDITING

Make sure your definition will be clear to your readers and gets the point across without grammatical errors. See Chapter 10 for advice on writing correct and effective sentences.

PROOFREADING

Read through the definition slowly, making sure you have written what you wanted to write. Get help from others. See Appendix, Part C, for proofreading tips.

3. **Pay close attention to key terms.** Be sure to carefully define terms that are essential for understanding the document. If, for instance, your document is about angioplasty, you will want to be especially careful when defining it.

4. **Use graphics to help readers understand a term or concept.** Graphics are particularly helpful to readers who speak different languages, and they reduce the cost of translating text from one language to another.

Think, too, about your purpose. For readers who need only a basic understanding of a concept—say, travelers researching lodging options who want to learn more about *time-sharing vacation resorts*—a brief, informal definition is usually sufficient. However, readers who need to understand an object, process, or concept thoroughly and be able to carry out tasks related to it need a more formal and elaborate definition. For example, the definition of a "Class 2 Alert" written for operators at a nuclear power plant must be comprehensive, specific, and precise.

DETERMINING THE KIND OF DEFINITION TO WRITE

Your audience and purpose will also determine the length and formality of your definitions. There are three basic types of definitions: parenthetical, sentence, and extended.

Writing Parenthetical Definitions A *parenthetical definition* is a brief clarification within an existing sentence. Sometimes, a parenthetical definition is simply a word or phrase that is enclosed in parentheses or commas or introduced by a colon or a dash. In the following examples, the term being defined is shown in italics, and the definition is underscored:

> The computers were infected by a *Trojan horse* (<u>a destructive program that appears to be benign</u>).

> Before the metal is plated, it is immersed in the *pickle*: <u>an acid bath that removes scales and oxides from the surface.</u>

Parenthetical definitions are not meant to be comprehensive; rather, they serve as quick and convenient ways of introducing terms. But make sure your definition is clear. You have gained nothing if readers don't understand it:

> Next, check for blight on the *epicotyl*, <u>the stem portion above the cotyledons.</u>

Readers who need a definition of *epicotyl* are unlikely to know the meaning of *cotyledons*. To solve this problem, think carefully about your readers' understanding of your subject before including technical terms specific to that subject.

Writing Sentence Definitions A *sentence definition*—a one-sentence clarification—is more formal than a parenthetical definition. A sentence definition usually follows a standard pattern: the item to be defined is placed in a category of similar items and then distinguished from them.

ITEM	=	CATEGORY	+	DISTINGUISHING CHARACTERISTICS
Open-source software	is	computer software		whose programming code is freely available to users.
Hypnoanalysis	is	a psychoanalytical technique		in which hypnosis is used to elicit information from a patient's unconscious mind.

In many cases, a sentence definition also includes a graphic. For example, a definition of an electron microscope would probably include a photograph, diagram, or drawing.

Writers often use sentence definitions to present a working definition for a particular document: "In this report, *electron microscope* refers to any microscope that uses electrons rather than visible light to produce magnified images." Such definitions are sometimes called *stipulative definitions* because the writer is stipulating how the term will be used in the context of the document rather than offering a general definition of the term.

◢
GUIDELINES Writing Effective Sentence Definitions

The following suggestions can help you write effective sentence definitions.

▶ **Be specific in stating the category and the distinguishing characteristics.** If you write, "A Bunsen burner is a burner that consists of a vertical metal tube connected to a gas source," the imprecise category—"a burner"—ruins the definition: many types of large-scale burners use vertical metal tubes connected to gas sources.

▶ **Don't describe a specific item if you are defining a general class of items.** If you wish to define *catamaran*, don't describe a particular catamaran. The catamaran you see on the beach in front of you might be made by Hobie and have a white hull and blue sails, but those characteristics are not features of catamarans in general.

▶ **Avoid writing circular definitions—that is, definitions that merely repeat the key words or the distinguishing characteristics of the item being defined in the category.** The definition "A required course is a course that is required" is useless: required of whom, by whom? However, in defining electron microscopes, you can repeat *microscope* because *microscope* is not the difficult part of the item. The purpose of defining *electron microscope* is to clarify *electron* as it applies to a particular type of microscope.

▶ **Be sure the category contains a noun or a noun phrase rather than a phrase beginning with *when*, *what*, or *where*.**

INCORRECT   A brazier is what is used to . . .
CORRECT   A brazier is a metal pan used to . . .

INCORRECT   Hypnoanalysis is when hypnosis is used to . . .
CORRECT   Hypnoanalysis is a psychoanalytical technique in which . . .

Writing Extended Definitions An *extended definition* is a more detailed explanation—usually one or more paragraphs—of an object, process, or idea. Often an extended definition begins with a sentence definition, which is then elaborated. For instance, the sentence definition "An electrophorus is a laboratory instrument used to generate static electricity" tells you the basic function of the device, but it doesn't explain how it works, what it is used for, or its strengths and limitations. An extended definition would address these and other topics.

There is no one way to "extend" a definition. Your analysis of your audience and the purpose of your communication will help you decide which method to use. In fact, an extended definition sometimes employs several of the eight techniques discussed here.

Graphics Perhaps the most common way to present an extended definition in technical communication is to include a graphic and then explain it. Graphics are useful in defining not only physical objects but also concepts and ideas. A definition of *temperature inversion*, for instance, might include a diagram showing the forces that create temperature inversions. The extended definition of *hydraulic fracturing* in Figure 20.1 is made up of both words and graphics.

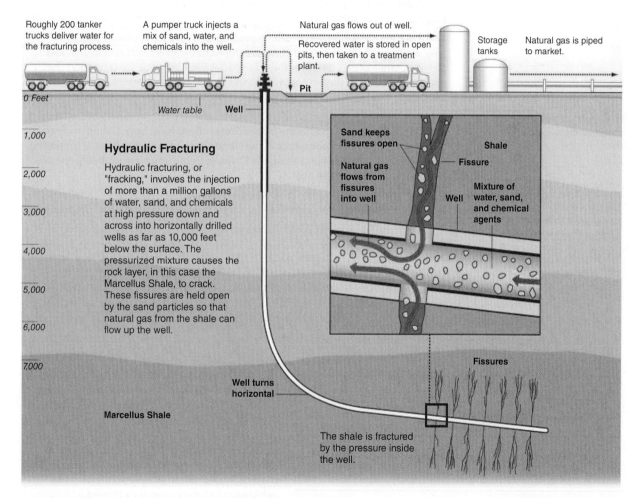

FIGURE 20.1   An Extended Definition with Graphics

The graphic provides important visual information that clarifies the concept of hydraulic fracturing.

ProPublica, 2016: www.propublica.org/special/hydraulic-fracturing-national.

ProPublica.

Examples Examples are particularly useful in making an abstract or difficult-to-explain term easier to understand. The following excerpt is an extended definition of *marine protected areas* from the website of the National Oceanic and Atmospheric Administration (NOAA.gov, 2016).

> Marine protected areas (MPAs) in the U.S. come in a variety of forms and are established and managed by all levels of government. There are marine sanctuaries, estuarine research reserves, ocean parks, and marine wildlife refuges. Each of these sites differ. MPAs may be established to protect ecosystems, preserve cultural resources such as shipwrecks and archaeological sites, or sustain fisheries production.
>
> There is often confusion and debate regarding what the term "marine protected area" really means. Some people interpret MPAs to mean areas closed to all human activities, while others interpret them as special areas set aside for recreation (e.g., national parks) or to sustain commercial use (e.g., fishery management areas). These are just a few examples of the many types of MPAs.

This extended definition includes examples of the many types of MPAs.

> In reality, "marine protected area" is a term that encompasses a variety of conservation and management methods in the United States. If you have been fishing in central California, diving near a shipwreck in the Florida Keys, camping in Acadia, snorkeling in the Virgin Islands, or hiking along the Olympic Coast, you were probably one of thousands of visitors to an MPA.
>
> In the U.S., MPAs span a range of habitats, including the open ocean, coastal areas, intertidal zones, estuaries, and the Great Lakes. They also vary widely in purpose, legal authorities, agencies, management approaches, level of protection, and restrictions on human uses.

Principle of Operation Describing the principle of operation—the way something works—is an effective way to develop an extended definition, especially for an object or a process. The following excerpt from an extended definition of *adaptive cruise control* (Canadian Association, 2009) is based on the mechanism's principle of operation.

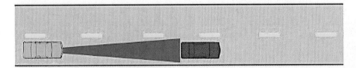

The ACC system in the green car detects the slower-moving red car.

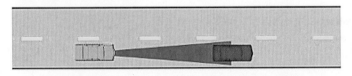

ACC reduces the green car's speed and maintains the preset headway.

Adaptive cruise control (ACC) employs sensing and control systems to monitor the vehicle's position with respect to any vehicle ahead. When a vehicle equipped with ACC approaches a slower moving vehicle, the ACC system reduces the vehicle speed in order to maintain a preset following distance (headway). However, when the traffic ahead clears, the ACC system automatically accelerates the vehicle back to the preset travel speed.

ACC systems use forward-looking radar or laser detection (lidar) systems to monitor the vehicle's position with respect to any vehicle in front and change the speed in order to maintain a preset following distance (headway).

High-tech vehicle safety systems. Used with permission from Canadian Association of Road Safety Professionals.

The system typically allows the driver to preset a "following time," for example a two-second gap between vehicles. The ACC computer makes calculations of speed, distance, and time based on the sensor inputs and makes appropriate adjustments to the vehicle's speed to maintain the desired headway.

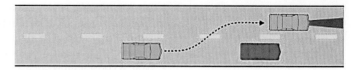

The green car overtakes the red car. The road ahead is clear. The ACC system resumes the vehicle's preset cruising speed.

High-tech vehicle safety systems. Used with permission from Canadian Association of Road Safety Professionals.

Partition Partitioning is the process of dividing a thing or an idea into smaller parts so that readers can understand it more easily. Figure 20.2 uses partition to define the components of a roof.

For more about partitioning, see Ch. 7.

Comparison and Contrast Using comparison and contrast, a writer discusses the similarities or differences between the item being defined and an item with which readers are more familiar. The following definition of VoIP (Voice over Internet Protocol) contrasts this new form of phone service to the form we all know.

For more about comparison and contrast, see Ch. 7.

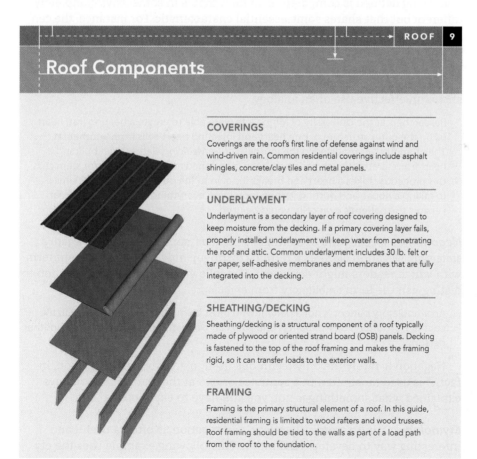

FIGURE 20.2 Definition by Partition

An excerpt from an architectural guide on constructing wind-resistant frame structures.

Source: Federal Alliance for Safe Homes, 2016: http://aiad8.prod.acquiasites.com /sites/default/files/2016-04/Res-Resilient -Design-Guide-HighWind-WoodFrame -Constr_0.pdf.

In this excerpt, the second and third paragraphs briefly compare VoIP and traditional phone service. Notice that this passage is organized according to the part-by-part comparison-and-contrast pattern. For more about this organizational pattern, see Ch. 7.

Voice over Internet Protocol is a form of phone service that lets you connect to the internet through your cable or DSL modem. VoIP service uses a device called a telephony adapter, which attaches to the broadband modem, transforming phone pulses into IP packets sent over the internet.

VoIP is considerably cheaper than traditional phone service: for as little as $20 per month, users get unlimited local and domestic long-distance service. For international calls, VoIP service is only about three cents per minute, about a third the rate of traditional phone service. In addition, any calls from one person to another person with the same VoIP service provider are free.

However, sound quality on VoIP cannot match that of a traditional land-based phone. On a good day, the sound is fine on VoIP, but frequent users comment on clipping and dropouts that can last up to a second. In addition, sometimes the sound has the distant, tinny quality of some of today's cell phones.

Analogy An *analogy* is a specialized kind of comparison. In a traditional comparison, the writer compares one item to another, similar item: an electron microscope to a light microscope, for example. In an analogy, however, the item being defined is compared to an item that is in some ways completely different but that shares some essential characteristic. For instance, the central processing unit of a computer is often compared to a brain. Obviously, these two items are very different, except that the relationship of the central processing unit to the computer is similar to that of the brain to the body.

The following example from a definition of *decellularization* (Falco, 2008) shows an effective use of an analogy.

The writer of this passage uses the analogy of gutting a house to clarify the meaning of *decellularization*.

Researchers at the University of Minnesota were able to create a beating [rat] heart using the outer structure of one heart and injecting heart cells from another rat. Their findings are reported in the journal *Nature Medicine*. Rather than building a heart from scratch, which has often been mentioned as a possible use for stem cells, this procedure takes a heart and breaks it down to the outermost shell. It's similar to taking a house and gutting it, then rebuilding everything inside. In the human version, the patient's own cells would be used.

Negation A special kind of contrast is *negation*, sometimes called *negative statement*. Negation clarifies a term by distinguishing it from a different term with which readers might confuse it. The following example uses negation to distinguish the term *ambulatory* from *ambulance*.

An ambulatory patient is not a patient who must be moved by ambulance. On the contrary, an ambulatory patient is one who can walk without assistance from another person.

Negation is rarely the only technique used in an extended definition; in fact, it is used most often in a sentence or two at the start. Once you have explained what something is not, you still have to explain what it is.

Etymology Citing a word's *etymology*, or derivation, is often a useful and interesting way to develop a definition. The following example uses the etymology of *spam*—unsolicited junk email—to define it.

For many decades, Hormel Foods has manufactured a luncheon meat called Spam, which stands for "Shoulder Pork and hAM"/"SPiced hAM." Then, in the 1970s, the English comedy team Monty Python broadcast a skit about a restaurant that served Spam with every dish. In describing each dish, the waitress repeats the word *Spam* over and over, and several Vikings standing in the corner chant the word repeatedly. In the mid-1990s, two businessmen hired a programmer to write a program that would send unsolicited ads to thousands of electronic newsgroups. Just as Monty Python's chanting Vikings drowned out other conversation in the restaurant, the ads began drowning out regular communication online. As a result, people started calling unsolicited junk email *spam*.

Etymology is a popular way to begin definitions of *acronyms*, which are abbreviations pronounced as words:

RAID, which stands for redundant array of independent (or inexpensive) disks, refers to a computer storage system that can withstand a single (or, in some cases, even double) disk failure.

Etymology, like negation, is rarely used alone in technical communication, but it provides an effective way to introduce an extended definition.

A Sample Extended Definition Figure 20.3 on page 560 is an example of an extended definition addressed to a general audience.

DECIDING WHERE TO PLACE THE DEFINITION

If you are writing a sentence definition or an extended definition, you need to decide where to put it. A definition is typically placed in one of these six locations:

- **In the text.** The text is an appropriate place for sentence definitions that many or most of your readers will need and for extended definitions of important terms.

- **In a marginal gloss.** Sentence definitions placed in the margin are easy to see, and they don't interrupt readers who don't need them.

- **In a hyperlink.** In a web page, definitions can be put in a separate file and displayed.

- **In a footnote.** A footnote is a logical place for an occasional sentence definition or extended definition. The reader who doesn't need it will ignore it. However, footnotes can slow readers down by interrupting the flow of the discussion. If you think you will need more than one footnote for a definition on every two to three pages, consider including a glossary.

- **In a glossary.** A glossary—an alphabetized list of definitions—can accommodate sentence definitions and extended definitions of fewer than three or four paragraphs in one convenient location. A glossary can be placed at the beginning of a document (for example, after the executive summary in a report) or at the end, preceding the appendixes.

- **In an appendix.** An appendix is appropriate for an extended definition of a page or more, which would be cumbersome in a glossary or footnote.

For more about glossaries and appendixes, see Ch. 18.

FIGURE 20.3 An
Extended Definition
GPS.gov, 2013: www.gps.gov/systems
/gps/

What is GPS?

The first paragraph of this extended
definition of GPS begins with a
sentence definition.

The Global Positioning System (GPS) is a U.S.-owned utility that
provides users with positioning, navigation, and timing (PNT)
services. This system consists of three segments: the space
segment, the control segment, and the user segment. The U.S. Air
Force develops, maintains, and operates the space and control
segments.

The second sentence serves as an
advance organizer for the definition, explaining that the definition
will be extended by partition: GPS
consists of three segments.

Space Segment
The space segment consists of a nominal
constellation of 24 operating satellites that
transmit one-way signals that give the current
GPS satellite position and time. *LEARN MORE...* ➡

The body of this extended definition consists of three sections, each
of which is introduced by a graphic
and a topic sentence explaining the
segment.

Control Segment
The control segment consists of worldwide
monitor and control stations that maintain the
satellites in their proper orbits through
occasional command maneuvers, and adjust the
satellite clocks. It tracks the GPS satellites,
uploads updated navigational data, and
maintains health and status of the satellite
constellation. *LEARN MORE...* ➡

Links lead the reader to much more
information about each segment,
including more text, diagrams, and
videos.

User Segment
The user segment consists of the GPS receiver
equipment, which receives the signals from the
GPS satellites and uses the transmitted
information to calculate the user's three-
dimensional position and time. *LEARN HOW GPS IS
USED...* ➡

Writing Descriptions

Technical communication often requires descriptions: verbal and visual representations of the physical or operational features of objects, mechanisms, and processes.

- **Objects.** An object is anything from a natural physical site, such as a volcano, to a synthetic artifact, such as a battery. A tomato plant is an object, as is an automobile tire or a book.

- **Mechanisms.** A mechanism is a synthetic object consisting of a number of identifiable parts that work together. A cell phone is a mechanism, as is a voltmeter, a lawnmower, or a submarine.

- **Processes.** A process is an activity that takes place over time. Species evolve; steel is made; plants perform photosynthesis. *Descriptions of processes,* which explain how something happens, differ from *instructions,* which explain how to do something. Readers of a process description want to *understand* the process; readers of instructions want a step-by-step guide to help them *perform* the process.

Descriptions of objects, mechanisms, and processes appear in virtually every kind of technical communication. For example, an employee who wants to persuade management to buy some equipment includes a description of the equipment in the proposal to buy it. A company manufacturing a consumer product provides a description and a photograph of the product on its website to attract buyers. A developer who wants to build a housing project includes in his proposal to municipal authorities descriptions of the geographical area and of the process he will use in developing that area.

Typically, a description is part of a larger document. For example, a maintenance manual for an air-conditioning system might begin with a description of the system to help the reader understand first how it operates and then how to fix or maintain it.

The writing process for a description is similar to that for any other type of technical communication. The Focus on Process box that follows outlines this process.

ANALYZING THE WRITING SITUATION FOR DESCRIPTIONS

Before you begin to write a description, consider carefully how the audience and the purpose of the document will affect what you write. What does the audience already know about the general subject? For example, if you want to describe how the next generation of industrial robots will affect car manufacturing, you first have to know whether your readers understand the current process and whether they understand robotics.

Your sense of your audience will determine not only how technical your vocabulary should be but also how long your sentences and paragraphs

FOCUS ON PROCESS: Descriptions

When writing descriptions, pay special attention to these steps in the writing process.

PLANNING
Analyze your audience and determine your purpose to decide how much description is necessary. Consider whether your description would be most effective in the form of text to be read, a script for a voice-over, a visual guide, or some combination of these formats.

DRAFTING
Draft your object, mechanism, or process description with your audience and purpose in mind. Clearly introduce the description, provide the appropriate level of detail, and include a brief conclusion. Also review the writing advice in Chapter 3.

REVISING
Think again about your audience and purpose, and then make appropriate changes to your draft. See the section on "Descriptions of Objects and Mechanisms" or the section on "Process Descriptions" in the Writer's Checklist at the end of this chapter.

EDITING
Make sure your description will be clear to your readers and gets the point across without grammatical errors. See Chapter 10 for advice on writing correct and effective sentences.

PROOFREADING
Read through the description slowly, making sure you have written what you wanted to write. Get help from others. See Appendix, Part C, for proofreading tips.

should be. Another audience-related factor is your use of graphics. Less knowledgeable readers need simple graphics; they might have trouble understanding sophisticated schematics or decision charts. As you consider your audience, think about whether any of your readers are from other cultures and might therefore expect different topics, organization, or writing style in the description.

Consider, too, your purpose. What are you trying to accomplish with this description? If you want your readers to understand how a personal computer works, write a *general description* that applies to several brands and sizes of computers. If you want your readers to understand how a specific computer works, write a *particular description*. A general description of personal computers might classify them by size, then go on to describe desktops, laptops, and tablets in general terms. A particular description, however, will describe only one model of personal computer, such as a Millennia 2500. Your purpose will determine every aspect of the description, including its length, the amount of detail, and the number and type of graphics.

There is no single organization or format used for descriptions. Because descriptions are written for different audiences and different purposes, they can take many shapes and forms. However, the following four suggestions will guide you in most situations:

1. Indicate clearly the nature and scope of the description.
2. Introduce the description clearly.
3. Provide appropriate detail.
4. End the description with a brief conclusion.

INDICATING CLEARLY THE NATURE AND SCOPE OF THE DESCRIPTION

If the description is to be a separate document, give it a title. If the description is to be part of a longer document, give it a section heading. In either case, clearly state the subject and indicate whether the description is general or particular. For instance, a general description of an object might be entitled "Description of a Minivan," and a particular description, "Description of the 2020 Honda Odyssey." A general description of a process might be called "Description of the Process of Designing a New Production Car," and a particular description, "Description of the Process of Designing the Chevrolet Malibu."

For more about titles and headings, see Ch. 9.

INTRODUCING THE DESCRIPTION CLEARLY

Provide any information that readers need in order to understand the detailed information that follows. Most introductions to descriptions are general: you want to give readers a broad understanding of the object, mechanism, or process. You might also provide a graphic that introduces your readers to the overall concept. For example, for a process, you might include a flowchart summarizing the steps in the body of the description; for an object, such as a robot, you might include a photograph or a drawing showing the major components you will describe in detail in the body.

Table 20.1 (on p. 564) shows some of the basic kinds of questions you might want to answer in introducing object, mechanism, and process descriptions. If the answer is obvious, simply move on to the next question.

Figure 20.4 (on p. 564) shows the introductory graphic accompanying a description of a robot.

PROVIDING APPROPRIATE DETAIL

In the body of a description—the part-by-part or step-by-step section—treat each major part or step as a separate item. In describing an object or a mechanism, define each part and then, if applicable, describe its function, operating principle, and appearance. In discussing the appearance, include shape, dimensions, material, and physical details such as texture and color (if essential). Some descriptions might include other qualities, such as weight or hardness.

In describing a process, treat each major step as if it were a separate process. Do not repeat your answer to the question about who or what performs the

TABLE 20.1 Questions To Answer in Introducing a Description

FOR OBJECT AND MECHANISM DESCRIPTIONS	FOR PROCESS DESCRIPTIONS
• **What is the item?** You might start with a sentence definition.	• **What is the process?** You might start with a sentence definition.
• **What is the function of the item?** If the function is not implicit in the sentence definition, state it: "Electron microscopes magnify objects that are smaller than the wavelengths of visible light."	• **What is the function of the process?** Unless the function is obvious, state it: "The main purpose of performing a census is to obtain current population figures, which government agencies use to revise legislative districts and determine revenue sharing."
• **What does the item look like?** Sometimes an object is best pictured with both graphics and words. Include a photograph or drawing if possible. (See Chapter 12 for more about incorporating graphics into your text.) If you cannot use a graphic, use an analogy or comparison: "The USB drive is a plastic- or metal-covered device, much smaller than a pack of gum, often with a removable cap that covers the type-A USB connection." Mention the material, texture, color, and other physical characteristics, if relevant.	• **Where and when does the process take place?** "Each year the stream is stocked with hatchery fish in the first week of March." Omit these facts only if your readers already know them.
	• **Who or what performs the process?** If there is any doubt about who or what performs the process, state that information.
• **How does the item work?** In a few sentences, define the operating principle. Sometimes objects do not "work"; they merely exist. For instance, a ship model has no operating principle.	• **How does the process work?** "The four-treatment lawn-spray plan is based on the theory that the most effective way to promote a healthy lawn is to apply different treatments at crucial times during the growing season. The first two treatments — in spring and early summer — consist of . . ."
• **What are the principal parts of the item?** Limit your description to the principal parts. A description of a bicycle, for instance, would not mention the many nuts and bolts that hold the mechanism together; it would focus on the chain, gears, pedals, wheels, and frame.	• **What are the principal steps in the process?** Name the steps in the order in which you will describe them. The principal steps in changing an automobile tire, for instance, are jacking up the car, replacing the old tire with the new one, and lowering the car back to the ground. Changing a tire also includes secondary steps, such as placing chocks against the tires to prevent the car from moving once it is jacked up. Explain or refer to these secondary steps at the appropriate points in the description.

FIGURE 20.4 Graphic with Linked Descriptions

This web-based description includes overview videos on four main topics: Form, Function, Movement, and Intelligence. Within each main topic, more specific information is given. For example, the Form tab includes specifics about features such as size, composition, and power source. Clicking on any of the links provides more detailed information about the robot's features.
Honda, 2016: http://asimo.honda.com /inside-asimo/.
Honda.

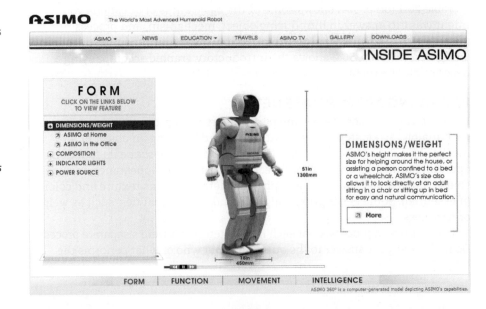

action unless a new agent performs it, but do answer the other important questions: what the step is; what its function is; and when, where, and how it occurs.

A description can have not only parts or steps but also subparts or substeps. A description of a computer system includes a keyboard as one of its main parts, and the description of the keyboard includes the numeric keypad as one of its subparts. And the description of the numeric keypad includes the arrow keys as one of its subparts. The level of detail depends on the complexity of the item and the readers' needs. The same principle applies in describing processes: if a step has substeps, you need to describe who or what performs each substep (if that is not obvious) as well as what the substep is, what its function is, and when, where, and how it occurs.

◢

GUIDELINES Providing Appropriate Detail in Descriptions

Use the following techniques to flesh out your descriptions.

FOR MECHANISM AND OBJECT DESCRIPTIONS

▶ **Choose an appropriate organizational principle.** Descriptions can be organized in various ways. Two organizational principles are common:

— Functional: how the item works or is used. In a radio, the sound begins at the receiver, travels into the amplifier, and then flows out through the speakers.

— Spatial: based on the physical structure of the item (from top to bottom, east to west, outside to inside, and so forth).

The description of a house, for instance, could be organized functionally (covering the different electrical and mechanical systems) or spatially (top to bottom, inside to outside, east to west, and so on). A complex description can use different patterns at different levels.

▶ **Use graphics.** Present a graphic for each major part. Use photographs to show external surfaces, drawings to emphasize particular items on the surface, and cutaways and exploded diagrams to show details beneath the surface. Other kinds of graphics, such as graphs and charts, are often useful supplements (see Chapter 12).

FOR PROCESS DESCRIPTIONS

▶ **Structure the step-by-step description chronologically.** If the process is a closed system — such as the cycle of evaporation and condensation — and therefore has no first step, begin with any principal step.

▶ **Explain causal relationships among steps.** Don't present the steps as if they had nothing to do with one another. In many cases, one step causes another. In the operation of a four-stroke gasoline engine, for instance, each step creates the conditions for the next step.

▶ **Use the present tense.** Discuss steps in the present tense unless you are writing about a process that occurred in the historical past. For example, use the past tense in describing how the Snake River aquifer was formed: "The molten material condensed . . ." However, use the present tense in describing how steel is

(continued)

made: "The molten material is then poured into . . ." The present tense helps readers understand that, in general, steel is made this way.

▶ **Use graphics.** Whenever possible, use graphics to clarify each point. Consider flowcharts or other kinds of graphics, such as photographs, drawings, and graphs. For example, in a description of how a four-stroke gasoline engine operates, use diagrams to illustrate the position of the valves and the activity occurring during each step.

ENDING THE DESCRIPTION WITH A BRIEF CONCLUSION

A typical description has a brief conclusion that summarizes it and prevents readers from overemphasizing the part or step discussed last.

A common technique for concluding descriptions of mechanisms and of some objects is to state briefly how the parts function together. At the end of a description of how the Apple iPhone touch screen works, for example, the conclusion might include the following paragraph:

> When you touch the screen, electrical impulses travel from the screen to the iPhone processor, which analyzes the characteristics of the touch. These characteristics include the size, shape, and location of the touch, as well as whether you touched the screen in several places at once or moved your fingers. The processor then begins to process this data by removing any background noise and mapping and calculating the touch area or areas. Using its gesture-interpreting software, which combines these data with what it already knows about which function (such as the music player) you were using, the processor then sends commands to the music-player software and to the iPhone screen. How long does this process take? A nanosecond.

Like an object or mechanism description, a process description usually has a brief conclusion: a short paragraph summarizing the principal steps. Here, for example, is the concluding section of a description of how a four-stroke gasoline engine operates:

> In the intake stroke, the piston moves down, drawing the air–fuel mixture into the cylinder from the carburetor. As the piston moves up, it compresses this mixture in the compression stroke, creating the conditions necessary for combustion. In the power stroke, a spark from the spark plug ignites the mixture, which burns rapidly, forcing the piston down. In the exhaust stroke, the piston moves up, expelling the burned gases.

For descriptions of more than a few pages, a discussion of the implications of the process might be appropriate. For instance, a description of the Big Bang might conclude with a discussion of how the theory has been supported and challenged by recent astronomical discoveries and theories.

A LOOK AT SEVERAL SAMPLE DESCRIPTIONS

A look at some sample descriptions will give you an idea of how different writers adapt basic approaches for a particular audience and purpose.

Figure 20.5 shows the extent to which a process description can be based on a graphic. The topic is a household solar array. The audience is the general reader.

FIGURE 20.5
A Process Description
Based on a Graphic
"How Solar Works" from Vanguard
Energy Partners. Used with permission.

How Our Solar Electric System Works

Your solar electric system is most likely to be what is called a **direct grid-tie system**. This means it is connected into the electricity system provided by your utility company.

Here's how it works . . .

The sun strikes the panels of your **solar array** and a flow of **direct current (DC)** electricity is produced. This is the only type of current produced by solar cells.

Appliances and machinery, however, are run on higher voltage **alternating current (AC)** electricity as supplied by your utility.

The lower voltage DC is fed into an **inverter** that transforms it into alternating current. The AC feeds into the **main electrical panel** from which it powers your household's or your business's electrical needs.

Your electrical panel is also connected to a **specially installed bi-directional utility meter**. This is **connected to the electrical grid**, which is the utility's means of delivering electricity. This set up allows AC electricity to flow both into, and out of, your home or business.

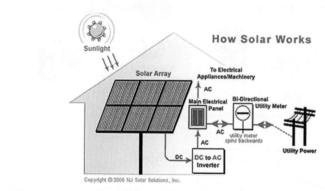

Copyright © 2006 NJ Solar Solutions, Inc.

During the day, your solar electric system will be providing some, or all, of your electrical needs.

How much will depend, firstly, on the intensity of the sunlight; the system produces less power on cloudy days and during the winter months. It will also depend on the appliances or machinery you are running at the time.

If your solar system is not providing all the power you need at any time, the **balance is automatically provided by your utility**.

On days when sunlight is intense, **your system may well produce more than you need**. The excess is automatically fed into the grid. This is registered on your bi-directional meter which will spin backwards, **giving you credit for the electricity you are providing**. (This is known as net metering.)

At night, your utility company automatically provides your electrical needs.

If there is a utility power outage, your grid-tie system will shut down immediately for safety reasons. Your power will be reinstated moments after grid power is restored.

A grid-tie solar electric system does not provide power during outages **unless it incorporates a battery storage system**. If your home or business has critical needs that require an uninterrupted power supply, we'll be happy to take you through the various alternatives available to you.

Off-grid, or stand-alone, solar systems produce power independently of the utility grid. They are most appropriate for remote or environmentally sensitive areas; stand-alone systems may effectively provide farm lighting, fence charging or solar water pumps. Most of these systems rely on battery storage so that power produced during the day can be used at night.

This description begins with an informal definition of "direct grid-tie system."

In the next section, the writer presents the steps of the process in chronological order.

The description uses boldfaced text to emphasize key terms, most of which appear in the graphic.

The description focuses on the operating principle of the system. It does not seek to explain the details of how the system works. Accordingly, the graphic focuses on the logic of the process, not on the particulars of what the components look like or where they are located in the house.

FIGURE 20.6 Excerpt from a Mechanism Description

Hybrids Under the Hood (Part 2): Drivetrains from Union of Concerned Scientists. www.ucsusa.org. Reprinted by permission.

This excerpt from a mechanism description begins with an advance organizer that helps the reader make the transition from the previous section (a basic description of hybrid technology) to the present section, which discusses the three types of drivetrains.

The interactive graphic enables the reader to view the principle of operation of three types of hybrid drivetrains, each during five modes. Here, the graphic shows how the components of the series drivetrain work together as the car operates at slow speeds. On the UCS website, the red and green striped lines are animated to highlight the components operating during the mode the reader has selected.

For each of the three types of drivetrains, the text begins with a description of the operating principle, followed by explanations of the strengths and weaknesses of the drivetrain. Notice that the audience and purpose of this description determine the kind of information it contains. Because this description seeks to explain the operating principle behind each of the three types of drivetrains, it focuses on the drivetrains' functions, not on the materials they are made of or on their technical specifications.

Drivetrains

Now that we've covered the basic technology that defines hybrid vehicles, let's take a look at how they are put together to move the vehicle. The drivetrain of a vehicle is composed of the components that are responsible for transferring power to the drive wheels of your vehicle. With hybrids there are three possible setups for the drivetrain: the series drivetrain, the parallel drivetrain, and the series/parallel drivetrain.

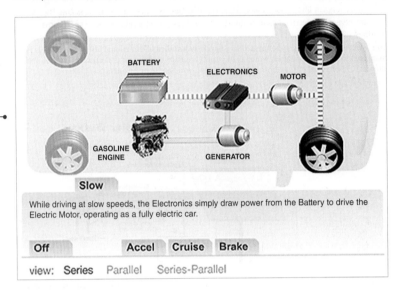

While driving at slow speeds, the Electronics simply draw power from the Battery to drive the Electric Motor, operating as a fully electric car.

Off   Accel   Cruise   Brake

view: **Series**   Parallel   Series-Parallel

Series Drivetrain

This is the simplest hybrid configuration. In a series hybrid, the electric motor is the only means of providing power to get your wheels turning. The motor receives electric power from either the battery pack or from a generator run by a gasoline engine. A computer determines how much of the power comes from the battery or the engine/generator set. Both the engine/generator and regenerative braking recharge the battery pack . . . . While the engine in a conventional vehicle is forced to operate inefficiently in order to satisfy varying power demands of stop-and-go driving, series hybrids perform at their best in such conditions. This is because the gasoline engine in a series hybrid is not coupled to the wheels. This means the engine is no longer subject to the widely varying power demands experienced in stop-and-go driving and can instead operate in a narrow power range at near optimum efficiency. . . .

Parallel Drivetrain

Some up-and-coming hybrid models use a second electric motor to drive the rear wheels, providing electronic all-wheel drive that can improve handling and driving in bad weather conditions.

With a parallel hybrid electric vehicle, both the engine and the electric motor generate the power that drives the wheels. The addition of computer controls and a transmission allow these components to work together. This is the technology in the Insight, Civic, and Accord hybrids from Honda. Honda calls it their Integrated Motor Assist (IMA) technology. . . . Since the engine is connected directly to the wheels in this setup, it eliminates the inefficiency of converting mechanical power to electricity and back, which makes these hybrids quite efficient on the highway. Yet the same direct connection between the engine and the wheels that increases highway efficiency compared to a series hybrid does reduce, but not eliminate, the city driving efficiency benefits (i.e., the engine operates inefficiently in stop-and-go driving because it is forced to meet the associated widely varying power demands).

Series/Parallel Drivetrains
This drivetrain merges the advantages and complications of the parallel and series drivetrains. By combining the two designs, the engine can both drive the wheels directly (as in the parallel drivetrain) and be effectively disconnected from the wheels so that only the electric motor powers the wheels (as in the series drivetrain). The Toyota Prius has made this concept popular, and a similar technology is also in the new Ford Escape Hybrid. As a result of this dual drivetrain, the engine operates at near optimum efficiency more often. . . .

Conclusion •
Knowing what's under the hood of hybrid electric vehicles will help you evaluate the available choices in the market. Considering most major auto manufacturers plan to release HEVs in the next few years, you'll be ready to choose the right one for you. Enjoy driving into the future.

This section of the description ends with a brief conclusion.

FIGURE 20.6   **Excerpt from a Mechanism Description** (*continued*)

Figure 20.6 on shows an excerpt from a mechanism description of three different types of hybrid drivetrains used in automobiles: series, parallel, and series/parallel.

Figure 20.7 on page 570 shows an excerpt from a set of specifications for Logitech headphones.

Figure 20.8 on page 571 is a description of the process of turning biomass into useful fuels and other products.

Writing Instructions

This section discusses *instructions*, which are process descriptions written to help readers perform a specific task—for instance, installing a water heater in a house.

Although written instructions are still produced today, the growth of social media has radically changed how organizations instruct people on how to use their products and services. Now that technology has made it easy for

FIGURE 20.7
Specifications
Courtesy of Logitech.

An important kind of description is called a *specification*. A typical specification (or spec) consists of a graphic and a set of statistics about the device and its performance characteristics. Specifications help readers understand the capabilities of an item. You will see specifications on devices as small as transistors and as large as aircraft carriers.

Because this web-based spec sheet accompanies a consumer product, the arrangement of the specs is geared toward the interests of the likely purchasers. The audio specs are presented before the power specs because potential purchasers of high-end headphones will be most interested in the sound quality.

Wireless Headset H600

NOTE: Information is for reference only and may be subject to change.

General Product Information	[Compliance Certification (CE) Link]
Warranty / Self Help	Please see product support page for warranty duration and frequently asked questions.
Category	Headset
Intended Usage	Desktop PC, Notebook PC
Wireless Protocol	Bluetooth 2.1
Wireless Range	Up to 30 Feet or 10 Meters
Bluetooth Support	Class 2, Supports A2DP , HFP profiles
Software Support (at release)	Pairing Utility (use only when re-pairing is needed)
	NOTE: If software is available, check website for latest software release.
OS Support (at release)	Windows XP, Windows XP x64, Windows Vista, Windows Vista x64, Windows 7, Windows 7 x64, Mac OS X 10.5+

Headset Specifications	
Available Image(s)	
Connection Type	Wireless
Headset Type	Stereo
Headset Design	Over-the-head
USB VID_PID	VID_046D & PID_0A29
USB Protocol	USB 2.0
USB Speed	High-speed
Frequency Response	40Hz-10KHz
Input Impedance	32ohms
Indicator Lights (LED)	Green (Solid - connected/full battery. Blinking - not connected). Red (Solid - battery low). Orange (Slow Blinking - charging. Solid - charging complete)
Adjustable Headband	Yes
Inline Audio Controls	N/A
Earcup Audio Controls	Mute, Volume control, Power On/Off
Battery Details	Removable/Not Replaceable, Rechargeable, Size: Proprietary, Quantity: 1, Type: Li-Ion
Battery Life	Recharge time 3 hours, Discharge time up to 6 hours
Cable Length	4 feet or 1.2 meters

Microphone Specifications	
Microphone Type	Rotating Boom
Connection Type	Wireless
Noise Canceling	Yes
Frequency Response	200Hz-6.5KHz
Input Sensitivity	N/A

Receiver Specifications	
Available Image(s)	
Connector Type	USB
USB VID_PID	VID_046D & PID_0A29
USB Protocol	USB 2.0
USB Speed	High-speed
Receiver Size	Nano USB Receiver
Connect Button	No
Indicator Lights	No

Package Contents	
Available Image(s)	No images
What is in the box	Headset, Wireless Receiver, User documentation, Charging Cable

Product Dimensions				
Product component	Width	Depth/Length	Height	Weight
Unit	148 mm (5.8 inch)	67 mm (2.6 inch)	172 mm (6.7 inch)	105 g (3.7 ounce)

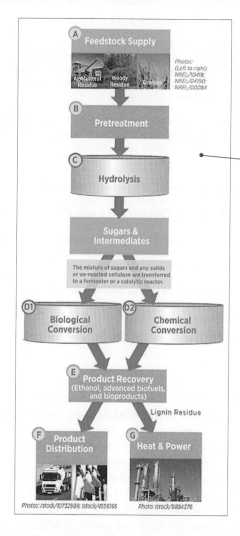

Photos:
(Left to right)
NREL/10418;
NREL/04190;
NREL/00084

The mixture of sugars and any solids or un-reacted cellulose are transferred to a fermenter or a catalytic reactor.

Lignin Residue

Photos: Istock/10732939; Istock/4556166

Photo: Istock/8894376

Biochemical conversion uses biocatalysts, such as enzymes, in addition to heat and other chemicals, to convert the carbohydrate portion of the biomass (hemicellulose and cellulose) into an intermediate sugar stream. These sugars are intermediate building blocks that can then be fermented or chemically catalyzed into ethanol, other advanced biofuels, and value-added chemicals. The overall process can be broken into the following essential steps:

A. Feedstock Supply: Feedstocks for biochemical processes are selected for optimum composition, quality, and size. Feedstock handling systems tailored to biochemical processing are essential to cost-effective, high-yield operations.

B. Pretreatment: Biomass is heated (often combined with an acid or base) to break the tough, fibrous cell walls down and make the cellulose easier to hydrolyze (see next step).

C. Hydrolysis: Enzymes (or other catalysts) enable the sugars in the pretreated material to be separated and released over a period of several days.

D1. Biological Conversion: Microorganisms are added, which then use the sugars to generate other molecules suitable for use as fuels or building-block chemicals.

D2. Chemical Conversion: Alternatively, the sugars can be converted to fuels or an entire suite of other useful products using chemical catalysis.

E. Product Recovery: Products are separated from water, solvents, and any residual solids.

F. Product Distribution: Fuels are transported to blending facilities, while other products and intermediates may be sent to traditional refineries or processing facilities for use in a diverse slate of consumer products.

G. Heat & Power: The remaining solids are mostly lignin, which can be burned for heat and power.

FIGURE 20.8
An Effective Process Description

U.S. Department of Energy, 2013: www1 .eere.energy.gov/bioenergy/pdfs /biochemical_four_pager.pdf.

This description begins with an overview of the process of biochemical conversion: the process of using fermentation and catalysis to make fuels and products.

The description includes a flowchart explaining the major steps in the process. The designers included photographs to add visual interest to the flowchart.

The lettered steps in the flowchart correspond to the textual descriptions of the steps in the process.

Most of the description is written in the passive voice (such as "Feedstocks for biochemical processes are selected . . ."). The passive voice is appropriate because the focus of this process description is on what happens to the materials, not on what a person does. By contrast, in a set of instructions the focus is on what a person does.

FOCUS ON PROCESS: Instructions

When writing instructions, pay special attention to these steps in the writing process.

PLANNING
Analyze your audience and determine your purpose to decide how much and what type of instruction should be provided. Envision how the instructions will most likely be used to determine the best format or formats — text, graphics, videos, or some combination of these.

DRAFTING
Draft your instructions with your audience and purpose in mind. Be sure to provide a clear organizational structure that readers can follow and include any appropriate safety information. Also review the writing advice in Chapter 3.

REVISING
Test your instructions to make sure users can follow them. See Chapter 13 on usability testing. Also go through the "Instructions" section in the Writer's Checklist at the end of this chapter.

EDITING
Make sure your instructions will be clear to your readers and get the point across without grammatical errors. See Chapter 10 for advice on writing correct and effective sentences.

PROOFREADING
Read through the instructions slowly, making sure you have written what you wanted to write. Get help from others. See Appendix, Part C, for proofreading tips.

people to participate in writing instructions and to view and make videos, most organizations try to present instructional material not only as formal written text but also through discussion forums, wikis, and videos. And users do not rely exclusively on the organizations themselves to create and present instructions. Rather, they create their own text and videos.

Your first job, then, in presenting instructions is to devise a strategy for incorporating user participation in the process and to choose the best mix of media for encouraging that participation. Written instructions (whether presented online or printed and put in the box with the product) will always have a role because they are portable and can include as much detail as necessary for even the most complex tasks and systems. But consider whether your users will also benefit from access to other people's ideas (in a discussion forum or wiki) or from watching a video. On page 573, help forum moderator Suzanne Barnhill discusses her strategies for giving instructions that respond to the needs and knowledge level of each person posting to the forum. The Focus on Process box above outlines additional steps in the process of writing instructions.

STRATEGIES FOR ONLINE COMMUNICATION

Suzanne Barnhill on Moderating User Forums

Technical communicators moderate user forums for all types of products and services. User forums are online discussion spaces that supplement manuals, instruction sets, descriptions, and other support documents. If users cannot solve their problems with the support documents that come with a product or service, online discussion spaces can serve as a secondary source of help. A major benefit of user forums is that the posted questions are answered by actual people, who themselves can ask questions if needed and even orchestrate an extended dialogue about the issue. In addition, the technical communicators who moderate user forums often have knowledge that goes beyond the life of a particular product or service, providing a longer-term view that can aid problem solving. Suzanne Barnhill is a moderator in the user forum for Microsoft Word. She illustrates the added value of user forums in technical communication contexts.

Courtesy of Suzanne Barnhill

SUZANNE BARNHILL

Suzanne Barnhill has been a moderator in the Microsoft Word user forum since 2011, and in fact has consistently earned Microsoft's Most Valuable Professional (MVP) award, which is given to people who actively share their knowledge with relevant communities. As you can imagine, the user forum for Word is quite lively, seeing hundreds of posts on a typical day. Barnhill is not the only moderator in the forum, so she can focus much of the time on her areas of expertise: creating and formatting large documents, including typesetting for print. She answers a lot of questions about tables of contents, indexes, page numbers, headers and footers, and the like, but she also has shareable knowledge about other Word features. In this example, Barnhill responds to a user who is struggling to create a Word form with fill-in fields. Moderators will work in any area in which they feel confident.

he original post (OP) is om a user who is having a oblem creating fill-in fields a Word form. Technical mmunicators use fill-in lds, for example, to collect ormation from users allow users to request ormation from a company.

e user attempts to scribe the problem. One ature of user forums is at they require people describe their problems writing, making them olicit, which is an portant step in trying to derstand what's going on.

The user also shares the solutions they've already tried. When faced with a problem, users have several options beyond the documents that come with a product or service. In typical fashion, this user tried to find answers using an internet search engine. Internet searches can provide solutions, but sometimes you need to involve human beings.

Figure 20.9 Moderating a User Forum for Microsoft Word

The moderator explains how to solve the problem but also recommends an entirely different approach to the task. The moderator's knowledge of older versions of Word is crucial here.

The moderator also links to a third-party document, drawing on a wider circle of experts to help provide solutions.

In addition to answering questions, moderators also merge and split threads to keep them on topic and prevent duplication, report spam, and keep discussions civil and productive.

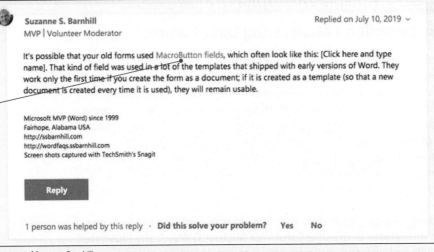

The moderator provides a description of the legacy method the user seems to be describing, with a link to a third-party document explaining how to use that method, and adds advice for best practices using the method. The moderator's knowledge of older versions of Word is crucial here, but the moderator concludes by recommending a more modern method that has already been suggested by another Word MVP.

Courtesy of Suzanne Barnhill

Figure 20.9 Moderating a User Forum for Microsoft Word (*continued*)

UNDERSTANDING THE ROLE OF INSTRUCTIONAL VIDEOS

The explosive growth of YouTube and other video-hosting sites has revolutionized how instructions are created and used. Product manufacturers and users alike make videos to help people understand how to perform tasks.

If you are producing instructional videos on behalf of your company, think about what style of video will be most effective for your audience, purpose, and subject. Companies often use simple, cartoon-style videos for basic conceptual information ("what can you do with a microblog?"), screenshot-based videos for computer-based tasks ("how to use master slides in PowerPoint"), and live-action videos for physical tasks ("how to install a ground-fault interrupter").

Video is particularly useful for communicating about physical tasks that call for subtle physical movements or that involve both sight and sound. For instance, a video would be more effective than written instructions in communicating how a guitarist uses the tremolo bar to create different sonic effects. The viewer can focus on the way the guitarist holds his or her hand on the tremolo and on the range of movement that he or she uses. In addition, the viewer can hear how these physical actions change the sound.

Although there are many software tools available for making videos, making professional-quality videos calls for professional skills, experience, and tools. If you are going to be making many videos, it makes sense to learn the process and acquire professional tools and equipment; otherwise, consult your company's media department or consider hiring freelance video producers. They can help you create videos that reflect positively on your organization.

Instructional videos tend to be brief. Whereas a reader of a document can navigate easily among various parts or steps, viewers of a video can only hit play, pause, and stop. For this reason, you should break long tasks into a series of brief videos: ideally 2–3 minutes, but no more than 12–15 minutes. Give each one a clear, specific title so viewers can easily tell whether they want to view it.

Similarly, you should make your instructional videos simple and uncluttered. Software makes it easy to add a lot of cinematic effects, but less is often more. Your purpose is not to win an Academy Award; it is to help your audience learn how to carry out a task. The fewer distractions in the video, the easier it will be for viewers to see what to do. And remember that video is a warm medium. Connect with the viewer by being friendly, informal, and direct. Don't say, "Next, the right mouse button is pushed." Say, "Press the right mouse button." But do not confuse being warm and informal with not needing to prepare. You *do* need to plan, write a script, and rehearse.

Be sure to build in the time and resources to revise the video. As discussed in Chapters 3 and 13, good technical communication calls for reviewing, revising, and testing. This concept applies to video. Start testing even before production. Make sure your script and visuals are right for your audience and purpose. And repeat the process after you have created the rough cut of the video and after each major revision.

For more about usability testing, see Ch. 13.

Use other sources responsibly. You need to obtain written permission to use any copyrighted text, images, videos, or music that will appear in your video. Because this process can be lengthy, difficult, and expensive, many organizations have a simple standing rule: do not use any copyrighted material. Instead, they generate their own images and text, and even their own music.

DESIGNING A SET OF WRITTEN INSTRUCTIONS

As you plan to write instructions, think about how readers will use them. Analyzing your audience and purpose and gathering and organizing your information will help you decide whether you should write a one-page set of instructions or a longer document that needs to be bound. You might realize that the information would work better as a web-based document that can include videos, be updated periodically, and provide readers with links to the information they need. Or you might decide to write several versions of the information: a brief printed set of instructions and a longer, web-based document with links.

As always in technical communication, imagining how readers will use what you write will help you plan your document. For example, having decided that your audience, purpose, and subject call for a printed set of instructions of perhaps 1,000 words and a dozen drawings and photographs, you can start to design the document. You will need to consider your resources, especially your budget: long documents cost more than short ones; color costs more than black and white; heavy paper costs more than light paper; secure bindings cost more than staples.

For more about planning, see Ch. 3.

Designing a set of instructions is much like designing any other kind of technical document. As discussed in Chapter 11, you want to create a document that is attractive and easy to use. When you design a set of instructions, you need to consider a number of issues related to document design and page design:

- **What are your readers' expectations?** For a simple, inexpensive product, such as a light switch, readers will expect to find instructions written on the back of the package or printed in black and white on a small sheet of paper folded inside the package. For an expensive consumer product, such as a high-definition TV, readers will expect to find instructions in a more sophisticated full-color document printed on high-quality paper.

- **What are your readers' abilities?** If you're creating an instructional video on how to use a smartphone for banking transactions, will you need to include closed captioning for people with hearing impairments? In addition to closed captioning, you might also want to provide a stand-alone transcript of the video narration.

- **Do you need to create more than one set of instructions for different audiences?** If you are writing about a complex device such as an electronic thermostat, you might decide to create one set of instructions for electricians (who will install and maintain the device) and one set for homeowners (who will operate the device). In addition to producing paper copies of the documents, you might want to post them on the internet, along with a brief video of the tasks you describe.

- **What languages should you use?** In most countries, several languages are spoken. You might decide to include instructions in two or more languages. Doing so will help you communicate better with more people, and it can help you avoid legal problems. In liability cases, U.S. courts sometimes find that if a company knows that many of its customers speak only Spanish, for example, the instructions should appear in Spanish as well as in English. You have two choices for presenting information in multiple languages: simultaneous presentation or sequential presentation. In a *simultaneous design*, you might use a multicolumn page on which one column presents the graphics, another has the text in English, and another has the text in Spanish. Obviously, this won't work if you need to present information in more than two or three languages. But it is efficient because you include each graphic only once. In a *sequential design*, you present all the information in English (say, on pages 1–8), then all the information in Spanish (on pages 9–16). The sequential design is easier for readers to use because they are not distracted by text in other languages, but you will have to include the graphics more than once, which will make the instructions longer.

- **Will readers be anxious about the information?** If readers will find the information intimidating, make sure the design is not intimidating. For instance, if you are writing for general readers about how to set up a wireless network for home computers, create open pages with a lot of white space and graphics. Use large type and narrow text columns so that each page contains a relatively small amount of information. Figure 20.10 (on p. 577) illustrates the advantages of an open design.

- **Will the environment in which the instructions are read affect the document design?** If people will be using the instructions outdoors, you will need to use a coated paper that can tolerate moisture or dirt. If people will be reading the instructions while sitting in a small, enclosed area, you might select a small paper size and a binding that allows the reader to fold the pages over to save space. If people have a lot of room, you might decide to create poster-size instructions that can be taped to the wall and that are easy to read from across the room.

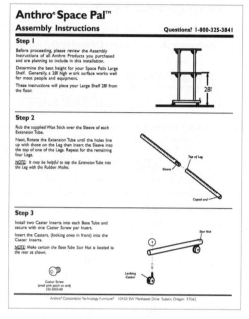

FIGURE 20.10 Cluttered and Attractive Page Designs for Instructions

a. Cluttered design

This page is cluttered, containing far too much information. In addition, the page is not chunked effectively. As a result, the reader's eyes don't know where to focus. Would you look forward to using these instructions to assemble a cabinet?

b. Attractive design

This page is well designed, containing an appropriate amount of information presented in a simple two-column format. Notice the effective use of white space and the horizontal rules separating the steps.

 GUIDELINES Designing Clear, Attractive Pages

To design pages that are clear and attractive, follow these guidelines:

▶ **Create an open, airy design.** Do not squeeze too much information onto the page. Build in space for wide margins and effective line spacing, use large type, and chunk the information effectively.

▶ **Clearly relate the graphics to the text.** In the step-by-step portion of a set of instructions, present graphics to accompany every step or almost every step. Create a design that makes it clear which graphics go with each text passage. One easy way to do this is to use a table, with the graphics in one column and the text in the other. A horizontal rule or extra line spacing separates the text and graphics for one step from the text and graphics for the next step.

For more about chunking, see Ch. 11.

PLANNING FOR SAFETY

If the subject you are writing about involves safety risks, your most important responsibility is to do everything you can to ensure your readers' safety.

ETHICS NOTE

ENSURING YOUR READERS' SAFETY

To a large extent, the best way to keep your readers safe is to be honest and write clearly. If readers will encounter safety risks, explain what those risks are and how to minimize them. Doing so is a question of rights. Readers have a right to the best information they can get.

Ensuring your readers' safety is also a question of law. People who get hurt can sue the company that made the product or provided the service. As discussed in Chapter 2, this field of law is called *liability law*. Your company is likely to have legal professionals on staff or on retainer whose job is to ensure that the company is not responsible for putting people at unnecessary risk.

When you write safety information, be clear and concise. Avoid complicated sentences.

COMPLICATED   It is required that safety glasses be worn when inside this laboratory.

SIMPLE   You must wear safety glasses in this laboratory.

SIMPLE   Wear safety glasses in this laboratory.

Sometimes a phrase works better than a sentence: "Safety Glasses Required."

Because a typical manual or set of instructions can contain dozens of comments—some related to safety and some not—experts have devised *signal words* to indicate the seriousness of the advice. Unfortunately, signal words are not used consistently. For instance, the American National Standards Institute (ANSI) and the U.S. military's MILSPEC publish definitions that differ significantly, and many private companies have their own definitions. Table 20.2 (on p. 579) presents the four most commonly used signal words. The first three signal words are accompanied by symbols showing the color combinations endorsed by ANSI in its standard Z535.4.

Whether safety information is printed in a document or on machinery or equipment, it should be prominent and easy to read. Many organizations use visual symbols to represent levels of danger, but these symbols are not standardized.

Organizations that create products that are used only in the United States design safety information to conform with standards published by ANSI and by the federal Occupational Safety and Health Administration (OSHA). Organizations that create products that are also used outside the United States design safety information to conform with standards published by the International Organization for Standardization (ISO). Figure 20.11 (on p. 579) shows a safety label that incorporates both ANSI and ISO standards.

Part of planning for safety is determining the best location for safety information. This question has no easy answer because you cannot control how your audience reads your document. Be conservative: put safety information

TABLE 20.2 Signal Words		
SIGNAL WORD	**EXPLANATION**	**EXAMPLE**
Danger ![A DANGER]	*Danger* is used to alert readers about an immediate and serious hazard that will likely be fatal. Writers often use all uppercase letters for danger statements.	DANGER: EXTREMELY HIGH VOLTAGE. STAND BACK.
Warning ![AWARNING]	*Warning* is used to alert readers about the potential for serious injury or death or serious damage to equipment. Writers often use all uppercase letters for warning statements.	WARNING: TO PREVENT SERIOUS INJURY TO YOUR ARMS AND HANDS, YOU MUST MAKE SURE THE ARM RESTRAINTS ARE IN PLACE BEFORE OPERATING THIS MACHINE.
Caution ![A CAUTION]	*Caution* is used to alert readers about the potential for anything from moderate injury to serious equipment damage or destruction.	Caution: Do not use nonrechargeable batteries in this charging unit; they could damage the charging unit.
Note	*Note* is used for a tip or suggestion to help readers carry out a procedure successfully.	Note: Two kinds of washers are provided — regular washers and locking washers. Be sure to use the locking washers here.

wherever you think the reader is likely to see it, and don't be afraid to repeat yourself. A reasonable amount of repetition—such as including the same safety comment at the top of each page—is effective. But don't repeat the same piece of advice in each of 20 steps, because readers will stop paying attention to it. If your company's format for instructions calls for a safety section near the beginning of the document, place the information there and repeat it just before the appropriate step in the step-by-step section.

Figure 20.11 shows one industry association's guidelines for placing safety information on conveyor belts.

The yellow triangle on the left is consistent with the ISO approach. Because ISO creates standards for international use, its safety labels use icons, not words, to represent safety hazards.

The signal word "Danger" and the text are consistent with the ANSI approach. The information is presented in English.

FIGURE 20.11 A Typical Safety Label

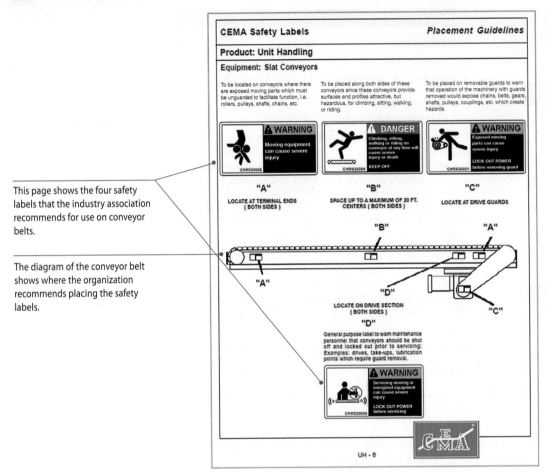

This page shows the four safety labels that the industry association recommends for use on conveyor belts.

The diagram of the conveyor belt shows where the organization recommends placing the safety labels.

FIGURE 20.12   **Placement of Safety Information on Equipment**
Reprinted by permission of Conveyor Equipment Manufacturers Association.

DRAFTING EFFECTIVE INSTRUCTIONS

Instructions can be brief (a small sheet of paper) or extensive (20 pages or more). Brief instructions might be produced by a writer, a graphic artist, and a subject-matter expert. Longer instructions might call for the assistance of others, such as marketing and legal personnel.

Regardless of the size of the project, most instructions are organized like process descriptions. The main difference is that the conclusion of a set of instructions is not a summary but an explanation of how readers can make sure they have followed the instructions correctly. Most sets of instructions contain four elements: a title, a general introduction, step-by-step instructions, and a conclusion.

Drafting Titles A good title for instructions is simple and clear. Two forms are common:

- **How-to.** This is the simplest: "How to Install the J112 Shock Absorber."
- **Gerund.** The gerund form of a verb is the *-ing* form: "Installing the J112 Shock Absorber."

One form to avoid is the noun string, which is awkward and difficult for readers to understand: "J112 Shock Absorber Installation Instructions."

For more about noun strings, see Ch. 10.

Drafting General Introductions The general introduction provides the preliminary information that readers will need to follow the instructions safely and easily.

GUIDELINES Drafting Introductions for Instructions

Every set of instructions is unique and therefore calls for a different introduction. Consider answering the following questions, as appropriate:

▶ **Who should carry out this task?** Sometimes you need to identify or describe the person or persons who are to carry out a task. Aircraft maintenance, for example, may be performed only by those certified to do it.

▶ **Why should the reader carry out this task?** Sometimes the reason is obvious: you don't need to explain why a backyard barbecue grill should be assembled. But you do need to explain the rationale for many tasks, such as changing antifreeze in a car's radiator.

▶ **When should the reader carry out this task?** Some tasks, such as rotating tires or planting seeds, need to be performed at particular times or at particular intervals.

▶ **What safety measures or other concerns should the reader understand?** In addition to the safety measures that apply to the whole task, mention any tips that will make the job easier:

> NOTE: For ease of assembly, leave all nuts loose. Give only three or four complete turns on bolt threads.

▶ **What items will the reader need?** List necessary tools, materials, and equipment so that readers will not have to interrupt their work to hunt for something. If you think readers might not be able to identify these items easily, include drawings next to the names.

For more about graphics, see Ch. 12.

▶ **How long will the task take?** Consider stating how long the task will take readers with no experience, some experience, and a lot of experience.

Drafting Step-by-Step Instructions The heart of a set of instructions is the step-by-step information.

▰▰▰ **GUIDELINES** Drafting Steps in Instructions

Follow these six suggestions for writing steps that are easy to understand.

▶ **Number the instructions.** For long, complex instructions, use two-level numbering, such as a decimal system:

1
   1.1
   1.2
2
   2.1
   2.2
etc.

If you need to present a long list of steps, group the steps logically into sets and begin each set with a clear heading. A list of 50 steps, for example, could be divided into six sets of 8 or 9 steps each.

▶ **Present the right amount of information in each step.** Each step should define a single task the reader can carry out easily, without having to refer back to the instructions.

TOO MUCH INFORMATION
1. Mix one part cement with one part water, using the trowel. When the mixture is a thick consistency without any lumps bigger than a marble, place a strip of the mixture about 1" high and 1" wide along the face of the brick.

TOO LITTLE INFORMATION
1. Pick up the trowel.

RIGHT AMOUNT OF INFORMATION
1. Mix one part cement with one part water, using the trowel, until the mixture is a thick consistency without any lumps bigger than a marble.
2. Place a strip of the mixture about 1" high and 1" wide along the face of the brick.

For more about the passive voice, see Ch. 10.

▶ **Use the imperative mood.** The imperative mood expresses a request or a command—for example, "Attach the red wire." The imperative is more direct and economical than the indicative mood ("You should attach the red wire" or "The operator should attach the red wire"). Avoid the passive voice ("The red wire is attached"), because it can be ambiguous: is the red wire already attached?

▶ **Do not confuse steps and feedback statements.** A *step* is an action that the reader is to perform. A *feedback statement* describes an event that occurs in response to a step. For instance, a step might read "Double-click on the install .cmd file." That step's feedback statement might read "The system will now install your software." Do not present a feedback statement as a numbered step. Present it as part of the step to which it refers. Some writers give feedback statements their own design.

(continued)

> ▸ **Include graphics.** When appropriate, add a photograph or a drawing to show the reader what to do. Some activities — such as adding two drops of a reagent to a mixture — do not need an illustration, but they might be clarified by a chart or a table.
>
> ▸ **Do not omit articles (*a, an, the*) to save space.** Omitting articles can make the instructions unclear and hard to read. In the sentence "Locate midpoint and draw line," for example, the reader cannot tell if "draw line" is a noun (as in "locate the draw line") or a verb and its object (as in "draw a line").

Drafting Conclusions Instructions often conclude by stating that the reader has now completed the task or by describing what the reader should do next. For example:

> Now that you have replaced the glass and applied the glazing compound, let the window sit for at least five days so that the glazing can cure. Then, prime and paint the window.

Some conclusions end with *maintenance tips* or a *troubleshooting guide*. A troubleshooting guide, usually presented as a table, identifies common problems and explains how to solve them.

REVISING, EDITING, AND PROOFREADING INSTRUCTIONS

You know, of course, to revise, edit, and proofread all the documents you write to make sure they are honest, clear, accurate, comprehensive, accessible, concise, professional in appearance, and correct. When you write instructions, you should be extra careful, for two reasons.

First, your readers rely on your instructions to carry out a task. If they can't complete it—or they do complete it, but they don't achieve the expected outcome—they'll be unhappy. Nobody likes to spend a few hours assembling a garage-door opener, only to find half a dozen parts left over. Second, your readers rely on you to help them complete the task safely. To prevent injuries and liability actions, build time into the budget to revise, edit, and proofread the instructions carefully. Then, if you can, carry out usability testing on the instructions.

For more about usability testing, see Ch. 13, pp. 347–66.

A LOOK AT SEVERAL SAMPLE SETS OF INSTRUCTIONS

Figure 20.12 is an excerpt from a set of instructions. Figure 20.14 on page 585 shows a list of tools and materials from a set of instructions. Figure 20.15 on page 586 is an excerpt from the safety information in a set of instructions. Figure 20.16 on page 587 is a portion of the troubleshooting guide in the instructions for a lawnmower. Figure 20.9 on page 573 is an excerpt from a thread in a discussion forum.

This page from the user's manual for a tablet computer used in health-care environments discusses how to use the barcode scanner.

Note that the writer uses a gerund (*-ing* verb) in the major heading to describe the action ("Using the bar-code scanner").

The writer explains why readers might want to scan barcodes.

The writer lists the types of bar-codes the tablet can scan and then explains how to enable the tablet to scan additional types. Note that the more conceptual information about the task precedes the instructional information. Why? Because readers want to understand the big picture before getting into the details.

The writer presents the steps. Note that the writer numbers the steps and uses the imperative mood for each one.

The drawing helps readers under-stand how to hold the tablet and aim it at the barcode. In cases such as this, simple drawings work better than photographs because they do not distract readers with unneces-sary detail.

Using the barcode scanner

Your C5te/F5te is available with an optional integrated 1D and 2D barcode scanner that you can use to retrieve information from barcodes. Many applications use barcodes for asset tracking, identification, and process controls.

Supported barcode types

The C5te/F5te barcode scanner supports several different types of barcodes—a minimum set of barcodes is enabled at the factory.

The following symbologies are enabled by default:

- Aztec Code
- EAN-128
- Code 39
- UPC-A
- EAN-8
- Interleaved 2 of 5
- Micro PDF417
- RSS Limited

- Code 128
- EAN-UCC-CC-AB
- DataMatrix
- UPC-E
- EAN-13
- PDF417
- RSS-14

Other barcode types can be enabled by using EasySet® by Intermec. This application can be installed by running **setup**, which is located here: **C:\Motion\Software\EasySet.**

To use the barcode scanner:

1. Open the application that you want to receive the barcode data and place the insertion point in the appropriate field.

2. Hold the unit by the handle with the scanner lens in front of you.

3. Aim the scanner lens at the barcode.

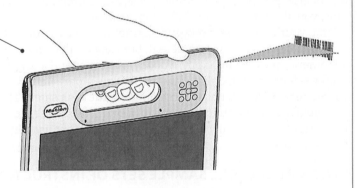

Chapter 2 Using your C5te/F5te   Using the barcode scanner   38

FIGURE 20.13   Excerpt from a Set of Instructions
Courtesy of Xplore.

Installation Instructions

PREPARE TO INSTALL THE RANGE

FOR YOUR SAFETY:

All rough-in and spacing dimensions must be met for safe use of your range. Electricity to the range can be disconnected at the outlet without moving the range if the outlet is in the preferred location (remove lower drawer).

To reduce the risk of burns or fire when reaching over hot surface elements, cabinet storage space above the cooktop should be avoided. If cabinet storage space is to be provided above the cooktop, the risk can be reduced by installing a range hood that sticks out at least 5" beyond the front of the cabinets. Cabinets installed above a cooktop must be no deeper than 13".

Be sure your appliance is properly installed and grounded by a qualified technician.

Make sure the cabinets and wall coverings around the range can withstand the temperatures (up to 200°F.) generated by the range.

MATERIALS YOU MAY NEED

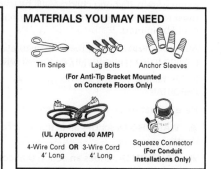

Tin Snips   Lag Bolts   Anchor Sleeves

(For Anti-Tip Bracket Mounted on Concrete Floors Only)

(UL Approved 40 AMP)

4-Wire Cord **OR** 3-Wire Cord
4' Long   4' Long

Squeeze Connector **(For Conduit Installations Only)**

PARTS INCLUDED

Anti-Tip Bracket Kit

TOOLS YOU WILL NEED

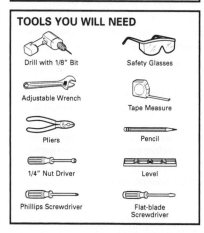

Drill with 1/8" Bit   Safety Glasses

Adjustable Wrench   Tape Measure

Pliers   Pencil

1/4" Nut Driver   Level

Phillips Screwdriver   Flat-blade Screwdriver

1 REMOVE SHIPPING MATERIALS

Remove packaging materials. Failure to remove packaging materials could result in damage to the appliance.

Drawings of tools, materials, and parts are more effective than lists.

FIGURE 20.14   List of Tools and Materials

Prepare to Install the Range from General Electric, INSTALLATION INSTRUCTIONS: FREE-STANDING ELECTRIC RANGES (Manual 229C4053P545-1 31-10556-1 04-03 JR). Used with permission.

FIGURE 20.15 Excerpt from Safety Information

This excerpt from a user manual for a video-game player that displays 3D images describes two of the safety risks associated with playing video games.

Notice that the excerpt uses mandatory language: "You must . . ." Although politeness is desirable most of the time, you don't want to sound as if you are making suggestions or asking readers to do you favors. For instance, if a task calls for using safety goggles, do not write "You should consider wearing safety goggles." Instead, write "You must wear safety goggles when operating this equipment."

This set of safety information defines the keywords *warning*, *caution*, and *important*.

The safety information goes on to discuss eyestrain and motion sickness, repetitive motion injuries, and radio frequency interference.

HEALTH AND SAFETY INFORMATION

You **must** read the following warnings before you set up or use the Orion 35 3D game system. If young children will be using this product, a competent adult **must** read and explain this safety information to them. Otherwise, these children could be injured.

Also, you **must** carefully read the instruction booklet for the game you are playing to learn additional health and safety information.

In this manual, you will see this symbol ▲ followed by WARNING, CAUTION, or IMPORTANT.

Here is what these three words mean:

▲ **WARNING** Describes an action that could lead to a serious personal injury or death.

▲ **CAUTION** Describes an action that could lead to personal injury or damage to the Orion 35 3D game system, games, or accessories.

▲ **IMPORTANT** Describes an action that could lead to damage to the Orion 35 3D game system, games, or accessories.

▲ **WARNING** The 3D Feature May Be Used Only by Children 7 and Older

Children age 6 or younger who watch 3D images can suffer vision damage. You must use the Parental Control feature (see page 36) to prevent the system from displaying 3D images when children 6 or younger are using the system.

▲ **WARNING** Seizures

For a small percentage of people (approximately 1 in 4000), light flashes and patterns can cause seizures or blackouts. TV programs and videos can include these light flashes and patterns.

Anybody who has ever had a seizure, loss of awareness, or any other symptom linked to epilepsy **must** check with a physician before playing any video game.

Always watch your children when they play video games. Stop the game and consult a physician if your child has any of the following symptoms:

- Convulsions
- Eye or muscle twitching
- Loss of awareness
- Altered vision
- Involuntary movements
- Disorientation

To reduce the chance that you or a child will have a seizure while playing video games:

1. Sit or stand as far as possible from the screen.
2. Play the game on the smallest screen that is available.
3. Do not play any video game if you are tired.
4. Keep the room well-lit.
5. Every hour, take a break for 10 or 15 minutes.

PROBLEM	CAUSE	CORRECTION
The mower does not start.	1. The mower is out of gas. 2. The gas is stale. 3. The spark plug wire is disconnected from the spark plug.	1. Fill the gas tank. 2. Drain the tank and refill it with fresh gas. 3. Connect the wire to the plug.
The mower loses power.	1. The grass is too high. 2. The air cleaner is dirty. 3. There is a buildup of grass, leaves, or trash in the underside of the mower housing.	1. Set the mower to a "higher cut" position. See page 10. 2. Replace the air cleaner. See page 11. 3. Disconnect the spark plug wire, attach it to the retainer post, and clean the underside of the mower housing. See page 8.

FIGURE 20.16   Excerpt from a Troubleshooting Guide

Writing Manuals

There is no absolute distinction between a set of instructions and a manual. Typically, the two share a main purpose: to explain how to carry out a task safely, effectively, and efficiently. Both kinds of documents can include safety information. For example, a set of instructions on how to use an extension ladder explains how to avoid falling off the ladder. A manual for a laptop explains how to avoid electrocution when you open the case. However, a set of instructions (which can be anywhere from 1 to 20 or more pages) is typically shorter than a manual and more limited in its subject. Obviously, using a laptop requires knowing about many more topics than does using a ladder.

A manual likely also includes some sections not found in a set of instructions. For instance, it typically has a title page. The main difference between the two is that a manual has more elaborate front matter and back matter.

- **Front matter.** The introduction, sometimes called a *preface*, often contains an *overview of the contents*, frequently in the form of a table, which explains the main contents of each section and chapter. It also contains a *conventions* section, which explains the typography of the manual. For instance, *italics* are used for the titles of books, boldface for keyboard keys, and so forth. It also might include a *where to get help* section, referring readers to other sources of information, such as the company's website and customer-support center. And it might contain a section listing the *trademarks* of the company's own products and those of other companies.

  For more about typography, see Ch. 11.

  For more about trademarks, see Ch. 2.

- **Back matter.** Manuals typically include a set of *specifications* of the device or system, a list of relevant government *safety regulations* and *industry standards* that the device or system supports, *tips on maintenance and servicing* the device, a *copyright page* listing bibliographic information about the manual, and an *index*. Many manuals also include *glossaries*.

Because they typically are longer and more complex than a set of instructions, manuals are almost always written collaboratively. Often, the writing team uses a wiki or other shared document workspace to make it easy for various subject-matter experts to contribute. When the manual is finished,

DOCUMENT ANALYSIS ACTIVITY

Presenting Clear Instructions

This page is from a set of instructions in an e-reader user's manual. The questions below ask you to think about the discussion of instructions earlier in this chapter.

1. This page includes no graphics. Point out two or three passages on the page that might be easier to understand if they included graphics. Describe the graphics you would include.

2. Is the amount of information presented in each step appropriate?

3. How effectively has the designer used typography to distinguish the various kinds of information presented on this page?

Reading on Your NOOK

Reading a Book

To read a book on your NOOK, tap on its cover.

Turning Pages

To turn to the next page, tap along the right side of the screen. You can also turn to the next page by swiping to the left.

To turn to the previous page, tap along the left side of the screen. You can also turn to the previous page by swiping to the right.

Moving from One Part of a Book to Another

To move quickly through the book, do this:

1. Tap the center of the page to open the Reading Tools.
   Two panels of tools appear at the bottom of the page.

2. Use the Reading Tools to move through the book.

   - Drag your finger along the scrollbar to scroll through the book.
     A bubble appears above the scrollbar, telling you which chapter and page you have reached.

   - To go to a specific page, tap *Go to Page*. A dialog box appears. Type the page number you want, and press the Go button (an arrow).

3. When you have reached the page you want, tap the middle of the page to close the Reading Tools and continue reading.

Using the Table of Contents

To see the Table of Contents of the book, or to jump to a chapter or section listed in the Table of Contents, do this:

1. Tap the center of the page to open the Reading Tools.

2. Tap the Contents icon (a stack of horizontal lines).
   A panel opens with three tabs: *Table of Contents*, *Highlights and Notes*, and *Bookmarks*.

3. Tap the *Table of Contents* tab if it is not already highlighted.
   Your NOOK displays the Table of Contents for the book.

4. Tap on the chapter or section you want to read next.
   Your NOOK closes the Reading Tools and displays the page you selected.

Barnes & Noble NOOK HD+ User Guide   45

the writing team often uses collaborative tools to enable users to evaluate and comment on it or even contribute to future versions of it.

Organizations work hard to make their instructions and manuals appropriate for multicultural readers. Because important instructions and manuals might be read by readers from any number of cultures, you need to answer three important questions as you plan the documents:

- **In what language should the information be written?** You can either translate the document into readers' native languages or try to make the English easy to understand. Although translation is sometimes the best or only alternative, companies often use Simplified English or some other form of English with a limited grammar and vocabulary. Many organizations translate their manuals into various languages and post the translations on their websites as PDF documents for download.

For more about Simplified English, see Ch. 10.

- **Do the text and graphics need to be modified?** As discussed in Chapter 5, communicators need to be aware of cultural differences. For example, one printer manual aimed at an Italian audience presented nude models with strategically placed rectangles showing the various colors the machine could reproduce. Nudity would be inappropriate in almost all other countries. A software manual in the United States showed an illustration of a person's left hand. Because the left hand is considered unclean in many countries in the Middle East, the manual would need to be modified for those countries.

- **What is the readers' technological infrastructure?** If your readers don't have internet access, there is no point in making a web version of the information. If your readers pay by the minute for internet access, you will want to create web-based information that downloads quickly.

WRITER'S CHECKLIST

Parenthetical, Sentence, and Extended Definitions

☐ Are all necessary terms defined? *(p. 551)*

Are the parenthetical definitions
☐ appropriate for the audience? *(p. 553)*
☐ clear? *(p. 553)*
☐ smoothly integrated into the sentences? *(p. 553)*

Does each sentence definition
☐ contain a sufficiently specific category and distinguishing characteristics? *(p. 554)*
☐ avoid describing one particular item when a general class of items is intended? *(p. 554)*

☐ avoid circular definition? *(p. 554)*
☐ identify a category with a noun or a noun phrase? *(p. 554)*

☐ Are the extended definitions developed logically and clearly? *(p. 554)*
☐ Are the definitions placed in the location most useful to readers? *(p. 559)*

Descriptions of Objects and Mechanisms

☐ Are the nature and scope of the description clearly indicated? *(p. 563)*

In introducing the description, did you answer, if appropriate, the following questions:

☐ What is the item? *(p. 564)*

☐ What is its function? *(p. 564)*

☐ What does it look like? *(p. 564)*

☐ How does it work? *(p. 564)*

☐ What are its principal parts? *(p. 564)*

☐ Is there a graphic identifying all the principal parts? *(p. 564)*

In providing detailed information, did you

☐ answer, for each of the major components, the questions listed above in the section on introducing the description? *(p. 564)*

☐ choose an appropriate organizational principle? *(p. 565)*

☐ include graphics for each of the components? *(p. 566)*

In concluding the description, did you

☐ summarize the major points in the part-by-part description? *(p. 566)*

☐ include (where appropriate) a description of the item performing its function? *(p. 566)*

Process Descriptions

☐ Are the nature and scope of the description clearly indicated? *(p. 563)*

In introducing the description, did you answer, if appropriate, the following questions:

☐ What is the process? *(p. 564)*

☐ What is its function? *(p. 564)*

☐ Where and when does it take place? *(p. 564)*

☐ Who or what performs it? *(p. 564)*

☐ How does it work? *(p. 564)*

☐ What are its principal steps? *(p. 564)*

☐ Is there a graphic identifying all the principal steps? *(p. 564)*

In providing detailed information, did you

☐ answer, for each of the major steps, the questions listed above in the section on introducing the description? *(p. 564)*

☐ discuss the steps in chronological order or some other logical sequence? *(p. 565)*

☐ make clear the causal relationships among the steps? *(p. 565)*

☐ include graphics for each of the principal steps? *(p. 566)*

In concluding the description, did you

☐ summarize the major points in the step-by-step description? *(p. 566)*

☐ discuss, if appropriate, the importance or implications of the process? *(p. 566)*

Instructions

☐ In planning the instructions, did you consider other media, such as wikis, discussion forums, and videos? *(p. 572)*

☐ Are the instructions designed effectively, with adequate white space and a clear relationship between the graphics and the accompanying text? *(p. 576)*

☐ Do the instructions have a clear title? *(p. 581)*

Does the introduction to the set of instructions

☐ state the purpose of the task? *(p. 581)*

☐ describe safety measures or other concerns that readers should understand? *(p. 581)*

☐ list necessary tools and materials? *(p. 581)*

Are the step-by-step instructions

☐ numbered? *(p. 582)*

☐ expressed in the imperative mood? *(p. 582)*

☐ simple and direct? *(p. 582)*

☐ accompanied by appropriate graphics? *(p. 583)*

Does the conclusion

☐ include any necessary follow-up advice? *(p. 583)*

☐ include, if appropriate, a troubleshooting guide? *(p. 583)*

EXERCISES

1. Add a parenthetical definition for the italicized term in each of the following sentences:

   a. Reluctantly, he decided to *drop* the physics course.

   b. The Anthropology Club decided to use *crowdfunding* to finance the semester's dig in Utah.

   c. The department is using *shareware* in its drafting course.

2. Write a sentence definition for each of the following terms:

   a. catalyst

   b. job interview

   c. website

3. Revise any of the following sentence definitions that need revision:

   a. A thermometer measures temperature.

   b. The spark plugs are the things that ignite the air–gas mixture in a cylinder.

   c. Parallel parking is where you park next to the curb.

   d. A strike is when the employees stop working.

   e. Multitasking is when you do two things at once while you're on the computer.

4. Write a 500- to 1,000-word extended definition of one of the following terms or of a term used in your field of study. In a brief note at the start, indicate the audience and purpose for your definition. If you do secondary research, cite your sources clearly and accurately (see Appendix, Part B, for documentation systems). Check that any graphics you use are appropriate for your audience and purpose.

   a. flextime

   b. binding arbitration

   c. robotics

   d. an academic major (don't focus on any particular major; instead, define what a major is)

   e. bioengineering

5. Write a 500- to 1,000-word description of one of the following items or of a piece of equipment used in your field. In a note preceding the description, specify your audience and indicate the type of description (general or particular) you are writing. Include appropriate graphics, and be sure to cite their sources correctly if you did not create them (see Appendix, Part B, for documentation systems).

   a. GPS device

   b. MP3 player

   c. waste electrical and electronic equipment

   d. automobile jack

   e. bluetooth technology

6. Write a 500- to 1,000-word description of one of the following processes or a similar process with which you are familiar. In a note preceding the description, specify your audience and indicate the type of description (general or particular) you are writing. Include appropriate graphics. If you use secondary sources, cite them properly (see Appendix, Part B, for documentation systems).

   a. how a wind turbine works

   b. how a food co-op works

   c. how a suspension bridge is constructed

   d. how people see

   e. how a baseball player becomes a free agent

7. Study a set of instructions from www.wikihow.com. Write a memo to your instructor evaluating the quality of the instructions. Attach a screen shot or a printout of representative pages from the instructions. For more about memos, see Ch. 14, p. 386.

8. You work in the customer-relations department of a company that makes plumbing supplies. The head of product development has just handed you a draft (below) of installation instructions for a sliding tub door. She wants you to comment on their effectiveness. Write a memo to her, evaluating the instructions and suggesting improvements.

9. Write a brief manual for a process familiar to you. For example, you might write a procedures manual for a school activity or a part-time job, such as your work as the business manager of the school newspaper or as a tutor in the writing center.

10. **TEAM EXERCISE** Write instructions for one of the following activities or for a process used in your field. In a brief note preceding the instructions, indicate your audience and purpose. Include appropriate graphics.

    a. how to change a bicycle tire

    b. how to convert a WAV file to an MP3 file

    c. how to find an online discussion forum and subscribe to it

    d. how to synchronize files and folders across two devices

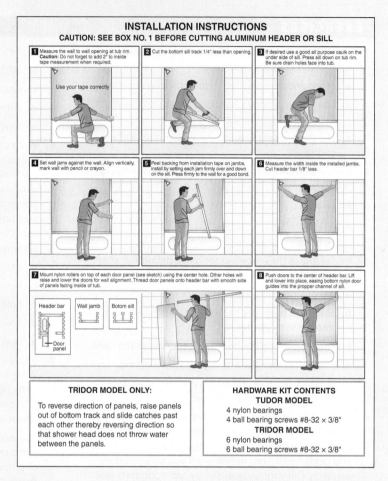

Exchange instructions with a partner. Each of you should observe the other person and take notes as he or she attempts to carry out the instructions. Then revise your instructions and share the revised version with your partner; discuss whether the revised instructions are easier to understand and apply and, if so, what made the difference. Submit the final version of your instructions to your instructor.

CASE 20: Writing Instructions

You work for the U.S. Department of Energy, which maintains an informational website called ENERGY STAR. One feature of the site is a series of videos on energy conservation produced for the general public. Your supervisor, concerned that few people are viewing most of the videos, has asked you to investigate the problem. Your assignment is to sample one of the videos and then develop a revised script that addresses any problems you see in the original video. If your instructor has assigned it, go to Achieve to get started.

Making Oral Presentations

A RECENT SEARCH FOR "death by PowerPoint" on Google returned millions of hits. Apparently, a lot of people have been on the receiving end of boring presentations built around bullet slides. But an oral presentation — with or without slides — doesn't have to be deadly dull.

And the process of creating and delivering a presentation doesn't have to be frightening. You might not have had much experience in public speaking, and perhaps your few attempts have been difficult. However, if you approach it logically, an oral presentation is simply another application you need to master in your role as a technical communicator. Once you learn that the people in the room are there to hear what you have to say — not to stare at you or evaluate your clothing or catch you making a grammar mistake — you can calm down and deliver your information effectively while projecting your professionalism.

There are four basic types of presentations:

- **Impromptu presentations.** You deliver the presentation without advance notice. For instance, at a meeting, your supervisor calls on you to speak for a few minutes about a project you are working on.

- **Extemporaneous presentations.** You plan and rehearse the presentation, and you might refer to notes or an outline, but you create the sentences as you speak. At its best, an extemporaneous presentation is clear and sounds spontaneous.

- **Scripted presentations.** You read a text that was written out completely in advance (by you or someone else). You sacrifice naturalness for increased clarity and precision.

- **Memorized presentations.** You speak without notes or a script. Memorized presentations are not appropriate for most technical subjects because most people cannot memorize presentations longer than a few minutes.

This chapter discusses extemporaneous and scripted presentations.

Understanding the Role of Oral Presentations

An oral presentation has one big advantage over a written one: it enables a dialogue between the speaker and the audience. Listeners can make comments or ask questions, and the speaker and listeners can talk before and after the presentation. As a technical communicator, you can expect to give oral presentations to several types of audiences:

- **Clients and customers.** You present the features of your products or services and their advantages over those of the competition. After concluding the sale or landing the contract, you might provide oral operating instructions and maintenance tips to users.

- **Colleagues in your organization.** You might instruct co-workers on a subject you know well. After you return from an important conference or an out-of-town project, you might brief your supervisors. If you have an idea for improving operations at your organization, you might write an informal proposal and then present it orally to a small group of managers. Your presentation helps them determine whether to study the idea.

- **Fellow professionals at technical conferences.** You might speak about your own research project or about a team project to professionals in your field or in other fields.

- **Government agencies.** You might speak before local, state, or federal government officials to explain a project your organization carried out. Or you might explain a proposed project so that the government officials can assess its implications. For instance, if you represent a developer, you might need to speak about the possible environmental impacts of a project your organization is proposing.

- **The public.** You might deliver oral presentations to civic organizations and the general public to help these audiences understand your organization's activities and plans. Oral presentations can help your organization reinforce its brand.

Understanding the Process of Preparing and Delivering an Oral Presentation

The Focus on Process box that follows presents an overview of the process of preparing and delivering an oral presentation. The rest of this chapter discusses this process, beginning with how to prepare a presentation.

Preparing the Presentation

When you see an excellent 20-minute presentation, you are seeing only the last 20 minutes of a process that took many hours. Experts recommend devoting 20 to 60 minutes of preparation time for each minute of the finished presentation (Nienow, 2013). That means that the average 20-minute presentation might take more than 13 hours to prepare. Obviously, there are many variables, including your knowledge of the subject and your experience creating graphics and giving presentations on that subject. But the point is that good presentations don't just happen.

FOCUS ON PROCESS: Oral Presentations

When preparing an oral presentation, pay special attention to these steps.

PLANNING	Think about how you can best prepare effective presentation graphics that are visible, legible, simple, clear, and correct. Choose the appropriate technology based on the speaking situation and the available resources.
DRAFTING	Choose effective and memorable language. Your listeners will not be able to read your presentation to help them understand your message.
REVISING	Rehearse at least three times, making any necessary changes to your transitions, the order of your slides, or your graphics. Get feedback from others on ways to improve your presentation. See the Speaker's Checklist at the end of this chapter.
EDITING	Make sure your spoken words and slides are well written. See Chapter 10 for advice on writing correct and effective sentences.
PROOFREADING	Make sure that your slides are free of errors. See Appendix, Part C, for proofreading tips.

As you start to prepare a presentation, think about ways to enlist others to help you prepare and deliver it. If possible, you should rehearse the presentation in front of others. You can also call on others to help you think about your audience and purpose, the organization of the information, the types of graphics to use, appropriate designs for slides, and so forth. The more extensively you work with other people as you plan, assemble, and rehearse, the more successful the presentation is likely to be.

Preparing an oral presentation requires the following steps:

- analyzing the speaking situation
- organizing and developing the presentation
- preparing presentation graphics
- choosing effective language
- rehearsing the presentation

ANALYZING THE SPEAKING SITUATION

First, analyze your audience and purpose. Also determine how much information you can deliver in the allotted time, and consider matters of setting, such as where the presentation will take place and what tools will be available to you.

Analyzing Your Audience and Purpose In planning an oral presentation, consider audience and purpose, just as you would in writing a document.

- **Audience.** What does the audience know about your subject? Your answer will help you determine the level of technical vocabulary and concepts you will use, as well as the types of graphics. Why are audience members listening to your presentation? Are they likely to be hostile, enthusiastic, or neutral? A presentation on the benefits of free trade, for instance, will be received one way by conservative economists and another way by U.S. steelworkers. Does your audience include nonnative speakers of English? If so, prepare to slow down the pace of the delivery and avoid unfamiliar slang or idioms.

- **Purpose.** Are you attempting to inform or to both inform and persuade? If you are explaining how wind-turbine farms work, you will describe a process. If you are explaining why your company's wind turbines are an economical way to generate power, you will compare them with other power sources.

Your analysis of your audience and purpose will affect the content and the form of your presentation. For example, you might have to emphasize some aspects of your subject and ignore others altogether. Or you might have to arrange topics to accommodate an audience's needs.

Budgeting Your Time At most professional meetings, each speaker is given a maximum time, such as 20 minutes. If the question-and-answer period is part of your allotted time, plan accordingly. Even for an informal presentation, you will probably have to work within an unstated time limit that you must determine from the speaking situation. If you take more than the appropriate amount of time, eventually your listeners will resent you or simply stop paying attention.

For a 20-minute presentation, the time allotment shown in Table 21.1 is typical. For scripted presentations, most speakers need a little over a minute to deliver a double-spaced page of text effectively.

TABLE 21.1 Time Allotment for a 20-Minute Presentation

TASK	TIME (MINUTES)
• Introduction	2
• Body	
– First Major Point	4
– Second Major Point	4
– Third Major Point	4
• Conclusion	2
• Questions	4

Considering Setting You may be delivering your presentation in person or remotely, with or without technical aids, to an audience ranging from 1 person to 1,000 or more people. All of these variables will affect the type of presentation you prepare and the way you prepare it. For example, if you will be speaking without technical aids to a small group of people, you may want to prepare handouts for them to take along. If you are preparing a remote online presentation on a platform such as WebEx or JoinMe, keep in mind that viewers will be focused on the materials they see on their computer or tablet screens — so your presentation materials will be perhaps even more important than the words you speak.

ORGANIZING AND DEVELOPING THE PRESENTATION

The speaking situation will help you decide how to organize and develop the information you will present.

For more about organizational patterns, see Ch. 7.

Start by considering the organizational patterns used typically in technical communication. One of them might fit the speaking situation. For instance, if you are a quality-assurance engineer for a computer-chip manufacturer and must address your technical colleagues on why one of the company's products is experiencing a higher-than-normal failure rate, think in terms of cause and effect: the high failure rate is the effect, but what is the cause? Or think in terms of problem–method–solution: the high failure rate is the problem; the research you conducted to determine its cause is the method; your recommended action is the solution. Of course, you can combine and adapt several organizational patterns.

As you create an effective organizational pattern for your presentation, note the kinds of information you will need for each section of the presentation. Some of this information will be data; some of it will be graphics that you can use in your presentation; some might be objects that you want to pass around in the audience.

Some presenters like to outline their presentations on paper or in a word-processing document. However, more and more, people are outlining with their presentation software.

As you organize your presentation, you will want to plan the introduction and the conclusion.

Planning the Introduction Like an introduction to a written document, an introduction to an oral presentation helps your audience understand what you are going to say, why you are going to say it, and how you are going to say it.

◢

GUIDELINES Introducing the Presentation

In introducing a presentation, consider these five suggestions.

▶ **Introduce yourself.** Unless you are speaking to colleagues you work with every day, begin with an introduction: "Good morning. My name is Omar Castillo, and I'm the Director of Facilities here at United." If you are using slides, include your name and position on the title slide.

▶ **State the title of your presentation.** Like all titles, titles of presentations should name the subject and purpose, such as "Replacing the HVAC System in Building 3: Findings from the Feasibility Study." Include the title of your presentation on your title slide.

▶ **Explain the purpose of the presentation.** This explanation can be brief: "My purpose today is to present the results of the feasibility study carried out by the Facilities Group. As you may recall, last quarter we were charged with determining whether it would be wise to replace the HVAC system in Building 3."

▶ **State your main point.** An explicit statement can help your audience understand the rest of the presentation: "Our main finding is that the HVAC system should be replaced as soon as possible. Replacing it would cost approximately $120,000. The payback period would be 2.5 years. We recommend that we start soliciting bids now, for an installation date in the third week of November."

(continued)

▶ **Provide an advance organizer.** Listeners need an advance organizer that specifically states where you are going: "First, I'd like to describe our present system, highlighting the recent problems we have experienced. Next, I'd like to . . . Then, I'd like to . . . Finally, I'd like to invite your questions."

Planning the Conclusion Like all conclusions, a conclusion to an oral presentation reinforces what you have said and looks to the future.

◢
GUIDELINES Concluding the Presentation

In concluding a presentation, consider these four suggestions.

▶ **Announce that you are concluding.** For example, "At this point, I'd like to conclude my talk with . . ." This statement helps the audience focus on your conclusions.

▶ **Summarize the main points.** Because listeners cannot replay what you have said, you should briefly summarize your main points. If you are using slides, you should present a slide that lists each of your main points in one short phrase.

▶ **Look to the future.** If appropriate, speak briefly about what you think (or hope) will happen next: "If the president accepts our recommendation, you can expect the renovation to begin in late November. After a few hectic weeks, we'll have the ability to control our environment much more precisely than we can now — and start to reduce our expenses and our carbon footprint."

▶ **Invite questions politely.** You want to invite questions because they help you clarify what you said or communicate information that you did not present in the formal presentation. You want to ask politely to encourage people to speak up.

PREPARING PRESENTATION GRAPHICS

Graphics clarify or highlight important ideas or facts. Statistical data, in particular, lend themselves to graphical presentation, as do abstract relationships and descriptions of equipment or processes. Researchers have known for decades that audiences remember information better if it is presented to them verbally and visually rather than only verbally. One other advantage of using presentation graphics is that the audience is not always looking at you. Giving the audience another visual focus can reduce your nervousness.

Most speakers use presentation software to develop graphics. By far the most popular program is PowerPoint, but other programs are becoming popular as well. One that has gained a lot of attention is Prezi, which takes a different approach from PowerPoint. Whereas PowerPoint uses a linear organization — the speaker presents each slide in sequence — Prezi uses a network or web pattern of organization. Figure 21.1 shows an example of a Prezi slide.

For more about creating graphics, see Ch. 12.

When the speaker clicks on any object on this overview slide, the software zooms in to reveal more objects within or next to that object. After discussing an object, the speaker can zoom out to the overview or zoom in to another object.

This capability of Prezi not only makes it easy for the speaker to navigate within the presentation but also helps audience members remember the big picture because they see the overview graphic frequently as the speaker moves from point to point. Whereas PowerPoint is linear like a book — page 6 always precedes page 7 — Prezi is more like a website in that the speaker can easily jump from one object to another.

Although the speaker can present each slide in sequence using the arrows at the bottom of the screen, Prezi makes it simple for the speaker to create a new sequence each time he or she delivers the presentation or to come back to a particular slide or set of slides during the question-and-answer period.

The free version of Prezi is cloud-based; that is, you have to be connected to the internet to use it. This feature means that you can deliver your Prezi presentation from any computer with an internet connection, that your team members can collaborate from remote locations, and that your presentation is stored in the cloud. However, your presentation is visible to all who visit the Prezi site, so you should be sure that it contains no confidential information or information you do not wish to share with those beyond your original audience.

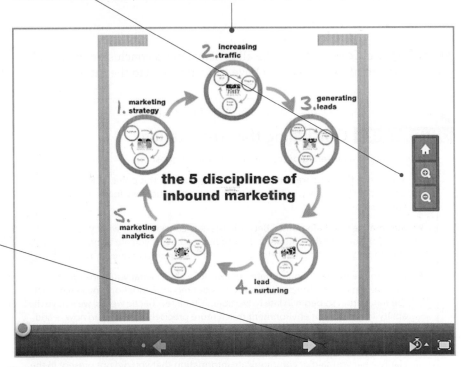

FIGURE 21.1   The Network Organization of Prezi
Shade Wilson, Scalability Project LLC.

Characteristics of an Effective Slide An effective presentation graphic has five characteristics:

- **It presents a clear, well-supported claim.** In a presentation slide, the best way to present a claim and to support it is to put the claim in the headline section of the slide and the support in the body of the slide. Engineering professor and presentation specialist Michael Alley (2007) recommends the structure shown in Figure 21.2 (on page 601).

- **It is easy to see.** The most common problem with presentation graphics is that they are too small. In general, text has to be in 24-point type or larger to be visible on a screen. Figure 21.3 on page 602 shows a slide that contains so much information that most of it is too small to see easily.

For more about typefaces, see Ch. 11. For more about using color in graphics, see Ch. 12.

```
Main claim goes here.


—Support in the form of text
and visuals is included
below claim.
```

a. The structure of a typical slide

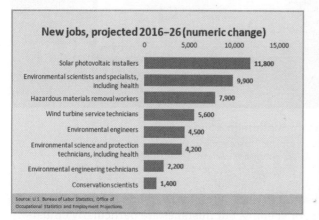

b. A slide with a claim and a single large graphic
This slide is structured like a paragraph. The headline is the topic sentence; the graphic is the support.
U.S. Bureau of Labor Statistics

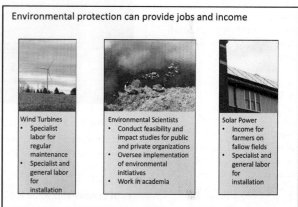

c. A slide with a claim, several graphics, and explanatory text
In this slide, the headline functions as an advance organizer, introducing three careers in environmental protection. Each panel has a title, a photograph, and bullet points that describe the specific career and income benefits.
©2020 Macmillan, Photos by Sherry Mooney

FIGURE 21.2 Michael Alley's Claim-and-Support Structure for Presentation Graphics

- **It is easy to read.** Use clear, legible lines for drawings and diagrams; black on white works best. Use legible typefaces for text; a boldface sans-serif typeface such as Arial or Helvetica is effective because it reproduces clearly on a screen. Avoid shadowed and outlined letters.

- **It is simple.** Text and drawings must be simple. Each graphic should present only one idea. Your listeners have not seen the graphic before and will not be able to linger over it.

This slide attempts to compare too many types of data at once, including differences between first-class and standard mail, between consumer and business mail, and among various types of mail within those segments. The main point of the slide — the overall decline in the volume of mail — is difficult for the audience to see.

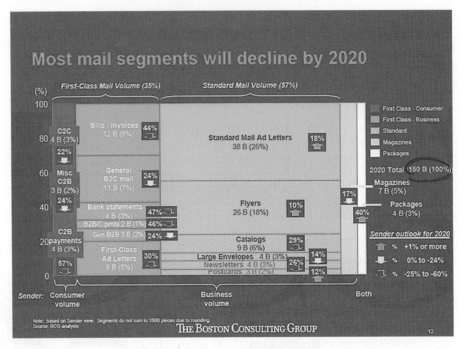

FIGURE 21.3 Too Much Information on a Slide

Most of the information on this slide is too small to see easily.

Information from Boston Group, 2010: www.usps.com/strategicplanning/_pdf/BCG_Detailedpresentation.pdf.

- **It is correct.** Proofread your graphics carefully. Everyone makes mistakes in grammar, punctuation, or spelling, but mistakes are particularly embarrassing when they are 10 inches tall on a screen.

When preparing a presentation using a program such as PowerPoint or Prezi, it may be best to create your own simple design rather than relying on preexisting templates. (For more on creating templates in PowerPoint and Prezi, see the TechTip on page 604.)

Presentation software programs contain many fancy animation effects. For example, you can set the software so that when a new slide appears, it is accompanied by the sound of applause or of breaking glass, and the heading text spins around like a pinwheel. Do not use animation effects that are unrelated to your subject. They undercut your professionalism and quickly become tiresome.

However, one animation effect in PowerPoint, sometimes called *appear and dim*, is useful. When you create a bulleted list, you can set the software to show just the first bullet item and then make the next bullet item appear when you click the mouse. When you do so, the previous bullet item dims. This feature is useful because it focuses the audience's attention on the bullet item you are discussing.

Regardless of whether you are using the appear-and-dim feature, set the software so that you use the mouse (or a colleague does) to advance from one graphic to the next. If you set the software so that the graphics advance automatically at a specified interval, such as 60 seconds, you will have to speed up or slow down your presentation to keep up with the graphics.

One more point: you cannot use copyrighted material—images, text, music, video, or other material—in your presentation without written permission to do so. (Your presentations in class, however, do not require permission because they are covered by the fair-use exemption.)

Graphics and the Speaking Situation To plan your graphics, analyze four aspects of the speaking situation:

- **Length of the presentation.** How many slides should you have? Smith (1991) suggests showing a different slide approximately every 30 seconds of the presentation. This figure is only a guideline; base your decision on your subject and audience. Still, the general point is valid: it is far better to have a series of simple slides than to have one complicated one that stays on the screen for five minutes.

- **Audience aptitude and experience.** What kinds of graphics can your audience understand easily? You don't want to present scatter plots, for example, if your audience does not know how to interpret them.

- **Setting.** What size images are most appropriate for the presentation context? Graphics suitable for a remote online WebEx presentation differ from those suitable for presentation in a small conference room or a 500-seat auditorium. In WebEx or other webcasting platforms, you can provide more detail because viewers will most likely be sitting close to their computer or tablet screen as they watch your presentation. For use in a large auditorium, by contrast, your slides should have larger, more simplified text and graphics.

- **Equipment.** Find out what kind of equipment will be available to you. Ask about backups in case of equipment failure. If possible, bring your own equipment—then you can be confident that the equipment works and you know how to use it. Some speakers bring graphics in two media just in case; that is, they have slides, but they also have handouts of the same graphics. If your presentation is going to be recorded to be made available on a website or as a podcast, try to arrange to have the recording technicians visit the site beforehand to see if there are any problems they will need to solve.

> **TECH TIP**

Why To Create a Presentation Template

Master slides and templates allow you to maintain a consistent look throughout your presentation graphics without needing to design each individual slide. Although the templates provided by Prezi and PowerPoint can be useful, they often violate basic design principles, and they may not fit the needs of your presentation. When possible, create an original design that suits your topic and will appear fresh and original to your audience members, who have probably seen many of the predesigned templates used before.

How To Create a Presentation Template

PowerPoint

In PowerPoint, select **Slide Master** from the **Master Views** group on the **View** tab.

By selecting elements on the master slide and then using the commands on the **Slide Master** tab, you can add a background, choose a color scheme, and choose type styles and sizes.

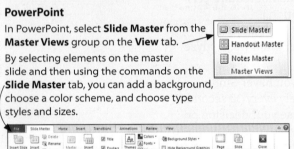

To add graphics to the master slide, use the **Images** and **Illustrations** groups on the **Insert** tab.

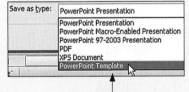

To save your page design so that you can use this design for another presentation, select **Save As** from the **File** tab, and then select **PowerPoint Template** from the drop-down menu.

Prezi

In Prezi, select **Start blank prezi** on the **Choose your template** page.

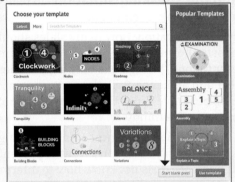

Click on the **Customize** option to launch the **Customize** panel, where you can choose the background colors and insert your own background images or content from your computer.

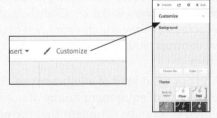

More background options are available from the **Advanced** button at the bottom of the **Customize** panel.

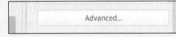

To save your customized background theme, choose **Save current theme**.

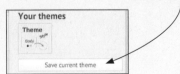

Why To Set List Items To Appear and Dim During a Presentation

To help your audience focus on the point you are discussing, you can apply PowerPoint's custom animation feature to the **Master Page** so that a list item appears and then dims when the next item appears.

How To Set List Items To Appear and Dim During a Presentation

1. To apply a **custom animation**, select the **Title and Content Layout** slide in the **Slide Master** view, and then highlight the list on the slide.

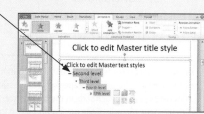

3. Select the **Animation Pane** button in the **Advanced Animation** group. In the **Animation Pane**, click the drop-down menu and select **Effect Options**.

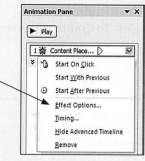

4. On the **Effect** tab in the **Appear** dialog box, click the **After Animation** drop-down menu and select a dim color.

2. In the **Advanced Animation** group, select **Add Animation**, and then select the **Entrance** category and the **Appear** effect.

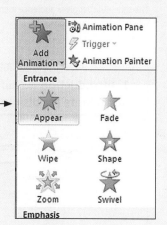

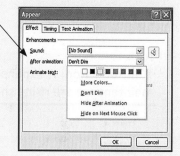

Using Graphics To Signal the Organization of a Presentation Used effectively, graphics can help you communicate how your presentation is organized. For example, you can use the transition from one graphic to the next to indicate the transition from one point to the next. Figure 21.4 shows the slides for a presentation that accompanied the report in Chapter 18 on tablet computer use at Rawlings Regional Medical Center (see Figure 18.8 on pp. 504–27.)

Selecting a Tablet Computer for the
Clinical Staff at Rawlings Regional
Medical Center:
A Recommendation Report

Prepared by:

Jeremy Elkins, Director of IT

Eloise Carruthers, Director of Nursing

December 15, 2018

Recommendation Report Outline

 1. Introduction
   2. Major Results
      2.1 Clinical-staff knowledge and attitudes
      2.2 BYOD v. hospital-owned model
      2.3 Determining criteria
      2.4 Assessing tablets
   3. Conclusions
   4. Recommendation

December 15, 2018   Tablet-Use Recommendation Report   2

The title slide shows the title of the presentation and the name and affiliation of each speaker. You might also want to include the date of the presentation.

The next slide presents an overview, which outlines the presentation. The arrow identifies the point the speaker is addressing.

At the bottom of each slide in the body of the presentation is a footer with the date, the title of the presentation, and the number of the slide. The slide number gives audience members a way to refer to the slide when they ask questions.

1. Introduction: IT expenses for tablet maintenance are rising sharply

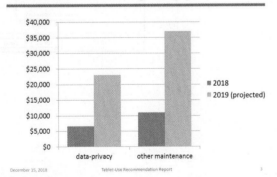

December 15, 2018   Tablet-Use Recommendation Report   3

1. Introduction (cont'd)**:** We cannot certify our tablets for disinfection

December 15, 2018   Tablet-Use Recommendation Report   4

This slide uses a simple bar graph created in PowerPoint. Don't try to present a lot of information on a single slide.

The title of this slide uses the numbering system introduced in the previous slide. This cue helps the audience understand the structure of the presentation. Following the colon is an independent clause that presents the claim that will be supported in the slide.

If the images in your presentation are your own intellectual property or are clip art that comes with the software, you can legally display them anywhere. If they are not, you need to cite their sources and obtain written permission. You have three choices for placing the source statements: at the bottom of the appropriate slides, in a sources slide that you show at the end of the presentation, or on a paper handout that you distribute at the end of the presentation.

BeeBright/Shutterstock.com

FIGURE 21.4   Sample PowerPoint Presentation (*continued*)

1. Introduction (cont'd): We lack a policy for making tablets available

For second and subsequent slides within the same section of the presentation, use the "continued" abbreviation shown here. Notice that the speakers use one color for the generic term ("Introduction") and a different color for the claim.

Photo: kurhan/Shutterstock.com

Recommendation Report Outline

1. Introduction
2. Major Results
   2.1 Clinical-staff knowledge and attitudes
   2.2 BYOD v. hospital-owned model
   2.3 Determining criteria
   2.4 Assessing tablets
3. Conclusions
4. Recommendation

This slide is identical to Slide 2, except that the arrow has moved. Use this organizing slide to help your audience remember the overall organization of your presentation. Don't overdo it; if you presented this organizing slide just a few slides ago, don't use it again until you make the transition to the next major unit in the presentation.

2.1 Results: Clinical staff own iPads and Androids

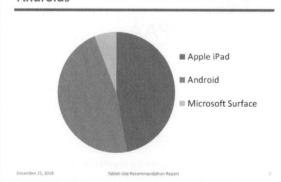

- Apple iPad
- Android
- Microsoft Surface

A pie chart is a logical choice for representing a small number of components (usually seven or fewer) that add up to 100 percent.

Note that the speakers use conservative blues for all their graphics on the slide set. You don't need a rainbow full of colors. You need just enough difference so that the audience can distinguish between the different slices.

2.1 Results (cont'd): Clinical staff with tablets consider themselves expert users

"I'm an expert user"

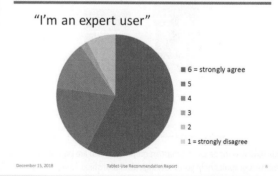

- 6 = strongly agree
- 5
- 4
- 3
- 2
- 1 = strongly disagree

Slides work best if the text is brief. The speaker will explain that here are the responses to the statement "I consider myself an expert user of my tablet."

FIGURE 21.4   Sample PowerPoint Presentation (*continued*)

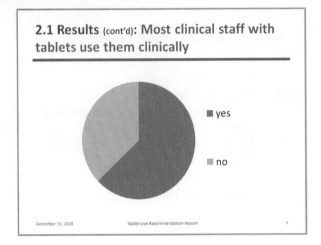

2.1 Results (cont'd): Most clinical staff with tablets use them clinically

- yes
- no

December 15, 2018 · Tablet-Use Recommendation Report · 9

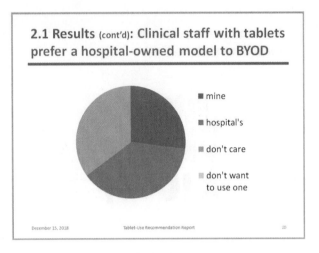

2.1 Results (cont'd): Clinical staff with tablets prefer a hospital-owned model to BYOD

- mine
- hospital's
- don't care
- don't want to use one

December 15, 2018 · Tablet-Use Recommendation Report · 10

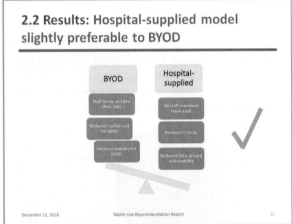

2.2 Results: Hospital-supplied model slightly preferable to BYOD

BYOD

- Staff know and like their tabs
- Reduced capital cost for RRMC
- Reduced liability for RRMC

Hospital-supplied

- All staff members have a tab
- Reduced IT costs
- Reduced data-privacy vulnerability

December 15, 2018 · Tablet-Use Recommendation Report · 11

2.3 Results: We set four *necessary* criteria for tablet study

HIPAA
Health Insurance Portability and Accountability Act

December 15, 2018 · Tablet-Use Recommendation Report · 12

This slide was made using SmartArt graphics, which are part of PowerPoint. SmartArt graphics help you show logical relationships. Here, the relationship is that the hospital-supplied model is "heavier"—that is, has more to recommend it—than the BYOD model.

The speakers added the checkmark to emphasize that the hospital-supplied model is preferable to the BYOD model.

If the images you show are not your own intellectual property, you can legally display them in a college classroom because they are covered by the fair-use provisions of U.S. copyright law. However, if you display them in a business presentation, you would need formal written permission from the copyright holders. See Ch. 2, pp. 24–26, for more information.

Money: Bureau of Engraving and Printing. Chains on laptop: Elnur/Shutterstock.com. Disinfecting wipes: BeeBright/Shutterstock.com.

FIGURE 21.4   **Sample PowerPoint Presentation** (*continued*)

2.3 Results (cont'd): We set two *desirable* criteria for tablet study

December 15, 2018   Tablet-Use Recommendation Report   13

2.4 Results: Medical-grade tablets are too expensive

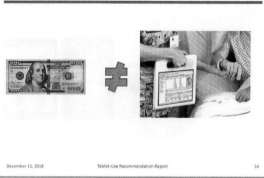

December 15, 2018   Tablet-Use Recommendation Report   14

The speakers used the "appear" animation to display first the picture of the tablet and then the picture of the battery. This feature lets the speakers display on the screen only what they are discussing so that the audience is not distracted by other images.

TMT-1830-10 MEDICAL TABLET PC: Courtesy Teguar Corporation. Battery: oxanaart/Shutterstock.com.

Money: Bureau of Engraving and Printing. Photo of Motion C5: Courtesy of Xplore.

2.4 Results (cont'd): General-purpose tablets meet our data-privacy criterion

December 15, 2018   Tablet-Use Recommendation Report   15

2.4 Results (cont'd): General-purpose tablets meet our other security criteria

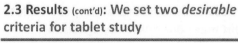

December 15, 2018   Tablet-Use Recommendation Report   16

HootSuite App for iPod: HootSuite.

Chains on laptop: Elnur/Shutterstock.com. HootSuite App for iPad: HootSuite.

FIGURE 21.4 Sample PowerPoint Presentation (*continued*)

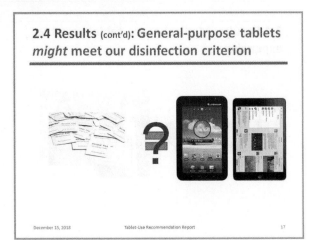

2.4 Results (cont'd): General-purpose tablets *might* meet our disinfection criterion

December 15, 2018   Tablet-Use Recommendation Report   17

2.4 Results (cont'd): General-purpose tablets *might* meet our durability criterion

December 15, 2018   Tablet-Use Recommendation Report   18

The formatting that appears throughout the slide set — the background color, the horizontal rule, and the footer — is created in the Slide-Master view. This formatting appears in every slide unless you modify or delete it for that slide.

Note that the speakers use color — sparingly — for emphasis.

Disinfecting wipes: BeeBright/Shutterstock.com. HootSuite App for iPad: HootSuite.

TMT-1830-10 MEDICAL TABLET PC: Courtesy Teguar Corporation. HootSuite App for iPad: HootSuite.

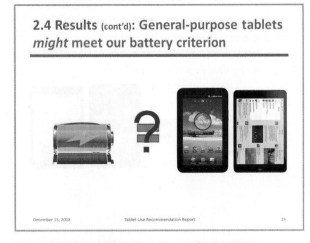

2.4 Results (cont'd): General-purpose tablets *might* meet our battery criterion

December 15, 2018   Tablet-Use Recommendation Report   19

Recommendation Report Outline

1. Introduction
2. Major Results
   2.1 Clinical-staff knowledge and attitudes
   2.2 BYOD v. hospital-owned model
   2.3 Determining criteria
   2.4 Assessing tablets
➤ 3. Conclusions
4. Recommendation

December 15, 2018   Tablet-Use Recommendation Report   20

Battery: oxanaart/Shutterstock.com. HootSuite App for iPad: HootSuite.

FIGURE 21.4   Sample PowerPoint Presentation (*continued*)

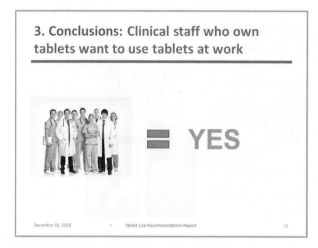

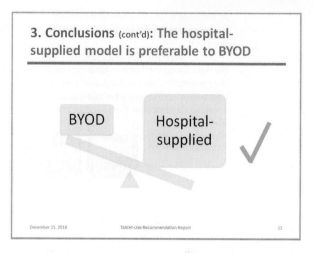

As discussed in Ch. 18, conclusions are inferences you draw from results.
Photo: kurhan/Shutterstock.com.

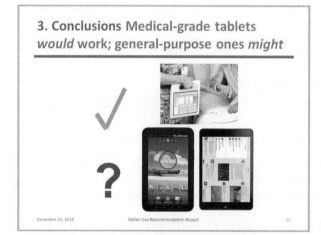

Photo of Motion C5: Courtesy of Xplore. HootSuite App for iPad: HootSuite.

FIGURE 21.4   Sample PowerPoint Presentation (*continued*)

As discussed in Ch. 19, recommendations are statements about what you think should be done next.

Some speakers like to make a final slide with the word "Questions?" on it to signal the end of the presentation. You can also display contact information (such as your email address) to encourage audience members to get in touch with you.

Photo of Motion C5: Courtesy of Xplore. HootSuite App for iPad: HootSuite.

4. Recommendation: We recommend one of two options

1. Reconsider budget, study medical-grade tablets.

2. Test general-purpose tablets on-site.

December 15, 2018   Tablet-Use Recommendation Report   25

FIGURE 21.4   Sample PowerPoint Presentation (*continued*)

Presentation software allows you to create two other kinds of documents—*speaking notes* and *handouts*—that can enhance a presentation. Figure 21.5 (on p. 613) shows a page of speaking notes. Figure 21.6 (on p. 613) shows a page from a handout created from PowerPoint slides.

CHOOSING EFFECTIVE LANGUAGE

Delivering an oral presentation is more challenging than writing a document for two reasons:

1. Listeners can't reread something they didn't understand.

2. Because you are speaking live, you must maintain your listeners' attention, even if they are hungry or tired or the room is too hot.

Using language effectively helps you meet these two challenges.

Using Language To Signal Advance Organizers, Summaries, and Transitions   Even if you use graphics effectively, listeners cannot "see" the organization of a presentation as well as readers can. For this reason, use language to alert your listeners to advance organizers, summaries, and transitions.

- **Advance organizers.** Use an advance organizer (a statement that tells the listener what you are about to say) in the introduction. In addition, use advance organizers when you introduce main ideas in the body of the presentation.

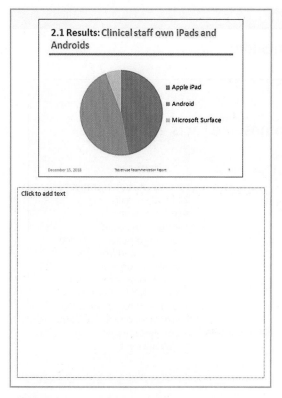

FIGURE 21.5   Speaking Notes

To create speaking notes for each slide, type the notes in the box under the picture of the slide, and then print the notes pages. You can print the slides on your notes pages in color or black and white. The problem with using speaking notes is that you cannot read your notes and maintain eye contact at the same time.

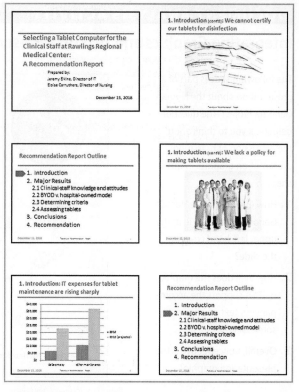

FIGURE 21.6   Handout

In PowerPoint, you use the Page Setup tab to configure the file for printing. You can set the software to display from one to nine slides on a page.

Disinfecting wipes: BeeBright/Shutterstock.com. Photo of health-care workers: kurhan/Shutterstock.com.

- **Summaries.** The major summary is in the conclusion, but you might also summarize at strategic points in the body of the presentation. For instance, after a three- to four-minute discussion of a major point, you might summarize it in one sentence before going on to the next major point. Here is a sample summary from a conclusion:

  > Let me conclude by summarizing my three main points about the implications of the new RCRA regulations on the long-range waste-management strategy for Radnor Township. The first point is . . . The second point is . . . The third point is . . . I hope this presentation will give you some ideas as you think about the challenges of implementing the RCRA.

DOCUMENT ANALYSIS ACTIVITY

Integrating Graphics and Text on a Presentation Slide

The following slide is part of a presentation about the Human Genome Project. The questions below ask you to think about the discussion of preparing presentation graphics in this chapter.

1. How effective is the Human Genome Project logo in the upper left-hand corner of the slide?

2. How well does the graphic of DNA support the accompanying text on chromosome facts?

3. Overall, how effective is the presentation graphic?

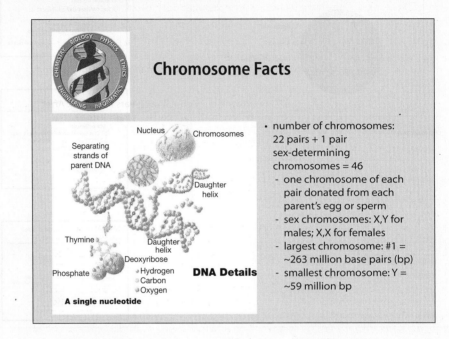

- **Transitions.** As you move from one point to the next, signal the transition clearly. Summarize the previous point, and then announce that you are moving to the next point:

  > It is clear, then, that the federal government has issued regulations without indicating how it expects county governments to comply with them. I'd like to turn now to my second main point. . . .

Using Memorable Language Effective presentations require memorable language.

◢
GUIDELINES Using Memorable Language
in Oral Presentations

Draw on these three techniques to help make a lasting impression on your audience.

▶ **Involve the audience.** People are more interested in their own concerns than in yours. Talk to the audience about their problems and their solutions. In the introduction, establish a link between your topic and the audience's interests. For instance, a presentation to a city council about waste management might begin like this:

> Picture yourself on the Radnor Township Council two years from now. After exhaustive hearings, proposals, and feasibility studies, you still don't have a waste-management plan that meets federal regulations. What you do have is a mounting debt: the township is being fined $1,000 per day until you implement an acceptable plan.

▶ **Refer to people, not to abstractions.** People remember specifics; they forget abstractions. To make a point memorable, describe it in human terms:

> What could you do with that $365,000 every year? In each computer lab in each school in the township, you could replace each laptop every three years instead of every four years. Or you could expand your school-lunch program to feed every needy child in the township. Or you could extend your after-school programs to cover an additional 3,000 students.

▶ **Use interesting facts, figures, and quotations.** Search the internet for interesting information about your subject. For instance, you might find a brief quotation from an authoritative figure in the field or a famous person not generally associated with the field (for example, Theodore Roosevelt on waste management and the environment).

A note about humor: only a few hundred people in the United States make a good living being funny. Don't plan to tell a joke. If something happens during the presentation that provides an opening for a witty remark and you are good at making witty remarks, fine. But don't *prepare* to be funny.

REHEARSING THE PRESENTATION
Even the most gifted speakers need to rehearse. It is a good idea to set aside enough time to rehearse your speech thoroughly.

Rehearsing the Extemporaneous Presentation Rehearse your extemporaneous presentation at least three times.

- **First rehearsal.** Don't worry about posture or voice projection. Just deliver your presentation aloud with your presentation slides. Your goal is to see if the speech makes sense—if you can explain all the points and create effective transitions. If you have trouble, stop and try to figure out the problem. If you need more information, get it. If you need a better transition, create one. You are likely to learn that you need to revise the order of your slides. Pick up where you left off and continue the rehearsal, stopping again where necessary to revise.

- **Second rehearsal.** This time, the presentation should flow more easily. Make any necessary changes to the slides. When you have complete control over the organization and flow, check to see if you are within the time limit.

- **Third rehearsal.** After a satisfactory second rehearsal, try the presentation under more realistic circumstances—if possible, in front of others. The listeners might offer questions or constructive advice about your speaking style. If people aren't available, record a video of the presentation on your computer or phone, and then evaluate your own delivery. If you can visit the site of the presentation to rehearse there, you will find giving the actual speech a little easier.

Rehearse again until you are satisfied with your presentation, but don't try to memorize it.

Rehearsing the Scripted Presentation Rehearsing a scripted presentation is a combination of revising and editing the text and rehearsing your delivery. As you revise, read the script aloud to hear how it sounds. Once you think the presentation says what you want to say, try recording yourself with an audio or video recorder as you read. Revise the presentation until you are satisfied, and then rehearse in front of real people. Do not memorize the presentation. There is no need to; you will have your script in front of you on the podium.

Delivering the Presentation

When giving your presentation, you will concentrate on what you have to say. However, you will have three additional concerns: staying calm, using your voice effectively, and using your body effectively.

CALMING YOUR NERVES

Most professional actors admit to being nervous before a performance, so it is no wonder that most technical speakers are nervous. You might well fear that you will forget everything or that no one will be able to hear you. These fears are common. But keep in mind three facts about nervousness:

- **You are much more aware of your nervousness than the audience is.** They are farther away from your trembling hands.

- **Nervousness gives you energy and enthusiasm.** Without energy and enthusiasm, your presentation will be flat. If you seem bored and listless, your audience will become bored and listless.

- **After a few minutes, your nervousness will pass.** You will be able to relax and concentrate on the subject.

This advice is unlikely to make you feel much better if you are distracted by nerves as you wait to give your presentation. Experienced speakers offer three tips for coping with nervousness:

- **Realize that you are prepared.** If you have done your homework, prepared the presentation carefully, and rehearsed it several times, you'll be fine.

- **Realize that the audience is there to hear you, not to judge you.** Your listeners want to hear what you have to say. They are much less interested in your nervousness than you are.

- **Realize that your audience is made up of individual people who happen to be sitting in the same room.** You'll feel better if you realize that audience members are like the people you talk to every day and they also get nervous before making presentations.

When it is time to begin, don't jump up to the podium and start speaking quickly. Walk up slowly and arrange your text, outline, or note cards before you. If water is available, take a sip. Look out at the audience for a few seconds before you begin. Begin with "Good morning" (or "Good afternoon" or "Good evening"), and refer to any officers and dignitaries present. If you have not been introduced, introduce yourself. In less formal contexts, just begin your presentation.

So that the audience will listen to you and have confidence in what you say, use your voice and your body to project an attitude of restrained self-confidence. Show interest in your topic and knowledge about your subject.

◢
GUIDELINES Releasing Nervous Energy

Experienced speakers suggest the following strategies for dealing with nervousness before a presentation.

▶ **Walk around.** A brisk walk of a minute or two can calm you by dissipating some of your nervous energy.

▶ **Go off by yourself for a few minutes.** Having some time alone can help you compose your thoughts and realize that you can handle your nervousness.

▶ **Talk with someone for a few minutes.** For some speakers, distraction works best. Find someone to talk to.

▶ **Take several deep breaths, exhaling slowly.** Doing so will help you control your nerves.

USING YOUR VOICE EFFECTIVELY

Inexperienced speakers often have problems with the following aspects of vocalizing.

- **Volume.** Because acoustics vary greatly from room to room and with different equipment, you won't know how well your voice will carry in a particular setting until you have heard someone speaking there. In some rooms, speakers can use a conversational volume. Other rooms require greater voice projection. Because more people speak too softly than too loudly, you might ask if the people in the back of the room can hear you. However, even soft-spoken people tend to speak too loudly when they speak into microphones. If you are using a mic, glance at your audience to see if you need to adjust your volume. The body language of audience members will be clear. If you are using a remote online platform such as WebEx or JoinMe, experiment with your microphone before the presentation to find the speaking volume that produces the most clarity.

- **Speed.** Nervousness makes people speak quickly. Even if you think you are speaking at the right rate, you might be going a little too fast for some listeners. Although you know your subject well, your listeners are trying to understand new information. For particularly difficult points, slow down for emphasis. After finishing one major point, pause before introducing the next one.

- **Pitch.** In an effort to control their voices, many speakers end up flattening their pitch. The resulting monotone is boring and, for some listeners, distracting. Try to let the pitch of your voice go up or down as it would in a normal conversation.

- **Articulation.** Nervousness can lead to sloppy pronunciation and a confused audience. If you want to say *environment*, don't say *envirament*. A related problem occurs with technical words and phrases, especially the important ones. When a speaker uses a phrase over and over, it tends to get clipped and become difficult to understand. Unless you articulate carefully, *Scanlon Plan* will end up as *Scanluhplah*.

- **Nonfluencies.** Avoid such meaningless fillers as *you know*, *like*, *okay*, *right*, *uh*, and *um*. These fillers do not hide the fact that you aren't saying anything. A thoughtful pause is better than an annoying verbal tic.

USING YOUR BODY EFFECTIVELY

Besides listening to you, the audience members at in-person presentations will be looking at you. Effective speakers use their body language to help listeners follow the presentation.

◢ GUIDELINES Facing an Audience

As you give a presentation, keep in mind these four guidelines about physical movement.

▶ **Maintain eye contact.** Eye contact helps you see how the audience is receiving the presentation. You will see, for instance, if listeners in the back are having trouble hearing you. With small groups, look at each listener randomly; with larger groups, look at each segment of the audience frequently during your speech. Do not stare at the screen, the floor, your notes, or out the window. If you are giving an online presentation, maintain eye contact with the camera when you are on.

▶ **Use natural gestures.** When people talk, they often gesture with their hands. Most of the time, gestures make a presentation look natural and improve

(continued)

listeners' comprehension. You can supplement your natural gestures by using your arms and hands to signal pauses and to emphasize important points. When referring to graphics, walk toward the screen and point to direct the audience's attention. Avoid mannerisms — physical gestures that serve no useful purpose, such as jiggling the coins in your pocket or pacing back and forth. Like verbal mannerisms, physical mannerisms are often unconscious. Constructive criticism from friends can help you pinpoint them.

▶ **Don't block the audience's view of the screen.** Stand off to the side of the screen. Use a pointer to indicate key words or images on the screen.

▶ **Control the audience's attention.** People will listen to and look at anything that is interesting. If you hand out photocopies at the start of the presentation, some people will start to read them and stop listening to you. If you leave an image on the screen after you finish talking about it, some people will keep looking at it instead of listening to you. When you want the audience to look at you and listen to you, remove the graphics or make the screen blank.

PRESENTING TO ALL AUDIENCES

If your audience includes people of different cultures and languages, keep in mind the following suggestions:

• **Hire translators and interpreters if necessary.** If many people in the audience do not understand your language, hire interpreters (people who translate your words as you speak them) and translators (people who translate your written material in advance).

• **Use graphics effectively to reinforce your points.** Try to devise ways to present information using graphics — flowcharts, diagrams, and so forth — to help your listeners understand you. Putting more textual information on graphics will allow your listeners to see as well as hear your points.

• **Be aware that gestures can have culturally based meanings.** As discussed in Ch. 12, American hand gestures (such as the thumbs-up sign or the "okay" gesture) have different — and sometimes insulting — meanings in other cultures. Therefore, it's a good idea to avoid the use of these gestures. You can't go wrong with an arms-out, palms-up gesture that projects openness and inclusiveness.

If your audience includes people with varying abilities, keep in mind the following suggestions:

• Provide handouts in accessible formats ahead of time for audience members to study and review.

• Hire a sign-language specialist who can translate your presentation for audience members with hearing impairments.

• Make a transcript of your talk available for audience members with hearing impairments.

• Provide a recording of the presentation for audience members who can't take notes.

Answering Questions After a Presentation

When you finish a presentation, thank the audience simply and directly: "Thank you for your attention." Then invite questions. Don't abruptly ask, "Any questions?" This phrasing suggests that you don't really want any questions. Instead, say something like this: "If you have any questions, I'll be happy to try to answer them now." If invited politely, people will be much more likely to ask questions, and you will be more likely to succeed in communicating your information effectively.

When you respond to questions, you might encounter any of these situations:

- **You're not sure everyone heard the question.** Ask if people heard it. If they didn't, repeat or paraphrase it, perhaps as an introduction to your response: "Your question is about the efficiency of these three techniques." Some speakers always repeat the question, which gives them an extra moment to prepare an answer.

- **You don't understand the question.** Ask for clarification. After responding, ask if you have answered the question adequately.

- **You have already answered the question during the presentation.** Restate the answer politely. Begin your answer with a phrase such as the following: "I'm sorry I didn't make that point clear in my talk. I wanted to explain how . . ." Never insult an audience member by pointing out that you already answered the question.

- **A belligerent member of the audience rejects your response and insists on restating his or her original point.** Politely offer to discuss the matter further after the presentation. If you are lucky, the person won't continue to bore or annoy the rest of the audience.

If it is appropriate to stay after the session to talk individually with members of the audience, offer to do so.

ETHICS NOTE

ANSWERING QUESTIONS HONESTLY

If an audience member asks a question to which you do not know the answer, admit it. Simply say, "I don't know" or "I'm not sure, but I think the answer is . . ." Smart people know that they don't know everything. If you have some ideas about how to find out the answer — by checking a particular reference source, for example — share them. If the question is obviously important to the person who asked it, you might offer to meet with him or her to discuss ways for you to provide a more complete response later, perhaps by email.

Sample Evaluation Form

Figure 21.7 (on p. 621) is a form that can help you focus your thoughts as you watch and listen to presentations by your classmates or others.

Oral Presentation Evaluation Form

Speaker(s)_____   Topic_____

The left-hand column lists statements about different aspects of the presentation. In the middle column, rate the speaker(s) on each aspect of the presentation by writing a number from 1 to 6, with 1 signifying that you strongly disagree with the statement and 6 signifying that you strongly agree with the statement. In the right-hand column, write any comments you wish the speaker(s) to see.

Aspect of the Presentation	Rating (1 = strongly disagree; 6 = strongly agree)	Comments
Organization and Development		
1. In the introduction, the speaker related the topic to the audience's concerns.		
2. In the introduction, the speaker explained the main points he or she wanted to make in the presentation.		
3. In the introduction, the speaker explained the organization of the presentation.		
4. I found it easy to understand the organization of the presentation.		
5. The speaker used appropriate and sufficient evidence to clarify the subject.		
6. In the conclusion, the speaker summarized the main points effectively.		
7. In the conclusion, the speaker invited questions politely.		
8. In the conclusion, the speaker answered questions effectively.		
9. The speaker used the allotted time effectively.		
Verbal and Physical Presence		
10. The speaker used interesting, clear language to get the points across.		
11. The speaker used clear and distinct enunciation.		
12. The speaker seemed relaxed and poised.		

FIGURE 21.7   Sample Evaluation Form (*continued*)

Aspect of the Presentation	Rating (1 = strongly disagree; 6 = strongly agree)	Comments
Verbal and Physical Presence		
13. The speaker exhibited no distracting vocal mannerisms.		
14. The speaker exhibited no distracting physical mannerisms.		
15. The speaker made eye contact effectively.		
16. The speaker was enthusiastic.		
Use of Graphics		
17. The speaker used graphics effectively to reinforce and explain the main points.		
18. The speaker used appropriate kinds of graphics.		
19. The speaker used graphics effectively to highlight the organization of the presentation.		
20. The graphics were easy to see.		
21. The graphics were easy to understand.		
22. The graphics looked correct and professional.		
23. The graphics helped me understand the organization of the presentation.		
For Group Presentations		
24. The group seemed well rehearsed.		
25. The graphics were edited so that they looked consistent from one group member to the next.		
26. The transitions from one group member to the next were smooth.		
27. Each group member seemed to have done an equal amount of work in preparing and delivering the presentation.		

On the other side of this sheet, answer the following two questions.
28. What did you particularly like about this presentation?
29. What would you have done differently if you had been the speaker?

FIGURE 21.7 Sample Evaluation Form (*continued*)

SPEAKER'S CHECKLIST

☐ Did you analyze the speaking situation — the audience and purpose of the presentation? *(p. 596)*

☐ Did you determine how much information you can communicate in your allotted time? *(p. 597)*

☐ Did you consider the variables of your presentation setting? *(p. 597)*

☐ Did you choose an appropriate organizational pattern and determine what kinds of information to present? *(p. 597)*

☐ Did you create an outline? *(p. 598)*

☐ Did you plan your introduction and your conclusion? *(p. 598)*

Does each presentation graphic have these five characteristics?

☐ It presents a clear, well-supported claim. *(p. 600)*

☐ It is easy to see. *(p. 600)*

☐ It is easy to read. *(p. 601)*

☐ It is simple. *(p. 601)*

☐ It is correct. *(p. 602)*

☐ In planning your graphics, did you consider the length of your presentation, your audience's aptitude and experience, the presentation setting, and the equipment available? *(p. 603)*

☐ Did you plan your graphics to help the audience understand the organization of your presentation? *(p. 605)*

☐ Did you use language to signal advance organizers, summaries, and transitions? *(p. 612)*

☐ Did you choose language that is vivid and memorable? *(p. 614)*

☐ Did you rehearse your presentation several times, recording it or using a live audience? *(p. 615)*

☐ Did you consider the needs of all audience members, including those from other cultures and those with varying physical abilities? *(p. 619)*

EXERCISES

1. Learn some of the basic functions of a presentation software program. For instance, modify a template, create your own original design, add footer information to a master slide, insert a graphic on a slide, and set the animation feature so that at first just the first bullet item on a slide appears and then a mouse click brings up the second bullet item.

2. Using PowerPoint, design a master slide for a presentation for one of your classes. If you are unfamiliar with how to create a master slide, consult PowerPoint's help files. Be prepared to explain the design to your classmates.

3. Prepare a five-minute presentation, including graphics, on one of the following topics. The audience for your presentation will consist of the other students in your class, and your purpose will be to introduce them to an aspect of your academic field.

   a. Define a key term or concept in your field.

   b. Describe how a particular device or technology is used in your field.

   c. Describe how to carry out a procedure common in your field.

   Your instructor and the other students will evaluate the presentation by filling out the form in Figure 21.7.

4. **TEAM EXERCISE** Prepare a five-minute presentation based either on the proposal for a research project that you prepared in Chapter 16 or on your recommendation report for that project. Your audience will consist of the other students in your class, and your purpose will be to introduce them to your topic. The instructor and the other students will evaluate your presentation by filling out the form in Figure 21.7. Your instructor might have you work on this assignment collaboratively.

CASE 21: Writing an Oral Presentation

You have been invited to a student conference to make an oral presentation of a paper you wrote for a class. You run a few ideas by a friend, who offers great pointers. She's offered to look at your revised speaking notes, so you need to get to work. If your instructor has assigned it, go to Achieve to get started.

Appendix:
Reference Handbook

Part A: Skimming Your Sources and Taking Notes

To record the information that will eventually go into your document, you need to skim your potential sources and take notes. Don't try to read every potential source. A careful reading of a work that looks promising might prove disappointing. You might also get halfway through a book and realize that you must start writing immediately in order to submit your document on time.

Skimming will not always tell you whether a book or article is going to be useful, but it can tell you if a work is *not* going to be useful—because it doesn't cover your subject, for example, or because it is too superficial or too advanced. Eliminating the sources you don't need will give you more time to spend on the ones you do.

◢❙ **GUIDELINES** Skimming Books and Articles

To skim effectively, look at the following parts of books and articles.

In a book, skim

▶ **the preface and introduction:** to understand the writer's approach and methods

▶ **the acknowledgments section:** to learn about help the author received from other experts in the field or about the author's use of primary research or other resources

▶ **the table of contents:** to understand the book's scope and organization

▶ **the notes at the end of chapters or at the end of the book:** to understand the nature and extent of the author's research

▶ **the index:** to determine the extent of the coverage of the information you need

▶ **a few paragraphs from different portions of the text:** to gauge the quality and relevance of the information

In an article, skim

▶ **the abstract:** to get an overview of the article's content

▶ **the introduction:** to understand the article's purpose, main ideas, and organization

▶ **the notes and references:** to understand the nature and extent of the author's research

▶ **the headings and several of the paragraphs:** to understand the article's organization and the quality and relevance of the information

Note taking is often the first step in writing a document. The best way to take notes is electronically. If you can download files from the internet, download bibliographic references from a database, and take notes on a computer, tablet, or smartphone, you will save a lot of time and prevent many errors. If you do not have access to these electronic tools, get a pack of note cards.

Most note taking involves three kinds of activities: paraphrasing, quoting, and summarizing. Knowing how to paraphrase, quote, and summarize is important for two reasons:

- To a large extent, your note taking will determine the quality of your finished product. You want to record information accurately and clearly. Mistakes made at this point can be hard to catch later, and they can ruin your document.

- Using your sources responsibly helps you to avoid unintentional plagiarism.

For a discussion of plagiarism, see Appendix, Part B, p. 632.

◢
GUIDELINES Recording Bibliographic Information

Record the bibliographic information for each source from which you take notes.

Information to record for a book

▶ author

▶ title

▶ publisher

▶ place of publication

▶ year of publication

▶ call number or URL

Information to record for an article

▶ author

▶ title of article

▶ title of periodical

▶ volume

▶ number

▶ date of publication

▶ pages on which article appears

▶ call number or URL of periodical

For electronic sources, record any additional relevant information such as identifying numbers, database name, and retrieval data.

Paraphrasing

A paraphrase is a restatement, in your own words, of someone else's words. If you simply copy someone else's words—even a mere two or three in a row if the phrasing is distinctive—you must use quotation marks.

In taking notes, what kind of material should you paraphrase? Any information that you think might be useful: background data, descriptions of mechanisms or processes, test results, and so forth.

Figure A.1 shows a paraphrased passage based on the following discussion. The author is explaining the concept of performance-centered design.

Original Passage

Roughly a decade has elapsed since the introduction of commodity level activity trackers such as the Fitbit™. Currently there is a thriving industry and a fast-growing research field concerned with the development of wearable systems for personal health monitoring. The majority of available devices are wrist worn, placed inside pockets, or clipped onto clothing. As electronics are further miniaturized and as e-textiles are becoming increasingly available, it also becomes more feasible to integrate electronics into "smart" garments to support healthy living and rehabilitation. This emerging application area presents opportunities and corresponding challenges pertaining to industrial design, interaction design, and ensuring the potential effectiveness of these solutions. This paper presents a design driven investigation that combines these perspectives for the design and evaluation of BackUp: a smart garment to support occupational low back pain prevention for nurses.

Low back pain is widespread; the lifetime prevalence of low back pain in the developed world ranges between 60 and 70% and is a major cause of activity limitation and work absence worldwide (Poitras et al., 2005). Costs relating to reduced productivity of workers and to treating low back pain are high; for example, Wenig et al. (2009) estimate an average cost of €1322 (95%) per patient per year in Germany. Such observations motivate the development of technologies to help prevent and treat low back pain.

FIGURE A.1   Inappropriate and Appropriate Paraphrased Notes

Bootsman, et al., "Wearable Technology for Posture Monitoring in the Workplace"
https://doi.org/10.1016/j.ijhcs.2019.08.003

reasons to address lower back pain:

- Lifetime prevalence of low back pain in the developed world ranges between 60 and 70% and is a major cause of activity limitation and work absence world-wide (Poitras et al., 2005)
- Wenig et al. (2009) estimate an average cost of €1322 (95%) per patient per year in Germany
- Costs relating to reduced productivity of workers and to treating low back pain are high

---

a. Inappropriate paraphrase

This paraphrase is inappropriate because the three bulleted points are taken word for word from the original. The fact that the student omitted the context from the original and that they cite third part sources is irrelevant. These are direct quotes, not paraphrases.

Bootsman, et al., "Wearable Technology for Posture Monitoring in the Workplace"l
https://doi.org/10.1016/j.ijhcs.2019.08.003

reasons to address lower back pain:
Bootsman, et al. argue that there are compelling reasons for exploring wearable technology as a way to address lower back pain. They cite two key sources (Poitras et al. and Wenig et al.) to support their claims that:

- Back pain costs companies a significant amount of money every year in treatment and lost productivity.
- Every year in Germany, problems related to back pain cost companies an average of over €1300.
- Back pain is a global problem, showing up in 60–70% of working people in the developed world sometime in their lifetimes.
- As the user gets smarter about using the system, the system gets smarter, making it faster to complete the task.

---

b. Appropriate paraphrase

This paraphrase is appropriate because the words are different from those used in the original.

When you turn your notes into a document, you are likely to reword your paraphrases. As you revise your document, check a copy of the original source document to be sure you haven't unintentionally reverted to the wording from the original source.

Source: Information from Bootsman, et al., "Wearable Technology for Posture Monitoring in the Workplace" https://doi.org/10.1016/j.ijhcs.2019.08.003

◢
GUIDELINES Paraphrasing Accurately

▸ **Study the original until you understand it thoroughly.**

▸ **Rewrite the relevant portions of the original.** Use complete sentences, fragments, or lists, but don't compress the material so much that you'll have trouble understanding it later.

▸ **Title the information so that you'll be able to identify its subject at a glance.** The title should include the general subject and the author's attitude or approach to it, such as "Criticism of open-sea pollution-control devices."

▸ **Include the author's last name, a short title of the article or book, and the page number (if any) of the original.** You will need this information later in citing your source.

Quoting

Sometimes you will want to quote a source, either to preserve the author's particularly well-expressed or emphatic phrasing or to lend authority to your discussion. Avoid quoting passages of more than two or three sentences; otherwise, your document will look like a mere compilation. Your job is to integrate an author's words and ideas into your own thinking, not merely to introduce a series of quotations.

Although you probably won't be quoting long passages in your document, recording a complete quotation in your notes will help you recall its meaning and context more accurately when you are ready to integrate it into your own work.

For more about formatting quotations, see "Quotation Marks," "Ellipses," and "Square Brackets" in Appendix, Part C. For a discussion of how to document quotations, see Appendix, Part B.

The simplest form of quotation is an author's exact statement:

As Jones states, "Solar energy won't make much of a difference for at least a decade."

To add an explanatory word or phrase to a quotation, use brackets:

As Nelson states, "It [the oil glut] will disappear before we understand it."

Use ellipses (three spaced dots) to show that you are omitting part of an author's statement:

ORIGINAL STATEMENT	"The generator, which we purchased in May, has turned out to be one of our wisest investments."
ELLIPTICAL QUOTATION	"The generator . . . has turned out to be one of our wisest investments."

According to the documentation style recommended by the Modern Language Association (MLA), if the author's original statement has ellipses, you should add brackets around the ellipses that you introduce:

ORIGINAL STATEMENT	"I think reuse adoption offers . . . the promise to improve business in a number of ways."
ELLIPTICAL QUOTATION	"I think reuse adoption offers . . . the promise to improve business [. . .] ."

Summarizing

Summarizing is the process of rewriting a passage in your own words to make it shorter while still retaining its essential message. Writers summarize to help them learn a body of information or to create a draft of one or more of the summaries that will go into the document.

Most long technical documents contain several kinds of summaries:

- a letter of transmittal (see page 495) that provides an overview of the document
- an abstract (see page 495), a brief technical summary
- an executive summary (see page 499), a brief nontechnical summary directed to a manager
- a conclusion (see page 494) that draws together a complicated discussion

The guidelines and examples in this section explain how to summarize the information you uncover in your research.

GUIDELINES Summarizing

The following advice focuses on extracting the essence of a passage by summarizing it.

▶ **Read the passage carefully several times.**

▶ **Underline key ideas.** Look for them in the titles, headings, topic sentences, transitional paragraphs, and concluding paragraphs.

▶ **Combine key ideas.** Study what you have underlined. Paraphrase the underlined ideas. Don't worry about your grammar, punctuation, or style at this point.

▶ **Check your draft against the original for accuracy and emphasis.** Check that you have recorded statistics and names correctly and that your version of a complicated concept faithfully represents the original. Check that you got the proportions right; if the original devotes 20 percent of its space to a particular point, your draft should not devote 5 percent or 50 percent to that point.

▶ **Record the bibliographic information carefully.** Even though a summary might contain all your own words, you still must cite your source, because the main ideas are someone else's. If you don't have the bibliographic information in an electronic form, put it on a note card.

Figure A.2 on page 630 is a narrative history of electric cars addressed to the general reader. Figure A.3 on page 631 is a summary that includes the key terms. This summary is 25 percent of the length of the original.

FIGURE A.2   Original Passage
Adapted from U.S. Department of Energy, 2014: www.energy.gov/articles/history-electric-car.

THE HISTORY OF THE ELECTRIC CAR

The Early Rise and Fall of the Electric Car

In the nineteenth century, French and English inventors built some of the first practical electric cars. Here in the U.S., the first successful electric car made its debut around 1890 thanks to William Morrison, a chemist who lived in Des Moines, Iowa. His six-passenger vehicle capable of a top speed of 14 miles per hour was little more than an electrified wagon, but it helped spark interest in electric vehicles. Over the next few years, electric vehicles from different automakers began popping up across the U.S. New York City even had a fleet of more than 60 electric taxis. By 1900, electric cars were at their heyday, accounting for around a third of all vehicles on the road.

Electric cars didn't have any of the issues associated with steam or gasoline. They were quiet, easy to drive, and didn't emit a smelly pollutant like the other cars of the time. They quickly became popular with urban residents—especially women. They were perfect for short trips around the city, and poor road conditions outside cities meant few cars of any type could venture farther. As more people gained access to electricity in the 1910s, it became easier to charge electric cars, adding to their popularity with all walks of life.

Many innovators at the time took note of the electric vehicle's high demand, exploring ways to improve the technology. For example, Ferdinand Porsche developed an electric car called the P1 in 1898. Around the same time, he created the world's first hybrid electric car—a vehicle that is powered by electricity and a gas engine. Thomas Edison, one of the world's most prolific inventors, thought electric vehicles were the superior technology and worked to build a better electric vehicle battery. Even Henry Ford partnered with Edison to explore options for a low-cost electric car in 1914.

Yet, it was Henry Ford's mass-produced Model T that dealt a blow to the electric car. Introduced in 1908, the Model T made gasoline-powered cars widely available and affordable. By 1912, the gasoline car cost only $650, while an electric roadster sold for $1,750.

Other developments also contributed to the decline of the electric vehicle. By the 1920s, the U.S. had a better system of roads connecting cities. With the discovery of Texas crude oil, gas became cheap and readily available for rural Americans, and filling stations began popping up across the country. In comparison, very few Americans outside of cities had electricity at that time. In the end, electric vehicles all but disappeared by 1935.

Gas Shortages Spark Interest in Electric Vehicles

Fast forward to the late 1960s and early 1970s. Soaring oil prices and gasoline shortages—peaking with the 1973 Arab Oil Embargo—created a growing interest in lowering the U.S.'s dependence on foreign oil and finding homegrown sources of fuel. Around this same time, many automakers began exploring options for alternative fuel vehicles, including electric cars. Yet, the vehicles developed and produced in the 1970s still suffered from drawbacks compared to gasoline-powered cars. Electric vehicles during this time had limited performance—usually topping at speeds of 45 miles per hour—and their typical range was limited to 40 miles before needing to be recharged.

(continued)

FIGURE A.2   Original
Passage (*continued*)

Environmental Concern Drives Electric Vehicles Forward

Fast forward again—this time to the 1990s. The passage of the 1990 Clean Air Act Amendment and the 1992 Energy Policy Act—plus new transportation emissions regulations issued by the California Air Resources Board—helped create a renewed interest in electric vehicles in the U.S. But the true revival of the electric vehicle didn't happen until around the start of the twenty-first century. Depending on whom you ask, it was one of two events that sparked the interest we see today in electric vehicles.

The first turning point was the introduction of the Toyota Prius. Released in Japan in 1997, the Prius became the world's first mass-produced hybrid electric vehicle. In 2000, the Prius was released worldwide, and it became an instant success with celebrities, helping to raise the profile of the car. To make the Prius a reality, Toyota used a nickel metal hydride battery. Rising gasoline prices and growing concern about carbon pollution helped Prius become the best-selling hybrid worldwide.

The other event that helped reshape electric vehicles was the announcement in 2006 that a small Silicon Valley startup, Tesla Motors, would start producing a luxury electric sports car that could go more than 200 miles on a single charge. In 2010, Tesla received a $465 million loan from the Department of Energy's Loan Programs Office to establish a manufacturing facility in California. By 2014 Tesla had won wide acclaim for its cars and had become the largest auto industry employer in California.

FIGURE A.3   Summary
of the Original Passage

Summary: The History of the Electric Car

Electric cars were first developed in Europe in the nineteenth century. In the United States, they became popular in the 1890s after William Morrison invented one that could travel up to 14 miles an hour. Other automakers improved the technology, including Ferdinand Porsche, who created the P1 electric car and developed the first hybrid car.

Electric cars were well suited to city environments, where people had access to roads and electricity and where long trips were unnecessary. However, their popularity waned after Henry Ford released the Model T in 1908—a mass-produced, gasoline-powered car that was less than half the price of electric cars of that time.

Electric cars experienced a brief resurgence around the time of the Arab Oil Embargo in 1973, but they tended to have limited range and speed compared to gasoline-powered cars. In the 1990s, environmental issues generated interest in electric cars once again. The 1997 release of the Toyota Prius, the first mass-produced hybrid car, and the 2006 development of Tesla's luxury electric car, which had a range of 200 miles, were both significant turning points in the popularity of electric cars. The Prius became the world's bestseller, and Tesla Motors became an industry leader.

Part B: Documenting Your Sources

Documentation identifies the sources of the ideas and the quotations in your document. Documentation consists of the citations in the text throughout your document and the reference list (or list of works cited) at the end of your document. Documentation serves three basic functions:

- **It helps you acknowledge your debt to your sources.** Complete and accurate documentation is a professional obligation, a matter of ethics. Failure to document a source, whether intentional or unintentional, is plagiarism. At most colleges and universities, plagiarism can mean automatic failure of the course and, in some instances, suspension or expulsion. In many companies, it is grounds for immediate dismissal.

- **It helps you establish credibility.** Effective documentation helps you place your document within the general context of continuing research and helps you define it as a responsible contribution to knowledge in the field. Knowing how to use existing research is one mark of a professional.

- **It helps your readers find your source in case they want to read more about a particular subject.**

Three kinds of material should always be documented:

For more about quoting and paraphrasing sources, see Appendix, Part A.

- **Any quotation from a written source or an interview, even if it is only a few words.**

- **A paraphrased idea, concept, or opinion gathered from your reading.** There is one exception. An idea or concept so well known that it has become general knowledge, such as Einstein's theory of relativity, needs no citation. If you are unsure about whether an item is general knowledge, document it, just to be safe.

For more about using graphics from other sources, see Ch. 12, p. 309.

- **Any graphic from a written or an electronic source.** Cite the source for a graphic next to the graphic or in the reference list. For an online source, be sure to include a retrieval statement, URL, or DOI in the bibliographic entry. If you are publishing your work, you must also obtain permission to use any graphic protected by copyright unless your use falls under the Fair Use clause.

Just as organizations have their own rules for formatting and punctuation, many organizations also have their own documentation styles. For documents prepared in the workplace, find out your organization's style and abide by it. Check with your instructor to see which documentation system to use in the documents you write for class. The documentation systems included in this section of the appendix are based on the following style manuals:

- *Publication manual of the American Psychological Association* (7th ed.). (2019). Washington, DC: APA. This system, referred to as *APA style*, is used widely in the social sciences.

- *IEEE editorial style manual.* (2019). Piscataway, NJ: IEEE. This manual provides editorial guidelines for IEEE transactions, journals, and letters, but it is often used for the production of technical documents in areas ranging from computer engineering, biomedical technology, and telecommunications to electric power, aerospace, and consumer electronics.

- *MLA handbook* (8th ed.). (2016). New York: Modern Language Association. This system, referred to as *MLA style*, is used widely in the humanities.

Other organizations may prefer one of the following published style guides.

GENERAL

University of Chicago. *Chicago manual of style* (17th ed.). (2017). See also http://www.chicagomanualofstyle.org/home.html

BUSINESS

American Management Association. (2010). *The AMA style guide for business writing*. AMACOM. See also http://www.amanet.org

CHEMISTRY

American Chemical Society. (2006). *ACS style guide: Effective communication of scientific information* (3rd ed.). Oxford University Press. See also http://www.acs.org

GEOLOGY

Adkins-Heljeson, M., Bates, R. L., & Buchanan, R. (Eds.). (1995). *Geowriting: A guide to writing, editing, and printing in earth science* (5th rev. ed.). American Geological Institute. See also http://www.agiweb.org

GOVERNMENT DOCUMENTS

U.S. Government Printing Office. (2008). *Style manual* (30th ed.). See also http://www.gpo.gov

JOURNALISM

Kent, T., Schwartz, J., Minthorn, D., & Froke, P. (Eds.). (2016). *Associated Press stylebook 2016*. Associated Press. See also http://www.ap.org

LAW

Columbia Law Review, Harvard Law Review, University of Pennsylvania Law Review, and Yale Law Journal. (2015). *The bluebook: A uniform system of citation* (20th ed.). Harvard Law Review Association. See also http://www.legalbluebook.com

MATHEMATICS

Higham, N. J. (1998). *Handbook of writing for the mathematical sciences* (2nd ed.). Society for Industrial and Applied Mathematics. See also http://www.siam.org

MEDICINE

American Medical Association. (2020). *American Medical Association manual of style* (11th ed.). Oxford University Press. See also http://www.amamanualofstyle.com

NATURAL SCIENCES

Council of Science Editors. (2014). *Scientific style and format: The CSE manual for authors, editors, and publishers* (8th ed.). Cambridge University Press. See also http://www.councilscienceeditors.org

PHYSICS

American Institute of Physics, Publication Board. (1990). *Style manual for guidance in the preparation of papers* (4th ed.). Author. See also http://www.aip.org

POLITICAL SCIENCE

American Political Science Association. (2018). *Style manual for political science* (rev. 2018 ed.). See also http://www.apsanet.org

SCIENCE AND TECHNICAL WRITING

National Information Standards Organization. (2005). *Scientific and technical reports — Preparation, presentation and preservation.* See also http://www.niso.org

Rubens, P. (Ed.). (2000). *Science and technical writing: A manual of style* (2nd ed.). Routledge.

SOCIOLOGY

American Sociological Association. (2019). *American Sociological Association style guide* (6th ed.). See also http://www.asanet.org

APA Style

APA (American Psychological Association) style consists of two elements: citations in the text and a list of references at the end of the document.

APA Style for Reference List Entries

APA TEXTUAL CITATIONS

In APA style, a textual citation typically includes the name of the source's author and the date of its publication. Textual citations vary depending on the type of information cited, the number of authors, and the context of the citation. The following models illustrate a variety of common textual citations; for additional examples, consult the *Publication Manual of the American Psychological Association*.

1. Summarized or Paraphrased Material For material or ideas that you have summarized or paraphrased, include the author's name and the publication date in parentheses immediately following the borrowed information.

> This phenomenon was identified almost 70 years ago (Wilkinson, 1948).

If your sentence already includes the source's name, do not repeat it in the parenthetical notation.

> Wilkinson (1948) identified this phenomenon almost 70 years ago.

2. Quoted Material or Specific Fact If the reference is to a specific fact, idea, or quotation, add the page number(s) from the source to your citation.

> This phenomenon was identified almost 70 years ago (Wilkinson, 1948, p. 36).

> Wilkinson (1948) identified this phenomenon almost 70 years ago (p. 36).

3. Source with Multiple Authors For a source written by two authors, cite both names. Use an ampersand (&) in the parenthetical citation itself, but use the word *and* in regular text.

> (Tyshenko & Paterson, 2020)

> Tyshenko and Paterson (2020) argued . . .

For a source written by three or more authors, include only the last name of the first author followed by *et al.*

> **Citation**
> Cashman et al. (2020) found . . .

4. Source Authored by an Organization If the author is an organization rather than a person, use the name of the organization.

> There is ongoing discussion of the scope and practice of nursing informatics (American Nurses Association, 2019).

> In a policy statement, the American Nurses Association (2019) discusses the scope and practice of nursing informatics.

If the organization name is commonly abbreviated, you may include the abbreviation in the first citation and use it in any subsequent citations.

> **First Text Citation**
> (International Business Machines [IBM], 2018)

> **Subsequent Citations**
> (IBM, 2018)

5. Source with an Unknown Author If the source does not identify an author, use a shortened version of the title in your parenthetical citation.

> Hawking made the discovery that under precise conditions, thermal radiation could exit black holes ("World Scientists," 2016).

If the author is identified as anonymous—a rare occurrence—treat *Anonymous* as a real name.

> (Anonymous, 2020)

6. Multiple Authors with the Same Last Name Use first initials if two or more sources have authors with the same last name.

> B. Porter (2019) created a more stable platform for database transfers, while A. L. Porter (2017) focused primarily on latitudinal peer-to-peer outcome interference.

7. Multiple Sources in One Citation When you refer to two or more sources in one citation, present the sources in alphabetical order, separated by a semicolon.

> This phenomenon has been well documented (Houlding, 2019; Jessen, 2014).

8. Personal Communication When you cite personal interviews, phone calls, letters, memos, and emails, include the words *personal communication* and the date of the communication.

> D. E. Walls (personal communication, April 3, 2019) provided the prior history of his . . .

9. Electronic Document Cite the author and date for an electronic source as you would for other kinds of documents. If the author is unknown, give a shortened version of the title in your parenthetical citation. If the date is unknown, use *n.d.* (for *no date*).

> Interpersonal relationships are complicated by differing goals (Hoffman, n.d.).

If the document is posted as a PDF file, include the page number in the citation. If a page number is not available, give the paragraph number. If the source does not number its paragraphs, you may need to count them yourself.

> (Tong, 2017, para. 4)

If no page number is available and the source has headings, cite the appropriate heading and paragraph.

> The CDC (2017) warns that babies born to women who smoke during pregnancy are 30% more likely to be born prematurely (The Reality section, para. 3).

THE APA REFERENCE LIST

A reference list provides the information your readers will need in order to find each source you have cited in the text. It should not include sources you read but did not use.

For a sample APA-style reference list, see p. 650.

Following are some guidelines for an APA-style reference list.

- **Arranging entries.** Arrange the entries alphabetically by author's last name. If two or more works are by the same author, arrange them by date, earliest to latest. If two or more works are by the same author in the same year, list them alphabetically by title and include a lowercase letter after the date: 2010a, 2010b, and so on. Alphabetize works by an organization by the first significant word in the name of the organization.

- **Book titles.** Italicize titles of books. Capitalize only the first word of the book's title, the first word of the subtitle, and any proper nouns.

- **Publication information.** For books, give the publisher's name in as brief a form as is intelligible; retain the words *Books* and *Press*.

- **Periodical titles.** Italicize titles of periodicals and capitalize all major words.

- **Article titles.** Do not italicize titles of articles or place them in quotation marks. Capitalize only the first word of the article's title and subtitle and any proper nouns.

- **Electronic sources.** Include as much information as you can about electronic sources, such as author, date of publication, identifying numbers, and retrieval information. Include the digital object identifier (DOI) when one exists. Remember that electronic information changes frequently. If the content of an electronic source is likely to change, be sure to record the date you retrieved the information.

- **Indenting.** Use a hanging indent, with the first line of each entry flush with the left margin and all subsequent lines indented one-half inch:

> Ganegoda, D. B., & Bordia, P. (2019). I can be happy for you, but not all the time: A contingency model of envy and positive empathy in the workplace. *Journal of Applied Psychology, 104*(6), 776–795.

Your instructor may prefer a paragraph indent, in which the first line of each entry is indented one-half inch:

> Ganegoda, D. B., & Bordia, P. (2019). I can be happy for you, but not all the time: A contingency model of envy and positive empathy in the workplace. *Journal of Applied Psychology, 104*(6), 776–795.

- **Spacing.** Double-space the entire reference list. Do not add extra space between entries.

- **Page numbers.** When citing a range of page numbers for an article, always give the complete numbers (for example, 121–124, *not* 121–24 or 121–4). If an article continues on subsequent pages after being interrupted by other articles or advertisements, use a comma to separate the page numbers. Use the abbreviation *p.* or *pp.* only with articles in newspapers, chapters in edited books, and articles from proceedings published as a book.

- **Dates.** Follow the format year, month, day, with a comma after only the year: (2020, October 31).

    Following are models of reference list entries for a variety of sources. For further examples of APA-style entries, consult the *Publication Manual of the American Psychological Association.*

BOOKS

10. Book by One Author Begin with the author's last name, followed by the first initial or initials. Include a space between initials. Place the year of publication in parentheses, then give the title of the book, followed by the name of the publisher.

> Treuer, D. (2019). *The heartbeat of Wounded Knee: Native America from 1890 to the present.* Riverhead Books.

11. Book by Multiple Authors When citing a work from two to twenty authors, separate the authors' names with a comma or commas, and use an ampersand (&) instead of *and* before the final author's name.

> Natterson-Horowitz, B., & Bowers, K. (2019). *Wildhood: The epic journey from adolescence to adulthood in humans and other animals.* Scribner.

To cite more than 20 authors, list only the first 19, followed by three dots (an ellipsis) and the last author's name.

12. Multiple Books by the Same Author Arrange the entries by date, with the earliest date first. If you use multiple works by the same author written in the same year, arrange the books alphabetically by title and include *a, b,* and so forth after the year—both in your reference list and in your parenthetical citations.

> Gladwell, M. (2019a). *Talking to strangers: What we should know about the people we don't know.* Little, Brown and Company.

> Gladwell, M. (2019b, January 14). Is marijuana as safe as we think? *The New Yorker.* https://www.newyorker.com/magazine/2019/01/14/is-marijuana -assafe-as-we-think

> Agger, B. (2007a). *Fast families, virtual children: A critical sociology of families and schooling.* Paradigm.

> Agger, B. (2007b). *Public sociology: From social facts to literary acts.* Rowman & Littlefield.

13. Book Authored by an Organization Use the full name of the organization in place of an author's name. If the organization is also the publisher, use the word *Author* in place of the publisher's name.

> Human Rights Watch. (2018). *World report 2019: Events of 2018.* Seven Stories Press.

APA: CITING A BOOK BY ONE AUTHOR

When citing a book, use the information from the title page and the copyright page (on the reverse side of the title page), not from the book's cover or a library catalog.

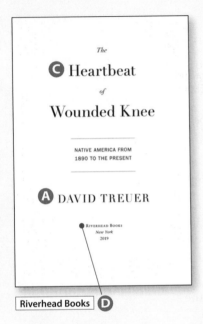

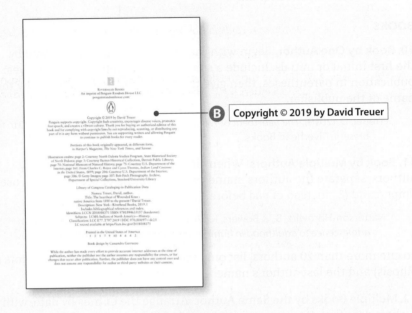

B Copyright © 2019 by David Treuer

Riverhead Books **D**

Record the following information:

A. The author. Give the last name first, followed by a comma and initials for first and middle names. Separate initials with a space (Tufte, E. R.). Separate the names of multiple authors with a comma or commas; use an ampersand (&) before the final author's name.

B. The date of publication. Put the most recent copyright year in parentheses and end with a period (outside the parentheses).

C. The title. Give the full title; include the subtitle (if any), preceded by a colon. Italicize the title and subtitle, capitalizing only the first word of the title, the first word of the subtitle, and any proper nouns. End with a period.

D. The publisher. Give the publisher's name, omitting words such as *Inc.* and *Co.* Include and do not abbreviate terms such as *University* and *Press.* End with a period.

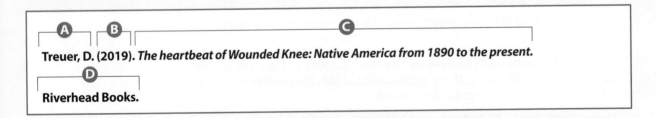

A **B** **C**

Treuer, D. (2019). *The heartbeat of Wounded Knee: Native America from 1890 to the present.*

D

Riverhead Books.

For more APA-style models for citing other types of books, see pp. 639 and 641.

14. Book by an Unknown Author If the author of the book is unknown, begin with the title in italics.

> *Atlas of the world.* (2019). Oxford University Press.

15. Edited Book Place the abbreviation *Ed.* (singular) or *Eds.* (plural) in parentheses after the name(s), followed by a period.

> Yeh, K.-H. (Ed.). (2019). *Asian indigenous psychologies in the global context.* Palgrave.

16. Chapter or Section in an Edited Book

> Pettigrew, D. (2018). The suppression of cultural memory and identity in Bosnia and Herzegovina. In J. Lindert & A. T. Marsoobian (Eds.), *Multidisciplinary perspectives on genocide and memory* (pp. 187–198). Springer.

17. Book in an Edition Other Than the First Include the edition number in parentheses following the title.

> Dessler, A. E., & Parson, E. A. (2019). *The science and politics of global climate change: A guide to the debate* (3rd ed.). Cambridge University Press.

18. Multivolume Work Include the number of volumes after the title.

> Zeigler-Hill, V., & Shackelford, T. K. (Eds.). (2018). *The SAGE handbook of personality and individual differences* (Vols. I–III). SAGE Publications.

19. Translated Book Name the translator after the title.

> Calasso, R. (2019). *The unnamable present* (R. Dixon, Trans.). Farrar, Straus and Giroux. (Original work published 2017)

20. Non-English Book Give the original title, then the English translation in brackets.

> Hernandez, G. H., Moreno, A. M., Zaragoza, F. G., & Porras, A. C. (Eds.). (2010). *Tratado de medicina farmacéutica* [Treaty of pharmaceutical medicine]. Editorial Médica Panamericana.

21. Entry in a Reference Work Begin with the title of the entry if it has no author.

> Synthetic food colors (2018). In P. Varelis, L. Melton, & F. Shahidi (Eds.), *Encyclopedia of food chemistry* (pp. 291–296). Elsevier.

PERIODICALS

22. Journal Article Follow the author's name and the year of publication with the article title; then give the journal title, followed by a comma. For all journals, include the volume number (italicized). For journals that begin each issue with page 1, also include the issue number in parentheses (not italicized). Insert a comma and end with the page number(s).

> Ganegoda, D. B., & Bordia, P. (2019). I can be happy for you, but not all the time: A contingency model of envy and positive empathy in the workplace. *Journal of Applied Psychology, 104*(6), 776–795.

APA: CITING AN ARTICLE FROM A PERIODICAL

Periodicals include journals, magazines, and newspapers. This page gives an example of a citation for a print journal article.

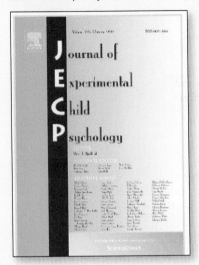

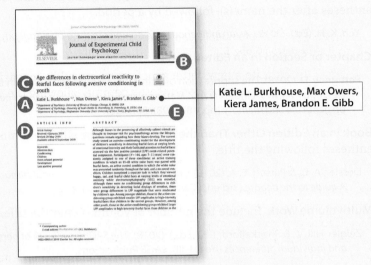

Katie L. Burkhouse, Max Owers, Kiera James, Brandon E. Gibb

Record the following information:

A. The author. Give the last name first, followed by a comma and initials for first and middle names. Separate initials with a space (Tufte, E. R.). Separate the names of multiple authors with a comma or commas; use an ampersand (&) before the final author's name.

B. The date of publication. Put the year in parentheses and end with a period (outside the parentheses). For magazines and newspapers, include the month and, if given, the day (2020, May 23).

C. The article title. Give the full title; include the subtitle (if any), preceded by a colon. Do not underline or italicize the title or put it in quotation marks. Capitalize only the first word of the title, the first word of the subtitle, and any proper nouns. End with a period.

D. The periodical title. Italicize the periodical title and capitalize all major words. Follow the periodical title with a comma.

E. The volume number and issue number. Include the volume number (italicized). Include the issue number in parentheses (not italicized) for magazines and for journals that begin each issue at page 1. Insert a comma.

F. Inclusive page numbers. (Not shown.) Give all the numbers in full (316–337, *not* 316–37). For newspapers, include the section letter, if relevant (D4). End with a period.

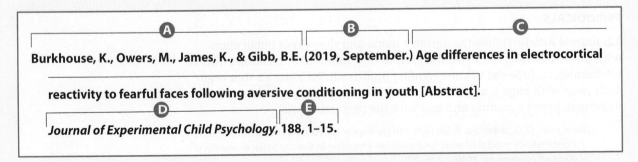

Burkhouse, K., Owers, M., James, K., & Gibb, B.E. (2019, September.) Age differences in electrocortical

reactivity to fearful faces following aversive conditioning in youth [Abstract].

Journal of Experimental Child Psychology, 188, 1–15.

For more APA-style models for citing other types of periodical articles, see pp. 631 and 643.

23. Magazine Article Include the month after the year. If it's a weekly magazine, include the day. Give the volume and issue numbers, if any, after the magazine title.

> Koch, C. (2019, October). Is death reversible? *Scientific American, 321*(4), 34–37.

24. Newspaper Article Include the specific publication date following the year.

> Finucane, M. (2019, September 25). Americans still eating too many low-quality carbs. *The Boston Globe*, B2.

25. Newsletter Article Cite a newsletter article as you would a magazine article. If the date is given as a season, insert a comma following the year and then include the season.

> Bond, G. (2018, Fall). Celebrities as epidemiologists. *American College of Epidemiology Online Member Newsletter*, 4–5.

ELECTRONIC SOURCES

Generally, include all the same elements for electronic sources as you would for print sources. Include any information required to locate the item. Many scholarly publishers are now assigning a digital object identifier (DOI) to journal articles and other documents. A DOI is a unique alphanumeric string assigned by a registration agency. It provides a persistent link to unchanging content on the internet. When available, substitute the DOI for a URL. If the content is subject to change, include the retrieval date before the URL. Use the exact URL wherever possible; use the home-page or menu-page URL for subscription-only material or content presented in frames, which make exact URLs unworkable. Long URLs may be shortened using a site such as bitly.com or shortdoi.org. Break URLs before a punctuation mark, and avoid using punctuation after a URL or DOI so as not to confuse the reader.

26. Nonperiodical Web Document To cite a nonperiodical web document, provide as much of the following information as possible: author's name, date of publication or most recent update (use *n.d.* if there is no date), document title (in italics), and URL (or DOI, if available) for the document.

> Berchick, E. R., Barnett, J. C., & Upton, R. D. (2019, September 10). *Health insurance coverage in the United States: 2018* (Report No. P60-267). U.S. Census Bureau. https://www.census.gov/library/publications/2019/demo/p60-267.html

If the author of a document is not identified, begin the reference with the title of the document. If the document is from a university program's website, identify the host institution and the program or department, followed by a colon and the URL for the document.

> *Safety manual.* (2018, October 31). Retrieved from Harvard University, Center for Nanoscale Systems website: https://cns1.rc.fas.harvard .edu/documents/2018/06/cns-safety-manual.pdf

APA: CITING A NONPERIODICAL WEB DOCUMENT WITH NO DOI

You will likely need to search the website where a document appears in order to find some of the citation information you need. For some sites, all of the details may not be available; find as many as you can. Remember that the citation you provide should allow readers to retrace your steps electronically to locate the source.

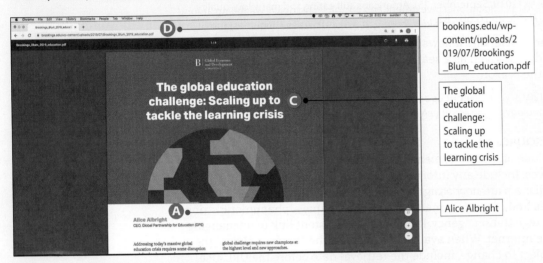

bookings.edu/wp-content/uploads/2019/07/Brookings _Blum_education.pdf

The global education challenge: Scaling up to tackle the learning crisis

Alice Albright

Record the following information:

A. The author. Give the last name first, followed by a comma and initials for first and middle names. Separate initials with a space (Tufte, E. R.). Separate the names of multiple authors with a comma or commas; use an ampersand (&) before the final author's name.

B. The date of publication or most recent update. Put the date in parentheses and end with a period (outside the parentheses). If there is no date, use *n.d.*

C. The document title. Give the full title; include the subtitle (if any), preceded by a colon. Italicize the title and subtitle, capitalizing only the first word of the title, the first word of the subtitle, and any proper nouns. End with a period.

D. The publisher. Give the publisher's name. End with a period.

E. The URL. Insert a retrieval date before the word *from* only for material that is likely to change (e.g., wikis). Omit final punctuation.

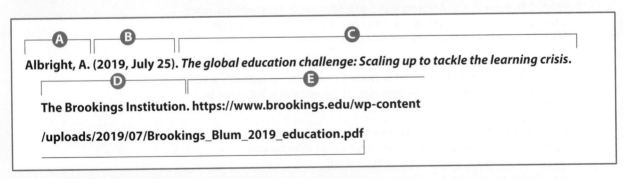

A **B** **C**

Albright, A. (2019, July 25). *The global education challenge: Scaling up to tackle the learning crisis.*

D **E**

The Brookings Institution. https://www.brookings.edu/wp-content

/uploads/2019/07/Brookings_Blum_2019_education.pdf

For more APA-style models for citing other types of web sources, see pp. 643 and 645.

Journal Articles

27. Article with DOI Assigned

Le Texier, T. (2019). Debunking the Stanford prison experiment. *American Psychologist, 74*(7), 823–839. https://doi.org/10.1037/amp0000401

28. Article with No DOI Assigned

Hung, J. (2018). Educational investment and sociopsychological wellbeing among rural Chinese women. *Inquiries Journal, 10*(05). http://www.inquiriesjournal.com/a?id=1736[AJ2]

29. Preprint Version of Article

Wang, T. J., Larson, M. G., Vasan, R. S., Cheng, S., Rhee, E. P., McCabe, E., Lewis, G. D., Fox, S., Jacques, P. F., Fernandez, C., O'Donnell, C. J., Carr, S. A., Mootha, V. K., Florez, J. C., Souza, A., Melander, O., Clish, C. B., & Gerszten, R. E. (2011). Metabolite profiles and the risk of developing diabetes. *Nature Medicine*. Advance online publication. https://doi//10.1038/nm.2307

Electronic Books

30. Entire Book Use "Retrieved from" if the URL leads to the information itself and "Available from" if the URL leads to information on how to obtain the content.

Einstein, A. (n.d.). *Relativity: The special and general theory*. Project Gutenberg. Retrieved from: http://www.gutenberg.org/etext/5001

Dissertations and Theses

31. Dissertation Retrieved from Database For a commercial database, include the database name, followed by the accession number. For an institutional database, include the URL.

Degli-Esposti, M. (2019). *Child maltreatment and antisocial behaviour in the United Kingdom: Changing risks over time* [Doctoral dissertation, University of Oxford]. Oxford University Research Archive. https://ora.ox.ac.uk/objects/uuid:6d5a8e55-bd19-41a1-8ef5-ef485642af89

Reference Materials

Give the home-page or index-page URL for reference works. If the entry has a DOI, include that instead.

32. Online Encyclopedia

Brue, A. W., & Wilmshurst, L. (2018). Adaptive behavior assessments. In B. B. Frey (Ed.), *The SAGE encyclopedia of educational research, measurement, and evaluation* (pp. 40–44). SAGE Publications. https://doi.org/10.4135/9781506326139.n21

33. Online Dictionary

Merriam-Webster. (n.d.). Adscititious. In *Merriam-Webster.com dictionary*. Retrieved September 5, 2019, from https://www.merriam-webster.com/dictionary/adscititious

APA: CITING AN ARTICLE WITH A DOI

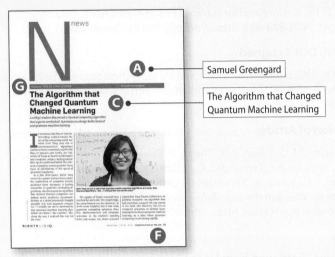

Samuel Greengard

The Algorithm that Changed Quantum Machine Learning

Record the following information:

A. The author. Give the last name first, followed by a comma and initials for first and middle names. Separate initials with a space (Tufte, E. R.). Separate the names of multiple authors with a comma or commas; use an ampersand (&) before the final author's name.

B. The date of publication. Put the year in parentheses and end with a period (outside the parentheses). For magazines and newspapers, include the month and, if relevant, the day (2020, May 23).

C. The article title. Give the full title; include the subtitle (if any), preceded by a colon. Do not underline or italicize the title or put it in quotation marks. Capitalize only the first word of the title, the first word of the subtitle, and any proper nouns. End with a period.

D. The periodical title. Italicize the periodical title and capitalize all major words. Follow the periodical title with a comma.

E. The volume number and issue number. For journals and magazines, include the volume number (italicized). Include the issue number in parentheses (not italicized) for magazines and for journals that begin each issue at page 1. Insert a comma.

F. Inclusive page numbers. Give all the numbers in full (316–337, *not* 316–37). For newspapers, include the abbreviation *p.* for *page* (or *pp.* for *pages*) and the section letter, if relevant (p. D4). End with a period.

G. The DOI. If the DOI is assigned to a preprint version of the article, include the expression *Advance online publication*, which is followed by a period. End with *https://doi/* followed by the DOI. Omit final punctuation.

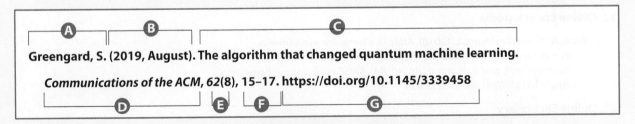

Greengard, S. (2019, August). The algorithm that changed quantum machine learning.

Communications of the ACM, 62(8), 15–17. https://doi.org/10.1145/3339458

For more APA-style models for citing other types of electronic sources, see pp. 645, 647, and 648.

34. Wiki

> Behaviorism. (2019, October 11). In *Wikipedia*. https://en.wikipedia.org/w/index
> .php?title=Behaviorism&oldid=915544724

Raw Data

35. Data Set

> Reid, L. (2019). *Smarter homes: Experiences of living in low carbon homes 2013–2018*
> [Data set]. UK Data Service. http://doi.org/10.5255/UKDA-SN-853485

36. Graphic Representation of Data

> Pew Research Center. (2018, November 15). *U.S. public is closely divided about
> overall health risk from food additives* [Chart]. https://www.pewinternet
> .org/2018/11/19/public-perspectives-on-food-risks/ps_2018-11
> -19_food_0-01/

37. Qualitative Data

> Jaques, C. (2010). They called it slums but it was never a slum to me [Audio stream].
> StoryCorps. http://storycorps.org/listen/stories/category/historias

Other Electronic Documents

38. Technical or Research Report

> Berchick, E. R., Barnett, J. C., & Upton, R. D. (2019, September 10). *Health insurance
> coverage in the United States: 2018* (Report No. P60-267). U.S. Census Bureau.
> https://www.census.gov/library/publications/2019/demo/p60-267.html

39. Presentation Slides

> Centers for Disease Control and Prevention. (2019, April 16). *Building local response
> capacity to protect families from emerging health threats* [Presentation slides].
> CDC Stacks. https://stacks.cdc.gov/view/cdc/77687

General-Interest Media and Alternative Presses

40. Newspaper Article

> Daly, J. (2019, August 2). Duquesne's med school plan part of national trend to train
> more doctors. *Pittsburgh Post-Gazette*. https://bit.ly/2Vzrm2l

41. Audio Podcast Include the presenter, producer, or other authority, if known; date; episode title; any episode or show identifier in brackets, such as *[Show 13]*; show name; the words *Audio podcast* in brackets; and retrieval information.

> West, S. (Host). (2003–present). *Philosophize this!* [Audio podcast].
> https://philosophizethis.org/category/episode

42. Online Magazine Content Not Found in Print Version

> Vlahos, J. (2019, March). Alexa, I want answers. *Wired*. https://www.wired.com
> /story/amazon-alexa-search-for-the-one-perfect-answer/

Online Communities

43. Message Posted to an Electronic Mailing List, Online Forum, or Discussion Group If an online posting is not archived and therefore is not retrievable, cite it as a personal communication and do not include it in the reference list. If the posting can be retrieved from an archive, provide the author's name (or the author's screen name if the real name is not available), the exact date of the posting, the title or subject line or thread name, and a description of the type of post in brackets. Finish with the address.

> ScienceModerator. (2018, November 16). *Science discussion: We are researchers working with some of the largest and most innovative companies using DNA to help people* [Online forum post]. Reddit. https://www.reddit.com/r/science /comments/9xlnm2/science_discussion_we_are_researchers_working/

44. Blog Post

> Fister, B. (2019, February 14). Information literacy's third wave. *Library Babel Fish.* https://www.insidehighered.com/blogs/library-babel-fish/information -literacy%E2%80%99s-third-wave
>
> Mollie F. (2019, February 14). It's a daunting task, isn't it? Last year, I got a course on Scholarly Communication and Information Literacy approved for [Comment on the blog post "Information literacy's third wave"]. *Library Babel Fish.* http://disq .us/p/1zr92uc

45. Email Message or Real-Time Communication Do not cite email messages in the reference list. Instead, cite them in the text as personal communications. (See item 8 on p. 637.)

OTHER SOURCES

46. Technical or Research Report Include an identifying number in parentheses after the report title. If appropriate, include the name of the service used to locate the item in parentheses after the publisher.

> Tahseen, M., Ahmed, S., & Ahmed, S. (2018). *Bullying of Muslim youth: A review of research and recommendations.* The Family and Youth Institute.

47. Government Document For most government agencies, use the abbreviation *U.S.* instead of spelling out *United States.* Include any identifying document number after the publication title.

> National Park Service. (2019, April 11). *Travel where women made history: Ordinary and extraordinary places of American women.* U.S. Department of the Interior. https://www.nps.gov/subjects/travelwomenshistory/index.htm

48. Brochure or Pamphlet After the title of the document, include the word *Brochure* or *Pamphlet* in brackets.

> National Council of State Boards of Nursing. (2018). *A nurse manager's guide to substance use disorder in nursing* [Brochure].

49. Article from Conference Proceedings After the proceedings title, give the page numbers on which the article appears.

Sebastianelli, R., Tamimi, N., Gnanendran, K., & Stark, R. (2010). An examination of factors affecting perceived quality and satisfaction in online MBA courses. In *Proceedings of the 41st Annual Meeting of the Decision Sciences Institute* (pp. 1641–1646). Decision Sciences Institute.

50. Lecture or Speech

Grigas, A. (2019, October 8). *The new geopolitics of energy* [Address]. Freeman Spogli Institute for International Studies, Stanford University, Stanford, CA, United States.

51. Audio Recording Give the role (narrator, producer, director, or the like) of the person whose name appears at the beginning of the entry in parentheses after the name. Give the medium in brackets after the title.

Nielsen, C. (Composer). (2014). *Carl Nielsen: Symphonies 1 & 4* [Album recorded by the New York Philharmonic Orchestra]. Dacapo Records. (Original work published 1892–1916)

52. Motion Picture Give the name of at least one primary contributor, such as the producer or director, and follow the film's title with the words *Motion picture* in brackets. List the studio's name. If the film was not widely distributed, give instead the distributor's name and address in parentheses.

Peele, J. (Director). (2017). *Get out* [Film]. Universal Pictures.

53. Television Program Start with the director, producer, or other principal contributor and the date the program aired. Include the words *Television broadcast* or *Television series* in brackets after the program title.

Waller-Bridge, P., Williams, H., & Williams, J. (Executive Producers). (2016–2019). *Fleabag* [Television series]. Two Brothers Pictures; BBC.

For a single episode in a television series, start with the writer and director of the episode or other relevant production personnel. Include the words *Television series episode* in brackets after the episode title. Also include information about the series. End with the name of the station or network.

Waller-Bridge, P. (Writer), & Bradbeer, H. (Director). (2019, March 18). The provocative request (Season 2, Episode 3) [TV series episode]. In P. Waller-Bridge, H. Williams, & J. Williams (Executive Producers), *Fleabag*. Two Brothers Pictures; BBC.

54. Published Interview If it is not clear from the title that the entry is an interview, or if there is no title, include the words *Interview with* and the subject's name in brackets.

Parrado, N. (2011, March 27). *Nando Parrado, plane crash survivor* [Interview with C. Gracie; audio file]. The Interview Archive; BBC World Service. https://www .bbc.co.uk/programmes/p00fhjnb

55. Personal Interview Consider interviews you conduct, whether in person or over the telephone, as personal communications, and do not include them in the reference list. Instead, cite them in the text. (See item 8 on p. 637.)

56. Personal Correspondence Like emails, personal letters and memos should not be included in the reference list. Instead, cite them in the text. (See item 8 on p. 637.)

57. Unpublished Data Where the title would normally appear, include a description of the data in brackets.

> Standifer, M. (2007). [Daily temperatures, 2007, Barton Springs municipal pool, Austin, TX]. Unpublished raw data.

SAMPLE APA REFERENCE LIST

Following is a sample reference list using the APA citation system.

<table>
<tr><td></td><td>References</td></tr>
<tr><td>Nonperiodical web document with no DOI</td><td>Albright, A. (2019, July 25). The global education challenge: Scaling up to tackle the learning crisis. The Brookings Institution. https://www.brookings.edu/wp-content/uploads/2019/07/Brookings_Blum_2019_education.pdf</td></tr>
<tr><td>Journal article, paginated by volume</td><td>Ganegoda, D. B., & Bordia, P. (2019). I can be happy for you, but not all the time: A contingency model of envy and positive empathy in the workplace. Journal of Applied Psychology, 104(6), 776–795.</td></tr>
<tr><td>Online article with a DOI</td><td>Le Texier, T. (2019). Debunking the Stanford Prison Experiment. American Psychologist, 74(7), 823–839. https://doi.org/10.1037/amp0000401</td></tr>
<tr><td>Chapter in an edited book</td><td>Pettigrew, D. (2018). The suppression of cultural memory and identity in Bosnia and Herzegovina. In J. Lindert & A. T. Marsoobian (Eds.), Multidisciplinary perspectives on genocide and memory (pp. 187–198). Springer.</td></tr>
<tr><td>Book in an edition other than the first</td><td>Dessler, A. E., & Parson, E. A. (2019). The science and politics of global climate change: A guide to the debate (3rd ed.). Cambridge University Press.</td></tr>
<tr><td>Online article, paginated by issue, with no DOI</td><td>Hung, J. (2018). Educational investment and sociopsychological wellbeing among rural Chinese women. Inquiries Journal, 10(05). http://www.inquiriesjournal.com/a?id=1736[AJ2]</td></tr>
</table>

IEEE Style

IEEE style consists of two elements: citations in the text and a reference list at the end of the document.

IEEE Style for Reference List Entries

BOOKS

1. Book by One Author   653
2. Book by Multiple Authors   653
3. Book Authored by an Organization   653
4. Edited Book   653
5. Chapter or Section in an Edited Book   653
6. Book in an Edition Other Than the First   653

PRINT PERIODICALS

7. Journal Article   653
8. Magazine Article   655
9. Newspaper Article   655

ELECTRONIC SOURCES

10. Article in an Online Journal or Magazine   655
11. Website   655
12. Document on a Government Website   655

OTHER SOURCES

13. Thesis or Dissertation   655
14. Standard   655
15. Scientific or Technical Report   655
16. Paper Published in Conference Proceedings   658
17. Government Document   658
18. Unpublished Document   658

IEEE TEXTUAL CITATIONS

In the IEEE (originally, Institute of Electrical and Electronics Engineers) documentation system, citations in the text are bracketed numbers, keyed to a numbered list of references that appears at the end of the document. Entries in the list are arranged in the order in which they are cited in the text and are numbered sequentially. Once a reference has been listed, the same number is used in all subsequent citations of that source.

To cite references in the text, place the reference number or numbers immediately after the author's name, in square brackets, before any punctuation. Use *et al.* if there are more than six author names.

> A recent study by Goldfinkel [5] shows that this is not an efficient solution. Murphy [8]–[10] comes to a different conclusion.

You can also use the bracketed citation number or numbers as a noun.

> In addition, [5] shows that this is not an efficient solution; however, [8]–[10] come to a different conclusion.

NOTE: Because references are listed *in the order in which they first appear in the text*, if you add a new citation within the text while rewriting or editing, you will need to renumber the reference list as well as the citations in the text. For example, if in rewriting you were to add a new reference between the first citations of the Murphy references originally numbered [8] and [9], the previous example would then read

> [8], [10], [11] come to a different conclusion.

To make a reference more precise, you can provide extra information.

A recent study by Goldfinkel [5, pp. 12–19] shows that this is not an efficient solution.

THE IEEE REFERENCE LIST

For a sample IEEE-style reference list, see p. 658.

The following guidelines will help you prepare IEEE-style references. For additional information on formatting entries, consult the latest edition of the *IEEE Editorial Style Manual* available at www.ieee.org.

- **Arranging entries.** Arrange the entries in the order in which they first are cited in the text, and then number them sequentially. Place the numbers in square brackets and set them flush left in a column of their own, separate from the body of the references. Place the entries in the next column, with no indents for turnovers.

- **Authors.** List the author's first initial (or first and middle initials, separated by spaces), followed by the last name. In the case of multiple authors, use up to six names; use *et al.* after the first author's name if there are more than six. If an entry has an editor in place of an author, add the abbreviation *Ed.* (or *Eds.* for *editors*) following the name.

- **Book titles.** Italicize titles of books. In English, capitalize the first word and all major words. In foreign languages, capitalize the first word of the title and subtitle, as well as any words that would be capitalized in that language.

- **Publication information.** For books, give the city of publication, the state abbreviation (if in the United States), the country, the publisher's name (abbreviated), and the year of publication. When two or more cities are given on a book's copyright page, include only the first.

- **Periodical titles.** Italicize and abbreviate titles of periodicals. Capitalize all major words in the title.

- **Article titles.** Place titles of articles in quotation marks. Capitalize the first word of the title and subtitle. Do not capitalize the remaining words unless they are proper nouns.

- **Electronic sources.** Provide the same information you would for a print source, including city, state, country, and page range, if available. You may include a date of access (*Accessed:*) or a DOI, if available. Always include the medium in square brackets (*[Online]*) and the URL or file path.

- **Spacing.** Single-space the reference list, and do not add extra space between entries.

- **Page numbers.** To give a page or a range of pages for a specific article in a book or periodical, use the abbreviation *p.* or *pp.* Write numbers in full (152–159, *not* 152–59 or 152–9).

- **Dates.** Follow the format month (abbreviated), day, year (for example, Apr. 3, 2020 or Feb. 22–23, 2018). Do not abbreviate May, June, or July.

BOOKS

1. Book by One Author Include the author's first initial and middle initial (if available), the author's last name, the book title (in italics), the place of publication, the publisher (abbreviated), the year of publication, and the page range of the material referenced.

> [1] M. Lee, *How to Grow a Robot: Developing Human-Friendly, Social AI.* Cambridge, MA, USA: MIT Press, 2020, pp. 22–28.

2. Book by Multiple Authors List all the authors' names. Use *et al.* after the first author's name if there are more than six authors. Do not invert names, and include a comma before *and* only if there are three or more names.

> [2] E. Karsh and A.S. Fox, *The Only Grant-Writing Book You'll Ever Need.* New York , NY, USA: Basic Books, 2019, pp. 254–255.

3. Book Authored by an Organization The organization takes the place of the author.

> [3] World Bank, *World Development Report 2020: Trading for Development in the Age of Global Value Chains.* Washington, DC, USA: World Bank, 2019, pp. 25–31.

4. Edited Book Include the abbreviation *Ed.* (singular) or *Eds.* (plural) after the name(s).

> [4] S. Kean, Ed., *The Best American Science and Nature Writing 2018.* New York, NY, USA: Houghton Mifflin Harcourt, 2018, pp. 157–162.

5. Chapter or Section in an Edited Book Give the author and the title of the chapter or section first (enclosed in quotation marks and with only the first word capitalized), followed by the word *in*, the book title, and the book editor(s). Then give the publication information for the book and the page numbers where the chapter or section appears.

> [5] E. Castronova, "The changing meaning of play," in *Online Communication and Collaboration: A Reader,* H. M. Donelan, K. L. Kear, and M. Ramage, Eds. New York, NY, USA: Routledge, 2010, pp. 184–189.

6. Book in an Edition Other Than the First The edition number follows the title of the book and is preceded by a comma.

> [6] L. Xinju, *Laser Technology*, 2nd ed. Boca Raton, FL, USA: CRC Press, 2018, pp. 203–205.

PRINT PERIODICALS

7. Journal Article Include the author, the article title, and the journal title (abbreviated where possible), followed by the volume number, issue number, page number(s), abbreviated month, and year (or abbreviated month, day, and year for weekly periodicals).

> [7] R. C. Weber, P.-Y. Lin, E. J. Garnero, Q. Williams, and P. Lognonne, "Seismic detection of the lunar core," *Science*, vol. 331, no. 6015, pp. 309–312, Jan. 21, 2011.

IEEE: CITING A BOOK BY ONE AUTHOR

When citing a book, use the information from the title page and the copyright page (on the reverse side of the title page), not from the book's cover or a library catalog.

State University of New York Press, Albany

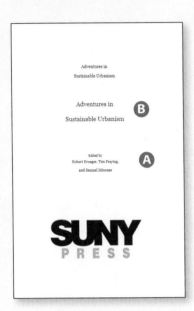

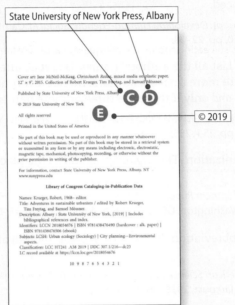

© 2019

Record the following information:

A. The author. Give the initials for the first and middle names, followed by the last name. Separate initials with a space. End with a comma.

B. The title. Give the full title in italics; include the subtitle (if any), preceded by a colon. Capitalize the first word of the title, the first word of the subtitle, and all major words. End with a period.

C. The place of publication. If more than one city is given, use the first one listed. Include the abbreviation

of the state (if in the United States) and the country: Sweetwater, TX, USA. Insert a colon.

D. The publisher. Use a concise version of the publisher's name. End with a comma.

E. The date of publication. Use the publication date, if given. Otherwise, use the copyright date. End with a comma.

F. The pages referenced. (Not shown.) If referring to only a portion of the book, give the page range of the material, preceded by *p.* or *pp.*

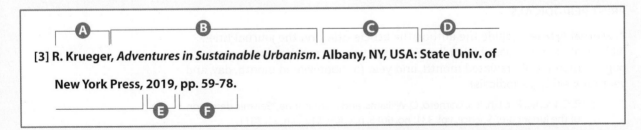

[3] R. Krueger, *Adventures in Sustainable Urbanism.* Albany, NY, USA: State Univ. of

New York Press, 2019, pp. 59-78.

For more IEEE-style models for citing other types of books, see p. 653.

8. Magazine Article List the author, the article title, and the magazine title (abbreviated where possible), followed by the page number(s) and the issue date.

> [8] C. Koch, "Is death reversible?," *Scientific Amer.*, pp. 34–37, Oct. 2019.

9. Newspaper Article List the author, the article title, and the newspaper name, followed by the section and the date.

> [9] M. Finucane, "Americans still eating too many low-quality carbs," *Boston Globe*, sec. B, Sept. 25, 2019.

ELECTRONIC SOURCES

10. Article in an Online Journal or Magazine

> [10] R. Marani and A. G. Perri, "An electronic medical device for preventing and improving the assisted ventilation of intensive care unit patients," *Open Elect. Electron. Eng. J.*, vol. 4, pp. 16–20, 2010. [Online]. Available: http://www.benthamscience.com/open/toeej/openaccess2.htm

11. Website

> [11] American Institute of Physics, "History of AIP." Accessed on: Aug. 17, 2020. [Online]. Available: https://www.aip.org/aip/history

12. Document on a Government Website

> [12] U.S. Department of Health and Human Services, Centers for Disease Control and Prevention. *Preparation and Planning for Bioterrorism Emergencies.* [Online]. Available: http://emergency.cdc.gov/bioterrorism/prep.asp

OTHER SOURCES

13. Thesis or Dissertation

> [13] M.J. Polo, "Chill responses to post-tonal music: Musical structures and physiological reactions," Ph.D. dissertation, Dept. Philos., Univ. of Florida, Gainesville, FL, 2017.

14. Standard For standards, include the title in italics, the standard number, and the date.

> [14] *Testing and Evaluation Protocol for Spectroscopic Personal Radiation Detectors (SPRDs) for Homeland Security*, ANSI Standard T&E Protocol N42.48, 2010.

15. Scientific or Technical Report

> [15] E. G. Fernando, "Investigation of rainfall and regional factors for maintenance cost allocation," Texas Transportation Inst. Texas A&M, College Station, TX, USA, Report 5-4519-01-1, Aug. 2010.

IEEE: CITING AN ARTICLE FROM A PRINT PERIODICAL

Periodicals include journals, magazines, and newspapers. This page gives an example of a citation for a print journal article.

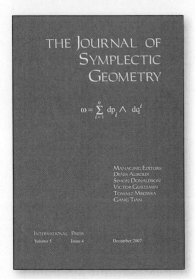

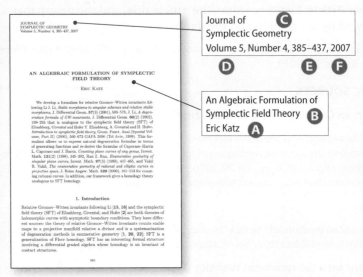

Record the following information:

A. The author. Give the initials for the first and middle names, followed by the last name. Separate initials with a space. End with a comma.

B. The article title. Give the full title; include the subtitle (if any), preceded by a colon. Capitalize only the first word of the title, the first word of the subtitle, and proper nouns. End with a comma. Enclose all in quotation marks.

C. The periodical title. Give the abbreviated title, in italics, with each word capitalized. End with a comma.

D. The volume number and issue number. Include the volume and issue numbers, using the abbreviations *vol.* and *no.* Follow each number with a comma.

E. Inclusive page numbers. Give the page range for the article. End with a comma.

F. The date of publication. Give the abbreviated month, followed by the year or the day and year. End with a period.

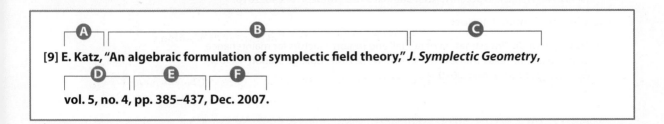

For more IEEE-style models for citing other types of periodical articles, see pp. 653–655.

IEEE: CITING AN ARTICLE FROM AN ONLINE DATABASE

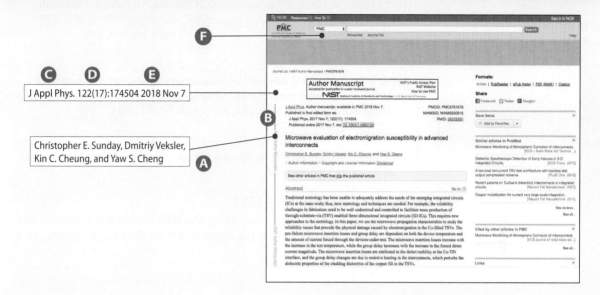

J Appl Phys. 122(17):174504 2018 Nov 7

Christopher E. Sunday, Dmitriy Veksler, Kin C. Cheung, and Yaw S. Cheng

Record the following information:

A. The author. Give the initials for the first and middle names, followed by the last name. Separate initials with a space. End with a comma.

B. The article title. Include the title, followed by a comma. Capitalize only the first word of the title, the first word of the subtitle, and proper nouns. Enclose all in quotation marks.

C. The periodical title. Give the abbreviated journal title in italics, followed by a comma.

D. The volume number, issue number, and pages. Include the volume and issue numbers, using the abbreviations *vol.* and *no.* Follow each number with a comma.

E. The date of publication. Give the abbreviated month, the day (if available), and the year. If necessary, include the words *Accessed:* and your date of access. End with a period.

F. Medium and retrieval information. Include the DOI, if any, and a comma. Place the medium in square brackets, followed by a period: [Online]. After the word *Available:* and a space, include the URL for the database or the article. Do not add a period after the URL.

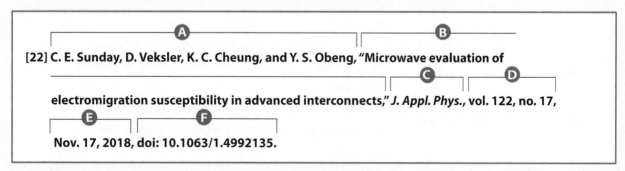

[22] C. E. Sunday, D. Veksler, K. C. Cheung, and Y. S. Obeng, "Microwave evaluation of electromigration susceptibility in advanced interconnects," *J. Appl. Phys.*, vol. 122, no. 17, Nov. 17, 2018, doi: 10.1063/1.4992135.

For more IEEE-style models for citing other types of electronic sources, see p. 655.

16. Paper Published in Conference Proceedings

[16] T. O'Brien, A. Ritz, B. J. Raphael, and D. H. Laidlaw, "Gremlin: An interactive visualization model for analyzing genomic rearrangements," in *Proc. IEEE Information Visualization Conf.*, 2010, vol. 16, no. 6, pp. 918–926.

17. Government Document

[17] W. R. Selbig and R. T. Bannerman, "Characterizing the size distribution of particles in urban stormwater by use of fixed-point sample-collection methods," U.S. Geological Survey, Open-File Report 2011-1052, 2011.

18. Unpublished Document

[18] S. Reed, "An approach to evaluating the autistic spectrum in uncooperative adolescents," unpublished.

SAMPLE IEEE REFERENCE LIST

Following is a sample reference list using the IEEE numbered reference system. The references are listed in the order in which they might appear in a fictional document.

Reference List

Article in an online magazine

[1] [8] C. Koch, "Is death reversible?," *Sci. Am.*, pp. 34–37, Oct. 2019.

Chapter in an edited book

[2] E. Castronova, "The changing meaning of play," in *Online Communication and Collaboration: A Reader,* H. M. Donelan, K. L. Kear, and M. Ramage, Eds. New York, NY, USA: Routledge, 2010, pp. 184–189.

Book in an edition other than the first

[3] L. Xinju, *Laser Technology,* 2nd ed. Boca Raton, FL, USA: CRC Press, 2018, pp. 203–205.

Online journal article

[4] R. Marani and A. G. Perri, "An electronic medical device for preventing and improving the assisted ventilation of intensive care unit patients," *Open Elect. Electron. Eng. J.*, vol. 4, pp. 16–20, 2010. [Online]. Available: http://www.benthamscience.com/open/toeej/openaccess2.htm

Standard

[5] *Testing and Evaluation Protocol for Spectroscopic Personal Radiation Detectors (SPRDs) for Homeland Security,* ANSI Standard T&E Protocol N42.48, 2010.

Journal article

[6] R. C. Weber, P.-Y. Lin, E. J. Garnero, Q. Williams, and P. Lognonne, "Seismic detection of the lunar core," *Science,* vol. 331, no. 6015, pp. 309–312, Jan. 21, 2011.

MLA Style

MLA (Modern Language Association) style consists of citations in the text as well as a list of works cited at the end of the document. In-text citations and works-cited entries are made up of elements (such as author, title, and publication date) from the original source work.

MLA Style for Textual Citations

MLA Style for Works-Cited Entries

(continued)

MLA Style for Works-Cited Entries (*continued*)

MLA TEXTUAL CITATIONS

In MLA style, the textual citation typically includes the name of the source's author and the number of the page being referred to. Textual citations vary depending on the type of source cited and the context of the citation. The following models illustrate a variety of common situations; for additional examples, consult the *MLA Handbook*.

1. Entire Work If you are referring to the whole source, not to a particular page or pages, use only the author's name.

> Harwood's work gives us a framework for understanding the aging process and how it affects communication.

2. Specific Page(s) Immediately following the material you are quoting or paraphrasing, include a parenthetical reference with the author's name and the page number(s) being referred to. Do not add a comma between the name and the page number, and do not use the abbreviation *p.* or *pp.*

> Each feature evolves independently, so there can't be a steady progression of fossils representing change (Prothero 27).

If your sentence already includes the author's name, put only the page number in the parenthetical citation.

> Prothero explains why we won't find a steady progression of human fossils approaching modern humans, as each feature evolves independently (27).

3. Work Without Page Numbers Give a paragraph, section, or screen number only if the number is provided in the source. Use *par.* (singular) or *pars.* (plural) to indicate paragraph numbers. Either spell out or use standard abbreviations (such as *col.*, *fig.*, *pt.*, *ch.*, or *l.*) for other identifying words. Use a comma after the author's name if it appears in the parenthetical citation.

> Under the right conditions, humanitarian aid forestalls health epidemics in the aftermath of natural disasters (Bourmah, pars. 3–6).

> Maternal leave of at least three months has a significantly positive effect on the development of attachment in the infant (Ling, screen 2).

4. Multiple Sources by the Same Author If you cite two or more sources by the same author, either include the full source title in the text or add the first noun phrase of the title to the parenthetical citation to prevent confusion.

Chatterjee believes that diversification in investments can take many forms (*Diversification* 13).

Risk is a necessary component of a successful investment strategy (Chatterjee, *Failsafe* 25).

5. Source with Multiple Authors For a source written by two authors, cite both names.

Grendel and Chang assert that . . .

This phenomenon was verified in the late 1970s (Grendel and Chang 281).

For a source written by three or more authors, give only the first author, followed by the abbreviation *et al.* Follow the same format as in the works-cited list.

Studies show that incidences of type 2 diabetes are widespread and rising quickly (Gianarikas et al.).

6. Source Quoted Within Another Source Give the source of the quotation in the text. In the parenthetical citation, give the author and page number(s) of the source in which you found the quotation, preceded by *qtd. in.*

Freud describes the change in men's egos as science proved that the earth was not the center of the universe and that man was descended from animals (qtd. in Prothero 89–90).

Only the source by Prothero will appear in the list of works cited.

7. Source Authored by an Organization If the author is an organization rather than a person, use the name of the organization. When giving the organization's name in parentheses, abbreviate common words.

In a recent booklet, the Association of Sleep Disorders discusses the causes of narcolepsy (2–3).

The causes of narcolepsy are discussed in a recent booklet (Assn. of Sleep Disorders 2–3).

8. Source with an Unknown Author If the source does not identify an author, shorten the title to the first noun phrase in your parenthetical citation.

Multidisciplinary study in academia is becoming increasingly common ("Interdisciplinary Programs" 23).

In a web document, the author's name is often at the end of the document or in small print on the home page. Do some research before assuming that a website does not have an author. Remember that an organization may be the author. (See item 7.)

9. Multiple Sources in One Citation When you refer to two or more sources at the same point, separate the sources with a semicolon.

Much speculation exists about the origin of this theory (Brady 42; Yao 388).

10. Multiple Authors with the Same Last Name If the authors of two or more sources have the same last name, spell out the first names of those authors in the text and use the authors' first initials in the parenthetical citations.

In contrast, Albert Martinez has a radically different explanation (29).

The economy's strength may be derived from its growing bond market (J. Martinez 87).

11. Chapter or Section in an Edited Book Cite the author of the work, not the editor of the anthology.

> Wolburg and Treise note that college binge drinkers include students with both high and low GPAs (4).

12. Multivolume Work If you use only one volume of a multivolume work, list the volume number in the works-cited list only. If you use more than one volume of a multivolume work, indicate the specific volume you are referring to, followed by a colon and the page number, in your parenthetical citation.

> Many religious organizations opposed the Revolutionary War (Hazlitt 2: 423).

13. Entry in a Reference Work If the entry does not have an author, use the word or term you looked up. You do not need to cite page numbers for entries in encyclopedias and dictionaries because they are arranged alphabetically.

> The term *groupism* is important to understand when preparing to communicate with Japanese business counterparts ("Groupism").

14. Electronic Source When citing electronic sources, follow the same rules as for print sources, providing author names and page numbers, if available. If an author's name is not given, use either the full title of the source in the text or the first noun phrase of the title in the parenthetical citation. (See item 8 on p. 637.) If no page numbers appear, include other identifying numbers, such as paragraph or section numbers, only if they are provided in the source.

> Twenty million books were in print by the early sixteenth century (Rawlins).

THE MLA LIST OF WORKS CITED

For a sample MLA-style list of works cited, see p. 675.

A list of works cited provides the information your readers will need to find each source you have cited in the text. It should not include sources you consulted for background reading. For each works-cited entry, include as many of the following elements as apply:

- The author.
- The title of the work.
- The title of the larger work in which the source is located, such as a collection, a journal, or a website. MLA calls this larger work a "container." If you are citing an entire book, journal, website, or other large work, there will be no separate container.
- The editor, translator, director, producer, or other important contributor.
- The version number.

- The volume and issue numbers.
- The publisher or sponsor.
- The date of publication.
- The location of the source (page numbers, DOI, or URL).
- A second container, such as the database from which a journal was accessed, as well as any available information about it (for example, version number, publisher or sponsor, and URL).

For an example of a works-cited entry with no container, see page 664; for an entry with one container, see page 667; for an entry with two containers, see page 671.

Following are some guidelines for an MLA-style list of works cited.

- **Arranging entries.** Arrange the entries alphabetically by the author's last name. If two or more works are by the same author, arrange them alphabetically by title. Alphabetize works by an organization by the first significant word in the name of the organization.
- **Book titles.** Italicize titles of books and capitalize all major words. Note that in MLA style, prepositions are not capitalized.
- **Publishers.** Give the full name of the publisher, including any words such as *Books* or *Publisher*. Omit terms such as *Inc.* or *Company*. If the publisher is a university press, you may use the abbreviation *UP*. If a source lists two equal publishers, use both names separated by a slash (/). For imprints, use the name of the parent company. For divisions, use the division name.
- **Periodical titles.** Italicize titles of periodicals and capitalize all major words. Omit any initial article.
- **Article titles.** Place titles of articles and other short works in quotation marks and capitalize all major words.
- **Electronic sources.** Include as much information as you can about electronic sources, such as author, date of publication, identifying numbers, and retrieval information. If no date of publication is provided, include the date you accessed the information at the end of the citation. If no author is known, start with the title of the website. Italicize titles of entire websites; treat titles of works within websites, such as articles and video clips, as you would titles of works within print sources. Include the URL for any sources you access on the internet. If you access a source through a database, include the DOI (digital object identifier), if provided, or a stable URL.
- **Indenting.** Use a hanging indent, with the first line of each entry flush with the left margin and all subsequent lines indented one-half inch.
- **Spacing.** Double-space the entire works-cited list. Do not add extra space between entries.

MLA: CITING A BOOK BY ONE AUTHOR

When citing a book, use the information from the title page and the copyright page (on the reverse side of the title page), not from the book's cover or a library catalog.

Chelsea Green Publishing

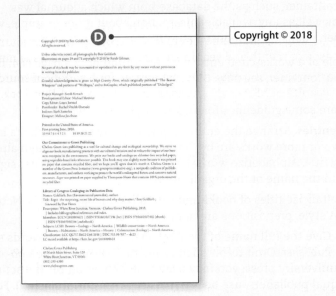

Copyright © 2018

Record the following information:

A. The author. Give the last name first, followed by a comma, the first name, and the middle initial (if given). Don't include titles such as *MD*, *PhD*, or *Sir*; include suffixes after the name, preceded by a comma (Jones, Durham F., Jr.). End with a period.

B. The title. Give the full title; include the subtitle (if any), preceded by a colon. Italicize the title and subtitle, capitalizing all major words. End with a period.

C. The publisher. Give the publisher's full name, omitting only terms such as *Inc.* and *Company*. If there is an imprint, give the name of the parent company. If there is a division, use the division name. For a university press, use the abbreviation *UP*.

D. The date of publication. If more than one copyright date is given, use the most recent one. End with a period.

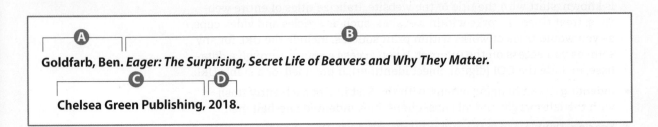

A **B**

Goldfarb, Ben. *Eager: The Surprising, Secret Life of Beavers and Why They Matter.*

C **D**

Chelsea Green Publishing, 2018.

For more MLA-style models for citing other types of books, see pp. 665 and 666.

- **Page numbers.** Use the abbreviation *p.* or *pp.* when giving page numbers in the works-cited list. For a range of pages, give only the last two digits of the second number if the previous digits are identical (for example, 243–47, *not* 243–247 or 243–7). Use a plus sign (+) to indicate that an article continues on subsequent pages, interrupted by other articles or advertisements.

- **Dates.** Follow the format day, month, year, with no commas (for example, 20 Feb. 2020). Spell out *May*, *June*, and *July*; abbreviate all other months (except *Sept.*) using the first three letters followed by a period. For journals, give the season or month and year in addition to volume and issue numbers.

Following are models of works-cited-list entries for a variety of sources. For further examples of MLA-style citations, consult the *MLA Handbook*.

BOOKS

15. Book by One Author Include the author's full name, in reverse order, followed by the book title. Next give the name of the publisher, followed by the year of publication.

> Demm, Eberhard. *Censorship and Propaganda in World War I: A Comprehensive History.* Bloomsbury Academic, 2019.

16. Book by Multiple Authors For a book by two authors, present the names in the sequence in which they appear on the title page. Use reverse order for the name of the first author only. Use a comma to separate the names of the authors.

> Baier, Bret, and Catherine Whitney. *Three Days at the Brink: FDR's Daring Gamble to Win World War II.* William Morrow, 2019.

For a book by three or more authors, use the abbreviation *et al.* after the first author's name.

> Feng, Kuishuang, et al. *Local Consumption and Global Environmental Impacts: Accounting, Trade-Offs and Sustainability.* Routledge, 2020.

17. Multiple Books by the Same Author For the second and subsequent entries by the same author, use three hyphens followed by a period in place of the name. Arrange the entries alphabetically by title, ignoring *An* or *The*.

> Gladwell, Malcolm. *Talking to Strangers: What We Should Know about the People We Don't Know.* Little, Brown and Company, 2019.

> ---. *Outliers: The Story of Success.* Little, Brown and Company, 2008.

18. Book Authored by an Organization The organization takes the position of the author.

> Mental Health America. "Position Statement 21: Rights of Persons with Mental Health and Substance Use Conditions." *Mental Health America*, nmha.org/go/position-statements/21. Accessed 30 Sept. 2019.

19. Book by an Unknown Author If the author of the book is unknown, begin with the title.

> *The World Almanac and Book of Facts 2019.* World Almanac, 2018.

Note that you would ignore *The* in alphabetizing this entry.

20. Edited Book List the book editor's name, followed by *editor* or *editors* (if more than one), in place of the author's name.

> Valentine, Scott Victor, et al., editors. *After Tobacco: What Would Happen If Americans Stopped Smoking?* Columbia UP, 2011.

21. Chapter or Section in an Edited Book Give the author and title of the chapter or section first, followed by the book title and editor. Present the editor's name in normal order, preceded by *edited by* and followed by a comma. After the publication information, give the pages on which the material appears.

> Marx, Karl. "Proletarians and Communists." *Marx Today: Selected Works and Recent Debates*, edited by John F. Sitton, Macmillan, 2010, pp. 51–56.

22. Book in an Edition Other Than the First List the edition number after the title of the book.

> Geary, Patrick, editor. *Readings in Medieval History*. 5th ed., U of Toronto P, 2015.

23. Multivolume Work If you use two or more volumes from a multivolume work, indicate the total number of volumes (for example, 4 *vols.*) after the publication date. If you use only one volume, give the volume number before the publisher, and give the total number of volumes after the date.

> Zeigler-Hill, Virgil and Todd K. Shackelford. *The SAGE Handbook of Personality and Individual Differences*. SAGE Publications, 2018. 3 vols.

24. Book That Is Part of a Series End the entry with the series name as it appears on the title page (but use common abbreviations, such as *Ser.*), followed by the series number, if any. Do not italicize the series name.

> Narayanan, Vasudha, editor. *The Wiley Blackwell Companion to Religion and Materiality*. Wiley-Blackwell, 2020. Blackwell Companions to Religion.

25. Translated Book After the title, present the translator's name in normal order, preceded by *translated by*.

> Patrick Modiano. *Sleep of Memory*. Translated by Mark Polizzotti, Yale UP, 2018.

26. Book in a Language Other Than English You may give a translation of the book's title in brackets.

> Moine, Fabienne. *Poésie et identité féminines en Angleterre: le genre en jeu, 1830–1900* [Poetry and Female Identity in England: Genre/Gender at Play]. L'Harmattan, 2010.

27. Entry in a Reference Work If entries are listed alphabetically, you do not need to include a page number.

> "Desdemona." *Women in Shakespeare: A Dictionary*, edited by Alison Findlay, Bloomsbury, 2014. Arden Shakespeare Dictionary Series.

MLA: CITING AN ARTICLE FROM A PRINT PERIODICAL

Periodicals include journals, magazines, and newspapers. This page gives an example of a citation for an article from a print journal.

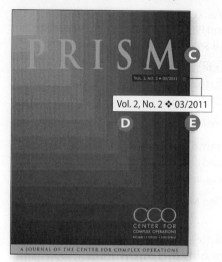

Vol. 2, No. 2 ❖ 03/2011

By James Douglas Orton with Christopher J. Lamb

Record the following information:

A. The author. Give the last name first, followed by a comma, the first name, and the middle name or initial (if given). Don't include titles such as *MD*, *PhD*, or *Sir*; include suffixes after the name, preceded by a comma (Jones, Durham F., Jr.). End with a period.

B. The article title. Give the full title; include the subtitle (if any), preceded by a colon. Enclose the title in quotation marks, capitalizing all major words. Insert a period inside the closing quotation mark, unless the title includes its own punctuation.

C. The periodical title. Italicize the title. Omit any initial article and capitalize all major words. Follow with a comma.

D. The volume number and issue number. For journals, give the volume number and then the issue number,

each followed by a comma. Use the abbreviations *vol.* for volume and *no.* for number.

E. The date of publication. For journals, give the month or season, if available, and the year. For monthly magazines, give the month and year. For weekly magazines and newspapers, give the day, month, and year (in that order). Abbreviate the names of all months except May, June, and July. Put a comma after the year.

F. Inclusive page numbers. (Not shown.) Use the abbreviation *p.* or *pp.* For a range of page numbers 100 and above, give only the last two digits of the second number if the previous digits are identical (for example, 243–47, *not* 243–247 or 243–7). Include section letters for newspapers, if relevant. If the article skips pages, use the first page and a plus sign (+). End with a period.

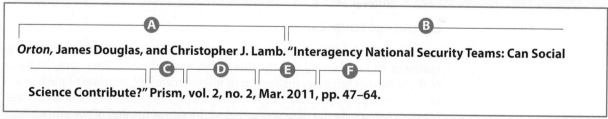

Orton, James Douglas, and Christopher J. Lamb. "Interagency National Security Teams: Can Social Science Contribute?" Prism, vol. 2, no. 2, Mar. 2011, pp. 47–64.

For more MLA-style models for citing other types of periodical articles, see p. 668.

PRINT PERIODICALS

28. Journal Article List the author's name, the article title (in quotation marks), and the journal title (italicized), followed by the volume number, issue number, month or season, year, and page number(s).

> Ganegoda, Deshani B. and Prashant Bordia. "I Can Be Happy For You, But Not All the Time: A Contingency Model of Envy and Positive Empathy in the Workplace." *Applied Psychology,* vol. 104, no. 6, 2019, pp. 776–795.

29. Magazine Article List the author's name, the article title (in quotation marks), and the magazine title (italicized), followed by the issue date and page number(s).

> Vlahos, James. "Alexa, I Want Answers." *Wired,* Mar. 2019, pp. 58–65.

30. Newspaper Article List the author's name, the article title (in quotation marks), and the newspaper name (italicized), followed by the issue date and the page number(s) (which might include a section letter).

> Finucane, Martin. "Americans Still Eating Too Many Low-Quality Carbs" *The Boston Globe*, 25 Sept. 2019, p. B2.

31. Unsigned Article If the author of an article is not indicated, begin with the title. Alphabetize the work by title, ignoring any initial article.

> "Denver Men Charged in Case Involving 2-Pound Brick of Fentanyl." *The Denver Post,* 16 Feb. 2019, p. 5A.

32. Article That Skips Pages Give the page on which the article starts, followed by a plus sign (+) and a period.

> Kennicott, Philip. "Out-Vermeering Vermeer." *The Washington Post,* 10 Apr. 2011, pp. E1+.

33. Review For a book or film review, give the author of the review and the title of the review (in quotation marks), followed by the words *Review of* and the title of the work reviewed (italicized). Insert a comma and the word *by*, then give the name of the author of the work reviewed. (Instead of *by*, you might use *edited by*, *translated by*, or *directed by*, depending on the work.) End with the publication information for the periodical in which the review was published.

> Wynne, Clive. "Our Conflicted Relationship with Animals." Review of *Some We Love, Some We Hate, Some We Eat*, by Hal Herzog, *Nature*, vol. 467, no. 7313, 16 Sept. 2010, pp. 275–76.

ELECTRONIC SOURCES

34. Entire Website If you are citing an entire website, begin with the name of the author or editor (if given) and the title of the site (italicized). Then give the name of the publisher (often an institution or an organization), the date of publication or most recent update, and the URL, followed by a period. If no publication date is available, include the date you accessed the site at the end of the entry.

> *Poets.org.* Academy of American Poets, www.poets org. Accessed 12 Jan. 2020.

MLA: CITING A SHORT WORK FROM A WEBSITE

You will likely need to search the website to find some of the citation information you need.

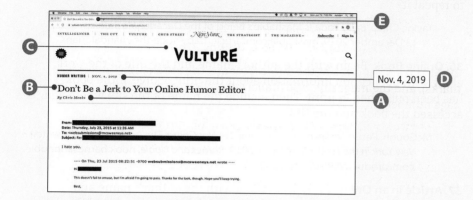

Record the following information:

A. The author. Give the last name first, followed by a comma, the first name, and the middle initial (if given). Don't include titles such as *MD*, *PhD*, or *Sir*; include suffixes after the name, preceded by a comma (Jones, Durham F., Jr.). End with a period.

B. The document title. Give the full title; include the subtitle (if any), preceded by a colon. Enclose the title in quotation marks, capitalizing all major words. Place a period inside the closing quotation mark, unless the title includes its own punctuation.

C. The title of the website. Italicize the title of the website. If there is no clear title and it is a personal home page, use *Home page*, not italicized. Follow with a comma.

D. The date of publication or most recent update. Use the day, month, year format; abbreviate all months except May, June, and July. If you can't identify the date of publication or most recent update, omit it.

E. The URL. Do not include *http://* or *https://*.

F. The retrieval date (optional). Include a retrieval date if you cannot include a date of publication or most recent update. Give the most recent date you accessed the site.

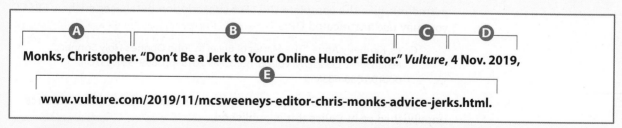

Monks, Christopher. "Don't Be a Jerk to Your Online Humor Editor." *Vulture*, 4 Nov. 2019,

www.vulture.com/2019/11/mcsweeneys-editor-chris-monks-advice-jerks.html.

For more MLA-style models for citing other types of web sources, see pp. 668, 670, and 672.

35. Short Work from a Website If you are citing a portion of a website, begin with the author, the title of the material (in quotation marks), and the title of the site (italicized). Then include the publisher, the date of publication, and the URL. If the publisher name is the same as the site title, you do not need to repeat it.

> Taylor, Chris. "Baby Yoda Is Mashable's Being of the Decade." *Mashable*,
> 13 December 2019, mashable.com/article/baby-yoda-the-mandalorian/.

36. Online Book Begin with the author's name and the title of the work, along with publication information about the print source, if the book has been published in print. Then include the name of the site where you accessed the book and the URL.

> McGough, Peter. *I've Seen the Future and I'm Not Going: The Art Scene and Downtown
> New York in the 1980's*. Pantheon, 2019. *Barnes and Noble*, nook.barnesandnoble
> .com/products/9781524747053/.

37. Article in an Online Periodical Begin with the author's name and include the title of the document, the name of the periodical, and the date of publication. If the periodical is a scholarly journal, include relevant identifying numbers, such as volume, issue, and page numbers, before the date. End with the URL.

> Torpy, Janet M., et al. "Panic Disorder." *Journal of the American Medical Association*,
> vol. 305, no. 12, 2011, pp. 20–30, jama.jamanetwork.com/article
> .aspx?articleid=646264.

For magazine and newspaper articles found online, give the author, the title of the article (in quotation marks), the title of the magazine or newspaper (italicized), the date of publication, and the URL.

> Blakemore, Erin. "Idealistic and tough, Catherine the Great sought to modernize
> Russia." *National Geographic*, Nov. 2019, www.nationalgeographic.com/history
> /reference/people/who-was-catherine-great/.

38. Article from a Database or Subscription Service After giving the print article information, give the name of the database (italicized) and the DOI of the article. If no DOI is available and the database provides a stable URL or permalink, give the complete URL. For subscription databases such as EBSCO, you may use a truncated URL.

> Coles, Kimberly Anne. "The Matter of Belief in John Donne's Holy Sonnets."
> *Renaissance Quarterly*, vol. 68, no. 3, Fall 2015, pp. 899–931. *JSTOR*,
> doi:10.1086/683855.

39. Dissertation The title appears in quotation marks if the dissertation is unpublished or in italics if it is published.

> Zimmer, Kenyon. *The Whole World Is Our Country: Immigration and Anarchism in the
> United States, 1885–1940*. Dissertation, U of Pittsburgh, 2010.

MLA: CITING AN ARTICLE FROM A DATABASE

Libraries subscribe to services such as LexisNexis, ProQuest, InfoTrac, and EBSCOhost, which provide access to databases of electronic texts.

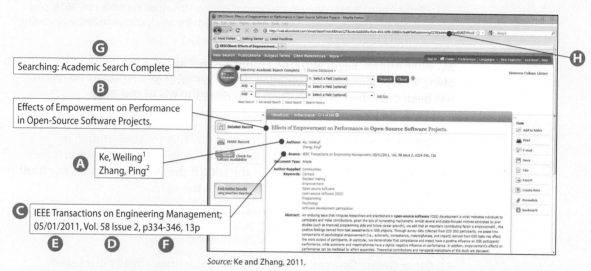

G Searching: Academic Search Complete

B Effects of Empowerment on Performance in Open-Source Software Projects.

A Ke, Weiling[1]
Zhang, Ping[2]

C IEEE Transactions on Engineering Management; 05/01/2011, Vol. 58 Issue 2, p334-346, 13p

E **D** **F**

Source: Ke and Zhang, 2011.

Record the following information:

A. **The author.** Give the last name first, followed by a comma, the first name, and the middle initial (if given). Don't include titles such as *MD*, *PhD*, or *Sir*; include suffixes after the name, preceded by a comma (Jones, Durham F., Jr.). End with a period.

B. **The article title.** Give the full title; include the subtitle (if any), preceded by a colon. Enclose the title in quotation marks, capitalizing all major words. Place a period inside the closing quotation mark, unless the title includes its own punctuation.

C. **The periodical title.** Italicize the title. Omit any initial article, and capitalize all major words.

D. **The volume number and issue number (if appropriate).**

E. **The date of publication.** For journals, give the month or season and year. For monthly magazines, give the month and year. For weekly magazines and newspapers, give the day, month, and year (in that order).

F. **Inclusive page numbers.** If only the first page number is given, follow it with a plus sign and a period.

G. **The name of the database.** Italicize the name.

H. **The DOI or URL.** Give the DOI, if available, or a complete, stable URL. For subscription databases that do not use DOIs or permalinks, you may truncate the URL if the complete URL is extremely long.

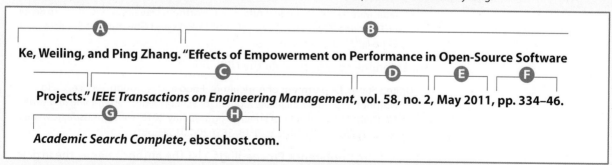

A **B**

Ke, Weiling, and Ping Zhang. "Effects of Empowerment on Performance in Open-Source Software

C **D** **E** **F**

Projects." *IEEE Transactions on Engineering Management,* **vol. 58, no. 2, May 2011, pp. 334–46.**

G **H**

Academic Search Complete, **ebscohost.com.**

For more MLA-style models for citing other types of electronic sources, see pp. 668, 670, and 672.

40. Audio File Treat audio files as you would if they were in print form and include a descriptive term at the end of the entry (for example, *Podcast* or *Song*. That is, if the source is a single piece of a larger item, like a selection from a book, treat it as you would a selection from a book.

> Yorke, Thom. "I Am a Very Rude Person." *Anima*, Unsustainabubble Ltd, 2019, play.
> google.com/store/music/album/ANIMA?id=Biptxw23d5oufctd2fe2uvqnczi&hl
> =en_US. Song.

41. Email Message Use the email's subject line as the title. Include the words *Received by* followed by the name of the recipient (if you were the recipient, use the phrase *the author*). End with the date the email was sent.

> Lange, Frauke. "Data for Genealogical Project." Received by the author, 26 Dec. 2020.

42. Online Posting List the author's name, the title (or subject line) in quotation marks, the name of the discussion forum or newsgroup in italics, the publisher, the posting date, and the URL. If the posting includes the time when it was posted, list the time along with the date.

> Curiosity Rover. "Can you see me waving? How to spot #Mars in the night sky:
> https://youtu.be/hv8hVvJlcJQ." *Twitter*, 5 Nov. 2015, 11:00 a.m., twitter.com
> /marscuriosity/status/672859022911889408.

43. Other Online Sources Follow the MLA guidelines already discussed, adapting them as appropriate to the electronic medium. The following examples are for a podcast and a blog post, respectively.

> "Episode 128: A Hole in the Head." *Lore*. Narrated by Aaron Mahnke, 28 Oct. 2019,
> www.lorepodcast.com/episodes/128. Podcast.

> Cimons, Marlene. "Why Cities Could Be the Key to Solving the Climate Crisis."
> *Thinkprogress.org*, Center for American Progress Action Fund, 10 Dec. 2015,
> thinkprogress.org/climate/2015/12/10/3730938/cities-key-to-climate-crisis/.

OTHER SOURCES

44. Government Document Begin with the author. If the author is a government agency, begin with the name of the country and the agency. Follow with the document title, publisher, and date.

> Canada, Minister of Aboriginal Affairs and Northern Development. *2015–16 Report
> on Plans and Priorities*. Minister of Public Works and Government Services
> Canada, 2015.

For an online source, include the URL.

> United States, Department of Agriculture, Food and Nutrition Service, Child
> Nutrition Programs. *Eligibility Manual for School Meals: Determining and Verifying
> Eligibility*. National School Lunch Program, July 2015, www.fns.usda.gov/sites
> /default/files/cn/SP40_CACFP18_SFSP20-2015a1.pdf.

45. Article from Conference Proceedings List the author's name, the article title, the proceedings title, and the editor's name, followed by the publication information.

Glicksman, Robert. "Climate Change Adaptation and the Federal Lands." *The Past, Present, and Future of Our Public Lands: Celebrating the 40th Anniversary of the Public Land Law Review Commission's Report,* edited by Gary C. Bryner, Natural Resources Law Center, 2010.

46. Pamphlet Cite a pamphlet as you would a book.

A Nurse Manager's Guide to Substance Use Disorder in Nursing. National Council of State Boards of Nursing, 2018.

47. Report Cite a report as you would a book.

Liebreich, Michael, et al. *Green Investing 2010: Policy Mechanisms to Bridge the Financing Gap.* World Economic Forum, 2010.

48. Interview For a published interview, begin with the name of the person interviewed. If the interview has a title, enclose it in quotation marks. Insert the words *Interview by* and give the interviewer's name followed by the information on the work in which the interview was published.

Caro, Robert. "Robert Caro Reflects on Robert Moses, L.B.J., and His Own Career in Nonfiction." Interview by David Remnick, *The New Yorker*, 1 Jul. 2019, www.newyorker.com/culture/the-new-yorker-interview /robert-caro-reflects-on-robert-moses-lbj-and-his-own-career-in-nonfiction

If you conducted the interview yourself, include the interviewee's name, the words *Personal interview*, and the date.

Youngblood, Adelaide. Personal interview, 5 Jan. 2020.

49. Letter or Memo If the letter or memo was addressed to you, include the writer's name, the words *Letter* [or *Memo*] *to the author*, and the date it was written.

Jakobiak, Ursula. Letter to the author, 27 Oct. 2019.

If the letter or memo was addressed to someone other than you, give the recipient's name in place of the words *the author*.

50. Lecture or Speech Give the speaker's name, the title of the lecture or speech (if known), the event and sponsoring organization (if applicable), and the place and date. End with a descriptive term such as *Lecture* or *Keynote speech*.

Wang, Samuel. "Neuroscience and Everyday Life." Freshman Assembly, Princeton University, Princeton, NJ, 12 Sept. 2010. Lecture.

51. Map or Chart Give the author (if known), the title (in quotation marks), and the publication information. For an online source, include the name of the website (italicized), the name of the site's publisher, the date of publication, and the URL.

"Malaysia." *Lonely Planet*, 2019. www.lonelyplanet.com/maps/asia/malaysia/

52. Photograph or Work of Art Give the name of the artist; the title of the artwork, italicized; the date of composition; and the institution and city in which the artwork can be found. For artworks found online, include the title of the website on which you found the work, the publisher, and the URL.

> Smedley, W. T. *On the Beach at Narragansett Pier.* 1900, *Cabinet of American Illustration,* Library of Congress, Prints and Photographs Division, www.loc.gov /pictures/collection/cai/item/2010718015/.

53. Legal Source For a legal case, give the name of the first plaintiff and first defendant, the law report number, the name of the court, and the year of the decision, followed by the publication information.

> Utah v. Evans. 536 US 452. Supreme Court of the US. 2002. *Legal Information Institute,* Cornell U Law School, www.law.cornell.edu/supremecourt /text/536/452.

For a legislative act, give the name of the act, the Public Law number, the Statutes at Large volume and page numbers, and the date the law was enacted.

> Protect America Act of 2007. Pub. L. 110-55. 5 Stat. 121–552. 5 Aug. 2007.

54. Radio or Television Program Give the title of the episode or segment, if applicable, and the title of the program. Include relevant information about the narrator, director, or performers. Then give the network and the broadcast date. If you accessed the program on the web, include the URL.

> "Aircraft Safety." *Nightline,* narrated by Cynthia McFadden, ABC, 4 Apr. 2011.

> "The Cathedral." *Reply All*, narrated by Sruthi Pinnamaneni, episode 50, Gimlet Media, 7 Jan. 2016, gimletmedia.com/episode/50-the-cathedral/.

55. Film, Video, or DVD Give the title of the film and the name of the director. You may also give the names of major performers (*performances by*) or the narrator (*narrated by*). Give the distributor and the year of the original release.

> Eggers, Robert, director. *The Lighthouse.* Performances by Robert Pattinson and Willem Dafoe, A24, 2019.

56. Advertisement Include the name of the product, organization, or service being advertised, and the publication information. At the end of the entry, add the descriptive term *Advertisement.*

> oVertone Coloring Conditioner. *oVertone.* https://overtone.co/. Accessed 30 Oct. 2019. Advertisement.

SAMPLE MLA LIST OF WORKS CITED

Following is a sample list of works cited using the MLA citation system.

Works Cited

Ke, Weiling, and Ping Zhang. "Effects of Empowerment on
   Performance in Open-Source Software Projects." *IEEE Transactions on
   Engineering Management*, vol. 58, no. 2, May 2011, pp. 334–46. *Academic
   Search Complete*, ebscohost.com.

Finucane, Martin. "Americans Still Eating Too Many Low-Quality
   Carbs." *The Boston Globe*, 25 Sept. 2019, p. B2.

Geary, Patrick, editor. *Readings in Medieval History*. 5th ed., U of
   Toronto P, 2015.

Marx, Karl. "Proletarians and Communists." *Marx Today: Selected
   Works and Recent Debate*, edited by John F. Sitton, Macmillan, 2010,
   pp. 51–56.

Mooney, William. "Sex, Booze, and the Code: Four Versions of
   The Maltese Falcon." *Literature/Film Quarterly*, vol. 39, no. 1, Jan. 2011,
   pp. 54–72.

Article from a database

Article in a newspaper

Book in an edition other than the first

Chapter in an edited book

Journal article

Part C: Editing and Proofreading Your Documents

This part of the handbook contains advice on editing your documents for grammar, punctuation, and mechanics. If your organization or professional field has a style guide with different recommendations about grammar and usage, you should follow those guidelines.

Your instructor might use the following abbreviations to refer you to specific topics in the text and in Parts C and D of this Appendix.

Abbreviation	Topic	Page Number	Abbreviation	Topic	Page Number
abbr	abbreviation	691	**ref**	ambiguous pronoun reference	222
adj	adjective (ESL)	224, 707	**rep**	repeated word (ESL)	709
adv	adverb (ESL)	707	**run**	run-on sentence	221
agr p/a	pronoun-antecedent agreement	225	**sent**	sentence part (ESL)	697
agr s/v	subject-verb agreement (ESL)	225, 704	**sub**	subordinating clause (ESL)	699
art	article (*a, an, the*) (ESL)	706	**t**	verb tense	225
cap	capitalization	692	**vb**	verb tense (ESL)	700
comp	comparison of items	223	**.**	period	682
cond	conditional sentence (ESL)	705	**!**	exclamation point	682
coor	coordinating clause (ESL)	669	**?**	question mark	682
cs	comma splice	221	**,**	comma	677
frag	sentence fragment	220	**;**	semicolon	680
help	helping verb and main verb (ESL)	703	**:**	colon	681
inf	infinitive form of the verb (ESL)	702	**—**	dash	683
-ing	*-ing* form of the verb (ESL)	702	**( )**	parentheses	683
ital	italics (underlining)	687	**-**	hyphen	688
num	number	689	**'**	apostrophe	684
omit	omitted word or words (ESL)	708	**" "**	quotation marks	685
			...	ellipses	687
			[ ]	square brackets	687

Punctuation

, COMMAS

The comma is the most frequently used punctuation mark, as well as the one about whose usage writers most often disagree. Examples of common misuses of the comma accompany the following guidelines. The section concludes with advice about editing for unnecessary commas.

1. **Use a comma in a compound sentence to separate two independent clauses linked by a coordinating conjunction (*and, or, nor, but, so, for,* or *yet*).**

INCORRECT	The mixture was prepared from the two premixes and the remaining ingredients were then combined.
CORRECT	The mixture was prepared from the two premixes, and the remaining ingredients were then combined.

2. **Use a comma to separate items in a series composed of three or more elements.**

    The manager of spare parts is responsible for ordering, stocking, and disbursing all spare parts for the entire plant.

    Despite the presence of the conjunction *and*, most technical-communication style manuals require a comma after the next-to-last item. The comma clarifies the separation and prevents misreading.

CONFUSING	The report will be distributed to Operations, Research and Development and Accounting.
CLEAR	The report will be distributed to Operations, Research and Development, and Accounting.

3. **Use a comma to separate introductory words, phrases, and clauses from the main clause of the sentence.**

    However, we will have to calculate the effect of the wind.

    To facilitate trade, the government holds a yearly international conference.

    In the following example, the comma actually prevents misreading:

    Just as we finished eating, the rats discovered the treadmill.

    NOTE: Writers sometimes make errors by omitting commas following introductory words, phrases, or clauses. A comma is optional only if the introductory text is brief and cannot be misread.

CORRECT	First, let's take care of the introductions.
CORRECT	First let's take care of the introductions.

INCORRECT   As the researchers sat down to eat the laboratory rats awakened.

CORRECT   As the researchers sat down to eat, the laboratory rats awakened.

4. Use a comma to separate a dependent clause from the main clause.

Although most of the executive council saw nothing wrong with it, the advertising campaign was canceled.

Most tablet computers use green technology, even though it is relatively expensive.

5. Use commas to separate nonrestrictive modifiers (parenthetical clarifications) from the rest of the sentence.

Jones, the temporary chairman, called the meeting to order.

For more about restrictive and nonrestrictive modifiers, see Ch. 10, p. 231.

NOTE: Writers sometimes introduce an error by dropping one of the commas around a nonrestrictive modifier.

INCORRECT   The data line, which was installed two weeks ago had to be disconnected.

CORRECT   The data line, which was installed two weeks ago, had to be disconnected.

6. Use a comma to separate interjections and transitional elements from the rest of the sentence.

Yes, I admit that your findings are correct.

Their plans, however, have great potential.

NOTE: Writers sometimes introduce an error by dropping one of the commas around an interjection or a transitional element.

INCORRECT   Our new statistician, however used to work for Konaire, Inc.

CORRECT   Our new statistician, however, used to work for Konaire, Inc.

7. Use a comma to separate coordinate adjectives.

The finished product was a sleek, comfortable cruiser.

The heavy, awkward trains are still being used.

The commas in these examples take the place of the conjunction *and*.

For more about coordinate adjectives, see Ch. 10, p. 224.

If the adjectives are not coordinate—that is, if one of the adjectives modifies the combined adjective and noun—do not use a comma:

They decided to go to the first general meeting.

8. Use a comma to signal that a word or phrase has been omitted from a sentence because it is implied.

Smithers is in charge of the accounting; Harlen, the data management; Demarest, the publicity.

The commas after *Harlen* and *Demarest* show that the phrase *is in charge of* has not been repeated.

9. **Use a comma to separate a proper noun from the rest of the sentence in direct address.**

> John, have you seen the purchase order from United?
>
> What I'd like to know, Betty, is why we didn't see this problem coming.

10. **Use a comma to introduce most quotations.**

> He asked, "What time were they expected?"

11. **Use a comma to separate cities or towns, states, and countries.**

> Bethlehem, Pennsylvania, is the home of Lehigh University.
>
> He attended Lehigh University in Bethlehem, Pennsylvania, and the University of California at Berkeley.
>
> Note that a comma precedes and follows Pennsylvania.

12. **Use a comma to set off the year in a date.**

> August 1, 2019, is the anticipated completion date.

If the month separates the date and the year, you do not need to use commas because the numbers are not next to each other:

> The anticipated completion date is 1 August 2019.

13. **Use a comma to clarify numbers.**

> 12,013,104

NOTE: European practice is to reverse the use of commas and periods in writing numbers: periods separate hundreds and thousands, thousands and millions, and so on, while commas separate whole numbers from decimals.

> 12.013,4

14. **Use a comma to separate names from professional or academic titles.**

> Harold Clayton, PhD
>
> Marion Fewick, CLU
>
> Joyce Carnone, PE

A comma also follows the title in a sentence:

> Harold Clayton, PhD, is the featured speaker.

Unnecessary Commas

Writers often introduce errors by using unnecessary commas. Commas are not used in the following situations:

- Commas are not used to link two independent clauses without a coordinating conjunction (an error known as a "comma splice"). For more about comma splices, see Ch. 10, p. 221.

INCORRECT	All the motors were cleaned and dried after the water had entered, had they not been, additional damage would have occurred.
CORRECT	All the motors were cleaned and dried after the water had entered; had they not been, additional damage would have occurred.
CORRECT	All the motors were cleaned and dried after the water had entered. Had they not been, additional damage would have occurred.

- Commas are not used to separate the subject from the verb in a sentence.

INCORRECT	Another of the many possibilities, is to use a "first in, first out" sequence.
CORRECT	Another of the many possibilities is to use a "first in, first out" sequence.

- Commas are not used to separate the verb from its complement.

INCORRECT	The schedules that have to be updated every month are, numbers 14, 16, 21, 22, 27, and 31.
CORRECT	The schedules that have to be updated every month are numbers 14, 16, 21, 22, 27, and 31.

- Commas are not used with a restrictive modifier.

INCORRECT	New and old employees, who use the processed order form, do not completely understand the basis of the system.
	The phrase *who use the processed order form* is a restrictive modifier necessary to the meaning: it defines which employees do not understand the system.
CORRECT	New and old employees who use the processed order form do not completely understand the basis of the system.
INCORRECT	A company, that has grown so big, no longer finds an informal evaluation procedure effective.
	The clause *that has grown so big* is a restrictive modifier.
CORRECT	A company that has grown so big no longer finds an informal evaluation procedure effective.

- Commas are not used to separate two elements in a compound subject.

INCORRECT	Recent studies, and reports by other firms confirm our experience.
CORRECT	Recent studies and reports by other firms confirm our experience.

;   SEMICOLONS

Use semicolons in the following instances:

1. **Use a semicolon to separate independent clauses not linked by a coordinating conjunction.**

The second edition of the handbook is more up-to-date; however, it is also more expensive.

2. Use a semicolon to separate items in a series that already contains commas.

The members elected three officers: Jack Resnick, president; Carol Wayshum, vice president; Ahmed Jamoogian, recording secretary.

Here the semicolon acts as a "supercomma," grouping each name with the correct title.

Misuse of Semicolons

Sometimes writers incorrectly use a semicolon when a colon is called for:

INCORRECT   We still need one ingredient; luck.

CORRECT   We still need one ingredient: luck.

COLONS

Use colons in the following instances:

1. Use a colon to introduce a word, phrase, or clause that amplifies, illustrates, or explains a general statement.

The project team lacked one crucial member: a project leader.

Here is the client's request: we are to provide the preliminary proposal by November 13.

We found three substances in excessive quantities: potassium, cyanide, and asbestos.

The week was productive: 14 projects were completed, and another dozen were initiated.

NOTE: The text preceding a colon should be able to stand on its own as a sentence:

INCORRECT   We found: potassium, cyanide, and asbestos.

CORRECT   We found the following: potassium, cyanide, and asbestos.

CORRECT   We found potassium, cyanide, and asbestos.

2. Use a colon to introduce items in a vertical list if the sense of the introductory text would be incomplete without the list.

For more about constructing lists, see Ch. 9, pp. 202–207.

We found the following:

- potassium
- cyanide
- asbestos

3. Use a colon to introduce long or formal quotations.

The president began: "In the last year . . . ."

Misuse of Colons

Writers sometimes incorrectly use a colon to separate a verb from its complement:

INCORRECT   The tools we need are: a plane, a level, and a T square.

CORRECT   The tools we need are a plane, a level, and a T square.

CORRECT   We need three tools: a plane, a level, and a T square.

. PERIODS

Use periods in the following instances:

1. Use a period at the end of sentences that do not ask questions or express strong emotion.

The lateral stress still needs to be calculated.

For more about abbreviations, see p. 691.

2. Use a period after some abbreviations.

U.S.A.

etc.

3. Use a period with decimal fractions.

4.056

$6.75

75.6 percent

! EXCLAMATION POINTS

The exclamation point is used at the end of a sentence that expresses strong emotion, such as surprise.

The nuclear plant, which was originally expected to cost $1.6 billion, eventually cost more than $8 billion!

In technical documents, which require objectivity and a calm, understated tone, exclamation points are rarely used.

? QUESTION MARKS

The question mark is used at the end of a sentence that asks a direct question.

What did the commission say about effluents?

NOTE: When a question mark is used within quotation marks, no other end punctuation is required.

She asked, "What did the commission say about effluents?"

Misuse of Question Marks

Do not use a question mark at the end of a sentence that asks an indirect question.

He wanted to know whether the procedure had been approved for use.

▬ DASHES

To make a dash, use two uninterrupted hyphens (—). Do not add a space before or after the dash. Some word-processing programs turn two hyphens into a dash, but with others, you have to use a special combination of keys to make a dash; there is no dash key on the keyboard.

Use dashes in the following instances:

1. Use a dash to set off a sudden change in thought or tone.

> The committee found—can you believe this?—that the company bore full responsibility for the accident.

> That's what she said—if I remember correctly.

2. Use a dash to emphasize a parenthetical element.

> The managers' reports—all 10 of them—recommend production cutbacks for the coming year.

> Arlene Kregman—the first woman elected to the board of directors—is the next scheduled speaker.

3. Use a dash to set off an introductory series from its explanation.

> Wetsuits, weight belts, tanks—everything will have to be shipped in.

NOTE: When a series follows the general statement, a colon replaces the dash.

> Everything will have to be shipped in: wetsuits, weight belts, and tanks.

Misuse of dashes

Sometimes writers incorrectly use a dash as a substitute for other punctuation marks:

INCORRECT	The regulations—which were issued yesterday—had been anticipated for months.
	There would be no reason to emphasize this parenthetical element.
CORRECT	The regulations, which were issued yesterday, had been anticipated for months.
INCORRECT	Many candidates applied—however, only one was chosen.
CORRECT	Many candidates applied; however, only one was chosen.

( ) PARENTHESES

Use parentheses in the following instances:

1. Use parentheses to set off incidental information.

> Please call me (x3104) when you get the information.
> Galileo (1564–1642) is often considered the father of modern astronomy.
> The cure rate for lung cancer almost doubled in thirty years (Capron, 2019).

2. **Use parentheses to enclose numbers or letters that label items listed in a sentence.**

> To transfer a call within the office, (1) place the party on HOLD, (2) press TRANSFER, (3) press the extension number, and (4) hang up.

Use both a left and a right parenthesis—not just a right parenthesis—in this situation.

Misuse of Parentheses

For more about square brackets, see p. 687.

Sometimes writers incorrectly use parentheses instead of brackets to enclose their insertion within a quotation:

INCORRECT	He said, "The new manager (Farnham) is due in next week."
CORRECT	He said, "The new manager [Farnham] is due in next week."

' APOSTROPHES

Use apostrophes in the following instances:

1. **Use an apostrophe to indicate possession.**

> the manager's goals   the employees' credit union
> the workers' lounge   Charles's T square

For joint possession, add an apostrophe and an s only to the last noun or proper noun:

> Watson and Crick's discovery

For separate possession, add an apostrophe and an **s** to each of the nouns or pronouns:

> Newton's and Galileo's theories

NOTE: Do not add an apostrophe or an s to possessive pronouns: *his, hers, its, ours, yours, theirs.*

2. **Use an apostrophe to indicate possession when a noun modifies a gerund.**

> We were all looking forward to Bill's joining the company.

> The gerund *joining* is modified by the proper noun *Bill.*

3. **Use an apostrophe to form contractions.**

> I've   shouldn't
> can't   it's

The apostrophe usually indicates an omitted letter or letters:

> can(no)t = can't
> it (i)s = it's

NOTE: Some organizations discourage the use of contractions. Find out what the policy of your organization is.

4. **Use an apostrophe to indicate special plurals.**

> three 9's
>
> two different JCL's
>
> the why's and how's of the problem

NOTE: For plurals of numbers and abbreviations, some style guides omit the apostrophe: *9s, JCLs*. Because usage varies considerably, check with your organization.

Misuse of Apostrophes

Writers sometimes incorrectly use the contraction *it's* in place of the possessive pronoun *its*.

INCORRECT	The company's management does not believe that the problem is it's responsibility.
CORRECT	The company's management does not believe that the problem is its responsibility.

QUOTATION MARKS

Use quotation marks in the following instances:

1. **Use quotation marks to indicate titles of short works, such as articles, essays, or chapters.**

> Smith's essay "Solar Heating Alternatives" was short but informative.

2. **Use quotation marks to call attention to a word or phrase used in an unusual way or in an unusual context.**

> A proposal is "wired" if the sponsoring agency has already decided who will be granted the contract.

NOTE: Do not use quotation marks to excuse poor word choice:

INCORRECT	The new director has been a real "pain."

3. **Use quotation marks to indicate a direct quotation.**

> "In the future," he said, "check with me before authorizing any large purchases."
>
> As Breyer wrote, "Morale *is* productivity."

NOTE: Quotation marks are not used with indirect quotations:

INCORRECT	He said that "third-quarter profits will be up."
CORRECT	He said that third-quarter profits will be up.
CORRECT	He said, "Third-quarter profits will be up."

For more about quoting sources, see Appendix, Part A, p. 628.

Also note that quotation marks are not used with quotations that are longer than four lines; instead, set the quotation in block format. In a word-processed manuscript, a block quotation is usually introduced by a complete sentence followed by a colon and indented one-half inch from the left-hand margin.

Different style manuals recommend variations on the basic rules; the following example illustrates APA style.

McFarland (2020) writes:

> The extent to which organisms adapt to their environment is still being charted. Many animals, we have recently learned, respond to a dry winter with an automatic birth control chemical that limits the number of young to be born that spring. This prevents mass starvation among the species in that locale. (p. 49)

Hollins (2017) concurs. She writes, "Biological adaptation will be a major research area during the next decade" (p. 2).

Using Quotation Marks with Other Punctuation

- If the sentence contains a *tag*—a phrase identifying the speaker or writer—a comma separates it from the quotation:

  Wilson replied, "I'll try to fly out there tomorrow."

  "I'll try to fly out there tomorrow," Wilson replied.

  Informal and brief quotations require no punctuation before a quotation mark:

  She asked herself "Why?" several times a day.

- In the United States (unlike most other nations where English is spoken), commas and periods following quotations are placed within the quotation marks:

  The project engineer reported, "A new factor has been added."

  "A new factor has been added," the project engineer reported.

- Question marks, dashes, and exclamation points are placed inside quotation marks when they are part of the quoted material:

  He asked, "Did the shipment come in yet?"

- When question marks, dashes, and exclamation points apply to the whole sentence, they are placed outside the quotation marks:

  Did he say "This is the limit"?

- When a punctuation mark appears inside a quotation mark at the end of a sentence, do not add another punctuation mark:

  INCORRECT Did she say "What time is it?"?

  CORRECT Did she say "What time is it?"

... ELLIPSES

Ellipses (three spaced periods) indicate the omission of material from a direct quotation.

SOURCE	My team will need three extra months for market research and quality-assurance testing to successfully complete the job.
QUOTE	She responded, "My team will need three extra months . . . to successfully complete the job."

Insert an ellipsis after a period if you are omitting entire sentences that follow:

Larkin refers to the project as "an attempt . . . to clarify the issue of compulsory arbitration. . . . We do not foresee an end to the legal wrangling . . . but perhaps the report can serve as a definition of the areas of contention."

The writer has omitted words from the source after *attempt* and after *wrangling*. After *arbitration*, the writer has inserted an ellipsis after a period to indicate that a sentence or more has been omitted.

NOTE: If the author's original statement has ellipses, MLA style recommends that you insert brackets around an ellipsis that you introduce in a quotation.

Sexton thinks "reuse adoption offers . . . the promise to improve business [. . .] worldwide."

[] SQUARE BRACKETS

Use square brackets in the following instances:

1. Use square brackets around words added to a quotation.

As noted in the minutes of the meeting, "He [Pearson] spoke out against the proposal."

A better approach would be to shorten the quotation:

The minutes of the meeting note that Pearson "spoke out against the proposal."

2. Use square brackets to indicate parenthetical information within parentheses.

(For further information, see Charles Houghton's *Civil Engineering Today* [2016].)

Mechanics

ital ITALICS

Although italics are generally preferred, you may use underlining in place of italics. Whichever method you choose, be consistent throughout your document. Use italics (or underlining) in the following instances:

1. Use italics for words used as words.

In this report, the word *operator* will refer to any individual who is in charge of the equipment, regardless of that individual's certification.

2. **Use italics to indicate titles of long works (books, manuals, and so on), periodicals and newspapers, long films, long plays, and long musical works.**

   See Houghton's *Civil Engineering Today*.

   We subscribe to the *Wall Street Journal*.

   Note that *the* is not italicized or capitalized when the title is used in a sentence.

   NOTE: The MLA style guide recommends that the names of websites be italicized.

   The Library of Congress maintains *Thomas*, an excellent site for legislative information.

3. **Use italics to indicate the names of ships, trains, and airplanes.**

   The shipment is expected to arrive next week on the *Penguin*.

4. **Use italics to set off foreign expressions that have not become fully assimilated into English.**

   Grace's *joie de vivre* makes her an engaging presenter.

   Check a dictionary to determine whether a foreign expression has become assimilated.

5. **Use italics to emphasize words or phrases.**

   Do not press the red button.

- HYPHENS

Use hyphens in the following instances:

1. **Use hyphens to form compound adjectives that precede nouns.**

   general-purpose register

   meat-eating dinosaur

   chain-driven saw

   NOTE: Hyphens are not used after adverbs that end in -ly.

   newly acquired terminal

   Also note that hyphens are not used when the compound adjective follows the noun:

   The Woodchuck saw is chain driven.

For more about compound adjectives, see p. 224.

Many organizations have their own policy about hyphenating compound adjectives. Check to see if your organization has a policy.

2. **Use hyphens to form some compound nouns.**

> once-over
>
> go-between

NOTE: There is a trend away from hyphenating compound nouns (*vice president*, *photomicroscope*, *drawbridge*); check your dictionary for proper spelling.

3. **Use hyphens to form fractions and compound numbers.**

> one-half
>
> fifty-six

4. **Use hyphens to attach some prefixes and suffixes.**

> post-1945
>
> president-elect

5. **Use hyphens to divide a word at the end of a line.**

> We will meet in the pavilion in one hour.

Whenever possible, however, avoid such line breaks; they slow the reader down. Even when your word processor is determining the line breaks, you may have to check the dictionary occasionally to make sure a word has been divided between syllables. If you need to break a URL at the end of a line, do not add a hyphen. Instead, break the URL before a single slash or before a period or other punctuation mark:

> http://www.stc.org
>
> /ethical.asp

num NUMBERS

Ways of handling numbers vary considerably. Therefore, in choosing between words and numerals, consult your organization's style guide. Many organizations observe the following guidelines:

1. **Express technical quantities of any size in numerals, especially if a unit of measurement is included.**

> 3 feet   43,219 square miles
>
> 12 grams   36 hectares

2. **Express nontechnical quantities of fewer than 10 in words.**

> three persons
>
> six whales

3. **Express nontechnical quantities of 10 or more in numerals.**

> 300 persons
>
> 12 whales

4. **Write out approximations.**

   approximately ten thousand people

   about two million trees

5. **Express round numbers over nine million in a combination of words and numerals.**

   14 million light-years

   $64 billion

6. **Express decimals in numerals.**

   3.14

   1,013.065

   Decimals of less than one should be preceded by a zero:

   0.146

   0.006

7. **Write out fractions, unless they are linked to units of measurement.**

   two-thirds of the members

   3½ hp

8. **Express time of day in numerals if A.M. or P.M. is used; otherwise, write it out.**

   6:10 A.M.

   six o'clock

   the nine-thirty train

9. **Express page numbers and figure and table numbers in numerals.**

   Figure 1

   Table 13

   page 261

10. **Write back-to-back numbers using a combination of words and numerals.**

    six 3-inch screws

    fourteen 12-foot ladders

    3,012 five-piece starter units

In general, the quantity linked to a unit of measurement should be expressed with the numeral. If the nontechnical quantity would be cumbersome in words, however, use the numeral for it instead.

11. **Use both words and numerals to represent numbers in legal contracts or in documents intended for international readers.**

> thirty-seven thousand dollars ($37,000)
>
> five (5) relays

12. **Use both words and numerals in some street addresses.**

> 3801 Fifteenth Street

Special Cases

- A number at the beginning of a sentence should be spelled out:

  > Thirty-seven acres was the size of the lot.

  Many writers would revise the sentence to avoid spelling out the number:

  > The lot was 37 acres.

- Within a sentence, numbers with the same unit of measurement should be expressed consistently in either numerals or words:

  INCORRECT   On Tuesday, the attendance was 13; on Wednesday, eight.

  CORRECT   On Tuesday, the attendance was 13; on Wednesday, 8.

  CORRECT   On Tuesday, the attendance was thirteen; on Wednesday, eight.

- In general, months should not be expressed as numbers. In the United States, 3/7/20 means March 7, 2020; in many other countries, it means July 3, 2020. The following forms, in which the months are written out, are preferable:

  > March 7, 2020
  >
  > 7 March 2020

abbr ABBREVIATIONS

Abbreviations save time and space, but you should use them carefully because your readers may not understand them. Many companies and professional organizations provide lists of approved abbreviations.

Analyze your audience to determine whether and how to abbreviate. If your readers include a general audience unfamiliar with your field, either write out the technical terms or attach a list of abbreviations. If you are new to an organization or are publishing in a field for the first time, find out which abbreviations are commonly used. If for any reason you are unsure about a term, write it out.

The following are general guidelines about abbreviations:

1. **When an unfamiliar abbreviation is introduced for the first time, give the full term, followed by the abbreviation in parentheses. In subsequent**

references, the abbreviation may be used alone. For long works, the full term and its abbreviation may be written out at the start of major units, such as chapters.

> The heart of the new system is the self-loading cartridge (SLC).

> The liquid crystal display (LCD) is your control center.

2. **To form the plural of an abbreviation, add an s, either with or without an apostrophe, depending on the style used by your organization.**

> GNP's or GNPs

> PhD's or PhDs

Abbreviations for most units of measurement do not take plurals:

> 10 in.

> 3 qt

3. **Do not use periods with most abbreviations in scientific writing.**

> lb

> cos

> dc

If an abbreviation can be confused with another word, however, a period should be used:

> in.

> Fig.

4. **If no number appears with a unit of measurement, do not use an abbreviation.**

> INCORRECT   How many sq meters is the site?

> CORRECT   How many square meters is the site?

cap CAPITALIZATION

For the most part, the conventions of capitalization in general writing apply in technical communication:

1. **Capitalize proper nouns, titles, trade names, and names of places, languages, religions, and organizations.**

> William Rusham

> Director of Personnel

> Quick-Fix Erasers

Bethesda, Maryland

Italian

Methodism

Society for Technical Communication

In some organizations, job titles are not capitalized unless they refer to specific people.

Valerie Cruz, Director of Personnel, is interested in being considered for vice president of marketing.

2. Capitalize headings and labels.

A Proposal to Implement the Wilkins Conversion System

Mitosis

Table 3

Section One

The Problem

Rate of Inflation, 2007–2017

Figure 6

Proofreading Symbols and Their Meanings

MARK IN MARGIN	INSTRUCTIONS	MARK ON MANUSCRIPT	CORRECTED TYPE
ℓ	Delete	$10 billion dollars	$10 billion
∧	Insert	enviroment	environment
stet	Let stand	let it stand	let it stand
cap	Capitalize	the english language	the English language
lc	Make lowercase	the English Language	the English language
—	Italicize	Technical Communication	*Technical Communication*
tr	Transpose	recieve	receive
⌒	Close up space	diagnostic ultra sound	diagnostic ultrasound
sp	Spell out	Pres Smithers	President Smithers
#	Insert space	3amp light	3 amp light
¶	Start paragraph	. . . the results. These results	. . . the results. These results
run in	No paragraph	. . . the results. For this reason,	. . . the results. For this reason,
sc	Set in small capitals	Needle-nose pliers	NEEDLE-NOSE PLIERS
bf	Set in boldface	Needle-nose pliers	**Needle-nose pliers**
⊙	Insert period	Fig 21	Fig. 21
⸚	Insert comma	the plant which was built	the plant, which was built
=	Insert hyphen	menu driven software	menu-driven software
⊙	Insert colon	Add the following	Add the following:
⸎	Insert semicolon	. . . the plan however, the committee	. . . the plan; however, the committee
⸍	Insert apostrophe	the users preference	the user's preference
❝/❞	Insert quotation marks	Furthermore, she said . . .	"Furthermore," she said . . .
(/)	Insert parentheses	Write to us at the Newark office	Write to us (at the Newark office)
[/]	Insert brackets	President John Smithers	President [John] Smithers
⟂N	Insert en dash	1984 2001	1984–2001
⟂M	Insert em dash	Our goal victory	Our goal—victory
⌄	Make superscript	4,000 ft2	4,000 ft^2
⌃	Make subscript	H2O	H_2O
//	Align	$123.05 $86.95	$123.05 $86.95
[	Move to the left	PVC piping	PVC piping
]	Move to the right	PVC piping	PVC piping
⌐	Move up	PVC piping	PVC piping
⌊⌋	Move down	PVC piping	PVC piping

Part D: Guidelines for Multilingual Writers (ESL)

Cultural and Stylistic Communication Issues

Just as native speakers of English must learn how to communicate with those with a different first language, technical communicators in the United States whose first language is not English must learn how to communicate effectively with native speakers.

For more about communicating across cultures, see Ch. 5, pp. 101–107.

If you want to communicate effectively with native speakers, you need to understand U.S. culture. Specifically, you need to understand how U.S. readers expect writers to select, organize, and present information and what writers expect from their readers. Speakers and listeners in the United States also have expectations. Indeed, cultural values affect all styles of communication. Of course, no two communicators are exactly alike. Still, if you know how culture affects communicators in general, you can analyze your communication task and communicate effectively.

Readers, writers, speakers, and listeners in the United States tend to value the following qualities:

- **Directness.** Audiences in the United States expect writers and speakers to get to the point quickly and to communicate information clearly. So when you write a claim letter, for example, clearly state what you want the individual you are addressing to do to correct the situation. Related to directness is *task orientation*. Do not begin a letter with a comment about the weather or family. Instead, communicate immediately about business.

For more about claim letters, see Ch. 14, p. 380.

- **Independence.** In spite of the increasingly significant role of collaborative writing, U.S. audiences still value individualism and people who can work independently. Therefore, when you write a letter to an individual in an organization, be aware that the recipient sees you as one person, too, not merely as a mouthpiece of an organization. Use the pronoun I rather than *we*.

For more about writing collaboratively, see Ch. 4.

- **Time consciousness.** Try to meet deadlines and to arrive on time for appointments. Audiences in the United States consider slowness in responding to issues a sign of disrespect.

To become familiar with the U.S. style of communication, study documents, talk to people, and ask for feedback from U.S. readers and listeners. Following are some specific guidelines for applying the preceding general cultural values as you listen, speak, and write to U.S. audiences.

LISTENING

Speakers in the United States expect you, their audience, to listen actively. They assume that you will ask questions and challenge their points—but not interrupt them unless you are invited to do so. To become a better listener, try the following strategies:

- **Look at the speaker's eyes or at least at the speaker's face.** Lean forward or nod your head to encourage the speaker. If you avoid looking at the speaker, he or she could think that you are not interested in the message.

- **Do not interrupt the speaker.** Interrupting shows the speaker that you do not value his or her opinion. Give the speaker enough time to complete the presentation.

- **Do not become indignant.** Be prepared to hear the speaker state clearly what he or she likes and dislikes, often without considering other people's personal feelings.

- **Assume that the speaker values your opinion.** Form responses and, at the appropriate time, express your opinions openly.

- **Ask questions.** If you have questions, ask them. If you do not ask questions, the speaker might assume that you not only understand but also agree with the message of the presentation. It is altogether appropriate to ask questions such as these: "Do you mean . . . ?" "Did I understand you to say . . . ?" "Would you repeat . . . ?"

SPEAKING

For more about claims, see Ch. 8, p. 182. For more about introductions, see Ch. 19, p. 535.

As suggested in Chapter 21, U.S. audiences expect speakers to control the situation, keep listeners interested, address listeners directly, and speak with authority. Do not apologize for your fluency or for problems in your content. Doing so could diminish your credibility and make listeners think you are wasting their time. To become a better speaker, try the following strategies:

- **Start and end your presentation on time.** If you start late or speak too long, you send the message "Your time is less valuable than mine."

- **Make eye contact and smile.** If you make eye contact with people, you look friendly and confident, and you send the message "You are important."

- **Speak up.** If you speak with your head bowed or in too low a voice, audience members could become distracted or think you are hiding something.

- **Make friendly gestures.** Invite the audience to ask questions. It is appropriate to say "Please feel free to ask me questions at any time" or "If you have questions, I'd be glad to answer them at the conclusion of my talk." Also, try to break the invisible barrier between you and your audience. For example, step out from behind the podium or move toward the audience.

WRITING

In the United States, technical communicators generally state their claims early and clearly. They support their claims by presenting the most important information first and by using numerical data. To become a better writer, try the following strategies:

- **State your claims directly.** In most cases, state your purpose directly in the first paragraph of a memo or letter, as well as at the start of any other document and at the start of each section within it.

- **Avoid digressions.** Focus on your task. If a piece of information is interesting but does not help you make your point, do not include it.

- **Move from one point to the next systematically.** Use an appropriate pattern of organization, and use transitions and other devices to ensure a smooth flow within a paragraph and between paragraphs.

For more about organizing information, see Ch. 7. For more about writing coherent paragraphs, see Ch. 9, pp. 207–214.

- **Use logic and technical information rather than allusion, metaphor, or emotion.** Western readers are persuaded more by numerical data—that is, by statistics, whether raw scores, dollar amounts, or percentages—than by an emotional appeal or an argument from authority.

For more about persuasion, see Ch. 8.

- **Use an appropriate level of formality.** Consider your audience, your subject, and your purpose. In the United States, email messages and memos tend to be less formal than reports and proposals. In most cases, avoid overly formal words, such as *pursuant*, *aforementioned*, and *heretofore*, in favor of clear, concise writing.

For more about choosing the right words and phrases, see Ch. 10, pp. 234–247.

Sentence-Level Issues

sent   BASIC CHARACTERISTICS OF A SENTENCE

A sentence has five characteristics.

1. **It starts with an uppercase letter and ends with a period, a question mark, or (rarely) an exclamation point attached to the final word.**

    I have a friend.

    Do you have a friend?

    I asked, "Do you have a friend?"

    The question mark is part of the quoted question.

    Did you write "Ode to My Friend"?

    The question mark is part of the question, not part of the title in quotation marks.

    Yes! You are my best friend!

2. **It has a subject, usually a noun. The subject performs the action(s) mentioned in the sentence or exists in a certain condition according to the rest of the sentence.**

SUBJECT
↓
My friend speaks five languages fluently.

The subject performs an action—*speaks*.

SUBJECT
↓
My friend is fluent in five languages.

The subject exists as (is) a fluent person.

3. **It has a verb, which tells what the subject does or states its existence.**

VERB
↓
My friend speaks five languages fluently.

The verb tells what the subject does.

VERB
↓
My friend is fluent in five languages.

The verb states that the subject exists.

4. **It has a standard word order.**

The most common sequence in English is subject–verb–object:

SUBJECT VERB OBJECT
↓   ↙   ⌐————————⌐
We hired a consulting firm.

You can add information in various places.

Yesterday we hired a consulting firm.

Information was added to the start of the sentence.

Yesterday we hired a consulting firm: *Sanderson & Associates.*

Information was added to the end of the sentence.

Yesterday we hired *the city's most prestigious* consulting firm: Sanderson & Associates.

Information was added in the middle of the sentence.

In fact, any element of a sentence can be expanded.

For more about subordinating words and phrases, see p. 699.

5. **It has an independent clause (a subject and verb that can stand alone—that is, a clause that does not begin with a subordinating word or phrase).**

The following is a sentence:

SUBJECT VERB
↓   ↓
The pump failed because of improper maintenance.

The following is also a sentence:

SUBJECT VERB
↓   ↓
The pump failed.

But the following is not a sentence because it lacks a subject with a verb and because it begins with a subordinating phrase:

Because of improper maintenance.

An independent clause is required to complete this sentence:

Because of improper maintenance, the pump failed.

coor LINKING IDEAS BY COORDINATION

One way to connect ideas in a sentence is by coordination. Coordination is used when the ideas in the sentence are roughly equal in importance. There are three main ways to coordinate ideas:

1. **Use a semicolon (;) to coordinate ideas that are independent clauses.**

   The information for bid was published last week; the proposal is due in less than a month.

2. **Use a comma and a coordinating conjunction (*and, but, or, nor, so, for,* or *yet*) to coordinate two independent clauses.**

   The information for bid was published last week, but the proposal is due in less than a month.

   In this example, *but* clarifies the relationship between the two clauses: the writer hasn't been given enough time to write the proposal.

3. **Use transitional words and phrases to coordinate two independent clauses. You can end the first independent clause with a semicolon or a period. If you use a period, begin the transitional word or phrase with a capital letter.**

   The Intel 6 Series chipset has already been replaced; *as a result*, it is hard to find an Intel 6 Series in a new computer.

   The Intel 6 Series chipset has already been replaced. *As a result*, it is hard to find an Intel 6 Series in a new computer.

For more about transitional words and phrases, see Ch. 9, pp. 212–213.

sub LINKING IDEAS BY SUBORDINATION

Two ideas can also be linked by subordination—that is, by deemphasizing one of them. There are two basic methods of subordination:

For more about restrictive and nonre-strictive modifiers, see Ch. 10, p. 231.

1. **Use a subordinating word or phrase to turn one idea into a subordinate clause.**

after	because	since	until	while
although	before	so that	when	who
as	even though	that	where	whom
as if	if	unless	which	whose

Start with two independent clauses:

The bridge was completed last year. The bridge already needs repairs.

Then choose a subordinating word and combine the clauses:

Although the bridge was completed last year, it already needs repairs.

Although subordinates the first clause, leaving *it already needs repairs* as the independent clause.

Note that a writer could reverse the order of the ideas:

The bridge already needs repairs *even though* it was completed last year.

Another way to subordinate one idea is to turn it into a nonrestrictive clause using the subordinating word *which*:

The bridge, which was completed last year, already needs repairs.

This version deemphasizes *was completed last year* by turning it into a nonrestrictive clause and emphasizes *already needs repairs* by leaving it as the independent clause.

2. **Turn one of the ideas into a phrase modifying the other.**

Completed last year, the bridge already needs repairs.

Completed last year was turned into a phrase by dropping the subject and verb from the independent clause. Here the phrase is used to modify *the bridge*.

For more about verb tenses, see Ch. 10, pp. 225–226.

vb VERB TENSES

The four tenses used most often in English are simple, progressive, perfect, and perfect progressive.

1. **SIMPLE: an action or state that was, is, or will be static or definite**

SIMPLE PAST (*VERB* + *ed* [or irregular past])

Yesterday we *subscribed* to a new ecology journal.

The action of subscribing happened at a specific time. The action of subscribing definitively happened regardless of what happens today or tomorrow.

SIMPLE PRESENT (*VERB* or *VERB* + *s*)

We *subscribe* to three ecology journals every year.

The action of subscribing never changes; it's regular, definite.

SIMPLE FUTURE (*will* + *VERB* or simple present of *be* + *going to* + *VERB*)

We *will subscribe* to the new ecology journal next year.

We *are going to subscribe* to the new ecology journal next year.

The action of subscribing next year (a specific time) will not change; it is definite.

2. PROGRESSIVE: an action in progress (continuing) at a known time

PAST PROGRESSIVE (simple past of *be* + *VERB* + *ing*)

We *were updating* our directory when the power failure occurred.

The action of updating was in progress at a known time in the past.

PRESENT PROGRESSIVE (simple present of *be* + *VERB* + *ing*)

We *are updating* our directory now.

The action of updating is in progress at a known time, this moment.

FUTURE PROGRESSIVE (simple future of *be* + *VERB* + *ing*)

We *will be updating* our directory tomorrow when you arrive.

The action of updating will be in progress at a known time in the future.

3. PERFECT: an action occurring (sometimes completed) at some indefinite time before a definite time

PAST PERFECT (simple past of *have* + *VERB* + *ed* [or irregular past])

We *had* already *written* the proposal when we got your call.

The action of writing began and ended at some indefinite past time before a definite past time.

PRESENT PERFECT (simple present of *have* + *VERB* + *ed* [or irregular past])

We *have written* the proposal and are proud to hand it to you.

The action of writing began at some indefinite past time and is being commented on in the present, a definite time.

FUTURE PERFECT (simple future of *have* + *VERB* + *ed* [or irregular past])

We *will have written* the proposal by the time you arrive.

The action of writing will have begun and ended at some indefinite time in the future before the definite time in the future when you arrive.

4. PERFECT PROGRESSIVE: an action in progress (continuing) until a known time

PAST PERFECT PROGRESSIVE (simple past of *have* + *been* + *VERB* + *ing*)

We *had been working* on the reorganization when the news of the merger became public.

The action of working continued until a known time in the past.

PRESENT PERFECT PROGRESSIVE (simple present of *have* + *been* + *VERB* + *ing*)

We *have been working* on the reorganization for over a year.

The action of working began at some indefinite past time and is continuing in the present, when it is being commented on.

FUTURE PERFECT PROGRESSIVE (simple future of *have* + *been* + *VERB* + *ing*)

We *will have been working* on the reorganization for over a year by the time you become CEO.

In the future, the action of working will have been continuing before another future action.

ing FORMING VERBS WITH -*ING*

English uses the -ing form of verbs in three major ways:

1. **As part of a progressive or perfect progressive verb (see numbers 2 and 4 in the previous "Verb Tenses" section)**

   We are *shipping* the materials by UPS.

   We have been *waiting* for approval since January.

2. **As a present participle, which functions as an adjective either by itself**

   the *leaking* pipe

   or as part of a participial phrase

   The sample *containing* the anomalies appears on Slide 14.

3. **As a gerund, which functions as a noun either by itself**

   Writing is the best way to learn to write.

   or as part of a gerund phrase

   The designer tried *inserting* the graphics by hand.

inf INFINITIVES

Infinitives consist of the word *to* plus the base form of the verb (*to write, to understand*). An infinitive can be used in three main ways:

1. **As a noun**

   The editor's goal for the next year is *to publish* the journal on schedule.

2. **As an adjective**

   The company requested the right *to subcontract* the project.

3. **As an adverb**

   We established the schedule ahead of time *to prevent* the kind of mistake we made last time.

help HELPING VERBS AND MAIN VERBS

Instead of a one-word verb, many English sentences contain a *verb phrase*.

> The system *meets* code.

This sentence has a one-word verb, *meets*.

> The new system *must meet* all applicable codes.

This sentence has a two-word verb phrase, *must meet*.

> The old system *must have met* all applicable codes.

This sentence has a three-word verb phrase, *must have met*.

In a verb phrase, the verb that carries the main meaning is called the *main verb*. The other words in the verb phrase are called *helping verbs*. The following discussion explains four categories of helping verbs.

1. **Modals**

There are nine modal verbs: *can, could, may, might, must, shall, should, will,* and *would*. After a modal verb, use the base form of the verb (the form of the verb used after *to* in the infinitive).

> BASE FORM
> ↓
> The system *must meet* all applicable codes.

2. **Forms of *do***

After a helping verb that is a form of *do—do, does,* or *did*—use the base form of the verb.

> BASE FORM
> ↓
> Do we *need* to include the figures for the recovery rate?

3. **Forms of *have* plus the past participle**

To form one of the perfect tenses (past, present, or future), use a form of *have* as the helping verb plus the past participle of the verb (usually the *-ed* form of the verb or the irregular past).

PAST PERFECT	We *had written* the proposal before learning of the new RFP.
PRESENT PERFECT	We *have written* the proposal according to the instructions in the RFP.
FUTURE PERFECT	We *will have written* the proposal by the end of the week.

4. **Forms of *be***

To describe an action in progress, use a form of *be* (*be, am, is, are, was, were, being, been*) as the helping verb plus the present participle (the *-ing* form of the verb).

For more about active and passive voice, see Ch. 10, pp. 235–240.

We *are testing* the new graphics tablet.

The company *is considering* flextime.

To create the passive voice, use a form of *be* plus the past participle.

The piping *was installed* by the plumbing contractor.

agr s/v AGREEMENT OF SUBJECT AND VERB

The subject and the verb in a clause or sentence must agree in number. That is, if the noun is singular, the verb must be singular.

The *valve needs* replacement.

Note the s that marks a singular present-tense verb.

If the noun is plural, the verb must be plural.

The *valves need* replacement.

Note the s that marks a plural noun.

Here are additional examples of subject–verb agreement.

The new *valve is* installed according to the manufacturer's specifications.

The new *valves are* installed according to the manufacturer's specifications.

When you edit your document for subject–verb agreement, keep in mind the following guidelines:

1. **When information comes between the subject and the verb, make sure the subject and verb agree.**

   The *result* of the tests *is* included in Appendix C.

   The *results* of the test *are* included in Appendix C.

2. **Certain pronouns and quantifiers always require singular verbs. Pronouns that end in -one or -body—*everyone, everybody, someone, somebody, anyone, anybody, no one,* and *nobody*—are singular. In addition, quantifiers such as *something, each,* and *every* are singular.**

   SINGULAR   *Everybody is* invited to the preproposal meeting.

   SINGULAR   *Each* of the members *is* asked to submit billable hours by the end of the month.

3. **When the clause or sentence contains a compound subject, the verb must be plural.**

   COMPOUND SUBJECT   *The contractor and the subcontractor want* to meet to resolve the difficulties.

4. **When a relative pronoun such as *who, that,* or *which* begins a clause, make sure the verb agrees in number with the noun that the relative pronoun refers to.**

The *numbers* that *are* used in the formula do not agree with the ones we were given at the site.

Numbers is plural, so the verb in the *that* clause (*are*) is also plural.

The *number* that *is* used in the formula does not agree with the one we were given at the site.

Number is singular, so the verb in the *that* clause (*is*) is also singular.

cond CONDITIONS

The word *if* in English can introduce four main types of conditions:

1. **Conditions of fact**

   Conditions of fact usually—but not always—call for the same verb tense in both clauses. In most cases, use a form of the present tense:

   > If rats *eat* as much as they want, they *become* obese.

   > If you *see* "Unrecoverable Application Error," the program *has crashed*.

   Here the present perfect is needed, because the crashing is over when you see the message.

2. **Future prediction**

   For prediction, use the present tense in the *if* clause. Use a modal (*can, could, may, might, must, shall, should, will,* or *would*) plus the base form of the verb in the independent clause.

   > If we *win* this contract, we *will need* to add three more engineers.

   > If this weather *keeps* up, we *might postpone* the launch.

3. **Present–future speculation**

   The present–future speculation usage suggests a condition contrary to fact. Use *were* in the *if* clause if the verb is *be*; use the simple past in the *if* clause if it contains another verb. Use *could, might,* or *would* plus the base form of the verb in the independent clause.

   > If I *were* president of the company, I *would be* much more aggressive.

   > If I *took* charge of the company, I *would be* much more aggressive.

   The example sentences imply that you are not president of the company and have not taken charge of it.

   The past tense in the example *if* clauses shows distance from reality, not distance in time.

4. **Past speculation**

   Use the past perfect in the *if* clause. Use *could, might,* or *would* plus the present perfect in the independent clause.

If we *had won* this contract, we *would have needed* to add three engineers.

This sentence implies that the condition is contrary to fact: the contract wasn't won, so the engineers were not needed.

art ARTICLES

Few aspects of English can be as frustrating to the nonnative speaker as the correct usage of the articles *a, an,* and *the* before nouns. Although there are a few rules that you should try to learn, remember that there are many exceptions and special cases.

Here are some guidelines to help you look at nouns and decide whether they may or must take an article—or not. As you will see, to make the decision about an article, you must determine

- whether a noun is proper or common
- for a common noun, whether it is countable or uncountable
- for a countable common noun, whether it is specific or nonspecific, and if it is nonspecific, whether it is singular or plural
- for an uncountable common noun, whether it is specific or nonspecific

Specific in this context means that the writer and the reader can both identify the noun—"which one" it is.

1. **Proper nouns**

   Singular proper nouns usually take no article but occasionally take *a* or *an*:

   > James Smith, but not John Smith, contributed to the fund last year. *A* Smith will contribute to the fund this year.

   The speaker does not know which Smith will make the contribution, so an article is necessary. Assuming that there is only one person with the name *Quitkin,* the sentence "Quitkin will contribute to the fund this year" is clear, so the proper noun takes no article.

   Plural proper nouns often, but not always, take *the:*

   > *The* Smiths have contributed for the past 10 years.

   > There are Smiths on the class roster again this year.

2. **Countable common nouns**

   Singular and plural specific countable common nouns take *the:*

   > *The* microscope is brand new.

   > *The* microscopes are brand new.

   Singular nonspecific countable common nouns take *a* or *an:*

   > *A* microscope will be available soon.

   > *An* electron was lost.

Plural nonspecific countable common nouns take no article but must have a plural ending:

> Microscopes must be available for all students.

3. Uncountable common nouns

Specific uncountable common nouns take *the*:

> *The* research started by Dr. Quitkin will continue.

> The subject under discussion is specific research.

Nonspecific uncountable common nouns generally take no article:

> Research is always critical.

> The subject under discussion is nonspecific—that is, research in general.

adj ADJECTIVES

Adjectives are modifiers. They modify—that is, describe—nouns and pronouns. Keep in mind four main points about adjectives in English:

1. Adjectives do not have a plural form.

> a *complex* project
>
> three *complex* projects

2. Adjectives can be placed either before the nouns they modify or after linking verbs.

> The *critical* need is to reduce the drag coefficient.
>
> The need to reduce the drag coefficient is *critical*.

3. Adjectives of one or two syllables usually take special endings to create the comparative and superlative forms.

Positive	Comparative	Superlative
big	bigger	biggest
heavy	heavier	heaviest

4. Adjectives of three or more syllables take the word more for the comparative form and the words the most for the superlative form.

Positive	Comparative	Superlative
qualified	more qualified	the most qualified
feasible	more feasible	the most feasible

adv ADVERBS

Like adjectives, adverbs are modifiers. They modify—that is, describe—verbs, adjectives, and other adverbs. Their placement in a sentence is somewhat more complex than the placement of adjectives. Remember five points about adverbs:

1. **Adverbs can modify verbs.**

   Management terminated the project *reluctantly*.

2. **Adverbs can modify adjectives.**

   The executive summary was *conspicuously* absent.

3. **Adverbs can modify other adverbs.**

   The project is going *very* well.

4. **Adverbs that describe how an action takes place can appear in different locations in a sentence—at the beginning of a clause, at the end of a clause, right before a one-word verb, or between a helping verb and a main verb.**

   Carefully the inspector examined the welds.

   The inspector examined the welds *carefully*.

   The inspector *carefully* examined the welds.

   The inspector was *carefully* examining the welds.

   NOTE: The adverb should not be placed between the verb and the direct object.

   INCORRECT   The inspector examined *carefully* the welds.

5. **Adverbs that describe the whole sentence can also appear in different locations in the sentence—at the beginning of the sentence, before an adjective, or at the end of the sentence.**

   Apparently, the inspection was successful.

   The inspection was *apparently* successful.

   The inspection was successful, *apparently*.

omit   OMITTED WORDS

For more about expletives, see Ch. 10, p. 229.

Except for imperative sentences, in which the subject *you* is understood (*Get the correct figures*), all sentences in English require a subject.

The company has a policy on conflict of interest.

Do not omit the expletive *there* or *it*.

INCORRECT	Are four reasons for us to pursue this issue.
CORRECT	*There* are four reasons for us to pursue this issue.
INCORRECT	Is important that we seek his advice.
CORRECT	*It* is important that we seek his advice.

REPEATED WORDS

1. **Do not repeat the subject of a sentence.**

   INCORRECT   The company we are buying from *it* does not permit us to change our order.

   CORRECT   The company we are buying from does not permit us to change our order.

2. **In an adjective clause, do not repeat an object.**

   INCORRECT   The technical communicator does not use the same software that we were writing in *it*.

   CORRECT   The technical communicator does not use the same software that we were writing in.

3. **In an adjective clause, do not use a second adverb.**

   INCORRECT   The lab where we did the testing *there* is an excellent facility.

   CORRECT   The lab where we did the testing is an excellent facility.

Selected Bibliography

Technical Communication

Alley, M. (2018). *The craft of scientific writing* (4th ed.). Springer Science and Business Media.

Alred, G. J., Brusaw, C. T., & Oliu, W. E. (2018). *Handbook of technical writing* (12th ed.). Bedford/St. Martin's.

Barnum, C. (2011). *Usability testing essentials: Ready, set . . . test.* Elsevier.

Beech, J. R. (2009). *How to write in psychology: A student guide.* Wiley-Blackwell.

Beer, D. F., & McMurrey, D. F. (2019). *A guide to writing as an engineer* (5th ed.). Wiley.

Etter, A. (2016). *Modern technical writing: An introduction to software documentation* [Kindle version]. Retrieved from Amazon.com

Gastel, B., & Day, R. A. (2016). *How to write and publish a scientific paper* (8th ed.). Greenwood.

Heath, R. L., & O'Hair, H. D. (Eds.). (2009). *Handbook of risk and crisis communication.* Routledge.

Kontaxis, J. M. (2008). *Rapid documentation of policies and procedures—The handbook: Proven secrets from consulting practitioners for developing benchmark manuals efficiently.* Benchmark Technologies International.

Lundgren, R. E., & McMakin, A. H. (2018). *Risk communication: A handbook for communicating environmental, safety, and health risks* (6th ed.). IEEE Press/Wiley.

Neuliep, J. W. (2018). *Intercultural communication: A contextual approach* (7th ed.). Sage.

Robinson, M. S., Stoller, F. L., Costanza-Robinson, M. S., & Jones, J. K. (2008). *Write like a chemist: A guide and resource.* Oxford University Press.

Rude, C. D., & Eaton, A. (2011). *Technical editing* (5th ed.). Longman.

Smith, C. F. (2019). *Writing public policy: A practical guide to communication in the policy making process* (5th ed.). Oxford University Press.

Tullis, T., & Albert, B. (2013). *Measuring the user experience: Collecting, analyzing, and presenting usability metrics* (2nd ed.). Morgan Kaufmann.

Van Laan, K. (2012). *The insider's guide to technical writing.* XML Press.

Varner, I., & Beamer, L. (2011). *Intercultural communication in the global workplace* (5th ed.). McGraw-Hill/Irwin.

Ethics and Legal Issues

Arnold, D. G., Beauchamp, T. L., & Bowie, N. E. (2012). *Ethical theory and business* (9th ed.). Pearson.

Ess, C. (2020). *Digital media ethics* (3rd ed.). Polity Press.

Klein, B., Moss, G., & Edwards, L. (2015). *Understanding copyright: Intellectual property in the digital age.* Sage.

Netanel, N. W. (2018). *Copyright: What everyone needs to know.* Oxford University Press.

Velasquez, M. G. (2017). *Business ethics: Concepts and cases* (8th ed.). Pearson.

Willerton, R. (2015). *Plain language and ethical action: A dialogic approach to technical content in the twenty-first century.* Routledge.

Wilson, L. (2013). *Fair use, free use and use by permission: How to handle copyrights in all media.* Allworth Press.

Collaborative Writing and Project Management

Davis, B. (Ed.). (2009). *97 things every project manager should know: Collective wisdom from the experts.* O'Reilly.

Dinsmore, P. C., & Cabanis-Brewin, J. (Eds.). (2018). *The AMA handbook of project management* (5th ed.). Amacom.

Eikenberry, K., & Turmel, W. (2018). *The long-distance leader: Rules for remarkable remote leadership.* Berrett-Koehler Publishers.

Hackos, J. T. (2007). *Information development: Managing your documentation projects, portfolio, and people.* Wiley.

Hamilton, R. L. (2009). *Managing writers: A real world guide to managing technical documentation.* XML Press.

Hewett, B. L., & Robidoux, C. (Eds.). (2010). *Virtual collaborative writing in the workplace: Computer-mediated communication technologies and processes.* Information Science Reference.

Kurtzberg, T. R. (2014). *Virtual teams: Mastering communication and collaboration in the digital age.* Praeger.

Meredith, J. R., Mantel, S. J., Jr., & Shafer, S. M. (2017). *Project management in practice* (6th ed.). Wiley.

Pullan, P. (2016). *Virtual leadership: Practical strategies for getting the best out of virtual work and virtual teams.* Kogan Page.

Stellman, A., & Greene, J. (Eds.). (2009). *Beautiful teams: Inspiring and cautionary tales from veteran team leaders.* O'Reilly.

Research Techniques

Cargill, M., & O'Connor, P. (2013). *Writing scientific research articles: Strategy and steps* (2nd ed.). Wiley-Blackwell.

Collins, D. (Ed.). (2015). *Cognitive interviewing practice.* Sage.

Fink, A. (2017). *How to conduct surveys: A step-by-step guide* (6th ed.). Sage.

Flick, U. (2018). *Managing quality in qualitative research* (2nd ed.). Sage.

Gentle, A. (2012). *Conversation and community: The social web for documentation* (2nd ed.). XML Press.

Gray, D. E. (2018). *Doing research in the real world* (4th ed.). Sage.

Mathewson, J., Donatone, F., & Fishel, C. (2010). *Audience, relevance, and search: Targeting web audiences with relevant content.* IBM Press.

Rubin, H. J., & Rubin, I. S. (2012). *Qualitative interviewing: The art of hearing data* (3rd ed.). Sage.

Wolcott, H. F. (2009). *Writing up qualitative research* (3rd ed.). Sage.

Usage and General Writing

Elster, C. H. (2010). *The accidents of style.* St. Martin's.

Garner, B. A. (2016). *Garner's modern English usage* (4th ed.). Oxford University Press.

Hale, C. (2013). *Sin and syntax: How to craft wicked good prose* (Rev. ed.). Random House.

Kohl, J. R. (2008). *The global English style guide: Writing clear, translatable documentation for a global market.* SAS Institute.

Lynch, J. (2009). *The lexicographer's dilemma: The evolution of "proper" English from Shakespeare to South Park.* Walker.

O'Conner, P. T. (2019). *Woe is I: The grammarphobe's guide to better English in plain English* (4th ed.). Random House.

Strunk, W., Jr., & White, E. B. (2000). *The elements of style* (4th ed.). Allyn & Bacon.

Waddingham, A. (Ed.). (2014). *New Hart's rules: The Oxford style guide* (2nd ed.). Oxford University Press.

Weiss, E. H. (2005). *The elements of international English style: A guide to writing correspondence, reports, technical documents, and Internet pages for a global audience.* M. E. Sharpe.

Williams, J. M., & Bizup, J. (2017). *Style: Lessons in clarity and grace* (12th ed.). Pearson.

Graphics, Design, and Web Pages

Amare, N., & Manning, A. (2013). *A unified theory of information design: Visuals, text & ethics.* Baywood.

Bergstrom, J. R., & Schall, A. J. (Eds.). (2014). *Eye tracking in user experience design.* Morgan Kaufmann.

Brumberger, E. R., & Northcut, K. M. (Eds.). (2013). *Designing texts: Teaching visual communication.* Baywood.

Cairo, A. (2012). *The functional art: An introduction to information graphics and visualization.* New Riders.

Colborne, G. (2018). *Simple and usable web, mobile, and interaction design* (2nd ed.). New Riders.

Dabner, D., Stewart, S., & Vickress, A. (2017). *Graphic design school: The principles and practice of graphic design* (6th ed.). Wiley.

DeLoach, S. (2013). *CSS to the point.* ClickStart.

Dougherty, B., & Celery Design Collaborative. (2008). *Green graphic design.* Allworth Press.

Eccher, C. (2015). *Professional web design: Techniques and templates* (5th ed.). Cengage Learning.

Few, S. (2012). *Show me the numbers: Designing tables and graphs to enlighten* (2nd ed.). Analytics Press.

Horton, S., & Quesenbery, W. (2014). *A web for everyone: Designing accessible user experiences.* Rosenfeld.

Johansson, K., Lundberg, P., & Ryberg, R. (2011). *A guide to graphic print production* (3rd ed.). Wiley.

Kirkham, H., & Duman, R. C. (2009). *The right graph: A manual for technical and scientific authors.* Wiley.

Kostelnick, C., & Roberts, D. D. (2010). *Designing visual language: Strategies for professional communicators* (2nd ed.). Allyn & Bacon.

Krug, S. (2014). *Don't make me think: A common sense approach to web usability* (3rd ed.). New Riders.

Lehr, D. (2009). *Technical and professional communication: Integrating text and visuals.* Focus Publishing/R. Pullins.

Lupton, E. (2010). *Thinking with type: A critical guide for designers, writers, editors, & students* (2nd ed.). Princeton Architectural Press.

Lupton, E. (Ed.). (2014). *Type on screen: A critical guide for designers, writers, developers, & students.* Princeton Architectural Press.

Lynch, P. J., & Horton, S. (2016). *Web style guide: Foundations of user experience design* (4th ed.). Yale University Press.

MacDonald, M. (2015). *Creating a website: The missing manual* (4th ed.). O'Reilly.

Mazza, R. (2009). *Introduction to information visualization.* Springer.

Obendorf, H. (2009). *Minimalism: Designing simplicity.* Springer.

Pullin, G. (2011). *Design meets disability.* MIT Press.

Robbins, J. N. (2018). *Learning web design: A beginner's guide to HTML, CSS, JavaScript, and web graphics* (5th ed.). O'Reilly.

Rosenfeld, L., Morville, P., & Arango, J. (2015). *Information architecture: For the web and beyond* (4th ed.). O'Reilly.

Shneiderman, B., Plaisant, C., Cohen, M., Jacobs, S., & Elmqvist, N. (2017). *Designing the user interface: Strategies for effective human-computer interaction* (6th ed.). Pearson.

Sklar, J. (2015). *Principles of web design* (6th ed.). Cengage Learning.

Tufte, E. R. (1990). *Envisioning information.* Graphics Press.

Tufte, E. R. (1997). *Visual explanations: Images and quantities, evidence and narrative.* Graphics Press.

Tufte, E. R. (2001). *The visual display of quantitative information* (2nd ed.). Graphics Press.

Williams, R. (2015). *The non-designer's design book: Design and typographic principles for the visual novice* (4th ed.). Peachpit.

Woolman, M. (2009). *100s visual ideas: Color combinations.* Angela Patchell Books.

Web 2.0 and Social Media

Bacon, J. (2012). *The art of community: Building the new age of participation* (2nd ed.). O'Reilly.

Barker, M. S., Barker, D. I., Bormann, N. F., Roberts, M. L., & Zahay, D. (2017). *Social media marketing: A strategic approach* (2nd ed.). Cengage Learning.

Deckers, E., & Lacy, K. (2018). *Branding yourself: How to use social media to invent or reinvent yourself* (3rd ed.). Que Publishing.

Handley, A. (2014). *Everybody writes: Your go-to guide to creating ridiculously good content.* Wiley.

Miller, D. (2017). *Building a story brand: Clarifying your message so customers will listen.* HarperCollins Leadership.

Millington, R. (2018). *The indispensable community: Why some brand communities thrive when others perish.* FeverBee.

Sagolla, D. (2009). *140 characters: A style guide for the short form.* Wiley.

Tasker, S. (2019). *Hashtag authentic: Finding creativity and building a community on Instagram and beyond.* White Lion Publishing.

Tuten, T. L., & Solomon, M. R. (2018). *Social media marketing* (3rd ed.). Sage.

Job-Application Materials

Bolles, R. N. (2019). *What color is your parachute? 2020: A practical manual for job-hunters and career-changers.* Ten Speed Press.

Davis, G. (2019). *How to land a tech job: Insider advice on landing a job at Instagram, Snapchat, Facebook, Google, or any tech company.* Bowker.

Fletcher, M. (2017). *Constructing the persuasive portfolio: The only primer you'll ever need.* Routledge.

Greene, B. (2008). *Get the interview every time: Proven strategies from Fortune 500 hiring professionals* (Rev. ed.). Kaplan.

Myers, D. R. (2014). *The graphic designer's guide to portfolio design* (3rd ed.). Wiley.

Oral Presentations

Atkinson, C. (2010). *The backchannel: How audiences are using Twitter and social media and changing presentations forever.* New Riders.

Bradbury, A. (2010). *Successful presentation skills: Build confidence; understand body language; use visual aids effectively* (4th ed.). Kogan Page.

Bunzel, T. (2010). *Tools of engagement: Presenting and training in a world of social media.* San Pfeiffer.

Chilcutt, A. S., & Brooks, A. J. (2019). *Engineered to speak: Helping you create and deliver engaging technical presentations.* IEEE Press/Wiley.

Gallo, C. (2010). *The presentation secrets of Steve Jobs: How to be insanely great in front of any audience.* McGraw-Hill.

Proposals and Grants

Freed, R. C., Romano, J. D., & Freed, S. (2011). *Writing winning business proposals* (3rd ed.). McGraw-Hill.

Hamper, R. J., & Baugh, L. S. (2011). *Handbook for writing proposals* (2nd ed.). McGraw-Hill.

Miner, J. T., & Ball, K. C. (2019). *Proposal planning & writing* (6th ed.). Greenwood.

O'Neal-McElrath, T., Kanter, L., & English, L. (2019). *Winning grants step by step: The complete workbook for planning, developing, and writing successful proposals* (5th ed.). Wiley.

References

CHAPTER 1:
Introduction to Technical Communication

Adecco Staffing. (2013). *Lack of soft skills negatively impacts today's workforce.* Retrieved September 23, 2019, from http://www.adeccousa.comabout/press /Pages/20130930-lack-of-soft-skills-negatively -impacts-todays-us-workforce.aspx

Carlaw, P. (2010, January 7). *The business case for first call resolution.* Retrieved May 17, 2013, from www.impactlearning.com /the-business-case-for-first-call-resolution

Freifeld, L. (Ed.). *The Industry Report, 2018,* p. 20. Retrieved August 29, 2019 from trainingmag.com /trgmag-article/2018-training-industry-report/

Hart Research Associates. (2015, January 20). *Falling short? College learning and career success.* Retrieved November 5, 2016, from www.aacu.org/leap /public-opinion-research/2015-survey-results

National Association of Colleges and Employers. (2019). *Job outlook 2019,* p. 30. Retrieved August 29, 2019, from www.naceweb.org/talent-acquisition/candidate -selection/employers-want-to-see-these-attributes -on-students-resumes/

TIME. (2013). *The real reason new college grads can't get hired.* Retrieved September 23, 2019, from http://business.time.com/2013/11/10 /the-real-reason-new-college-grads-cant-get-hired/

CHAPTER 2:
Understanding Ethical and Legal Considerations

Bettinger, B. (2010). *Social media implications for intellectual property law.* Retrieved May 23, 2013, from www. slideshare.net/blaine_5/social-media-implications-for- intellectual-property-law

Donaldson, T. (1991). *The ethics of international business.* Oxford University Press.

Ethics and Compliance Initiative. (2018). *2018 Global Business Ethics Survey.* Retrieved August 30, 2019, from https://www.ethics.org/knowledge-center/2018-gbes-2/

Ethics Resource Center. (2014). 2013 national business ethics survey: Workplace ethics in transition. Retrieved October 1, 2019, from www.ethics.org/nbes /files/FinalNBES-web.pdf

Federal Trade Commission. (2017, September). *The FTC's endorsement guides: What people are asking.* Retrieved August 30, 2019, from www .ftc.gov/tips-advice/business-center/guidance /ftcs-endorsement-guides-what-people-are-asking

Helyar, P. S. (1992). Products liability: Meeting legal standards for adequate instructions. *Journal of Technical Writing and Communication, 22*(2), 125–147.

Institute on Disability. (2017). *2017 Disability statistics annual report.* Retrieved October 1, 2019, from disabilitycompendium.org/sites/default/files/user -uploads/2017_AnnualReport_2017_FINAL.pdf

Lipus, T. (2006). International consumer protection: Writing adequate instructions for global audiences. *Journal of Technical Writing and Communication, 36*(1), 75–91.

Miranda-Hess, S. (2013, January 7). Interview with Brenda Heuttner: What every technical communicator should know about accessibility. *TechWhirl.* Retrieved September 25, 2016, from https://techwhirl.com /technical-communication-accessibility-brenda -huettner-interview/

Pew Research Center. (2014). *Workers use social media at work for many reasons; taking a mental break is one of the most common.* Retrieved October 1, 2019, from www.pewinternet .org/2016/06/22/social-media-and-the-workplace /pi_2016-06-22_social-media-and-work_0-01/

Proskauer Rose LLP. (2014). *Social media in the workplace around the world 3.0.* Retrieved September 21, 2016, from www.proskauer.com/files/News/4b7b2510 -9529-46ae-8832-1784ef8d2927/Presentation /NewsAttachment/a4678020-1e5e-4427-b157 -245425d994d5/social-media-in-the-workplace-2014.pdf

Ross, K. (2011). *Warnings and instructions: Updated U.S. standards and global requirements.* Retrieved September 21, 2016, from www.productliabilityprevention.com /images/DRI_Fall_2011_Strictly_Speaking_Warnings.pdf

Salary.com. (2013). *Your employees are wasting more time at work than ever.* Retrieved September 21, 2016, from http://business.salary.com /your-employees-wasting-time-2013/

Sigma Xi. (2000). *Honor in science.* New Haven, CT: Author.

Trillos-Decarie, J. (2012). Marketing + sales + communication + legal = social strategy (PowerPoint presentation). Retrieved May 23, 2013, from www.slideshare.net /JasmineTrillos-Decarie/jasmine-vegas-conf-final

U.S. Census Bureau. (2016). *U.S. international trade in goods and services: 2015.* Retrieved September 15, 2016, from www.census.gov/foreign-trade/Press-Release/current _press_release/exh1.pdf

U.S. Consumer Product Safety Commission. (2017). *2017 annual report to the president and Congress.* Retrieved August 30, 2019, from www.cpsc.gov/s3fs-public/FY17 -CPSC-Annual-Report.pdf?nuKsFE7Ex450hc9Efs2GU9E wYbBlPEFxU.S.

Velasquez, M. G. (2011). *Business ethics: Concepts and cases* (7th ed.). Pearson.

CHAPTER 4:
Writing Collaboratively

Cisco Systems, Inc. (2010). *Cisco 2010 midyear security report.* Retrieved July 22, 2010, from www.cisco.com /en/US/prod/collateral/vpndevc/security_annual _report _mid2010.pdf

Cross, R., and the Institute for Corporate Productivity. (2017). Top employers are 5.5x more likely to reward collaboration. *The i4cp productivity blog.* Retrieved October 1, 2019, from www.i4cp.com/productivity -blog/top-employers-are-5-5x-more-likely-to-reward -collaboration

Duin, A. H., Jorn, L. A., & DeBower, M. S. (1991). Collaborative writing—courseware and telecommunications. In M. M. Lay & W. M. Karis (Eds.), *Collaborative writing in industry: Investigations in theory and practice* (pp. 146–169). Baywood.

Karten, N. (2002). *Communication gaps and how to close them.* Dorset House.

Kaupins, G., & Park, S. (2010, June 2). Legal and ethical implications of corporate social networks. *Employee Responsibilities and Rights Journal.* Retrieved July 9, 2010, from www.springerlink.com /content/446x810tx0134588/fulltext.pdfDOI10.1007 /s10672-010-9149-8

Lustig, M. W., & Koester, J. (2012). *Intercultural competence: Interpersonal communication across cultures* (7th ed.). Allyn & Bacon.

Shaban, H. (2019). Twitter reveals its daily active user numbers for the first time. *The Washington Post.* Retrieved October 1, 2019, from www.washingtonpost .com/technology/2019/02/07/twitter-reveals-its-daily -active-user-numbers-first-time/

CHAPTER 5:
Analyzing Your Audience and Purpose

Bell, A. H. (1992). *Business communication: Toward 2000.* South-Western.

Centers for Disease Control and Prevention. (2013). *CDC .gov and social media metrics: April 2013.* Retrieved July 9, 2013, from www.cdc.gov/metrics/reports/2013 /oadcmetricsreportapril2013.pdf

Hoft, N. L. (1995). *International technical communication: How to export information about high technology.* Wiley.

Tebeaux, E., & Driskill, L. (1999). Culture and the shape of rhetoric: Protocols of international document design. In C. R. Lovitt & D. Goswami (Eds.), *Exploring the rhetoric of international professional communication: An agenda for teachers and researchers* (pp. 211–251). Baywood.

U.S. Census Bureau. (2019). *Foreign trade.* Retrieved October 1, 2019, from www.census.gov/foreign-trade /statistics/highlights/annual.html

U.S. Department of Homeland Security. (2019). *Table 1. Persons obtaining lawful permanent resident status: Fiscal years 1820 to 2017.* Retrieved October 1, 2019, from https://www.dhs.gov/immigration-statistics /yearbook/2017/table1#wcm-survey-target-id

Yan, S. (2015, September 24). Microsoft ditches Bing for Baidu in China. *CNN.* Retrieved September 8, 2016, from http://money.cnn.com/2015/09/24/technology /microsoft-baidu-xiaomi-china-deal/

CHAPTER 6:
Researching Your Subject

DeVault, G. (2013). *Market research case study—Nielsen Twitter TV rating metric.* Retrieved June 26, 2013, from http://marketresearch.about.com/od/market.research .social.media/a/Market-Research-Case-Study-Nielsen -Twitter-Tv-Rating-Metric.htm

McCaney, K. (2013, June 18). Energy lab team explores new ways of analyzing social media. *GCN.* Retrieved June 26, 2013, from http://gcn.com /articles/2013/06/18/Energy-lab-new-ways-analyzing -social-media.aspx

CHAPTER 8:
Communicating Persuasively

National Press Photographers Association. (2016). *NPPA code of ethics.* Retrieved October 20, 2016, from https://nppa.org/code_of_ethics

CHAPTER 10:
Writing Correct and Effective Sentences

ASD Simplified Technical English Maintenance Group. (2010). *ASD-STE100*. Retrieved August 2, 2010, from www.asd-ste100.org

Institute on Disability. (2017). *2017 Disability statistics annual report*. Retrieved October 1, 2019, from disabilitycompendium.org/sites/default/files/user -uploads/2017_AnnualReport_2017_FINAL.pdf.

Snow, K. (2009). *People first language*. Retrieved August 2, 2010, from www.disabilityisnatural.com/images/PDF /pfl-sh09.pdf

CHAPTER 11:
Designing Print and Online Documents

Haley, A. (1991). All caps: A typographic oxymoron. *U&lc, 18*(3), 14–15.

Horton, W. (1993). The almost universal language: Graphics for international documents. *Technical Communication, 40*, 682–693.

Internet World Stats. (2019). *Internet users in the world by regions*. Retrieved October 21, 2019, from www .internetworldstats.com/stats.htm

Lynch, P. J., & Horton, S. (2011). *Web style guide online* (3rd ed.). Retrieved July 12, 2013, from http://webstyleguide .com/index.html

Peterson, M. (2017). *Rhetoric of typography: Cross-cultural perceptions of typefaces for technical and visual communication*. Retrieved October 21, 2019, from https://pdfs.semanticscholar.org/ad48/04a32c8cf5d27c b0ae5bc28915d04fc4a5f7.pdf

Poulton, E. (1968). Rate of comprehension of an existing teleprinter output and of possible alternatives. *Journal of Applied Psychology, 52*, 16–21.

U.S. Department of Agriculture. (2002, March 5). *Thermometer usage messages and delivery mechanisms for parents of young children*. Retrieved April 4, 2002, from www.fsis.usda.gov/oa/research/rti_thermy.pdf

WebAIM. (2016). *Introduction to web accessibility*. Retrieved October 15, 2016, from http://webaim.org/intro/

Williams, R. (2015). *The non-designer's design book* (4th ed.). Peachpit Press.

Williams, T., & Spyridakis, J. (1992). Visual discriminability of headings in text. *IEEE Transactions on Professional Communication, 35*, 64–70.

CHAPTER 12:
Creating Graphics

Brockmann, R. J. (1990). *Writing better computer user documentation: From paper to hypertext*. Wiley.

Congressional Research Service. (2019). *Federal Research and Development (R&D) Funcing: FY2020*. Retrieved October 21, 2019, from https://fas.org/sgp/crs/misc /R45715.pdf

Gatlin, P. L. (1988). Visuals and prose in manuals: The effective combination. In *Proceedings of the 35th International Technical Communication Conference* (pp. RET 113–115). Society for Technical Communication.

Grimstead, D. (1987). Quality graphics: Writers draw the line. In *Proceedings of the 34th International Technical Communication Conference* (pp. VC 66–69). Society for Technical Communication.

Horton, W. (1992). Pictures please—presenting information visually. In C. Barnum & S. Carliner (Eds.), *Techniques for technical communicators*. Longman.

Horton, W. (1993). The almost universal language: Graphics for international documentation. *Technical Communication, 40*, 682–693.

Levie, W. H., & Lentz, R. (1982). Effects of text illustrations: A review of research. *Journal of Educational Psychology, 73*, 195–232.

Morrison, C., & Jimmerson, W. (1989, July). Business presentations for the 1990s. *Video Manager, 4*, 18.

Straker Translations. (2019). *Translation rates per word*. Retrieved October 21, 2019, from strakertranslations .com/translation-price-guide/rates-per-word/

Tufte, E. R. (1983). *The visual display of quantitative information*. Graphics Press.

White, J. V. (1984). *Using charts and graphs: 1000 ideas for visual persuasion*. R. R. Bowker.

White, J. V. (1990). *Color for the electronic age*. Watson-Guptill.

CHAPTER 13:
Evaluating and Testing Technical Documents

Bloom, B. (2016, September 30). Creating wall-sized interaction at the Smithsonian's National Air and Space Museum. *DigitalGov*. Retrieved November 18, 2016, from www.digitalgov.gov/2016/09/30/creating -wall-sized-interaction-at-the-smithsonians-national -air-and-space-museum/

Dumas, J. S., & Redish, J. C. (1999). *A practical guide to usability testing*. University of Chicago Press.

Johnson-Eilola, J., & Selber, S. A. (2007). Understanding usability approaches. In C. Selfe (Ed.), *Resources in technical communication: Outcomes and approaches* (pp. 195–219). Baywood.

Nielsen, J. (1994). Heuristic evaluation. In J. Nielsen & R. L. Mack (Eds.), *Usability inspection methods*. Wiley.

Nielsen, J. (1995). *How to conduct a heuristic evaluation.* Retrieved February 27, 2017, from www.nngroup.com /articles/how-to-conduct-a-heuristic-evaluation/

Nielsen, J. (2012). *Usability 101: Introduction to usability.* Retrieved July 25, 2013, from www.nngroup.com /articles/usability-101-introduction-to-usability/

Rubin, J., & Chisnell, D. (2008). *Handbook of usability testing: How to plan, design, and conduct effective tests* (2nd ed.). Wiley.

Selber, S. A., Johnson-Eilola, J., & Mehlenbacher, B. (1997). On-line support systems: Tutorials, documentation, and help. In A. B. Tucker, Jr. (Ed.), *The computer science and engineering handbook* (pp. 1619–1643). CRC Press.

CHAPTER 14:
Corresponding in Print and Online

Hall, S. (2009, August 21). Twitter fan companies say it helps them get closer to customers. *ITBusinessEdge.* Retrieved November 11, 2013, from www .itbusinessedge.com/cm/community/features/articles /blog/twitter-fan-companies-say-it-helps-them-get -closer-to-customers

Meyer, K. (2016, January 9). 2015: The year in social media disasters. *Medium.com.* Retrieved November 11, 2016, from https://medium.com/the-social -reader/2015-the-year-in-social-media-disasters -9cf0d53b60aa#.9xptx7afx

Sasaki, U. (2010). *Japanese business etiquette for email.* Retrieved September 3, 2010, from www.ehow.com /about_6523223_japanese-business-etiquette-email .html

CHAPTER 15:
Writing Job-Application Materials

Auerbach, D. (2012, August 29). *How to get that computer to send your résumé to a real person.* Retrieved August 4, 2013, from www.careerbuilder.com/Article/CB-3185 -Résumés-Cover-Letters-How-to-get-that-computer-to -send-your-résumé-to-a-real-person

Bowers, T. (2013, March 18). Would you hire someone with poor grammar skills? *TechRepublic.* Retrieved August 6, 2013, from www .techrepublic.com/blog/career-management /would-you-hire-someone-with-poor-grammar-skills/

Cohen, S. (2013, May 15). Online hiring tools are changing recruiting techniques. *New York Times.* Retrieved August 4, 2013, from www.nytimes.com/2013/05/16 /business/smallbusiness/online-recruiting-efforts -gain-ground.html

Halzack, S. (2013, August 4). Tips for using LinkedIn to find a job. *Washington Post.* Retrieved August 4,

2013, from www.washingtonpost.com/business /capitalbusiness/tips-for-using-linkedin-to-find-a -job/2013/08/01/7c50c418-e0ff-11e2-8ae9-5db15d3c0fca _story.html

Isaacs, K. (2012). *Lying on your résumé: What are the consequences?* Retrieved August 10, 2013, from http:// college.monster.com/training/articles/51-lying-on -your-resume-what-are-the-consequences

Lorenz, M. (2012, May 31). *Six ways hiring managers are spotting résumé lies.* Retrieved August 5, 2013, from www.careerbuilder.com/Article/CB-3077-Résumés -Cover-Letters-6-ways-hiring-managers-are-spotting -résumé-lies

Society for Human Resource Management. (2016, January 7). *SHRM survey findings: Using social media for talent acquisition—recruitment and screening.* Retrieved November 13, 2016, from www.shrm.org /hr-today/trends-and-forecasting/research-and -surveys/Documents/SHRM-Social-Media-Recruiting -Screening-2015.pdf

Tarpey, M. (2015, May 14). More employers checking out candidates on social media. *The HiringSite Blog.* Retrieved October 10, 2016, from http://thehiringsite.careerbuilder.com /employers-checking-candidates-social-media/

U.S. Department of Labor. (2019, February 12). Number of jobs held, labor market activity, and earnings growth among the youngest baby boomers: Results from a longitudinal survey summary. *Economic News Release* (Document USDL-15-0528), p. 1. Retrieved November 19, 2019, from https://www.bls.gov/nls /nlsfaqs.htm

CHAPTER 16:
Writing Proposals

Newman, L. (2011). *Proposal guide for business and technical professionals* (4th ed.). Shipley Associates.

Thrush, E. (2000, January 20). *Writing for an international audience: Part I. Communication skills.* Retrieved November 5, 2002, from www.suite101.com/article .cfm/5381/32233

USAspending.gov. (2019). *Advanced data search.* Retrieved November 4, 2019, from www.usaspending.gov/Pages /AdvancedSearch.aspx?sub=y&ST=C&FY=2015&A=0&S S=USA&AA=9700

CHAPTER 18:
Writing Recommendation Reports

Honold, P. (1999). Learning how to use a cellular phone: Comparison between German and Chinese users. *Technical Communication, 46*(2), 195–205.

CHAPTER 19:
Writing Lab Reports

Thomford, J. (2008). *Bile salts enhance lipase digestion of fats.* Unpublished document.

CHAPTER 20:
Writing Definitions, Descriptions, and Instructions

Canadian Association of Road Safety Professionals. (2009). *High-tech vehicle safety systems: Adaptive cruise control.* Retrieved August 29, 2013, from www.carsp.ca/hitech /hitech_acc.htm

Falco, M. (2008, January 14). *New hope may lie in lab-created heart.* Retrieved March 21, 2008, from www.cnn .com/2008/HEALTH/01/14/rebuilt.heart

National Oceanic and Atmospheric Administration. (2016, October 19). *What is a marine protected area?* Retrieved November 30, 2016, from http://oceanservice.noaa .gov/facts/mpa.html

CHAPTER 21:
Making Oral Presentations

Alley, M. (2007). *Rethinking the design of presentation slides.* Retrieved March 26, 2008, from www.writing.eng .vt.edu/slides.html

Nienow, S. (2013, July 6). *How long does it take to create a really great presentation?* Retrieved August 28, 2013, from http://redzestdesign.com/2013/10/how-long -does-it-take-to-create-a-really-great-presentation

Smith, T. C. (1991). *Making successful presentations: A self-teaching guide.* Wiley.

Index

Note: *f* indicates a figure and *t* indicates a table.

# of Selected Features

TECH TIPS

CHECKLISTS